Mee Young Namkoong

2002. 5-13~17. 전국 연합 대회 at La Vegas

찬 송 과 예 배

COME, LET US WORSHIP

COME, LET US WORSHIP
THE KOREAN-ENGLISH UNITED METHODIST HYMNAL
Book of United Methodist Worship

ISBN 0-687-08513-6

찬송과 예배

COME, LET US WORSHIP

Book of United Methodist Worship

연합감리교회 한영찬송가

THE KOREAN-ENGLISH
UNITED METHODIST HYMNAL

THE UNITED METHODIST PUBLISHING HOUSE
NASHIVLLE, TENNESSEE

머리말

한인교회 교인들은 찬송 부르기를 좋아한다. 기독교가 한국에 전파된 이래, 찬송은 교회 생활에서 대단히 중요한 활력소가 되어 왔다. 찬송은 하나님의 말씀을 사람들의 마음에 심어 주는 매개체 역할을 해주었을 뿐만 아니라 1910년에 신구약 한글성경 전체가 번역될 때까지 사람들에게 기독교의 가르침을 전파하는 역할을 하기도 했다.

한인교회는 성경에 기초한 예배를 선호한다. 찬송가를 출판할 준비가 되어있기 훨씬 전에도 교인들이 믿음 안에서 성장하는 데 큰 도움을 줄 수 있도록 성경말씀에 근거한 찬송가가 출판되면 도움이 되겠다는 말이 오고갔었다. 이 찬송가를 사용하는 분들은 성경책에 나오는 순서대로 말씀에 근거한 찬송을 부르게 되고, 교회력과 특별한 예배에 사용할 수 있도록 준비된 교독문을 사용함으로써 그들의 마음과 영혼을 하나님의 말씀을 들을 수 있도록 도와주게 될 것이다.

한국과 세계 곳곳에서 작사 작곡된 찬송이 이 찬송가에 실려있으며, 여기에 실려있는 찬송과 예문은 새로운 삶으로 초대하는 하나님의 은혜에 우리가 마음 문을 열고 응답할 수 있도록 도와줄 것이다. 뿐만 아니라 이 찬송가는 연합감리교회와 장로교회가 공동으로 출판하기 때문에, 이 두 신앙의 전통에서 사용되는 용어들을 수집하려고 노력했다. 이 두 교단은 같은 찬송을 부르게 되고, 예문은 각 교단 전통에 따라 준비된 예문을 별도로 사용하게 된다. 연합감리교회는 총회에서 인준한 성례전 예문과 다른 예문들을 사용하게 된다.

찬송가위원회는 현재 불려지고 있는 새로운 찬송들을 수집하여 준비하고, 새 가사와 곡조의 다양성을 반영시킬 수 있는 찬송가를 만드는 작업에 총 책임을 지고 일을 시작하였다. 위원회는 특별히 음악적인 기교를 필요로 하거나 선호하는 것보다는 현재 한인교회에서 많이 애창되거나 또는 앞으로 애창될 가능성이 많은 찬송들을 수집하였다. 또한 이민 1세대와 2세대들이 함께 사용할 수 있는 자료를 찾는 데 주력하였다. 이러한 모든 이유 때문에 김해종 감독을 중심으로 한인찬송가위원회와 자문위원회는 자료 조사, 수집, 검토, 경청을 하면서 부지런히 작업하였다. 그들이 수고한 결과, 결국 이와 같이 기존 자료와 새 자료를 골고루 갖춘 훌륭한 찬송가를 출판해 내게 되었다.

우리는 이 한영찬송가가 이민자들이 믿음 생활을 더욱 굳건하게 할 수 있도록 도움이 되기를 기도한다.

연합감리교회 한인찬송가위원회

김해종	위원장	백미영
이선경	찬송분과위원장	신영각
이승우	예문분과위원장	윤대섭
원달준	편집인	이경희
캐런 그린월드	총회제자훈련부 총무	전영호
닐 알렉싼더	총회연합감리교회출판사 발행인	함종택

미국장로교회 대표 (THE PRESBYTERIAN CHURCH U.S.A.)

김선배	허정갑
김승남	호러스 티 앨런

직원

총회제자훈련부
댄 베네딕트 예배
전상의 소수민족 교회

연합감리교회출판사
해리얼 제인 올슨 부사장/편집국장
강만희 찬송 편집인
리오 횔거슨 디자이너
엄은란 프로덕션 편집인

한인찬송가자문위원회

곽철환	박정찬	이창순
구본웅	백승배	이처권
김원기	유석종	이훈경
김옥남	유인순	장철우
김웅민	윤사무엘	정희수
김찬희	윤원경	진정우
김태근	이경식	차헬렌
박성호	이성현	홍혜성
박송자	이원화	

PREFACE

Korean Christians are a singing people. Since the beginning of the Christian movement in Korea, hymn singing has been a vital component of the worship life of the community. Hymn singing not only prepared the soil of the people's hearts for fruitful planting of the Word of God, but it also served as the primary instrument by which Christian teaching was transmitted until the whole Bible was translated into Korean in 1910.

Korean worship has long had a strong focus upon the Bible. Before the process of planning the hymnal project ever began, it was recognized that a scripture based hymnal reflecting distinctive Christian concepts would strengthen Korean Christian's spiritual journey. This hymnal helps to direct the users' hearts and minds to the Word of God through journeying with the order of the Bible and by the deep scriptural basis of each hymn text and responsive reading.

The hymnal shapes the language that our hearts use in responding to God's gracious invitation to new life. This hymnal seeks to bring some new hymns into that language—some hymns from Korean writers and some hymns from Christians around the world. It also seeks to be a collection that speaks in the idiom of two different faith traditions—The United Methodist Church and the Presbyterian Church (U.S.A.). It contains the same hymns and two different liturgical resources. The United Methodist liturgical resources have been adopted by the General Conference. Similarly, the Presbyterian edition contains the Lord's Day service, Psalms and Canticles, and other appropriate liturgical resources for use in its churches.

The Hymnal Committee accepted as its charge the responsibility to create a collection that would reflect the variety of new texts and tunes. The Committee was to create a collection that would be used and appreciated by the average worshiper in a Korean church, rather than seeking to serve a particular musical skill level or liturgical preference. It was also working to create a resource that would serve as a bridge for some of the differences between first and second generation Korean-Americans. For all of these reasons, the Committee and Bishop Hae Jong Kim, its chairperson, became convinced of the need for a broader Advisory Group who would be representative of some of the diversity within the church. These persons conducted diligent work—researching, collecting, checking, listening and finally shaping this collection. The Committee has achieved a wonderful blend of familiar and new resources.

We commend this hymnal to you and pray that it will strengthen and support the spiritual life of this generation of Korean-Americans.

THE KOREAN UNITED METHODIST HYMNAL COMMITTEE

HAE JONG KIM Chairperson

SUN KYUNG LEE Chair—Hymns

SEUNG WOO LEE Chair—Ritual

DAL JOON WON General Editor

KAREN GREENWALD
    General Secretary, General Board of Discipleship

NEIL ALEXANDER
    Publisher, The United Methodist Publishing House

YOUNG HO CHUN

JONG TAIK HAHM

KEYONG HEE LEE

MIYOUNG PAIK

DANIEL SHIN

DAE SOB YOON

THE PRESBYTERIAN CHURCH (U.S.A.)

PAUL JUNGGAP HUH

SUNBAE KIM

SEUNG NAM KIM

HORACE T. ALLEN, JR.

STAFF

General Board of Discipleship

DAN BENEDICT

SANG EUI CHUN

United Methodist Publishing House

HARRIETT JANE OLSON
    Senior Vice President/Book Editor

MAHN HEE KANG Music Editor

LEO FURGUSON Designer

EUN RAN UM Production Editor

ADVISORY GROUP

HELEN CHA

CHUL WOO CHANG

HYESUNG HONG

JUNG WOO JIN

HEE SOO JUNG

CHAN HIE KIM

OK NAM KIM

TAE KUN KIM

WON KIE KIM

WOONG MIN KIM

BON WOONG KOO

CHEOL HWAN KWAK

CHANG SOON LEE

CHOE KWON LEE

HOON KYUNG LEE

JONATHAN LEE

SAM LEE

SAMUEL LEE

WON HWA LEE

SEUNGBAE PAIK

ADNDREW PARK

JEREMIAH PARK

SONG JA PARK

IN SOON YU

SUK CHONG YU

WON KYUNG YUN

차 례

머리말 ……………………………………………………………………… iv-v

차례 ………………………………………………………………………… viii-ix

주일예배 기본 양식 …………………………………………………………… 1-4

성만찬 예문 I ………………………………………………………………… 9-16

성만찬 예문 II ……………………………………………………………… 24-25

세례 예문 I ………………………………………………………………… 28-38

세례 예문 II ………………………………………………………………… 49-53

창조주 하나님

　창조 ……………………………………………………………………… 59-70

　하나님 …………………………………………………………………… 71-78

출애굽과 구원

　출애굽과 구원 ………………………………………………………… 88-99

　인도 …………………………………………………………………… 100-107

말씀과 가르침 …………………………………………………………… 108-113

시와 찬미

　시편 …………………………………………………………………… 114-126

　찬미 …………………………………………………………………… 127-135

예언과 정의

　예언과 정의 …………………………………………………………… 136-146

　강림 …………………………………………………………………… 147-151

예수 그리스도

　탄생 …………………………………………………………………… 152-163

　성육신 ………………………………………………………………… 164-165

　주현 …………………………………………………………………… 166-167

예수의 생애와 사역

　예수의 생애와 사역 ………………………………………………… 168-179

　고난 …………………………………………………………………… 180-187

　부활 …………………………………………………………………… 188-197

예수 찬양 ………………………………………………………………… 198-211

성령 ……………………………………………………………………… 212-224

삼위일체 ………………………………………………………………… 225-229

성례

　세례 …………………………………………………………………… 230-232

　성찬 …………………………………………………………………… 233-240

감사 ··· 241-247
교회 ··· 248-257
전도와 선교 ·· 258-270
그리스도인의 삶
    죄와 고백 ··· 271-278
    신뢰와 확신 ··· 279-303
    시련과 극복 ··· 304-309
    헌신 ·· 310-321
    기도 ·· 322-334
    가정 ·· 335-340
    사랑 ·· 341-345
은혜와 평안
    은혜와 평안 ··· 346-347
    기도·축복송 ··· 348-368
아침과 저녁 ·· 369-376
새 하늘과 새 땅 ··· 377-392
교독문 ··· 393-493
결혼 예문 ··· 494-499
죽음과 부활 예문 (장례 예문) ·· 506-514
아침 찬양과 기도 ·· 524-525
저녁 찬양과 기도 ·· 528-529
신앙고백
    니케야 신조 ··· 532
    사도신경 ·· 534
    기독교대한감리회 신앙고백 ·· 535
    주기도문 ·· 537
색인
    판권 정보 ··· 538-543
    작사, 작곡, 편곡, 번역자 ·· 544-547
    성경 인용 ··· 548-549
    제목 분류 ··· 552-568
    가사 첫 줄 차례 ·· 587-590

CONTENTS

PREFACE .... vi–vii

CONTENTS .... x–xi

GENERAL SERVICES

The Basic Pattern of Worship 5–8

A SERVICE OF WORD AND TABLE I 17–23

A SERVICE OF WORD AND TABLE II 26–27

THE BAPTISMAL COVENANT I 40–48

THE BAPTISMAL COVENANT II 54–58

GOD THE CREATOR

Creation 59–70

God 71–87

EXODUS AND SALVATION

Exodus and Salvation 88–99

Guidance 100–107

THE WORD AND TEACHING 108–113

PSALMS AND PRAISE

Psalms 114–126

Praise 127–135

PROPHECY AND JUSTICE

Prophecy and Justice 136–146

Advent 147–151

JESUS CHRIST

Christmas 152–163

Incarnation 164–165

Epiphany 166–167

JESUS CHRIST: LIFE AND MINISTRY

Jesus Christ: Life and Ministry 168–179

Suffering 180–187

Resurrection 188–197

PRAISE JESUS CHRIST 198–211

THE HOLY SPIRIT 212–224

TRINITY 225–229

THE SACRAMENTS
    Baptism ·· 230-232
    Holy Communion ·· 233-240
THANKSGIVING ·· 241-247
CHURCH ·· 248-257
EVANGELISM AND MISSION ·· 258-270
THE CHRISTIAN LIFE
    Sins and Confession ·· 271-278
    Trust and Assurance ·· 279-303
    Affliction and Comfort ··· 304-309
    Commitment ··· 310-321
    Prayer ·· 322-334
    Home ··· 335-340
    Love ·· 341-345
GRACE AND CALMNESS
    Grace and Calmness ·· 346-347
    Service Music ··· 348-368
MORNING AND EVENING ··· 369-376
NEW HEAVEN AND A NEW EARTH ··· 377-392
PSALTER AND OTHER SCRIPTURES ··· 393-493
SERVICE OF CHRISTIAN MARRIAGE ·· 500-505
SERVICE OF DEATH AND RESURRECTION ···························· 515-523
ORDER FOR MORNING PRAYER ·· 526-527
ORDER FOR EVENING PRAYER ·· 530-531
AFFIRMATION OF FAITH
    The Nicene Creed ·· 533
    The Apostles' Creed ·· 534
    A Statement of Faith of the Korean Methodist Church ············ 536
    The Lord's Prayer ·· 537
INDEXES
    Acknowledgments ··· 538-5
    Authors, Composures, Arrangers, and Translators ··················· 544-
    Index of Scriptures ··· 550
    Topics And Categories ·· 56
    First Lines and Common Titles ·· 5

연합감리교회 예배문
Book of United Methodist Worship

주일예배 기본 양식에 관하여

이 주일예배 기본 양식은 성경과, 전통과, 경험에 뿌리를 내리고 있기 때문에 모든 예배를 위하여 기본적으로 사용될 수 있다. 이 예배 기본 양식은 예배를 준비하는 사람들을 위해 안내 역할을 하여 주고, 또한 회중으로 하여금 예배의 구조와 내용을 이해할 수 있도록 도와준다. 예배를 준비하는 사람은 이 주일예배 기본 양식에 기초하여 다른 순서를 다양하게 첨가할 수 있다.

부활하신 예수께서 엠마오로 향하여 가던 두 제자에게 나타나신 이야기는 주일예배에 대한 좋은 설교이자 가르침이 될 수 있다.

◆ 부활하신 후 첫 날, 예수께서 엠마오로 가던 두 제자와 동행하셨듯이, 부활 승천하신 예수께서는 우리가 모일 때마다 성령의 능력으로 늘 함께 하신다.

◆ 제자들이 그들의 슬픔을 예수님과 나누며 예수께서 하시는 말씀에 그들의 마음 문을 열었듯이, 우리도 우리의 마음 속에 있는 아픔을 예수님과 나눌 수 있다.

◆ 예수께서 "성경을 그들에게 풀어주실 때" 그들이 뜨거운 마음을 체험하였듯이, 성경이 우리의 마음 문을 열어줄 때에 그 체험을 통해 뜨거워진 마음으로 하나님을 찬양할 수 있다.

◆ 제자들이 결단을 내려야 했을 때 그들이 결단의 표시로 예수께 그들과 함께 머물자고 초청하였듯이, 우리도 예수께 우리와 함께 계셔 달라고 초청할 수 있다.

◆ 제자들이 부활하신 예수님과 식탁에 함께 둘러앉았듯이, 우리도 예수님과 함께 식탁에 둘러앉을 수 있다. 예수께서 떡(빵)을 가지사 (took), 축사하시고 (blessed), 떼어 (broke), 제자들에게 주었을 (gave) 때 그들이 삼일 전에 본 예수님을 만났듯이, 우리도 부활하신 예수님의 이름으로 떡과 잔을 가지고, 축사하고, 떼어 서로 나눌 때 예수께서 행하신 성만찬을 행하게 된다. 제자들이 떡(빵)을 뗌으로 그들의 눈이 밝아졌듯이, 우리도 성찬에 참여함으로 부활하고 승천하신 그리스도를 만나게 된다.

◆ 예수께서 제자들에게서 떠나며 믿음과 기쁨으로 그들을 세상으로 보내셨듯이, 예수께서는 우리를 세상으로 보내신다.

◆ 제자들이 저녁 늦게 예루살렘에 도착하였을 때 그리스도를 만났듯이, 우리도 어디에 가든지 그리스도를 만날 수 있다.

신약시대 이후, 주일예배 기본 양식은 계속 변형되어 왔다. 어떤 시기에는 이해하기 어려울 정도로 예배의 순수성을 잃은 때도 있었으나, 또 어떤 시기에는 예배의 순수성을 되찾기 위해 새롭고 활발하게 시도했던 때도 있었다. 감리교 전통에서는 복음을 세상에 전파하기 위하여 말씀을 전파하고, 찬송으로 찬양을 드리고, 성찬을 거행하면서 말씀과 성만찬을 동시에 계속해서 강조했다. 오늘날 연합감리교회는 "영과 진리"로 하나님께 예배드리기 위하여 주일예배 기본 양식을 회복하고자 성서적 역사적 전통을 재강조하고 있다.

주일예배 기본 양식

부름

예배준비

성도들은 주님의 이름으로 함께 모인다.
성도들 간의 인사나 대화는 예배실에 들어가기 전에 서로 간단히 나눈다.

전주

예배실에서는 찬송, 기도, 명상, 오르간, 혹은 다른 악기 연주에 따라 예배드리기 전에 마음준비를 한다.

예배로의 부름

집례자는 주님의 이름으로 인사하고 주님께서 우리 예배에 권능 주심을
회중에게 선포하고 그들을 환영한다. 성도들이 응답할 수도 있다.
적절한 성경구절을 사용할 수도 있다.
혹은 간단한 기도를 할 수도 있다.

찬송

찬송가에서 찬양과 경배 찬송으로 주님을 찬양한다.
입례송을 부를 경우에는 이를 예배로의 부름 이전에 둔다.

기도

다음의 기도들 가운데서 한두 가지 선택한다.

> 공동기도 (Collect)
> 참회와 용서의 기도
> 교독기도 (Litany)

예찬 (Act of Praise)

찬송가에 있는 교독문 중에서 그 주일에 적합한 것을 선택하여 교독한 후,
삼위일체 송영 중 하나를 함께 찬송한다.

말씀의 선포와 응답

말씀의 깨달음을 위한 기도 (Prayer for Illumination)

성경말씀을 읽고, 듣고, 행할 때에 성령께서 축복해 주시기를 간구하는 기도이다.
앞에 있는 예찬 순서를 생략하였을 경우에는 이 기도를 개회기도에 포함시켜도 좋다.

성경 봉독

설교를 위한 성경본문을 봉독한다.
시편이나 다른 연관된 성경구절을 봉독할 수 있다.
교회 절기별 성구집을 사용할 경우 해당 주일의 성구를 사용한다.

찬양

성가대 혹은 다른 그룹이 그 주일예배 주제에 적합한 찬양을 한다.

설교

하나님의 말씀을 선포한다.

말씀에 대한 응답

다음의 순서 중에서 한두 가지 선택한다.

초대 또는 응답이 있은 후에 그리스도인들로 하여금 제자가 되도록
결단하는 은혜의 수단으로 기도, 찬송, 또는 신앙고백을 할 수 있다.

성례전이 필요할 때에는 다음의 예식을 이 때에 행할 수 있다:
세례 예식
세례의 재확인
입교 예식
신조 혹은 신앙고백 (세례 예문에서 사용하지 않을 경우에 사용한다.)

중보의 기도

간략한 중보기도, 청원기도, 감사기도를 집례자가 인도하거나 성도들 가운데서
한 사람이 인도할 수도 있다. 이 기도가 끝나면 성도들은 "주님, 우리의 기도를
들어주소서" 하고 응답할 수도 있다.
또는 여기에서 목회기도를 할 수도 있다.

참회의 기도

지금까지 참회와 용서의 순서가 없었을 경우, 목사는 이 참회기도에 참여하는
성도들에게 용서하시는 하나님에 대하여 적절한 성경말씀을 인용하여 선포한다.

용서의 확증

목사: 이 기쁜 소식을 들으십시오.
우리가 아직 죄인이었을 때에
그리스도께서 우리를 위하여 죽으심으로
우리에게 대한 하나님의 사랑을 확증하셨습니다.
여러분이 용서받았음을 예수 그리스도의 이름으로 선포합니다.

찬송

평화의 인사

회중들은 화해와 사랑의 표시로 두 손을 서로 잡고
"주님의 사랑과 평화가 늘 함께 하시기를 원합니다" 하고 말한다.
광고를 이전에 안 했을 경우, 이 순서에서 할 수 있다.
새로 나온 신자를 소개한다.

봉헌

헌금을 드리는 동안 찬송이나 성가대의 찬양 또는 특별음악 순서를 가진다.

성만찬 (원하면 이 시간에 거행함)

보냄

찬송

축도

축도송

후주

오르간 또는 다른 악기를 연주한다.
서로 인사와 친교를 나눈 후, 성도들은 선교지인 세상을 향하여 나아간다.

INTRODUCTION TO AN ORDER OF SUNDAY WORSHIP

The Basic Pattern of Worship is rooted in Scripture and in the Christian heritage and experience. This Basic Pattern serves to guide those who plan worship and to help congregations understand the basic structure and content of our worship. The Basic Pattern of Worship described below makes plain the structure of all the General Services of the Church.

The Emmaus account can be used today in preaching and teaching the Basic Pattern of Worship.

- As on the first day of the week the two disciples were joined by the risen Christ, so in the power of the Holy Spirit the risen and ascended Christ joins us when we gather.
- As the disciples poured out to him their sorrow and in so doing opened their hearts to what Jesus would say to them, so we pour out to him whatever is on our hearts and thereby open ourselves to the Word.
- As Jesus "opened the Scriptures" to them and caused their hearts to burn, so we hear the Scriptures opened to us and out of the burning of our hearts praise God.
- As they were faced with a decision and responded by inviting Jesus to stay with them, we can do likewise.
- As they joined the risen Christ around the table, so can we. As Jesus *took, blessed, broke,* and *gave* the bread just as the disciples had seen him do three days previously, so in the name of the risen Christ we do these four actions with the bread and cup. As he was "made known to them in the breaking of the bread," so the risen and ascended Christ can be known to us in Holy Communion.
- As he disappeared and sent the disciples into the world with faith and joy, so he sends us forth into the world.
- And as those disciples found Christ when they arrived at Jerusalem later that evening, so we can find Christ with us wherever we go.

Since New Testament times, this Basic Pattern has had a long history of development. At times this pattern has been obscured and corrupted, and at times it has been recovered and renewed. The Wesleyan revival continued this emphasis on Word and Table, taking the gospel into the world by preaching and singing and by celebrating of the holy meal. Today The United Methodist Church is reclaiming our biblical and historic heritage, as we seek in this Basic Pattern to worship God "in spirit and in truth."

AN ORDER OF SUNDAY WORSHIP USING THE BASIC PATTERN

This order shows the variety that is possible within the basic pattern of worship. It is a guide for those who plan worship, not an order to be followed by the congregation. The congregation may be guided through the service by a bulletin or by announcement, whether or not Holy Communion is celebrated. This order is the basis of the following forms of service provided for congregations that wish to use this book for all or part of the service of Holy Communion.

ENTRANCE

GATHERING

The people come together in the Lord's name. While they are gathering,
one or more of the following may take place:

Informal greetings, conversation, and fellowship

Announcements and welcoming

Rehearsal of congregational music and other acts of worship

Informal prayer, singing, testimony

Quiet meditation and private prayer

Organ or other instrumental or vocal music

GREETING

Facing the people, the leader greets them in the Lord's name.
Scripture sentences or responsive acts between leader and people declare
that the Lord is present and empowers our worship.

OPENING HYMN

The leader and people declare the Lord's presence by singing.
The opening hymn may be sung before the greeting, if there is a processional.

OPENING PRAYER(S)

One or more of the following may be spoken or sung:

Prayer of the day, such as a collect

Prayer of confession and act of pardon

Litany, such as "Lord, have mercy."

ACT OF PRAISE

One or more of the following may be spoken or sung:
The Gloria Patri, a psalm or other scripture song, and an anthem

PROCLAMATION AND RESPONSE

PRAYER FOR ILLUMINATION

The blessing of the Holy Spirit is invoked upon the reading, preaching, hearing,
and doing of the Word. This may be included with the opening prayers,
if there has not been an act of praise.

SCRIPTURE

Two or three Scripture readings should be used. If there are not Old Testament, Epistle, and Gospel readings
at each service, care should be taken that over a period of time the people hear representative readings
from each.

The scripture readings may be interspersed with:

A psalm or psalm's portions after the first reading

A hymn or song related to the Scriptures of the day sung before the final reading

Gospel readings

SERMON

One or more of the Scripture readings is interpreted.

RESPONSE TO THE WORD

Responses may include one or more of the following:

Invitation to Christian discipleship, followed by
   a hymn of invitation or of response, or a baptism
     or confirmation hymn

Appropriate portions of the Baptismal Covenant:
   Holy Baptism, Confirmation,
   Reaffirmation of Faith
   Reception into The United Methodist Church
   Reception into the Local Congregation

A creed, except when already used in the Baptismal Covenant

CONCERNS AND PRAYERS

Joys and concerns to be included in the prayers may be expressed.
Prayer may take one or more of these forms:

Brief intercessions, petitions, and thanksgivings by the leader or members
   of the congregation. Each of these prayers may be followed by a common
   response, such as "Lord, hear our prayer," spoken or sung by all.
Pastoral prayer

CONFESSION

A prayer of confession and act of pardon are used here, if not used during the Entrance.

The people may offer one another signs of reconciliation and love, particularly when Holy Communion is celebrated.

WORDS OF ASSURANCE

The pastor and people may proclaim the word of God's forgiveness to each other.

Hear the good news:

Christ died for us while we were yet sinners;

that proves God's love toward us.

In the name of Jesus Christ, you are forgiven!

HYMN

PEACE

The people may offer one another signs of reconciliation and love by holding hands or shaking hands, and say, "May the love and peace of God be with you."

OFFERING

As the gifts are received and presented, there may be a hymn or an anthem.

THANKSGIVING

WITH HOLY COMMUNION

WITHOUT HOLY COMMUNION

SENDING FORTH

HYMN OR SONG

DISMISSAL WITH BLESSING

GOING FORTH

One or more of the following may be included:

Organ or other instrumental voluntary

After informal greetings, the people go into the world,

which is their mission field.

성만찬 예문 I

연합감리교회는 성만찬을 통하여 부활하신 예수 그리스도를 만날 수 있다고 믿는다. 이러한 의미에서 성만찬은 부활 축제에 참여하는 것이다. 연합감리교회는 은혜의 수단인 성만찬을 통해 하나님께서 역사하고 계시다는 사실을 믿기 때문에 어린이를 포함한 모든 사람들이 성만찬에 참여할 수 있다.

떡과 잔이 이미 제단에 놓여 있을 경우에는 성찬보를 벗기고 성만찬 예식에 임한다.

떡과 잔이 이미 제단에 놓여 있지 않을 경우에는 성찬위원들이 성만찬에 사용될 떡과 잔을 헌금위원들이 헌금을 봉헌하는 같은 시간에 제단 앞으로 가지고 나온다.

부름

전주

예배로의 부름

집례목사: 하나님께서 여러분과 함께 계시기를 바랍니다.

회　　중: **하나님께서 우리와 함께 계심을 믿습니다.**

집례목사: 여러분의 마음을 하나님께 드리십시오.

회　　중: **우리의 마음을 하나님께 드립니다.**

집례목사: 주 우리 하나님께 감사와 찬양을 드립시다.

회　　중: **기쁨으로 감사와 찬양을 드립니다.**

찬송

기도

다음과 같은 기도문이나 혹은 다른 기도문을 회중과 함께 읽는다.

전능하신 하나님,
이 시간 주님 앞에 숨김없이 우리의 마음 문을 엽니다.
성령의 인도하심으로 우리의 마음을 깨끗하게 하시고,
우리로 하여금 주님을 진정으로 사랑하게 하시며,
주님의 거룩한 이름에 합당한 찬양을 드리게 하소서.
예수 그리스도의 이름으로 기도합니다.
아멘.

[예찬]

[찬송가에 있는 교독문 중에서 선택하여 교독한 후, 삼위일체 송영 중에서 하나를 함께 찬송한다.]

[　] 부분은 경우에 따라 생략이 가능함

말씀의 선포와 응답

말씀의 깨달음을 위한 기도

주님, 성령의 능력으로 우리의 마음을 열어주셔서,
이 시간 성경말씀을 봉독하고 주님의 말씀이 선포될 때에,
우리에게 약속하신 은혜를 받을 수 있게 하소서. 아멘.

성경 봉독

구약성경

신약성경

시편

찬양

복음서 봉독

설교

말씀에 대한 응답

다음의 순서들 가운데서 한두 가지를 선택한다.
초대 또는 응답이 있은 후에 그리스도인들로 하여금 제자가 되도록 결단하는
은혜의 수단으로 기도, 찬송, 또는 신앙고백을 할 수 있다.
세례, 유아 세례 확증 (견신례) 혹은 입교식을 이 시간에 할 수 있다.

사도신경:

전능하사 천지를 만드신 하나님 아버지를 내가 믿사오며,
그 외아들 우리 주 예수 그리스도를 믿사오니,
이는 성령으로 잉태하사 동정녀 마리아에게 나시고,
본디오 빌라도에게 고난을 받으사, 십자가에 못박혀 죽으시고,
장사되어 죽은 자들에게 내려가셨다가 다시 살아나시며,
하늘에 오르사, 전능하신 하나님 우편에 앉아 계시다가,
저리로서 산 자와 죽은 자를 심판하러 오시리라.
성령을 믿사오며, 거룩한 공회와, 성도가 서로 교통하는 것과,
죄를 사하여 주시는 것과, 몸이 다시 사는 것과,
영원히 사는 것을 믿사옵나이다. 아멘.

(이 번역은 초대교회 때부터 사용되어진 사도신경을 참작하여 수정된 것임.)

중보의 기도

간략한 중보기도, 청원기도, 또는 감사기도를 집례자가 인도하거나
    성도들 가운데 한 사람이 할 수도 있다.
이 기도가 끝나면 성도들은 "주님, 우리의 기도를 들어주소서" 하고 응답할 수도 있다.
목회기도로 대신할 수도 있다.

성찬에로의 초대

우리 주 예수 그리스도께서는
주님을 사랑하며, 죄를 진정으로 회개하며,
    이웃과 평화롭게 살기로 결심하는 모든 사람들을
    성찬에 초대하십니다.
그러므로 이 성찬에 참여하기 위하여 먼저 하나님과
    모든 형제자매 앞에서 우리의 죄를 고백합시다.

공동 참회기도

자비로우신 하나님,
우리는 마음을 다하여 주님을 사랑하지 않았으며,
우리는 주님의 뜻을 따르지 않았으며,
우리는 주님의 계명을 어겼으며,
우리는 이웃을 사랑하지 않았으며,
우리는 궁핍한 자들이 부르짖는 소리를 들으려 하지도 않았습니다.
우리는 주님께 순종하는 교회가 되지 못했습니다.
이 시간 주님께 우리의 죄를 고백하오니 우리를 용서하여 주시고,
주님의 뜻에 기쁜 마음으로 순종할 수 있게 하소서.
예수 그리스도의 이름으로 기도합니다.   아멘.

개인 참회기도

공동 참회기도 후, 조용히 개인의 죄를 고백하는 기도를 드린다.

용서의 확증

집례목사: 이 기쁜 소식을 들으십시오:
            우리가 아직 죄인 되었을 때에 그리스도께서
                우리를 위하여 죽으심으로 하나님께서 우리에 대한
                자기의 사랑을 확증하셨습니다.
            여러분이 용서 받았음을 예수 그리스도의 이름으로 선포합니다.
회   중: 우리가 용서 받았음을 믿고 감사드립니다.
다 같 이: 하나님께 영광을 돌립니다.
            아멘.

평화의 인사

우리 서로 화해와 사랑의 표시를 주고받읍시다.

회중들은 두 손을 서로 잡고 "주님의 사랑과 평화가 늘 함께 하시기를 원합니다" 하고 말한다.

봉헌

용서받고 화해한 하나님의 자녀들로서 우리 자신과 삶을 하나님께 드립시다.

헌금을 드리는 동안 회중이 찬송을 하거나, 특송을 하거나, 또는 성가대의 찬양 순서를 가진다.
예물을 제단으로 가져올 때에 송영 또는 다른 응답송을 부른다.
만일 떡과 잔이 아직 제단에 놓여 있지 않을 경우에는 성찬위원들이 떡과 잔을 들고
헌금위원들과 함께 제단 앞으로 나와 준비한다.

성만찬

예식사

집례목사: 하나님께서 여러분과 함께 계시기를 바랍니다.
회   중: **하나님께서 우리와 함께 계심을 믿습니다.**
집례목사: 여러분의 마음을 하나님께 드리십시오.
회   중: **우리의 마음을 하나님께 드립니다.**
집례목사: 주 우리 하나님께 감사와 찬양을 드립시다.
회   중: **기쁨으로 감사와 찬양을 드립니다.**

집례목사:

하늘과 땅을 지으신 전능하신 창조주 하나님,
  우리가 언제, 어디서나 하나님께 감사를 드리는 것은
  지극히 마땅하며 기쁘고 즐거운 일입니다.
하나님께서는 우리를 자신의 형상대로 창조하시고
  생기를 불어넣어 주셨습니다.
우리가 하나님에게로부터 돌아서서 멀리 떠났을 때에도,
  하나님은 변함없이 우리를 사랑하셨습니다.
하나님께서는 우리가 포로 되었을 때에
  자유하게 하시어,
  우리의 구원자가 되어주실 것을 약속해 주셨으며,
  이를 선지자들을 통하여 우리에게 말씀해 주셨습니다.
그래서 우리는 땅 위의 사람들과
  하늘의 모든 권속과 함께
  하나님의 이름을 찬양하며 끊임없는 찬송을 드립니다.

회   중: **거룩 거룩 거룩 만군의 여호와여**
그의 영광이 온 땅에 충만하도다.
찬송하리로다 주의 이름으로 오시는 이여
가장 높은 곳에서 호산나.

집례목사:

하나님은 거룩하시고,
하나님의 아들 예수 그리스도는
마땅히 우리의 찬양을 받을 분이십니다.
성령께서 주님에게 기름을 부으시고,
가난한 자에게 복음을 전하게 하시고
포로 된 자에게 자유를,
눈먼 자에게 다시 보게 함을 전파하며
눌린 자를 자유롭게 하고
주의 은혜의 해를 전파하게 하셨습니다.
주님은 병든 자를 고치셨고, 배고픈 자를 먹이셨으며,
죄인들과 식탁을 함께 하셨습니다.
주님은 그의 고난과 죽음과 부활에 동참하는 이들로 하여금
교회를 세우셨고,
우리를 죄와 죽음의 결박에서 구원하여 주셨으며,
물과 성령으로 우리와 새 언약을 맺으셨습니다.
주님께서는 승천하실 때, 주님의 말씀과 성령의 능력 안에서
우리와 항상 함께 하시기로 약속하셨습니다.

성찬제정

(집례목사가 떡을 두 손으로 들고 말한다.)

예수께서 잡히시던 밤에 떡을 가지사
축사하시고 떼어 제자들에게 주며 말씀하시기를
"이것은 너희를 위하여 주는 내 몸이니
너희가 이를 행하여 나를 기념하라" 하시고,

(집례목사가 잔을 두 손으로 들고 말한다.)

식후에 또한 그와 같이 잔을 가지고 축사하시고
제자들에게 주며 말씀하시기를
"이 잔은 죄 사함을 얻게 하려고 너희와 많은 사람들의
죄를 위하여 흘리는 나의 새 언약의 피니
이것을 행하여 마실 때마다 나를 기념하라" 하고 말씀하셨습니다.

그러므로 우리는 그리스도를 통하여 이루신

하나님의 크신 구원의 은총 안에서 우리의 영혼과 몸을
　　주님께 거룩한 산 제물로 드려
　　자신을 내어주신 주님과 하나되어
　　하나님이 행하신 구원의 신비를 고백하면서
　　감사와 찬양을 드립시다.

다 같 이: 그리스도께서 죽으셨습니다.
　　　　　　그리스도께서 다시 사셨습니다.
　　　　　　그리스도께서 다시 오십니다.

성령 임재의 기원

자비하신 하나님,
여기에 모인 우리에게 성령을 부으시고,
주님의 선물인 떡과 잔 위에 임하사, 성별하시고,
우리로 하여금 그리스도의 보혈로 구원받아,
세상을 위한 그리스도의 몸이 되게 하소서.
성령으로 우리를 그리스도와 하나되게 하시고,
우리로 서로 하나되게 하소서.
그리스도께서 최후의 승리자로 오실 때까지
우리가 온 세상을 향하여 사역하는 데 하나되게 하소서.
우리가 주님의 천국잔치의 즐거움에 참여하게 하소서.
예수 그리스도의 이름으로 기도합니다.
아멘.

주기도문

이제는 하나님의 자녀가 된 확신을 가지고, 다함께 기도합시다.

하늘에 계신 우리 아버지여,
　이름이 거룩히 여김을 받으시오며,
　나라이 임하옵시며,
　뜻이 하늘에서 이룬 것 같이 땅에서도 이루어지이다.
오늘날 우리에게 일용할 양식을 주옵시고,
우리가 우리에게 죄지은 자를 사하여 준 것 같이
　우리 죄를 사하여 주옵시고,
우리를 시험에 들게 하지 마옵시고,
　다만 악에서 구하옵소서.
대개 나라와 권세와 영광이
아버지께 영원히 있사옵나이다.
아멘.

성찬분급

집례자는 다음과 같이 말을 하면서 떡과 잔을 분배한다.
이 성만찬에 참여하지 못하는 성도들이나 북한동포를 위하여 상징적으로 떡과 잔의 일부분을
떼어놓는 것도 좋다.

여러 밀 알이 한 덩어리의 떡이 된 것 같이,
　우리가 여럿이지만 주님의 성찬을 나눔으로,
　우리도 한 몸이 됩니다.
우리가 이 떡을 나눔은 그리스도의 몸을 나누는 것입니다.
그리스도께서 우리를 위하여 고난 받으신 몸을 기념하면서
이것을 받아 먹으며 감사하십시오.

여러 포도 알이 한 잔의 포도주가 된 것 같이,
　우리가 여럿이지만 주님의 성찬을 나눔으로
　우리도 한 몸이 됩니다.
우리가 이 잔을 나눔은 그리스도의 새 언약의 잔을
　나누는 것입니다.
우리 주 예수 그리스도께서
　우리를 위하여 그의 피를 흘리신 것은
　우리 하나 하나를 하늘나라 잔치에 초청하기 위함이며,
　우리의 영혼과 육신을 보전하여
　영생에 이르게 하기 위함입니다.

그리스도께서 우리를 위하여 피 흘리신 것을 기억하면서
　이것을 받아 마시고 감사하십시오.

당신을 위하여 주신 그리스도의 몸입니다.　**아멘**.
당신을 위하여 주신 그리스도의 피입니다.　**아멘**.

떡과 잔이 분배되는 동안 회중은 조용히 묵상을 하거나, 다같이 찬송을 부르거나,
　또는 집례자가 성경말씀으로 권면한다.
모두가 다 성찬을 분배 받은 후에, 집례자는 성찬보로 남은 떡과 잔을 덮는다.
그 후에 집례자와 회중은 다음과 같이 기도한다.

감사와 결단

긍휼과 자비가 풍성하신 우리의 하나님이시여,
하나님의 사랑과 능력을 힘입어,
　주의 겸비한 종된 우리들이 이 성례에 참여하였음에
　진실로 감사와 찬양을 드립니다.
주님께 진심으로 간구하오니

이 성례에 참여한 성도들로 하여금
예수 그리스도의 살과 피를 먹고 마심으로
주와 완전히 하나되게 하시고,
이제부터 주의 말씀에 순종하여 죽도록 충성하는
주님의 자녀들이 되게 하소서.
주여 우리들로 하여금 매일 매일의 생활이 성찬의 연속이 되어
주님께 드리는 거룩한 산 제물이 되도록 도와주소서.
또한 우리들이 하나님의 자녀된 본분과 제자된 의무를
충실히 감당하도록 성령이여 함께 하소서.
우리가 모든 존귀와 영광을
전능하신 성부 성자와 성령 삼위일체
하나님께 영원히 돌리나이다.
아멘.

보냄

찬송

축도

주 예수 그리스도의 은혜와
하나님의 사랑과
성령의 교통하심이
여러분과 함께 하시기를 축원합니다.
아멘.

축도송

후주

남은 떡과 잔은 병원이나 혹은 불가피한 사정으로 성찬에 참여하지 못한 이들을 방문하여
나누면 좋다.
집례목사의 지시에 따라 남은 떡과 포도주를 성찬위원들이 성스럽게 처리해야 한다.

A SERVICE OF WORD AND TABLE I

United Methodist Christians celebrate the Lord's Supper as an encounter with the risen Lord, Jesus Christ. For this reason its tone is an Easter celebration service. United Methodists celebrate the Lord's Supper as a means of grace. Therefore, in the American church, the practice is to open the table to all including children.

If the bread and wine are already in place, uncover the cover. If the bread and wine are not in place, representatives of the people bring them to the Lord's table with the other gifts.

ENTRANCE

GREETING

The Lord be with you.
And also with you.
Lift up your hearts.
We lift them up to the Lord.
Let us give thanks to the Lord our God.
It is right to give our thanks and praise.

HYMN OF PRAISE

OPENING PRAYER

The following or a prayer of the day is offered:

Almighty God,
to you all hearts are open, all desires known,
  and from you no secrets are hidden.
Cleanse the thoughts of our hearts
  by the inspiration of your Holy Spirit,
that we may perfectly love you,
and worthily magnify your holy name,
  through Jesus Christ our Lord.
Amen.

[ACT OF PRAISE]

PROCLAMATION AND RESPONSE

[ ] means optional

PRAYER FOR ILLUMINATION

Lord, open our hearts and minds
   by the power of your Holy Spirit,
that, as the Scriptures are read and your Word proclaimed,
we may hear with joy what you say to us today.
Amen.

SCRIPTURE LESSON

OLD TESTAMENT

NEW TESTAMENT

[PSALM] may be spoken

HYMN

GOSPEL LESSON

SERMON

RESPONSE TO THE WORD

Responses may include one or more of the following acts:
Invitation to Christian discipleship, followed by a hymn of invitation
   or of response, or a baptism or confirmation hymn
Baptism, confirmation, reaffirmation of faith, or other reception of members

The following or another creed:

I believe in God, the Father Almighty, Creator of heaven and earth.
I believe in Jesus Christ, his only Son, our Lord,
   who was conceived by the Holy Spirit,
   born of the Virgin Mary, suffered under Pontius Pilate,
   was crucified, died, and was buried; he descended to the dead.
   On the third day he rose again; he ascended into heaven,
   is seated at the right hand of the Father,
   and will come again to judge the living and the dead.
I believe in the Holy Spirit,
   the holy catholic church, the communion of saints,
   the forgiveness of sins, the resurrection of the body,
   and the life everlasting. Amen.

CONCERNS AND PRAYERS

Brief intercessions, petitions, and thanksgivings may be prayed by the leader,
or spontaneously by members of the congregation. To each of these, all may make a common response,
  such as: "Lord, hear our prayer."
Or, a litany of intercession and petition may be prayed.
Or, a pastoral prayer may be prayed.

INVITATION

Christ our Lord invites to his table all who love him,
  who earnestly repent of their sin
  and seek to live in peace with one another.
Therefore, let us confess our sin before God and one another.

CONFESSION OF SIN

Merciful God,
we confess that we have not loved you with our whole heart.
We have failed to be an obedient church.
We have not done your will,
we have broken your law,
we have rebelled against your love,
we have not loved our neighbors,
and we have not heard the cry of the needy.
Forgive us, we pray.
Free us for joyful obedience,
through Jesus Christ our Lord.   Amen.

SILENT PRAYER

WORDS OF ASSURANCE

Leader to people:

Hear the good news:
  Christ died for us while we were yet sinners;
  that proves God's love toward us.
In the name of Jesus Christ, you are forgiven!

People to leader:

In the name of Jesus Christ, you are forgiven!

Leader to people:

Glory to God.   **Amen.**

THE PEACE

All exchange signs and words of God's peace. and saying,
"May the love and peace of God be with you."

OFFERING

As forgiven and reconciled people,
let us offer ourselves and our gifts to God.

A hymn, psalm, or anthem may be sung as the offering is received.
The bread and wine are brought by representatives of the people to
the Lord's table with the other gifts, if the elements were not placed before
the service, or uncovered if already in place.
A hymn, doxology, or other response may be sung as the gifts are presented.

THANKSGIVING AND COMMUNION

TAKING THE BREAD AND CUP

The pastor takes the bread and cup, and the bread and wine are prepared for the meal.

THE GREAT THANKSGIVING

The Lord be with you.
And also with you.
Lift up your hearts.
We lift them up to the Lord.
Let us give thanks to the Lord our God.
It is right to give our thanks and praise.

It is right, and a good and joyful thing,
always and everywhere to give thanks to you,
Father Almighty, creator of heaven and earth.
You formed us in your image
and breathed into us the breath of life.
When we turned away, and our love failed,
your love remained steadfast.
You delivered us from captivity,
made covenant to be our sovereign God,
and spoke to us through your prophets.

And so,
with your people on earth and all the company of heaven
we praise your name and join their unending hymn:

Holy, holy, holy Lord, God of power and might,
heaven and earth are full of your glory.
   Hosanna in the highest.
Blessed is he who comes in the name of the Lord.
   Hosanna in the highest.

Holy are you, and blessed is your Son Jesus Christ.
Your Spirit anointed him to preach good news to the poor,
   to proclaim release to the captives
      and recovering of sight to the blind,
   to set at liberty those who are oppressed,
   and to announce that the time had come
      when you would save your people.
He healed the sick, fed the hungry, and ate with sinners.
By the baptism of his suffering, death, and resurrection
   you gave birth to your church,
   delivered us from slavery to sin and death,
   and made with us a new covenant by water and the Spirit.
When the Lord Jesus ascended, he promised to be with us always,
   in the power of your Word and Holy Spirit.
On the night in which he gave himself up for us,
   he took bread, gave thanks to you,
   broke the bread, gave it to his disciples,
and said:
"Take, eat; this is my body which is given for you.
Do this in remembrance of me."
When the supper was over, he took the cup,
   gave thanks to you, gave it to his disciples,
and said:
"Drink from this, all of you;
   this is my blood of the new covenant,
   poured out for you and for many for the forgiveness of sins.
Do this, as often as you drink it, in remembrance of me."
And so,
in remembrance of these your mighty acts in Jesus Christ,
we offer ourselves in praise and thanksgiving
   as a holy and living sacrifice,
   in union with Christ's offering for us,
as we proclaim the mystery of faith.

Christ has died;
Christ is risen;
Christ will come again.

Pour your Holy Spirit on us gathered here,
   and on these gifts of bread and wine.
Make them be for us the body and blood of Christ,
that we may be for the world the body of Christ,
   redeemed by his blood.
By your Spirit make us one with Christ,
   one with each other,
   and one in ministry to all the world,
until Christ comes in final victory
   and we feast at his heavenly banquet.
Through your Son Jesus Christ,
with the Holy Spirit in your holy church,
all honor and glory is yours, almighty Father,
now and for ever.
Amen.

THE LORD'S PRAYER

And now, with the confidence of children of God,
let us pray:

Our Father in heaven, hallowed be your name,
   your kingdom come, your will be done, on earth as in heaven.
Give us today our daily bread.
Forgive us our sins as we forgive those who sin against us.
Save us from the time of trial, and deliver us from evil.
For the kingdom, the power, and the glory are yours
   now and for ever.   Amen.

BREAKING THE BREAD

The pastor breaks the bread in silence, or while saying:

Because there is one loaf,
we, who are many, are one body,
for we all partake of the one loaf.
The bread which we break is a sharing in the body of Christ.

The pastor lifts the cup in silence, or while saying:

The cup over which we give thanks is a sharing
in the blood of Christ.

GIVING THE BREAD AND CUP

The bread and wine are given to the people, with these or other words being exchanged:

The body of Christ, given for you.
Amen.
The blood of Christ, given for you.
Amen.

The congregation may sing hymns while the bread and cup are given.
When all have received, the Lord's table is put in order.
The following prayer is then offered by the pastor or by all:

Eternal God, we give you thanks for this holy mystery
in which you have given yourself to us.
Grant that we may go into the world
in the strength of your Spirit,
to give ourselves for others,
in the name of Jesus Christ our Lord.
Amen.

SENDING FORTH

HYMN

DISMISSAL WITH BLESSING

Go forth in peace.
The grace of the Lord Jesus Christ,
and the love of God,
and the communion of the Holy Spirit
be with you all.
Amen.

GOING FORTH

성만찬 예문 II

이 예문은 주일예배 때 성만찬 예문 I을 대신하여 사용하거나, 결혼식과 장례식을 포함하여 성만찬이 필요로 되는 모든 예배를 위하여 사용할 수 있다.

연합감리교회는 성만찬을 통하여 부활하신 예수 그리스도를 만날 수 있다고 믿는다. 이러한 의미에서 성만찬은 부활 축제에 참여하는 것이다. 연합감리교회는 은혜의 수단인 성만찬을 통해 역사하시는 하나님의 임재를 믿기 때문에 어린이를 포함한 모든 사람들이 성만찬에 참여할 수 있다.

성만찬

떡과 잔이 놓여 있는 성찬보를 벗기고 성만찬에 임한다.

집례목사: 하나님께서 여러분과 함께 계십니다.

회   중: **하나님께서 우리와 함께 계심을 믿습니다.**

집례목사: 여러분의 마음을 하나님께 드리십시오.

회   중: **우리의 마음을 하나님께 드립니다.**

집례목사: 주 우리 하나님께 감사와 찬양을 드립시다.

회   중: **기쁨으로 감사와 찬양을 드립니다.**

집례목사는 이 특별한 날을 허락하여 주신 하나님의 구원의 역사에 감사한 후, 기도를 한다.

혹은 성만찬 예문 I(9-16쪽)에서 적절한 내용을 선택하여 읽는다. 요한복음 6:51; 고린도전서 10:16-17; 요한1서 4:7-9; 요한계시록 3:20에 있는 성경말씀 중 몇 절을 선택하여 읽은 후, 다음과 같이 결말을 짓는다:

그래서,
     우리는 땅 위의 사람들과 하늘의 모든 권속과 함께
     하나님의 이름을 찬양하며 끊임없는 찬송을 드립니다.

회   중: **거룩 거룩 거룩 만군의 여호와여 그의 영광이 온 땅에 충만하도다.**
          찬송하리로다 주의 이름으로 오시는 이여 가장 높은 곳에서 호산나.

성찬제정

(집례목사가 떡을 두 손으로 들고 말한다.)

예수께서 잡히시던 밤에 떡을 가지사 축사하시고
   떼어 제자들에게 주며 말씀하시기를
"이것은 너희를 위하여 주는 내 몸이니 너희가 이를 행하여 나를 기념하라" 하시고,

(집례목사가 잔을 두 손으로 들고 말한다.)

식후에 또한 그와 같이 잔을 가지고 축사하시고 제자들에게 주며 말씀하시기를
"이 잔은 죄 사함을 얻게 하려고 너희와 많은 사람들의 죄를 위하여 흘리는 나의
   새 언약의 피니 이것을 행하여 마실 때마다 나를 기념하라" 하고 말씀하셨습니다.
그러므로 우리는 그리스도를 통하여 이루신 하나님의 크신 구원의 은총 안에서
   우리의 영혼과 몸을 주님께 거룩한 산 제물로 드려 자신을 내어주신 주님과
   하나되어 하나님이 행하신 구원의 신비를 고백하면서 감사와 찬양을 드립시다.

다 같 이: **그리스도께서 죽으셨습니다.**
그리스도께서 다시 사셨습니다.
그리스도께서 다시 오십니다.

집례목사는 성령의 임재를 위해 기도를 하며 삼위일체 하나님을 찬양한 후,
다음과 같은 말로 결말을 짓는다. (성만찬 예문 I을 참조하면 된다.)

존귀와 영광이 아버지께 영원히 있사옵나이다.
아멘.

주기도문

성찬분급

집례자는 다음과 같이 말을 하면서 떡과 잔을 분배한다.
떡과 잔을 나누는 동안 회중은 찬송을 부른다. 성만찬이 끝나면 제단을 정리한다.

여러 밀 알이 한 덩어리의 떡이 된 것 같이,
우리가 여럿이지만 주님의 성찬을 나눔으로 우리도 한 몸이 됩니다.
우리가 이 떡을 나눔은 그리스도의 몸을 나누는 것입니다.
그리스도께서 우리를 위하여 고난 받으신 몸을 기념하면서
이것을 받아 먹으며 감사하십시오.

여러 포도 알이 한 잔의 포도주가 된 것 같이,
우리가 여럿이지만 주님의 성찬을 나눔으로 우리도 한 몸이 됩니다.
우리가 이 잔을 나눔은 그리스도의 새 언약의 잔을 나누는 것입니다.
우리 주 예수 그리스도께서 우리를 위하여 그 피를 흘리신 것은
우리 하나 하나를 하늘나라 잔치에 초청하기 위함이며,
우리의 영혼과 육신을 보전하여 영생에 이르게 하기 위함입니다.
그리스도께서 우리를 위하여 피 흘리신 것을 기념하면서
이것을 받아 마시고 감사하십시오.

당신을 위하여 주신 그리스도의 몸입니다. **아멘.**
당신을 위하여 주신 그리스도의 피입니다. **아멘.**

보냄

찬송

축도

후주

A SERVICE OF WORD AND TABLE II

The service through the Entrance and the Proclamation and Response is guided by a bulletin or by announcement. This text may also be used in Sunday worship as an alternative to Word and Table I. This text may be used when a Service of Christian Marriage or a Service of Death and Resurrection includes Holy Communion.

THANKSGIVING AND COMMUNION

TAKING THE BREAD AND CUP

The pastor takes the bread and cup, and the bread and wine are prepared for the meal.

THE GREAT THANKSGIVING

The Lord be with you.
And also with you.
Lift up your hearts.
We lift them up to the Lord.
Let us give thanks to the Lord our God.
It is right to give our thanks and praise.

Here the pastor says to supplement these texts with impromptu thanks appropriate to the occasion, remembering God's act of salvation when written texts as on pages 17-23, or addressing God the Father remembering creation, covenant, and God's love when humanity has been unfaithful. Or one or two of the following lessons may be read: John 6:51; 1 Corinthians 10:16-17; 1 John 4:7-9; Revelation 3:20. and concludes:

And so,
with your people on earth and all the company of heaven
we praise your name and join their unending hymn:

Holy, holy, holy Lord, God of power and might,
heaven and earth are full of your glory.
  Hosanna in the highest.
Blessed is he who comes in the name of the Lord.
  Hosanna in the highest.

The pastor continues the thanksgiving remembering the work and ministry of Jesus that addresses, liberates, and heals the world. The pastor recalls institution of the Lord's Supper, saying:

On the night in which he gave himself up for us,
  he took bread, gave thanks to you, broke the bread,
    gave it to his disciples, and said:
"Take, eat; this is my body which is given for you.
Do this in remembrance of me."

When the supper was over, he took the cup,
  gave thanks to you, gave it to his disciples, and said:
"Drink from this, all of you:
  this is my blood of the new covenant,
  poured out for you and for many for the forgiveness of sins.
Do this, as often as you drink it, in remembrance of me."

And so,
in remembrance of these your mighty acts in Jesus Christ,
we offer ourselves in praise and thanksgiving
  as a holy and living sacrifice, in union with Christ's offering for us,
as we proclaim the mystery of faith.

Together: **Christ has died;**
           Christ is risen;
           Christ will come again.

The pastor invokes the present work of the Holy Spirit and then praises the Trinity, concluding:

All honor and glory is yours, almighty Father (God),
now and for ever.
Amen.

THE LORD'S PRAYER

BREAKING THE BREAD

The pastor breaks the bread and then lifts the cup, in silence or with appropriate words.

GIVING THE BREAD AND CUP

The bread and wine are given to the people, with appropriate words being exchanged.
The congregation may sing hymns while the bread and cup are given.
When all have received, the Lord's table is put in order.
The pastor or congregation may give thanks after Communion.

SENDING FORTH

HYMN

DISMISSAL WITH BLESSING

GOING FORTH

세례에 관하여

세례는 하나님께서 그의 은총으로 우리를 자녀로 삼으신다고 선포하는 하나님의 말씀이며, 우리가 믿음과 사랑으로 살겠다고 하나님께 응답하는 우리의 약속이다. 그러므로 특별한 경우를 제외하고는 세례 받을 사람은 입교할 교회에서 대중예배 시간에 세례를 받게 되어 있다.

사람들은 연령에 제한 없이 누구나 세례를 받을 수 있다. 스스로 세례 문답에 답할 수 없는 유아나 다른 사람들은 부모나 보호자들이 대신 문답에 답을 할 수 있다. 이 때 부모나 보호자는 교회의 입교인이어야 한다.

비상시에는 목사가 서약 부분을 읽은 후, 세례 후보자에게 물을 세 번 끼얹으며 성부와 성자와 성령의 이름으로 세례를 준다고 말하면 된다. 대중예배 시간에 세례를 받지 않은 사람은, 후에 필히 대중예배에 참석시켜서 회중에게 소개해 주어야 한다.

스스로 세례 문답을 할 수 있기 전에 세례를 받은 사람들은 유아 세례 확증 예식(견신례)을 통하여 신앙을 고백하는 입교인이 될 수 있도록 지도해 주어야 한다. 스스로 세례 문답을 할 수 있는 사람들은 세례를 받을 때 입교인이 된다.

유아 세례 확증 (견신례) 예식을 통하여 입교인이 된 사람이나 스스로 세례 문답에 참여하여 세례를 받은 후, 입교인이 된 사람들은 그들이 받은 세례를 재확인할 수 있도록 권장해 주는 것이 좋다. 그러나 이 세례를 재확인하는 예배는 성례가 아니라는 사실을 명심해야 한다. 세례 받은 이에게 세례를 다시 베풀 수는 없다. 인간인 우리의 서약이 불완전하여 믿을 수 없는 것이라 할지라도, 하나님께서 성례를 통하여 약속하시는 것은 확실한 것이기 때문이다.

전 회중이 그리스도와 함께 죽고 다시 사는 것을 생각나게 하는 부활절기 때 세례를 재확인해 주는 예배를 드리는 것이 적절하다. 그리고 다른 교회에서 교적을 옮겨오는 사람들이 있다면 세례를 재확인해 주는 예배를 드리는 것이 의미 있다.

세례 예문 I

스스로 세례 문답을 할 수 있는
사람들을 위한 예문
유아 세례 확증, 교적이전, 입교식

목사가 세례 받을 사람(들)을 앞에 세울 때에 아래 사항을 참작하도록 한다.
교회 대표가 세례 받을 사람(들)을 소개할 수도 있다.
세례 받은 교인들 중 두 명의 증인을 택하여 세례 받을 사람(들)을 앞으로 인도할 수도 있다.
가족이 다함께 세례 받을 사람(들)을 앞으로 인도한다.

예식사

그리스도 안에서 한 형제자매가 된 성도 여러분,
성경에 교회는 하나님의 집이요,
그리스도는 교회의 머리요,
우리는 그 지체라고 하였습니다.
교회는 말씀을 선포하며, 가르치고, 성례를 행하며,
　성도의 교제와 봉사로 하나님의 뜻을
　이 땅에 이루어야 합니다.
우리는 이 일을 위하여 기도와 시간과 재능과 재물을 바치고
　한 마음 한 뜻이 되어
　힘을 모아 교회를 온전하게 해야 합니다.
또 우리는 우리의 말과 행동으로
　다른 사람들에게 주님의 복음을 전하여
　그들을 주님 앞으로 인도하여야 합니다.
교회는 모든 사람이 필요로 하는
　하나님의 은혜를 베푸는 공동체입니다.

기도

모든 사람이 죄를 범하여 하나님의 영광에 이르지 못하게 되어
우리 구주 예수 그리스도께서 말씀하시기를
　"사람이 물과 성령으로 나지 아니하면 하나님의 나라에 들어갈 수 없다"고
　하셨습니다.

기도합시다.

전능하시고 영원하신 하나님,
세례 받기를 원하여 오늘 이 자리에 서 있는
　성도(들을)를 위하여 기도합니다.

이 성도(들)의 죄를 씻어 주시고,
　성령으로 충만하게 하여 주소서.
주님께서 약속하신 대로 이 사람(들)을 받아 주시고,
　이들이 생명이 다하는 날까지
하나님께 충성을 다할 수 있도록 은혜를 베풀어 주시고,
　주님께서 사랑하는 아들을 통하여 약속하신 영원한 나라에
　이를 수 있도록 항상 인도하여 주소서.
우리 주 예수 그리스도의 이름으로 기도합니다.
아멘.

세례 후보자 소개

목사가 다음과 같이 세례 후보자 이름을 부르며 소개한다.
교회 대표가 다음과 같이 이름을 부르며 소개할 수도 있다.

○○○는 세례 받기를 원합니다.

문답

목사가 세례 받을 사람(들)에게 묻는다.

사랑하는 성도여,
당신(여러분)이 거룩한 세례를 받고자 나왔으니
하나님과 성도들 앞에서 거룩한 세례를 받는 뜻과
세례 받기를 원하는 증거로
이제 내가 온 교회를 대표하여
묻는 말에 대답하시기 바랍니다:

문: 당신(여러분)은 생각과 말과 행동에 있어서
　　하나님의 뜻에 어긋나는 것들을 회개하고,
　　이 세상의 악한 세력을 물리치겠습니까?
답: **예, 그렇게 하겠습니다.**

　　　[혹은, 북쪽, 남쪽, 서쪽과 동쪽을 (제단이 동쪽을 향해 있지 않은 경우에는
　　　제단 쪽을 맨 마지막으로) 향하여 다음과 같이 네 번에 걸쳐 대답하게 한다.
　　　옛 교회 전통에서는 이러한 예식을 행했었다.

　　　하나님의 뜻에 어긋나는 것들을 회개하고,
　　　이 세상의 악한 세력을 버리고
　　　하나님의 뜻에 순종하겠습니다.]

[　] 부분은 경우에 따라 생략이 가능함

문: 당신(여러분)은 하나님께서 주시는 자유와 능력으로
　　남을 억압하는 모든 악한 세력과 불의에 대항하시겠습니까?

답: **예, 그렇게 하겠습니다.**

문: 당신(여러분)은 예수 그리스도가 당신(여러분)의 구세주이심을 믿으며,
　　그의 은혜를 의지하여 국적, 인종, 성별, 연령, 계급의
　　차별 없이 모든 사람을 사랑하신 예수 그리스도를
　　당신의 주님으로 섬기겠습니까?

답: **예, 그렇게 하겠습니다.**

문: 당신(여러분)은 하나님 아버지를 믿습니까?

답: **전능하사 천지를 만드신 하나님 아버지를 믿습니다.**

문: 당신(여러분)은 예수 그리스도를 믿습니까?

답: **하나님의 외아들 우리 주 예수 그리스도를 믿습니다.**
　　[이는 성령으로 잉태하사 동정녀 마리아에게 나시고,
　　본디오 빌라도에게 고난을 받으사,
　　십자가에 못박혀 죽으시고,
　　장사되어 죽은 자들에게 내려가셨다가
　　사흘만에 다시 살아나시며,
　　하늘에 오르사, 전능하신 하나님 우편에 앉아 계시다가,
　　저리로서 산 자와 죽은 자를 심판하러 오시는 분이심을
　　믿습니다.]

문: 당신(여러분)은 성령을 믿습니까?

답: **성령을 믿습니다.**
　　[거룩한 공회와, 성도가 서로 교통하는 것과
　　죄를 사하여 주시는 것과,
　　몸이 다시 사는 것과, 영원히 사는 것을 믿습니다.]

문: 당신(여러분)은 성경을 정기적으로 읽으며 성경의 가르침에 따라
　　신앙생활을 하시겠습니까?

답: **예, 그렇게 하겠습니다.**

성별의 기도

이 시간에 목사가 물을 회중이 볼 수 있도록 세례대에 따르고, 다음과 같이 기도한다.

기도합시다.

영원하신 창조주 하나님,
　　태초에 땅이 혼돈하고 공허하며 어두움이 깊을 때에,
　　하나님께서는 어두움을 몰아내시고 빛을 창조하셨습니다.

공의로 심판하시는 하나님,
노아 시대에 물로 심판하실 때에
   노아의 방주를 통해 구원하시고
   홍수 후에 무지개를 보여주셔서
   약속의 증표로 삼으셨습니다.
당신의 구속된 백성들을
당신께서는 이스라엘 백성들이 애굽에서
   노예로 고통을 당할 때에도,
   그들에게 자유를 주시기 위하여
   홍해를 갈라 인도하셨고,
   요단 강을 건너 약속의 땅에 이르게 하셨습니다.
하나님께서는 때가 차매 그의 아들 예수를 보내시어
   어머니의 태 안에서 자라게 하셨습니다.
그는 세례 요한에게서 물로 세례를 받으시고
   성령을 충만하게 받으셨습니다.
예수께서는 제자들을 부르시고
   그들로 하여금 그의 세례와 죽음과 부활을 증거하고
   모든 족속을 제자로 삼아
   아버지와 아들과 성령의 이름으로
   세례를 베풀라 하셨습니다.
주님의 영을 부으셔서 이 물을 성별하시고
   그 물로 우리의 모든 죄를 씻어주시고
   우리의 삶이 의의 옷을 입게 하소서.
그리하여 그리스도와 함께 죽고, 그리스도와 함께 부활하여
   최후의 승리에 임하게 하소서.

세례

목사가 세례 후보자에게 물을 세 번 끼얹으며 다음과 같이 말한다.

○○○, 내가 성부와 성자와 성령의 이름으로 세례를 주노라.
아멘.

세례를 베풀고 세례 받은 이의 머리에 손을 얹은 후, 목사가 다음과 같이 말한다.

성령이여,
이 시간 물과 성령으로 세례를 받아
   새롭게 당신의 자녀가 된 ○○○에게 임하시어
   예수 그리스도의 진실한 제자가 되게 하소서.
아멘.

입교식 예문

세례 예식이 있은 후, 목사가 교적을 옮겨온 교인이나, 오늘 세례 받은 사람이나, 전에 세례를 받았으나 입교를 하지 않고 있다가 오늘 입교하려는 사람(들)의 이름을 불러 앞에 세우고 소개한다.

000는 _____교회에서 교적을 옮겨왔습니다.
000는 입교인이 되기를 원합니다.

연합감리교회로 교적이전

다른 교단에서 연합감리교회로 교적을 옮겨오는 사람이 있으면,
목사가 이 시간에 소개하며 말한다.

문: 그리스도께서 세우신 교회의 일원으로서,
연합감리교회에 충성을 다하며,
연합감리교회의 장정을 지키고,
연합감리교회가 하는 사역에 적극 참여하겠습니까?
답: **예, 그렇게 하겠습니다.**

개체교회에 등록

다른 연합감리교회에서 교적을 옮겨오는 사람이나,
세례를 통해서 입교인이 되는 사람(들)에게 목사가 말한다.

문: 당신(여러분)은 우리 교회의 장정과 성례를 지키고,
기도와 재물과 시간과 재능을 바쳐 그리스도께서 세우신
교회를 위하여 교인된 의무를 힘써 다하겠습니까?
답: **예, 제가 그렇게 하겠습니다.**

환영

목사가 세례 받고 입교인이 된 사람(들로)으로 하여금 회중을 향하게 한다.
그리고 회중으로 하여금 입교인(들)을 환영하도록 한다.

목사가 회중에게 말한다:
하나님 안에서 한 식구가 된 여러분,
이 성도(들을)를 여러분이 사랑하여 주시고
보살펴 주기 바랍니다.
이 성도(들)의 믿음이 자라나고,
이 성도(들이)가 바라는 소망이 확증되며,
사랑 안에서 온전해질 수 있도록
힘이 닿는 데까지 도와주시기 바랍니다.

회중으로 하여금 입교인(들)을 환영하도록 한다.

우리는 하나님께서 여러분에게 주신
  모든 것을 감사드립니다.
그리고 그리스도인의 한 사람으로
  여러분을 환영합니다.
우리는 그리스도의 몸된 연합감리교회
  회중의 한 일원으로서 신앙생활을 하면서
  기도와 재물과 시간과 재능을 바쳐
  교회의 선교를 위하여 함께 봉사하면서
예수 그리스도의 이름으로
  하나님께 영광 돌리는 일에
  적극 참여할 것을 새롭게 다짐합니다.

축도

그리스도 안에서 여러분을 부르사
자기의 영원한 영광에 들어가게 하신 이가
잠깐 고난을 당한 여러분을
친히 온전하게 하시며 굳건하게 하시며
강하게 하시며 터를 견고하게 하시고
그리스도 안에 있는 여러분에게
은혜와 평강이 늘 있게 하시기를 축원합니다.
                    (베드로전서 5:10 참조)

목사가 세례 받은 이(들)에게 세례증서를 주고, 교회 대표들이 나와서
세례 받은 이와 가족을 환영한다.

찬송

다음 예배 순서로 연결한다.

유아 세례 확증 예문
(견신례)

목사가 유아 세례 확증 예식에 참여할 젊은이들을 불러 앞에 세우고 회중을 향하여 말한다.

예식사

사랑하는 성도 여러분,
이 젊은이(들은)는 유아 세례를 받은 후,
성장하여 교회의 한 지체가 되려고
특별히 마련된 교육과 훈련을 통해
　세례 받을 때에 우리에게 주셨던 언약을
　새롭게 재확인하였습니다.
그리고 하나님께서 우리를 위하여
　지금도 역사하고 계심을 고백하였습니다.

교회는 하나님의 집이요,
그리스도는 교회의 머리요,
우리는 그 지체입니다.
교회는 말씀을 선포하며, 가르치고, 성례를 행하며
　성도의 교제와 봉사로 하나님의 뜻을
　이 땅에 이루어야 합니다.
우리는 이 일을 위하여 재물을 바치고
한 마음 한 뜻이 되어
　힘을 모아 교회를 온전하게 해야 합니다.
또 우리는 우리의 말과 행동으로
　다른 사람들에게 주님의 복음을 전하여
　그들을 주님 앞으로 인도하여야 합니다.
여러분은 이 일을 위하여
기도하여 주시기 바랍니다.

유아 세례 확증 후보자 소개

목사나 혹은 교회 대표가 다음과 같이 이름을 부르며 소개한다.

000는 유아 세례 확증 예식을 통해 입교인이 되기를 원합니다.

[기도]

[ ] 부분은 경우에 따라 생략이 가능함

[은혜로우신 하나님,
이 젊은이(들)의 가정을 주님께서 축복하시어
　저들로 하여금 어려서부터 주님을 알게 하시고,
　세례를 받게 한 후, 지금까지 주님의 사랑과 은혜로
　인도하여 주심을 감사드립니다.
주님께서 이 젊은이(들)의 지나간 날들을 지켜주신 것 같이
　앞으로도 돌보아 주셔서 이 성도(들이)가 성장할수록
　주님의 신실한 자녀가 되게 하시고, 믿음으로 모든 유혹을
　물리칠 수 있는 온전한 그리스도인이 되게 하소서.
예수 그리스도의 이름으로 기도합니다.　**아멘.**]

문답

목사가 세례 받고 유아 세례 확증(견신례)을 통하여 입교할 젊은이(들)에게 다음에 있는 질문이나,
[ ] 안에 있는 질문을 더 첨가하여 묻는다.

당신(여러분)은 거룩한 세례를 받은 후, 특별히 마련된 훈련을 통하여
우리 교회에 입교하고자 나왔습니다.
하나님과 교우들 앞에서 거룩한 세례를 받은 뜻을 기억하며
우리 교회에 입교하기를 약속하는 증거로
묻는 말에 대답하시기 바랍니다:

문:　당신(여러분)은 하나님과 회중 앞에서 세례 받을 때에 서약하고
　　약속했던 것을 다시 새롭게 서약하고 약속하시겠습니까?
답:　**예, 그렇게 하겠습니다.**

문:　당신(여러분)은 진정으로 죄를 회개합니까?
답:　**예, 회개합니다.**

[문:　당신(여러분)은 생각과 말과 행동에 있어서
　　하나님의 뜻에 어긋나는 것들을 회개하고,
　　이 세상의 악한 세력을 물리치겠습니까?
답:　**예, 그렇게 하겠습니다.**

문:　당신(여러분)은 하나님께서 주시는 자유와 능력으로
　　남을 억압하는 모든 악한 세력과 불의에 대항하시겠습니까?
답:　**예, 그렇게 하겠습니다.**

문:　당신(여러분)은 예수 그리스도가 당신(여러분)의 구세주이심을
　　믿으며, 그의 은혜를 의지하여 국적, 인종, 성별, 연령, 계급의
　　차별 없이 모든 사람을 사랑하신 예수 그리스도를
　　당신(여러분)의 주님으로 섬기겠습니까?
답:　**예, 그렇게 하겠습니다.**]

문: 당신(여러분)은 하나님 아버지를 믿습니까?
답: **전능하사 천지를 만드신 하나님 아버지를 믿습니다.**

문: 당신(여러분)은 예수 그리스도를 믿습니까?
답: **하나님의 외아들 우리 주 예수 그리스도이심을 믿습니다.**
　　[이는 성령으로 잉태하사 동정녀 마리아에게 나시고,
　　본디오 빌라도에게 고난을 받으사, 십자가에 못박혀 죽으시고,
　　장사되어 죽은 자들에게 내려가셨다가
　　사흘만에 다시 살아나시며,
　　하늘에 오르사, 전능하신 하나님 우편에 앉아 계시다가,
　　저리로서 산 자와 죽은 자를 심판하러 오시는 분이심을 믿습니다.]

문: 당신(여러분)은 성령을 믿습니까?
답: **성령을 믿습니다.**
　　[거룩한 공회와, 성도가 서로 교통하는 것과
　　죄를 사하여 주시는 것과, 몸이 다시 사는 것과,
　　영원히 사는 것을 믿습니다.]

유아 세례 확증 (견신례) 후보자 머리에 손을 얹은 후 목사가 다음과 같이 말한다:

OOO 군/양,
하나님께서 OOO를 은혜로 보호해 주시기를 원하며,
예수님을 따르는 모든 신실한 성도들의 믿음과
교제 안에서 성령의 이름으로 유아 세례 확증 예식(견신례)을 행합니다.

연합감리교회로 교적이전

다른 교단에서 연합감리교회로 교적을 옮겨오는 사람이 있으면,
목사가 이 시간에 소개하며 말한다.

문: 그리스도께서 세우신 교회의 일원으로서,
　　연합감리교회에 충성을 다하며,
　　연합감리교회의 장정을 지키고,
　　연합감리교회가 하는 사역에 적극 참여하겠습니까?
답: **예, 그렇게 하겠습니다.**

개체교회에 등록

문: 당신(여러분)은 우리 교회의 장정과 성례를 지키고,
　　기도와 재물과 시간과 재능을 바쳐
　　그리스도께서 모든 사람을 위하여 세우신
　　교회를 위하여 교인된 의무를 힘써 다하겠습니까?
답: **예, 교인된 의무를 힘써 다하겠습니다.**

환영

목사가 회중에게 말한다:

하나님 안에서 한 식구가 되신 여러분,
이 젊은이(들을)를 여러분들이 사랑하여 주시고
　보살펴 주시기 바랍니다.
이 젊은이(들)의 믿음이 자라나고,
　바라는 소망이 확증되며, 사랑 안에서 온전해질 수 있도록
　힘이 닿는 데까지 도와주시기 바랍니다.

회중이 응답한다:

우리는 하나님께서 여러분에게 주신
　모든 것을 감사드립니다.
그리고 그리스도인의 사랑으로 여러분을 환영합니다.
우리는 그리스도의 몸된 연합감리교회 회중의 한 일원으로
　신앙생활을 하면서
기도와 재물과 시간과 재능을 바쳐
교회의 선교를 위하여 함께 봉사하고
예수 그리스도의 이름으로 하나님께 영광 돌리는 일에
적극 참여할 것을 새롭게 다짐합니다.

축도

성부 성자 성령의 하나님께서
영원토록 축복하여 주시고, 보살펴 주시고,
지켜 주시기를 축원합니다.

목사와 교회 대표들이 앞에 나와 견신례 받은 젊은이들을 환영한다.

CONCERNING THE SERVICE OF
THE BAPTISMAL COVENANT

The Baptismal Covenant is God's word to us, proclaiming our adoption by grace, and our word to God promising our response of faith and love. Those within the covenant constitute the community we call the church; therefore, the services of the Baptismal Covenant are conducted during the public worship of the congregation where the person's membership is to be held, except in very limited circumstances. These services are best placed in the order of worship as a response following the reading of Scripture and its exposition in the sermon.

Persons of any age are suitable candidates. Infants and others unable to take the vows for themselves are presented by parents and/or sponsors. There may also be sponsors when candidates can speak for themselves. Parents or sponsors should be members of Christ's holy church.

In case of emergency the essential acts in baptism are the vows and the baptism with water in the name of the Father, and of the Son, and of the Holy Spirit. A candidate baptized outside of a congregational worship service should, if possible, be presented at a later time to the congregation.

Those baptized before they are old enough to take the vows for themselves make their personal profession of faith in the service called confirmation. Those who are able to take the vows for themselves at their baptism are not confirmed, for they have made their public profession of faith at the font.

After confirmation, or after baptism when candidates take the vows for themselves, Christians are encouraged to reaffirm the Baptismal Covenant from time to time. Such reaffirmation is not, however, to be understood as the Sacrament of Baptism. Baptism is not administered to any person more than once, for while our baptismal vows are less than reliable, God's promise to us in the sacrament is steadfast.

Reaffirmation of the Baptismal Covenant is particularly appropriate by an entire congregation at Easter, which recalls our death and resurrection with Christ. It is also especially appropriate for persons who are transferring into a congregation.

THE BAPTISMAL COVENANT I

HOLY BAPTISM
FOR THOSE WHO CAN ANSWER FOR THEMSELVES
CONFIRMATION,
RECEPTION INTO THE UNITED METHODIST CHURCH,
RECEPTION INTO A LOCAL CONGREGATION

INTRODUCTION TO THE SERVICE

The pastor makes the following statement to the congregation:

The church is of God,
and will be preserved to the end of time,
for the conduct of worship and the due administration of
    God's Word and Sacraments,
the maintenance of Christian fellowship and discipline,
the edification of believers, and the conversion of the world.
All, of every age and station, stand in need of the means of grace
    which it alone supplies.

PRAYER FOR THOSE TO BE BAPTIZED

Forasmuch as all have sinned
    and fallen short of the glory of God, our Christ said,
    "Unless one is born of water and the Spirit,
    one cannot enter the kingdom of God."

Let us pray.

Almighty and everlasting God,
we call upon you for these your *servants*,
that *they*, coming to your holy baptism,
    may receive remission of *their* sins
    and be filled with the Holy Spirit.
Receive *them*, O Lord,
    as you have promised by your well-beloved Son,
and grant that *they* may be faithful to you
    all the days of *their lives*,
and finally come to the eternal kingdom
    which you have promised;
through Jesus Christ our Lord. **Amen.**

PRESENTATION OF CANDIDATES

A representative of the congregation presents the candidate with the appropriate statement:

I present *Name(s)* for baptism.

RENUNCIATION OF SIN AND PROFESSION OF FAITH

The pastor addresses candidates:

On behalf of the whole church, I ask you:
Do you renounce the spiritual forces of wickedness,
   reject the evil powers of this world,
   and repent of your sin?
I **do.**

Do you accept the freedom and power God gives you
   to resist evil, injustice, and oppression
   in whatever forms they present themselves?
I **do.**

Do you confess Jesus Christ as your Savior,
put your whole trust in his grace,
and promise to serve him as your Lord,
in union with the church which Christ has opened
   to people of all ages, nations, and races?
I **do.**

Do you believe in God the Father?
I **believe in God, the Father Almighty,**
   Creator of heaven and earth.

Do you believe in Jesus Christ?
I **believe in Jesus Christ, his only Son, our Lord,**
   [who was conceived by the Holy Spirit,
   born of the Virgin Mary, suffered under Pontius Pilate,
   was crucified, died, and was buried;
   he descended to the dead.
   On the third day he rose again;
   he ascended into heaven,
   is seated at the right hand of the Father,
   and will come again to judge the living and the dead.]

[ ] means optional

Do you believe in the Holy Spirit?
I believe in the Holy Spirit,
[the holy catholic church, the communion of saints,
the forgiveness of sins, the resurrection of the body,
and the life everlasting.]

Do you receive and profess the Christian faith
as contained in the Scriptures of the Old and New Testaments?
I do.

THANKSGIVING OVER THE WATER

The water may be poured into the font at this time, and the following prayer is offered:

Let us pray.

Eternal Father,
When nothing existed but chaos,
you swept across the dark waters
and brought forth light.
In the days of Noah
you saved those on the ark through water.
After the flood you set in the clouds a rainbow.
When you saw your people as slaves in Egypt,
you led them to freedom through the sea.
Their children you brought through the Jordan
to the land which you promised.
In the fullness of time you sent Jesus,
nurtured in the water of a womb.
He was baptized by John and anointed by your Spirit.
He called his disciples to share
in the baptism of his death and resurrection
and to make disciples of all nations.

Pour out your Holy Spirit,
to bless this gift of water and *those* who *receive* it,
to wash away *their* sin
and clothe *them* in righteousness throughout *their lives*,
that, dying and being raised with Christ,
they may share in his final victory.
Amen.

[ ] means optional

BAPTISM WITH LAYING ON OF HANDS

As each candidate is baptized, the pastor says:

Name, I baptize you in the name of the Father,
and of the Son, and of the Holy Spirit. **Amen.**

As the pastor, and others if desired, place hands on the head of each person
who has been baptized, the pastor says to each:

Name, the Lord defend you with his heavenly grace
and by his Spirit confirm you in the faith and fellowship
of all true disciples of Jesus Christ.
Amen.

RECEPTION INTO THE UNITED METHODIST CHURCH
RECEPTION INTO A LOCAL CONGREGATION

PRESENTATION OF CANDIDATES

The pastor or a representative of the congregation presents the candidate with
the appropriate statements:

I present *Name(s)* who come(s) to this congregation of
The United Methodist Church from the _____Church.
I present *Name(s)* who want(s) to join this congregation.

RECEPTION INTO THE UNITED METHODIST CHURCH

If there are persons coming into membership in The United Methodist Church from other
denominations who have not yet been presented, they may be presented at this time,
and the pastor may say:

As members of Christ's universal church,
will you be loyal to The United Methodist Church,
and do all in your power to strengthen its ministries?
I will.

RECEPTION INTO THE LOCAL CONGREGATION

If there are persons joining this congregation from other United Methodist
congregations who have not yet been presented, they may be presented at
this time.

The pastor addresses all those transferring membership into the congregation
and those who have just professed their own faith through baptism:

As members of this congregation,
will you faithfully participate in its ministries
by your prayers, your presence,
your gifts, and your service?
I will.

COMMENDATION AND WELCOME

The pastor addresses the congregation:

Members of the household of God,
I commend these persons to your love and care.
Do all in your power to increase their faith,
confirm their hope, and perfect them in love.

The congregation responds:

**We give thanks for all
that God has already given you
and we welcome you in Christian love.
As members together with you
in the body of Christ
and in this congregation of The United Methodist Church,
we renew our covenant faithfully to participate
in the ministries of the church
by our prayers, our presence, our gifts, and our service,
that in everything God may be glorified
through Jesus Christ.**

The pastor addresses those received:

The God of all grace, who has called us to eternal glory in Christ,
establish you and strengthen you by the power of the Holy Spirit
that you may live in grace and peace.
Amen.

Appropriate thanksgivings and intercessions for those who have participated in these acts should be included in the concerns and prayers that follow.

It is most fitting that the service continue with Holy Communion, in which the union of the new members with the body of Christ is most fully expressed. The new members may receive first.

Or the service may continue with the next act of worship.

CONFIRMATION

INTRODUCTION TO THE SERVICE

The pastor makes the following statement to the congregation:

Through confirmation,
   we renew the covenant declared at our baptism,
   acknowledge what God is doing for us,
   and affirm our commitment to Christ's holy church.

The pastor may add:

The church is of God,
and will be preserved to the end of time,
for the conduct of worship and the due administration of
   God's Word and sacraments,
the maintenance of Christian fellowship and discipline,
the edification of believers,
and the conversion of the world.
All, of every age and station,
   stand in need of the means of grace
   which it alone supplies.

PRESENTATION OF CANDIDATES

The pastor or a representative of the congregation presents the candidate
with the appropriate statement:

I present *Name(s)* for confirmation.

RENUNCIATION OF SIN AND PROFESSION OF FAITH

The pastor may use the following questions or/and the questions included in the bracket:

On behalf of the whole church, I ask you:

Do you in the presence of God and this congregation
renew the solemn vow and promise made at your baptism?
I do.

Do you truly and earnestly repent of your sins?
I do.

[Do you renounce the spiritual forces of wickedness,
  reject the evil powers of this world,
  and repent of your sin?
I do.

Do you accept the freedom and power God gives you
  to resist evil, injustice, and oppression
  in whatever forms they present themselves?
I do.

Do you confess Jesus Christ as your Savior,
put your whole trust in his grace,
and promise to serve him as your Lord,
in union with the church which Christ has opened
  to people of all ages, nations, and races?
I do.]

Do you believe in God the Father?
**I believe in God, the Father Almighty,
  creator of heaven and earth.**

Do you believe in Jesus Christ?
**I believe in Jesus Christ, his only Son, our Lord,
  [who was conceived by the Holy Spirit,
  born of the Virgin Mary,
  suffered under Pontius Pilate, was crucified, died,
  and was buried; he descended to the dead.
  On the third day he rose again;
  he ascended into heaven,
  is seated at the right hand of the Father,
  and will come again to judge the living and the dead.]**

Do you believe in the Holy Spirit?
**I believe in the Holy Spirit,
  [the holy catholic church,
  the communion of saints,
  the forgiveness of sins,
  the resurrection of the body,
  and the life everlasting.]**

[ ] means optional

LAYING ON OF HANDS

As the pastor, and others if desired, place hands on the head of each person
who is being confirmed, the pastor says to each:

Name, the Lord defend you with his heavenly grace
and by his Spirit confirm you
  in the faith and fellowship
  of all true disciples of Jesus Christ.
Amen.

RECEPTION INTO THE UNITED METHODIST CHURCH

The pastor, addressing the people, may say:

Let those persons
  who are members of other communions
  in Christ's holy church,
and who now desire to enter
  into the fellowship of this congregation,
present themselves
  to be received into the membership
  of The United Methodist Church.

As *members* of Christ's universal church,
will you be loyal to The United Methodist Church,
and do all in your power to strengthen its ministries?
I will.

RECEPTION INTO THE LOCAL CONGREGATION

As members of this congregation,
will you faithfully participate in its ministries
  by your prayers, your presence,
  your gifts, and your service?
I will.

COMMENDATION AND WELCOME

Members of the household of God,
I commend *this person (these persons)*
  to your love and care.
Do all in your power to increase *their* faith,
confirm *their* hope, and perfect *them* in love.

The congregation responds:

We give thanks
for all that God has already given you
and we welcome you in Christian love.
As members together with you
in the body of Christ and in this congregation
of The United Methodist Church,
we renew our covenant faithfully
to participate in the ministries of the church
by our prayers, our presence,
our gifts, and our service,
that in everything God may be glorified
through Jesus Christ.

The pastor addresses those confirmed:

God the Father,
God the Son,
and God the Holy Spirit
bless, preserve, and keep you,
now and for evermore.
Amen.

세례 예문 II

스스로 세례 문답을
할 수 없는 사람들이나
혹은 유아를 위한 예문

목사가 세례 받을 유아(들을)를 앞에 세울 때에 아래 사항을 참작하도록 한다.
교회 대표가 세례 받을 유아를 소개할 수 있다.
세례 받은 교인들 중 두 명의 증인을 택하여 세례 받을 유아를 부모와 가족과
  (혹은 보호자와) 함께 앞으로 인도할 수 있다.
부모(혹은 보호자)가 세례 받을 유아를 데리고 앞으로 나온다.

예식사

목사가 회중을 향하여 다음과 같이 말한다:

그리스도 안에서 한 형제자매가 된 성도 여러분,
우리는 성례전인 세례를 통하여
  그리스도의 거룩한 교회의 새 가족으로 인정을 받습니다.
그리고 우리는 물과 성령의 세례를 통하여
  전능하신 하나님의 구원의 역사에 참여하며
  새 삶을 얻게 됩니다.
이 모든 것은 값없이 주시는 하나님의 선물입니다.

[기도]

[목사가 다음과 같이 기도한다:

전능하신 하나님,
주의 사랑하는 독생자 예수 그리스도로 말미암아
  우리에게 명하시어 온 세상에 나아가
  모든 백성으로 제자를 삼아
  아버지와 아들과 성령의 이름으로
  세례를 주라 하셨습니다.
지금 주께 간구하오니
  주의 무한하신 자비와 은혜로
이 아이(들을)를 돌보시고 구원하사
믿음에 굳게 서고 소망 중에 즐거워하며
사랑에 뿌리를 내림으로 모든 악을 이기게 하소서.
예수 그리스도의 이름으로 기도합니다. **아멘.**]

[ ] 부분은 경우에 따라 생략이 가능함

[성경]

목사가 다음의 성경말씀 중에서 한두 구절을 읽는다.

[어린 아이들이 내게 오는 것을 용납하고 금하지 말라
　하나님의 나라가 이런 자의 것이니라 (마가복음 10:14).

삼가 이 작은 자 중의 하나도 업신여기지 말라
　너희에게 말하노니 그들의 천사들이 하늘에서
　하늘에 계신 내 아버지의 얼굴을 항상 뵈옵느니라
　　　　　　　　　　　　　　(마태복음 18:10).

아비들아 너희 자녀를 노엽게 하지 말고
　오직 주의 교훈과 훈계로 양육하라 (에베소서 6:4).]

세례 후보자 소개

목사가 세례 받을 후보자의 이름을 부르며 소개한다.
교회 대표(혹은 중인, 보호자)가 세례 받을 후보자(들)의 이름을 부르며
　소개할 수도 있다.

오늘 000가 세례를 받습니다.

문답

목사가 세례 받을 아이(들)의 부모나 보호자(들)에게 묻는다.

사랑하는 여러분,
여러분들은 오늘 000에게 세례 베풀기를 원합니다.
하나님께 이 아이를 바쳐 주님의 교훈을 가르치기를 결심하는 뜻으로
하나님과 성도들 앞에서 이제 내가 온 교회를 대표하여
묻는 말에 대답하시기 바랍니다:

문: 당신(여러분)은 생각과 말과 행동에 있어서
　　하나님의 뜻에 어긋나는 것들을 회개하고,
　　이 세상의 악한 세력을 물리치겠습니까?
답: **예, 그렇게 하겠습니다.**

　　[혹은, 북쪽, 남쪽, 서쪽과 동쪽을 (제단이 동쪽을 향해 있지 않은 경우에는
　　제단 쪽을 맨 마지막으로) 향하여 다음과 같이 네 번에 걸쳐 대답하게 한다.
　　옛 교회 전통에서는 이러한 예식을 행했다.

　　하나님의 뜻에 어긋나는 것들을 회개하고,
　　이 세상의 악한 세력을 버리고
　　하나님의 뜻에 순종하겠습니다.]

[ ] 부분은 경우에 따라 생략이 가능함

문: 당신(여러분)은 하나님께서 주시는 자유와 능력으로
남을 억압하는 모든 악한 세력과 불의에 대항하시겠습니까?

답: **예, 그렇게 하겠습니다.**

문: 당신(여러분)은 예수 그리스도가 여러분의 구세주이심을 믿으며,
그의 은혜를 의지하여 국적, 인종, 성별, 연령, 계급의 차별 없이
모든 사람을 사랑하신 예수 그리스도를
당신(여러분)의 주님으로 섬기시겠습니까?

답: **예, 그렇게 하겠습니다.**

문: 당신(여러분)은 이 아이(들이)가 자라는 동안 그리스도의 몸된 교회 안에서
이 성례의 뜻을 가르치고, 성경을 읽고 기도하며,
예배에 참여하는 것과 그리스도인의 생활에 대하여
몸소 행하여 가르치시겠습니까?

답: **예, 그렇게 하겠습니다.**

문: 당신(여러분)은 하나님 아버지를 믿습니까?

답: **전능하사 천지를 만드신 하나님 아버지를 믿습니다.**

문: 당신(여러분)은 예수 그리스도를 믿습니까?

답: **하나님의 외아들 우리 주 예수 그리스도를 믿습니다.**
[성령으로 잉태하사 동정녀 마리아에게 나시고,
본디오 빌라도에게 고난을 받으사, 십자가에 못박혀 죽으시고,
장사되어 죽은 자들에게 내려가셨다가
사흘만에 다시 살아나시며,
하늘에 오르사, 전능하신 하나님 우편에 앉아 계시다가,
저리로서 산 자와 죽은 자를
심판하러 오시는 분이심을 믿습니다.]

문: 당신(여러분)은 성령을 믿습니까?

답: **성령을 믿습니다.**
[거룩한 공회와, 성도가 서로 교통하는 것과
죄를 사하여 주시는 것과, 몸이 다시 사는 것과,
영원히 사는 것을 믿습니다.]

목사가 회중에게 묻는다.

문: 여러분은 이 아이(들이)가 그리스도인의 신앙 안에서
성장할 수 있도록 돌보시겠습니까?

답: **우리들은 사랑과 용서하는 공동체로서**
이 아이(들이)가 하나님을 사랑하고
이웃을 사랑하며 교회생활을 충실히 할 수 있도록
사랑하고 용서하는 공동체로서 돌보겠습니다.

성별의 기도

이 시간에 목사가 물을 회중이 볼 수 있도록 세례대에 따르고, 다음과 같이 기도한다.

기도합시다.

영원하신 창조주 하나님,
　태초에 땅이 혼돈하고 공허하며
　어두움이 깊을 때에,
　하나님께서는 어두움을 몰아내시고
　빛을 창조하셨습니다.
공의로 심판하시는 하나님,
노아 시대에 물로 심판하실 때에
　노아의 방주를 통해 구원하시고
　홍수 후에 무지개를 보여주셔서
　약속의 증표로 삼으셨습니다.
당신께서는 이스라엘 백성들이 애굽에서
　노예로 고통을 당할 때에도,
　그들에게 자유를 주시기 위하여
　홍해를 갈라 인도하셨고,
　요단 강을 건너 약속의 땅에 이르게 하셨습니다.
하나님께서는 때가 차매 그의 아들 예수를 보내시어
　　어머니의 태 안에서 자라게 하셨습니다.
그는 세례 요한에게서 물로 세례를 받으시고
　성령을 충만하게 받으셨습니다.
예수께서는 제자들을 부르시고
　그들로 하여금 그의 세례와 죽음과 부활을 증거하고
　모든 족속을 제자로 삼아 아버지와 아들과 성령의
　이름으로 세례를 베풀라 하셨습니다.
주님의 영을 부으셔서 이 물을 성별하시고
　그 물로 우리의 모든 죄를 씻어주시고
　우리의 삶이 의의 옷을 입게 하소서.
그리하여 그리스도와 함께 죽고,
　그리스도와 함께 부활하여
　최후의 승리에 임하게 하소서.

세례

목사가 세례 후보자에게 물을 세 번 끼얹으며 다음과 같이 말한다.

OOO, 내가 성부와 성자와 성령의 이름으로 세례를 주노라.
아멘.

세례를 베풀고 세례 받은 이의 머리에 손을 끼얹은 후, 목사와 이 세례 예식에 참여하도록 초청
받은 이들이 손을 얹은 후 목사가 다음과 같이 말한다:

성령이여, 이 시간 물과 성령으로 세례를 받아
새롭게 당신의 자녀가 된 OOO에게 임하시어
예수 그리스도의 진실한 제자가 되게 하소서.
아멘.

세례를 베푼 후, 목사가 세례 받은 아이(들)로 하여금 회중을 향하게 한다.
그리고 회중으로 하여금 세례 받은 아이(들을)를 환영하도록 한다.

우리는 하나님께서 여러분에게 주신
모든 것을 위하여 감사드립니다.
그리고 그리스도인의 한 사람으로 여러분을 환영합니다.
우리는 그리스도의 몸된 연합감리교회
회중의 한 일원으로서 신앙생활을 하면서
기도와 재물과 시간과 재능을 바쳐
교회의 선교를 위하여 함께 봉사하면서
예수 그리스도의 이름으로 하나님께 영광 돌리는 일에
적극 참여할 것을 새롭게 다짐합니다.

축도

그리스도 안에서 여러분을 부르사
자기의 영원한 영광에 들어가게 하신 이가
잠깐 고난을 당한 여러분을 친히 온전하게 하시며
굳건하게 하시며 강하게 하시어
그리스도 안에 있는 여러분에게
은혜와 평강이 늘 있게 하시기를 축원합니다.
(베드로전서 5:10 참조)

목사가 세례 받은 이(들)에게 세례증서를 주고, 교회 대표들이 나와서 세례 받은 이와 가족을 환영한다.

찬송

다음 예배 순서로 연결한다.

THE BAPTISMAL COVENANT II

HOLY BAPTISM
FOR CHILDREN AND OTHERS UNABLE TO ANSWER FOR THEMSELVES

This service is to be used only when children or others unable to take the vows themselves are being baptized, and when there is not a youth or adult baptism, confirmation, or reaffirmation of faith.

INTRODUCTION TO THE SERVICE

As persons are coming forward, an appropriate hymn of baptism may be sung. The pastor makes the following statement to the congregation:

Brothers and sisters in Christ:
Through the Sacrament of Baptism
  we are initiated into Christ's holy church.
We are incorporated into God's mighty acts of salvation
  and given new birth through water and the Spirit.
All this is God's gift, offered to us without price.

PRESENTATION OF CANDIDATES

The pastor or a representative of the congregation presents the candidates:

I present *Name(s)* for baptism.

RENUNCIATION OF SIN AND PROFESSION OF FAITH

The pastor addresses parents or other sponsors:

On behalf of the whole church, I ask you:
Do you renounce the spiritual forces of wickedness,
  reject the evil powers of this world,
  and repent of your sin?
I **do.**

Do you accept the freedom
  and power God gives you
    to resist evil, injustice, and oppression
    in whatever forms they present themselves?
I **do.**

Do you confess Jesus Christ as your Savior,
put your whole trust in his grace,
and promise to serve him as your Lord,
in union with the church which Christ has opened
    to people of all ages, nations, and races?
I do.

Will you nurture *this child (these children, persons)*
   in Christ's holy church,
that by your teaching and example *he* or *she (they)* may be guided
  to accept God's grace for *himself* or *herself* (*themselves*),
  to profess *his* or *her (their)* faith openly,
  and to lead a Christian life?
I will.

Do you believe in God the Father?
I believe in God, the Father Almighty,
  creator of heaven and earth.

Do you believe in Jesus Christ?
I believe in Jesus Christ, his only Son, our Lord,
  [who was conceived by the Holy Spirit,
  born of the Virgin Mary,
  suffered under Pontius Pilate,
  was crucified, died, and was buried;
  he descended to the dead.
  On the third day he rose again;
  he ascended into heaven,
  is seated at the right hand of the Father,
  and will come again to judge the living
    and the dead.]

Do you believe in the Holy Spirit?
I believe in the Holy Spirit,
  [the holy catholic church,
  the communion of saints,
  the forgiveness of sins,
  the resurrection of the body,
  and the life everlasting.]

[ ] means optional

The pastor addresses the congregation:

Will you nurture one another in the Christian faith and life
and include *these persons* now before you in your care?

**With God's help we will proclaim the good news
and live according to the example of Christ.
We will surround *these persons*
with a community of love and forgiveness,
that *they* may grow in *their* service to others.
We will pray for *them*,
that *they* may be true disciples
who walk in the way that leads to life.**

THANKSGIVING OVER THE WATER

The water may be poured into the font at this time, and the following prayer offered:.

Let us pray.

Eternal Father:
When nothing existed but chaos,
you swept across the dark waters and brought forth light.
In the days of Noah
you saved those on the ark through water,
After the flood you set in the clouds a rainbow.
When you saw your people as slaves in Egypt,
you led them to freedom through the sea.
Their children you brought through the Jordan
to the land which you promised.
In the fullness of time you sent Jesus,
nurtured in the water of a womb.
He was baptized by John and anointed by your Spirit.
He called his disciples
to share in the baptism of his death and resurrection
and to make disciples of all nations.

Pour out your Holy Spirit,
to bless this gift of water and *those* who *receive* it,
to wash away *their* sin and clothe *them* in righteousness
throughout *their lives*,
that, dying and being raised with Christ,
they may share in his final victory.   **Amen.**

BAPTISM WITH LAYING ON OF HANDS

As each candidate is baptized, the pastor says:

Name, I baptize you in the name of the Father,
and of the Son,
and of the Holy Spirit.
Amen.

Immediately after the administration of the water, the pastor, and others if desired,
place hands on the head of each candidate, as the pastor says to each:

The Holy Spirit work within you,
that being born through water and the Spirit
you may be a faithful disciple of Jesus Christ.
Amen.

When all candidates have been baptized, the pastor invites the congregation to
welcome them:

Now it is our joy to welcome
our new *sisters and brothers* in Christ.

Through baptism
you are incorporated by the Holy Spirit
into God's new creation
and made to share in Christ's royal priesthood.
We are all one in Christ Jesus.
With joy and thanksgiving we welcome you
as *members* of the family of Christ.

COMMENDATION AND WELCOME

The pastor addresses the congregation:

Members of the household of God,
I commend *these persons* to your love and care.
Do all in your power to increase *their* faith,
confirm *their* hope, and perfect *them* in love.

The congregation responds:

We give thanks for
all that God has already given you
and we welcome you in Christian love.
As members together with you in the body of Christ

and in this congregation of
The United Methodist Church,
we renew our covenant
faithfully to participate
in the ministries of the church
by our prayers, our presence,
our gifts, and our service,
that in everything God may be glorified
through Jesus Christ.

DISMISSAL WITH BLESSING

The God of all grace,
who has called us to eternal glory in Christ,
establish you and strengthen you
by the power of the Holy Spirit,
that you may live in grace and peace.

One or more lay leaders may join with the pastor in acts of welcome
and peace.

Appropriate thanksgivings and intercessions for those who have participated in these acts should be included
in the concerns and prayers that follow.

It is most fitting that the service continue with Holy Communion, in which the union of the new members
with the body of Christ is most fully expressed. The new members may receive first.

HYMN

The service may continue with the next act of worship.

찬 송 과 예 배

COME, LET US WORSHIP

연합감리교회 한영찬송가
THE KOREAN-ENGLISH
UNITED METHODIST HYMNAL

하늘의 새와 물고기

Unison

1. 하늘의 새같이 와 물고기같이 들이다라네 주
2. 늘 풍지언 이 진 셨 나 별 유 의
3. 무 벗 자 적 계 다 구 만
4. 헐 웃 과 이 약 들 이 신

별 들 의 반 짝 임 면 하 나 님 지 은 솜 때 셨 하 하
주 십 나 울 리 나 님 재 앙 이 덤 이 할 이 래 래 뻐
탕 자 가 하 나 나 님 빈 무 이 물 보 노 하
공 사 랑 의 한 하 나 님 만 물 이 들 기

[1-5]
씨 에 어 떻 게 찬 양 할 까 서 리
에 네 우 리 어 찌 다 의 의 주 우 리 님
네 네 네 리 어 찌 생 명 구 하 하 리 님
네 네 평 화 주 님 은 우 리 고

[6]
향

WORDS: Jaroslav J. Vajda; Korean trans. The United Methodist Korean Hymnal Committee
MUSIC: Carl F. Schalk
Words © 1983 Concordia Publishing; music © 1983 GIA Publications, Inc.

ROEDER
546.77

God of the Sparrow God of the Whale **59**

Unison

1. God of the spar - row God of the whale
2. God of the earth - quake God of the storm
3. God of the rain - bow God of the cross
4. God of the hun - gry God of the sick
5. God of the neigh - bor God of the foe
6. God of the a - ges God near at hand

God of the swirl - ing stars	How does the crea-ture say
God of the trum - pet blast	How does the crea-ture cry
God of the emp - ty grave	How does the crea-ture say
God of the prod - i - gal	How does the crea-ture say
God of the prun - ing hook	How does the crea-ture say
God of the lov - ing heart	How do your chil-dren say

awe	How does the crea-ture say	praise
woe	How does the crea-ture cry	save
grace	How does the crea-ture say	thanks
care	How does the crea-ture say	life
love	How does the crea-ture say	peace
joy	How do your chil-dren say	home

*last time

WORDS: Jaroslav J. Vajda
MUSIC: Carl F. Schalk
Words © 1983 Concordia Publishing; music © 1983 GIA Publications, Inc.

ROEDER
546.77

높이 계신 주 찬양해

WORDS: Johann J. Schütz (Dt. 32:3); Korean trans. The United Methodist Korean Hymnal Committee
MUSIC: Bohemian Brethren's *Kirchengesänge*, 1566; harm. Maurice F. Bell
Korean trans. © 2001 The United Methodist Publishing House, admin. The Copyright Co.

MIT FREUDEN ZART
87.87.887

Sing Praise to God Who Reigns Above

1. Sing praise to God who reigns a-bove, the God of all cre-a-tion, the God of power, the God of love, the God of our sal-va-tion. With heal-ing balm my soul is filled and ev-ery faith-less mur-mur stilled: to God all praise and glo-ry.

2. The Lord is nev-er far a-way, but through all grief dis-tress-ing, an ev-er pres-ent help and stay, our peace and joy and bless-ing. As with a moth-er's ten-der hand, God gent-ly leads the cho-sen band: to God all praise and glo-ry.

3. Thus, all my toil-some way a-long, I sing a-loud thy prais-es, that earth may hear the grate-ful song my voice un-wea-ried rais-es. Be joy-ful in the Lord, my heart, both soul and bod-y bear your part: to God all praise and glo-ry.

4. Let all who name Christ's ho-ly name give God all praise and glo-ry; let all who own his power pro-claim a-loud the won-drous sto-ry! Cast each false i-dol from its throne, for Christ is Lord, and Christ a-lone: to God all praise and glo-ry.

WORDS: Johann J. Schütz (Dt. 32:3); English trans. Frances E. Cox
MUSIC: Bohemian Brethren's *Kirchengesänge*, 1566; harm. Maurice F. Bell

MIT FREUDEN ZART
87.87.887

61

주 하나님 지으신 모든 세계

WORDS: Stuart K. Hine; Korean trans. The United Methodist Korean Hymnal Committee
MUSIC: Stuart K. Hine
© 1953 Stuart K. Hine, renewed 1981 Manna Music, Inc.; Korean trans. © 2001 Manna Music, Inc.

HOW GREAT THOU ART
Irr. with Refrain

후렴

주님의 높 고 위 대 하심을

내 영혼 이 - 찬 양 하 네

주님의 높 고 위 대 하심 을

내 영혼 이 - 찬 양 하 네

61

1. O Lord my God! When I in awe-some won-der
2. When thru the woods and for-est glades I wan-der,
3. And when I think that God, his Son not spar-ing,
4. When Christ shall come with shout of ac-cla - ma-tion

con-sid-er all the *worlds thy hands have made,
and hear the birds sing sweet-ly in the trees;
sent him to die, I scarce can take it in;
and take me home, what joy shall fill my heart.

I see the stars, I hear the *roll-ing thun-der,
when I look down from loft-y moun-tain gran-deur
that on the cross, my bur-den glad-ly bear-ing,
Then I shall bow in hum-ble ad-o - ra-tion,

thy power through-out the un-i-verse dis-played.
and hear the brook, and feel the gen-tle breeze;
he bled and died to take a-way my sin;
and there pro-claim, my God, how great thou art!

*Author's original words are "works" and "mighty."

WORDS: Stuart K. Hine
MUSIC: Stuart K. Hine
© 1953 Stuart K. Hine, renewed 1981 Manna Music, Inc.

HOW GREAT THOU ART
Irr. with Refrain

Refrain

Then sings my soul, my Sav - ior God to thee;

how great thou art, how great thou art!

Then sings my soul, my Sav - ior God to thee;

how great thou art, how great thou art!

참 아름다와라

1. 참 아름다와라 주님의세계는
2. 참 아름다와라 주님의세계는
3. 참 아름다와라 주님의세계는

저 솔로몬의 옷보다더 고운백합 화별
저 아침해와 저녁놀밤 하늘빛난 화별
저 산에부는 바람과잔 잔한시냇 물

주 찬송하는 듯 저늘맑은새 소리니
망 망한바다와 저늘푸른봉 우리니
그 소리가운데 주음성들리 니

내 아버지의 지으신그 솜씨깊도 다다
다 주하나님의 영광을잘 드러내도 다다
주 하나님의 큰뜻을나 알듯하도 다

WORDS: Maltbie D. Babcock (Ps. 24:1); Korean trans. The Christian Literature Society of Korea
MUSIC: Trad. English melody; adapt. Franklin L. Sheppard
Korean trans. © The Christian Literature Society of Korea

TERRA BEATA
SMD

This Is My Father's World

1. This is my Father's world, and to my list'ning ears
2. This is my Father's world, the birds their car-ols raise,
3. This is my Father's world, O let me ne'er for - get

all na - ture sings, and round me rings the mu - sic of the spheres.
the morn-ing light, the lil - y white, de - clare their mak-er's praise.
that though the wrong seems oft so strong, God is the rul - er yet.

This is my Fa-ther's world: I rest me in the thought
This is my Fa-ther's world: he shines in all that's fair;
This is my Fa-ther's world: why should my heart be sad?

of rocks and trees, of skies and seas; his hand the won-ders wrought.
in the rust - ling grass I hear him pass; he speaks to me ev-ery-where.
The Lord is King; let the heav-ens ring! God reigns; let the earth be glad!

WORDS: Maltbie D. Babcock (Ps. 24:1)
MUSIC: Trad. English melody; adapt. Franklin L. Sheppard

TERRA BEATA
SMD

아름다운 모든 것

후렴 (Unison)

아 름 다 운 모 든 것 크 고 작 은 만 물

슬 기 로 운 모 든 것 다 주 가 만 든 것

1. 저 피 어 나 는 꽃 들 또 노 래 하 는 새 물 해
2. 저 화 려 한 산 들 과 또 호 르 는 강 름 해
3. 한 겨 울 추 운 바 람 또 밝 은 여 름 해
4. 볼 수 있 는 두 눈 과 말 하 는 입 술 도

참 고 운 색 깔 들 입 히 그 날 주 셨 네 놀 것 해
저 저 아 침 에 익 은 밝 히 고 는 살 가 만 든 양
다 주 님 께 서 주 신 것 창 조 주 찬 양 해

WORDS: Cecil Frances Alexander (Gen. 1:31);
Korean trans. The United Methodist Korean Hymnal Committee
MUSIC: 17th cent. English melody; arr. Martin Shaw
Korean trans. © 2001 The United Methodist Publishing House, admin. The Copyright Co.

ROYAL OAK
76.76 with Refrain

All Things Bright and Beautiful

Refrain (Unison)

All things bright and beau - ti - ful, all crea-tures great and small,

Fine

all things wise and won - der - ful: the Lord God made them all.

1. Each lit - tle flower that o - pens, each lit - tle bird that sings,
2. The pur-ple-head-ed moun-tains, the riv - er run-ning by,
3. The cold wind in the win - ter, the pleas -ant sum-mer sun,
4. God gave us eyes to see them, and lips that we might tell

D.C.

God made their glow-ing col - ors, and made their ti - ny wings.
the sun - set and the morn - ing that bright-ens up the sky.
the ripe fruits in the gar - den: God made them ev - ery one.
how great is God al - might - y, who has made all things well.

WORDS: Cecil Frances Alexander (Gen. 1:31)
MUSIC: 17th cent. English melody; arr. Martin Shaw

ROYAL OAK
76.76 with Refrain

64

찬란하고 빛난 하늘
God, Who Stretched the Spangled Heavens

WORDS: Catherine Cameron; Korean trans. The United Methodist Korean Hymnal Committee
MUSIC: William Moore
Words © 1967, Korean trans. © 2001 Hope Publishing Co.

HOLY MANNA
87.87. D

주 하나님의 능력

1. 주 하 나 님 의 능 력 을 나 찬 송 합 니
2. 주 하 나 님 의 선 하 심 나 찬 송 합 니
3. 이 모 든 꽃 과 나 무 들 주 영 광 보 이

다 저 산 과 하 늘 만 들 고 바 다 펼 치 셨 네
다 만 물 을 창 조 하 시 고 선 하 다 하 셨 네
고 저 구 름 과 큰 폭 풍 도 주 명 령 따 르 네

주 명 령 따 라 는 빛 나 는 저 해 와 달 과 별 도
내 발 길 닿 는 모 든 곳 저 하 늘 까 지 도
주 허 락 하 신 생 명 을 늘 돌 봐 주 시 고

그 다 스 리 는 지 혜 를 나 찬 송 합 니 다
그 신 비 로 운 주 솜 씨 잘 드 러 내 도 다
또 어 느 곳 에 있 든 지 주 함 께 계 시 네

WORDS: Isaac Watts; Korean trans. The United Methodist Korean Hymnal Committee
MUSIC: Trad. English melody; arr. Ralph Vaughan Williams
Korean trans. © 2001 The United Methodist Publishing House, admin. The Copyright Co.; arr. © Oxford University Press

FOREST GREEN
CMD

I Sing the Almighty Power of God

1. I sing the al-might-y power of God, that made the moun-tains
2. I sing the good-ness of the Lord, who filled the earth with
3. There's not a plant or flower be-low, but makes thy glo-ries

rise, that spread the flow-ing seas a-broad, and built the loft-y skies.
food, who formed the crea-tures thru the Word, and then pro-nounced them good.
known, and clouds a-rise, and tem-pests blow, by or-der from thy throne;

I sing the wis-dom that or-dained the sun to rule the day;
Lord, how thy won-ders are dis-played, wher-e'er I turn my eye,
while all that bor-rows life from thee is ev-er in thy care;

the moon shines full at God's com-mand, and all the stars o-bey.
if I sur-vey the ground I tread, or gaze up-on the sky.
and ev-ery-where that we can be, thou, God, art pres-ent there.

WORDS: Isaac Watts
MUSIC: Trad. English melody; arr. Ralph Vaughan Williams
Arr. © Oxford University Press

FOREST GREEN
CMD

66

아버지의 사랑으로
Of the Father's Love Begotten

Unison

1. 아 버 지 의 사 랑 으 - 로　이 세 상 이 창 조 되 니
2. 높 은 하 늘 찬 미 하 - 며　천 사 들 이 찬 양 하 네
3. 성 부 성 자 성 령 주 - 님　삼 위 일 체 하 나 님 께

1. Of the Fa-ther's love be-got - ten, e'er the worlds be-gan　to be,
2. O ye heights of heaven a-dore　him; an-gel hosts, his prais - es sing;
3. Christ, to thee with God the Fa - ther, and, O Ho-ly Ghost,　to thee,

그 는 알 파 와 오 메　가　처 음 이 요 나 중 이 라
모 든 나 라 경 배 하　네　우 리 의 왕 하 나 님 께
감 사 찬 미 노 래 하　며　끊 임 없 이 찬 양 하 리

he is Al-pha and O-meg - a,　he the source, the end - ing he,
powers, do-min-ions, bow be - fore　him,　and ex-tol our God　and King;
hymn and chant and high thanks giv - ing　and un-wea-ried prais - es be:

WORDS: Aurelius Clemens Prudentius (348-413); English trans. John Mason Neale
and Henry Williams Maker; Korean trans. The United Methodist Korean Hymnal Committee
MUSIC: 11th Century *Sanctus* trope; arr. C. Winfred Douglas
Korean trans. © 2001 The United Methodist Publishing House, admin. The Copyright Co.; arr. © 1943 Church Pension Fund

DIVINUM MYSTERIUM
8.7.8.7.8.7.7

지난 날과 장래 일 — 을 모 두 주 장 하 시 네
모 든 입 술 열 어 찬 — 양 목 소 리 를 합 하 여
존 귀 영 광 주 의 권 — 세 영 원 하 신 승 리 를

of the things that are, that have been, and that fu-ture years shall see,
let no tongue on earth be si - lent, ev-ery voice in con-cert ring,
hon-or, glo-ry, and do-min - ion, and e-ter-nal vic-to-ry,

영 원 토 록 영 원 토 록
영 원 토 록 영 원 토 록
영 원 토 록 영 원 토 록 아 — 멘 —

ev-er-more and ev-er-more!
ev-er-more and ev-er-more!
ev-er-more and ev-er-more! A - men.

주 찬양 드리세
Let's Sing unto the Lord

Unison

1. 주 찬 양 드 리 세 – 즐 거 운 찬 송
2.   찬 양 드 리 세 – 경 배 의 찬 송

1. Let's sing un-to the Lord   a hymn of glad re-
2.   sing un-to the Lord   a hymn of ad o-

불 러 – 이 신 선 한 아 침 주 의
불 러 – 믿 음 소 망 사 랑 모 두

joic-ing.   Let's sing   a hymn   of love,   at the
ra-tion,   which shows our love   and faith   and the

사 랑 찬 양 하 세 – 저 하 늘 과 바
담 아 찬 양 하 세 – 온 세 상 만 물

new day's fresh   be-gin-ning.   God made   the sky   a-
hope   of all   cre-a-tion.   Thru all   that has   been

다 – 해 와 별 만 드 셨 네 – 주 큰
들 – 위 대 하 신 주 찬 양 – 큰

bove,   the stars,   the sun,   the o-ceans;   and
made,   the Lord   is praised   for great-ness,   and

WORDS: Carlos Rosas (Ps.19); English trans. Roberto Escamilla, Elise S. Eslinger, and George Lockwood;
Korean trans. The United Methodist Korean Hymnal Committee
MUSIC: Carlos Rosas; arr. Raquel Mora Martinez
English trans. © 1989, Korean trans. © 2001 The United Methodist Publishing House, admin. The Copyright Co.;
music © 1976 Resource Publications, Inc.; arr. © 1983 The United Methodist Publishing House

ROSAS
67.68 D with Refrain

다 찬양하여라

1. 다 찬양 하 여 라 전능왕 창조의 주 께
2. 다 찬양 하 여 라 놀라운 만유의 주 께께
3. 다 찬양 하 여 라 온 몸과 마음을 바 처

내 혼 아 주 찬양 평강과 구원의 주 님
포 근 한 날개 밑 늘품어 주시는 주 님
온 세 상 만물아 주 앞에 다 나와 찬 양

성 도 들 아 주 앞 에 모 두 나 와
성 도 들 아 아 주 님 의 뜻 안 에 에 서 여
성 도 들 아 기 쁘 게 소 리 높

즐 겁 게 찬 양 하 여 리 라 라
네 소 원 다 이 하 루 리 라
영 원 히 찬 양 하 여 라 라

WORDS: Joachim Neander (Ps. 103:1-6;150); Korean trans. The Christian Literature Society of Korea
MUSIC: *Erneuerten Gesangbuch*, 1665; harm. William Sterndale Bennett
Korean trans. © The Christian Literature Society of Korea

LOBE DEN HERREN
14 14.478

Praise to the Lord, the Almighty

1. Praise to the Lord, the Al-might-y, the King of cre - a - tion!
2. Praise to the Lord, who o'er all things so won-drous-ly reign - ing
3. Praise to the Lord, O let all that is in me a - dore him!

O my soul, praise him, for he is thy health and sal - va - tion!
bears thee on ea-gle's wings, e'er in his keep-ing main-tain - ing.
All that hath life and breath, come now with prais-es be - fore him!

All ye who hear, now to his tem - ple draw near;
God's care en - folds all, whose true good he up - holds.
Let the a - men sound from his peo - ple a - gain;

join me in glad ad - o - ra - tion!
Hast thou not known his sus - tain - ing?
glad - ly for - ev - er a - dore him.

WORDS: Joachim Neander (Ps. 103:1-6;150); sts. 1 and 3 English trans. Catherine Winkworth;
st. 2 S. Paul Schilling
MUSIC: *Erneuerten Gesangbuch*, 1665; harm. William Sterndale Bennett
English trans. St. 2 © 1989 The United Methodist Publishing House, admin. The Copyright Co.

LOBE DEN HERREN
14 14.478

빛 있으라

WORDS: Hae-Jong Kim
MUSIC: Sunkyung Lee
© 2001 The United Methodist Publishing House, admin. The Copyright Co.

LET THERE BE LIGHT

Irr.

빨갛사주산동 갖랑님소서 게의의망와 물그은되남 든빛혜신북 저자선주구 녁유포를별 늘시때축다 빛네에해네 ----- -----

서가무빛무 로난지과지 다한개사개 른자빛랑빛 사위모십우 람하두자리 들여다가는 지복품능주 으음어력의 --- 신주주으백 주머는로성

보눈주평주 시먼님화님 기자의의께 에에교나서 참게회라늘 좋광탄함새 다명생께롭 하주했이게 셨시도루하 네네다세리 -----

69

Let There Be Light

1. "Let there be light," and there were ma - ny co - lors;
2. "Let there be love," th'e - ter - nal God so de - clared;
3. "Let there be hearts," af - ter the lo - ving im - age;
4. "Let there be hope," says our God of the rain - bow;
5. "Let there be songs," in me - lo - dies of na - tions;

the Tech - ni - co - lor world, God cre - a - ted;
a child was born, whose name was al - so "Light."
one day a heart was strange - ly warmed, en - larged.
sus - pend - ed from the cross to emp - ty tomb.
let us all dance, in rhy - thm of our own.

blue seas, green trees, and beau - ti - ful red sun - set.
Walk in this light and you shall not see dark - ness;
In love em - braced, served this world as "my pa - rish";
The Eas - ter dawn is gi - ving hope to all;
Let us u - nite in Christ, the light to na - tions;

WORDS: Hae-Jong Kim
MUSIC: Sunkyung Lee
© 2001 The United Methodist Publishing House, admin. The Copyright Co.

LET THERE BE LIGHT
Irr.

I - mage of light, God made hu-ma - ni - ty;
by this great light, hu - ma - ni -ty was freed.
prea - ching God's grace, set - ting all pris'-ners free,
we ce - le - brate, the light, the li - ving hope.
in whom there is no east, west, north, or south,

male and fe - male, all ra-ces in all co - lors;
Blind re-ceived sight, and to the poor good news came;
God's church was born, in-clu-sive as the rain - bow;
'Cause of the light, the cross and lo - ving hearts;
nor black or white, but one true rain - bow peo - ple;

and then God said, "It is so ve - ry good."
love's li - be - ra - ting work has now be - gun.
one peo - ple of the Tech - ni - co - lor world.
world of sha - lom, to - ge - ther let us build.
for God makes all things new and e - ver good.

70

온 세상 우리 주님 손 안에
He's Got the Whole World in His Hands

WORDS: African American spiritual; Korean trans. The United Methodist Korean Hymnal Committee
MUSIC: African American spiritual; arr. Gary Alan Smith
Korean trans. © 2001 The United Methodist Publishing House, admin. The Copyright Co.; arr. © 2001 Gamut Music Productions

WHOLE WORLD
Irr.

하늘과 땅을 지으신 주
Many and Great, O God

71

1. 하 늘 과 땅 을 지 으 신 주 창 조 주
2. 주 님 과 교 통 케 하 소 서 하 늘 에

1. Man-y and great, O God, are thy things, Mak-er of
2. Grant un-to us com-mun-ion with thee, thou star a-

하 나 님 하 늘 의 별 을 만 드 시 고
계 신 주 우 리 와 함 께 거 하 소 서

earth and sky. Thy hands have set the heav-ens with stars;
bid-ing one; come un-to us and dwell with us;

산 과 들 지 어 펼 치 셨 네 주 께 서
생 명 의 선 물 주 시 는 주 주 님 과

thy fin-gers spread the moun-tains and plains. Lo, at thy
with thee are found the gifts of life. Bless us with

말 씀 하 시 니 바 다 가 되 었 네
함 께 거 하 -는 영 생 을 주 소 서

word the wa-ters were formed; deep seas o-bey thy voice.
life that has no end, e-ter-nal life with thee.

WORDS: Joseph R. Renville (Ps. 104:24-30; Jer. 10:12-13); para. Philip Frazier;
Korean trans. The United Methodist Korean Hymnal Committee
MUSIC: Native American melody; harm. Richard Proulx
Korean trans. © 2001 The United Methodist Publishing House, admin. The Copyright Co.; harm. © 1986 GIA Publications, Inc.

LACQUIPARLE
Irr.

72

주의 백성 찬양

후렴 Unison

주의백성찬양 찬양 만국의하나님

주의백성찬양 찬양 영원하신주께

1. 아름답고 놀라운날 기쁨의빛넘치네
2. 크신축복 온갖은혜 베푸시는우리왕

주의사랑 주의능력 널리전하네
주의영광 주의승리 노래부르네

주의백성찬양 찬양 영원히찬양

WORDS: Kate Steams Page; Korean trans. The United Methodist Korean Hymnal Committee
MUSIC: Franz Joseph Haydn; arr. Edith Lowell Thomas; alt.
Korean trans. © 2001 The United Methodist Publishing House, admin. The Copyright Co.;
arr. © renewed 1963 Abingdon Press, admin. The Copyright Co.

ST. ANTHONY'S CHORALE

Irr.

We, Thy People, Praise Thee

Refrain Unison

We, thy peo-ple, praise thee, praise thee, God of ev-ery na-tion!

We, thy peo-ple, praise thee, praise thee, Lord of Hosts e-ter-nal!

1. Days of won-der, days of beau-ty, days of rap-ture filled with light
2. For thy bless-ings, for thy boun-ty, joy-ful songs to thee we sing,

tell thy good-ness, tell thy mer-cies, tell thy glo-rious might.
songs of glo-ry, songs of tri-umph to our God and King.

We thy peo-ple, praise thee, praise thee, praise thee ev-er-more!

WORDS: Kate Steams Page
MUSIC: Franz Joseph Haydn; arr. Edith Lowell Thomas; alt.
Arr. © renewed 1963 Abingdon Press, admin. The Copyright Co.

ST. ANTHONY'S CHORALE

Irr.

사랑으로 다스리는

WORDS: William Boyd Grove; Korean trans. The United Methodist Korean Hymnal Committee
MUSIC: John Goss
Words © 1980, Korean trans. © 2001 William Boyd Grove

LAUDA ANIMA
87.87.87

God, Whose Love Is Reigning o'er Us

1. God, whose love is reign-ing o'er us, source of all, the
2. Word of God from na-ture bring - ing spring-time green and
3. Ho - ly God of an-cient glo - ry, choos-ing man and
4. Cove-nant, new a - gain in Je - sus, Star-child born to
5. Lift we then our hu-man voic - es in the songs that

end - ing true; hear the u - ni - ver-sal cho - rus
au - tumn gold; moun-tain streams like chil-dren sing - ing,
wom - an, too; A-br'am's faith and Sa - rah's sto - ry
set us free; sent to heal us, sent to teach us
faith would bring; live we then in hu - man choic - es

raised in joy - ful praise to you:
o - cean waves like thun - der bold: Al - le - lu - ia,
formed a peo - ple bound to you.
how love's chil - dren we might be.
lives that, like our mu - sic, sing:

wor - ship an - cient, wor - ship new.
Al - le - lu - ia, to your cove-nant keep us true.
ris - en Christ, our Sav - ior he!
joined in love our prais - es ring!

WORDS: William Boyd Grove
MUSIC: John Goss
Words © 1980 William Boyd Grove

LAUDA ANIMA
87.87.87

신비롭고 영원한 지혜의 주

WORDS: Walter Chalmers Smith (1 Tim. 1:17);
Korean trans. The United Methodist Korean Hymnal Committee
MUSIC: Welsh melody from John Roberts' *Canaidau y Cyssegr*
Korean trans. © 2001 The United Methodist Publishing House, admin. The Copyright Co.

ST. DENIO
11 11.11 11

Immortal, Invisible, God Only Wise

1. Im - mor - tal, in - vis - i - ble, God on - ly wise,
2. Un - rest - ing, un - hast - ing, and si - lent as light,
3. To all, life thou giv - est, to both great and small;
4. Thou reign - est in glo - ry; thou dwell - est in light;

in light in - ac - ces - si - ble hid from our eyes,
nor want - ing, nor wast - ing, thou rul - est in might;
in all life thou liv - est, the true life of all;
thine an - gels a - dore thee, all veil - ing their sight;

most bless - ed, most glo - rious, the An - cient of Days,
thy jus - tice like moun - tains high soar - ing a - bove
we blos - som and flour - ish as leaves on the tree,
all laud we would ren - der; O help us to see

al - might - y, vic - to - rious, thy great name we praise.
thy clouds which are foun - tains of good - ness and love.
and with - er and per - ish, but naught chang - eth thee.
'tis on - ly the splen - dor of light hid - eth thee.

WORDS: Walter Chalmers Smith (1 Tim. 1:17)
MUSIC: Welsh melody from John Roberts' *Canaidau y Cyssegr*

ST. DENIO
11 11.11 11

75

기뻐하며 경배하세

WORDS: Henry Van Dyke; st. 4 alt. 1989; Korean trans. The United Methodist Korean Hymnal Committee
MUSIC: Ludwig van Beethoven; arr. Edward Hodges
Korean trans. © 2001 The United Methodist Publishing House, admin. The Copyright Co.

HYMN TO JOY
87.87.D

Joyful, Joyful, We Adore Thee

1. Joy-ful, joy-ful, we a-dore thee, God of glo-ry, Lord of love;
2. All thy works with joy sur-round thee, earth and heav'n re-flect thy rays;
3. Thou art giv-ing and for-giv-ing, ev-er bless-ing, ev-er blest,
4. Mor-tals join the might-y cho-rus which the morn-ing stars be-gan;

hearts un-fold like flow'rs be-fore thee, open-ing to the sun a-bove.
stars and an-gels sing a-round thee, cen-ter of un-bro-ken praise.
well-spring of the joy of liv-ing, o-cean depth of hap-py rest!
love di-vine is reign-ing o'er us, bind-ing all with-in its span.

Melt the clouds of sin and sad-ness; drive the dark of doubt a-way; Giv
Field and for-est, vale and moun-tain, flow-ery mead-ow, flash-ing sea, chant
Thou our Fa-ther, Christ our broth-er, all who live in love are thine; teach
Ev-er sing-ing, march we on-ward, vic-tors in the midst of strife; joy

-er of im-mor-tal glad-ness, fill us with the light of day!
-ing bird and flow-ing foun-tain, call us to re-joice in thee.
us how to love each oth-er, lift us to the joy di-vine.
-ful mu-sic leads us sun-ward, in the tri-umph song of life.

WORDS: Henry Van Dyke; st. 4 alt. 1989
MUSIC: Ludwig van Beethoven; arr. Edward Hodges

HYMN TO JOY
87.87.D

76

하나님을 찬양하세
Praise to the Lord

1. 하 나 님 을 찬 양 하 세
2. 평 화 의 왕 임 하 소 서
1. Praise to the Lord and glo-ry to God, we
2. Be with us, Lord, as we come to you, you

무 릎 꿇 어 경 배 해
사 랑 의 주 오 소 서
ga - ther in wor-ship and fall up-on our knees,
are the King of peace, the God of love,

그 의 사 랑 그 의 은 혜
우 리 모 두 주 안 에 서
raise high your voi - ces, sing to the Lord, give
u - nite us, Lord, that we would be one; your

소 리 높 여 찬 양 해
하 나 되 게 하 소 서
thanks for God's love and grace, praise to the Lord!
love is the bond of peace, praise to the Lord!

WORDS: Sung Mo Moon and Sung Won Park; English trans. Edward Poitras
MUSIC: Sung Mo Moon
© Kyung Dong Presbyterian Church

엘샤다이
El Shaddai

WORDS: Michael Card and John Thompson; Korean trans. The United Methodist Korean Hymnal Committee
MUSIC: Michael Card and John Thompson
© 1981, Korean trans. © 2001 Mole End Music, admin. Word Music

EL SHADDAI
Irr.

하나님께 영광을
To God Be the Glory

1. 하 나 님 께 영 광 을 돌 리 어 라
2. 온 전 하 신 주 님 의 대 속 함 은

1. To God be the glo - ry, great things he hath done!
2. O per - fect re-demp-tion, the pur-chase of blood,

이 세 상 을 이 처 럼 사 랑 하 사
주 보 혈 로 베 푸 신 약 속 이 라

So loved he the world that he gave us his Son,
to ev - ery be - liev - er the prom-ise of God;

독 생 자 를 우 리 게 주 셨 으 니
죄 중 에 서 헤 매 는 모 든 사 람

who yield - ed his life an a - tone-ment for sin,
the vil - est of-fend - er who tru - ly be - lieves,

주 믿 는 자 영 생 을 얻 으 리 라
주 앞 으 로 나 오 면 사 함 받 네

and o - pened the life - gate that all may go in.
that mo - ment from Je - sus a par-don re - ceives.

WORDS: Fanny J. Crosby; Korean trans. The United Methodist Korean Hymnal Committee
MUSIC: William H. Doane
Korean trans. © 2001 The United Methodist Publishing House, admin. The Copyright Co.

TO GOD BE THE GLORY
11 11.11 11 with Refrain

주 찬 양 주 찬 양 큰 소 리 로 찬 양
Praise the Lord, praise the Lord, let the earth hear his voice!

주 찬 양 주 찬 양 기 쁨 으 로 찬 양
Praise the Lord, praise the Lord, let the peo - ple re joice!

다 주 앞 에 나 와 서 찬 양 하 라
O come to the Fa - ther thru Je - sus the Son,

그 크 신 일 이 루 신 하 나 님 께
and give him the glo - ry, great things he hath done!

3. 위대하신 행함과 가르치심
그 크신 일 인하여 기뻐하나
더 놀라운 기쁨과 참된 영화
주 예수님 뵈올 때 얻으리라

3. Great things he hath taught us,
great things he hath done,
and great our rejoicing thru Jesus the Son;
but purer, and higher, and greater will be
our wonder, our transport, when Jesus we see.

거룩 거룩 거룩

WORDS: Reginald Heber (Rev. 4:8-11); Korean trans. The Christian Literature Society of Korea
MUSIC: John B. Dykes
Korean trans. © The Christian Literature Society of Korea

NICAEA
11 12.12 10

Holy, Holy, Holy! Lord God Almighty

1. Ho-ly, ho-ly, ho - ly! Lord God Al-might - y!
Ear - ly in the morn - ing our song shall rise to thee.
Ho - ly, ho-ly, ho - ly! Mer-ci - ful and might - y!
God in three per - sons, bless - ed Trin - i - ty!

2. Ho-ly, ho-ly, ho - ly! All the saints a - dore thee,
cas - ting down their gold-en crowns a - round the glass - y sea;
cher - u-bim and ser - a-phim fall-ing down be - fore thee,
which wert, and art, and ev - er-more shalt be.

3. Ho-ly, ho-ly, ho - ly! Tho' the dark-ness hide thee,
tho' the eye of sin - ful man thy glo-ry may not see,
on - ly thou art ho - ly; there is none be - side thee,
per - fect in pow'r, in love and pu - ri - ty.

4. Ho-ly, ho-ly, ho - ly! Lord God Al-might - y!
All thy works shall praise thy name, in earth and sky and sea.
Ho - ly, ho-ly, ho - ly! Mer-ci - ful and might - y!
God in three per - sons, bless - ed Trin - i - ty!

WORDS: Reginald Heber (Rev. 4:8-11)
MUSIC: John B. Dykes

NICAEA
11 12.12 10

80

거룩하신 하나님 이름 높여
Holy God, We Praise Thy Name

WORDS: Ignaz Franz, 18th cent.; English trans. Clarence Walworth;
Korean trans. The United Methodist Korean Hymnal Committee
MUSIC: *Katholisches Gesangbuch*
Korean trans. © 2001 The United Methodist Publishing House, admin. The Copyright Co.

GROSSER GOTT
78.78.77

81

오 신실하신 주
Great Is Thy Faithfulness

1. 오 신 실 하 신 주 내 아 버 지 여
2. 봄 철 과 또 여 름 가 을 과 겨 울
3. 내 죄 를 사 하 여 안 위 하 시 고

1. Great is thy faith - ful-ness, O God my Fa - ther;
2. Sum - mer and win - ter and spring-time and har - vest,
3. Par - don for sin and a peace that en - dur - eth,

늘 함 께 계 시 니 두 렴 없 네
해 와 달 별 들 도 다 주 의 것
주 친 히 오 셔 서 인 도 하 네

there is no shad - ow of turn - ing with thee;
sun, moon, and stars in their cours - es a - bove
thine own dear pres - ence to cheer and to guide;

그 사 랑 변 찮 고 날 지 키 시 며
만 물 이 하 나 로 드 러 낸 증 거
오 늘 의 힘 되 고 내 일 의 소 망

thou chang-est not, thy com - pas-sions, they fail not
join with all na - ture in man - i fold wit - ness,
strength for to - day and bright hope for to - mor - row,

WORDS: Thomas O. Chisholm (Lam. 3:22-23);
Korean trans. The United Methodist Korean Hymnal Committee
MUSIC: William M. Runyan
© 1923, renewed 1951, Korean trans. © 2001 Hope Publishing Co.

FAITHFULNESS
11 10.11 10 with Refrain

82

거룩 거룩 거룩하신 주
Holy, Holy, Holy Is the Lord

1. 거 룩 거 룩 거 룩하신 주
2. 존 귀 존 귀 존 귀하신 주
3. 영 광 영 광 영 광돌리세

1. Ho - ly, ho - ly, ho - ly is the Lord;
2. Wor - thy, wor - thy, wor - thy is the Lord;
3. Glo - ry, glo - ry, glo - ry to the Lord;

전 능 하신 주 하 나 님 - -
전 능 하신 주 하 나 님 - -
전 능 하신 주 하 나 님

ho - ly is the Lord God Al - migh - ty! ty!
wor - thy is the Lord God Al - migh - ty! ty!
glo - ry to the Lord God Al - migh - ty! ty!

영 원 부 터 영 원 까 지
Who was, and is, and is to come!

거 룩 거 룩 거 룩 하 신 주 -
존 귀 존 귀 존 귀 하 신 주 -
영 광 영 광 영 광 돌 리 세 -

Ho - ly, ho - ly, ho - ly is the Lord!
Wor - thy, wor - thy, wor - thy is the Lord!
Glo - ry, glo - ry, glo - ry to the Lord!

WORDS: From Revelation 4; Korean trans. The United Methodist Korean Hymnal Committee
MUSIC: Anonymous; arr. Bill Newton
Korean trans. © 2001 The United Methodist Publishing House, admin. The Copyright Co.; arr. © 1991 McKinney, Inc.

JUBILATE
Irr.

주 너를 독수리 날개 위에
On Eagle's Wings
(And God Will Raise You Up)

주 너를 독 수 리 날 개 위 에
And God will raise you up on ea - gle's wings,

태 우 사 날 게 하 고 해 처럼 빛 나게 하 며 - 주
bear you on the breath of dawn, make you to shine like the sun, and

손 으로 잡 아 - 주시 리 -
hold you in the palm of God's hand.

WORDS: Michael Joncas (Ex. 19:4); Korean trans. The United Methodist Korean Hymnal Committee
MUSIC: Michael Joncas; harm. Carlton R. Young
© 1979, 1989, Korean trans. © 2001 North American Liturgy Resources

ON EAGLE'S WINGS
Irr. with Refrain

84

하늘에 가득 찬 영광의 하나님

1. 하늘에 가득 찬 영광의 하나님
2. 사랑이 넘치는 자비하신 하나님
3. 연약한 심령을 굳게 세워 주시고
4. 주 앞에 나올 때 우리 맘이 기쁘고

온 땅에 충만한 존귀하신 하나님
은혜가 풍성한 구원의 은혜롭게 하나님
우둔한 마음을 지혜 희망 솟아 오른다
그 말씀 힘 되어 회망 솟아 오른다

생명과 빛으로에어 지혜와를 권능으로고며
참회의 심판 안을 주살으시가시
주난도 슬픔도 참이게 하옵시

언제나 나허리를 지키시는 하나님 나소서서
제악나의 우게을서 용감아 하하하 나소서서
주말쏨따라잇대살아 가가 하하 소서

WORDS: Jung Joon Kim (Jn. 4:23-24)
MUSIC: Sang Soo Kwak
© The Korean Hymnal Society

ACCEPT OUR WORSHIP

Irr.

성 부 와 성 자 와 성 령
찬 송 과 영 광 과 생 명
권 능 리 의 지 혜 과 사 기쁨

구 원 의 하 나 님 우 - 리

예 배 를 받 아 주 시 옵 소 서

84

Lord God, Thy Glory

1. Lord God, thy glo - ry doth spread a-cross the un - i-verse,
2. God of a - bun - dant love, thou for - giv - est all our sins;
3. To us the fee - ble souls, comes thy strength from up a - bove;
4. What a great joy it is, as we come in to your court;

thy di - vine ma - jes - ty co - vers all the earth a - round.
thy bound-less grace thus re - deems us from all our debts.
en - light - en fool - ish hearts with thy bright di - vine wis - dom.
thy words pour strength in us, build us with hope a - new.

Rich in life, bright in light, mighty in wis - dom and po-wer,
Lord, grant thy las - ting peace un - to re - pent -ant hearts;
Help us to know thy will, that we be lov - ing and true;
No dis -tress and sor- row will e - ver con-quer us;

he holds us fast and firm, he leads us in his mer - cy.
heal us from wretch-ed wounds, re- store all; our strength in thee.
thou fillest me with cour-age, with pa-tience and with thy strength.
grant that we may ex-tend our lives to e - ter - nal life.

WORDS: Jung Joon Kim (Jn. 4:23-24)
MUSIC: Sang Soo Kwak
© The Korean Hymnal Society

ACCEPT OUR WORSHIP
Irr.

O Fa - ther, Son, Ho - ly Spir - it;
To thee be praise and all glo - ry;
Thine is the wis - dom and pow - er;
Thou art our hap - pi - ness and pride;

Sa - vior of all, our Lord, we praise thee,

wor - ship thee, with all of our hearts and souls.

사랑하는 나의 아버지

사 랑 하 는 나 의 아 버 지 -

이 름 높 여 드 립 니 다

주 의 나 라 찬 양 속 에 임 하 시 니 -

능 력 의 주 께 찬 송 하 네

전 능 하 - 신 하 나 님 찬 양

언 제 나 동 일 하 신 주 -

전 능 하 - 신 하 나 님 찬 양

영 원 히 다 스 리 네

WORDS: Bob Fitts; Korean trans. The United Methodist Korean Hymnal Committee
MUSIC: Bob Fitts
© 1984, Korean trans. © 2001 Scripture in Song (a div. of Integrity Music, Inc.)

Father in Heaven, How We Love You
(Blessed Be the Lord God Almighty)

Fa-ther in heav-en, how we love you, we lift your name in all the earth.

May your king-dom be es-tab-lished in our prais-es, as your people de-clare your might-y works.

Bless-ed be the Lord God Al-migh-ty, who was, and is, and is to come.

Bless-ed be the Lord God Al-migh-ty, who reigns for-ev-er-more.

WORDS: Bob Fitts
MUSIC: Bob Fitts

그 크신 하나님의 사랑

1. 그 크신 하나님의 사랑 말로 다 형용 못하네 저 높고 높은 별을 넘어 이 낮고 낮은 땅 위에 죄범한 영혼 구원하려 그 아들 보내사 화목제를 삼으시고 죄 용서하셨네

an, stz. 3 Meir Ben Isaac (Jn. 3:16);
thodist Korean Hymnal Committee

Methodist Publishing House, admin. The Copyright Co.

THE LOVE OF GOD
9.8.9.8.8.6

86

The Love of God

1. The love of God is great - er far than tongue or
2. When hoar - y time shall pass a - way, and earth - ly
3. Could we with ink the o - cean fill, and were the

pen can ev - er tell; it goes be - yond the high - est
thrones and king - doms fall; when men who here re - fuse to
skies of parch - ment made, were ev - ery stalk on earth a

star and reach - es to the low - est hell. The guilt - y
pray, on rocks and hills and moun - tains call; God's love, so
quill and ev - ery man a scribe by trade; to write the

pair bowed down with care, God gave his Son to win;
sure, shall still en - dure, all meas - ure - less and strong;
love of God a - bove would drain the o - cean dry;

WORDS: Frederick M. Lehman, stz. 3 Meir Ben Isaac (Jn. 3:16)
MUSIC: Frederick M. Lehman

THE LOVE OF GOD
9.8.9.8.8.6

his err - ing child he rec - on - ciled. And par - doned
re - deem - ing grace to Ad - am's race, the saints' and
nor could the scroll con - tain the whole, tho' stretched from

from his sin.
an - gels' song. Oh, love of God, how rich and
sky to sky.

Refrain

pure! How meas-ure - less and strong! It shall for-

ev - er-more en - dure, the saints' and an - gels' song.

87

왕이신 나의 하나님
My Savior, My King

왕 이 신 - 나 의 하 나 님 - 내
I bless you, my God and my King. I

가 - 주 를 높 이 고 - 영
bless - ex-tol and a-dore. For-

원 히 - 주 의 이 름 을 - 송
e-ver my God, I will praise, ex-

축 하 나 이 다 -
alt your ho-ly name.

WORDS: Stephen Hah (Ps. 145:1)
MUSIC: Stephen Hah
© 1989 All Nations Music, admin. CopyCare Korea

다 오라 복음 잔치에
Come, Sinners, to the Gospel Feast

1. 다 오라 복음 잔 - 치에 주 께 서 죄 - 인 부르시네 온 세 상 모 든 사 람 들 다 오 라 말 씀 하 시 네
2. 주 께 서 나 - 를 보 - 내 사 모 두 다 부 르 라 명 하 시 네 모 든 것 준 비 하 시 고 다 오 라 말 씀 하 시 네
3. 죄 짐에 눌 - 린 영 - 혼 들 안 식 을 찾 - 아 헤 - 맬 때 병 들 고 가 난 한 자 들 주 께 서 맞 아 주 시 리

1. Come, sin - ners, to the gos - pel feast; let ev - ery soul be Je - sus' guest. Ye need not one be left be - hind, for God hath bid all hu - man-kind.
2. Sent by my Lord, on you I call; the in - vi - ta - tion is to all. Come, all the world! Come, sin - ner, thou! All things in Christ are read - y now.
3. Come, all ye souls by sin op-pressed, ye rest - less wan - derers af - ter rest; ye poor, and maimed, and halt, and blind, in Christ a heart - y wel - come find.

4. 주께서 말씀하시네 내게 와 생명 얻으라
   나 위해 죽은 그 사랑 헛되지 않게 하소서

5. 지금 곧 주께 나오라 은혜의 때니 지체 말라
   온 세상 위해 죽으신 주님을 위해 살 때라

4. My message as from God receive;
   ye all may come to Christ and live.
   O let his love your hearts constrain,
   nor suffer him to die in vain.

5. This is the time, no more delay!
   This is the Lord's accepted day.
   Come thou, this moment, at his call,
   and live for him who died for all.

WORDS: Charles Wesley (Lk. 14:16-24); Korean trans. The United Methodist Korean Hymnal Committee
MUSIC: Katholisches Gesangbuch; adapt. from Metrical Psalter
Korean trans. © 2001 The United Methodist Publishing House, admin. The Copyright Co.

HURSLEY
LM

지금까지 지내 온 것

WORDS: Att. Tetusaburo Sasao (Rom. 8:28)
MUSIC: Chai Hoon Park
Words © The Korean Hymnal Society; music © Chai Hoon Park

GRACE
8.7.8.7

O, the Help That God Has Given

1. O, the help that God has gi-ven, thru his grace un-to this hour,
2. I am weak of frame and spir-it, but the Lord has strengthened me,
3. O, the time we'll meet our Sav-ior, it draws clos-er day by day,

O, his love which nev-er fail-eth, wond-rous grace and wond-rous pow'r,
he has poured his grace up-on me, so that I can want no more.
he will take our heav-y bur-dens and will car-ry them a-way,

day and night, he ev-er guides us, keeps us in his lov-ing care.
Thru the val-ley and the de-sert, I am sing-ing as I go,
in-to rest which he has prom-ised in our heav'n-ly home a-bove,

Yes, in him all things are possi-ble for the glo-ry of our God.
for my Mas-ter walks be-side me, hold-ing my hand where'er we go.
in the bo-som of our Fa-ther for-e'er in his per-fect love.

WORDS: Att. Tetusaburo Sasao (Rom. 8:28)
MUSIC: Chai Hoon Park
Words © The Korean Hymnal Society; music © Chai Hoon Park

GRACE
8.7.8.7

주 호숫가에 오셔서
Lord, You Have Come to the Lakeshore

Unison

1. 주 – 호숫가에 오 셔 서 –
2. 내 – 작은고깃배안 에 –
3. 내 – 손과발드립니 다 –

1. Lord, you have come to the lake - shore
2. You know so well my pos - ses - sions;
3. You need my hands, full of car - ing

내 게 오 라 – 날부르시네 –
금 과 무 기 – 없을지라도 –
나 의 이 웃 – 돌보아주고 –

look - ing nei - ther for wealth-y nor wise ones;
my boat car - ries no gold and no weap - ons;
through my la - bors to give oth-ers rest,

– 겸 손 히 주 를 – 따르라하네 –
– 그 물 과 수 고 – 있음아시네 –
– 나 끊임 없 이 – 사랑하리라 –

you on - ly asked me to fol - low hum - bly.
you will find there my nets and la - bor.
and cons - tant love that keeps on lov - ing.

4. 주 우리 바다에 오사 갈급하던 뭇 영혼에게 큰사랑 주사 친구 되셨네

4. You who have fished other oceans, ever longed for by souls
who are waiting, my loving friend, as thus you call me. *Refrain*

WORDS: Cesareo Gabaraín (Mt. 4:18-22; Mk. 1:16-20; Lk. 5:1-11); English trans. Gertrude C. Suppe, George
Lockwood, and Raquel Gutiérrez-Achon; Korean trans. The United Methodist Korean Hymnal Committee
MUSIC: Cesareo Gabaraín; harm. Skinner Chávez-Melo
© 1979, Korean trans. © 2001 Ediciones Paulinas; English trans. © 1989 The United Methodist Pulishing House,
admin. The Copyright Co.; harm. © 1987 Skinner Chávez-Melo

PESCADOR DE HOMBRES
Irr. with Refrain

후렴 (Refrain)

오 주 - 나를 바라 보 시 고
O Lord, with your eyes you have searched me,

- 다 정 하 게 - 날 부르셨 네 -
and while smil - ing have spo-ken my name;

- 이 제 나 의 - 배는뒤에남기 고
now my boat's left on the shore-line be-hind me;

- 주 님 의 - 바다향하리 라 -
by your side I will seek oth-er seas.

주님의 사랑과 그 영이
Spirit Song
(O Let the Son of God)

1. 주님의 사랑과 그 영이 너를
   찬양드리어라 맘에

1. O let the Son of God en-fold you with his
   sing this song with glad-ness as your

감 싸주시고 너의맘 과영 혼
기 쁨넘치니 두손높 이들 고
Spir-it and his love. Let him fill your heart and
hearts are filled with joy. Lift your hands in sweet sur-

채 워주시 니 모든것 주 께맡 기
주 이름찬 양 네슬픈 눈 물쌓 인
sat-is-fy your soul. O let him have the things that
ren-der to his name. O give him all your tears and

어 라 그의영 이도 우 사 너의
아 픔 모두주 께아 뢰 면 그의
hold you, and his Spir-it like a dove will de-
sad-ness; give him all your years of pain,   and you'll

WORDS: John Wimber; Korean trans. The United Methodist Korean Hymnal Committee
MUSIC: John Wimber
© 1979, Korean trans. © 2001 Mercy/Vineyard Publishing

SPIRIT SONG
9 7 11 D

난 들었네 주 예수

WORDS: Eugene M. Bartlett; Korean trans. The United Methodist Korean Hymnal Committee
MUSIC: Eugene M. Bartlett
ⓒ 1939 Eugene M. Bartlett, renewed 1967 Mrs. Eugene M. Bartlett, assigned to Albert E. Brumley & Sons, Inc.,
admin. ICG; Korean trans. ⓒ 2001 Albert E. Brumley & Sons, Inc.

HARTFORD
Irr. with Refrain

후럼

얻 었 네 네   오   예 수 안 의   승 리 영
노   래 를

원 한 내 구 주 그   대 속 의 피 로

날   사 신 구 세 주   나   주 를 알 기

전 에 날   먼 저 사 랑 했 네 그

물 로 날   씻 으 사 승   리 를 주 셨 네

92

I Heard an Old, Old Story
(Victory in Jesus)

1. I heard an old, old story, how a Sav-ior came from glory, how he gave his life on Cal-va-ry to save a wretch like me; I heard a-bout his groan-ing, of his pre-cious blood's a-ton-ing, then I re-pent-ed of my sins and won the

2. I heard a-bout his heal-ing, of his cleans-ing power re-veal-ing, how he made the lame to walk a-gain and caused the blind to see; and then I cried, "Dear Je-sus, come and heal my bro-ken spir-it," and some-how Je-sus came and brought to me the

3 I heard a-bout a man-sion he has built for me in glory, and I heard a-bout the streets of gold be-yond the crys-tal sea; a-bout the an-gels sing-ing and the old re-demp-tion sto-ry, and some sweet day I'll sing up there the song of

WORDS: Eugene M. Bartlett
MUSIC: Eugene M. Bartlett
© 1939 Eugene M. Bartlett, renewed 1967 Mrs. Eugene M. Bartlett,
assigned to Albert E. Brumley & Sons, Inc., admin. ICG

HARTFORD
Irr. with Refrain

Refrain

vic - to - ry.
vic - to - ry. O   vic - to-ry   in   Je - sus,   my
vic - to - ry.

Sav - ior   for - ev - er!   He   sought me   and   bought me

with   his   re - deem-ing   blood;   he   loved me ere   I

knew him,   and   all   my love   is   due him;   he

plunged me   to   vic - to-ry   be - neath the cleans-ing   flood.

저 나사렛 예수 앞에
I Stand Amazed in the Presence

1. 저 나 사 렛 예 수 앞 에 나
2. 내 뜻 대 로 마 옵 시 고 주
3. 내 불 쌍 한 영 혼 위 해 주

1. I stand a-mazed in the pres - ence of
2. For me it was in the gar - den he
3. In pit - y an-gels be-held him, and

놀 라 며 서 있 네 영 죽 을
뜻 대 로 하 소 서 날 위 해
슬 퍼 하 시 던 밤 저 천 사

Je - sus the Naz - a - rene, and won - der
prayed: "Not my will, but thine." He had no
came from the world of light to com - fort

더 러 운 죄 인 어 찌 사 랑 하 셨 나 네
피 땀 을 흘 려 주 서 님 기 도 하 셨 네
들 내 려 와 서 주 님 위 로 하 였 네

how he could love me, a sin - ner, con-demned, un - clean.
tears for his own griefs, but sweat-drops of blood for mine.
him in the sor - rows he bore for my soul that night.

WORDS: Charles H. Gabriel (Lk. 22:41-44);
Korean trans. The United Methodist Korean Hymnal Committee
MUSIC: Charles H. Gabriel
Korean trans. © 2001 The United Methodist Publishing House, admin. The Copyright Co.

MY SAVIOR'S LOVE
87.87 with Refrain

후렴 (Refrain)

오 놀랍고 오 놀랍네 영원히 찬 양 하 리
How mar-vel-ous! How won-der-ful! And my song shall ev-er be:
(오 참 놀 랍 고 오 참 놀 랍 네)
(O how mar-vel-ous! O how won-der-ful!)

오 놀랍고 오 놀랍네 나를 위한 그 사 랑
How mar-vel-ous! How won-der-ful is my Sav-ior's love for me!
(오 참 놀 랍 고 오 참 놀 랍 네)
(O how mar-vel-ous! O how won-der-ful!)

4. 내 슬픔과 모든 죄악 몸소
   담당하시고 주 갈보리
   십자가에 죽임 당하셨도다

5. 그 언젠가 영광 중에 나
   주 얼굴 뵈올 때 날 구하신
   그의 사랑 기뻐 찬양하리라

4. He took my sins and my sorrows,
   he made them his very own;
   he bore the burden to Calvary,
   and suffered and died alone.

5. When with the ransomed in glory
   his face I at last shall see,
   'twill be my joy through the ages
   to sing of his love for me.

나 같은 죄인 살리신

WORDS: John Newton (Eph. 2:5); Korean trans. The Christian Literature Society of Korea
MUSIC: 19th cent. American melody; harm. Edwin O. Excell
Korean trans. © The Christian Literature Society of Korea

AMAZING GRACE
8.6.8.6.

Amazing Grace! How Sweet the Sound

1. A - maz - ing grace! How sweet the sound
2. 'Twas grace that taught my heart to fear,
3. Thru man - y dan - gers, toils, and snares,
4. When we've been there ten thou - sand years,

that saved a wretch like me! I
and grace my fears re - lieved; how
I have al - read - y come; 'tis
bright shin - ing as the sun, we've

once was lost, but now am found;
pre - cious did that grace ap - pear
grace hath brought me safe thus far,
no less days to sing God's praise

was blind, but now I see.
the hour I first be - lieved.
and grace will lead me home.
than when we'd first be - gun.

WORDS: John. Newton (Eph. 2:5)
MUSIC: 19th cent. American melody; harm. Edwin. O. Excell

AMAZING GRACE
8.6.8.6.

우리가 지금은 길가는 나그네
I Am a Stranger Here

1. 우리가 지금은 길가는 나그네
2. 주 예수 말씀이 온 세상 만민들
3. 영원한 생명과 기쁨이 넘치는

1. I am a strang-er here, with-in a for-eign land;
2. This is the King's com-mand; that all men, ev-'ry where,
3. My home is bright-er far than Shar-on's ro-sy plain,

화려한 천국에 머 잖아 가리니
흉악한 죄에서 떠나라 하시니
저 밝은 본향에 우리가 가리니

my home is far a-way, up-on a gold-en stand;
re-pent and turn a-way, from sin's se-duc-tive snare;
e-ter-nal life and joy thru'-out its vast do-main;

온 세상 향하여 주 말씀 전하라리
주 말씀 따르면 새 생명 얻으리리
만 백성 알도록 이 복음 전하라

am-bas-sa-dor to be of realms be-yond the sea,
that all who will o-bey, with him shall reign for aye,
my sov-'reign bids me tell how mor-tals there may dwell,

WORDS: F. H. Cassel; Korean trans. The United Methodist Korean Hymnal Committee
MUSIC: F. H. Cassel
Korean trans. © 2001 The United Methodist Publishing House, admin. The Copyright Co.

BUSINESS
12.12.12.8

주 께서 부 탁 하 셨 네 -
이 기쁜 소식 전 하 셨 세 -
주 께서 부 탁 하 셨 네 -

I'm here on busi-ness for my King.
and that's my busi-ness for my King.
and that's my busi-ness for my King.

후렴 (Refrain)

주 내 게 부 - 탁 하 신 일 - 천 사 도
This is the mes - sage that I bring, a mes -sage

찬 송 하 겠 네 - 하 늘 의 주 님 과 화 목 케
an-gels fain would sing: "Oh, be ye rec-on-ciled," thus saith my

하 라 신 주 말 씀 널 리 전 하 세 -
Lord and King, "Oh, be ye rec-on-ciled to God."

풍랑 이는 바다 위로

WORDS: Cecil Frances Alexander (Mt. 4:18-22); Korean trans. The United Methodist Korean Hymnal Committee
MUSIC: William H. Jude
Korean trans. © 2001 The United Methodist Publishing House, admin. The Copyright Co.

GALILEE
87.87

Jesus Calls Us

1. Je - sus calls us o'er the tu - mult of our
2. As of old the a - pos - tles heard it by the
3. Je - sus calls us from the wor - ship of the
4. In our joys and in our sor - rows, days of
5. Je - sus calls us! By thy mer - cies, Sav - ior,

life's wild, rest-less sea; day by day his sweet voice
Gal - i - le - an lake, turned from home and toil and
vain world's gold-en store, from each i - dol that would
toil and hours of ease, still he calls, in cares and
may we hear thy call, give our hearts to thine o -

sound - eth, say - ing, "Chris - tian, fol - low me!"
kin - dred, leav - ing all for Je - sus' sake.
keep us, say - ing, "Chris - tian, love me more!"
plea - sures, "Chris-tian, love me more than these!"
be - dience, serve and love thee best of all.

WORDS: Cecil Frances Alexander (Mt. 4:18-22)
MUSIC: William H. Jude

GALILEE
87.87

꽃이 필 때 믿음으로

WORDS: Anders Frostenson (Heb. 11); English trans. Fred Kaan;
Korean trans. The United Methodist Korean Hymnal Committee
MUSIC: V. Earle Copes
Words © 1976, Korean trans. © 2001 Hope Publishing Co.; music © 1960, renewed 1988 Hope Publishing Co.

FOR THE BREAD
87.87

Faith, While Trees Are Still in Blossom 97

1. Faith, while trees are still in blos - som, plans the pick-ing of the fruit; faith can feel the thrill of har - vest when the buds be - gin to sprout.
2. Long be - fore the dawn is break - ing, faith an - tic - i - pates the sun. Faith is ea - ger for the day - light, for the work that must be done.
3. Long be - fore the rains were com - ing, No - ah went and built an ark. A - bra - ham, the lone - ly mi - grant, saw the light be - yond the dark.
4. Faith, up - lift - ed, tamed the wa - ter of the un - di - vid - ed sea, and the peo - ple of the He - brews found the path that made them free.
5. Faith be - lieves that God is faith - ful: God will be what God will be! Faith ac - cepts the call, re - spond - ing, "I am will - ing, Lord, send me."

WORDS: Anders Frostenson (Heb. 11); English trans. Fred Kaan
MUSIC: V. Earle Copes
Words © 1976 Hope Publishing Co.; music © 1960, renewed 1988 Hope Publishing Co.

FOR THE BREAD
87.87

향유가 있는 길르앗
There Is a Balm in Gilead

후렴 (Refrain)

향 유가 있 는 길르앗 맘
There is a balm in Gil-e-ad to

상 처고치 네 - 향 유가 있 는
make the wound-ed whole; there is a balm in

Fine

길르앗 내 영 혼고 치 네
Gil-e-ad to heal the sin-sick soul.

1. 때 때 로 낙 심 되 고 큰 너
2. 주 예 수 친 구 시 니 너
3. 베 드 로 바 울 같 이 너

1. Some-times I feel dis-cour-aged, and
2. Don't ev-er feel dis-cour-aged, for
3. If you can't preach like Pe-ter, if

WORDS: African American spiritual (Jer. 8:22); Korean trans. The United Methodist Korean Hymnal Committee
MUSIC: African American spiritual; adapt. and arr. William Farley Smith
Adapt. and arr. © 1989, Korean trans. © 2001 The United Methodist Publishing House, admin. The Copyright Co.

BALM IN GILEAD
Irr.

실 망 하 여 도 주 성 령 께 서
낙 심 말 아 라 너 지 혜 구 할
할 수 없 어 도 널 위 해 돌 아
think my work's in vain. But then the Ho - ly
Je - sus is your friend, and if you look for
you can't pray like Paul, just tell the love of

D. S.

내 영 소 생 시 키 도 다 - -
때 에 주 응 답 하 시 리 - -
가 신 그 사 랑 전 하 라 - -
Spir - it re - vives my soul a - gain.
knowl - edge he'll ne'er re - fuse to lend.
Je - sus, and say he died for all.

99

주 예수님 내 맘에 오사
Come into My Heart, Blessed Jesus

1. 주 예수님 내 맘에 오오 사사
2. 주 예예수님 내 맘에 오오 사사
3. 주 예예수님 내 맘에 오오 사사
4. 주 예예수님 내 맘에 오 사

1. Come in - to my heart, bless - ed Je - sus,
2. Come in - to my heart, bless - ed Je - sus,
3. Come in - to my heart, bless - ed Je - sus,
4. Come in - to my heart, bless - ed Je - sus,

날 붙들어 어 주 - 시고 -
내 소원 다아 - 시고 -
날 정결케인 하 - 시고 -
내 앞길 인도 - 하여 -

come in - to my heart, I pray;
I need thee thro' life's dreary way;
and take all my guilt a - way;
O cleanse and il - lu - mine my soul;

내 마음 음에 새 힘을 주 사사
내 무은 거기운로 짐맡아 주채 워에
그 이세 혜상을 내심판할 때 에
이 세 상을 심판할 주 채 때에

my soul is so troub - led and wea - ry,
the bur - den of sin is so heav - y,
then spot - less I'll stand in thy pres - ence,
fill me with thy won - der - ful Spir - it,

WORDS: Harry D. Clarke (Eph. 3:17-19); Korean trans. The United Methodist Korean Hymnal Committee
MUSIC: Harry D. Clarke
© 1924, renewed 1952, Korean trans. © 2001 Hope Publishing Co.

INTO MY HEART
9.7.9.7.8.8.8.8.

늘 기 쁘 게 합 소 서 -
맘 편 충 하 게 합 소 서
늘 흠 만 게 합 소 서
날 없 케 합 소 서

come in - to my heart to - day.
come in - to my heart to stay.
when breaks thine e - ter - nal day.
come in and take full con - trol.

후렴 (*Refrain*)

사 랑 의 주 사 랑 의 주 내 맘 속 에 찾 아
In - to my heart, in - to my heart, come in - to my heart, Lord

오 사 내 모 든 죄 사 하 시 고 내
Je - sus; come in to-day, come in to stay, come

상 한 맘 고 치 소 서
in - to my heart, Lord Je - sus.

100

주여 나를 이끄사
Dear Lord, Lead Me Day by Day

1. 주여 나를 이끄사 힘과 지혜
2. 주여 나를 이끄사 순종하게
3. 주께 확신 가지고 기쁜 찬양

1. Dear Lord, lead me day by day; make me stead-fast,
2. Dear Lord, lead me day by day; make me fol-low
3. Now with con-fi-dence I sing joy-ous prais-es

주시고 나를 사랑하심을 항상
하시고 변치 않는주사랑의지
드리며 맘과 정성다하여 나의

wise, and strong; hap-py most of all to know that my
and o - bey faith-ful - ly your words of life, that your
to our God, and with up - right heart I give ten - der

후렴 (Refrain)

알게 하소서
하게 하소서 찬양해 주님께
이웃 돌보네

dear Lord loves me so.
love ev - er a - bide. Praise to God, fount of love,
care and sym - pa - thy.

WORDS: Francisca Asuncion; Korean trans. The United Methodist Korean Hymnal Committee
MUSIC: Philippine folk melody; arr. Francisca Asuncion
© 1983, Korean trans. © 2001 The United Methodist Publishing House, admin. The Copyright Co.

COTTAGE GROVE
77.77 with Refrain

언제든지 찬양해 사랑의
praise from morn till the set of sun; praise at home,

주 님 께 어 디 서 나 찬 양 해
praise in church; praise to God ev-ery-where on earth.

101

나의 갈 길 다 가도록
All the Way My Savior Leads Me

1. 나 의 갈 길 다 가 도 록 예 수 인 도 하 시 니
2. 나 의 갈 길 다 가 도 록 예 수 인 도 하 시 니
3. 나 의 갈 길 다 가 도 록 예 수 인 도 하 시 니

1. All the way my Sav-ior leads me; what have I to ask be-side?
2. All the way my Sav-ior leads me; cheers each wind-ing path I tread;
3. All the way my Sav-ior leads me; O the full-ness of his love!

내 주 안 에 있는 궁 휼 어 찌 의 심 하 리 요
어 려 운 일 당 할 때도 족 한 은 혜 주 시 네
그 의 사 랑 어 찌 큰 지 말 로 할 수 없 도 다

Can I doubt his ten-der mer-cy, who thru life has been my guide?
gives me grace for ev-ery tri-al, feeds me with the liv-ing bread;
Per-fect rest to me is prom-ised in my Fa-ther's house a-bove;

믿 음 으 로 사 는 자 는 하 늘 위 로 받 겠 네
나 는 심 히 고 단 하 고 나 의 영 혼 갈 하 나
나 를 위 해 예 비 하 신 하 늘 나 라 갈 때 에

Heaven-ly peace, di-vin-est com-fort, here by faith in him to dwell;
though my wea-ry steps may fal-ter, and my soul a-thirst may be,
when my spir-it clothed, im-mor-tal, wings its flight to realms of day,

WORDS: Fanny J. Crosby; Korean trans. The United Methodist Korean Hymnal Committee
MUSIC: Robert Lowry
Korean trans. © 2001 The United Methodist Publishing House, admin. The Copyright Co.

ALL THE WAY
8.7.8.7.D

102

주의 빛 따르기 원합니다

1. 주 의 빛 따 르 기 원 합 니 다
2. 주 님 의 빛 보 기 원 합 니 다
3. 곧 오 실 주 님 을 기 다 리 네

예 수 를 따 라 라 가 리
예 수 를 바 라 라 보 리
예 수 와 함 께 살 리

하 나 님 세 상 에 빛 주 셨 네 내
의 우 리 운 태 양 빛 길 밝 동 서 날
우 리 의 인 생 길 가 는 는 안 주

생 명 의 별 이 주 예 수 서 네
주 께 로 이 끄 소 네
기 쁨 을 맛 보 겠

WORDS: Kathleen Thomerson; Korean trans. The United Methodist Korean Hymnal Committee
MUSIC: Kathleen Thomerson
© 1970, 1975, Korean trans. © 2001 Celebration

HOUSTON
10 7. 10 8 with Refrain

후렴

주 안에 어둠 전혀 없네 또

밤 낮이 구 - 분 없다네 저

천 국의 빛 되신 주 - 예 수 여.

내 마음 밝히 소 - 서

102 I Want to Walk as a Child of the Light

1. I want to walk as a child of the light.
2. I want to see the bright-ness of God.
3. I'm look-ing for the com-ing of Christ.

I want to fol - low Je - sus.
I want to look at Je - sus.
I want to be with Je - sus.

God set the stars to give light to the world. The
Clear sun of Righ-teous-ness, shine on my path, and
When we have run with pa-tience the race we

star of my life is Je - sus.
show me the way to the Fa - ther.
shall know the joy of Je - sus.

WORDS: Kathleen Thomerson
MUSIC: Kathleen Thomerson
© 1970, 1975 Celebration

HOUSTON
10 7. 10 8 with Refrain

이 마음 주께로

1. 이 마음 주께로 이 이끄소서
2. 내 걸음 주께로 이 이끄소서
3. 세 상을 주께로 이 이끄소서

빛 나 는 새 뜻 을 을 주 가 옵 소 서 다서
주 가 신 과 그 길 을 을 셋 오 기 소 서
허 물 과 죄 악 을 을 셋 오 기 소

그 크 신 사 랑 에서 내 마 음 녹 아 서며지
새 힘 을 받 아 서 내 마 음 녹 아 서며지
이 땅 에 천 국 이 바 임 하 는 걸 날 까

주 님 의 귀 한 뜻 빛 내 리리 다라다
인 생 의 의 참 된 길 보 이 르리 다라다
구 원 의 노 래 를 부 르리

WORDS: Lucy Arcom (Lk. 17:5); Korean trans. The Christian Literature Society of Korea
MUSIC: Arthur S. Sullivan
Korean trans. © The Christian Literature Society of Korea

ST. EDMUND
6.4.6.4.6.6.6.4

Draw Thou My Soul, O Christ

1. Draw thou my soul, O Christ, clos - er to thine;
2. Lead forth my soul, O Christ, one with thine own,
3. Not for my - self a - lone may my prayer be;

breathe in - to ev - ery wish thy will di - vine!
joy - ful to fol - low thee through paths un - known!
lift though thy world, O Christ, clos - er to thee!

Raised my low self a - bove, won by thy death-less love;
In thee my strength re - new; give me my work to do!
Cleanse it from guilt and wrong; teach it sal - va - tion's song,

ev - er, O Christ, thru mine let thy life shine.
Through me thy truth be shown, thy love made known.
till earth, as hea - ven, ful - fills God's ho - ly will.

WORDS: Lucy Larcom (Lk. 17:5)
MUSIC: Arthur S. Sullivan

ST. EDMUND
6.4.6.4.6.6.6.4

나와 함께 걸으소서

1. 나 와 함 께 – 걸 으 소 서 (예 수 여)
2. 내 가 시 험 – 당 할 때 에 (예 수 여)
3. 내 가 괴 롬 – 당 할 때 에 (예 수 여)

나 와 함 께 – 걸 으 소 서 (예 수 여)
나 와 함 께 – 걸 으 소 서 (예 수 여)
나 와 함 께 – 걸 으 소 서 (예 수 여)

나 의 평 생 – 순 – 례 길 을 때
나 의 가 슴 – 찢 – 어 질 때
내 가 슬 퍼 – 낙 – 심 될 때

주 – 님 나 와 함 께 – 걸 으 소 서 (예 수 여)

WORDS: African American spiritual; Korean trans. The United Methodist Korean Hymnal Committee
MUSIC: African American spiritual; adapt. William Farley Smith
Adapt. © 1989, Korean trans. © 2001 The United Methodist Publishing House, admin. The Copyright Co.

SOJOURNER
888.9

I Want Jesus to Walk with Me

104

1. I want Je - sus to walk with me. (walk with me)
2. In my tri - als, Lord, walk with me. (walk with me)
3. When I'm trou - bled, Lord, walk with me. (walk with me)

I want Je - sus to walk with me. (walk with me)
In my tri - als, Lord, walk with me. (walk with me)
When I'm trou - bled, Lord, walk with me. (walk with me)

All a - long my pil - grim jour - ney,
When my heart is al - most break - ing,
When my head is bowed in sor - row,

Lord, I want Je - sus to walk with me. (walk with me)

WORDS: African American spiritual
MUSIC: African American spiritual; adapt. William Farley Smith
Adapt. © 1989 The United Methodist Publishing House, admin. The Copyright Co.

SOJOURNER
888.9

105

예수 내 주께
(싸라남 싸라남)

후렴

예 수 내 주 께 나 아 갑 니 다

싸 라 남 싸 라 남 싸 라 남
(예 수 는 우 리 의 피 난 처)

주 는 나 의 반 석 과 피 난 처

싸 라 남 싸 라 남 싸 라 남
(예 수 는 우 리 의 피 난 처)

Saranam: 피난처 (파키스탄어)

WORDS: Trad. Pakistani (Ps. 61: Heb. 13:8); Korean trans. The United Methodist Korean Hymnal Committee
MUSIC: Trad. Punjabi melody; arr. Shanti Rasanayagam
Arr. by permission of Chistian Conference of Asia

PUNJABI
Irr. with Refrain

105

Jesus, Savior, Lord
(Saranam, Saranam)

Refrain

Je - sus, Sav - ior, Lord, lo, to thee I fly:

Sar - a - nam, Sar - a - nam, Sar - a - nam;

thou the Rock, my ref - uge that's higher than I:

Sar - a - nam, Sar - a - nam, Sar - a - nam.

Saranam: Refuge
WORDS: Trad. Pakistani (Ps. 61: Heb. 13:8); English trans. D. T. Niles
MUSIC: Trad. Punjabi melody; arr. Shanti Rasanayagam
Trans. and arr. by permission of Christian Conference of Asia

PUNJABI
Irr. with Refrain

1. In the midst of foes I cry to thee,
2. In thy tent give me a dwell - ing place,
3. O that I my vows to thee may pay,
4. Yes - ter - day, to - day, for - e'er the same,

from the ends of earth wher- ev - er I may be;
and be - neath thy wings may I find shel - tering grace;
and that by thy faith - ful - ness to me each day
lo, the her - i - tage of all who bear thy name;

my strength in help - less - ness, O an - swer me:
O lift on me the sun - shine of thy face:
may live, and on thy love my bur - dens lay:
to ran - som them from sin the Sav - ior came:

Sar - a - nam, Sar - a - nam, Sar - a - nam.

캄캄한 밤중에 빈들에서

1. 캄 캄 한 밤 중 에 빈 들 에 서 죄
2. 조 상 의 허 물 과 내 지 은 죄
3. 이 길 은 나 에 게 살 길 이 요

갈 바 리 를 의 모 살 르 길 고 을 애 늘 쓰 다 는 가 데 라
우 이 리 빛 의 은 나 길 에 게 참 막 복 이 라

어 둠 을 쫓 는 해 떠 오 를 때 가
참 이 생 빛 명 을 찾 따 으 라 서 늘 앞 으 로

생 명 을 주 는 길 나 나 찾 보 았 다 다
예 수 의 밝 은 성 에 나 나 가 려 다 다
끝 까 지 천 빛 나 보 가 련 다

WORDS: Bin Oh (Jn. 8:12)
MUSIC: Woon Young Na
Music © Woon Young Na

In Deepest Darkness I Wandered Alone   106

1. In deep-est dark-ness I wan-dered a - lone,
2. Sins of our an - ces - tors block - ing the way,
3. This way has led me to new - ness of life,

lost in the wild - er - ness, year - ning for home;
my sins have al - so led me a - stray;
sho - wers of bles - sing now rain on my head;

I found the way of life as the sun a - rose
I saw the light of life, Je - sus shone on me
I found the way of light, this will lead me on,

chas-ing the dark, show-ing the way,
I tried in vain, he res-cued me, I found the way.
I will go forth in Je-sus' light,

WORDS: Bin Oh (Jn. 8:12); English trans. Edward Poitras
MUSIC: Woon Young Na
English trans. © 2001 The United Methodist Publishing House, admin. The Copyright Co.;
music © Woon Young Na

LIGHT OF THE WORLD
10.10

온종일 예수와 함께

1. 온 종 일 - 예 수 와 함 께
2. 온 종 일 - 예 예 수 와 함 께
3. 당 신 도 - 예 수 와 함 께

즐 겁 게 - 지 내 었 네 -
이 야 기 - 나 누 었 네 네 -
행 하 지 - 않 으 려 나 -

한 걸 음 - 더 높 이 올 - 라 라
한 걸 음 - 더 높 이 올 - 라 나
모 든 죄 - 슬 픔 을 떠 - 나

주 의 거 룩 한 길 걸 으 으 리 리 -
주 의 거 룩 한 길 걸 으 리 -
주 의 거 룩 한 길 걸 으 리

WORDS: African folk hymn (Ps. 23:6); Korean trans. The United Methodist Korean Hymnal Committee
MUSIC: Traditional; arr. Marie Gray
Korean trans. © 2001 The United Methodist Publishing House, admin. The Copyright Co.;
arr. © 1991 McKinney Music, Inc., admin. Genevox Music Group

ALL DAY LONG
Irr.

All Day Long

1. All day long   I've been with Je - sus,
2. All day long   I've been with Je - sus,
3. Won't you come   and walk with Je - sus?

it has been   a glo - rious day.
it has been   a glo - rious day.
It will be   a glo - rious day.

I've just moved   up one step high - er,
It has moved   me one step high - er
You can leave   your sin and sor - row,

and I'm walk - ing on the King's high - way.
on my walk a - long the King's high - way.
you can walk up - on the King's high - way.

WORDS: African folk hymn (Ps. 23:6)
MUSIC: Traditional; arr. Marie Gray
Arr. © 1991 McKinney Music, Inc., admin. Genevox Music Group

ALL DAY LONG
Irr.

예수 말씀 듣고자

WORDS: Tobias Clausnitzer; Korean trans. The United Methodist Korean Hymnal Committee
MUSIC: Johann R. Ahle
Korean trans. © 2001 The United Methodist Publishing House, admin. The Copyright Co.

LIEBSTER JESUS
78.78.88

Blessed Jesus, at Thy Word

1. Bless-ed Je-sus, at thy Word we are gath-ered
2. All our knowl-edge, sense, and sight lie in deep-est
3. Glo-rious Lord, thy-self im-part! Light of light, from

all to hear thee; let our hearts and souls be stirred
dark-ness shroud-ed, till thy spir-it breaks our night
God pro-ceed-ing, o-pen thou our ears and heart;

now to seek and love and fear thee, by thy teach-ings
with the beams of truth un-cloud-ed. Thou a-lone to
help us by thy spir-it's plead-ing; hear the cry thy

sweet and ho-ly, drawn from earth to love thee sole-ly.
God canst win us; thou must work all good with-in us.
peo-ple rais-es; hear, and bless our prayers and prais-es.

WORDS: Tobias Clausnitzer; English trans. Catherine Winkworth
MUSIC: Johann R. Ahle

LIEBSTER JESU
78.78.88

주 말씀은 나의 발에 등

WORDS: Amy Grant (Ps. 119:105); Korean trans. The United Methodist Korean Hymnal Committee
MUSIC: Michael W. Smith; arr. Keith Phillips
© 1984 Meadowgreen Music Co., Word Music, Inc.

THY WORD
Irr. with Refrain

Thy Word Is a Lamp

WORDS: Amy Grant (Ps. 119:105)
MUSIC: Michael W. Smith; arr. Keith Phillips
© 1984 Meadowgreen Music Co., Word Music, Inc.

THY WORD
Irr. with Refrain

110

거룩하다 성경은
Holy Bible, Book Divine

1. 거룩하다 성경은 나의 귀한 보배요
2. 내가 방황할 때에서 주의 사랑 깨우치고
3. 성경의 힘입어서 깊은 진리 깨닫고
4. 모든 기쁜 소식이 이 책 중에 실리고

1. Ho-ly Bi-ble, book di-vine, pre-cious trea-sure, thou art mine:
2. Mine to chide me when I rove, mine to show a Sa-vior's love;
3. Mine to com-fort in dis-tress, suf-fering in this wil-der-ness;
4. Mine to tell of joys to come, and the re-bel sin-ner's doom:

나의 근본 길 어딘지 서서 밝히 알게 해 주고 고
나의 믿음으로 살아서 모진 고난 견디고고
거역하는 사람은 경계함을 받으니

ho-ly Bi-ble, book di-vine, pre-cious trea-sure, thou art mine:
mine to chide me when I rove, mine to show a Sa-vior's love;
mine to com-fort in dis-tress, suf-fering in this wil-der-ness;
mine to tell of joys to come, and the re-bel sin-ner's doom:

나의 할 일 판세 깨달 게 어서 밝영 히생 일전길가 러을 주보 도인른 다다다
주사망하다 성경은 거룩하

mine to tell me whence I came; mine to teach me what I am.
mine thou art to guide and guard; mine to pun-ish or re-ward.
mine to show by li-ving faith, we can tri-umph o-ver death.
O thou ho-ly book di-vine, pre-cious trea-sure, thou art mine.

WORDS: John Burton (Ps. 119:11); Korean trans. The Christian Literature Society of Korea
MUSIC: H. H. Blackith
Korean trans. © The Christian Literature Society of Korea

ALETTA
7.7.7.7.

주 하나님의 말씀이

1. 주 - 하 나 님의 말씀이 씨 - 뿌 려졌으 니 -
2. 그 - 거 룩 하신 씨앗을 늘 - 지 켜주시 고 -
3. 이 - 세 상 많은 유혹에 빠 - 지 지않으 며 -

공 - 의 의열 매 맺도록 이슬 내 려주소 서
사 - 랑 의열 매 맺도록 뿌리 내 려주소 서
평 - 화 의열 매 풍성히 맺 - 도 록하소 서

Almighty God, Your Word Is Cast   111

1. Al - might - y God, your Word is cast like seed in-to the ground;
2. Let not the sly sa - tan- ic foe this ho - ly seed re - move,
3. Let not the world's de -ceit-ful cares the ris - ing plant de - stroy,

now let the dew of heav'n de-scend and righ-teous fruits a-bound.
but give it root in ev-'ry heart to bring forth fruits of love.
but let it yield a hun-dred-fold the fruits of peace and joy.

WORDS: Phoebe H. Brown (Phil. 1:11); Korean trans. The United Methodist Korean Hymnal Committee
MUSIC: Alonzo J. Abbey
Korean trans. © 2001 The United Methodist Publishing House, admin. The Copyright Co.

COOLING
8.6.8.7

이슬을 내리시듯 말씀을 내리소서

1. 이 슬 을 내리시듯 말 씀 을 내리소서
2. 단 비 를 내리시듯 맑은 혜 를 내리소서
3. 햇 빛 을 비추시듯 평 화 를 내리소서

생 명 의의 주 예 수 님 말 씀 을 내 리 시 면
사 랑 의의 주 예 수 님 맑은 혜 를 내 리 시 면
구 원 의 주 예 수 님 평 화 를 내 리 시

죄 악 에 시 든 영혼 새 생 명 얻 으 리 니
마 르 고 주 린 영혼 새 새 힘 을 얻 으 리 니
상 하 고 찢 긴 영혼 위 로 를 받 으 리 니

말 은 씀 을 내 리 소 서 생 명 의의 주 예 수 여
맑은 혜 를 내 리 소 서 사 랑 의의 주 예 수 여
평 화 를 내 리 소 서 사 랑 의 의 주 예 수 여

WORDS: Hee Bo Kim (Dt. 32:2)
MUSIC: Soon Sae Kim
Words © Korean Hymnal Society; music © Soon Sae Kim

AS DEW FALLS
7.8.8.8.

As Dew Falls Gently at Night

1. As dew falls gent-ly at night speak to us your beautiful word,
2. As rain falls feed-ing the earth send the bless-ings of your great love,
3. As light shines forth from the sun, breathe on us your spir-it of peace,

Je - sus, Lord, when you send your word, word of life, your won-der-ful word
Je - sus, Lord, when you send your grace, grace un-bound-ed fill-ing our souls
Sa - vior Je - sus, send us your peace, calm our wound-ed souls from with - in

all we who wan-der in sin find strength and new-ness of life.
all we who hun-ger and thirst find strength and new-ness of life.
all we who suf-fer and sigh find strength and new-ness of life.

Je-sus, Lord, when you send your word morn-ing breaks and we walk in light.
Je-sus, Lord, when you send your love we a-rise and fol-low your way.
Je-sus, Lord, when you send your love we go forth in heavenly peace.

WORDS: Hee Bo Kim (Dt. 32:2); English trans. Edward Poitras
MUSIC: Soon Sae Kim
Words and English trans. © The Korean Hymnal Society; music © Soon Sae Kim

AS DEW FALLS
7.8.8.8.

주의 말씀 내리소서
Send Your Word

1. 주 의 말 씀 내 리 소 서
2. 주 의 말 씀 내 리 소 서

1. Send your Word, O Lord, like the rain,
2. Send your Word, O Lord, of the wind,

떨 어 지 는 빗 물 처 럼 오 주 여
불 어 오 는 바 람 처 럼 오 주 여

fall- ing down up - on the earth. Send your Word.
blow-ing down up - on the earth. Send your Word.

한 없 는 주 은 혜 력
놀 라 운 주 능 력

We seek your end - less grace,
We seek your won - drous power,

주 리 고 목 마 름 에 는
모 든 죄 물 리 치 는

with souls that hun - ger and thirst,
pure - ness that re - jects all sins,

WORDS: Yasushige Imakoma; English trans. Nobuaki Hanaoka
MUSIC: Shozo Koyama
English trans. © 1983, Korean trans. © 2001 The United Methodist Publishing House, admin. The Copyright Co.;
© 1967 The Hymnal Committee of The United Church of Japan

MIKOTOBA
Irr.

애 타 - 게 구 하 네
완 전 - 한 그 능 력
sor - row and ag - o - nize.
though they per - sist and cling.

주 의 참 빛 없 이 는
승 리 하 게 하 소 서
We would all be lost in dark
Bring us to com - plete vic - tory;

어 둠 속 헤 매 리
자 유 케 하 소 서
with - out your guid - ing light.
set us all free in - deed.

3. 주의 말씀 내리소서
부드러운 이슬처럼
오 주여 한없는 주 사랑
고통과 상처받은 영혼들
위하여 주 사랑의 능력을
베풀어주소서

3. Send your Word, O Lord, like the dew,
coming gently upon the hills.
Send your Word. We seek your endless love.
For life that suffers in strife with adversities
and hurts, send your healing power of love;
we long for your new world.

114

내가 환난 당할 때에

1. 내가 환난 당할 때에 주가 보호하시고
2. 주가 구원하셨으니 기쁘고도 고마와
3. 어떤 이는 세상 권세 믿고 의지하여도

거룩한 산 시온에서 도우심을 원하네
주의 이름 위하여서 기를 들어 세우리
우리들은 주의 이름 의지하고 바라네

모든 죄를 통회하고 나의 몸을 드리니
하나님이 구세주를 하늘에서 보내사
저이들은 넘어져도 우리 굳게 서리라

믿음으로 구한 것을 이뤄 주심 바라네
피를 흘려 구려 우리들을 구원하여 주셨네
우리 주여 구원하고 내게 응답하소서

WORDS: A. A. Pieters (Ps. 20:1); Korean trans. The Christian Literature Society of Korea
MUSIC: J. H. Willcox
Korean trans. © The Christian Literature Society of Korea

FABEN
8.7.8.7.D

The Lord H...

1. The Lord hear thee in af-flic-tion; the Lord guard thee i...
2. For the sav - ing grace be-stow'd us hymns of joy and thanks we...
3. Let who will re - ly on rich-es, name or sta - tion, strength or swor...

from his ho - ly hill of Zi - on be thy staff and stay in-deed.
while we lift a - loft the ban - ner of our Sa-vior's ho-ly name.
As for us, our full re - li-ance shall be on - ly on the Lord.

When the soul turns in re-pent-ance from the sin we so de-plore,
God sent down his Son from heav-en his re-bel-lious world to win;
On the day they fall and per - ish, still shall we in him stand fast.

may he grant his full sal - va-tion and his peace on Ca-naan's shore.
Christ the Son, his blood out-pour-ing, wro't sal-va-tion for our sin.
O, our God, be swift to save us! Hear and an-swer us at last!

WORDS: A. A. Pieters (Ps. 20:1)
MUSIC: J. H. Willcox

FABEN
8.7.8.7.D

나의 목자 되시니
The Lord's My Shepherd, I'll Not Want

1. 주 나 의 목 자 되 시 니 부 족 함 없 도 다
2. 내 영 혼 소 생 시 키 며 그 이 름 위 하 여
3. 나 어 둠 골 짝 지 나 도 두 려 움 없 겠 네

1. The Lord's my shep - herd, I'll not want. He makes me down to lie
2. My soul he doth re - store a-gain, and me to walk doth make
3. Yea, though I walk in death's dark vale, yet will I fear no ill;

푸 른 풀 밭 호 숫 가 로 날 인 도 하 시 네
늘 의 로 운 길 걷 도 록 날 인 도 하 시 네
주 막 대 기 와 지 팡 이 날 안 위 하 시 네

in pas - tures green; he lead - eth me the qui - et wa - ters by.
with - in the paths of righ - teous-ness, e'en for his own name's sake.
for thou art with me, and thy rod and staff me com-fort still.

4. 주 나의 원수 앞에서 내 상을 베푸사
   머리에 기름 부으니 내 잔이 넘치네

5. 선함과 인자하심이 내 평생 따르리
   여호와 전에 영원히 나 거하리로다

4. My table thou hast furnished in presence of my foes;
   my head thou dost with oil anoint, and cup overflows.

5. Goodness and mercy all my life shall surely follow me;
   and in God's house forevermore my dwelling place shall be.

WORDS: *Scottish Psalter*, 1650 (Ps. 23); Korean trans. The United Methodist Korean Hymnal Committee
MUSIC: Jesse Seymour Irvine; harm. TCL. Pritchard
Korean trans. © 2001 The United Methodist Publishing House, admin. The Copyright Co.; harm. © Oxford University Press

CRIMOND
CM

목마른
As the

MS AND PRAISE

1. 목 마 른 사 슴 시 냇 물 을
2. 금 보 다 귀 한 나 의 주 님 내
1. As the deer pant-eth for the wa-ter, so my
2. I want you more than gold or sil-ver, on-ly

헤 매 이 듯 이 며 갈 급 한 나 의
만 족 주 시 며 눈 동 자 처 럼
soul longs af-ter you. You a - lone are my
you can sat-is-fy. You a - lone are the

영 혼 주 를 찾 아 부 르 나 이 다
귀 한 주 님 참 된 기 쁨 주 시 네
heart's de-sire, and I long to wor - ship you.
real joy gi-ver and the ap - ple of my eye.

후렴 (Refrain)

주 님 만 이 나 의 힘 나 의 방 패 나 의
You a - lone are my strength, my shield; to you a - lone may my

참 소 망 나 의 맘 정 성
spir - it yield. You a - lone are my

다 바 쳐 서 주 님 경 배 합 니 다
heart's de-sire, and I long to wor - ship you.

WORDS: Martin Nystrom (Ps. 42:1); Korean trans. The United Methodist Korean Hymnal Committee
MUSIC: Martin Nystrom
© 1984, Korean trans. © 2001, Maranatha! Praise, Inc., admin. The Copyright Co.

주여 우리 무리를

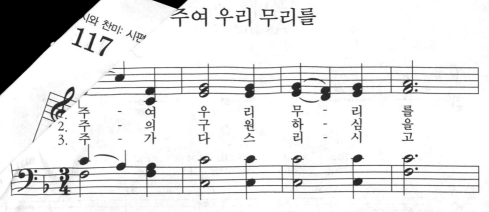

4. 땅에 나는 모든 것 주의 크신 은혜니 천하 만국 백성들 주께 찬송합니다
5. 하나님이 우리게 복을 내려주시니 땅의 모든 만물이 주를 경외합니다

WORDS: Anonymous (Ps. 67:1); Korean trans. The Christian Literature Society of Korea
MUSIC: W. B. Bradbury
Korean trans. © The Christian Literature Society of Korea

ALETTA
7.7.7.7.

God, Be Merciful to Us

1. God, be merciful to us,
   in the greatness of your grace,
   and to us who are but dust,
   grant the joy to see your face.

2. By the world-wide message giv'n,
   you have made salvation known,
   and all peoples under heav'n,
   lift their praises to your throne.

3. You do gov'rn in holiness,
   truth in judgment do employ;
   while the nations you do bless,
   bless your name with holy joy.

4. All that comes to pass on earth,
   Lord, your bounteous grace supplies;
   and we laud your matchless worth
   from all nations 'neath the skies.

5. Blest of God who names us his,
   raining bounties from above,
   earth and all that in it is
   fears the Lord with joy and love!

WORDS: Anonymous (Ps. 67:1)
MUSIC: W. B. Bradbury

ALETTA
7.7.7.7.

118

온 땅의 모든 사람들
All People That on Earth Do Dwell

WORDS: Attr. William Kethe (Ps. 100); Korean trans. The United Methodist Korean Hymnal Committee
MUSIC: Attr. Louis Bourgeois
Korean trans. © 2001 The United Methodist Publishing House, admin. The Copyright Co.

OLD 100th
LM

내가 산을 향하여
To the High and Kindly Hills

내 가 산 을 향 하 여　　눈 을 드 니 -
To the high and kind-ly hills　I lift my eyes;

장고 (Chang-go/Drum)

나 의 도 움 이 어 디 서　　오 는 - 가 -
where is some-one to res-cue me　in my plight?

나 의 도 움 이 천 지 를　　지 으 - 신 -
Tru-ly from the dear Lord a-bove　help will come.

여 호 와 하 나 님 에 게 서　　오 - 네 -
God is the mak-er of heav'n and earth:　all is well.

WORDS: Song-suk Im; para. James Minchin (Ps. 121)
MUSIC: Song-ch'on Lee
© 1990 *Sound The Bamboo*

NA-UI DO-UM
7.4.8.3

120

찬양하여라
Bless the Lord

회중 *(Cong.)*

찬 양 하 여 라　　　　주 찬 양 하 여 라 -
Bless the Lord, my soul,　　and bless God's ho-ly name.

찬 양 하 여 라　　　　생 명 의 하 나 님　(1. 용서)
Bless the Lord, my soul,　　who leads me in-to life.　(1. It is)

WORDS: Jacques Berthier (Ps. 103); Korean trans. The United Methodist Korean Hymnal Committee
MUSIC: Jacques Berthier and The Taizé Community
© 1984, Korean trans. © 2001 Les Presses de Taizé (France), admin. GIA Publications, Inc.

회중 찬송이 반복될 때 독창자가 부르는 시편 가사 (Superimposed on ostinato chorale)

독창 (Solo(s))

1. 용서 하 시 는 주 하 나 님 네
1. It is God who for- gives all your guilt who

아 픔 을 씻 으 시 네 사 랑 으 로 인 도 하
heals ev-'ry one of your ills, who re-deems your life from the

고 그 큰 사 랑 베 푸 시 도 다
grave, who crowns you with love and com-pas-sion.

2. 하 나 님 은 사 랑 이 라 분 노
2. The Lord is com-pas-sion and love, slow to

하 기 를 더 디 하 사 우 리 의 모 든 죄용서하시
an-ger and rich in mer-cy. God does not treat us ac-cord-ing to our

고 크 신 자 비 를 베 푸 시 도 다
sins nor re-pay us ac-cord-ing to our faults.

3. 아 버 지 가 자 녀 사 랑 하 심 같 이 우 리 를
3. As a Fa-ther has com-pas-sion on his chil-dren, the Lord has

불 쌍 히 여 기 심 은 그 가 우 리 연 약 함
pit-y on those who fear him; for God knows of what we are

을 항 상 기 억 하 심 이 라
made; God re-mem-bers that we are dust.

121

주 찬양하여라
Sing, Praise and Bless the Lord

WORDS: Taizé Community (Ps. 117; 47:1; 100:2-3); Korean trans. The United Methodist Korean Hymnal Committee
MUSIC: Jacques Berthier
© 1980, Korean trans. © 2001 Les Presses de Taizé (France), admin. GIA Publications, Inc.

회중 찬송이 반복될 때 독창자가 부르는 시편 가사 (Superimposed on ostinato chorale)

독창 (Solo(s))

1. 찬 - 양 해 모 든 나 라 찬 양 모 든
1. Praise - the Lord, all you na - tions; praise him, all you

백 성 알 - 렐 루 야 주 님 의 크 신
peo - ples; al - le - lu - ia. Strong is his love and

사 랑 주 의 영 원 한 자 비 알 - 렐 루 야
mer - cy, God is faith-ful for - ev - er, al - le - lu - ia.

2. 땅 들 아 주 께 외 쳐 라 알 렐 루 야 알 렐
2. Let the earth shout to God with joy, al - le - lu - ia, al - le -

루 - 야 기 쁨 의 소 리 로 경 - 배
lu - ia. Let the earth wor-ship with sounds of

하 라 알 렐 루 야 알 렐 루 야
glad - ness, al - le - lu - ia, al - le - lu - ia.

3. 기 쁨 의 노 래 로 주 께 오 네 알 렐 루
3. We come be - fore you with joy - ful songs, al - le - lu -

야 알 렐 루 - 야 창 조 의 주 하 나
ia, al - le - lu - ia. You are our God, you have

님 께 알 렐 루 야 알 렐 루 야 알 렐 루 야
made us, al - le - lu - ia, al - le - lu - ia, al - le - lu - ia.

122

내가 깊은 곳에서
From the Depths, O Lord, I Cry

1. 내 - 가 깊 은 곳 - 에 서
2. 주 - 가 죄 를 살 - 피 면
3. 파 - 수 꾼 이 새 - 벽 을
4. 이 - 스 라 엘 백 - 성 아

1. From the depths, O Lord, I cry;
2. Lord, if thou shouldst mark our sin,
3. As the watch - man waits the dawn,
4. Is - ra - el, God's cho - sen race,

주 - 께 불 러 아 - 뢰 리 요
누 - 가 다 리 고 바 - 라 듯
기 - 다 만 믿 고 바 - 라 라
주 - 만

hear me when I pray to thee.
who could then be - fore thee stand?
dark - ness done and light re - stored.
look to him and trust his name;

주 - 여 나 의 간 - 구 를
오 - 직 주 만 모 - 든 죄 만
나 - 의 영 혼 은 - 님 에
주 - 의 깊 은 은 - 충 만

Migh - ty, help - er, ev - er nigh,
But all sins, with - out, with - in,
Yearns my soul, the dark - ness gone,
for on his un - fath - om'd grace,

WORDS: Anonymous (Ps. 130:1); Korean trans. The Christian Literature Society of Korea
MUSIC: D. S. Bortniansky (1752-1825)
Korean trans. © The Christian Literature Society of Korea

WELLS
7.7.7.7.7.7.

숨 쉬는 동안 주 찬양

WORDS: Isaac Watts (Ps. 146); alt. John Wesley; alt.;
Korean trans. The United Methodist Korean Hymnal Committee
MUSIC: Attr. Matthäus Greiter; harm. V. Earle Copes
Harm. © 1964, Korean trans. © 2001 The United Methodist Publishing House, admin. The Copyright Co.

OLD 113th
888.888

I'll Praise My Maker While I've Breath 123

Unison

1. I'll praise my Mak - er while I've breath; and when my voice is
2. Hap - py are they whose hopes re - ly on Is - rael's God, who
3. The Lord pours eye - sight on the blind; the Lord sup - ports the
4. I'll praise my God who lends me breath; and when my voice is

lost in death, praise shall em - ploy my no - bler powers.
made the sky and earth and seas, with all their train;
faint - ing mind and sends the la - boring con-science peace.
lost in death, praise shall em - ploy my no - bler powers.

My days of praise shall ne'er be past, while life, and thought, and
whose truth for - ev - er stands se - cure, who saves th'op-pressed and
God helps the stran - ger in dis - tress, the wid - ow and the
My days of praise shall ne'er be past, while life, and thought, and

be - ing last, or im - mor - tal - i - ty en - dures.
feeds the poor, for none shall find God's prom - ise vain.
fa - ther - less, and grants the pris - oner sweet re - lease.
be - ing last, or im - mor - tal - i - ty en - dures.

WORDS: Isaac Watts (Ps. 146); alt. John Wesley; alt.
MUSIC: Attr. Matthäus Greiter; harm. V. Earle Copes
Harm. © 1964 The United Methodist Publishing House, admin. The Copyright Co.

OLD 113th
888.888

높은 곳에 계신 주님

1. 높은 곳에 계신 주님 찬양하여라
2. 영원하신 하나님을 찬양하여라
3. 주님 안의 만물들아 찬양하여라

거룩하신 사랑의 주 찬양하여라
소 고치시며 제금 울려 찬양하여라
우리의 왕 창조주께 영광 돌리자

고귀하신 주 사랑은 위대하신 주 능력
마음에서 울리는 아름다운 곡조로
온 하늘과 온 땅에 거룩하신 주 이름

복의 근원 하나님을 경배하여라
모든 악기 소리 모아 찬양하여라
호흡 있는 만물들아 찬양하여라

WORDS: Charles Wesley (Ps.150); Korean trans. The United Methodist Korean Hymnal Committee
MUSIC: Foundery Collection, 1742
Korean trans. © 2001 The United Methodist Publishing House, admin. The Copyright Co.

AMSTERDAM
76.76.77.76

Praise the Lord Who Reigns Above

1. Praise the Lord who reigns a-bove and keeps his court be-low;
2. Cel - e - brate th'e - ter - nal God with harp and psal - ter - y,
3. God, in whom they move and live, let ev - ery crea - ture sing,

praise the ho - ly God of love and all his great-ness show;
tim - brels soft and cym - bals loud in this high praise a - gree;
glo - ry to their Mak - er give, and hom-age to their King.

praise him for his no - ble deeds, praise him for his match-less power;
praise with ev - ery tune - ful string; all the reach of heaven-ly art,
Hallow-ed be thy name be-neath, as in heaven on earth a - dored;

him from whom all good pro-ceeds let earth and heaven a - dore.
all the powers of mu - sic bring, the mu - sic of the heart.
praise the Lord in ev - ery breath, let all things praise the Lord.

WORDS: Charles Wesley (Ps. 150)
MUSIC: Foundery Collection, 1742

AMSTERDAM
76.76.77.76

125

어하라디야 상사디야
Hallelujah, in God's Temple

인도자 (Leader)　　　　　　　회중 (Congregation)

어 하 라 디 야 - 상 사 디 야 - 어 하 라 디 야 - 상 사 디 야 -
Ŏ hŏ ra di ya - sang sa di ya - Ŏ hŏ ra di ya - sang sa di ya -
(Hal - le-lu-jah　Hal-le-lu-jah　Hal - le-lu-jah　Hal-le-lu-jah

1. 성 소 에 서 - 찬 양 하 라 -
2. 하 나 님 을 - 찬 양 하 라 -
1. In God's tem-ple, praise to Yah-weh!
2. In the heav-ens, praise to Yah-weh!

어 하 라 디 야 - 상 사 디 야 -
Ŏ hŏ ra di ya - sang sa di ya -
(Hal - le-lu-jah　Hal-le-lu-jah)

3. 하 늘 에 서 - 찬 양 하 라 -
4. 그 권 능 을 - 찬 양 하 라 -
3. God has act-ed, praise to Yah-weh!
4. Great the won-ders, praise to Yah-weh!

어 하 라 디 야 - 상 사 디 야 -
Ŏ hŏ ra di ya - sangsa di ya -
(Hal - le-lu-jah　Hal-le-lu-jah)

어 하 라 디 야 - 상 사 디 야 - 어 하 라 디 야 - 상 사 디 야 -
Ŏ hŏ ra di ya - sang sa di ya - Ŏ hŏ ra di ya - sang sa di ya -
(Hal - le-lu-jah　Hal-le-lu-jah　Hal - le-lu-jah　Hal-le-lu-jah)

5. 엄 청 난 일 - 하 - 셨 다 -
6. 그 지 없 이 - 높 으 시 다 -
5. Praise to Yah-weh, God, the high-est!
6. Praise to Yah-weh, God, most ho-ly!

어 하 라 디 야 - 상 사 디 야 -
Ŏ hŏ ra di ya - sangsa di ya -
(Hal - le-lu-jah　Hal-le-lu-jah)

빠르게 (Faster)

어 화 디 야 상 사 디 야 어 화 디 야 상 사 디 야
Ŏ hwa di ya sang sa di ya Ŏ hwa di ya sang sa di ya
(Hal -le - lu -jah　Hal-le -lu-jah　Hal - le - lu -jah　Hal - le - lu -jah)

WORDS: Psalm 150
MUSIC: Geonyong Lee
© Geonyong Lee

OHORADIYA
Irr.

7. 나 팔소리 우 렁차게 어 화 디 야 상 사 디 야
8. 거 문고와 비 파타며 (Hal - le - lu - jah Hal - le - lu - jah)
7. Blow the fan-fare on the trum-pet! Ŏ hwa di ya sang sa di ya
8. Pluck the zith-er, harp and ly-re! (Hal - le - lu-jah Hal - le - lu-jah)

9. 북 을 치며 춤 을 추며 어 화 디 야 상 사 디 야
10. 현 금 타고 피 리불며 (Hal - le - lu - jah Hal - le - lu - jah)
9. Sound the drum beat, join the dan-cing! Ŏ hwa di ya sang sa di ya
10. Strings and pipes, give praise to Yah-weh! (Hal - le - lu-jah Hal - le - lu-jah)

어 화 디 야 상 사 디 야 어 화 디 야 상 사 디 야
Ŏ hwa di ya sang sa di ya Ŏ hwa di ya sang sa di ya
(Hal - le - lu-jah Hal - le- lu-jah Hal - le - lu-jah Hal - le - lu-jah)

11. 깽 매 깽 깽 매 깽 꽹 과 리 치 면서 어 화 디 야 상 사 디 야
12. 칭 칭 칭 칭 징 을 치 면서 (Hal - le - lu-jah Hal - le - lu - jah)
11. Ting-a-ling, ting-a-ling, ring out the fing-er bells. Ŏ hwa di ya sang sa di ya
12. Bang-ing and clash-ing the cym-bals and sound-ing gongs. (Hal-le-lu-jah Hal-le-lu-jah)

인도자 (Leader) 6-8회 반복 (repeat 6-8 times) 회중 (Cong) 인도자 (Leader)

어 화 디 야 상 사 디 야 어 화 디 야 상 사 디 야
Ŏ hwa di ya sang sa di ya Ŏ hwa di ya sang sa di ya
(Hal - le - lu-jah Hal - le - lu-jah Hal - le - lu-jah Hal - le - lu-jah)

회중 (Cong) 인도자 (Leader) 천천히 (Slower) 회중 (Cong)

어 화 디 야 상 사 디 야 어 하 라 디 야 - 상 사 디 야 -
Ŏ hwa di ya sang sa di ya Ŏ hŏ ra di ya - sang sa di ya -
(Hal-le-lu-jah Hal-le-lu-jah Hal - le -lu-jah Hal-le- lu- jah)

인도자 (Leader)

13. 숨 쉬 는 모 든 것 들 아 - - 야 훼 를 찬 양 하 여 라
13. Let ev-'ry-thing that lives and breathes come and give praise to Yah-weh, God.

126

온 천하 거하는 만물아
From All That Dwell Below the Skies

1. 온　천하　거하는　만물아님－어
2. 영원한　자비의　하나님－어
3. 귀하신　주이름높이어
4. 만백성　즐거운찬송이

1. From all that dwell be - low the skies,
2. E - ter - nal are thy mer - cies, Lord;
3. Your loft - y themes, ye mor - tals, bring,
4. In ev - ery land be - gin the song;

창조의　주를　찬양해　온　민족모든소리
진리의말씀영원해　온　땅의이끝에서
거룩한찬송부르네　구원의기쁜소식
온　땅에울려퍼지네　큰소리함께외쳐

let the Cre - a - tor's praise a - rise; let the Re - deem - er's
e - ter - nal truth at - tends thy word. Thy praise shall sound from
in songs of praise di - vine - ly sing; the great sal - va - tion
to ev - ery land the strains be - long; in cheer - ful sounds all

합－하여　구세주이름찬양해
저－끝까지　주찬송울려퍼지네
선－포하며　구세주이름외치네네
부르－며　온세상찬송하겠네

name be sung, through ev - ery land by ev - ery tongue.
shore to shore, till suns shall rise and set no more.
loud pro - claim, and shout for joy the Sav - ior's name.
voic - es raise, and fill the world with loud - est praise.

WORDS: Sts. 1-2, Isaac Watts; sts. 3-4, anon. (Ps. 117);
Korean trans. The United Methodist Korean Hymnal Committee
MUSIC: Attr. John Hatton
Korean trans. © 2001 The United Methodist Publishing House, admin. The Copyright Co.

DUKE STREET
LM

복의 근원 강림하사
Come, Thou Fount of Every Blessing

1. 복의 근원 강림하사 찬송하게 하소서니
2. 주의 크신 도움 받아 이때까지 왔으니
3. 주의 귀한 은혜 받고 일생 빚진 자 되네

1. Come, thou Fount of ev-'ry bless-ing, tune my heart to sing thy grace;
2. Here I raise mine Eb-en-e-zer; hith-er by thy help I'm come;
3. O to grace how great a debt-or dai-ly I'm con-strained to be!

끊임없는 주의 자비 높이 찬송합니다
이와 같이 천국에도 높이르기를 바라네
주의 은혜 사슬 되사 나를 주께 매소서

streams of mer - cy, nev-er ceas-ing, call for songs of loud-est praise.
and I hope, by thy good plea-sure, safe-ly to ar-rive at home.
Let thy good-ness, like a fet-ter, bind my wan-d'ring heart to thee.

천사들의 찬송 가를 내게 가르치소서 때니
하나님의 의의 품을 떠나 위험한 길 쉬 맬우
사랑하는 주를 떠나 방황하기 쉬운

Teach me some me-lo-dious son-net, sung by flam-ing tongues a - bove.
Je-sus sought me when a stran-ger, wan-d'ring from the fold of God;
Prone to wan-der, Lord, I feel it, prone to leave the God I love;

구속하신 주구의 하 사랑 항상 찬송합니다네
나를 찾아 신아을 받아 주사 천국인 혈을 흘렸네서
나의 맘을 받아 주사 천국 인을 치소서

Praise the mount! I'm fixed up - on it, mount of thy re-deem-ing love.
he, to res-cue me from dan-ger, in-ter-posed his pre-cious blood.
here's my heart, O take and seal it, seal it for thy courts a - bove.

WORDS: Robert Robinson (1 Sam. 7:12); Korean trans. The United Methodist Korean Hymnal Committee
MUSIC: Wyeth's *Repository of Sacred Music, Part Second*, 1813
Korean trans. © 2001 The United Methodist Publishing House, admin. The Copyright Co.

NETTLETON
87.87 D

128

주님의 사람들

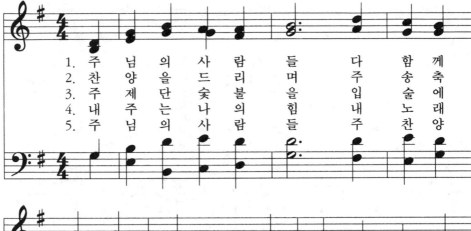

```
1. 주   님   의   사   람   들   며   을   힘   다   함   께
2. 찬   송   양   제   주   리   불   의   사   드   숯   나
3. 주   내   주   님   의   을   단   는   들   입   송   술
4. 찬   양   제   주   의   람   리   불   다   주   노   찬
5. 주   님   의   사   드   숯   나   람   주   래   양   축
```

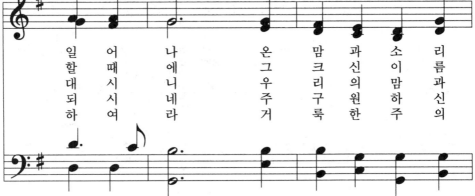

```
일   어   나   온   맘   과   소   리
할   때   에   그   크   신   이   름
할   대   시   니   우   신   맘   과
되   시   시   네   주   의   하   신
하   여   라   거   룩   한   주   의
```

```
합   하   여   주   찬   양   하   라
높   이   각   이   경   배   드   세
생   사   이   을   늘   로   치   여
이   랑   을   다   선   포   하   해
           영   원   히   찬
```

WORDS: James Montgomery (Neh. 9:5); Korean trans. The United Methodist Korean Hymnal Committee
MUSIC: Genevan Psalter, 1551; adapt. William Crotch
Korean trans. © 2001 The United Methodist Publishing House, admin. The Copyright Co.

ST. MICHAEL
SM

Stand Up and Bless the Lord

1. Stand up and bless the Lord, ye peo - ple of his choice; stand up and bless the Lord your God with heart and soul and voice.

2. Though high a - bove all praise, a - bove all bless - ing high, who would not fear his ho - ly name, and laud and mag - ni - fy?

3. O for the liv - ing flame from his own al - tar brought, to touch our lips, our minds in - spire, and wing to heaven our thought!

4. God is our strength and song, and his sal - va - tion ours; then be his love in Christ pro - claimed with all our ran - somed powers.

5. Stand up and bless the Lord; the Lord your God a - dore; stand up and bless his glo - rious name, hence - forth for - ev - er - more.

WORDS: James Montgomery (Neh. 9:5)
MUSIC: *Genevan Psalter*, 1551; adapt. William Crotch

ST. MICHAEL
SM

129

노래로 주께 영광 돌리며

WORDS: Fred Pratt Green (Mk. 14:26);
Korean trans. The United Methodist Korean Hymnal Committee
MUSIC: Charles Villiers Stanford
Words © 1972, Korean trans. © 2001 Hope Publishing Co.

ENGELBURG
10 10 10 with Alleluias

When in Our Music God Is Glorified

Unison

1. When in our mu - sic God is glo - ri - fied,
2. How of - ten, mak - ing mu - sic, we have found
3. So has the church in lit - ur - gy and song,
4. And did not Je - sus sing a psalm that night
5. Let ev - ery in - stru-ment be tuned for praise!

and ad - o - ra - tion leaves no room for pride,
a new di - men - sion in the world of sound,
in faith and love, through cen - tu - ries of wrong,
when ut - most e - vil strove a - gainst the light?
Let all re - joice who have a voice to raise!

it is as though the whole cre - a - tion cried
as wor - ship moved us to a more pro - found
borne wit - ness to the truth in ev - ery tongue,
Then let us sing, for whom he won the fight:
And may God give us faith to sing al - ways

[1 ~ 4] Al - le - lu - ia!

[5] Al - le - lu - ia!

WORDS: Fred Pratt Green (Mk. 14:26)
MUSIC: Charles Villiers Stanford
Words © 1972 Hope Publishing Co.

ENGELBURG
10 10 10 with Alleluias

맘 정결한 자들

WORDS: Edward H. Plumptre (Ps. 20:4; 147:1; Phil. 4:4);
Korean trans. The United Methodist Korean Hymnal Committee
MUSIC: Arthur H. Messiter
Korean trans. © 2001 The United Methodist Publishing House, admin. The Copyright Co.

MARION
SM with Refrain

Rejoice, Ye Pure in Heart

1. Re - joice, ye pure in heart; re - joice, give
2. Your clear ho - san - nas raise, and al - le -
3. Yes, on through life's long path, still chant - ing
4. At last the march shall end; the wea - ried
5. Praise God who reigns on high, the Lord whom

thanks, and sing; your glo - rious ban - ner
lu - ias loud; whilst an - swering ech - oes
as ye go; from youth to age, by
ones shall rest; the pil - grims find their
we a - dore, the Fa - ther, Son, and

wave on high, the cross of Christ your King.
up - ward float, like wreaths of in - cense cloud.
night and day, in glad - ness and in woe.
heaven - ly home, Je - ru - sa - lem the blest.
Ho - ly Ghost, one God for - ev - er - more.

Refrain

Re - joice, re - joice, re - joice, give thanks and sing.

Re - joice, re - joice

WORDS: Edward H. Plumptre (Ps. 20:4; 147:1; Phil. 4:4)
MUSIC: Arthur H. Messiter

MARION
SM with Refrain

131

다 나와서 노래하자
Come One and All, Come Join in Song

1. 다 나와서 노래하자 즐거이 노래를 부르자
2. 전능하신 주 하나님 처음이요 나중 되신 주
3. 우리들을 사랑하는 하나님 아버지 찬양해
4. 거룩하신 삼위일체 영광을 받으시옵소서

1. Come one and all, come join in song, come let us sing a joy-ful song
2. Al -migh-ty God, God our Lord, God the be-gin-ning and the end
3. Praise to our God, praise to the Lord, God who comes down to us in love
4. Ho - ly God, three in one, glo - ry to you, re - ceive our praise

주님 앞에 모두 나와 소리높여 노래해네
어디든지 계신 주님 이자리에 계시네
우리들을 구원하신 성자예수 찬양해
맘과 뜻과 정성다해 주께예배 하오니

come be-fore the Lord with prais-es, come and bless God's ho - ly name;
God is with us in the place and God is pre-sent eve-ry-where
praise to Je-sus, one with God, who saves us all from the power of sin,
with our hearts and minds and souls we wor-ship you, O God our Lord,

성도들아 모두나와 손뼉치며 노래해네
어디든지 계신 주님 나와함께 계시네
우리들을 지키시는 성령님을 찬양해
우리들의 이예배를 받아주시옵소서

come you saints and sing to-geth-er, clap your hands in God's ac-claim.
God, the Lord of earth and heav-en, has come down ho-ly life to share.
prais-es to the Ho - ly Spir-it who gives com-fort and leads with-in.
take we pray this hum-ble offer-ing, may it glo-ri - fy your name.

WORDS: Anonymous (Ps. 95:1-2); Korean trans. The United Methodist Korean Hymnal Committee
MUSIC: Traditional Hebrew melody; arr. Lonnie Goode
Korean trans. © 2001 The United Methodist Publishing House, admin. The Copyright Co.;
arr. © 2001 Abingdon Press, admin. The Copyright Co.

KOMMT HERBEI
8.8

눈을 들어
Open Your Eyes

눈 을 들 어　　　영광 의 왕을 보 라
Op - en your eyes,　　　see the glo - ry of the King.

소 　리높 여　　　주를 찬 - 양 하 라
Lift　up your voice　and his prais - es sing.

사 랑 해 요　　　선 포 하 리
I love you, Lord,　　　I will pro-claim.

알 렐 루 - 야　　　주 송 축 해
Al - le - lu - ia,　　　I bless your name.

WORDS: Carl Tuttle; Korean trans. The United Methodist Korean Hymnal Committee
MUSIC: Carl Tuttle
© 1985, Korean trans. © 2001 Mercy/Vineyard Publishing

133

좋은 날 기쁜 날

1. 좋 은 날 기 쁜 날 주 님 을 뵈 옵 는 날
2. 좋 은 날 기 쁜 날 주 님 을 뫼 시 옵 고
3. 좋 은 날 기 쁜 날 성 전 에 모 여 서

성 도 들 함 께 모 여 주 님 을 찬 양 하 자
생 명 수 주 님 말 씀 다 함 께 마 시 자
떡 과 잔 을 나 누 니 주 님 의 살 과 피 라

후렴

찬 양 찬 양 다 찬 양 하 자

성 도 들 아 다 오 라 주 님 찬 양 하 자

WORDS: Chul Joo Lee
MUSIC: Young Jo Lee
© Young Jo Lee

BLESSED DAY
6.7.7.7.

Blessed Day, Happy Day

1. Bless-ed day, hap-py day, when we come to the Lord,
2. Bless-ed day, hap-py day, day that we spend with the Lord,
3. Bless-ed day, hap-py day, day in the tem-ple of God,

of one ac-cord, saints of the Lord, gath-er to praise and a - dore.
wa-ter of life, God's liv-ing word, free-ly we drink of God's love.
shar-ing the bread, sha-ring the cup, one in the bo - dy and blood.

Refrain

Sing praise, all praise, sing praise to the Lord,

saints of the Lord, gath-ered in love, sing your prais-es to God.

WORDS: Chul Joo Lee; English trans. Edward Poitras
MUSIC: Young Jo Lee
© Young Jo Lee

BLESSED DAY
6.7.7.7.

사랑으로 천지만물
God Who Created All

1. 사 랑 으 로 천 지 만 물
2. 사 람 되 어 우 중 안 에
3. 사 랑 하 는 그 품 안 에
4. 세 분 이 자 사 랑 으 로

1. God who cre - at - ed all by your Word,
2. God our Sav - ior in hu - man form,
3. God our com - fort, Spir - it di - vine,
4. God in three per - sons, God un-di - vi - ded,

창 조 하 신 하 나 님
내 려 오 신 하 나 님
살 게 되 신 성 령 님
한 몸 되 신 하 나 님

you who cre - at - ed all things in love,
Word e - ter - nal, born on this earth,
safe in your bo - som, give us new life,
one in your being, one by your love,

우 주 만 물 그 속 에 서
삶 과 죽 음 다 바 쳐 서
단 힌 마 음 열 게 하 여
새 하 늘 과 새 땅 을

in heav'n and earth, all you have made,
you gave your life, suf - fered and died
you take our hearts, o - pen them wide
you will bring new heav - en and earth

당 신 모 습 뵈 옵 니 다
우 리 구 원 하 시 셨 네
하 나 되 게 하 시 시 네
하 약 속 게 주 시 시 네

we see your hand - work, we find your face,
that you might save, O cru - ci - fied,
lead - ing our spir - its, mak - ing us one,
where we will praise and wor - ship the Lamb,

WORDS: Won Yong Kang; English trans. Edward Poitras
MUSIC: Unsu Kang
© Kyung Dong Presbyterian Church

CREATED ALL
8.7.8.7.8.7.8.7.

135

두 손 들고 찬양합니다
I Lift My Hands

두 손 들고　　　　찬양 합 니 다　　　　다시
I lift my hands　　　to the coming King,　　　to the

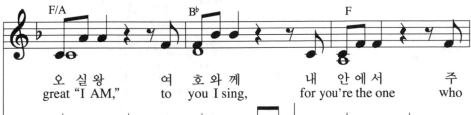

오 실 왕　　　　여 호와 께　　　　내 안에 서　　　　주
great "I AM,"　　　to you I sing,　　　for you're the one　　　who

다 스 리 시 네　　　　　　　　나 모든우상
reigns with-in my heart.　　　　And I will serve no

버 리 고　　　　　　주 님만을 섬　　기 리
for - eign god,　　　or a-ny o-ther trea　- sure;

WORDS: Andre Kempen; Korean trans. The United Methodist Korean Hymnal Committee
MUSIC: Andre Kempen
Korean trans. © 2001 The United Methodist Publishing House, admin. The Copyright Co.

내 마 음 의 소   원 은   -   한 이 없 는
you're my heart's de - si   - re,   Spir- it with-out

주   성   령   -   주   님   앞   에   나   의
mea   - sure.   Un - to   your   name   I   would

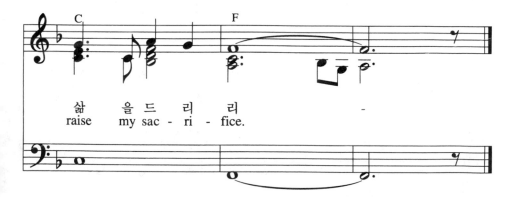

삶   을   드   리   리   -
raise   my   sac - ri - fice.

136

너희는 먼저 주의 나라와

1. 너 희 는 먼 저 – 주 의 나 라 와
2. 구 하 면 네 게 – 주 실 것 이 요

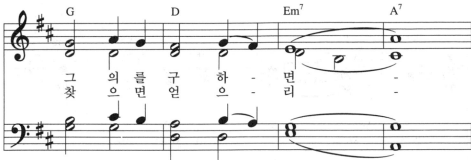

그 의 를 구 하 – 면 –
찾 으 면 얻 으 – 리 –

이 모 든 것 네 게 더 하 시 리 라
두 드 리 면 네 게 열 릴 것 이 라

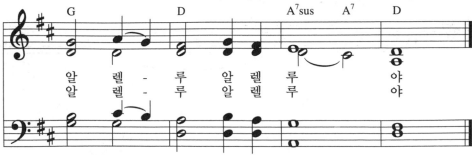

알 렐 – 루 알 렐 루 야
알 렐 – 루 알 렐 루 야

WORDS: Karen Lafferty (Mt. 6:33; 7:7); Korean trans. The United Methodist Korean Hymnal Committee
MUSIC: Karen Lafferty
© 1972 Maranatha Music, admin.The Copyright Co.

SEEK YE
Irr.

Seek Ye First

WORDS: Karen Lafferty (Mt. 6:33; 7:7)
MUSIC: Karen Lafferty

SEEK YE
Irr.

이 땅에 주의 평화
Let There Be Peace on Earth

Let there be peace on earth, and let it be-gin with
me; let there be peace on earth, the peace that was
meant to be. With God our cre-a-tor,
chil-dren all are we. Let us
walk with each oth-er in per-fect har-mo-ny.

*이 땅에 주의 평화 나에게 주소
서 이 땅에 주의 평화 주시기
원하네 *창조 주 하나님
우 린 그 자 녀 모 두
한 마음 되어 다 함께 걸으리

Original words: With God as our Father, brothers all are we.
Let me walk with my brother in perfect harmony.

WORDS: Sy Miller and Jill Jackson; Korean trans. The United Methodist Korean Hymnal Committee
MUSIC: Sy Miller and Jill Jackson; harm. Charles H. Webb
© 1955, assigned to Jan-Lee Music; renewed 1983; Korean trans. © 2001 Jan-Lee Music

WORLD PEACE
Irr.

이 시 간 주 의 평 화 나 에게 주 소
Let peace be - gin with me; let this be the mo - ment

서 - 매 순 간 걸 어 갈 때
now. With ev - ery step I take, let

평 화 를 주 소 서 - 나 사 는 동 안 에
this be my sol - emn vow: to take each mo-ment and

평 화 이 루 며 살 아 가 리 니 -
live each mo-ment in peace e - ter - nal - ly.

이 땅 에 주 의 평 화 나 에게 주 소 서.
Let there be peace on earth, and let it be - gin with me.

가난해도 이웃에게
When the Poor Ones

Unison — Dm — A7 — Bb

1. 가난 해도 - 이웃 에게 - 나눠 주고 -
2. 고통 받는 - 모든 자들 - 위로 받고 -
3. 우리 삶에 - 참된 기쁨 - 넘쳐 나고 -

1. When the poor ones who have noth-ing share with strang-ers,
2. When at last all those who suf-fer find their com-fort,
3. When our joy fills up our cup to o-ver-flow-ing,

D7 — Gm — C7 — F

- 목말 라도 - 생명 수 나눠주 며 -
- 절망 중에 - 있어 도 소망하 며 -
- 우리 입술 - 진리 만 얘기하 며 -

when the thirst-y wa-ter give un-to us all,
when they hope though e-ven hope seems hope-less-ness,
when our lips can speak no words oth-er than true,

F — E7 — A7 — Dm

연약 해도 - 이웃 에게 - 힘을 줄때 -
온세 상이 - 미워 해도 - 사랑 할때 -
만족 하는 - 참된 행복 - 깨달 을때 -

when the crip-pled in their weak-ness strength-en oth-ers,
when we love though hate at times seems all a-round us,
when we know that love for sim-ple things is bet-ter,

WORDS: J. A. Olivar and Miguel Manzano (Mt. 25:31-46); English trans. George Lockwood;
Korean trans. The United Methodist Hymnal Committee
MUSIC: J. A. Olivar and Miguel Manzano; arr. Alvin Schutmaat

EL CAMINO
12 11 12 with Refrain

4.우리 가정 선한 일이 넘쳐나고
싸움대신 참 평화 이루면서
나그네도 이웃이라 불러줄 때
후렴

4. When our homes are filled with goodness in abundance,
when we learn how to make peace instead of war,
when each stranger that we meet is called a neighbor,
Refrain

139 주 하나님의 음성 우리를 부르네

WORDS: John Haynes Holmes (Is. 6:8); Korean trans. The United Methodist Korean Hymnal Committee
MUSIC: William Lloyd
Korean trans. © 2001 The United Methodist Publishing House, admin. The Copyright Co.

MEIRIONYDD
76.76 D

The Voice of God Is Calling

1. The voice of God is call - ing its sum-mons in our day;
2. "I hear my peo-ple cry - ing in slum and mine and mill;
3. We heed, O Lord, your sum-mons, and an-swer: Here are we!
4. From ease and plen-ty save us; from pride of place ab - solve;

I - sa-iah heard in Zi - on, and we now hear God say;
no field or mart is si - lent, no cit - y street is still.
Send us up - on your er - rand, let us your ser-vants be.
purge us of low de - sire; lift us to high re - solve;

"Whom shall I send to suc - cor my peo-ple in their need?
I see my peo - ple fall - ing in dark-ness and de - spair.
Our strength is dust and ash - es, our years a pass-ing hour;
take us, and make us ho - ly; teach us your will and way.

Whom shall I send to loos - en the bonds of shame and greed?"
Whom shall I send to shat - ter the fet-ters which they bear?"
but you can use our weak - ness to mag-ni - fy your power.
Speak, and be-hold! we an - swer; com-mand, and we o - bey!

WORDS: John Haynes Holmes (Is. 6:8)
MUSIC: William Lloyd

MEIRIONYDD
76.76 D

140

승리하리라
We Shall Overcome

1. 승리하리라 - 승리하리라 -
1. We shall o - ver - come, we shall o - ver - come,

승리하리라 그 날 - 에
we shall o - ver - come some - day!

오 - 가슴깊이 나는믿네 -
Oh, deep in my heart I do be - lieve

우 리 승 리 하 리 라
we shall o - ver - come some - day!

2. 손잡고 가리 (손을 잡고 가리라)   2. We'll walk hand in hand.
3. 자유하리라 (모두 자유 하리라)   3. We shall all be free.
4. 평화 이루리 (우리 평화 이루리)   4. We shall live in peace.
5. 함께 하시리 (주님 함께 하시리)   5. The Lord will see us through.

WORDS: African American spiritual; Korean trans. The United Methodist Korean Hymnal Committee
MUSIC: African American spiritual; adapt. William Farley Smith
Adapt. © 1989, Korean trans. © 2001 The United Methodist Publishing House, admin. The Copyright Co.

MARTIN
Irr.

주의 길 예비하라
Prepare the Way of the Lord
141

주 의 길 예비하 라　주 의 길 예비하 라
Pre - pare the way of the Lord.　Pre - pare the way of the Lord,

모 든 사람들 주 의 구 원 을보리 라 주
and all peo-ple will see the sal - va - tion of our God. Pre -

WORDS: Is. 40:3; 52:10; Korean trans. The United Methodist Korean Hymnal Committee
MUSIC: Jacques Berthier and the Taizé Community
© 1984, Korean trans. © 2001 Les Presses de Taizé, admin. GIA Publication, Inc.

PREPARE THE WAY
Irr.

주의 평화 내리소서
Dona Nobis Pacem
142

주 의 평화 내 리 소 서 우 리
Do - na no - bis pa - cem, pa-cem. Do - na

에 -게 내 리 소 서 평 화 내 - 리 소 서
no - bis pa - cem. Do - na no - bis pa-cem.

우 리 에 게 내 리 소 서 평 화
Do - na no - bis pa - cem. Do - na

내 - 리 소 서 우 리 에 게 내 리 소 서
no - bis pa-cem. Do - na no - bis pa - cem.

WORDS: Trad. Latin; Korean trans. The United Methodist Korean Hymnal Committee
MUSIC: Trad. melody
Korean trans. © 2001 The United Methodist Publishing House, admin. The Copyright Co.

DONA NOBIS PACEM
Irr.

시온의 영광이 빛나는 아침

WORDS: T. Hastings (Is. 60:1); Korean trans. The Christian Literature Society of Korea
MUSIC: Lowell Mason
Korean trans. © The Christian Literature Society of Korea

WESLEY
11.10.11.10

Hail to the Brightness

1. Hail to the bright-ness of Zi - on's glad morn-ing!
2. Hail to the bright-ness of Zi - on's glad morn-ing!
3. Lo, in the des - ert rich flow - ers are spring-ing,
4. See, from all lands, from the isles of the o - cean,

Joy to the lands that in dark - ness have lain!
Long by the proph - ets of Is - rael fore - told!
streams ev - er cop - ious are glid - ing a - long;
praise to Je - ho - vah as-cend - ing on high;

Hushed be the ac - cents of sor - row and mourn-ing;
Hail to the mil - lions from bon - dage re - turn-ing!
loud from the moun - tain tops ech - oes are ring-ing,
fall'n are the en - gines of war and com - mo - tion;

Zi - on in tri - umph be - gins her mild reign.
Gen - tiles and Jews the blest vis - ion be - hold.
wastes rise in ver - dure, and min - gle in song.
shouts of sal - va - tion are rend - ing the sky.

WORDS: T. Hastings (Is. 60:1)
MUSIC: Lowell Mason

WESLEY
11.10.11.10

큰 소망 중에 살리라

WORDS: Jane Parker Huber; Korean trans. The United Methodist Korean Hymnal Committee
MUSIC: Thomas Williams; harm. Lowell Mason
Words ©, Korean trans. © 2001 Jane Parker Huber

TRURO
LM

Live into Hope

1. Live in-to hope do cap-tives freed, of
2. Live in-to hope the blind shall see with
3. Live in-to hope of lib-er-ty, the
4. Live in-to hope of cap-tives freed from

sight re-gained, the end of greed. The op
in-sight and with clar-i-ty, re-
right to speak, the right to be, the
chains of fear or want or greed. God

-pressed shall be the first to see the
mov-ing shades of pride and fear a
right to have one's dai-ly bread, to
now pro-claims our full re-lease to

year of God's own ju-bi-lee!
vi-sion of our God brought near.
hear God's Word and thus be fed.
faith and hope and joy and peace.

WORDS: Jane Parker Huber
MUSIC: Thomas Williams; harm. Lowell Mason
Words © Jane Parker Huber

TRURO
LM

십자가 지라
Take Up Thy Cross

1. 십자가 지라 하 - 시네 너희는 주의 제 - 자라 너 자신 부 - 인력을 하고 서 - 겸손히 주 - 를 따 - 르라
2. 십자가 지라 하 - 시네 연약한 영혼 두 - 드리고 주 크신 신자가 - 를 으로 써 - 주너를 인 - 도하 - 시리네
3. 십자가 지라 하 - 시네 두려움 모두 버 - 리고 주 십자가 - 지시고 - 네영혼 구 - 원하 - 셨네
4. 십자가 지고 따르라 네생명 다 할때 - 까지 십자가지 - 고 가는자 영광의 면류관 얻 - 으리

1. "Take up thy cross," the Sav - ior said, "if thou wouldst my dis - ci - ple be; de - ny thy - self, the world for - sake, and hum - bly fol - low af - ter me."
2. Take up thy cross, let not its weight fill thy weak spir - it with a - larm; his strength shall bear thy spir - it up, and brace thy heart and nerve thine arm.
3. Take up thy cross, nor heed the shame, nor let thy fool - ish pride re - bel; thy Lord for thee the cross en - dured, to save thy soul from death and hell.
4. Take up thy cross, and fol - low Christ, nor think till death to lay it down; for on - ly those who bear the cross may hope to wear the glo - rious crown.

WORDS: Charles W. Everest (Mt. 16:24-25; Mk. 8:34-35; Lk. 9:23-24);
Korean trans. The United Methodist Korean Hymnal Committee
MUSIC: William Gardiner's *Sacred Melodies*
Korean trans. © 2001 The United Methodist Publishing House, admin. The Copyright Co.

GERMANY
LM

정의가 강물처럼
Justice Comes as River Waters Flow

1. 정 의 가 강 물 처 럼
2. 눈 물 과 씨 를 뿌 리 며
1. Jus-tice comes as riv-er wa-ters flow,
2. When we sowed 'twas a day for tears,

평 화 가 들 불 처 럼
지 나 온 수 난 의 세 월
peace spreads forth like wild-fire on the plain,
now the time of suf-fer-ing has passed,

사 랑 이 햇 빛 처 럼
보 아 라 우 리 눈 앞 에
love shines forth like sun-shine af-ter rain,
and be-fore our long-ing eyes we

하 나 님 주 신 생 명 보 듬 어
새 하 늘 이 활 짝 열 린 다
em-brac-ing all the life God has made.
see a new heav-en and the vic-to-ry.

희 년 을 향 해 함 께 가 는 길
We march on the road to the ju-bi-lee,

주 의 약 속 군 게 믿 으 며
the Lord's prom-ise lead-ing us to-day,

일 곱 번 씩 일 곱 번 넘 어 져 도
tho' we fail and fall sev-en times on our way,

약 속 을 군 게 믿 으 며
we trust God to set us all free.

WORDS: Hyung Sun Ryu; English trans. Edward Poitras
MUSIC: Hyung Sun Ryu
© Hyung Sun Ryu

147
구주여 오소서
While We Are Waiting, Come

1. 구 주 여 오 소 서 -
2. 구 주 여 오 소 서 -
3. 구 주 여 오 소 서

1. While we are wait - ing, come;
2. With pow'r and glo - ry, come;
3. Come, Sav - ior, quick - ly come;

갈 급 한 나 에 게 -
영 광 과 권 세 로 -
서 둘 러 오 소 서 -

while we are wait - ing, come.
with pow'r and glo - ry, come.
come, Sav - ior, quick - ly come.

후렴 (Refrain)

예 수 내 주 임 마 누 엘

Je - sus, our Lord, Em - man - u - el,

여 기 에 오 소 서 -

while we are wait - ing, come.

WORDS: Claire Cloninger (Rev. 22:12); Korean trans. The United Methodist Korean Hymnal Committee
MUSIC: Don Cason
© 1986, Korean trans. © 2001 Word Music, Inc.

WAITING
S.M.

오소서 (O-So-So)   148
Come Now, O Prince of Peace

1. 오 소 서   오 소 서 평 화 의   임 금
(O - so - so   o - so - so, pyong- hwa eui   im - geum)
2. 오 소 서   오 소 서 사 랑 의   임 금
3. 오 소 서   오 소 서 자 유 의   임 금
4. 오 소 서   오 소 서 통 일 의   임 금

1. Come now, O   Prince of Peace, make us   one   bod - y,
2. Come now, O   God   of   love, make us   one   bod - y,
3. Come now, and   set   us   free, O God our   Sa - vior,
4. Come, hope of   u - ni - ty,   make us   one   bod - y,

우 리 가   한 몸   이 루 게 하   소 서
(u - ri - ga   han - mom   i - ru - ge ha - so - so.)
come, O Lord   Je - sus,   re - con-cile all   peo - ple.

WORDS: Geonyong Lee; English paraph. Marion Pope
MUSIC: Geonyong Lee
© 1988 Geonyong Lee

O-SO-SO
6.5.5.6.

149

평화의 나라 임하시니
God Brings the Kingdom

1. 평화의 나라 임하시니
2. 사랑의 나라 임하시니
3. 자유의 나라 임하시니

1. God brings the king - dom, rul - ing in peace,
2. God brings the king - dom, rul - ing in love,
3. God brings the king - dom, mak - ing us free,

주 예수 그 나라 왕 일 세
주 예수 그 나라 다 스 리 네
주 예수 그 나라 통 치 하 네

Je - sus is ru - ler here, he is the King,
Je - sus is ru - ler here, he is the King,
Je - sus is ru - ler here, he is the King,

우 리 죄 를 - 사 하 시 고
구 원 의 문 에 - 열 어 주 고
율 법 명 문 에 - 풀 어 주 니

Je - sus par - dons all of our sins,
he has o - pened the way to new life,
Je - sus lifts the yoke of the law,

WORDS: Ki Tak Cho; English trans. Edward Poitras
MUSIC: Moon Seung Lee
© Moon Seung Lee; English trans. © 2001 The United Methodist Publishing House, admin. The Copyright Co

인생들아 잠잠하라

1. 인 생 들아 잠 잠 - 하 라 떨 림으로에 기 다 리 라 세 상 욕 심다 버 으 - 리 고 주 께 충 성 다 오 오 - 셨 시 네 강 우 림하 - 사 크 양어 주시 시 - 리 께

2. 왕 의 왕이 되 신 - 주 님서 마 리아호 위어 다 나 시 고 인 간 밤 이없 나 으 - 라 에 이 참 땅 된빛 이오 오 외 치 - 니 네 깨 알 렐루 - 고 야 높 이복 로리 신 주 님 - 께

3. 천 군 천사 하 늘 - 에 주 를호 위 어 리 고 상 욕 심다 입 나 - 라 에서려 찬 양 하네 그 날 개 로얼 굴 - 가 려 그 몸 악의알 렐 루 주 치 시 - 리 네

4. 천 사 들이 주 발 - 앞 에 엎 드 리 어 할 때 에에 그 날 개 로얼 굴 - 가 려 쉬 지 않고 외 치 - 네 알 렐 루 - 고 야 축 으물계 신 주 님 - 께

Let All Mortal Flesh Keep Silence

Unison

1. Let all mor-tal flesh keep si - lence, and with fear and
2. King of kings, yet born of Ma - ry, as of old on
3. Rank on rank the host of heav - en spreads its van-guard
4. At his feet the six - winged ser - aph, cher - u - bim, with

trem-bling stand; pon- der noth-ing earth - ly - mind - ed,
earth he stood, Lord of lords, in hu - man ves - ture,
on the way, as the Light of light de - scend-eth
sleep - less eye, veil their fac-es to the pres - ence,

for with bless-ing in his hand, Christ our God to
in the bod - y and the blood; he will give to
from the realms of end - less day, that the powers of
as with cease-less voice they cry: Al - le - lu - ia,

earth de - scend - eth, our full hom-age to de - mand.
all the faith - ful his own self for heaven-ly food.
hell may van - ish as the dark-ness clears a - way.
al - le - lu - ia, al - le - lu -ia, Lord Most High!

WORDS: Liturgy of St. James (Jn. 6:35-58; Rev. 4); English trans. Gerard Moultrie
MUSIC: French carol melody; harm. from *The English Hymnal*

PICARDY
87.87.87

저 동정녀 마리아

WORDS: Gracia Grindal (Lk. 1:26-38); Korean trans. The United Methodist Korean Hymnal Committee
MUSIC: Rusty Edwards
© 1984, Korean trans. © 2001 Hope Publishing Co.

ANNUNCIATION
76.76.76

To a Maid Engaged to Joseph

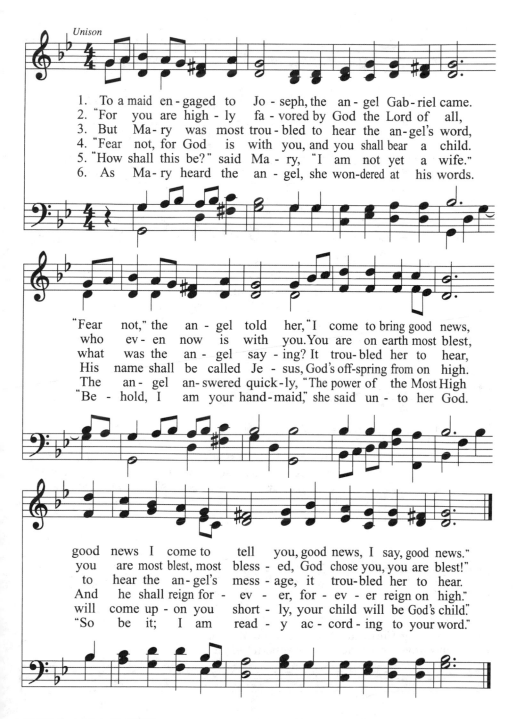

1. To a maid en-gaged to Jo-seph, the an-gel Gab-riel came.
2. "For you are high-ly fa-vored by God the Lord of all,
3. But Ma-ry was most trou-bled to hear the an-gel's word,
4. "Fear not, for God is with you, and you shall bear a child.
5. "How shall this be?" said Ma-ry, "I am not yet a wife."
6. As Ma-ry heard the an-gel, she won-dered at his words.

"Fear not," the an-gel told her, "I come to bring good news,
who ev-en now is with you. You are on earth most blest,
what was the an-gel say-ing? It trou-bled her to hear,
His name shall be called Je-sus, God's off-spring from on high.
The an-gel an-swered quick-ly, "The power of the Most High
"Be-hold, I am your hand-maid," she said un-to her God.

good news I come to tell you, good news, I say, good news."
you are most blest, most bless-ed, God chose you, you are blest!"
to hear the an-gel's mess-age, it trou-bled her to hear.
And he shall reign for-ev-er, for-ev-er reign on high."
will come up-on you short-ly, your child will be God's child."
"So be it; I am read-y ac-cord-ing to your word."

WORDS: Gracia Grindal (Lk. 1:26-38)
MUSIC: Rusty Edwards
© 1984 Hope Publishing Co.

ANNUNCIATION
76.76.76

거룩하신 아기 예수
Infant Holy, Infant Lowly

Unison

1. 거룩 하 신 아기 예 수 구 유 안 에 누 셨
2. 빈 들 에 서 새 벽 까 지 양 을 치 던 목 자

1. In-fant ho - ly, in-fant low - ly, for his bed a cat-tle
2. Flocks were sleep-ing, shep-herds keep-ing vig - il till the morn-ing

네 육 축 소 리 들 으 시 며 우 리 구 주 나 셨
주 의 영 광 바 라 볼 때 기 쁜 소 식 들 었

stall; ox-en low-ing, lit-tle know-ing, Christ the babe is Lord of
new saw the glo-ry, heard the sto-ry, tid-ings of a gos-pel

네 천 사 들 의 노 래 소 리 기 쁜 소 식 전 파
네 슬 픔 에 서 해 방 되 고 기 쁜 날 을 맞 이

all. Swift are wing-ing an-gels sing - ing, no-els ring-ing, tid-ings
true. Thus re-joic - ing, free from sor-row, prais-es voic-ing, greet the

간주, 후주 *(Interlude, Ending)*

하 네 우 리 구 주 나 셨 네
하 리 우 리 위 해 나 셨 네

bring-ing: Christ the babe is Lord of all.
mor-row: Christ the babe was born for you.

WORDS: Polish carol (Lk. 2:6-20); English trans. Edith M. G. Reed;
Korean trans. The United Methodist Korean Hymnal Committee
MUSIC: Polish carol; arr. Edith M. G. Reed
Korean trans. © 2001 The United Methodist Publishing House, admin. The Copyright Co.

W ZLOBIE LEZY
447.447.44447

고요히 그 아기 잠자네
Still, Still, Still

1. 고 - 요 - 히   그 아 기 잠 자 네   이
2. 자 장 자 - 장   주 깊 이 잠 자 네   저

1. Still, still, still,   he sleeps this night so chill!   The
2. Sleep, sleep, sleep,   he lies in slum-ber deep   while

추 운 밤 에 따 스 하 게 동 정 녀 의 팔 에 안 겨
천 사 들 이 내 려 와 서 기 쁜 노 래 부 를 때 에

Vir-gin's ten-der arms en-fold-ing, warm and safe the child are hold-ing.
an-gel hosts from heav-en come wing-ing, sweet-est songs of joy are sing-ing.

고 - 요 - 히   그 아 기 잠 자 네
자 장 자 - 장   주 깊 이 잠 자 네

Still, still, still,   he sleeps this night so chill.
Sleep, sleep, sleep,   he lies in slum-ber deep.

WORDS: Austrian carol; English trans. George K. Evans;
Korean trans. The United Methodist Korean Hymnal Committee
MUSIC: Austrian melody; arr. Walter Ehret
© 1963, 1980, Korean trans. © 2001 Walter Ehret and George K. Evans

STILL.STILL.STILL
3.6.9.3.6

마리아 무릎 위에
What Child Is This

1. 마 리 아 무 룹 위 에 누 워 잠 든
2. 왜 육 축 들 을 먹 이 는 저 구 유
3. 다 와 서 주 께 드 리 어 라 황 금

1. What child is this who, laid to rest, on Ma - ry's
2. Why lies he in such mean es - tate where ox and
3. So bring him in - cense, gold, and myrrh, come, peas - ant,

아 기 누 군 가 저 천 사 들 이
안 에 향 몰 약 을 만 왕 의 왕 께
유 향 몰 약 을 만 왕 의 왕 께

lap is sleep - ing? Whom an - gels greet with
ass are feed - ing? Good Chris - tians, fear, for
king, to own him; the King of kings sal -

찬 양 하 며 목 자 지 켜 보 네
입 고 오 사 죄 인 부 르 시 네
경 배 하 세 구 원 하 실 주 께

an - thems sweet, while shep - herds watch are keep - ing?
sin - ners here the si - lent Word is plead - ing.
va - tion brings, let lov - ing hearts en - throne him.

WORDS: William C. Dix (Lk. 2:6-20; Mt. 2:1-12);
Korean trans. The United Methodist Korean Hymnal Committee
MUSIC: 16th cent. English melody
Korean trans. © 2001 The United Methodist Publishing House, admin. The Copyright Co.

GREENSLEEVES
87.87 with Refrain

후렴 *(Refrain)*

왕 되 신 그 리 스 도 천 사 들 이 노 래 해
This, this is Christ the King, whom shep-herds guard and an - gels sing;

다 와 서 아 기 왕 께 찬 양 드 리 어 라
haste, haste to bring him laud, the babe, the son of Ma - ry.

탄생
155

성도여 기뻐 찬양해
Good Christian Friends, Rejoice

WORDS: 14th cent. Latin; English trans. John Mason Neale;
Korean trans. The United Methodist Korean Hymnal Committee
MUSIC: German melody; harm. Gary Alan Smith
Harm. © 1989, Korean trans. © 2001 The United Methodist Publishing House, admin. The Copyright Co.

IN DULCI JUBILO
66.727.78.55

절 하 네 저 구 유 안 에 계 신 주
여 시 고 영 원 한 축 복 주 시 려
부 르 사 영 원 한 천 국 주 시 려

fore him bow, and he is in the man - ger now.
heav - en's door, and ye are blest for - ev - er-more.
calls you all to gain his ev - er - last - ing hall.

오 늘 나 셨 네 - 구 주 나 셨 네 -

Christ is born to - day, Christ is born to - day!
Christ was born for this, Christ was born for this!
Christ was born to save, Christ was born to save!

탄생
156

아기 예수 나셨네
He Is Born

후렴 *(Refrain)* Unison

아 기 예 수 나 셨 네 악 기 소 리
He is born, the ho-ly Child, play the o-boe and

울 려 찬 양 해 아 기 예 수 나 셨 네
bag-pipes mer-ri-ly! He is born, the ho-ly Child,

Fine *Optional S.A.*

구 세 주 께 찬 양 해
sing we all of the Sav-ior mild.

1. 오 래 전 에
2. 아 름 답 고
3. 온 세 상 의

1. Thru long a - ges
2. O how love - ly,
3. Je - sus, Lord of

WORDS: Trad. 19th cent. French carol; English trans. anon.;
Korean trans. The United Methodist Korean Hymnal Committee
MUSIC: 18th cent. French carol; harm. Carlton R. Young
Harm. © 1989, Korean trans. © 2001 The United Methodist Publishing House, admin. The Copyright Co.

IL EST NÉ
78.77 with Refrain

선 지 자 구 주 오 심 예 언 했 네 오 랫
순 결 한 하 늘 에 서 오 신 아 기 아 름
주 예 수 우 리 중 에 오 시 었 네 온 세
of the past, proph-ets have fore-told his com-ing; thru long
O how pure is this per-fect child of heav-en; O how
all the world, com-ing as a child a-mong us, Je-sus,

D.C.

동 안 기 다 린 구 주 오 늘 나 셨 네
답 고 순 결 한 귀 한 선 물 되 셨 네
상 의 주 예 수 하 늘 평 화 주 소 서
a - ges of the past, now the time has come at last!
love - ly, O how pure, gra-cious gift to hu-man-kind!
Lord of all the world, grant to us thy heaven-ly peace.

그 어린 주 예수
Away in a Manger

1. 그 어린 주 예수 눌 자리 없어
2. 저 육축들 울어 그 아기 깨나
3. 주 예수 내 곁에 늘 계시어서

1. A - way in a man - ger, no crib for his bed,
2. The cat - tle are low - ing, the poor ba - by wakes,
3. Be near me, Lord Je - sus; I ask thee to stay

그 귀하신 몸이 구 유에 있네
그 어린 주 예수 울 지도 않네
그 한없는 사랑 늘 베푸소서

the lit - tle Lord Je - sus laid down his sweet head.
but lit - tle Lord Je - sus, no cry - ing he makes.
close by me for - ev - er and love me, I pray.

WORDS: Anonymous; Korean trans. The United Methodist Korean Hymnal Committee
MUSIC: William James Kirkpatrick
Korean trans. © 2001 The United Methodist Publishing House, admin. The Copyright Co.

CRADLE SONG
11.11.11.11

저 하늘 의 별 들 다 반 짝 일 때
내 사 랑 주 예 수 날 굽 어 보 사
온 세 상 어 린 이 다 축 복 하 사
The stars in the bright sky looked down where he lay,
I love thee, Lord Je - sus, look down from the sky,
Bless all the dear chil - dren in thy ten - der care,

그 어 린 주 예 수 꼴 위 에 자 네
새 벽 까 지 곁 에 계 시 옵 소 서
주 예 수 와 함 께 살 게 하 소 서
the lit - tle Lord Je - sus, a - sleep on the hay.
and stay by my side un - til morn-ing is nigh.
and fit us for heav-en to live with thee there.

구유 안에 누이신 마리아의 아기

1. 구유 안에 누이신 마리아의 아기
2. 천사 노래 울리고 영광 돌리었네
3. 구유 안에 누이신 마리아의 아기

이 세상이 모르던 순결하신 아기네
빛난 별을 따라서 순박사들이 왔네
세상 구원하시는 거룩하신 주님

낮고 천한 구유에 누워 계신 구주판
목자들이 보았네 밝게 빛난 구들
낮은 곳에 임하신 하나님의 아들

구원받은 백성들 주의 은혜 찬양
모든 산에 울리던 천사들의 찬양
그의 이름 찬양해 영광의 왕 찬양

WORDS: Joseph Simpson Cook; Korean trans. The United Methodist Korean Hymnal Committee
MUSIC: Piae Cantiones, 1582; arr. Ernest C. Macmillan
Words © 1956, 1958, Korean trans. © 2001 Gordon V. Thompson, Ltd.

TEMPUS ADEST FLORIDUM
7.6.7.6 D

Gentle Mary Laid Her Child

1. Gen-tle Ma-ry laid her child low-ly in a man-ger;
2. An-gels sang a-bout his birth, wise men sought and found him;
3. Gen-tle Ma-ry laid her child low-ly in a man-ger;

there he lay, the un-de-filed, to the world a stran-ger.
heav-en's star shone bright-ly forth, glo-ry all a-round him.
he is still the un-de-filed, but no more a stran-ger.

Such a babe in such a place, can he be the Sav-ior?
Shep-herds saw the won-drous sight, heard the an-gels sing-ing:
Son of God, of hum-ble birth, beau-ti-ful the sto-ry;

Ask the saved of all the race who have found his fa-vor.
all the plains were lit that night, all the hills were ring-ing.
praise his name in all the earth, hail the King of glo-ry!

WORDS: Joseph Simpson Cook
MUSIC: *Piae Cantiones*, 1582; arr. Ernest C. Macmillan
Words © 1956, 1958 Gordon V. Thompson, Ltd.

TEMPUS ADEST FLORIDUM
7.6.7.6 D

어느 옛날 다윗 성에

WORDS: Cecil Frances Alexander (Lk. 2:7); Korean trans. The United Methodist Korean Hymnal Committee
MUSIC: Henry J. Gauntlett
Korean trans. © 2001 The United Methodist Publishing House, admin. The Copyright Co.

IRBY
87.87.77

Once in Royal David's City

1. Once in roy - al Da - vid's cit - y stood a low - ly cat - tle
2. He came down to earth from heav-en who is God and Lord of
3. Je - sus is our child-hood's pat-tern; day by day, like us he
4. And our eyes at last shall see him, thru his own re - deem-ing

shed, where a moth - er laid her ba - by in a
all, and his shel - ter was a sta - ble, and his
grew; he was lit - tle, weak, and help - less, tears and
love; for that child so dear and gen - tle is our

man - ger for his bed; Ma - ry, lov - ing moth-er
cra - dle was a stall. With the poor, the scorned, the
smiles like us he knew; and he feel - eth for our
Lord in heaven a - bove; and he leads his chil-dren

mild, Je - sus Christ, her lit - tle child.
low - ly lived on earth our Sav - ior ho - ly.
sad - ness, and he shar - eth in our glad - ness.
on - to the place where he is gone.

WORDS: Cecil Frances Alexander (Lk. 2:7)
MUSIC: Henry J. Gauntlett

IRBY
87.87.77

고요한 밤 거룩한 밤

1. 고 요한 밤 거 룩한 밤 어 둠 에 묻 힌 밤
2. 고 요한 밤 거 룩한 밤 영 광 이 둘 린 밤
3. 고 요한 밤 거 룩한 밤 동 방 의 박 사 들
4. 고 요한 밤 거 룩한 밤 주 예 수 나 신 밤

주 의 부 모 앉 아 서 감 사 기 도 드 릴 때
천 군 천 사 나 타 나 기 뻐 노 래 불 러 네 네
별 을 보 고 찾 아 와 꿇 어 경 배 드 렸 네
그 의 얼 굴 광 채 가 세 상 빛 이 되 셨 네

아 기 잘 도 잔 다 - 아 기 잘 도 잔 다
왕 이 나 셨 도 다 - 왕 이 나 셨 도 다 다
왕 이 나 셨 도 다 - 왕 이 나 셨 도 다 다
왕 이 나 셨 도 다 - 왕 이 나 셨 도 다

WORDS: Jospeh Mohr; Korean trans. The Christian Literature Society of Korea
MUSIC: Franz Grüber
Korean trans. © The Christian Literature Society of Korea

STILLE NACHT
Irr.

Silent Night! Holy Night!

1. Si - lent night, ho - ly night, all is calm, all is bright
2. Si - lent night, ho - ly night, shep-herds quake at the sight;
3. Si - lent night, ho - ly night, Son of God, love's pure light;
4. Si - lent night, ho - ly night, won - drous star, lend thy light;

round yon vir - gin moth-er and child. Ho - ly in-fant, so tender and mild,
shep-herds hear the an - gels sing, Al - le - lu - ia! Hail the king!
see the east-ern wise men bring gifts and hom - age to our king;
ra-diant beams from thy ho-ly face with the dawn of re - deem - ing grace,

sleep in heav-en-ly peace, sleep in heav-en-ly peace.
Christ the Sav-ior is born, Christ the Sav-ior is born!
Je-sus, Lord, at thy birth, Je - sus, Lord, at thy birth.
Christ the Sav-ior is born, Christ the Sav-ior is born.

WORDS: Jospeh Mohr
MUSIC: Franz Gruber

STILLE NACHT
Irr.

기쁘다 구주 오셨네
Joy to the World

1. 기쁘다 구주 오셨네 만백찬성양맞으라 온교회상 여 - 다일어 나 - 다
2. 구세주 탄생했으니 다찬예수오셨네 이죄와슬 의 - 만물아 내고 - 다
3. 온세상 죄를 사하려 주성상슬 품 - 몰아 내고 - 다

1. Joy to the world, the Lord is come! Let earth re - ceive her King; let ev - ery heart pre - pare him room, and
2. Joy to the world, the Sav - ior reigns! Let all their songs em - ploy; while fields and floods, rocks, hills, and plains re -
3. No more let sins and sor - rows grow, nor thorns in - fest the ground; he comes to make his bless - ings flow far

WORDS: Isaac Watts (Ps. 98:4-9); Korean trans. The United Methodist Korean Hymnal Committee
MUSIC: Att. G. F. Handel; arr. Lowell Mason
Korean trans. © 2001 The United Methodist Publishing House, admin. The Copyright Co.

ANTIOCH
CM with Repeat

찬양하여라 　다 찬양하여라 　다
화답하여라 　다 화답하여라 　다
구원하시네 　다 구원하시네 　다

heav-en and nature sing, 　and heaven and na-ture sing, 　and
peat the soun-ding joy, 　re - peat the sound-ing joy, 　re -
as the curse is found, 　far as the curse is found, 　far

다 찬양하여라 　다 찬양하여
and heaven and na-ture sing, 　and heaven and na-ture

찬 - 양 찬 - 양 하 여 라
화 - 답 화 - 답 하 여 라
구 - 원 구 - 원 하 시 네

heaven, 　and heaven, 　and na - ture sing.
peat, 　re - peat 　the sound - ing joy.
as, 　far as 　the curse is found.

라 다
sing, and

4. 은혜와 진리 되신 주
　다 주관 하시니
　만국 백성 구주 앞에
　다 경배하여라 다 경배하여라
　다 경배 경배하여라

4. He rules the world with truth and grace,
　and makes the nations prove the glories
　of his righteousness, and wonders of his
　love, and wonders of his love, and wonders,
　wonders of his love.

베들레헴 작은 그 마을

1. 베들레헴 작은 그 마을에 한 아기 나셨네
2. 낮고 천한 구유에 나신 주 그 놀라운 사

네 거룩한 빛이 하늘 밝히며 아기
랑 완전하시고 거룩한 길을 주는

후렴

예 수 비 췄 네   알 렐 루 야 - 하 늘 의
걸 어 가 셨 네

천 사 들 알 렐 루 야 찬 양 해   거 룩

한 빛이 하늘 밝 혔네 아기 왕이 나 셨네

WORDS: William Harold Neidlinger (Jer. 23:5);
Korean trans. The United Methodist Korean Hymnal Committee
MUSIC: William Harold Neidlinger
Korean trans. © 2001 The United Methodist Publishing House, admin. The Copyright Co.

NEIDLINGER
Irr.

In the Little Village of Bethlehem

1. In the lit - tle vil-lage of Beth - le-hem, there lay   a child one
2. 'Twas a   hum - ble birth-place, but O how much God gave to us that

day,   and the sky   was bright with a   ho - ly light o'er the
day,   from the man - ger bed what a   path   has led, what a

Refrain

place where Je - sus   lay.   Al - le - lu - ia!   O how the
per - fect, ho - ly   way.

an - gels sang. Al - le - lu - ia!   How it   rang!   And the

sky   was bright with a   ho - ly light, 'twas the birth-day   of a   king.

WORDS: William Harold Neidlinger (Jer. 23:5)
MUSIC: William Harold Neidlinger

NEIDLINGER
Irr.

흰눈이 쌓이고 별 빛날 때

WORDS: Anglo-Irish carol; alt.; Korean trans. The United Methodist Korean Hymnal Committee
MUSIC: English melody; adapt. C. Winfred Douglas; harm. Leo Sowerby
Korean trans. © 2001 The United Methodist Publishing House, admin. The Copyright Co.;
harm. © 1941 Ronald Stalford

VENITE ADOREMUS
10.10.10.10 with Refrain

다 와 서 경 배 하 자 주 뉘 님 께 께 -
그 다 와 구 유 안 에 구 주 찬 였 네 해 -
성 다 부 서 경 배 하 자 령 주 양 께 -

후렴

다 와 서 경 배 하 자 주 님 께

다 와 서 경 배 하 자 주 님 께

The Snow Lay on the Ground

1. The snow lay on the ground, the stars shone bright,
2. 'Twas gen - tle Ma - ry maid, so young and strong,
3. Saint Jo - seph too was by to tend the child,
4. And thus that man - ger poor be - came a throne;

when Christ our Lord was born on Christ - mas night.
who wel - comed here the Christ - child with a song.
to guard him, and pro - tect his moth - er mild.
for he whom Ma - ry bore was God the Son.

Ve - ni - te a - do - re - mus Do - mi - num.
She laid him in a stall at Beth - le - hem;
The an - gels hov - ered round and sang this song:
O come, then, let us join the heaven - ly host;

WORDS: Anglo-Irish carol; alt.
MUSIC: English melody; adapt. C. Winfred Douglas; harm. Leo Sowerby
Harm. © 1941 Ronald Stalford

VENITE ADOREMUS
10.10.10.10 with Refrain

Ve - ni - te a - do - re - mus Do - mi - num.
the ass and ox - en shared the roof with them.
Ve - ni - te a - do - re - mus Do - mi - num.
to praise the Fa - ther, Son, and Ho - ly Ghost.

Refrain

Ve - ni - te a - do - re - mus Do - mi - num.

Ve - ni - te a - do - re - mus Do - mi - num.

하나님의 아들이 사람 몸을 입으사

1. 하 나 님 의 아 들 이 사 람 몸 을 입 으 사
2. 하 나 님 의 아 들 이 사 람 몸 을 입 으 사
3. 하 나 님 의 아 들 이 사 람 몸 을 입 으 사

이 땅 위 에 오 셨 다 모 두 나 와 영 접 하 자
우 리 안 에 오 셨 다 세 상 만 민 기 뻐 하 자
우 리 함 께 사 셨 다 소 리 높 여 찬 양 하 자

구 주 여 우 리 들 로 거 듭 나 게 하 시 어 사
구 주 여 크 신 사 랑 우 리 맘 에 채 우 사
구 주 여 우 리 맘 에 생 명 으 로 채 우 사

어 둠 을 - 밝 혀 주 는 - 빛 이 되 게 하 소 서
원 수 도 - 친 구 삼 아 - 화 평 하 게 하 소 서
님 께 - 영 광 돌 려 - 길 이 살 게 하 소 서

WORDS: Byung Joo Suh
MUSIC: Jung Hee Hahn
© The Korean Hymnal Society

God Almighty, Ruling the World

1. God Al-migh-ty, rul-ing the world, took hu-man form and came to this earth,
2. God Al-migh-ty, rul-ing the world, took hu-man form though being di-vine,
3. God Al-migh-ty, rul-ing the world, took hu-man form and lived in our ways,

let all peo-ples come and bow down, greet the Sav - ior, sing at this birth;
now with-in us Spir-it di-vine, God has come to be yours and mine;
let us raise our voi-ces in praise, God is with us and bless-es our days;

Lord of all, give us re-birth, we who come to off-er our praise,
Lord of all, send your great love, help our love to ev - er in-crease,
Lord of all, grant us new life, o - ver-flowing each of our hearts,

help us to shine as lights in the dark-ness sing-ing your praise all of our days.
help us to love those peo-ple who hate us, help us to bring your day of peace.
give us long days to sing and to praise you, in the love that ne - ver de-parts.

WORDS: Byung Joo Suh; English trans Edward Poitras
MUSIC: Jung Hee Hahn
© The Korean Hymnal Society

사랑의 주님 예수

1. 사랑의 주님 예수 세상에 오셨네 가난한 우리에게 새 기쁨 주시려 우리의 임마누엘 아기로 오셨네 사랑의 기쁜 소식 우리 맘 밝히리
2. 자비의 주님 예수 세상에 오셨네 눈이 먼 우리에게 새 빛을 주시려 우우리의 임마누엘 인자로 오셨네 자비의 귀한 놀라운 힘 우리 몸 살리
3. 정의의 주님 예수 세상에 오셨네 포로된 우리에게 자유를 주시려 우우리의 임마누엘 왕 구주로 오셨네 정의의 선한 싸움 우리 님 치히리
4. 은혜의 주님 예수 세상에 오셨네 주님의 크신 은혜 우리게 주시려 우리의 임마누엘 주로 오셨네 은혜의 의의 놀라운 살리

WORDS: Kae Joon Lee
MUSIC: Doo Wan Kim
© The Korean Hymnal Society

Loving Lord Jesus, Today

1. Lo-ving Lord Je-sus, to-day, came to world, in to world,
2. Gra-cious Lord Je-sus, to-day, came to world, in to world,
3. Righ-teous Lord Je-sus, to-day, came to world, in to world,
4. Grace-ful Lord Je-sus, to-day, came to world, in to world,

came to those in pov-er-ty, came to us, joys to give,
came to us that blind may see, came to us, light to give,
to us in cap-tiv-i-ty, to give us, li-ber-ty,
came that his grace to im-part, un-to us, gift of God,

Je-sus our Im-ma-nu-el, Je-sus, our lov-ing child.
Je-sus our Im-ma-nu-el, came as the Son of man.
Je-sus our Im-ma-nu-el, came as the King of kings.
Je-sus our Im-ma-nu-el, came as the Sav - ior.

The ti-dings of love and joy, our poor hearts, came to fill.
With his mer-ci-ful hand touch our eyes and now we see.
To fight the good fight vic-to-rious, to bring us sal-va-tion.
A-maz-ing grace that's so power-ful, brought to us re-demp-tion.

WORDS: Kae Joon Lee; English trans. Edward Poitras
MUSIC: Doo Wan Kim
© The Korean Hymnal Society

성탄 노래하세

WORDS: Trad. French carol (Lk. 2:8-20; Mt. 2:1-12);
Korean trans. The United Methodist Korean Hymnal Committee
MUSIC: Trad. French carol; harm. Martin Shaw
Korean trans. © 2001 The United Methodist Publishing House, admin. The Copyright Co.;
harm. by permission of Oxford University Press

FRENCH CAROL
11 10.10 11

Sing We Now of Christmas

1. Sing we now of Christ-mas, No - el, sing we here!
2. An-gels called to shep-herds, "Leave your flocks at rest,
3. In Beth-le-hem they found him; Jo - seph and Ma - ry mild,
4. From the east-ern coun-try came the kings a - far,
5. Gold and myrrh they took there, gifts of great-est price;

Hear our grate-ful prais - es to the babe so dear.
jour-ney forth to Beth - lehem, find the child so blest."
seat - ed by the man - ger, watch - ing the ho-ly child.
bear-ing gifts to Beth - lehem, guid-ed by a star.
there was never a sta - ble so like par-a - dise.

Refrain

Sing we No - el, the King is born, No - el!

Sing we now of Christ-mas, sing we now No - el!

WORDS: Trad. French carol (Lk. 2:8-20; Mt. 2:1-12)
MUSIC: Trad. French carol; harm. Martin Shaw
Harm. by permission of Oxford University Press

FRENCH CAROL
11 10.10 11

주현
167

새벽 별 오 기쁜 빛

WORDS: Johann Scheffler; Korean trans. The United Methodist Korean Hymnal Committee
MUSIC: F. F. Hagen
Korean trans. © 2001 The United Methodist Publishing House, admin. The Copyright Co.

HAGEN
7.7.3.3.7. (310 B)

Morning Star, O Cheering Sight!

1. Morn-ing Star, O cheer-ing sight! Ere thou cam'st how dark earth's night! Morn-ing Star, O cheer-ing sight! Ere thou cam'st how dark earth's night! Je-sus mine, in me shine; in me shine, Je-sus mine; fill my heart with light di-vine.

2. Morn-ing Star, thy glo-ry bright! Far ex-cels the sun's clear light: Morn-ing Star, thy glo-ry bright far ex-cels the sun's clear light. Je-sus be, con-stant-ly, con-stant-ly, Je-sus be more than thou-sand suns to me.

3. Thy glad beams, thou Morn-ing Star cheer the na-tions near and far. Thy glad beams, thou Morn-ing Star, cheer the na-tions near and far; thee we own, Lord a-lone, Lord a-lone, thee we own man's great Sav-ior, God's dear Son.

4. Morn-ing Star, my soul's true light, tar-ry not, dis-pel my night; Morn-ing Star, my soul's true light, tar-ry not, dis-pel my night; Je-sus mine, in me shine; in me shine, Je-sus mine fill my heart with light di-vine.

WORDS: Johann Scheffler; English trans. Bennet Harvey, Jr.
MUSIC: F. F. Hagen

HAGEN
7.7.3.3.7. (310 B)

예수를 보리

1. 예수를 보리 천사 노래 할 때
2. 예수를 보리 거룩하신 주님
3. 예수를 보리 높은 산위에서

마내모 굿삶여 간의든 위밝무 에은리 큰빛가 별이르 빛되치 나시시 네네네

말어하 구두늘 유운과 안곳꽃 에과 누워밝 계게신 신빛나 아래시 기는네

어생주 서명님 가과만 왕길의 께과지 예진하 물리는 드되축 리신복 세주을

4. 예수를 보리 해질 저녁 무렵 병든 자 치유하여 주시네
   육신을 입고 사람되신 주님 사랑의 본이 되어 주셨네

5. 예수를 보리 이른 새벽아침 날 따라 오라 말씀하시네
   다 일어나세 주님 것이오니 우리 몸 주께 드리옵니다

WORDS: J. Edgar Park; Korean trans. The United Methodist Korean Hymnal Committee
MUSIC: Herbert B. Turner
Korean trans. © 2001 The United Methodist Publishing House, admin. The Copyright Co.

CUSHMAN
11.10.11.10

We Would See Jesus

1. We would see Je - sus; lo! his star is shin - ing
2. We would see Je - sus, Ma - ry's son most ho - ly,
3. We would see Je - sus, on the moun-tain teach - ing,

a - bove the sta - ble while the an - gels sing;
light of the vil - lage life from day to day;
with all the lis-tening peo-ple gath - ered round;

there in a man - ger on the hay re - clin - ing;
shin - ing re - vealed through ev - ery task most low - ly,
while birds and flowers and sky a - bove are preach - ing

haste, let us lay our gifts be - fore the King.
the Christ of God, the life, the truth, the way.
the bless-ed - ness which sim - ple trust has found.

4. We would see Jesus, in his work of healing,
   at eventide before the sun was set;
   divine and human, in his deep revealing
   of God made flesh, in loving service met.

5. We would see Jesus, in the early morning,
   still as of old he calleth, "Follow me!"
   Let us arise, all meaner service scorning;
   Lord, we are thine, we give ourselves to thee.

WORDS: J. Edgar Park
MUSIC: Herbert B. Turner

CUSHMAN
11.10.11.10

오 놀랍고 아름다운

1. 오 놀 - 랍 고 아 름 - 다 운
2. 옛 날 부 - 터 들 려 - 오 타 는 나
3. 엘 리 - 야 모 세 나 - 오 타 는 나

영 광 - 스 런 주 님 이 - 모 야 습 기 다
저 주 변 은 - 화 혜 증 - 의 거 하 - 도 다
주 저 - 제 자 에 함 - 올 라 끼 올 신 라 주 가 성

저 세 산 - 에 올 함 라 가 신 주가
세 구 제 - 자 속 하 나 님 음 성

해 주 그 보 - 다 더 나 - 빛 나 - 셨 다 네 네
그 아 - 들 선 - 포 하 - 도 다

4. 그 옷과 얼굴 빛나며 주 밝히 나타내셨네 주안에 기뻐하는 자 그 훗날 천국 영광을
5. 그 신비로움 인하여 신실한 자 새 힘 얻네 기쁨의 소리 높여서 기도와 찬양드리네

WORDS: *Sarum Breviary*, 1495 (Mt. 17:1-8; Mk. 9:2-8; Lk. 9:28-36); English trans. John Mason Neale;
Korean trans. The United Methodist Korean Hymnal Committee
MUSIC: William Knapp; harm. from *Hymns Ancient and Modern*
Korean trans. © 2001 The United Methodist Publishing House, admin. The Copyright Co.

WAREHAM
LM

O Wondrous Sight! O Vision Fair

1. O won - drous sight! O vi - sion fair
2. From age to age the tale de - clares
3. The law and proph - ets there have place,

of glo - ry that the church shall share,
how with the three dis - ci - ples there
two cho - sen wit - ness - es of grace;

with Christ up - on the moun - tain shows,
where Mo - ses and E - li - jah meet,
the Fa - ther's voice from out the cloud

where bright - er than the sun he glows!
the Lord holds con - verse high and sweet.
pro - claims his on - ly Son a - loud.

4. With shining face and bright array, Christ deigns to manifest that day
   what glory shall be theirs above who joy in God with perfect love.

5. And faithful hearts are raised on high by this great vision's mystery;
   for which in joyful strains we raise the voice of prayer, the hymn of praise.

WORDS: *Sarum Breviary*, 1495 (Mt. 17:1-8; Mk. 9:2-8; Lk. 9:28-36);
English trans. John Mason Neale
MUSIC: William Knapp, 1738; harm. from *Hymns Ancient and Modern*

WAREHAM
LM

이 세상이 시작되던

WORDS: Sydney Carter; Korean trans. The United Methodist Korean Hymnal Committee
MUSIC: 19th cent. Shaker tune; adapt. Sydney Carter
Words and adapt. © 1963, Korean trans. © 2001 Stainer & Bell, Ltd., admin. Hope Publishing Co.

LORD OF THE DANCE
Irr. with Refrain

170
I Danced in the Morning
(Lord of the Dance)

Unison

1. I danced in the morn-ing when the world was be-gun, and I
2. I danced for the scribe and the Phar - i - see, but they
3. I danced on the sab-bath when I cured the lame, the
4. I danced on a Fri-day and the sky turned black; it's
5. They cut me down and I leapt up high,

danced in the moon and the stars and the sun, and I
would not dance and they would not fol - low me; I
ho - ly peo - ple said it was a shame; they
hard to dance with the dev - il on your back; they
I am the life that - 'll nev - er, nev - er die; I'll

came down from heav - en and I danced on the earth. At
danced for the fish - er-men, for James and John; they
whipped and they stripped and they hung me high; and they
bur - ied my bod - y and they thought I'd gone, but
live in you if you'll live in me;

WORDS: Sydney Carter
MUSIC: 19th cent. Shaker tune; adapt. Sydney Carter
Words and adapt. © 1963 Stainer & Bell, Ltd., admin. Hope Publishing Co.

LORD OF THE DANCE
Irr. with Refrain

Beth - le - hem I had my birth.
came to me and the dance went on.
left me there on a cross to die. Dance, then, wher-
I am the dance and I still go on.
I am the Lord of the Dance, said he.

ev - er you may be; I am the Lord of the

dance, said he. And I'll lead you all wher-ev-er you may

be, and I'll lead you all in the dance, said he.

주 예수님 갈릴리 지나실 때

5. 저 귀신 들린 자와 나병환자 주여 고치소서
   저 등굽은 여인도 바로 섰네 고쳐주소서

6. 그 제자들 두 명씩 보내실 때 주여 고치소서
   병 고치며 주 복음 전하였네 고쳐주소서

7. 저 수많은 병자들 고통받네 주여 고치소서
   그 치유함 위하여 기도하니 고쳐주소서

WORDS: Peter D. Smith; Korean trans. The United Methodist Korean Hymnal Committee
MUSIC: Peter D. Smith
© 1978, Korean trans. © 2001 Stainer & Bell, Ltd., Hope Publishing Co.

HEALER
11 6.11 5

When Jesus the Healer Passed Through Galilee 171

1. When Je-sus the heal-er passed thru Gal-i-lee,
2. A par-a-lyzed man was let down through a roof.
3. The death of his daugh-ter caused Jai-rus to weep.
4. When blind Bar-ti-mae-us cried out to the Lord,

Heal us, heal us to-day!

the deaf came to hear and the
His sins were for-giv-en, his
The Lord took her hand, and he
His faith made him whole and his

blind came to see.
walk-ing the proof.
raised her from sleep. Heal us, Lord Je-sus!
sight was re-stored.

5. The lepers were healed and the demons cast out. Heal us, heal us today!
   A bent woman straightened to laugh and to shout. Heal us, Lord Jesus!

6. The twelve were commissioned and sent out in twos. Heal us, heal us today!
   To make the sick whole and to spread the good news. Heal us, Lord Jesus!

7. There's still so much sickness and suffering today. Heal us, heal us today!
   We gather together for healing and pray: Heal us, Lord Jesus!

WORDS: Peter D. Smith
MUSIC: Peter D. Smith
© 1979 Stainer & Bell, Ltd., Hope Publishing Co.

HEALER
11 6.11 5

주님 보좌와 영광

WORDS: Emily E. S. Elliott (Jn. 1:11); Korean trans. The United Methodist Korean Hymnal Committee
MUSIC: Timothy R. Matthews
Korean trans. © 2001 The United Methodist Publishing House, admin. The Copyright Co.

MARGARET
Irr.

Thou Didst Leave Thy Throne

1. Thou didst leave thy throne and thy king- ly crown, when thou cam- est to earth for me; but in Beth - le - hem's home was there found no room for thy ho - ly na-tiv - i - ty

2. Heav-en's arch - es rang when the an - gels sang, pro - claim - ing thy roy - al de - cree; but of low - ly birth didst thou come to earth, and in great hu - mil - i - ty.

3. The fox - es found rest, and the birds their nest in the shade of the for - est tree; but thy couch was the sod, O thou Son of God, in the des - erts of Gal - i - lee.

4. Thou cam - est, O Lord, with the liv - ing word that should set thy peo - ple free; but with mock-ing scorn, and with crown of thorn, they bore thee to Cal - va - ry.

5. When the heav - ens shall ring, and the an - gels sing, at thy com - ing to vic - to - ry, let thy voice call me home, say- ing "Yet there is room, there is room at my side for thee."

1-4. O come to my heart, Lord Je - sus, there is room in my heart for thee.
5. My heart shall re - joice, Lord Je - sus, when thou com-est and call-est for me.

WORDS: Emily E. S. Elliott (Jn. 1:11)
MUSIC: Timothy R. Matthews

MARGARET
Irr.

아멘 아멘

회중

아 - 멘 아 - 멘 아 - 멘 아 -

인도자

1. 구 유안 에계 신 - 아 기예 수보 라 - 이그 병피 내영영
2. 성 전안 의주 님 - 말 씀나 누실 때 - 그
3. 바 닷가 의주 님 - 복 음전 하시 며 - 피
4. 동 산위 의주 님 - 기 도하 실때 에 - 내
5. 고 통당 하시 는 - 십 자가 의주 님 - 영
6. 우 리위 해죽 고 - 부 활하 신주 님 - 영
7. (음~) 알 렐루 야 - 예 수나 의구 주 -

멘 아 - 멘 아 - 멘 아 -

성 탄 아 침 에 -
지 혜 놀 라 와 -
고 쳐 주 셨 네 -
땀 을 흘 리 셨 네 -
죄 를 지 셨 네 -
원 히 사 시 네 -
원 히 사 시 네 -

마지막절

멘 아 - 멘, 아 멘, 아 멘

WORDS: African American spiritual
MUSIC: African American spiritual; arr. Nelsie T. Johnson
Korean trans. © 2001 The United Methodist Publishing House, admin. The Copyright Co.

AMEN, AMEN
Irr.

Amen, Amen

Congregation

A - men, A - men, A - men, A - men, A - men! A - men, A -

Leader

1. See the lit-tle ba-by   ly-ing in a man-ger   on
2. See him in the tem-ple   talk-ing to the el-ders;   how
3. See him at the sea-shore   preach-ing to the peo-ple,
4. See him in the gar-den   pray-ing to the Fa-ther   in
5. See him on the cross   bear-ing all my sins   in
6. Yes, he died to save us   and he rose on Eas-ter;
7. (mm) Al-le-lu-ia!   Je-sus is my Sav-ior,

men, A - men, A -

Christ-mas morn-ing.
they all mar-veled!
heal-ing all the sick ones!
deep-est sor-row!
bit-ter ag-o-ny!
now he lives for-ev-er!
and he lives for-ev-er!

Last Time

men,   A - men, A - men, A - men!

WORDS: African American spiritual
MUSIC: African American spiritual; arr. Nelsie T. Johnson

AMEN, AMEN
Irr.

높이 들라 사랑의 십자가

후렴 (Unison)

높 이 들 라 사 랑 의 십 자 가

온 세 상 주 경배 할 때 까 지

Harmony

1. 성 도 들 모 두 로 하 거 나 되 어 서 들 승 그 약 주
2. 주 십 자 가 위 노 로 달 듭 난 종 던 리 주 셨
3. 십 자 리 의 노 래 영 원 히 불 러 주
4. 승 리 의 노 래 영 원 히 불 러 주

리 십 속 의 자 대 십 가 로 자 사 주 가 랑 께 함 증 인 께 인 도 따 되 하 르 었 소 여 세 네 서 라
십 십 자 가 승 리 찬 양 하

WORDS: George William Kitchin and Michael Robert Newbolt; alt.;
Korean trans. The United Methodist Korean Hymnal Committee
MUSIC: Sydney Hugo Nicholson
© 1974, Korean trans. © 2001 Hope Publishing Co.

CRUCIFER
10 10 with Refrain

Lift High the Cross

Refrain (Unison)

Lift high the cross, the love of Christ pro-claim

Fine

till all the world a - dore his sa - cred name.

Harmony

1. Come, Chris - tians, fol - low this tri - um-phant sign. The
2. Each new - born ser - vant of the Cru - ci - fied bears
3. O Lord, once lift - ed on the glo-rious tree, as
4. So shall our song of tri - umph ev - er be: Praise

D.C.

hosts of God in u - ni-ty com - bine.
on the brow the seal of him who died.
thou hast prom - ised, draw the world to thee.
to the Cru - ci - fied for vic - to - ry!

WORDS: George William Kitchin and Michael Robert Newbolt; alt.
MUSIC: Sydney Hugo Nicholson
© 1974 Hope Publishing Co.

CRUCIFER
10 10 with Refrain

내 마음 작은 갈릴리
(갈릴리 맑은 바다)

1. 갈 릴 리 맑 은 은 바 들 다 과
2. 기 름 진 넓 의 아 들
3. 능 력 의 신 의 아 들

푸 른 목 장 이 없 어 도 도
아 담 함 없 어 도 게
오 셔 서 의 로 어 울 게

주 님 찾 아 는 오 셔 서 서 로
순 종 하 신 오 맘 으 로 로
무 궁 하 신 사 랑 을

좌 정 하 시 오 니 리
따 라 사 가 지 오 은 곳
역 사 지 은 곳

WORDS: Chin Young Suck
MUSIC: Chai Hoon Park
© Chai Hoon Park

LITTLE GALILEE
7.7.

어 둡 던 내 마 음 상 에은
옛 날 처 럼 도 그 처 럼
어 옛 날 처 럼 내 도 그 처 럼
은 럼

생 어 명 의 석 빛 다 되 시 하 네
어 리 명 석 말 네
주 의 뜻 이 루 소 서

갈 릴 리 작 은 갈 릴 리 오

내 마 음 작 은 갈 릴 리

175

My Heart is Little Galilee

1. My heart is lit - tle Ga - li - lee,
2. My heart is lit - tle Ga - li - lee,
3. My heart is lit - tle Ga - li - lee,

where my Lord comes to vis - it;
where my heart re - ceives the Lord.
came the Son of God to dwell.

though there are no green pas - tures,
Bar - ren wil - der - ness, my heart,
Lone - li - ness and suf - fer - ing,

be - cause he is there.
hear and o - bey a call;
he came to con - quer.

WORDS: Chin Young Suck; English trans. Edward Poitras
MUSIC: Chai Hoon Park
© Chai Hoon Park

LITTLE GALILEE
7.7.

He's the light of the world that came,
th'world is still dark as an - cient days,
My lone - some soul here a - waits,

to give the light of life to all;
but Je - sus, true light, comes to save.
your will be done to save me.

Ga - li - lee, lit - tle Ga - li - lee, O

my heart is lit - tle Ga - li - lee.

176

예수님의 두 손 친절하신 손
Jesus' Hands Were Kind Hands

Unison

1. 예 수 님 의 두 손 친 절 하 신 손
2. 주 예 수 여 내 손 잡 아 주 셔 서

1. Je - sus' hands were kind hands, do - ing good to all,
2. Take my hands, Lord Je - sus, let them work for you;

병 을 고 치 시 며 축 복 하 시 네
주 의 손 과 같 이 되 게 하 소 서

heal-ing pain and sick - ness, bless-ing chil- dren small,
make them strong and gen - tle, kind in all I do.

발 을 씻 어 주 고 일 으 키 시 는
친 절 하 고 강 한 두 손 되 어 서

wash-ing tir - ed feet, and sav - ing those who fall;
Let me watch you, Je - sus, till I'm gen - tle too,

예 수 님 의 두 손 친 절 하 신 손
주 를 위 해 쓰 임 받 게 하 소 서

Je - sus' hands were kind hands, do - ing good to all.
till my hands are kind hands, quick to work for you.

WORDS: Margaret Cropper; Korean trans. The United Methodist Korean Hymnal Committee
MUSIC: Old French melody; harm. Carlton R. Young
Words © 1979, Korean trans. © 2001 Stainer & Bell, Ltd., admin. Hope Publishing Co.;
harm. © 1989 The United Methodist Publishing House, admin. The Copyright Co.

AU CLAIR DE LA LUNE
65.65 D

예수님 이야기 내게 들려주오
Tell Me the Stories of Jesus

177

Unison (Optional S. A.)

1. 예수님 이야기 내 게 들 려 주 오 —
1. Tell me the sto-ries of Je - sus I love to hear;

나 항상 그 말씀 들 기 즐 거 우 니 —
things I would ask him to tell me if he were here:

길 거 리 에 서 바 다 에 서 —
scenes by the way - side, tales of the sea,

행 하 신 일 들 들 려 주 오
sto - ries of Je - sus, tell them to me.

2. 예수님 앞으로 나온 어린이들 축복해 주시던 손길 나 느끼네
   다정한 말씀 크신 은혜 사랑의 빛을 담고 있네
3. 어린이 무리를 나도 따라가리 종-려가지를 높이 흔들면서
   큰 소리 외쳐 찬양하리 "주께 호산나 예수는 왕"

2. First let me hear how the children stood round his knee,
   and I shall fancy his blessing resting on me; words full of kindness,
   deeds full of grace, all in the lovelight of Jesus' face.
3. Into the city I'd follow the children's band, waving a branch of
   the palm tree high in my hand; one of his heralds, yes, I would
   sing loudest hosannas, "Jesus is King!"

WORDS: William H. Parker (Mt. 19:13-15; 21:8-9; Mk. 10:13-16; 11:8-10; Jn. 12:13)
MUSIC: Frederick A. Challinor
Korean trans. © 2001 The United Methodist Publishing House, admin. The Copyright Co.

STORIES OF JESUS
84.84.54.54

홍분한 군중들이
Filled with Excitement

1. 홍 분 한 군 중 들 이 거 리 에 -
2. 그 옛 날 예 루 살 렘 성 같 이 -

1. Filled with ex-cite-ment, all the hap-py throng
2. As in that en-trance to Je-ru-sa-lem,

겉 옷 과 종 려 가 지 깔 고 서 - 저 멀 리
우 리 도 호 산 나 를 부 르 네 - 지 금 도

spread cloaks and branch-es on the cit-y streets. There in the
we sing ho-san-nas to the Christ, our King, to the liv-ing

나 귀 타 고 오 시 는 - 하 나 님 아 들 맞 이
살 아 계 신 구 주 께 - 우 리 를 부 르 시 는

dis-tance they be-gin to see, rid-ing on a don-key, comes the
Sav-ior who still calls to-day, ask-ing us to fol-low him with

후렴 (Refrain)

한 다 네 - 곳 곳 에 서 모 두 찬 양 부 르 네
주 님 께 -

Son of God.
love and faith. From ev-ery cor-ner a thou-sand voic-es sing

WORDS: Rubén Ruiz Avila; English trans. Gertrude C. Suppe (Mt. 21:8-9; Mk. 11:8-10; Lk. 19:36-38; Jn. 2:12-13);
Korean trans. The United Methodist Korean Hymnal Committee
MUSIC: Rubén Ruiz Avila; arr. Alvin Schutmaat
© 1972, 1979, 1989, Korean trans. © 2001 The United Methodist Publishing House, admin. The Copyright Co.

HOSANNA
10 10.10 11 with Refrain

179

예수 예수
Jesu, Jesu

3. 우리가 섬기면서 우리가 사랑하는
   그들은 우리들의 이웃

4. 사랑과 봉사로써 우리가 섬길 때에
   주님과 동행하는 그 길

5. 우리도 무릎꿇고 이웃의 발을 씻는
   주님과 동행하는 그 길

3. These are the ones we should serve,
   these are the ones we should love;
   all these are neighbors to us and you.

4. Loving puts us on our knees,
   serving as though we are slaves,
   this is the way we should live with you.

5. Kneel at the feet of our friends,
   silently washing their feet,
   this is the way we should live with you.

WORDS: Tom Colvin (Jn. 13:1-17); Korean trans. The United Methodist Korean Hymnal Committee
MUSIC: Ghana folk song; adapt. Tom Colvin, 1969; harm. Charles H. Webb
© 1989, Korean trans. © 2001 Hope Publishing Co.

CHEREPONI
Irr. with Refrain

골짜기 외로운 길
Jesus Walked This Lonesome Valley

WORDS: African American spiritual; Korean trans. The United Methodist Korean Hymnal Committee
MUSIC: African American spiritual
Korean trans. © 2001 The United Methodist Publishing House, admin. The Copyright Co.

LONESOME VALLEY
8.8.10.8

사십일 동안

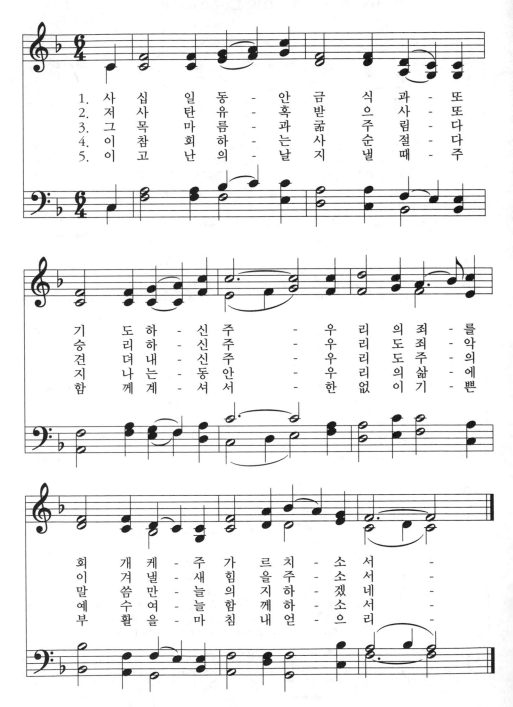

WORDS: Claudia F. Hernaman (Mt. 4:1-11; Mk. 1:12-13; Lk. 4:1-13);
Korean trans. The United Methodist Korean Hymnal Committee
MUSIC: USA folk melody; arr. Annabel Morris Buchanan; harm. Charles H. Webb
Harm. © 1989, Korean trans. © 2001 The United Methodist Publishing House, admin. The Copyright Co.

LAND OF REST
CM

Lord, Who Throughout These Forty Days 181

1. Lord, who through-out these for - ty days for
2. As thou with Sa - tan didst con - tend, and
3. As thou didst hun - ger bear, and thirst, so
4. And through these days of pen - i - tence, and
5. A - bide with us, that so, this life of

us didst fast and pray, teach us with thee to
didst the vic - tory win, O give us strength in
teach us, gra - cious Lord, to die to self, and
thru thy pas - sion - tide, yea, ev - er - more in
suf - fering o - ver past, an Eas - ter of un -

mourn our sins and close by thee to stay.
thee to fight, in thee to con - quer sin.
chief - ly live by thy most ho - ly word.
life and death, Je - sus, with us a - bide.
end - ing joy we may at - tain at last.

WORDS: Claudia F. Hernaman (Mt. 4:1-11; Mk. 1:12-13; Lk. 4:1-13)
MUSIC: USA folk melody; arr. Annabel Morris Buchanan; harm. Charles H. Webb
Harm. © 1989 The United Methodist Publishing House, admin. The Copyright Co.

LAND OF REST
CM

고난
182

다 이루었다

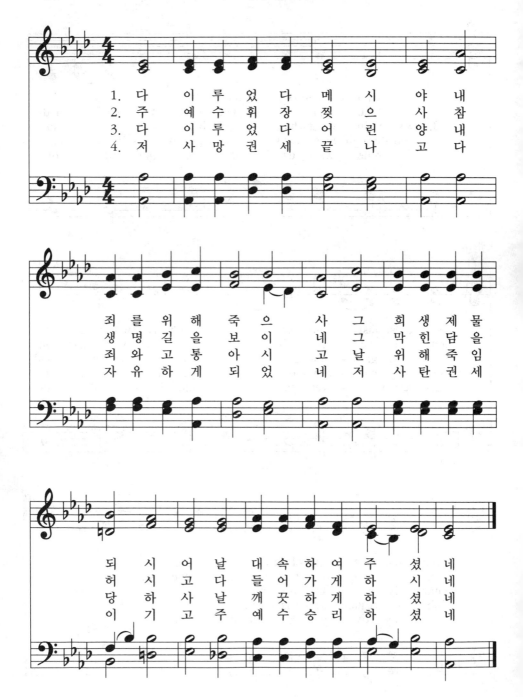

1. 다 이루었다 메시야 내
2. 주 예수 휘장 찢으사 참
3. 다 이루었다 어린 양 내
4. 저 사망 권세 끝나고 다

죄를 위해 죽으사 그 희생 제물
생명 길을 보이사네 그 막힌 담을
죄와 고통 아시고 날 위해 죽임
자유하게 되었네 저 사탄 권세

되시어날 대속하여 주셨네
허시고다 들어가게 하시네
당하사날 깨끗하게 하셨네
이기고주 예수 승리하셨네

WORDS: Charles Wesley (Jn. 19:30); Korean trans. The United Methodist Korean Hymnal Committee
MUSIC: William B. Bradbury
Korean trans. © 2001 The United Methodist Publishing House, admin. The Copyright Co.

OLIVE'S BROW
LM

'Tis Finished! The Messiah Dies

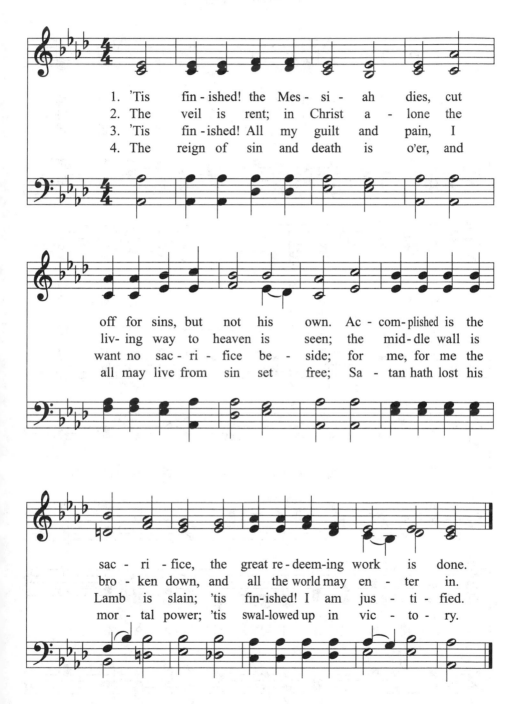

1. 'Tis fin-ished! the Mes-si-ah dies, cut
2. The veil is rent; in Christ a-lone the
3. 'Tis fin-ished! All my guilt and pain, I
4. The reign of sin and death is o'er, and

off for sins, but not his own. Ac-com-plished is the
liv-ing way to heaven is seen; the mid-dle wall is
want no sac-ri-fice be-side; for me, for me the
all may live from sin set free; Sa-tan hath lost his

sac-ri-fice, the great re-deem-ing work is done.
bro-ken down, and all the world may en-ter in.
Lamb is slain; 'tis fin-ished! I am jus-ti-fied.
mor-tal power; 'tis swal-lowed up in vic-to-ry.

WORDS: Charles Wesley (Jn. 19:30)
MUSIC: William B. Bradbury

OLIVE'S BROW
LM

183

예수 나를 위하여

1. 예 수 나 를 위 하 여 십 자 가 를 질 있 때 나
2. 십 자 가 를 지 심 은 무 죄 이 가 없 네
3. 피 와 같 이 붉 은 죄 없 는 이 가 없 네
4. 아 름 답 다 예 수 여 나 의 좋 은 친 구

세 상 죄 를 지 시 고 고 초 당 하 셨 네 네
어 리 석 은 무 리 들 고 메 시 과 같 이 되 시 네
십 자 가 의 공 로 로 나 를 구 하 시 네
주 의 은 혜 베 푸 사

후렴

예 수 여 예 수 여 나 의 죄 위 하 여

보 배 피 를 흘 리 니 죄 인 받 으 소 서

WORDS: Fanny J. Crosby (Eph. 2:16); Korean trans. The United Methodist Korean Hymnal Committee
MUSIC: William H. Doane
Korean trans. © 2001 The United Methodist Publishing House, admin. The Copyright Co.

NEAR THE CROSS
76.76 with Refrain

Jesus Shed His Blood for Me

1. Je-sus shed his blood for me, bore, for our sal-va-tion
2. For what crime should he be killed, for his kill-ers pray-ing?
3. None there lives who does not know sin, blood-ied as crim-son;
4. Je-sus, oh so fair art thou! My good friend, my Sav-ior,

on his cross, the ag-o-ny of a lost cre-a-tion.
Mad, that mind-less mob has willed their Mes-si-ah's slay-ing.
but the cross makes white as snow all in Christ's do-min-ion.
thy grace, on-ly, save me now, and from hell for-ev-er.

Refrain

Je-sus, Lord, Je-sus, Lord, for my sins they slew thee.

Now by thy dear blood re-stored, draw the sin-ner to thee.

WORDS: Fanny J. Crosby (Eph. 2:16)
MUSIC: William H. Doane

NEAR THE CROSS
76.76 with Refrain

고난

184

주 가시관을 쓰시고
To Mock Your Reign, O Dearest Lord

1. 주 가 시 관 을 쓰 시 고 조
2. 그 자 색 옷 을 입 히 사 조
3. 주 손 에 갈 대 들 리 워 조

1. To   mock your reign, O dear - est Lord, they
2. In   mock ac - claim, O gra - cious Lord, they
3. A   scep - tered reed, O pa - tient Lord, they

롱 당 하 시 며 놀 림 과 모 욕
롱 당 하 시 며 비 웃 는 군 병
롱 당 하 시 며 그 모 진 수 치

made a   crown of   thorns;   set   you with taunts a -
snatched a   pur - ple cloak;   your pas - sion turned, for
thrust in - to your   hand,   and act - ed out their

속 에 서 주 걸 어 가 셨 네
앞 에 서 주 고 통 당 했 네
모 욕 을 다 참 아 내 셨 네

long that road from which no   one   re - turns.
all   they cared, in - to a   sol - dier's joke.
grim cha - rade to its   ap - point - ed end.

WORDS: Fred Pratt Green (Mt. 27:27-31; Mk. 15:16-20; Jn. 19:1-5);
Korean trans. The United Methodist Korean Hymnal Committee
MUSIC: English melody; arr. Ralph Vaughan Williams
Words © 1973, Korean trans. © 2001 Hope Publishing Co.;
arr. © Oxford University Press

KINGSFOLD
CMD

거룩한 사랑의 주님

1. 거 룩 한 사 랑 의 주 님 날 위 해서
2. 우 리 와 화 목 하 시 려 는 주 께서
3. 피 흘 려 돌 아 가 시 는 구 세 주

돌 아 가 셨 네 내 모 든 죄 를 지 시 시
돌 아 가 셨 네 라 우 리 를 죄 용 서 하 시 시
바 라 보 아 라 생 명 과 평 화 주 신

고 십 자 가 달 리 셨 다 네 내 사 랑
고 예 수 의 피 로 사 셨 네 내 사 랑
왕 그 피 로 구 원 하 셨 네 내 사 랑

나 의 주 예 수 못 박 혀 돌 아 가 셨 네
나 의 주 예 수 못 박 혀 돌 아 가 셨 네
나 의 주 예 수 못 박 혀 돌 아 가 셨 네

WORDS: Charles Wesley; Korean trans. The United Methodist Korean Hymnal Committee
MUSIC: Isaac B. Woodbury
Korean trans. © 2001 The United Methodist Publishing House, admin. The Copyright Co.

SELENA
88.88.88.

O Love Divine, What Hast Thou Done

1. O Love di - vine, what hast thou done! Th'im - mor - tal God hath died for me! The Fa - ther's co - e - ter - nal Son bore all my sins up - on the tree. Th'im - mor - tal God for me hath died: my Lord, my Love, is cru - ci - fied!

2. Is cru - ci - fied for me and you, to bring us reb - els back to God. Be - lieve, be - lieve the rec - ord true, ye all are bought with Je - sus' blood. Par - don for all flows from his side: my Lord, my Love, is cru - ci - fied!

3. Be - hold him, all ye that pass by, the bleed - ing Prince of life and peace! Come, sin - ners, see your Sav - ior die, and say, "Was ev - er grief like his?" Come feel with me his blood ap - plied: my Lord, my Love, is cru - ci - fied!

WORDS: Charles Wesley
MUSIC: Isaac B. Woodbury

SELENA
88.88.88.

거룩한 예수 무슨 죄가 있어

WORDS: Johann Herrmann; English trans. Robert S. Bridges;
Korean trans. The United Methodist Korean Hymnal Committee
MUSIC: Johann Crüger
Korean trans. © 2001 The United Methodist Publishing House, admin. The Copyright Co.

HERZLIEBSTER JESU
11.11.11.5

Ah, Holy Jesus

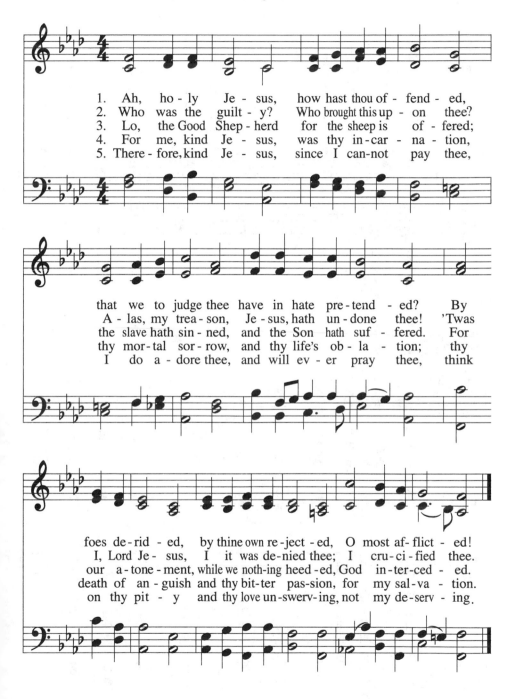

1. Ah, ho-ly Je-sus, how hast thou of-fend-ed,
2. Who was the guilt-y? Who brought this up-on thee?
3. Lo, the Good Shep-herd for the sheep is of-fered;
4. For me, kind Je-sus, was thy in-car-na-tion,
5. There-fore, kind Je-sus, since I can-not pay thee,

that we to judge thee have in hate pre-tend-ed? By
A-las, my trea-son, Je-sus, hath un-done thee! 'Twas
the slave hath sin-ned, and the Son hath suf-fered. For
thy mor-tal sor-row, and thy life's ob-la-tion; thy
I do a-dore thee, and will ev-er pray thee, think

foes de-rid-ed, by thine own re-ject-ed, O most af-flict-ed!
I, Lord Je-sus, I it was de-nied thee; I cru-ci-fied thee.
our a-tone-ment, while we noth-ing heed-ed, God in-ter-ced-ed.
death of an-guish and thy bit-ter pas-sion, for my sal-va-tion.
on thy pit-y and thy love un-swerv-ing, not my de-serv-ing.

WORDS: Johann Herrmann; English trans. Robert S. Bridges
MUSIC: Johann Crüger

HERZLIEBSTER JESU
11.11.11.5

겟세마네 동산의 구세주

WORDS: James Montgomery; alt.; Korean trans. The United Methodist Korean Hymnal Committee
MUSIC: Richard Redhead
Korean trans. © 2001 The United Methodist Publishing House, admin. The Copyright Co.

REDHEAD 76
77.77.77

Go to Dark Gethsemane

1. Go to dark Geth - sem - a - ne, ye that feel the
2. See him at the judg - ment hall, beat - en, bound, re -
3. Cal-vary's mourn-ful moun - tain climb; there, a - dor - ing
4. Ear - ly has - ten to the tomb where they laid his

temp - ter's power; your Re - deem - er's con - flict see,
viled, ar-raigned; O the worm - wood, and the gall!
at his feet, mark that mir - a - cle of time,
breath-less clay; all is sol - i - tude and gloom.

watch with him one bit - ter hour. Turn not from his
O the pangs his soul sus-tained! Shun not suf - fering,
God's own sac - ri - fice com-plete. "It is fin-ished!"
Who has tak - en him a - way? Christ is risen! He

griefs a - way; learn of Je - sus Christ to pray.
shame, or loss; learn of Christ to bear the cross.
Hear him cry; learn of Je - sus Christ to die.
meets our eyes; Sav - ior, teach us so to rise.

WORDS: James Montgomery; alt.
MUSIC: Richard Redhead

REDHEAD 76
77.77.77

주 부활하신 이 날

WORDS: John of Damascus; English trans. John Mason Neale;
Korean trans. The United Methodist Korean Hymnal Committee
MUSIC: Henry T. Smart
Korean trans. © 2001 The United Methodist Publishing House, admin. The Copyright Co.

LANCASHIRE
76.76 D

The Day of Resurrection

1. The day of res - ur - rec - tion! Earth, tell it out a - broad;
2. Our hearts be pure from e - vil, that we may see a - right
3. Now let the heavens be joy - ful! Let earth the song be - gin!

the pass - o - ver of glad - ness, the pass - o - ver of God.
the Lord in rays e - ter - nal of res - ur - rec - tion light;
Let the round world keep tri - umph, and all that is there - in!

From death to life e - ter - nal, from earth un - to the sky,
and lis - ten - ing to his ac - cents, may hear, so calm and plain,
Let all things seen and un - seen their notes in glad - ness blend,

our Christ hath brought us o - ver, with hymns of vic - to - ry.
his own "All hail!" and, hear - ing, may raise the vic - tor strain.
for Christ the Lord hath ris - en, our joy that hath no end.

WORDS: John of Damascus; English trans. John Mason Neale
MUSIC: Henry T. Smart

LANCASHIRE
76.76 D

주 예수 십자가에
(주 살아나셨네)

WORDS: African American spiritual; Korean trans. The United Methodist Korean Hymnal Committee
MUSIC: African American spiritual; adapt. and arr. William Farley Smith
Adapt. and arr. © 1989, Korean trans. © 2001 The United Methodist Publishing House, admin. The Copyright Co.

ASCENSIUS
76.76.76.9 with Refrain

They Crucified My Savior
(He Rose)

1. They cru - ci - fied my Sav - ior and nailed him to the tree, they cru - ci - fied my Sav - ior and nailed him to the tree, they cru - ci - fied my Sav - ior and nailed him to the tree,

2. Then Jo - seph begged his bod - y and laid it in the tomb, then Jo - seph begged his bod - y and laid it in the tomb, then Jo - seph begged his bod - y and laid it in the tomb,

3. Sis - ter Ma - ry she came run - ning, a - look - ing for my Lord, Sis - ter Ma - ry she came run - ning, a - look - ing for my Lord, Sis - ter Ma - ry she came run - ning, a - look - ing for my Lord,

4. An an - gel came from heav - en and rolled the stone a - way, an an - gel came from heav - en and rolled the stone a - way, an an - gel came from heav - en and rolled the stone a - way,

WORDS: African American spiritual;
Korean trans. The United Methodist Korean Hymnal Committee
MUSIC: African American spiritual; adapt. and arr. William Farley Smith
Adapt. and arr. © 1989 The United Methodist Publishing Housea, admin. The Copyright Co

ASCENSIUS
76.76.76.9 with Refrain

주 사셨다

WORDS: Brian Wren; alt.; Korean trans. The United Methodist Korean Hymnal Committee
MUSIC: *Psalmodia Evangelica*, 1789
Words © 1975, rev. 1995, Korean trans. © 2001 Hope Publishing Co.

TRURO
LM

Christ Is Alive

1. Christ is a - live! Let Chris-tians sing. The cross stands
2. Christ is a - live! No long - er bound to dis - tant
3. In ev - ery in - sult, rift, and war, where col - or,
4. Wo-men and men, in age and youth, can feel the
5. Christ is a - live, and comes to bring good news to

emp - ty to the sky. Let streets and homes with
years in Pal - es - tine, but sav - ing, heal - ing,
scorn, or wealth di - vide, Christ suf - fers still, yet
Spir - it, hear the call, and find the way, the
this and ev - ery age, till earth and sky and

prais - es ring. Love drowned in death, shall nev - er die.
here and now, and touch - ing ev - ery place and time.
loves the more, and lives, where e - ven hope has died.
life, the truth, re - vealed in Je - sus freed for all.
o - cean ring with joy, with jus - tice, love, and praise.

WORDS: Brian Wren; alt.
MUSIC: *Psalmodia Evangelica*, 1789
Words © 1975, rev. 1995 Hope Publishing Co.

TRURO
LM

주님은 죽음 이기고

WORDS: Michael Baughen; Korean trans. The United Methodist Korean Hymnal Committee
MUSIC: Traditional Israeli song; arr. Michael Baughen
© 1984, Korean trans. © 2001 Jubilate Hymns, Ltd., admin. Hope Publishing Co.

ISRAELI
8.8.8.12

Because He Died and Is Risen

1. Be-cause he died and is ris-en, be-cause he
2. stroys walls be-tween us, his peace de-
3. give you," said Je-sus, "my peace I
4. yond un - der-stand-ing, the peace be-

died and is ris-en, be-cause he died
stroys walls be-tween us, his peace de - stroys
give you," said Je-sus, "my peace I give
yond un - der-stand-ing, the peace be - yond

and is ris-en, we now have peace with God through
walls be - tween us, for on - ly he can rec - on -
you," said Je-sus, "don't let your heart be trou - bled;
un - der-stand-ing will guard the hearts and minds of

Je - sus Christ our Lord. 2. His peace de -
cile us both to God. 3. "My peace I
do not be a - fraid! 4. The peace be -

those who pray.

WORDS: Michael Baughen
MUSIC: Traditional Israeli song; arr. Michael Baughen
© 1984 Jubilate Hymns, Ltd., admin. Hope Publishing Co.

ISRAELI
8.8.8.12

무덤에 머물러
Low in the Grave He Lay

1. 무 덤 에 머 물 러 예 수 내 구 주
2. 헛 되 이 지 키 네 예 수 내 구 주
3. 거 기 못 가 두 네 예 수 내 구 주

1. Low in the grave he lay, Je - sus my Sav - ior!
2. Vain - ly they watch his bed, Je - sus my Sav - ior!
3. Death can - not keep its prey, Je - sus my Sav - ior!

새 벽 기 다 렸 네 예 수 내 주
헛 되 이 봉 하 네 예 수 내 주
우 리 를 살 리 네

Wait - ing the com - ing day, Jesus my Lord!
Vain - ly they seal the dead, Je - sus my Lord!
He tore the bars a - way,

후렴 *(Refrain)*

원 수 를 다 이 기 고 무 덤
Up from the grave he a - rose, with a

이 기 고
he a - rose,

WORDS: Robert Lowry (Mt. 28:1-10); Korean trans. The Christian Literature Society of Korea
MUSIC: Robert Lowry
Korean trans. © The Christian Literature Society of Korea

CHRIST AROSE
65.64 with Refrain

부활
193
예수 부활했으니
Christ the Lord Is Risen Today

1. 예 수 부 활　했 으 니 -　알 - 렐 루 - 야
2. 대 속 하 신　주 예 수 -

1. Christ the Lord is　risen to-day,　Al - le - lu - ia!
2. Lives a- gain our　glo-riousKing,

만 민 찬 송　하 여 라 -　알 - 렐 루 - 야
선 한 싸 움　이 겼 네 -

Sons of men and　an - gels say,　Al - le - lu - ia!
Where, O death, is　now thy sting?

천 사 들 이　즐 거 워　알 - 렐 루 - 야
사 망 권 세　이 기 고

Raise your joys and　tri-umphs high,　Al - le - lu - ia!
Once he died, our　souls to save,

WORDS: Charles Wesley; Korean trans. The Christian Literature Society of Korea
MUSIC: *Lyra Davidica*, 1708
Korean trans. © The Christian Literature Society of Korea

EASTER HYMN
77.77.D

기 쁜 찬 송 부 르 네 - 알 - 렐 루 - 야
하 늘 문 을 여 셨 네 -

Sing, ye heavens, and earth re-ply   Al - le - lu - ia!
Where's thy vic-tory, boast-ing grave?

3. 무덤 권세 이긴 주 알렐루야 왕의 왕이 되셨네 알렐루야
   높은 이름 세상에 알렐루야 널리 반포하여라 알렐루야

4. 길과 진리되신 주 알렐루야 우리 부활 하겠네 알렐루야
   부활 생명 되시니 알렐루야 우리 부활 하겠네 알렐루야

3. Love's redeeming work is done, Alleluia!
   Fought the fight, the battle won, Alleluia!
   Death in vain forbids him rise, Alleluia!
   Christ has opened paradise, Alleluia!

4. Soar we now where Christ has led, Alleluia!
   Following our exalted Head, Alleluia!
   Made like him, like him we rise, Alleluia!
   Ours the cross, the grave, the skies, Alleluia!

주님께 영광
Thine Be the Glory

1. 주 님 께 영 광 다 시 사 신 주
2. 부 활 의 주 님 나 타 나 시 사
3. 생 명 의 임 금 영 광 의 주 님

1. Thine be the glo - ry, ris - en, con-quering Son;
2. Lo! Je - sus meets thee, ris - en from the tomb;
3. No more we doubt thee, glo-rious Prince of life!

사 망 권 세 모 두 이 기 시 었 네
두 려 움 과 의 심 물 리 치 셨 네
주 님 없 는 삶 은 헛 될 뿐 이 라

end - less is the vic - tory thou o'er death hast won.
lov - ing - ly he greets thee, scat - ters fear and gloom.
Life is naught with - out thee; aid us in our strife.

흰 옷 입 은 천 사 돌 을 옮 겼 고
주 의 교 회 기 뻐 찬 송 하 여 라
주 의 사 랑 으 로 세 상 이 기 고

An - gels in bright rai - ment rolled the stone a - way,
Let the church with glad - ness hymns of tri-umph sing,
Make us more than con-querors, thru thy death-less love;

WORDS: Edmond L. Budry; English trans. Birch Hoyle;
Korean trans. The Christian Literature Society of Korea
MUSIC: G. F. Handel
Korean trans. © The Christian Literature Society of Korea

JUDAS MACCABEUS
55.65.65.65

누 우 셨 던 곳 은 비 어 있 었 네
다 시 사 신 주 님 죽 음 이 겼 네
요 단 건 너 본 향 가 게 하 소 서
kept the fold-ed grave-clothes where thy bod - y lay.
for our Lord now liv - eth; death hath lost its sting.
bring us safe thru Jor-dan to thy home a - bove.

후렴 *(Refrain)*

주 님 께 영 광 다 시 사 신 주
Thine be the glo - ry, ris - en, con-quering Son;

사 망 권 세 모 두 이 기 시 었 네
end - less is the vic - tory thou o'er death hast won.

사랑하는 우리 예수

1. 사랑 하는 우리 예수 무덤 속에 가둬놓고
2. 의로 우신 우리 예수 십자 가에 못을 박고
3. 죄악 권세 죽음 권세 한 꺼 번에 물리치고

죽음 권세 영원 토록 득세 할줄 알 았더 냐
악한 무리 힘을 합쳐 승리 할줄 알 았더 냐
승리 하신 우리 예수 사랑 으로 다 스린다

Unison

물 러가라 물 러가라 죽 음권세 물 러가라
가 소롭다 가 소롭다 사 탄권세 무 너졌다
부 활하신 예 수앞에 원 도한도 사 라지고

Chorus

생 명예수 부 활했 다 할 렐루야 찬 양하 자
구 주예수 승 리했다 할 렐루야 찬 양하 자
사 랑으로 하 나되 어 부 활예수 찬 양하 자

WORDS: Sung Ho Kim (Rom. 6:9)
MUSIC: Woon Young Na
Words © The Korean Hymnal Society; music © Woon Young Na

Jesus, Beloved Lord

Solo

1. Je-sus, be-loved Lord, shut with-in death's dark tomb of hea-vy stone,
2. Je-sus, our righ-teous Lord, for us sin-ners nailed to the cru-el tree,
3. Je-sus, vic-to-rious Lord, by your ris-ing from death we are now free,

will death pre-vail and hold, will evil's pow-er keep you in death a-lone?
will those who mock you now, in their e-vil de-feat you fi-nal-ly?
Je-sus, you rule in love, and your great love will reign e-ter-nal-ly.

Unison

Pow-ers of death, gone for-ev-er; pow-ers of death, gone for-ev-er!
Pow-ers of hell, gone for-ev-er; pow-ers of hell, shamed for-ev-er!
Je-sus now lives, lives for-ev-er; e-vil and sin, crushed for-ev-er!

Chorus

Je-sus now lives, he is ris-en, al-le-lu-ia, praise to the Lord!
Je-sus has won, he is the Christ, al-le-lu-ia, praise to the Lord!
One in his love, we have new life, Je-sus a-rose, praise to the Lord!

WORDS: Sung Ho Kim (Rom. 6:9); English trans. Edward Poitras
MUSIC: Woon Young Na
Words © The Korean Hymnal Society; music © Woon Young Na

알렐루야 찬양하라

WORDS: William C. Dix; alt. (Rev. 19:6-7); Korean trans. The United Methodist Korean Hymnal Committee
MUSIC: Rowland H. Prichard; arr. Ralph Vaughan Williams
Korean trans. © 2001 The United Methodist Publishing House, admin. The Copyright Co.;
music and arr. used by permission of Oxford University Press from *The English Hymnal*, 1906

HYFRYDOL
8.7.8.7. D

평화 로 운 시온 성 에 로
죄 십인 들의 친 구 되신

찬 송 울려 퍼지 니 때
중 이자 요구 실세 주

구 주 예 수 귀 한 보 혈 리
영 원 토 록 천 국 에 서

우 리 구 속 하 셨 네
주 기 도 들 어 주 소 서

Alleluia! Sing to Jesus

1. Al - le - lu - ia, sing to Je - sus!
2. Al - le - lu - ia! Not as or - phans
3. Al - le - lu - ia! Heav - enly High Priest,

his the scep - ter, His the throne:
are we left in sor - row now;
here on earth our help, our stay;

Al - le - lu - ia! His the tri - umph,
Al - le - lu - ia! He is near us;
Al - le - lu - ia! Hear the sin - ful

his the vic - to - ry a - lone.
faith be - lieves nor ques - tions how.
cry to you from day to day.

WORDS: William C. Dix; alt. (Rev. 19:6-7)
MUSIC: Rowland H. Prichard; arr. Ralph Vaughan Williams
Music and arr. used by permission of Oxford University Press from *The English Hymnal*, 1906

HYFRYDOL
8.7.8.7. D

Hark! The songs of peace - ful Zi - on
Though the cloud from sight re - ceived him
In - ter - ces - sor, friend of sin - ners,

thun - der like a might - y flood.
when the for - ty days were o'er,
earth's Re - deem - er, hear our plea,

Je - sus, out of ev - ery na - tion,
shall our hearts for - get his prom - ise,
where the songs of all the sin - less

has re - deemed us by his blood.
"I am with you ev - er - more."
sweep a - cross the crys - tal sea.

부활
197

알렐루야 예수 다시 사셨네
Alleluia! Christ Is Risen

*3부 돌림노래 *(3 Part Canon)*

①
알 렐 루 야 예 수 다 시 사 셨 네
Al - le - lu - ia! Christ is ris - en from the dead.

②
알 렐 루 야 주 의 말 씀 따 라 서
Al - le - lu - ia! He is ris - en as he said

③
알 렐 루 야 예 수 다 시 사 셨 네
Al - le - lu - ia! Christ is ris - en from the dead.

마지막 부분까지 부른 후 부르는 합창 마무리
Optional choral ending (to be sung after Part 3 completes canon)

알 렐 루 야 - 부 활 했 네 -
Al - le - lu - ia! He is ris - en!

WORDS: Gerald S. Henderson (Mt. 28:6-7);
Korean trans. The United Methodist Korean Hymnal Committee
MUSIC: German folk song; arr. Gerald S. Henderson
Words and arr. © 1986, Korean trans. © 2001 Word Music, Inc.

RESURRECTION CANON
11.11.11

내 사랑하는 그 이름
There Is a Name I Love
(O How I Love Jesus)

1. 내 사 랑 하 는 그 이 름 늘 노 래 부 르 네
2. 그 크 신 사 랑 베 푸 사 날 자 유 케 했 네
3. 내 깊 은 슬 픔 까 지 도 다 알 고 계 신 주

1. There is a name I love to hear, I love to sing its worth;
2. It tells me of a Sav-ior's love, who died to set me free;
3. It tells of one whose lov-ing heart can feel my deep-est woe;

내 귀 에 즐 거 운 그 이 름 다 정 한 그 이 름
이 죄 인 살 리 려 흘 리 신 귀 중 한 보 배 피
그 크 신 사 랑 의 맘 으 로 주 함 께 하 시 네

it sounds like mu-sic in my ear, the sweet-est name on earth.
it tells me of his pre-cious blood, the sin-ner's per-fect plea.
who in each sor-row bears a part that none can bear be-low.

후렴 (Refrain)

오 그 이 름 예 수 참 사 랑 합 니 다
O how I love Je-sus, O how I love Je-sus,

날 사 랑 한 예 수 참 사 랑 합 니 다
O how I love Je-sus, be-cause he first loved me!

WORDS: Frederick Whitfield; Korean trans. The United Methodist Korean Hymnal Committee
MUSIC: 19th cent. USA melody
Korean trans. © 2001 The United Methodist Publishing House, admin. The Copyright Co.

O HOW I LOVE JESUS
CM with Refrain

예수는 가장 높으신

4. 원수들 대적하여도 주 선포하겠네 영화로우신 주 이름 담대히 전하리
5. 주님의 공의 밝히며 구원의 진리를 이 세상 사는 동안에 나 선포하리라
6. 이 세상 떠나갈 때에 주 이름 부르리 숨질 때 나의 외칠 말 "어린양을 보라"

WORDS: Charles Wesley (Phil. 2:9-11); Korean trans. The United Methodist Korean Hymnal Committee
MUSIC: Johann Crüger
Korean trans. © 2001 The United Methodist Publishing House, admin. The Copyright Co.

GRÄFENBERG
CM

Jesus! the Name High over All

1. Je - sus! the name high o - ver all,
2. Je - sus! the name to sin - ners dear,
3. O that the world might taste and see

in hell or earth or sky;
the name to sin - ners given;
the rich - es of his grace!

an - gels and mor - tals pros - trate fall,
it scat - ters all their guilt - y fear,
The arms of love that com - pass me

and dev - ils fear and fly.
it turns their hell to heaven.
would all the world em - brace.

4. Thee I shall constantly proclaim, though earth and hell oppose;
   bold to confess thy glorious name before a world of foes.
5. His only righteousness I show, his saving truth proclaim;
   'tis all my business here below to cry, "Behold the Lamb!"
6. Happy, if with my latest breath I may but gasp his name,
   preach him to all and cry in death, "Behold, behold the Lamb!"

WORDS: Charles Wesley (Phil. 2:9-11)
MUSIC: Johann Crüger

GRÄFENBERG
CM

다 와서 찬양해
Come on and Celebrate

다 와 서 찬 양 해　　사 랑 을 주 신 주
Come on and ce - le - brate　　his gift of love we will

찬 양 해 -　　사 랑 의 우 리 주 - 님 -
ce - le - brate　　the Son of God who loved us

- 생 명 주 셨 네 -　　- 소 리 쳐
and gave us life.　　We'll shout your

찬 양 해 -　　기 쁨 을 주 시 는 우 리 왕 -
praise, O King,　　you give us joy no - thing else can bring,

찬 양 의 제 사 드 리 며　　- 주 님 께 경 배
we'll give to you our off - er - ing　　in ce - le - bra - tion

WORDS: Patricia Morgan; Korean trans. The United Methodist Korean Hymnal Committee
MUSIC: Patricia Morgan
© 1984, Korean trans. © 2001 Kingsway's Thankyou Music, admn. EMI Christian Music Group

알렐루야 알렐루야
Alleluia No. 1
(Alleluia, Alleluia)

후렴 (Refrain) Unison

알 렐 루 야 알렐 루 야 주께 감 사 를
Al - le - lu - ia, al-le-lu - ia! Give thanks to the

드 리 세 알 렐 루 야 알 렐 루 야 주 의
ris- en Lord. Al-le-lu - ia, al-le-lu - ia! Give

1~4

마지막 (Final ending)

이 름 찬 양 해 해
praise to his name. name.

WORDS: Donald Fishel; Korean trans. The United Methodist Korean Hymnal Committee
MUSIC: Donald Fishel
© 1973, Korean trans. © 2001 Word of God Music, admin. The Copyright Co.

ALLELUIA NO. 1
Irr.

함께 주의 이름으로

1. 함께 주의 이름으로 주의 전에 모여
2. 우리 모든 염려 잊고 주의 이름 높여

경배해 – 함께 주의 이름으로
경배해 – 우리 모든 염려 잊고

주의 전에 모 여 경배해 – 함께
주의 이름 높 여 경배해 – 우리

주의 이름으로 주의 전에 모 여
모든 염려 잊고 주의 이름 높 여

주께 경배해 구주께 경 – 배해 –
주께 경배해 구주께 경 – 배해 –

WORDS: Bruce Ballinger (Ps. 122:1); Korean trans. The United Methodist Korean Hymnal Committee
MUSIC: Bruce Ballinger
© 1976, Korean trans. © 2001 Universal-MCA Music Publishing

WORSHIP HIM
Irr.

We Have Come into His House

1. We have come in-to his house and gath-ered in his name to wor-ship him. We have come in-to his house and gath-ered in his name to wor-ship him. We have come in-to his house and gath-ered in his name to wor-ship Christ the Lord. Wor-ship him, Christ the Lord.

2. Let's for-get a-bout our-selves and mag-ni-fy his name and wor-ship him. Let's for-get a-bout our-selves and mag-ni-fy his name and wor-ship him Let's for-get a-bout our-selves and mag-ni-fy his name and wor-ship Christ the Lord. Wor-ship him, Christ the Lord.

WORDS: Bruce Ballinger (Ps. 122:1)
MUSIC: Bruce Ballinger
© 1976 Universal-MCA Music Publishing

WORSHIP HIM
Irr.

놀라운 그 이름
His Name Is Wonderful

놀 라 운 그 이름 놀 라 운 그 이름
His name is won-der-ful, his name is won-der-ful,

놀 라 운 그 이름 예 수 내 주
his name is won-der-ful, Je - sus, my Lord.

전 능 의 왕 이요 만 물 의 주 시니
He is the might-y King, mas - ter of ev-ery-thing;

놀 라 운 그 이름 예 수 내 주
his name is won-der-ful, Je - sus, my Lord.

WORDS: Audrey Mieir; Korean trans. The United Methodist Korean Hymnal Committee
MUSIC: Audrey Mieir
© 1959, renewed 1987, Korean trans. © 2001 Manna Music, Inc.

HIS NAME IS WONDERFUL
Irr.

경배해 위대한 주님께
Majesty, Worship His Majesty

경배해 - 위대한 주님께 -
Maj - es - ty, wor-ship his maj - es -ty;

모든 영광 존귀 찬양 드리어라 -
un - to Je - sus be all glo - ry, hon-or, and praise.

찬 양해 - 위대한 주 님께 -
Maj - es - ty, king-dom au - thor - i - ty,

주의 왕 권 보좌에 서 넘 쳐나 네 -
flow from his throne un-to his own; his an-them raise.

WORDS: Jack Hayford; Korean trans. The United Methodist Korean Hymnal Committee
MUSIC: Jack Hayford; arr. Eugene Thomas
© 1981, Korean trans. © 2001 Rocksmith Music, c/o Trust Music Management, Inc.

MAJESTY
Irr.

주 예수보다 더 귀한 것은 없네

1. 주 예수보다 더 귀한 것은 없네
2. 주 예수보다 더 귀한 것은 없네
3. 주 예수보다 더 귀한 것은 없네

이 세 상 부귀 와 바 꿀 수 없 네
이 이세 상 명예 와 바바 꿀 수수 없없 네네
이 세 상 행복 과 바 꿀 수 없 네

영 이 죽 을 내 대 신 던 돌 세 아 상 가 일 신 도
유 전 혹 에 과 즐 기 신 몰 려 와 도
유 전 혹 과 핍 박 이 세 몰 상 려 와 신 도 도

그 놀 라 운 사 랑 잊 지 지 못 해
주 사 랑 하 는 맘 뺏 지 지 못 못 해 해
주 섬 기 는 내 맘 변 치 못 해

WORDS: Rhea F. Miller (Ph. 3:8); Korean trans. The United Methodist Korean Hymnal Committee
MUSIC: G. B. Shea
Words © 1922, renewed 1950, Korean trans. © 2001; music © 1939, renewed 1968 Word Music, Inc.

I'D RATHER HAVE JESUS
12.11.10.10.

세상 즐 거 움 다 버 리 고

세 상 자 랑 다 버 렸 네 -

주 예 수보다 더 귀한 것 은 없 네

예 수 밖에 는 없 네 -

I'd Rather Have Jesus

1. I'd rath - er have Je - sus than sil - ver or gold;
2. I'd rath - er have Je - sus than men's ap - plause;
3. He's fair - er than lil - ies of rar - est bloom;

I'd rath - er be his than have rich - es un - told;
I'd rath - er be faith - ful to his dear cause;
he's sweet - er than hon - ey from out the comb;

I'd rath - er have Je - sus than houses or lands.
I'd rath - er have Je - sus than world - wide fame.
he's all that my hun - ger - ing spir - it needs.

I'd rath - er be led by his nail - pierced hand.
I'd rath - er be true to his ho - ly name.
I'd rath - er have Je - sus and let him lead.

WORDS: Rhea F. Miller (Ph. 3:8)
MUSIC: G. B. Shea
Words © 1922, renewed 1950; music © 1939, renewed 1968 Word Music, Inc.

I'D RATHER HAVE JESUS
12.11.10.10.

206

내 모든 장래 지난 날
Jesus Is Lord of All
(All My Tomorrows, All My Past)

1. 내 모 든 장 래 지 난 날
2. 내 모 든 갈 등 생 각 들
3. 내 모 든 열 망 모 든 꿈

1. All my to - mor - rows, all my past,
2. All of my con - flicts, all my thoughts,
3. All of my long - ings, all my dreams,

예 수 가 주 되 시 네 그
예 수 가 주 되 시 네
예 수 가 주 되 시 네

Je - sus is Lord of all.
Je - sus is Lord of all. His
Je - sus is Lord of all.

싸 움 이 끝 나 만 족 함 오 네
크 신 주 사 랑 승 리 하 시 네
쓰 러 질 때 에 새 힘 주 시 네

I've quit my strug - gles, con - tent - ment at last,
love wins the bat - tles I could not have fought,
All of my fail - ures his pow - er re - deems,

WORDS: Gloria Gaither and William J. Gaither (Mt. 6:24);
Korean trans. The United Methodist Korean Hymnal Committee
MUSIC: William J. Gaither
© 1973, Korean trans. © 2001 William J. Gaither, Inc., admin. Gaither Copyright Management

LORD OF ALL
Irr.

기뻐하며 왕께 노래 부르리
Shout for Joy and Sing

Unison

기 뻐 하 며 왕 께 노래 부르리 -
Shout for joy and sing your prais-es to the King,

소 리 높 여 할 렐 루 야 부르리 -
lift your voice and let your hal - le - lu-jahs ring;

주 님 앞 에 나 와 찬 양 드리며 -
come be-fore his throne to wor-ship and a-dore,

우 리 주 님 과 함 - 께 기 뻐 하 리 라 -
en - ter joy-ful-ly now the pre-sence of the Lord.

WORDS: David Fellingham; Korean trans. The United Methodist Korean Hymnal Committee
MUSIC: David Fellingham
© 1988, Korean trans. © 2001 Thankyou Music, admin. EMI Christian Music Group

SHOUT FOR JOY
Irr.

예수 사랑해요
Jesus, I Love You
(Alleluia)

예 - 수 사랑 해요 나 주 앞 에 엎드려 -
Je - sus, I love you, I bow down be - fore you.

경 - 배 와 찬 - 양 왕 께 드 리 네
Prais - es and wor - ship to our King.

알 - 렐 루 - 야 알 렐 루 야
Al - le - lu - ia, Al - le - lu - ia.

알 - 렐 루 - 야 알 렐 - 루
Al - le - lu - ia, Al - le - lu.

WORDS: Jude Del Hierro; Korean trans. The United Methodist Korean Hymnal Committee
MUSIC: Jude Del Hierro
© 1985, Korean trans. © 2001 Mercy/Vineyard Publishing

DEL HIERRO
Irr.

주 안에 평안 있고
In His Name

WORDS: Stephen Amerson; Korean trans. The United Methodist Korean Hymnal Committee
MUSIC: Stephen Amerson
© 1922 Universal

210

주를 찬양하리라
I Just Want to Praise You

WORDS: Arthur Tannous; Korean trans. The United Methodist Korean Hymnal Committee
MUSIC: Arthur Tannous
© 1984, 1987, Korean trans. © 2001 Acts Music, admin. EMI Christian Music Group

임마누엘 임마누엘
Emmanuel, Emmanuel

Unison

임 마 누 엘 -임 마 누 엘
Em-man-u-el, Em-man-u-el,

-그 의 이 름 -임 마 누 엘
his name is called Em-man-u-el.

-우 리 와 -함 께 계 신
God with us, re-vealed in us,

마지막 (Final)

-그 의 이 름 -임 마 누 엘 -
his name is called Em-man-u-el.

WORDS: Bob McGee (Mt. 1:23); Korean trans. The United Methodist Korean Hymnal Committee
MUSIC: Bob McGee
© 1976, Korean trans. © 2001 C. A. Music (div. of C. A. Records, Inc.)

McGEE
Irr.

영광스런 주님 전능하신 주

1. 영광스런 주님 전능하신 주라
2. 하나님의 모습 다양하셔라
3. 신선한 이 아침 새로운 이 밤

불안하여 떨 때 은혜 베풀어 주사네
사람 또한 달 사랑 창조하시네
끊임없는 사랑 창조하시네

많은 변화 중에도 찬양하게 하소서서
옛것 사라질 때에 두렴 떨쳐 주소서
많은 은사 주께서 우리에게 주시네

WORDS: Al Carmines; Korean trans. The United Methodist Korean Hymnal Committee
MUSIC: Al Carmines
© 1974, Korean trans. © 2001 Al Carmines

KATHERINE
65.65.77

Many Gifts, One Spirit

1. God of change and glo - ry, God of time and space,
2. God of man - y col - ors, God of man - y signs,
3. Fresh - ness of the morn - ing, new - ness of each night,

when we fear the fu - ture, give to us your grace.
you have made us dif - ferent, bless-ing man - y kinds.
you are still cre - at - ing end - less love and light.

In the midst of chang-ing ways give us still the grace to praise.
As the old ways dis - ap-pear, let your love cast out our fear.
This we see, as shad-ows part, man - y gifts from one great heart.

WORDS: Al Carmines
MUSIC: Al Carmines
© 1974 Al Carmines

KATHERINE
65.65.77

주의 성령 느낄 때
Every Time I Feel the Spirit

후렴 *(Refrain)*

주의 성령 - 느낄 때면 - 나는 주님께
Ev-ery time I feel the Spir-it mov-ing in my heart,

-기 도 해 - 주님의 성 령 - 느 낄
I will pray. Yes, ev-ery time I feel the

때 면 - 나 는 주님께 - 기 도 해 -
Spir-it mov-ing in my heart, I will pray.

Fine

1. 산 위의 주 님 - 불로 써 - 내 게
2. 요 단 강물 - 차 가 와 - 나 의

1. Up-on the moun-tain, my Lord spoke, out his
2. Jor-dan riv-er runs right cold, chills the

WORDS: African American spiritual (Rom. 8:15-17);
Korean trans. The United Methodist Korean Hymnal Committee
MUSIC: African American spiritual; adapt. and arr. William Farley Smith
Adapt. and arr. © 1989, Korean trans. © 2001 The United Methodist Publishing House, admin. The Copyright Co.

PENTECOST
Irr.

말 씀 - 하 셨 네 - 나 의 주 변 - 광 채
몸 은 - 추 워 도 - 주 님 향 한 - 내 영
mouth came   fire and smoke.   All a - round me   looks so
bod - y,   not the soul.   Ain't but   one train   on this

D. C.

는 - 주 님 내 게 - 주 셨 네 -
혼 - 성 령 으 로 - 뜨 겁 네 -
shine,   ask my Lord   if   all   was   mine.
track,   runs to heav - en   and   right   back.

214

살아계신 주 성령
Spirit of the Living God

살 아 계 신 주 성 령 내 게 오 소 서
Spir - it of the liv - ing God, fall a- fresh on me.

살 아 계 신 주 성 령 내 게 오 소 서
Spir - it of the liv - ing God, fall a- fresh on me.

빛 으 시 고 채 우 소 서 -
Melt me, mold me, fill me, use me.

살 아 계 신 주 성 령 내 게 오 소 서
Spir - it of the liv - ing God, fall a-fresh on me.

WORDS: Daniel Iverson (Acts 11:15); Korean trans. The United Methodist Korean Hymnal Committee
MUSIC: Daniel Iverson
© 1935, renewed 1963, Korean trans. © 2001 Birdwing Music, admin. EMI Christian Music Group

LIVING GOD
75.75.875

주님의 영이 여기 함께 하시니
Surely the Presence of the Lord

주 님 의 영 이 여 기 함 께 하 시 니
Sure - ly the pres-ence of the Lord is in this place;

그 의 능 력 과 은 혜 넘 치 네 -
I can feel his might-y pow-er and his grace.

천 사 들 의 날 개 소 리 와
I can hear the brush of an - gels' wings,

주 의 영 광 을 보 니 주 님 의
I see glo - ry on each face; sure - ly the

영 이 여 기 함 께 하 시 네
pres - ence of the Lord is in this place.

WORDS: Lanny Wolfe; Korean trans. The United Methodist Korean Hymnal Committee
MUSIC: Lanny Wolfe
© 1977, Korean trans. © 2001 Lanny Wolfe Music, admin Gaither Copyright Management

WOLFE
11 11.9 7 12

내 안에 계신 온유하신 주

WORDS: C. Eric Lincoln; Korean trans. The United Methodist Korean Hymnal Committee
MUSIC: Alfred Morton Smith
Words © 1989, Korean trans. © 2001 The United Methodist Publishing House, admin. The Copyright Co.

SURSUM CORDA
10 10.10 10

How Like a Gentle Spirit

Unison

1. How like a gen-tle spir-it deep with-in
2. Let God be God wher-ev-er life may be;
3. God like a moth-er ea-gle hov-ers near
4. When in our vain pre-ten-sions we con-spire
5. Through all our fret-ful claims of sex and race

God reins our fer-vent pas-sions day by day,
let ev-ery tongue bear wit-ness to the call;
on might-y wings of pow-er man-i-fest;
to shape God's im-age as we see our own,
the un-i-ver-sal love of God shines through,

and gives us strength to chal-lenge and to win
all hu-man-kind is one by God's de-cree;
God like a gen-tle shep-herd stills our fear,
hark to the voice a-bove our base de-sire;
for God is love tran-scend-ing style and place

de-spite the per-ils of our cho-sen way.
let God be God, let God be God for all.
and com-forts us a-gainst a peace-ful breast.
God is the sculp-tor, we the bro-ken stone.
and all the i-dle op-tions we pur-sue.

WORDS: C. Eric Lincoln
MUSIC: Alfred Morton Smith
Words © 1989 The United Methodist Publishing House, admin. The Copyright Co.

SURSUM CORDA
10 10.10 10

217

성령이여 진리 안에
Holy Spirit, Come, Confirm Us

1. 성 령 이 여 진 리 안 에 굳 게
2. 성 령 이 여 함 께 하 사 우 리
1. Ho - ly Spir - it, come, con - firm us in the
2. Ho - ly Spir - it, come, con - sole us, come as

서 게 하 소 - 서 도 우 시 는 주 의
위 로 하 시 - 고 사 랑 하 는 주 의
truth that Christ makes known; we have faith and un - der-
ad - vo-cate to plead; lov-ing Spir - it from the

성 령 우 리 믿 음 주 소 서
성 령 우 리 도 와 주 소 서
stand - ing through your help-ing gifts a - lone.
Fa - ther, grant in Christ the help we need.

3. 성령이여 우리 삶을 거듭나게
하소서 성령 함께 사심으로
거룩하게 하소서

4. 성령이여 사랑으로 우리
다스리소서 삼위일체 하나님의
거룩하신 주 성령

3. Holy Spirit, come, renew us, come
yourself to make us live; holy through
your loving presence, holy through the
gifts you give.

4. Holy Spirit, come, possess us, you the
love of Three in One, Holy Spirit of the
Father, Holy Spirit of the Son.

WORDS: Brian Foley; Korean trans. The United Methodist Korean Hymnal Committee
MUSIC: V. Earle Copes
Words © 1971, Korean trans. © 2001 Faber Music, Ltd.; music © 1960, renewed 1988 Hope Publishing Co.

FOR THE BREAD
87.87

오 성령이여 오소서
Come, Holy Ghost, Our Hearts Inspire

1. 오 성 령이 여 오 소 서 내 날
2. 오 성 령이 여 오 소 서 내 날
3. 주 크 신날 개 펼 치 사 날
4. 주 성 령으 로 내 안 에 그

1. Come, Ho - ly Ghost, our hearts in - spire, let
2. Come, Ho - ly Ghost, (for moved by thee the
3. Ex - pand thy wings, ce - les - tial Dove, brood
4. God, through the Spir - it we shall know if

맘 에 오 소 서 한 없 는 주 의
도 와 어 주 소 서 그 진 어 리 말 씀
품 빛 을 비 추 소 서 니 그 거 룩 하 운신

us thine in - fluence prove; source of the old pro -
proph - ets wrote and spoke), un - lock the truth, thy
o'er our na - ture's night; on our dis - or - dered
thou with - in us shine, and sound, with all thy

사 랑 이 샘 깨 솟 게 하 소 서 서라
펼 치 사령 에 참 다 달 빛 을 주 양 하 소 소 서 서
사 랑 을 을 찬 하 리 라

phet - ic fire, foun - tain of life and love.
self the key, un - seal the sa - cred book.
spir - its move, and let there now be light.
saints be - low, the depths of love di - vine.

WORDS: Charles Wesley; Korean trans. The United Methodist Korean Hymnal Committee
MUSIC: Est's *The Whole Booke of Psalmes*, 1592; harm. from *Hymns Ancient and Modern*, 1861
Korean trans. © 2001 The United Methodist Publishing House, admin. The Copyright Co.

WINCHESTER OLD
CM

믿음의 영이여
Spirit of Faith, Come Down

1. 믿음의 영이여을 하숨나님진않영리으이여를면여
2. 생명의말씀쓰씀 나쉬지의의영믿음을
3. 속죄의어린양 승믿음리의민음을
4. 산믿음주소서 승리의민음을

1. Spir - it of faith, come down, re - veal the things of God,
2. No one can tru - ly say that Je - sus is the Lord,
3. O that the world might know the all - a - ton - ing Lamb!
4. In - spire the liv - ing faith (which who-so - e'er re - ceive,

깨 달 아 무 상 하 시 고 증 거 주 케
그 온 세 한 라 예 수 름 다 나 타
확 실 에 증 주 이 를 지 나 라 게

and make to us the God-head known, and wit - ness
un - less thou take the veil a - way and breathe the
Spir - it of faith, de - scend and show the vir - tue
the wit - ness in them - selves they have and con - scious-

하 소 서 주 보 혈 흘 리 사
못 하 소 리 그 보 혈 힘 입 어
내 소 서 서 주 저 산 혜 베 푸 사

with the blood. 'Tis thine the blood to ap - ply
liv - ing Word. Then, on - ly then, we feel
of his name; the grace which all may find,
ly be - lieve), the faith that con - quers all,

WORDS: Charles Wesley; Korean trans. The United Methodist Korean Hymnal Committee
MUSIC: Sacred Harp (Mason)
Korean trans. © 2001 The United Methodist Publishing House, admin. The Copyright Co.

BEALOTH
SMD

우주 리 눈 여 시 고 죄 인 들 위 해 의
우 주 말 쏨 따 를 때 예 수 는 나 의
구 큰 원 의 능 력 을 온 세 상 사 람
and give us eyes to see, who did for ev - ery
our in - terest in his blood, and cry with joy un -
the sav - ing power, im - part, and tes - ti - fy to
and doth the moun - tain move, and saves who-e'er on

죽 으 심 깨 달 게 하 소 서
구 주 라 기 쁘 게 하 외 치 소 서
맘 속 에 증 거 해 주 소 서
우 리 를 온 전 케 하 소 서
sin - ner die hath sure - ly died for me.
speak - a - ble, "Thou art my Lord, my God!"
hu - man - kind, and speak in ev - ery heart.
Je - sus call, and per - fects them in love.

여기 성령 함께 계시니
There's a Sweet, Sweet Spirit

여 기 성 령 함께계시 니 - 주 의
There's a sweet, sweet Spir-it in this place, and I

다 정하신 성 령이 시 네 - 얼 굴
know that it's the Spir - it of the Lord; there are

마 다 기쁨넘치 니 - 주 의
sweet ex - pres-sions on each face, and I

임 재 하 심 우 리 느 끼 네 -
know they feel the pres - ence of the Lord.

WORDS: Doris Akers; Korean trans. The United Methodist Korean Hymnal Committee
MUSIC: Doris Akers
© 1962, renewed 1990, Korean trans. © 2001 Manna Music, Inc.

SWEET, SWEET SPIRIT
Irr. with Refrain

성 령
Spirit

성 령 은밀한 바람 - 참 자유 주시려
Spir - it, spir-it of gen-tle-ness, blow thru the wil-der-ness,

불어 오네 - 성 령 능력의 바람 -
call-ing and free, Spir - it, spir-it of rest-less-ness,

잠 잠한 내 영혼을 깨 우 시 네 - -
stir me from plac-id-ness, wind, wind on the sea.

1. 물 위 를 거 닐 며 손 내 미 시 네
2. 광 야 의 백 성 과 주 함 께 하 사
3. 구 유 안 의 노 래 산 위 의 말 씀
4. 주 앞 서 가 시 며 날 부 르 시 네

1. You moved on the wa - ters, you called to the deep,
2. You swept through the des - ert, you stung with the sand,
3. You sang in a sta - ble, you cried from a hill,
4. You call from to - mor - row, you break an - cient schemes,

- 깊 은 골 짜 기 에 서 주 님 부 르 시 네 네
- 갈 길 몰 라 헤 맬 때 임 우 말 씀 잠 시 었 우 네네
- 침 묵 속 의 속 삭 임 게 우 리 잠 깨 시 었 네네
- 슬 퍼 하 는 자 에 게 꿈 을 주 시 었 네

then you coaxed up the moun - tains from the val-leys of sleep,
and you gift-ed your peo - ple with a law and a land,
then you whis-pered in si - lence when the whole world was still,
from the bond-age of sor - row the cap-tives dream dreams;

WORDS: James K. Manley; Korean trans. The United Methodist Korean Hymnal Committee
MUSIC: James K. Manley
© 1978, Korean trans. © 2001 James K. Manley

SPIRIT
Irr.

222

주 믿는 성도들 날마다 기도해
Let Every Christian Pray

1. 주 믿는 성도들 - 날 마 다 기 도 해
2. 성 령의 역사는 - 잃 은 자 구 하 려
3. 성 령의 능력이 - 새 힘 을 주 시 네

1. Let ev-ery Chris-tian pray, this day and ev-ery day,
2. The Spir-it brought to birth the church of Christ on earth
3. On - ly the Spir-it's power can fit us for this hour:

주 성 령 오 소 서 우 리 의 교 회 는
주 교 회 세 웠 네 오 순 절 내 리 신
주 성 령 오 소 서 다 하 나 되 어 서

come, Ho - ly Spir - it, come! Was not the church we love
to seek and save the lost: God nev - er has with-drawn,
come, Ho - ly Spir - it, come! In - struct, in - spire, u - nite,

주 님 의 몸 이 니 주 성 령 어 오 소 서
성 령 의 은 혜 를 늘 부 어 주 시 네
참 빛 을 보 도 록 주 성 령 오 소 서

com - mis-sioned from a - bove? Come, Ho - ly Spir - it, come!
since that tre-men-dous dawn, the gifts at Pen - te - cost.
and help us see your light: come, Ho - ly Spir - it, come!

WORDS: Fred Pratt Green; Korean trans. The United Methodist Korean Hymnal Committee
MUSIC: Joseph Barnby
Words © 1971, Korean trans. © 2001 Hope Publishing Co.

LAUDES DOMINI
6.6.6 D

성령을 따라서 찬양하리
I'm Goin'a Sing When the Spirit Says Sing

1. 성 령 을 따 라 서 *찬 양 하 리 -
1. I'm goin' a sing* when the Spir- it says sing,

성 령 을 따 라 서 찬 양 하 리 -
I'm goin' a sing when the Spir - it says sing

성 령 을 따 라 서 찬 양 하 리 - 주 의
I'm goin' a sing when the Spir- it says sing, and o-

성 령 순 종 하 리 라 -
bey the Spir - it of the Lord.

*2. 기도하리   3. 슬퍼하리   4. 외치겠네
2. pray   3. moan   4. shout

WORDS: African American spiritual; Korean trans. The United Methodist Korean Hymnal Committee
MUSIC: African American spiritual; adapt. William Farley Smith
Adapt. © 1989, Korean trans. © 2001 The United Methodist Publishing House, admin. The Copyright Co.

I'M GOIN'A SING
Irr.

성령이여 오셔서 정결케 하소서

1. 성 - 령이여 오 셔 서   정 결 케 하 소 서 -
2. 성 - 령이여 오 셔 서   순 종 케 하 소 서 -
3. 성 - 령이여 오 셔 서   새 힘 을 주 소 서 -
4. 성 - 령이여 오 셔 서   주 님 것 만 드 사 -

내 맘 에 주 의 밝 은 빛 비 추 - 어 주 소 서 -
나 에 게 향 한 주 의 뜻 깨 달 - 게 하 소 서 -
사 랑 과 열 정 내 맘 에 불 붙 - 게 하 소 서 -
주 님 만 위 해 살 도 록 날 주 - 장 하 소 서 -

후렴

나 - 에게   오 - 소서   성 령 이 여 오 - 소서

나 의 마 음   정 결 하 게   성 - 령 이 - 여 오 소 서

WORDS: Edwin Hatch (Jn. 20:22); adapt. B. B. McKinney;
Korean trans. The United Methodist Korean Hymnal Committee
MUSIC: B. B. McKinney
Korean trans. © 2001 The United Methodist Publishing House, admin. The Copyright Co.
Music © 1937, renew. 1965 Broadman Press

TRUETT
7.6.8.6. with Refrain

Holy Spirit, Breathe on Me

1. Ho - ly Spir-it, breathe on me, un - til my heart is clean;
2. Ho - ly Spir-it, breathe on me, my stub-born will sub-due;
3. Ho - ly Spir-it, breathe on me, fill me with pow'r di-vine;
4. Ho - ly Spir-it, breathe on me, till I am all thine own,

let sun-shine fill its in - most part, with not a cloud be-tween.
teach me in words of liv - ing flame what Christ would have me do.
kin - dle a flame of love and zeal with - in this heart of mine.
un - til my will is lost in thine, to live for thee a - lone.

Refrain

Breathe on me, breathe on me, Ho - ly Spir-it, breathe on me;

take thou my heart, cleanse ev-'ry part, Ho - ly Spir - it, breathe on me.

WORDS: Edwin Hatch (Jn. 20:22); adapt. B. B. McKinney
MUSIC: B. B. McKinney
Music © 1937, renew. 1965 Broadman Press

TRUETT
7.6.8.6. with Refrain

나의 하나님 나의 삶을 다해 사랑해요
Father, I Adore You

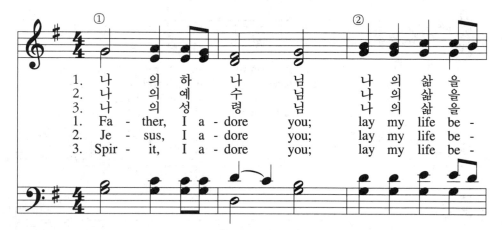

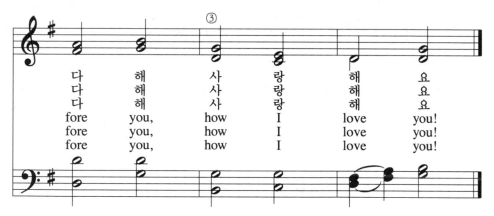

돌림노래 (May be sung as a canon)

WORDS: Terrye Coelho (Eph. 3:19); Korean trans. The United Methodist Korean Hymnal Committee
MUSIC: Terrye Coelho
© 1972, Korean trans. © 2001 Maranatha! Music, admin. The Copyright Co.

MARANATHA
Irr.

만 입이 내게 있으면
O for a Thousand Tongues

1. 만 입이 내게 있으면 그 날 날
2. 내 은 혜로 신한 하이 름이 날
3. 내 내 주의 귀한 이 이 름이 날
4. 내 죄의 권 세 깨 뜨 려 그

1. O for a thou-sand tongues to sing my
2. My gra-cious Mas-ter and my God, as -
3. Je - sus! the name that charms our fears, that
4. Hear him, ye deaf; his praise, ye dumb, your

입 다 가 지시 고사 내 구 주 크 신 름악
도 와 주 시시 내 주 내 크 신 이 음 신름악을
위 로 하 시시 니 내 주내 이 귀 에 한 맘
결 박 푸 시 고 이 추 한 맘 을

great Re-deem - er's praise, the glo - ries of my
sist me to pro - claim, to spread thru all the
bids my sor - rows cease; 'tis mu - sic in the
loos-ened tongues em - ploy; ye blind, be-hold your

은 총 을 늘 - 찬 송 하 하 겠 네 서 다
온 땅 에 전 - 하 게 하 소 도 다
같 으 며 참 - 평 안 되 도 네
피 로 써 정 - 결 케 하 셨 네

God and King, the tri-umphs of his grace!
earth a-broad the hon-ors of thy name.
sin-ner's ears, 'tis life, and health, and peace.
Sav-ior come, and leap, ye lame, for joy.

WORDS: Charles Wesley; Korean trans. The United Methodist Korean Hymnal Committee
MUSIC: Carl G. Gläser; arr. Lowell Mason
Korean trans. © 2001 The United Methodist Publishing House, admin. The Copyright Co.

AZMON
CM

하늘의 주님 내려주소서
O God in Heaven

Unison

1. 하늘의 주님 내려주소서 자비와
2. 대속자 예수 기억합니다 당신의
3. 은혜의 성령 축복의 성령 새 힘 주

1. O God in heav - en, grant to thy chil-dren mer - cy and
2. Je - sus, Re - deem-er, may we re - mem- ber thy gra-cious
3. Spir - it de - scend-ing, whose is the bless-ing, strength for the

축복 영원한 노래 연합의 사랑 대속의
죽음 당신의 부활 경배드리며 찬양합
시고 도와주시네 우리의 예배 받아주

bless - ing, songs nev - er ceas-ing, love to u - nite us, grace to re -
pas - sion, thy res - ur - rec - tion. Wor-ship we bring thee, praise we shall
wea - ry, help for the need - y; sealed in our kin-ship, thine be our

은 혜 하늘의 주님 주 하나 님
니 다 대속자 예수 주 예수 님
소 서 은혜의 성령 우리주 님

deem us, O God in heav - en, dear Lord, our God.
sing thee, Je-sus, Re - deem- er, Je - sus, our Lord.
wor - ship, Spir-it de - scend- ing, Spir - it a - dored.

WORDS: Elena G. Maquiso; English trans. D. T. Niles;
Korean trans. The United Methodist Korean Hymnal Committee
MUSIC: Elena G. Maquiso; harm. Charles H. Webb
English trans. by permission of Christian Conference of Asia;
Korean trans. © 2001 The United Methodist Publishing House, admin. The Copyright Co.

HALAD
55.55

하나님 사랑과 경배 드립니다
Glorify Thy Name
(Father, We Love You)

1. 하 나 님 사 랑 과 경 배 드 립 니 다
2. 예 수 님 사 랑 과 경 배 드 립 니 다
3. 성 령 님 사 랑 과 경 배 드 립 니 다

1. Fa - ther, we love you, we wor-ship and a - dore you.
2. Je - sus, we love you, we wor-ship and a - dore you.
3. Spir - it, we love you, we wor-ship and a - dore you.

온 땅 위 에 주 이 름 찬 양 -
Glo - ri - fy thy name, in all the earth.

영 광 돌 리 세 영 광 돌 리 세
Glo - ri - fy thy name, glo - ri - fy thy name,

온 땅 위 에 주 이 름 찬 양 -
glo - ri - fy thy name, in all the earth.

WORDS: Donna Adkins; Korean trans. The United Methodist Korean Hymnal Committee (Ps. 138:2)
MUSIC: Donna Adkins
© 1976, Korean trans. © 2001 Maranatha! Music, admin. The Copyright Co.

GLORIFY THY NAME
Irr.

거룩 거룩

WORDS: Jimmy Owens; Korean trans. The United Methodist Korean Hymnal Committee
MUSIC: Jimmy Owens
© 1972, Korean trans. © 2001 Bud John Songs, Inc., admin. EMI Christian Music Group

HOLY, HOLY
Irr.

Holy, Holy

1. Ho - ly, ho - ly, ho - ly, ho - ly, ho - ly,
2. Gra - cious Fa - ther, gra - cious Fa - ther, we're so
3. Pre - cious Je - sus, pre - cious Je - sus, we're so
4. Ho - ly Spir - it, Ho - ly Spir - it, come and

ho - ly, Lord God Al - might - y;
blest to be your chil - dren, gra - cious Fa - ther;
glad that you've re - deemed us pre - cious - Je - sus;
fill our hearts a - new, Ho - ly Spir - it;

and we lift our hearts be - fore you as a
and we lift our heads be - fore you as a
and we lift our hands be - fore you as a
and we lift our voice be - fore you as a

to - ken of our love, ho - ly, ho - ly, ho - ly, ho - ly.
to - ken of our love, gra - cious Fa - ther, gra - cious Fa - ther.
to - ken of our love, pre - cious Je - sus, pre - cious Je - sus.
to - ken of our love, Ho - ly Spir - it, Ho - ly Spir - it.

HOLY, HOLY
Irr.

창조주 하나님 감사 찬송하세

WORDS: H. Francis Yardley (Lk. 3:21-22);
Korean trans. The United Methodist Korean Hymnal Committee
MUSIC: *Paris Antiphoner*, 1681; harm. David Evans; alt.
Words © 1982, Korean trans. © 2001 H. Francis Yardley; harm. by permission of Oxford University Press

CHRISTE SANCTORUM
11 11 11.5

Praise and Thanksgiving Be to God

1. Praise and thanks-giv - ing be to God our mak - er,
2. Not our own ho - li - ness nor that we have striv - en
3. Come, Ho - ly Spir - it, come in vis - i - ta - tion;
4. Praise to the Fa - ther, Son, and Ho - ly Spir - it;

source of all bless - ing, prod - i - gal cre - a - tor.
brings us the peace which you, O Christ, have giv - en.
you are the truth, our hope, and our sal - va - tion.
one Lord, one faith, one source of ev - ery mer - it.

Bap - tized and made your own, now we come be -
Bap - tized and set a - part, strength - en us, O
Bap - tize with joy and power, give, O Dove de -
Here now re - new your church through this wa - ter

fore you, while we a - dore you.
Sav - ior, with grace and fa - vor.
scend - ing, life nev - er end - ing.
giv - en; grant peace from heav - en.

WORDS: H. Francis Yardley (Lk. 3:21-22)
MUSIC: *Paris Antiphoner*, 1681; harm. David Evans; alt.
Words © 1982 H. Francis Yardley; harm. by permission of Oxford University Press

CHRISTE SANCTORUM
11 11 11.5

사망의 모든 권세 이기고

WORDS: John Brownlow Geyer; Korean trans. The United Methodist
Korean Hymnal Committee (Rom. 6:3-11)
MUSIC: Charles Villiers Stanford

ENGELBERG
10 10 10 with Alleluias

We Know That Christ Is Raised

1. We know that Christ is raised and dies no more.
2. We share by wa-ter in his sav-ing death.
3. A new cre-a-tion comes to life and grows

Em-braced by death, he broke its fear-ful hold,
Re-born, we share with him an Eas-ter life
as Christ's new bod-y takes on flesh and blood.

and our de-spair he turned to blaz-ing joy.
as liv-ing mem-bers of a liv-ing Christ.
The un-i-verse re-stored and whole will sing:

Al-le-lu-ia! Al-le-lu-ia!

WORDS: John Brownlow Geyer (Rom. 6:3-11)
MUSIC: Charles Villiers Stanford
Words © 1981 John Brownlow Geyer

ENGELBERG
10 10 10 with Alleluias

축복하신 주의 자녀

WORDS: Ronald S. Cole-Turner; Korean trans. The United Methodist Korean Hymnal Committee
MUSIC: Attr. C. F. Witt; adapt. Henry J. Gauntlett
Words © 1981, Korean trans. © 2001 Ronald S. Cole-Turner

STUTTGART
87.87

Child of Blessing, Child of Promise

232

1. Child of bless-ing, child of prom-ise, bap-tized with the Spir-it's sign; with this wa-ter God has sealed you un-to love and grace di-vine.
2. Child of love, our love's ex-pres-sion, love's cre-a-tion, loved in-deed! Fresh from God, re-fresh our spir-its, in-to joy and laugh-ter lead.
3. Child of joy, our dear-est trea-sure, God's you are, from God you came. Back to God we hum-bly give you; live as one who bears Christ's name.
4. Child of God your lov-ing Par-ent, learn to know whose child you are. Grow to laugh and sing and wor-ship, trust and love God more than all.

WORDS: Ronald S. Cole-Turner
MUSIC: Attr. C. F. Witt; adapt. Henry J. Gauntlett
Words © 1981 Ronald S. Cole-Turner

STUTTGART
87.87

233 거룩 거룩 거룩 전능하신 주
Holy, Holy, Holy

거룩 거룩 거룩 전 능
Ho- ly, ho- ly, ho- ly Lord, God of

하 신 주 - 주 -
power and might. might

하 늘과 땅 에 가 득
주 님의 이 름 으 로
Heav - en and earth are full,
Bless - ed is he who comes

주 의 영 - 광 이 - 호
오 시 는 - 이 여
full of your glo - ry. Ho-
in the name of the Lord.

산 나 높 은 곳 에 호
san - na in the high - est, ho-

WORDS: From *Deutsche Messe* Franz Schubert; adapt. Richard Proulx;
Korean trans. The United Methodist Korean Hymnal Committee
MUSIC: From *Deutsche Messe* Franz Schubert; adapt. Richard Proulx
Adapt. © 1985, GIA Publications, Inc.; Korean trans. © 2001 The United Methodist Publishing House, admin. The Copyright Co.

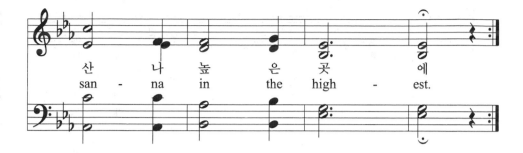

산　나　높　은　곳　에
san - na in the high - est.

기억하소서
Remember Me

234

기　억　하　소　서　기　억　하　소　서
Re - mem - ber me, re - mem - ber me,

주　여　기　억　하　소　서
O Lord, re - mem - ber me.

WORDS: Trad. (Lk. 23:42); Korean trans. The United Methodist Korean Hymnal Committee
MUSIC: Trad.; harm. J. Jefferson Cleveland
Korean trans. © 2001 The United Methodist Publishing House, admin. The Copyright Co.;
harm. © 1981 Abingdon Press, admin. The Copyright Co.

CLEVELAND
Irr.

주님 떼어 주신 떡

1. 주   님   떼   어   주   신   떡   과   며   내   게
2. 주   의   사   랑   베   푸   시   중   에   평   화   아
3. 하   늘   나   라   영   광   할   에   앉   아   리
4. 주   의   사   역   감   당   할   때   우   리

부   어   주   신   —   잔   주   님   주   신   생   명   리
회   복   하   시   —   고   하   늘   소   리   명   내   주   의
있   는   성   도   —   와   기   다   리   는   주   의
삶   을   지   키   —   사   보   내   주   신   세   상

말   씀   주   께   감   사   드   리   소   네   서   서
시   니   거   룩   하   게   하   소   소   서   서
교   회   하   나   되   게   하   소   소   서
안   에   천   국   이   뤄   주   소   소   서

WORDS: Louis F. Benson (Mt. 26:26-29; Mk. 14:22-25; Lk. 22:15-20; 1 Cor. 11:23-26);
Korean trans. The United Methodist Korean Hymnal Committee
MUSIC: V. Earle Copes
Korean trans. © 2001 The United Methodist Publishing House, admin. The Copyright Co.;
music © 1960, renewed 1988 Hope Publishing Co.

FOR THE BREAD
87.87

For the Bread Which You Have Broken 235

1. For the bread which you have bro - ken, for the
2. By this pledge that you do love us, by your
3. With our saint - ed ones in glo - ry seat - ed
4. In your ser - vice, Lord, de - fend us, in our

wine which you have poured, for the words which you have
gift of peace re - stored, by your call to heaven a -
at the heav - enly board, may the church that's wait - ing
hearts keep watch and ward; in the world where you have

spo - ken, now we give you thanks, O Lord.
bove us, hal - low all our lives, O Lord.
for you keep love's tie un - bro - ken, Lord.
sent us, let your king - dom come, O Lord.

WORDS: Louis F. Benson (Mt. 26:26-29; Mk. 14:22-25; Lk. 22:15-20; 1 Cor. 11:23-26)
MUSIC: V. Earle Copes
Music © 1960, renewed 1988 Hope Publishing Co.

FOR THE BREAD
87.87

함께 주님의 떡을 나누세
Let Us Break Bread Together

1. 함 께 주 님 의 떡을 나 누 세 (나 누 세)
　　　주 님 의 잔을 나 누 세 (나 누 세)
　　　주 님 께 찬 양 드 리 세 (드 리 세)

1. Let us break bread to-geth-er on our knees, (on our knees)
　　drink wine to-geth-er on our knees, (on our knees)
　　praise God to-geth-er on our knees, (on our knees)

함 께 주 님 의 떡을 나 누 세 (나 누 세)
함 께 주 님 의 잔을 나 누 세 (나 누 세)
함 께 주 님 께 찬 양 드 리 세 (드 리 세)

let us break bread to-geth-er on our knees. (on our knees)
let us drink wine to-geth-er on our knees. (on our knees)
let us praise God to-geth-er on our knees. (on our knees)

우 리 무 릎 꿇 고 주를 바 라 보 오 니
When I fall on my knees with my face to the ris-ing sun,

오 - 자 비 베 푸 소 서 (주 여) 2.3. 함 께
O Lord, have mer-cy on me. (on me) 2.3. Let us

*3절까지만 부르고 마칠수도 있음. (May end after stanza 3)

WORDS: African American spiritual (Acts 2:42);
Korean trans. The United Methodist Korean Hymnal Committee
MUSIC: African American spiritual; adapt. and arr. William Farley Smith
Adapt. and arr. © 1989, Korean trans. © 2001 The United Methodist Publishing House, admin. The Copyright Co.

LET US BREAK BREAD
10 10 with Refrain

237

한 떡을 떼며
One Bread, One Body

후렴 (Refrain) Unison

한 떡 -을 떼며 - 한 몸 되어
One bread, one bod-y, one Lord of all,

축복 의 잔 을 나누 세 - 한
one cup of bless - ing which we bless. And

주 -님 안에 - 한 몸 이룬
we, though man-y through-out the earth,

온 땅 에 사 는 주 의 백 성 -
we are one bod -y in this one Lord.

Fine

WORDS: John B. Foley (1 Cor. 10:16-17; Gal. 3:28; 1 Cor. 12);
Korean trans. The United Methodist Korean Hymnal Committee
MUSIC: John B. Foley; harm. Gary Alan Smith
© 1978, 1989, Korean trans. © 2001 John B. Foley, SJ and New Dawn Music

ONE BREAD, ONE BODY
44.6 with Refrain

238

우리 삶을 받아주소서
Take Our Bread

후렴 *(Refrain) Unison*

우 리 삶 을 받 아 주 소 서 주 사 랑
Take our bread, we ask you; take our hearts, we love you.

Fine

합 니 다 아 버 지 우 리 는 주 의 것
Take our lives, O Fa-ther, we are yours, we are yours.

1. 주 님 의 성 찬 을 받 을 때 에
2. 주 피 로 정 결 함 받 은 우 리
1. Yours as we stand at the ta - ble you set;
2. Your ho - ly peo-ple stand-ing washed in your blood,

우 리 는 주 의 것 임 기 억 하 네
베 푸 실 하 늘 양 식 기 다 리 네
yours as we eat the bread our hearts can't for-get.
Spir - it filled yet hun-gry we a - wait your food. We are

WORDS: Joe Wise; Korean trans. The United Methodist Korean Hymnal Committee
MUSIC: Joe Wise
© 1966, Korean trans. © 2001 GIA Publications, Inc.

TAKE OUR BREAD
Irr. with Refrain

우 리 와 늘 함 께 계 시 는 주
가 난 한 맘 으 로 나 왔 으 니
We are the sign of your life with us yet,
poor, but we've brought our-selves the best we could;

우 리 는 주 의 것
we are yours, we are yours.

D. C.

239

모든 은사와 언어로
Let Us Talents and Tongues Employ

Unison

1. 모 든 은 사 와 언 어 로 기 쁜 소 리 를
2. 만 찬 베 푸 신 주 예 수 우 릴 하 나 로
3. 우 릴 세 상 에 보 내 사 열 매 맺 으 라

1. Let us tal-ent and tongues em-ploy, reach-ing out with a
2. Christ is a-ble to make us one, at the ta-ble he
3. Je-sus calls us in, sends us out bear-ing fruit in a

외 치 세 주 의 몸 과 피 베 푸 사
묶 으 시 사 우 리 언 어 엘 의 행 실 로
하 시 네 임 마 누 엘 의 하 나 님

shout of joy: bread is bro-ken, the wine is poured,
sets the tone, teach-ing peo-ple to live to bless,
world of doubt, gives us love to tell, bread to share:

후렴 *(Refrain)*

그 의 사 랑 을 맛 보 네
사 랑 하 라 고 하 시 네 예 수 사 셨 네
떡 을 나 누 라 하 시 네

Christ is spo-ken and seen and heard.
love in word and in deed ex-press. Je-sus lives a-gain,
God (Im-man-u-el) ev-ery-where!

온 땅 숨 쉬 네 말 씀 풍 성 히 나 누 세
earth can breathe a-gain, pass the word a-round: loaves a-bound!

WORDS: Fred Kaan; Korean trans. The United Methodist Korean Hymnal Committee
MUSIC: Jamaican folk melody; adapt. Doreen Potter
© 1975, Korean trans. © 2001 Hope Publishing Co.

LINSTEAD
LM with refrain

자비로 그 몸 찢기시고
Bread of the World

1. 자 비 로 그 몸 찢 - 기 시 고 그의 피
2. 회 개 한 죄 인 상 - 한 가 슴 흐르는
1. Bread of the world in mer - cy bro - ken, wine of the
2. Look on the heart by sor - row bro - ken, look on the

흘 려 주 - 신 주 생 명의 말 씀 주 심
눈 물 보 - 시 고 은 혜로 내 영 먹 이
soul in mer - cy shed, by whom the words of life were
tears by sin - ners shed; and be thy feast to us the

으 로 우 리 죄 사 해 주 - 셨 네
시 는 큰 잔 치 되 게 하 - 소 서
spo-ken, and in whose death our sins are dead.
to - ken, that by thy grace our souls are fed.

WORDS: Reginald Heber (Jn. 6:35-58); Korean trans. The United Methodist Korean Hymnal Committee
MUSIC: John S. B. Hodges
Korean trans. © 2001 The United Methodist Publishing House, admin. The Copyright Co.

EUCHARISTIC HYMN
98.98

감사하는 성도여

WORDS: Henry Alford; alt. (Mk. 4:26-29; Mt. 13:36-43);
Korean trans. The United Methodist Korean Hymnal Committee
MUSIC: George J. Elvey
Korean trans. © 2001 The United Methodist Publishing House, admin. The Copyright Co.

ST. GEORGE'S WINDSOR
77.77 D

Come, Ye Thankful People, Come

1. Come, ye thank-ful peo-ple, come, raise the song of har-vest home;
2. All the world is God's own field, fruit as praise to God we yield;
3. For the Lord our God shall come, and shall take the har-vest home;
4. E - ven so, Lord, quick-ly come, bring thy fi - nal har-vest home;

all is safe-ly gath - ered in, ere the win-ter storms be - gin.
wheat and tares to - geth - er sown are to joy or sor-row grown;
from the field shall in that day all of-fens-es purge a - way,
gath - er thou thy peo - ple in, free from sor-row, free from sin,

God our Mak-er doth pro - vide for our wants to be sup-plied;
first the blade and then the ear, then the full corn shall ap - pear;
giv - ing an-gels charge at last in the fire the tares to cast;
there, for-ev - er pu - ri - fied, in thy pres-ence to a - bide;

come to God's own tem - ple, come, raise the song of har-vest home.
Lord of har-vest, grant that we whole-some grain and pure may be.
but the fruit-ful ears to store in the gar-ner ev - er - more.
come, with all thine an - gels, come, raise the glo-rious har-vest home.

WORDS: Henry Alford; alt. (Mk. 4:26-29; Mt. 13:36-43)
MUSIC: George J. Elvey

ST. GEORGE'S WINDSOR
77.77 D

하늘 나는 새를 보라
See the Birds As They Fly Thru The Air

1. 하 늘 나 는 새 를 보 라
2. 들 에 피 는 꽃 을 보 라
3. 너 는 먼 저 주 의 나 라

1. See the brids as they fly thru the air,
2. See the flowers that bloom in the field,
3. You who seek the king - dom of God

농 사 하 지 않 으 며
길 쌈 수 고 안 해 도
주 의 의 를 구 하 라

they have no need to plow or raise grain,
they have no need to spin or to weave,
and who hun - ger for God's righ-teous-ness,

곡 식 모 아 곳 간 안 에
솔 로 몬 의 의 모 복 보 을
하 나 님 이 모 든 것 을

though they do not har - vest in fall,
yet the gar - ments God gives them to wear
God will grant to you all that you need,

들 인 것 이 없 어 도
더 욱 아 름 답 도 다
너 회 에 게 주 시 리

they have no need to store or pre - pare,
would out - shine e - ven Sol - o-mon's robes,
be not anx - ious, trust and be - lieve,

WORDS: F. S. Miller (Mt. 6:26); English trans. Edward Poitras
MUSIC: Young Soo Na
Korean trans. © 2001 The United Methodist Publishing House, admin. The Copyright Co.;
music © Kyung Dong Presbyterian Church

산마다 불이 탄다 고운 단풍에

WORDS: Ok In Lim (Act. 14:17)
MUSIC: Chai Hoon Park
Words © The Christian Literature Society of Korea; music © Chai Hoon Park

Ev'ry Hill Seems to Be Aflame

1. Ev-'ry hill seems to be a-flame, au-tumn col-ors glow-ing,
2. Ev-'ry field where the seed was sown, prom-i-ses full mea-sure,
3. For the sweat of the farm-er's brow, in his good-ness giv-en
4. If we stand firm-ly on the Word, then up-on our sow-ing

ev-'ry dell pours it-self a-way, sil-ver stream-lets flow-ing.
ev-'ry tree in the or-chard grown prom-i-ses its trea-sure.
where the earth, wound-ed by the plow in the spring was riv-en,
dai-ly rains prom-ised of the Lord shall as-sure the grow-ing.

Gold-en fields like the gold-en sun, boun-ty are bring-ing.
Wind and rain and the sun are planned all for our bless-ing,
har-vest wealth shall be his re-ward, such is God's prom-ise;
Break the clods, plough the wast-ed field, all our strength spend-ing.

Rad-iant heav'n in di-vine de-light floods the earth with sing-ing!
pour-ing out in each o-pen hand boun-ty be-yond guess-ing.
all the good gifts of God out-poured lav-ish-ly up-on us.
When we see God's re-wards re-vealed we'll give thanks un-end-ing.

WORDS: Ok In Lim (Act. 14:17); English trans. John T. Underwood
MUSIC: Chai Hoon Park
Words © The Christian Literature Society of Korea; music © Chai Hoon Park

Refrain

To all dis - tan - ces where the eye can search,

in all crev - i - ces where the hand can touch;

see the fruits God's mer - cies af - ford and the grains his hand has out-poured!

Let us give thanks, then! Praise we the Lord! (to Him)

Let us give thanks, then! Praise we the Lord!

봄이 오면 밭고랑에

WORDS: Jong Rack Im (Jn. 15:8)
MUSIC: Sum Sook Lee

Soft Rains of Spring Flow

1. Soft rains of spring flow thru the fields,
2. Ten - der young shoots green in the sun
3. Our hearts are filled, God gives us grace,

earth a - wakes and greets a new year,
glis - ten with the beau - ty of spring,
o - ver-flow - ing we give our praise,

deep with - in the soil of our hearts
God will watch and care for each one,
we come hum-bly bring - ing our thanks,

seeds of love be - gin to take root,
bring the growth and strength to bear fruit,
bring our hearts and of - fer them back,

WORDS: Jong Rack Im; English trans. Edward Poitras (Jn. 15:8)
MUSIC: Sum Sook Lee
© The Korean Hymnal Society

주의 형상 따라서

1. 주의 형상 따 - 라서 지음받은 우리들이
2. 세상죄와 죽음에서 구원받은 우리들이
3. 하나님의 사랑안에 풍성하게 살았으니

크신은혜 감사하여 주께찬송 드립니다
건져주신 크신은혜 감사찬송 드립니다
복의근원 하나님께 감사찬송 드립니다

후렴

우리몸과 마음과 우리가진 모든것을

주님앞에 드리오니 주여받아 주옵소서

WORDS: Won Yong Na (Ps. 136:1)
MUSIC: Woon Young Na
Words © The Korean Hymnal Society; music © Woon Young Na

We Who Bear the Image of God

1. We who bear the im-age of God giv-en thru your won-der-ful word,
2. We who have sal-va-tion from God from the pow'r of sin and from death
3. We who live in love from our Lord, life a-bun-dant, bless-ed by grace,

bring our praise and of-fer our thanks for your love and in-fi-nite grace.
raise our grate-ful hymn to the Lord, for de-liv'r ance, in-fi-nite grace.
raise our grate-ful hymn to the Lord, God the one source, bles-sings a-bound.

Refrain

Lord, we bring our hearts and minds, bring-ing ev-'ry-thing that we have,

Lord, we of-fer, bo-dy and soul, take and bless us, hum-bly we pray.

WORDS: Won Yong Na (Ps. 136:1); English trans. Edward Poitras
MUSIC: Woon Young Na
Words and English trans. © The Korean Hymnal Society; music © Woon Young Na

대속하신 주께 감사

1. 대속하신 주께 감사 축복 베푸심 감사
2. 기도 응답하심 감사 응답 없어도 감사
3. 길가장 미꽃을 감사 가시 있음도 감사

지난 날의 은혜 감사 곁에 계심을 감사
역경 지켜주심 감사 사랑 베푸심 감사
화기애애 가정 감사 참는 지혜를 감사

향기 나는 봄날 감사 가을 쓸쓸함 감사
고통 감사 희락 감사 슬픔 위로함 감사
슬픔 감사 기쁨 감사 하늘 평화를 감사

눈물 닦아 주심 감사 영혼 평안함 감사
넓고 넓은 은혜 감사 깊은 사랑을 감사
내일 소망 주심 감사 주께 영원히 감사

WORDS: August Ludvig Storm; Korean trans. The United Methodist Korean Hymnal Committee
MUSIC: J. A. Haultman
Korean trans. © 2001 The United Methodist Publishing House, admin. The Copyright Co.

TACK O GUD
8.7.8.7.D.

Thanks to God for My Redeemer

1. Thanks to God for my Re-deem-er, thanks for all thou dost pro-vide!
2. Thanks for prayers that thou hast an-swered, thanks for what thou dost de-ny!
3. Thanks for ros-es by the way-side, thanks for thorns their stems con-tain!

Thanks for times now but a mem-'ry, thanks for Je-sus by my side!
Thanks for storms that I have weath-ered, thanks for all thou dost sup-ply!
Thanks for home and thanks for fire-side, thanks for hope, that sweet re-frain!

Thanks for pleas-ant, balm-y spring-time, thanks for dark and drea-ry fall!
Thanks for pain and thanks for pleas-ure, thanks for com-fort in de-spair!
Thanks for grace that none can meas-ure, thanks for love be-yond com-pare!

Thanks for tears by now for-got-ten, thanks for peace with-in my soul!
Thanks for grace that none can meas-ure, thanks for love be-yond com-pare!
Thanks for hope in the to-mor-row, thanks thru all e-ter-ni-ty!

WORDS: August Ludvig Storm; English trans. Carl E. Backstrom
MUSIC: J. A. Haultman

TACK O GUD
8.7.8.7.D.

거룩하신 하나님 주께 감사
Give Thanks

거 록 하신 하 나 님 - 주
의 맘과 뜻 다해 - 주
Give thanks with a grate - ful heart, give

께 감 사 드 리 세 - 날 위 해 - 이 땅에
를 사 랑 합 니 다 -
thanks to the Ho - ly One, give thanks because he's

오 신 - 독 생 자 - 예 수 나
giv- en Je - sus Christ, his Son. Give

WORDS: Henry Smith; Korean trans. The United Methodist Korean Hymnal Committee
MUSIC: Henry Smith
© 1978, Korean trans. © 2001 Integrity's Hosanna! Music

GIVE THANKS
Irr.

교회

248

은혜 작은 불꽃이
See How Great a Flame Aspires

1. 은 혜 작은 은 불 꽃 이 큰 불
2. 예 수 들구 역아 시찬 작양 은해 비 록
3. 성 도 아름 찬한 솟신 네 주 하 일 늘
4. 성 작은 들구 아름 한 조 각 하 일 늘

1. See how great a flame as - pires, kin - dled
2. When he first the work be - gun, small and
3. Saints of God, your Sav - ior praise, who the
4. Saw ye not the cloud a - rise, lit - tle

되 어 치 솟 네 주 예 수 의
미 약 했 으 나 그 의 하 말 에
문 을 여 신 신 주 은 혜 하 말 쓸
남 을 보 았 네 은 온 하 늘 에

by a spark of grace. Je - sus' love the
fee - ble was his day; now the Word doth
door hath o - pened wide; he hath given the
as a hu - man hand? Now it spreads a -

큰 사 랑 모 든 나 라 태 우 네
세 상 시 고 속 히 전 파 게 되 도 다
주 시 어 영 한 화 땅 되 셨 네
퍼 지 어 갈 한 땅 을 덮 도 다

na - tions fires, sets the king - doms on a blaze.
swift - ly run, now it wins its wid - ening way;
word of grace, Je - sus' word is glo - ri - fied;
long the skies, hangs o'er all the thirst - y land.

WORDS: Charles Wesley (Lk. 12:49; 1 Kg. 18:44-45);
Korean trans. The United Methodist Korean Hymnal Committee
MUSIC: Welsh hymn melody; harm. Carlton R. Young; alt.
Korean trans. © 2001 The United Methodist Publishing House, admin. The Copyright Co.;
harm. © 1964 Abingdon Press, admin. The Copyright Co.

ARFON (MAJOR)
77.77 D

오 하나님의 교회
O Church of God, United

1. 오 하 나 님 의 교 - 회 한 주 님
2. 온 땅 과 나 라 에 - 서 주 명 령

1. O church of God, u - nit - ed to serve one
2. From ev - ery land and na - tion the or - dered

섬 기 며 한 맘 으 로 한 복 - 음 다
받 은 자 한 주 님 섬 기 려 - 고 다

com - mon Lord, pro - claim to all one mes - sage, with
ranks ap - pear; to serve one val - iant lead - er they

선 포 하 도 다 주 항 상 앞 서
모 여 들 도 다 그 살 아 계 신

hearts in glad ac - cord. Christ ev - er goes be -
come from far and near. They chant their one con -

WORDS: Frederick B. Morley (Acts 2:5-11); Korean trans. The United Methodist Korean Hymnal Committee
MUSIC: Gesangbuch der H. W. k. Hofkappelle, 1784; alt.
Words © 1954, renewed 1982, Korean trans. © 2001 The Hymn Society, admin. Hope Publishing Co.

ELLACOMBE
76.76 D

가 - 니 그 뒤 를 따 라 서 늘
주 - 를 다 찬 양 하 면 서 주
fore us we fol - low day by day with
fes - sion, they praise one liv - ing Lord, and

힘 찬 걸 음 으 - 로 저 천 성 향 하 네
구 원 의 그 말 - 씀 다 의 지 하 도 다
strong and ea-ger foot - steps a - long the up-ward way.
place their sure de - pen - dence up - on his sav-ing word.

3. 교리와 우리 언어 혹 다를지라도 주 크신 사랑 안에 한 백성 되리라
   한 목표 가진 우리 충성을 다할 때 구세주 이름 권세 선포케 하소서

4. 주 예수 우리 위해 기도 하심같이 그 크신 사랑 안에 다하나 되어서
   주 진리 증거하고 길 밝게 비추어 저 어둠 속의 영혼 참 빛을 찾으리

3. Though creeds and tongues may differ, they speak, O Christ,
   of thee; and in thy loving spirit we shall one people be.
   Lord, may our faithful service and singleness of aim
   proclaim to all the power of thy redeeming name.

4. May thy great prayer be answered that we may all be one,
   close bound, by love united in thee, God's blessed Son:
   to bring a single witness, to make the pathway bright,
   that souls which grope in darkness may find the one true light.

완전하게 하시는 복의 근원 예수여

WORDS: Charles Wesley (1 Cor. 12:4-31; Gal. 3:27-28);
Korean trans. The United Methodist Korean Hymnal Committee
MUSIC: Adapt. from Orlando Gibbons
Korean trans. © 2001 The United Methodist Publishing House, admin. The Copyright Co.

CANTERBURY
77.77

Christ, from Whom All Blessings Flow

1. Christ, from whom all bless-ings flow, per-fect-ing the saints be-low, hear us, who thy mys-tic bod-y are, who thy mys-tic bod-y are.
2. Join us, in one spir-it join, let us still re-ceive of thine; still for more on thee we call, thou who fill-est all in all.
3. Move and ac-tu-ate and guide, di-verse gifts to each di-vide; placed ac-cord-ing to thy will, let us all our work ful-fill.
4. Nev-er from thy ser-vice move, need-ful to each oth-er prove; use the grace on each be-stowed, tem-pered by the art of God.
5. Man-y are we now, and one, we who Je-sus have put on; there is neith-er bond nor free, male nor fe-male, Lord, in thee.
6. Love, like death, hath all de-stroyed, ren-dered all dis-tinc-tions void; names and sects and par-ties fall; thou, O Christ, art all in all!

WORDS: Charles Wesley (1 Cor. 12:4-31; Gal. 3:27-28)
MUSIC: Adapt. from Orlando Gibbons

CANTERBURY
77.77

주의 종들 여기에 모여
Here, O Lord, Your Servants Gather

Unison

1. 주의 종들 여기에 - 모여 손잡 고
2. 우리 언어 다르고 - 멀리 있어 도

1. Here, O Lord, your ser-vants gath-er, hand we link with hand;
2. Man - y are the tongues we speak, scat-tered are the lands,

우 리 구 주 십 자 가 - 바 라 보 면 서
주 안 에 서 우 리 맘 - 하 나 되 었 네

look-ing toward our Sav-ior's cross, joined in love we stand.
yet our hearts are one in God, one in love's de - mands.

주 의 나 라 구 하 며 - 기 도 하 오 니
어 둠 속 에 있 어 도 - 소 망 있 으 니

As we seek the realm of God, we u - nite to pray:
E'en in dark-ness hope ap-pears, call - ing age and youth:

WORDS: Tokuo Yamaguchi; English trans. Everett M. Stowe;
Korean trans. The United Methodist Korean Hymnal Committee
MUSIC: Isao Koizumi
Words © 1958, Korean trans. © 2001 The United Methodist Publishing House, admin. The Copyright Co.

TOKYO
77.77

길 되 신 주 예 수 여　인 도 하 소 서
진 리 되 신 예 수 여　함 께 하 소 서

Je-sus, Sav-ior, guide our steps, for you are the Way.
Je-sus, teach-er, dwell with us, for you are the Truth.

3. 밝혀지는 신비와 끝없는 변화
   지친영혼 어디서 평안 얻을까
   상처입고 괴로운 모든 영혼들
   생명되신 예수여 치유하소서

4. 큰사랑의 새시대 허락하소서
   기도하고 일할때 우리도우사
   힘과용기 믿음을 내려주시고
   길과 진리 생명이 되어 주소서

3. Nature's secrets open wide, changes never cease.
   Where, Oh where, can weary souls find the source of peace?
   Unto all those sore distressed, torn by endless strife:
   Jesus, healer, bring your balm, for you are the Life.

4. Grant, O God, an age renewed, filled with deathless love;
   help us as we work and pray, send us from above
   truth and courage, faith and power, needed in our strife:
   Jesus, Master, be our Way, be our Truth, our Life.

나는 교회 너도 교회
I Am the Church!

후렴 *(Refrain)* Unison

나 는교회 너 도교회 우 리가모 두
I am the church! You are the church! We are the church to-

교 — 회 세 상 어 디 서 나
geth - er! All who fol - low Je - sus,

예 수 따 르 면 우 리 가 모 두 교 회
all a-round the world! Yes, we're the church to - geth - er!

Fine

WORDS: Richard K. Avery and Donald S. Marsh;
Korean trans. The United Methodist Korean Hymnal Committee
MUSIC: Richard K. Avery and Donald S. Marsh
© 1972, Korean trans. © 2001 Hope Publishing Co.

PORT JERVIS
77.87 with Refrain

1. 교 회 는 건 물 이 나   종   탑 이 아 니 라 네
2. 우 리 는 서 로 다 른   모   습 을 가 졌 다 네
3. 때 로 는 행 진 하 고   때   로 는 타 오 르 며
1. The church is not a build-ing,   the church is not a stee-ple,
2. We're man-y kinds of peo-ple,   with man-y kinds of fac-es,
3. Some-times the church is march-ing,   some-times it's brave-ly burn-ing,

또   쉬 는 곳 도 아 니 라 네   우 리 가 교 회
색   깔 과 나 이 모 두 다 른   우 리 가 교 회
또   달 릴 때 나 숨 을 때 도   늘 배 운 다 네
the   church is not a   rest-ing place, the church is a peo-ple.
all   col-ors and all   a-ges, too, from   all times and plac-es.
some-times it's rid-ing, some-times hid-ing,   al-ways it's learn-ing.

4. 다함께 모였을 땐 찬양과 기도하며
   웃기도 하고 때론 함께 울기도 하네

5. 그 옛날 오순절에 주 성령 받은자들
   온 세상 향해 주의 복음 전파했다네

4. And when the people gather, there's singing and there's praying
   there's laughing and there's crying sometimes, all of it saying:

5. At Pentecost some people received the Holy Spirit
   and told the Good News thru the world to all who would hear it.

주 우릴 받아주심 본받게

WORDS: Fred Kaan (Jn. 15:12); Korean trans. The United Methodist Hymnal Committee
MUSIC: John Ness Beck
Words © 1975, Korean trans. © 2001, music © 1977 Hope Publishing Co.

ACCEPTANCE
76.76 D

Help Us Accept Each Other

Unison

1. Help us ac - cept each oth-er as Christ ac - cept-ed us;
2. Teach us, O Lord, your les-sons, as in our dai - ly life
3. Let your ac - cep-tance change us, so that we may be moved
4. Lord, for to - day's en-coun-ters with all who are in need,

teach us as sis - ter, broth - er, each per - son to em - brace.
we strug - gle to be hu - man and search for hope and faith.
in liv - ing sit - u - a - tions to do the truth in love;
who hun - ger for ac - cep-tance, for righ - teous - ness and bread,

Be pres - ent, Lord, a-mong us, and bring us to be-lieve
Teach us to care for peo-ple, for all, not just for some,
to prac - tice your ac-cep-tance, un - til we know by heart
we need new eyes for see-ing, new hands for hold-ing on;

we are our - selves ac-cept-ed and meant to love and live.
to love them as we find them, or as they may be - come.
the ta - ble of for-give-ness and laugh-ter's heal - ing art.
re - new us with your Spir-it; Lord, free us, make us one!

WORDS: Fred Kaan (Jn. 15:12)
MUSIC: John Ness Beck
Words © 1975, music © 1977 Hope Publishing Co.

ACCEPTANCE
76.76 D

오 우릴 연합하시는

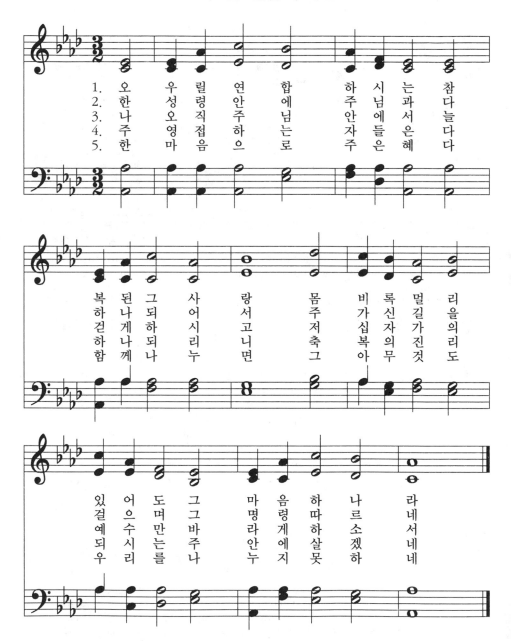

WORDS: Charles Wesley (1 Cor. 2:2); Korean trans. The United Methodist Korean Hymnal Committee
MUSIC: William Havergal; arr. Lowell Mason
Korean trans. © 2001 The United Methodist Publishing House, admin. The Copyright Co.

EVAN
CM

Blest Be the Dear Uniting Love

1. Blest be the dear u - nit - ing love that
2. Joined in one spir - it to our head, where
3. O may we ev - er walk in him, and
4. We all are one who him re - ceive, and
5. Par - tak - ers of the Sav - ior's grace, the

will not let us part; our bod - ies may far
he ap - points we go, and still in Je - sus'
noth - ing know be - side, noth - ing de - sire, noth -
each with each a - gree, in him the One, the
same in mind and heart, nor joy, nor grief, nor

off re - move, we still are one in heart.
foot - steps tread, and do his work be - low.
ing es - teem, but Je - sus cru - ci - fied!
truth, we live; blest point of u - ni - ty!
time, nor place, nor life, nor death can part.

WORDS: Charles Wesley (1 Cor. 2:2)
MUSIC: William Havergal; arr. Lowell Mason

EVAN
CM

교회의 참된 터는

1. 교회의 참된 터는 우리 주 예수라
2. 온 세계 모든 교회 한 몸을 이루며
3. 땅 위의 모든 교회 주 안에 있어서

그 귀한 말씀 위에 이 교회 세웠네
한 주님 섬기 위면서와 한 믿음 가지네
하늘의 성도들과 한 몸을 이루네

주 예수 강림하하사 피 흘려 사셨으니며
오 주여 복을 주사 저 성도들 같이
한 이름 찬송을 주 저 성경 읽으니

땅 위의 모든 교회 주님의 신부라다
다 같은 모든 소망 고 늘은 혜신반도
우리도 주와 함께 늘 살게 하소서

WORDS: Samuel J. Stone; Korean trans. The Christian Literature Society of Korea
MUSIC: Samuel Sebastian Wesley
Korean trans. © The Christian Literature Society of Korea

AURELIA
76.76 D

The Church's One Foundation

1. The church's one foun - da - tion is Je - sus Christ, her Lord;
2. E - lect from ev - ery na - tion, yet one o'er all the earth;
3. Yet she on earth hath un - ion with God the Three in One,

she is his new cre - a - tion by wa - ter and the Word.
her char - ter of sal - va - tion, one Lord, one faith, one birth;
and mys - tic sweet com - mu - nion with those whose rest is won.

From heav'n he came and sought her to be his ho - ly bride;
one ho - ly name she bless - es, par - takes one ho - ly food;
O hap - py ones and ho - ly! Lord, give us grace that we

with his own blood he bought her, and for her life he died.
and to one hope she press - es, with ev - ery grace en - dued.
like them, the meek and low - ly, on high may dwell with thee.

WORDS: Samuel J. Stone
MUSIC: Samuel Sebastian Wesley

AURELIA
76.76 D

시온성과 같은 교회

1. 시온성과 같은 교회 그의 영광 한 없다니
2. 생명샘이 흘러나와 모든 성도 마시니
3. 주의은혜 내가 받아 시온백성 되는 때

허락하신 말씀 대로 주가 친히 세웠다
언제든지 솟아나와 부족함이 없도다
세상사람 비방해도 주를 찬송 하리라

반석위에 세운교회 흔들자가 누구랴
이런물이 흘러가니 목마를자 누구랴
세상헛된 모든영광 아침안개 같으니

모든원수에 워싸도 아무근심 없도다
주의은혜 풍족하여 복은영원 토록궁
주의자녀 받을복은 영원무궁 하다다

WORDS: John Newton (Ps. 87:3; Is. 33:20-21; Ex. 13:22);
Korean trans. The United Methodist Korean Hymnal Committee
MUSIC: Croatian folk song; arr. Franz Joseph Haydn
Korean trans. © 2001 The United Methodist Publishing House, admin. The Copyright Co.

AUSTRIA
87.87. D

Glorious Things of Thee Are Spoken

1. Glo-rious things of thee are spok-en, Zi-on, cit-y of our God;
2. See, the streams of liv-ing wa-ters, spring-ing from e-ter-nal love,
3. Sav-ior, if of Zi-on's cit-y, I thru grace a mem-ber am,

God whose word can-not be bro-ken, formed thee for his own a-bode.
well sup-ply thy sons and daugh-ters, and all fear of want re-move.
let the world de-ride or pi-ty, I will glo-ry in thy name.

On the Rock of A-ges found-ed, what can shake thy sure re-pose?
Who can faint, while such a riv-er ev-er will their thirst as-suage?
Fad-ing is the world-ling's plea-sure, all its vaunt-ed pomp and show;

With sal-va-tion's walls sur-round-ed, thou may'st smile at all thy foes.
Grace which like the Lord, the giv-er, nev-er fails from age to age.
Sol-id joys and last-ing treas-ure, on-ly Zi-on's chil-dren know.

WORDS: John Newton (Ps. 87:3; Is. 33:20-21; Ex. 13:22)
MUSIC: Croatian folk song; arr. Franz Joseph Haydn

AUSTRIA
87.87. D

교회
257

성령 안에서 우리 하나
We Are One in the Spirit
(They'll Know We Are Christians by Our Love)

Unison

1. 성령 안 에서 우리하나 가 되었 네
2. 손에 손 잡고 가리함께 걸 어가 리
3. 우리 힘 모두 합해함께 일 하리 라

1. We are one in the Spir-it, we are one in the Lord,
2. We will walk with each oth-er, we will walk hand in hand,
3. We will work with each oth-er, we will work side by side,

주 님 안 에 서 우리하나 가 되었 네
손 에 손 잡 고 가리함께 걸 어가 리
우 리 힘 모 두 합해함께 일 하리 라

we are one in the Spir-it, we are one in the Lord,
we will walk with each oth-er, we will walk hand in hand,
we will work with each oth-er, we will work side by side,

모 두 하 나 가 되기위해 기도드 리 네
이 땅 에 계 신 하나님을 전파하 리 라
서 로 존 중 해 주고서로 지켜주 면 서

and we pray that all u-ni-ty may one day be re-stored:
and to-geth - er we'll spread the news that God is in our land:
and we'll guard each one's dig-ni-ty and save each one's pride:

WORDS: Peter Scholtes (Jn. 13:35); Korean trans. The United Methodist Korean Hymnal Committee
MUSIC: Peter Scholtes

ST. BRENDAN'S
Irr.

4. 창조주 하나님을 모두 찬양하라
   독생자 구주 예수 모두 찬양하라
   우릴 하나로 묶으시는 성령 찬양해
   후렴

4. All praise to the Father, from whom all things come,
   and all praise to Christ Jesus, his only Son,
   and all praise to the Spirit, who makes us one:
   Refrain

예수 이름으로
God Forgave My Sin
(Freely, Freely)

1. 예 수 이 름 으 로 나 의 죄 사 함
2. 땅과 하 늘 모 든 권 세 를 예수

1. God for- gave my sin in Je - sus' name, I've been
2. All power is given in Je - sus' name, in

받 고 거 듭 났 으 니 주의말 씀 대 로
이 름 으 로 주 시 니 주의말 씀 대 로

born a - gain in Je - sus' name, and in Je - sus' name I
earth and heaven in Je - sus' name, and in Je - sus' name I

그 사 랑 이 웃 과 나 누 기 원 하 네
그 능 력 이 웃 과 나 누 기 원 하 네

come to you, to share his love as he told me to.
come to you, to share his power as he told me to.

WORDS: Carol Owens (Mt. 10:8; 28:18-20); Korean trans. The United Methodist Hymnal Committee
MUSIC: Carol Owens

FREELY, FREELY
99.99 with Refrain

후렴 (Refrain)

너 도 주 - 께 거 - 저 받 았 으 니
He said, "Free - ly, free - ly you have re - ceived,

거 - 저 주 - 어 라 내 이름 세 상 에
free - ly, free - ly give. Go in my name, and be -

증 거 하 라 주 께서 명 하 시 네
cause you be - lieve, oth - ers will know that I live."

많은 사람들 참된 진리를
(예수가 좋다오)

1. 많 은 사람 들 참 된 진 리를모른 채
2. 무 거운짐진 자 다 내 게로오 라
3. 형 제 자매 여 참 행 복을찾거 든

주 님 곁을 떠 나 가 지만
내 가 너를 쉬 게 하 리라
예 수 님을 만 나 보 세요

내 가 만난주 님 은 참 사 랑 이었 고
이 길 만이생 명의 길 참 복 된 길이 라
그 분 으로인 하 여 참 평 안을얻으 면

진 리였 고 소 망 이었 소
항 상 내게 들 려 주 셨소
나 와 같 이 고 백 할거 요

후렴
난 예 수 가 좋 다 오

난 예 수 가 좋 다 오

주 를 사 랑 한 다던 베 드 로고 백처럼

난 예 수 를 사 랑 한 다 오

WORDS: Seog Kyun Kim
MUSIC: Seog Kyun Kim
© Seog Kyun Kim

Though So Many Have Gone Astray Far 259

1. Though so ma-ny have gone a-stray far from the Lord,
2. "All ye we-a-ry and hea-vy la-den,
3. If you have the heart to find true hap-pi-ness,

with-out un-der-stand ing the truth,
come to me and I will give you rest.
Je-sus is the one you ought to meet.

Je-sus came in-to my life, em-braced me with his love,
I'm the on-ly way of life, and way of ble-ssed-ness,"
When you find the heav'n-ly peace by trust-ing Je-sus' name,

showed to me the truth and gave me hope.
gent-ly he would whis-per to my heart.
my friend, you will sing this song with me.

Refrain

I, I love you, Je - sus Lord.

I, I love you, Je - sus Lord.

Just like Pe-ter who con-fessed his burn-ing love for his Lord,

I, I love you, Je-sus Christ, my Lord.

WORDS: Seog Kyun Kim; English trans. Edward Poitras
MUSIC: Seog Kyun Kim
© Soeg Kyun Kim

세상의 구주께

WORDS: Samuel Wolcott; Korean trans. The United Methodist Korean Hymnal Committee
MUSIC: Felice de Giardini
Korean trans. © 2001 The United Methodist Publishing House, admin. The Copyright Co.

ITALIAN HYMN
664. 6664

Christ for the World We Sing

1. Christ for the world we sing, the world to
2. Christ for the world we sing, the world to
3. Christ for the world we sing, the world to
4. Christ for the world we sing, the world to

Christ we bring, with lov-ing zeal; the poor, and
Christ we bring, with fer-vent prayer; the way-ward
Christ we bring, with one ac-cord; with us the
Christ we bring, with joy-ful song; the new-born

them that mourn, the faint and o - ver-borne,
and the lost, by rest-less pas - sions tossed,
work to share, with us re - proach to dare,
souls, whose days, re - claimed from er - ror's ways,

sin - sick and sor - row-worn, whom Christ doth heal.
re - deemed at count - less cost, from dark de - spair.
with us the cross to bear, for Christ our Lord.
in - spired with hope and praise, to Christ be - long.

WORDS: Samuel Wolcott
MUSIC: Felice de Giardini

ITALIAN HYMN
664. 6664

너 가서 모든 자로

WORDS: Leon M. Adkins (Mt. 28:19-20); alt.; Korean trans. The United Methodist Korean Hymnal Committee
MUSIC: Henry T. Smart
Words © 1964 Abingdon Press, admin. The Copyright Co.;
Korean trans. © 2001 The United Methodist Publishing House, admin. The Copyright Co.

LANCASHIRE
76.76 D

Go, Make of All Disciples

1. "Go, make of all dis - ci - ples." We hear the call, O Lord,
2. "Go, make of all dis - ci - ples." Bap - tiz - ing in the name
3. "Go, make of all dis - ci - ples." We at thy feet would stay
4. "Go, make of all dis - ci - ples." We wel - come thy com - mand.

that comes from thee, our Fa - ther, in thy e - ter - nal Word.
of Fa - ther, Son, and Spir - it, from age to age the same.
un - til each life's vo - ca - tion ac - cents thy ho - ly way.
"Lo, I am with you al - ways." We take thy guid - ing hand.

In - spire our ways of learn - ing through ear - nest, fer - vent prayer,
We call each new dis - ci - ple to fol - low thee, O Lord,
We cul - ti - vate the na - ture God plants in ev - ery heart,
The task looms large be - fore us; we fol - low with - out fear,

and let our dai - ly liv - ing re - veal thee ev - ery - where.
re - deem - ing soul and bod - y by wa - ter and the Word.
re - veal - ing in our wit - ness the mas - ter teach - er's art.
in heaven and earth thy pow - er shall bring God's king - dom here.

WORDS: Leon M. Adkins; alt. (Mt. 28:19-20)
MUSIC: Henry T. Smart
Words © 1964 Abingdon Press, admin. The Copyright Co.

LANCASHIRE
76.76 D

작은 불꽃 하나가
It Only Takes a Spark
(Pass It On)

Unison

1. 작은 불 꽃 하나 가 큰 불 을 일 으
2. 새 싹 이 돌 아 나 면 새 들 은 지 저
3. 친 구 여 당 신 께 이 행 복 드 리

1. It on - ly takes a spark to get a fire
2. What a won - drous time is spring, when all the trees are
3. I wish for you, my friend, this hap - pi - ness that

키 - 어 - 곧 주 위 사 람 들 그
귀 - 고 - 꽃 들 은 피 어 나 화
려 - 네 - 주 님 은 당 신 의 의

go - ing, and soon all those a-round can
bud - ding; the birds be-gin to sing, the
I've found; you can de-pend on him, it

불 에 몸 녹 이 듯 이 - 이 처 럼 주 의
창 한 봄 날 이 라 네 - 이 처 럼 주 의
지 할 구 세 주 라 오 - 산 위 에 올 라

warm up in its glow- ing. That's how it is with
flow - ers start their bloom-ing. That's how it is with
mat - ters not where you're bound. I'll shout it from the

WORDS: Kurt Kaiser; Korean trans. The United Methodist Korean Hymnal Committee
MUSIC: Kurt Kaiser
© 1969, Korean trans. © 2001 EMI Christian Music Group

PASS IT ON
Irr.

바다와 하늘의 주
(내가 여기 있나이다)
I, the Lord of Sea and Sky
(Here I Am, Lord)

Unison

1. 바다와 하늘의 주 어둔 죄악 속에서 리
   밤의 별을 만든든 주 어두움을 밝히 리
2. 눈과 비를 만든든 주 너희아픔 아노 라
   굳은 마음 녹이고 주 사랑심어 주리 니
3. 바람과 불꽃의 주 나의 백성 위하여
   생-명의 양식을 넘치도록 베풀 리

1. I, the Lord of sea and sky, I have heard my peo-ple cry.
   I who made the stars of night, I will make their dark-ness bright.
2. I, the Lord of snow and rain, I have borne my peo-ple's pain.
   I will break their hearts of stone, give them hearts for love a-lone.
3. I, the Lord of wind and flame, I will tend the poor and lame,
   Fin-est bread I will pro-vide till their hearts be sat-is-fied.

부르짖는 백성들 구하리 라
나의 빛을 가지고 울었노 라
너를사랑 함가지 고
나의 말씀 가지 고
아름다운 지만 찬을 니
목숨까지 주리 라 베풀리 라

All who dwell in dark and sin my hand will save.
Who will bear my light to them? They turn a-way.
I have wept for love of them.
I will speak my word to them.
I will set a feast for them. My hand will save.
I will give my life to them.

WORDS: Dan Schutte (Is. 6:8); Korean trans. The United Methodist Korean Hymnal Committee
MUSIC: Dan Schutte; adapt. Carlton R. Young
© 1981, 1983, 1989, Korean trans. © 2001 Daniel L. Schutte and New Dawn Music

HERE I AM, LORD
77.74 D with Refrain

누가 갈 까 —
누가 갈 까 —
누가 갈 까 —   내 가 여 기 —
Whom shall I send?
Whom shall I send?
Whom shall I send?   Here I am, Lord.

있 나 이 다 — 부 르 심 을 들 었 나 이
Is it I, Lord?   I have heard you   call-ing in the

다 — 인 도 하 사 — 보 내 소 서
night.   I will go, Lord,   if you lead me.

주 의 백   성 섬 기 오 리 다
I will hold   your peo - ple in my heart.

264

주여 사랑의 빛을 비추사
Lord, the Light of Your Love
(Shine, Jesus, Shine)

Unison

1. 주 여 사 랑의 빛 을 비추사 어 둠 밝히어
2. 주 여 내 모든 어 둠 헤치고 주 의 빛으로
3. 주 의 밝 은빛 바 라보오니 우 리 얼굴에

1. Lord, the light of your love is shin-ing, in the midst of the
2. Lord, I come to your awe-some pres-ence, from the shad-ows in
3. As we gaze on your king-ly bright-ness so our fac-es dis-

주 시옵소서 예 수세 상의 빛 되신 우리주
나 아옵니다 주 의보 혈로 날 정케하소서
기 쁨넘치네 주 의사 랑과 존 귀로 옷입고

dark-ness shin-ing; Je - sus, light of the world, shine up-on us,
to your ra-diance; by the blood I may en - ter your bright-ness;
play your like-ness, ev - er chang-ing from glo-ry to glo - ry:

후렴 (Refrain)

진 리로 우릴 자 유케하소서
나 의모 든죄 다 씻겨주소서 비 추소
주 의복 음을 전 하게하소서

set us free by the truth you now bring us;
search me, try me, con-sume all my dark - ness; shine on
mir - rored here, may our lives tell your sto - ry;

WORDS: Graham Kendrick; Korean trans. The United Methodist Korean Hymnal Committee
MUSIC: Graham Kendrick; arr. Tom Fettke
© 1987, Korean trans. © 2001 Make Way Music Ltd., admin. Music Services

SHINE, JESUS SHINE
Irr. with Refrain

서 비 추 소 서
me. Shine on me.

비 추 소 서 - 주 의 영 - 광 온
넘 치 소 서 - 주 의 은 - 혜 강
Shine, Je - sus, shine, fill this land with the
Flow, riv - er, flow, flood the na - tions with

땅 에 가 득 태 우 소 서 - 성 령
같 이 흘 러 비 추 소 서 - 말 씀
Fa - ther's glo - ry; blaze, Spir - it, blaze, set our
grace and mer - cy; send forth your Word, Lord, and

의 불 로
hearts on fire.

주 옵 소 서 -
let there be light.

주여 내가 여기 있나이다

1. 주 여 내 가 여기있 나 이 다 주 앞에
2. 주 여 내 가 여기있 나 이 다 귀 한성 령
3. 주 여 내 가 여기있 나 이 다 나 의맘 과

즐 거 이 나 아 오 니 서 갈 길 보 여
오 셔 서 채 우 소 서 서 힘 과 지 혜
나 의 뜻 받 으 소 서 나 의 음 성

주시고 날 보내주 시 며 길 잃을 때 밝 은 빛
주시고 끊임 없 으 신 주 의사랑 전 하 게
드 리니 주여 받 으 사 끊임 없 이 찬 양 케

주 소 서 오 주여날 보 내 소 서
하 소 서 서
하 소 서

WORDS: John Purifoy; Korean trans. The United Methodist Korean Hymnal Committee
MUSIC: John Purifoy
© 1977 Word Music, Inc.

SALLY TOWNSEND
Irr.

Here Am I, Send Me

Unison

1. Here am I, send me. Here am I, Lord, send me. Un-to thee,
2. Here am I, send me. Here am I, Lord, send me. Pre-cious Ho - ly
3. Here am I, send me. Here am I, Lord, send me. Take my heart, it

will-ing-ly, yield - ed I come. Show the path that
Spir-it, come, fill me a - new. Give me wis - dom,
is your own, my will is thine. Take my voice and

I must walk, com-pel me then to go, and if I stray bring back the
send me strength, grant that I may be a mir-ror of your nev-er-
let me sing al-ways un - to thee, so that my days shall flow in

light of day, for here am I, send me, I pray.
end - ing love, for here am I, send me, I pray.
cease - less praise. Lord, here am I, send me, I pray.

WORDS: John Purifoy
MUSIC: John Purifoy
© 1977 Word Music, Inc.

SALLY TOWNSEND
Irr.

빛의 사자들이여

1. 빛의 사자들이여 어 서 가내가 서서서지
2. 선한 역사 위하여 어여 힘너는 내가 서서서지
3. 제단 숯불 가지고 나 땅 끝 까 서서서지
4. 동서 남북 어디나 땅 끝 까 지

어 주주 둠사진님 을랑리만 물전전의 리파파지 치하하 고라라라
주주 진리 모하건자 르시너위 백힘힘 성주을 에시다 게리해며
죄로 눈 먼 자 해 기 도 하

복사진생 음랑리명 의의의의 빛빛빛빛 비비비비 취취취취 라라라라 (비 취 라)

WORDS: J. E. Lewis (Acts 1:8); Korean trans. The Christian Literature Society of Korea
MUSIC: J. E. Jones
Korean trans. © The Christian Literature Society of Korea

HERALD OF LIGHT
11.7.11.7 with Refrain

후렴 *Refrain*

빛 의 사 자 들 이 여

들 이 여

복 음 의 빛 비 춰 라

비 춰 라

죄 로 어 둔 밤 밝 게 비 춰 라

빛 의 사 자 들 이 여 (들 이 여)

266 Heralds of Light, Speed Away

1. Her-alds of the light, be swift, haste your go - ing;
2. Do the work of God, with pow'r of his giv - ing;
3. Bear the truth of God, the fire of his al - tar;
4. North and south and east and west, go, o - bey - ing,

shat - ter the fet - ters of night.
he your com - pan - ion will prove.
faint not in age or in youth.
God your sup - port in the strife.

Peo - ples still with-out the truth wait un - know - ing.
Tell the love God for all peo - ple liv - ing.
Cross-ing seas and moun-tains, rest not, nor fal - ter.
For the dead and blind in sin, go forth pray - ing.

Beam forth the gos - pel of light.
Beam forth the gos - pel of love.
Beam forth the gos - pel of truth.
Beam forth the gos - pel of life.

Gos - pel of light.

WORDS: J. E. Lewis (Acts 1:8)
MUSIC: J. E. Jones

HERALD OF LIGHT
11.7.11.7 with Refrain

Refrain

Her - alds   of light,   speed a - way!
speed   a - way

Let   shine   the bright   gos - pel   ray.
gos - pel   ray.

End   the night   of sin,   let   the bright-ness in!

Her - alds   of light,   speed the   day. (speed the way)

온 세상 위하여
Christ for the Whole Wide World!

1. 온 세 상 위하 여 나 복 음 전 하 리
2. 온 세 상 위하 여 주 복 음 전 하 리

1. Christ for the whole wide world! Our task has just be - gun,
2. Christ for the whole wide world! His mes - sage must be sent

온 땅의 모 든 백 성들 주 말 씀 기 다 려
죄 속에 죽 어 가는자 다 회 개 하 도 록

for mil - lions wait in ev - ery land the mes - sage of God's Son.
to mil - lions dy - ing in their sin to call them to re - pent.

주 예 수 모 르 고 다 죽 어 가 는 데
이 세 상 구 하 려 주 돌 아 가 신 것

Shall they be left in sin, to die with - out his Word
Christ Je - sus died to save, but they can nev - er know

나 어 찌 버 려 두 리요 주 복 음 전 하 리
나 증 거 하 지 않으면 그 사 랑 모 르 리

with - out the Sav - ior Je - sus Christ, be - cause they nev - er heard?
un - til we bring our gifts of love and bid his he - ralds go!

WORDS: H. B. Allen; Korean trans. The United Methodist Korean Hymnal Committee
MUSIC: B. B. McKinney
Korean trans. © 2001 The United Methodist Publishing House, admin. The Copyright Co.

CHRIST FOR THE WORLD
12.14.12.14.

후렴 (Refrain)

전 하 고   기 도 해   매 일 증 인 되 리   라
We will give,   we will pray,   we will wit-ness ev-ery   day.

즐 겨 전 하 고 매 일   기 도 해   되 리 라
We will glad-ly give, we will hum-bly pray.   ev-eryday

주 의   사 랑 모 든   사 람 들 다 알 게 되 도 록
That the   mil-lions of   the whole wide world may know our Sav-ior's love.

3. 온 세상 위하여 나 선포하리라
   주 예수 이름 믿으면 다 구원 얻으리
   먼 곳에 나가서 전하지 못해도
   나 어디서나 전하며 늘 기도 힘쓰리

3. Christ for the whole wide world! His heralds will proclaim
   salvation for men everywhere in Jesus' blessed name.
   And we who cannot go to bear his tidings far
   will pray for those who take the word and witness where we are.

나 비록 연약하지만
Even Though I'm Forever Weak

나 비 록 연 약 하 지 만 하 나 님 완 전 하 시 고
E- ven though I'm for-ev-er weak, God is per-fect, God is com - plete.

우 리 때 때 로 넘 어 져 도 - 주 님 일 으 키 시 네
And tho' time and a-gain I may fall he will raise me up a - gain.

주 께 서 함 께 하 시 네 우 리 는 언 약 의 백 성
He is here, he is here with us. We are his, the peo-ple of God.

성 령 으 로 역 사 하 시 네 - 우 리 의 걸 음 속 에
Our God works in our lives thru his Spir - it, and in ev-'ry step we take.

생 명 의 복 음 을 - 막 을 자 없 고 -
No one can keep from spread - ing the Word of life.

WORDS: Jang Hee Lee; English trans. Edward Poitras
MUSIC: Jang Hee Lee

거룩한 불꽃 주시려

WORDS: Charles Wesley (Lev. 6:13); Korean trans. The United Methodist Korean Hymnal Committee
MUSIC: Samuel Wesley
Korean trans. © 2001 The United Methodist Publishing House, admin. The Copyright Co.

HEREFORD
LM

O Thou Who Camest from Above

1. O thou who cam - est from a - bove,
the pure ce - les - tial fire to im - part,
kin - dle a flame of sa - cred love
up - on the mean al - tar of my heart.

2. There let it for thy glo - ry burn
with in - ex - tin - guish - a - ble blaze,
and trem - bling to its source re - turn,
in hum - ble prayer and fer - vent praise.

3. Je - sus, con - firm my heart's de - sire
to work and speak and think for thee;
still let me guard the ho - ly fire,
and still stir up thy gift in me.

4. Read - y for all thy per - fect will,
my acts of faith and love re - peat,
till death thy end - less mer - cies seal,
and make my sac - ri - fice com - plete.

WORDS: Charles Wesley (Lev. 6:13)
MUSIC: Samuel Wesley

HEREFORD
LM

270

예수 그리스도 모든 문제의 해결자
Jesus, He Is the Christ

예 수   그 리 스 도 모든 문제의해결 자
Je - sus,   he is the Christ. He's the ans-wer to ev-'ry - thing!

예 수   그 리 스 도 우리 모두 전 하 세
Je - sus,   he is the Christ, let us tell it to the world.

사 단 의 왕 국 을 - 깨 뜨 린 왕 의 왕
The King of kings who came to crush the de-vil's power,

하 나 님 만 나 는 - 길 되 신 주 의 주 -
the Lord of lords who is the on - ly way to God,

죄 에 서 해 방 하 - 신 어 린 양 예 - 수
the Lamb of God who set us free from sin and death,

감 사 하 세 찬 양 하 세 증 거 하 세
let us thank him, let us praise him, pro - claim to all!

WORDS: Jang Hee Lee; English trans. Edward Poitras
MUSIC: Jang Hee Lee

인애하신 구세주
Pass Me Not, O Gentle Savior

1. 인애하신 구세주 여에 앞하여 내가 비오시니
2. 자비하신 보좌 앞하여 주 쉬게 하가오고니
3. 주의 공로의 지한 예수 위로의 주여니
4. 생명보다 귀한 예수 위로의 주여

1. Pass me not, O gen-tle Sav-ior, hear my hum-ble cry;
2. Let me at thy throne of mer-cy find a sweet re-lief,
3. Trust-ing on-ly in thy mer-it, would I seek thy face;
4. Thou the spring of all my com-fort, more than life to me,

죄무상우 인를오라 하실때 에니 날부르소소서서까
인른한리 꿇영을 고회개치 하시신 고이 믿구어원디 있을
오라고와 같으 신 이 하수 디 하 있 을

1. while on oth-ers thou art call-ing, do not pass me by.
2. kneel-ing there in deep con-tri-tion; help my un-be-lief.
3. heal my wound-ed, bro-ken spir-it, save me by thy grace.
4. whom have I on earth be-side thee? Whom in heav'n but thee?

후렴 (Refrain)

주여 주여 내가 비오니
Sav-ior, Sav-ior, hear my hum-ble cry;

죄인오라하실때에 날부르소서
while on oth-ers thou art call-ing, do not pass me by.

WORDS: Fanny J. Crosby; Korean trans. The United Methodist Korean Hymnal Committee
MUSIC: William H. Doane
Korean trans. © 2001 The United Methodist Publishing House, admin. The Copyright Co.

PASS ME NOT
85.85 with Refrain

272

어서 돌아오오

1. 어 서 돌 – 아 오 오 어 서 돌 아 만 오 오
2. 어 서 돌 – 아 오 오 어 서 돌 아 만 오 오
3. 어 서 돌 – 아 오 오 어 서 돌 아 만 오 오

지 은 죄 가 아 무 리 무 겁 고 크 기 로
우 리 주 는 날 마 다 기 다 리 신 다 로
채 찍 맞 아 아 파 도 주 님 의 손 으 로

주 어 찌 못 담 당 하 고 못 받 으 시 리 요
밤 마 다 문 열 어 놓 고 마 음 졸 이 시 며
때 리 시 고 어 루 만 져 위 로 해 주 시 는

우 리 주 의 넓 은 가 슴 은 하 늘 보 다 넓 고 넓 어 서
나 간 자 식 돌 아 오 기 만 밤 새 기 다 리 신 다 오
우 리 주 의 넓 은 품 으 로 어 서 돌 아 오 오 어 서

WORDS: Young Taik Chun (Lk.15:11-32)
MUSIC: Chai Hoon Park
Korean trans. © 2001 The United Methodist Publishing House, admin. The Copyright Co.

KOREA
Irr.

Come Back Quickly to the Lord

1. Come back quick - ly to the Lord, just come back to the Lord.
2. Come back quick - ly to the Lord, just come back to the Lord.
3. Come back quick - ly to the Lord, just come back to the Lord.

Though how grave your sins may be, or how bur - den-some they seem,
Our Lord waits ev-ery day with his doors kept o - pen wide.
Though you think that you have sinned and aren't fit to be his child,

there is no sin he can-not bear, nor sin-ner not ac - cept,
He is anx - ious-ly wait-ing for you ev-ery day and ev - ery night.
God will cel - e-brate with a big feast, when re-pen-tance brings you home.

for the bo - som of our lov-ing Lord is much great-er than all the skies.
The Lord is wait-ing thru the night for a child who has gone a - stray.
So, come back to his o - pen arms, come back quick-ly un - to the Lord.

WORDS: Young Taik Chun (Lk. 15:11-32); English trans. Sang E. and Ivy G. Chun
MUSIC: Chai Hoon Park
Trans. © 1989, The United Methodist Publishing House, admin. The Copyright Co.

KOREA
Irr.

주의 깊은 그 자비

WORDS: Charles Wesley; Korean trans. The United Methodist Korean Hymnal Committee
MUSIC: Adapt. from Orlando Gibbons
Korean trans. © 2001 The United Methodist Publishing House, admin. The Copyright Co.

CANTERBURY
77.77

Depth of Mercy

1. Depth of mer - cy! Can there be mer - cy
2. I have long with - stood his grace, long pro -
3. I my Mas - ter have de - nied, I a -
4. There for me the Sav - ior stands, shows his
5. Now in - cline me to re - pent, let me

still re - served for me? Can my God his
voked him to his face, would not heark - en
fresh have cru - ci - fied, oft pro - faned his
wounds and spreads his hands, God is love! I
now my sins la - ment, now my foul re -

wrath for - bear, me, the chief of sin - ners, spare?
to his calls, grieved him by a thou - sand falls.
hal - lowed name, put him to an o - pen shame.
know, I feel; Je - sus weeps and loves me still.
volt de - plore, weep, be - lieve, and sin no more.

WORDS: Charles Wesley
MUSIC: Adapt. from Orlando Gibbons

CANTERBURY
77.77

274

살피소서 내 맘을

WORDS: J. Edwin Orr (Ps. 139:23); Korean trans. The United Methodist Korean Hymnal Committee
MUSIC: Maori melody; arr. Robert F. Douglas
Korean trans. © 2001 The United Methodist Publishing House, admin. The Copyright Co.;
arr. © 1986 Word Music, Inc.

MAORI
10.10.10.10.

274

Search Me, O God

Unison

1. Search me, O God, and
2. I praise thee, Lord, for
3. Lord, take my life, and
4. O Ho - ly Ghost, re -

know my heart to - day;
cleans - ing me from sin;
make it whol - ly thine;
viv - al comes from thee;

try me, O Sav - ior,
ful - fill thy word, and
fill my poor heart with
send a re - viv - al,

know my thoughts, I pray.
make me pure with - in.
thy great love di - vine.
start the work in me.

WORDS: J. Edwin Orr (Ps. 139:23)
MUSIC: Maori melody; arr. Robert F. Douglas
Arr. © 1986 Word Music, Inc.

MAORI
10.10.10.10.

See | if | there | be | | some
Fill | me | with | fire, | | where
Take | all | my | will, | | my
Thy | Word | de - clares, | | thou

wick - ed | way | in | me; | |
once | I | burned | with | shame; |
pas - sion, | self, | and | pride; |
wilt | sup - ply | our | need; |

cleanse | me | from | ev - ery | sin, | and
grant | my | de - sire | to | mag - ni -
I | now | sur - ren - der, | Lord, | in
for | bless - ings | now, | O | Lord, | I

set | me | free.
fy | thy | name.
me | a - bide.
hum - bly | plead.

여러 해 동안 주 떠나

1. 여 러 해 동 안 주 떠 나 세 상 연 락 을 즐 기 고
2. 죄 악 에 죽 을 인 생 을 심 히 불 쌍 히 여 기 사
3. 홍 포 를 입 은 구 주 는 가 시 면 류 관 쓰 시 고
4. 미 련 한 우 리 인 생 은 주 의 공 로 를 모 르 고

저 흉 악 한 죄 에 빠 져 서 그 은 혜 를 잊 었 네
저 하 늘 의 영 광 버 리 고 그 이 세 상 에 오 셨 네
그 십 자 가 높 이 달 리 사 그 아 픔 을 참 았 네
그 쓸 쓸 한 사 막 가 운 데 늘 헤 매 고 다 녔 네

후렴

오 사 랑 의 예 수 님 내 맘 을 곧 엽 니 다

곧 들 어 와 나 와 동 거 하 며 내 생 명 이 되 소 서

WORDS: Robert Lowry (Lk. 15:15-20); Korean trans. The Christian Literature Society of Korea
MUSIC: Robert Lowry
Korean trans. © The Christian Literature Society of Korea

WHERE IS MY BOY TONIGHT
8.8.9.7.

Far from the Lord I Wandered Long
275

1. Far from the Lord I wan-der'd long in en-chant-ments of time and place,
2. Griev-ing for Ad-am's dy-ing seed in the bond-age of sin and shame,
3. Mock-e-ry's crim-son cloth he wore, and his crown was a crown of thorn,
4. Fol-ly and sin of hu-man-kind! so un-will-ing our Lord to know

sunk deep in my sins, im-mers'd in wrong, for-get-ting a Sav-ior's grace.
from glo-ries of heav'n to meet our need, in pit-y the Sav-ior came.
and, high on the cross, the pains he bore, the sins of a world have borne!
we wan-der our de-serts, faint and blind! how long shall we scorn him so?

Refrain

O, Je-sus, dear Lord, my heart is o-pen-ing now the door.

Come in to-day, come for-ev-er to stay, my life to be, ev-er-more!

WORDS: Robert Lowry (Lk. 15:15-20)
MUSIC: Robert Lowry

WHERE IS MY BOY TONIGHT
8.8.9.7.

276

고통의 멍에 벗으려고
Out of My Bondage

1. 고통의 멍에 벗으려고 예수께로
2. 수치와 실망을 당한뒤에 예수께로
3. 교만한 맘을 내버리고 예수께로
4. 죽음의 길을 벗어나서 예수께로

1. Out of my bond-age, sor-row, and night, Je - sus, I come,
2. Out of my shame-ful fail - ure and loss, Je - sus, I come,
3. Out of un-rest and ar - ro-gant pride, Je - sus, I come,
4. Out of the fear and dread of the tomb, Je - sus, I come,

나 갑니다 자유와 기쁨에 베푸시는
나 갑니다 십자가 되신말씀 따르려고
나 갑니다 복영원한 집을 바라보고
나 갑니다 영원한 집을 바라보고

Je - sus, I come; in - to thy free - dom, glad - ness, and light,
Je - sus, I come; in - to thy glo - rious gain of thy cross,
Je - sus, I come; in - to thy bless - ed will to a - bide,
Je - sus, I come; in - to thy joy and light of thy home,

주께로 갑니다 — 병든 내 몸 이음몸구
주께로 갑니다 — 슬픔 던 망한 이음몸
주께로 갑니다 — 실멸 망의 한이포
주께로 갑니다 — 멸망의 포구

Je - sus, I come to thee out of my sick - ness
Je - sus, I come to thee out of earth's sor - rows
Je - sus, I come to thee out of my-self to
Je - sus, I come to thee out of the depths of

WORDS: William T. Sleeper; Korean trans. The Christian Literature Society of Korea
MUSIC: George C. Stebbins
Korean trans. © The Christian Literature Society of Korea

JESUS, I COME
Irr.

치 유 받 고 빈 궁 한 삶 이 부 해 지 며
위 로 받 고 이 예 수 의 의 풍 파 신 잔 잔 하 아
혜 어 나 와 평 화 의 나 라 다 다 라 서

into thy health, out of my want and in - to thy wealth,
in - to thy balm, out of life's storms and in - to thy calm,
dwell in thy love, out of de - spair into rap - tures a - bove,
ru - in un - told, in - to the peace of thy shel - ter -ing fold,

죄 악 을 벗 어 버 리 려 고 주 께 로 갑 니 다 -
하 영 광 의 찬 송 부 르 려 고 주 께 로 갑 니 다 -
영 광 의 주 를 뵈 오 려 고 주 께 로 갑 니 다 -

out of my sin and in - to thy-self, Je - sus, I come to thee.
out of dis-tress to ju - bi - lant psalm, Je - sus, I come to thee.
up - ward for aye on wings like a dove, Je - sus, I come to thee.
ev - er thy glo - rious face to be -hold, Je - sus, I come to thee.

구주의 십자가 보혈로

1. 구 주 의 십 자 가 보 혈 로 죄 씻 음 받 기 를 원 하 네
2. 죄 악 을 속 하 여 주 신 주 내 속 에 들 어 와 계 시 네
3. 귀 하 신 구 원 의 샘 물 에 들 어 간 내 영 혼 기 쁘 네
4. 구 주 의 발 앞 에 엎 드 려 이 샘 에 들 어 와 젖 으 라

내 죄 를 씻 으 신 주 이 름 찬 송 합 시 다
십 자 가 앞 에 서 서 주 이 이 름 찬 송 합 시 다
날 씻 어 정 결 케 하 신 주 찬 송 합 시 다
온 전 케 하 시 는 주 이 름 찬 송 합 시 다

후렴

찬 송 합 시 다 - 찬 송 합 시 다 -

내 죄 를 씻 으 신 주 이 름 찬 송 합 시 다

WORDS: Elisha A. Hoffman (Col. 1:20); Korean trans. The Christian Literature Society of Korea
MUSIC: John H. Stockton
Korean trans. © The Christian Literature Society of Korea

GLORY TO HIS NAME
Irr.

Down at the Cross

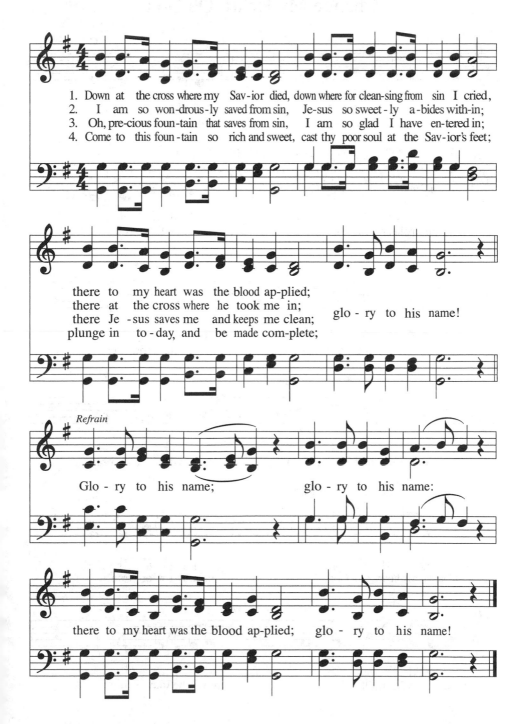

1. Down at the cross where my Sav-ior died, down where for clean-sing from sin I cried,
2. I am so won-drous-ly saved from sin, Je-sus so sweet-ly a-bides with-in;
3. Oh, pre-cious foun-tain that saves from sin, I am so glad I have en-tered in;
4. Come to this foun-tain so rich and sweet, cast thy poor soul at the Sav-ior's feet;

there to my heart was the blood ap-plied;
there at the cross where he took me in;
there Je-sus saves me and keeps me clean; glo-ry to his name!
plunge in to-day, and be made com-plete;

Refrain

Glo-ry to his name; glo-ry to his name:

there to my heart was the blood ap-plied; glo-ry to his name!

WORDS: Elisha A. Hoffman (Col. 1:20)
MUSIC: John H. Stockton

GLORY TO HIS NAME
Irr.

278

항상 진실케
Change My Heart, Oh God

항상 진실 케 -
Change my heart, Oh God,
내 맘 바 꾸 사 -
make it ev - er true.

주 님 의 모 습 -
Change my heart, Oh God,
닮 게 하 소 서 -
may I be like you.

주 는 토 기 장 이
You are the pot - ter,
나 는 진 흙
I am the clay,

날 빛 으 소 - 서
mold me and make me,
기 도 하 오 니
this is what I pray.

항 상 진 실 케 -
Change my heart, Oh God,
내 맘 바 꾸 사 -
make it ev - er true.

주 님 의 모 습 -
Change my heart, Oh God,
닮 게 하 소 서 -
may I be like you.

WORDS: Eddie Espinosa; Korean trans. The United Methodist Korean Hymnal Committee
MUSIC: Eddie Espinosa
© 1982, Korean trans. © 2001 Mercy/Vineyard Publishing

CHANGE MY HEART
Irr.

나의 삶 속에서
Through It All

나의 삶 - 속에서 -
Through it all,   through it all,

나 주 를 의 지 하는 그 믿음 배웠네
I've learned to trust in Je- sus,   I've learned to trust in God;

나 의 삶 - 속에서 -
through it all,   through it all,

말 씀 의 지 하 게 되 었 네 -
I've learned to de - pend up- on God's Word.

WORDS: Andraé Crouch; Korean trans. The United Methodist Korean Hymnal Committee
MUSIC: Andraé Crouch
© 1971, renewed 1999, Korean trans. © 2001 Manna Music, Inc.

THROUGH IT ALL
Irr.

구주 예수 피 흘리심

WORDS: Charles Wesley (Acts 16:26); Korean trans. The United Methodist Korean Hymnal Committee
MUSIC: Thomas Campbell
Korean trans. © 2001 The United Methodist Publishing House, admin. The Copyright Co.

SAGINA
88.88.88 with Repeat

And Can It Be that I Should Gain

1. And can it be that I should gain
2. He left his Fa - ther's throne a - bove,
3. Long my im - pris - oned spir - it lay,
4. No con - dem - na - tion now I dread;

an in - t'rest in the Sav - ior's blood!
so free, so in - fi - nite his grace!
fast bound in sin and na - ture's night;
Je - sus, and all in him, is mine;

Died he for me? Who caused his pain!
emp - tied him - self of all but love,
thine eye dif - fused a quick - ening ray;
a - live in him, my liv - ing Head,

For me? Who him to death pur - sued?
and bled for Ad - am's help - less race.
I woke, the dun - geon flamed with light;
and clothed in righ - teous - ness di - vine,

WORDS: Charles Wesley (Acts 16:26)
MUSIC: Thomas Campbell

SAGINA
88.88.88 with Repeat

281

온 하늘에 가득히 주의 영광
Christ, Whose Glory Fills the Skies

WORDS: Charles Wesley; Korean trans. The United Methodist Korean Hymnal Committee
MUSIC: J. G. Werner's *Choralbuch*, 1815; harm. William H. Havergal
© 1981, Korean trans. © 2001 The United Methodist Publishing House, admin. The Copyright Co.

RATISBON
77.77.77

두려움 떨치고 소망을 가지세
Give to the Winds Thy Fears

282

1. 두 려 움 떨 치 고 　 소 망 을 가 지 세
2. 인 생 길 험 하 나 　 주 평 탄 케 하 네
3. 선 택 과 명 령 을 　 주 님 께 맡 기 면
4. 살 든 지 죽 든 지 　 주 진 리 외 치 며

1. Give to the winds thy fears; hope and be un-dis-mayed.
2. Thru waves and clouds and storms, God gent - ly clears thy way;
3. Leave to God's sov-ereign sway to choose and to com-mand;
4. Let us in life, in death, thy stead - fast truth de-clare,

주 너 의 아 픔 아 시 고 새 힘 을 주 시 리
어 두 운 밤 이 지 나 면 기 쁜 날 밝 으 리
주 강 하 신 그 손 으 로 널 지 켜 주 시 리
숨 질 때 까 지 주 사 랑 전 하 게 하 소 서

God hears thy sighs and counts thy tears, God shall lift up thy head.
wait thou God's time; so shall this night soon end in joy-ous day.
so shalt thou, won-dering, own that way, how wise, how strong this hand.
and pub-lish with our lat - est breath thy love and guard-ian care.

WORDS: Paul Gerhardt (Ps. 37:5); English trans. John Wesley;
Korean trans. The United Methodist Korean Hymnal Committee
MUSIC: William H. Walter
Korean trans. © 2001 The United Methodist Publishing House, admin. The Copyright Co.

FESTAL SONG
SM

다 함께 오라

다 함께 오 라 ─ 우 리 가 ─ 변 론

하 자 다 함 께 오 라 ─ 주

1, 3   *Fine*   2

말 씀 하 시 네   네   주 홍 빛 같 은

네 죄   눈 과 같 이 되 리 라

D.C.

진 홍 빛 같 은 네 죄   희 어 지 리 라

WORDS: Ken Medema; Korean trans. The United Methodist Korean Hymnal Committee
MUSIC: Ken Medema; arr. David Allen
© 1972, Korean trans. © 2001 Word Music, Inc.

COME LET US REASON
Irr.

Come, Let Us Reason

"Come, let us rea-son to-geth-er," that's what God says. "Come, let us rea-son to-geth-er," says the Lord. Lord. "Tho' your sins be as scar-let, they shall be as white as snow; tho' they be red as crim-son, they shall be as wool."

1, 3 Fine *2*

D.C.

WORDS: Ken Medema
MUSIC: Ken Medema; arr. David Allen
© 1972 Word Music, Inc.

COME LET US REASON
Irr.

284

예수가 우리를 부르는 소리
Softly and Tenderly Jesus Is Calling

1. 예수가 우리를 부르는 소리 그 음성 가
2. 간절히 오라고 부르실 때에나 우리가
3. 세월이 살같이 빠르게 지나 어느덧 놀라운
4. 우리를 위하여 언약해 주신 놀라운

1. Soft - ly and ten - der - ly Je - sus is call - ing, call - ing for
2. Why should we tar - ry when Je - sus is plead - ing, plead - ing for
3. Time is now fleet - ing, the mo - ments are pass - ing, pass - ing from
4. O for the won - der - ful love he has prom - ised, prom - ised for

부지 드러하 워라 문주 앞에님의 나와서를이
지끝 체이의 나사 고랑 사망 의의의 그자비로

부드러워라 문주 앞님에의 나와서를이
지끝 주의 나사 고랑 사주 망님의 그자비로

you and for me; see, on the por - tals he's
you and for me? Why should we lin - ger and
you and from me; shad - ows are gath - er - ing,
you and for me! Though we have sinned, he has

사면을보며 우리를기다리려네나네
왜아니와내앞에 못들은게체다하가네나네
너아와내앞에 어둠게해주시겠네나네
우리의죄를 용서해 주시 겠네나네

wait - ing and watch - ing, watch - ing for you and for me.
heed not his mer - cies, mer - cies for you and for me?
death - beds are com - ing, com - ing for you and for me.
mer - cy and par - don, par - don for you and for me.

WORDS: Will L. Thompson; Korean trans. The United Methodist Korean Hymnal Committee
MUSIC: Will L. Thompson
Korean trans. © 2001 The United Methodist Publishing House, admin. The Copyright Co.

THOMPSON
11 7.11 7 with Refrain

주 하나님 독생자 예수

1. 주 하 나 님 – 독 생 자 예 – 수 –
2. 주 안 에 서 – 거 듭 난 생 – 명 –
3. 그 언 젠 가 – 주 뵐 때 까 – 지 –

날 위 하 여 – 오 시 었 네 –
참 만 족 과 – 기 쁨 있 네 –
주 를 위 해 – 싸 우 리 라 –

죽 음 으 로 – 날 대 속 한 주 –
더 욱 강 한 – 확 신 가 지 고 –
최 후 승 리 – 나 얻 을 때 에 –

빈 무 덤 그 – 의 사 심 증 거 하 도 다 –
주 님 의 도 – 우 심 을 믿 으 며 살 리 –
저 하 늘 영 – 광 의 빛 바 라 보 리 라 –

WORDS: Gloria and William J. Gaither; Korean trans. The United Methodist Korean Hymnal Committee
MUSIC: William J. Gaither
© 1971, Korean trans. © 2001 William. J. Gaither, Inc., admin. Gaither Copyright Management

RESURRECTION
98.9 11 with Refrain

후렴

나의 소망 - 살아계신 주 님 -

모든 두렴 -사 라 지 네 -

내 모든 삶 - - 주 장하 시 니 -

주께서 나의삶에 기쁨주시네 -

285

God Sent His Son
(Because He Lives)

1. God sent his Son, they called him Je - sus;
2. How sweet to hold a new- born ba - by,
3. And then one day I'll cross the riv - er;

he came to love, heal, and for - give;
and feel the pride and joy he gives;
I'll fight life's fi - nal war with pain;

he lived and died to buy my par - don,
but great - er still the calm as - sur - ance,
and then as death gives way to vic - tory,

an emp - ty grave is there to prove my Sav - ior lives.
this child can face un - cer - tain days be - cause he lives.
I'll see the lights of glo - ry and I'll know he reigns.

WORDS: Gloria and William J. Gaither
MUSIC: William J. Gaither
© 1971 William J. Gaither, Inc., admin. Gaither Copyright Management

RESURRECTION
98.9 11 with Refrain

Refrain

Be-cause he lives, I can face to-mor-row;
be-cause he lives, all fear is gone;
be-cause I know he holds the fu-ture,
and life is worth the liv-ing just be-cause he lives.

286

죄와 수치 무거운 짐
Shackled by a Heavy Burden
(He Touched Me)

1. 죄 와 수치 무 거 운 짐
2. 구 세주를 만 난 뒤에
1. Shack - led by a heav - y bur - den,
2. Since I met this bless - ed Sav - ior,

나 를 괴롭 힐 때 에
깨 끗하게 되 었 네
neath a load of guilt and shame,
since he cleansed and made me whole,

사 랑 스런 주 의 손 길
영 원 토록 찬 양 하 며
then the hand of Je - sus touched me,
I will nev - er cease to praise him;

날 구 원하여 주 시 었 네
그 이 름 높이 외 치 리 라
and now I am no long - er the same.
I'll shout it while e - ter - ni - ty rolls.

WORDS: William J. Gaither (Mt. 8:3; Mk. 1:41; Lk. 5:13);
Korean trans. The United Methodist Korean Hymnal Committee
MUSIC: William J. Gaither
© 1963, Korean trans. © 2001 William. J. Gaither, Inc., admin. Gaither Copyright Management

HE TOUCHED ME
Irr. with Refrain

후렴 *(Refrain)*

주 손 길   나 를 만 져 -
He touched me,   O   he touched me,

내 영 혼 기 쁨 넘 치 네 -
and O the joy that floods my soul!

나 의 -   삶 이 변 하 였 네
Some-thing hap-pened, and now I know,

주 손 길 날 구 - 했 네 -
he touched me and made me whole.

예수를 내가 주로 믿어
Blessed Assurance, Jesus Is Mine

1. 예수를 내 가 주로믿 어 성령과 피 로 써
2. 온 전 히 주 께 맡긴내 영 온 전 한 기 쁨 을
3. 예 수 께 맡 긴 나의영 혼 주 안 에 복 되 고

1. Bless-ed as - sur - ance, Je-sus is mine! O what a fore-taste of
2. Per-fect sub-mis - sion, per-fect de-light, vi-sions of rap-ture now
3. Per-fect sub-mis - sion, all is at rest; I in my Sav-ior am

거 듭 나 니 이 세 상 에 서 내 영 혼 이
누 리 면 서 자 비 와 사 랑 속 삭 이 는
평 안 하 니 세 상 도 없 고 나 도 없 고

glo-ry di - vine! Heir of sal - va - tion, pur-chase of God,
burst on my sight; an-gels de-scend-ing, bring from a - bove
hap-py and blest, watch-ing and wait - ing, look-ing, a - bove,

후렴 (Refrain)

하 늘 의 영 광 누 리 도 다
하 늘 의 천 사 보 리 로 다   이 것 이 나 의 간 증 이
사 랑 의 주 만 보 이 도 다

born of his Spir - it, washed in his blood.
ech-oes of mer - cy, whis-pers of love. This is my sto-ry, this is my
filled with his good-ness, lost in his love.

WORDS: Fanny J. Crosby; Korean trans. The United Methodist Korean Hymnal Committee
MUSIC: Phoebe P. Knapp
Korean trans. © 2001 The United Methodist Publishing House, admin. The Copyright Co.

ASSURANCE
9.10.9.9. with Refrain

요 이것이 나 의 찬 송 일 세 나 사 는 동 안
song, prais-ing my Sav - ior all the day long; this is my sto - ry,

끊 임 없 이 예 수 내 구 주 찬 송 하 리
this is my song, prais-ing my Sav- ior all the day long.

어찌 알 수 있나

1. 어찌 보고 알 수 있긴 나것여를 죄확주깨우다 용신돌달리변 서을아게게화
2. 나 찌 리를 느 위우 하리께품 세 세 세 세 세 세 세 세 세 세
3. 우 주 리 성 령 님 성 께 를 세 세 세 세 세 세 세 세 세 세
4. 주 보 성 령 우 님 성 께 서 이 세 세 세 세 세 세 세 세 세
5. 주 성 령 과 성 하 리 서 세 세 세 세 세 세 세 세 세 세
6. 온 맘 과 성 품 이 세 세 세 세 세 세 세 세 세 세

받 음 을 저 생 명 책 에
가 지 고 담 대 히 세 상
가 심 을 믿 는 자 마 다
하 시 시 주 우 리 에 게
주 시 네 그 온 유 의 영 과
되 었 네 우 리 하

내 이 름 기 록 되 었 음 을 네
끝 까 지 화 나 증 거 겠 시 을 네
참 평 신 주 내 신 사 랑 을
베 푸 한 그 크 의 마 음 을
겸 손 이 하 나 가 되 었
성 령 주 나 신 었 마 음

WORDS: Charles Wesley; Korean trans. The United Methodist Korean Hymnal Committee
MUSIC: Genevan Psalter, 1551; adapt. William Crotch
Korean trans. © 2001 The United Methodist Publishing House, admin. The Copyright Co.

ST. MICHAEL
SM

How Can We Sinners Know

1. How can we sin - ners know our sins on
2. What we have felt and seen, with con - fi -
3. We who in Christ be - lieve that he for
4. We by his Spir - it prove and know the
5. The meek and low - ly heart that in our
6. Our na - ture's turned, our mind trans - formed in

earth for - given? How can my gra - cious
dence we tell, and pub - lish to the
us hath died, we all his un - known
things of God, the things which free - ly
Sav - ior was, to us that Spir - it
all its powers, and both the wit - ness -

Sav - ior show my name in - scribed in heaven?
ends of earth the signs in - fal - li - ble.
peace re - ceive and feel his blood ap - plied.
of his love he hath on us be - stowed.
doth im - part and signs us with his cross.
es are joined, the Spirit of God with ours.

WORDS: Charles Wesley
MUSIC: *Genevan Psalter*, 1551; adapt. William Crotch

ST. MICHAEL
SM

289

내 맘속의 음악 소리는
There's Within My Heart a Melody

1. 내 맘 속 의 음 악 소 리 는
2. 죄 악 으 로 내 맘 아 프 고
3. 깊 은 강 을 건 널 때 에 나

1. There's with-in my heart a mel-o-dy
2. All my life was wrecked by sin and strife,
3. Though some-times he leads through wa-ters deep,

속 삭 이 는 주 음 성 — 너 와 항 상 함 께
고 통 중 에 헤 맬 때 — 예 수 나 의 상 처
어 려 운 일 당 할 때 — 나 의 길 이 때 론

Je-sus whis-pers sweet and low: Fear not, I am with thee,
dis-cord filled my heart with pain; Je-sus swept a-cross the
tri-als fall a-cross the way, though some-times the path seems

하 리 니 두 려 말 라 하 시 네
고 치 사 새 노 래 를 주 셨 네
험 해 도 주 님 함 께 하 시 네

peace, be still, in all of life's ebb and flow.
bro-ken strings, stirred the slum-bering chords a-gain.
rough and steep, see his foot-prints all the way.

WORDS: Luther B. Bridgers; Korean trans. The United Methodist Korean Hymnal Committee
MUSIC: Luther B. Bridgers
Korean trans. © 2001 The United Methodist Publishing House, admin. The Copyright Co.

SWEETEST NAME
97.97 with Refrain

후렴 (Refrain)

예 수 예 수 예 수 귀 한 그 이 름
Je - sus, Je - sus, Je - sus, sweet-est name I know,

소 망 채 우 시 며 찬 양 하 게 하 시 네
fills my ev - ery long - ing, keeps me sing-ing as I go.

4. 풍성하신 은혜 누리며
   날개 아래 쉬면서 주의 얼굴 항상
   뵈오니 기뻐 노래 부르네

5. 주님 이제 다시 오셔서
   나를 맞아 주시리 높은 하늘에서
   주 함께 다스리며 살겠네

4. Feasting on the riches of his grace,
   resting neath his sheltering wing,
   always looking on his smiling face,
   that is why I shout and sing.

5. Soon he's coming back to welcome me
   far beyond the starry sky;
   I shall wing my flight to worlds unknown;
   I shall reign with him on high.

290

아 하나님의 은혜로
I Know Not Why God's Wondrous Grace

1. 아 하 나 님 의 은 혜 로
2. 왜 주 의 말 씀 믿 을 때

1. I know not why God's won - drous grace
2. I know not how this sav - ing faith

이 쓸 데 없 는 자 며
참 평 안 주 시 며

to me he hath made known,
to me he did im - part,

왜 구 속 하 여 주 는 지
왜 굳 센 믿 음 주 는 지

nor why, un - wor - thy, Christ in love
nor how be - liev - ing in his word

난 알 수 없 으 나
난 알 수 없 으 나

re - deemed me for his own.
wrought peace with - in my heart.

WORDS: Daniel W. Whittle (2 Tim. 1:12); Korean trans. The United Methodist Korean Hymnal Committee
MUSIC: James McGranahan
Korean trans. © 2001 The United Methodist Publishing House, admin. The Copyright Co.

EL NATHAN
CM with Refrain

후렴 (Refrain)

내 가 믿 고 또 의 지 함 은 내 모 든 형 편
But I know whom I have be-liev-ed, and am per-suad-ed

잘 아 는 주 님 늘 돌 보 아 주 실
that he is a - ble to keep that which I've com -

것 을 나 는 확 실 히 아 네
mit - ted un - to him a-gainst that day.

3. 왜 내게 성령 주셔서
   내 맘을 감동해
   주 예수 믿게 하는지
   난 알수 없으나

3. I know not how the Spirit moves,
   convincing us of sin,
   revealing Jesus through the word,
   creating faith in him.

4. 주 언제 강림 하실지
   혹 밤에 혹 낮에
   또 주님 만날 그곳도
   난 알수 없으나

4. I know not when my Lord may come,
   at night or noonday fair,
   nor if I walk the vale with him,
   or meet him in the air.

291

주의 친절한 팔에 안기세
What a Fellowship, What a Joy Divine

1. 주 의 친 절 한 팔 에 안 기 세
2. 날 이 갈 수 록 주 의 사 랑 이
3. 주 의 보 좌 로 나 아 갈 때 에

1. What a fel - low - ship, what a joy di - vine,
2. O how sweet to walk in this pil - grim way,
3. What have I to dread, what have I to fear,

우 리 맘 이 평 안 하 리 니
두 루 광 명 하 게 비 치 고
기 뻐 찬 미 소 리 외 치 고

lean - ing on the ev - er - last - ing arms;
lean - ing on the ev - er - last - ing arms;
lean - ing on the ev - er - last - ing arms?

항 상 기 쁘 고 복 이 되 겠 네
천 성 가 는 길 밝 혀 주 리 니
겁 과 두 려 움 없 어 지 리 니

what a bless - ed - ness, what a peace is mine,
O how bright the path grows from day to day,
I have bless - ed peace with my Lord so near,

WORDS: Elisha A. Hoffman (Dt. 33:27); Korean trans. The United Methodist Korean Hymnal Committee
MUSIC: Anthony J. Showalter
Korean trans. © 2001 The United Methodist Publishing House, admin. The Copyright Co.

SHOWALTER
10 9.10 9 with Refrain

나는 주를 의지하리

WORDS: African American spiritual (Ps. 37:3); Korean trans. The United Methodist Korean Hymnal Committee
MUSIC: African American spiritual; adapt. and arr. William Farley Smith
Adapt. and arr. © 1989, Korean trans. © 2001 The United Methodist Publishing House, admin. The Copyright Co.

I WILL TRUST
Irr.

I Will Trust in the Lord

1. I will trust in the Lord, I will trust in the Lord,
2. Sis-ter, will you trust in the Lord, sis-ter, will you trust in the Lord,
3. Broth-er, will you trust in the Lord, broth-er, will you trust in the Lord,
4. Preach-er, will you trust in the Lord, preach-er, will you trust in the Lord,

I will trust in the Lord, till I die;
sis-ter, will you trust in the Lord, till you die;
broth-er, will you trust in the Lord, till you die;
preach-er, will you trust in the Lord, till you die;

I will trust in the Lord, I will trust in the Lord,
sis-ter, will you trust in the Lord, sis-ter, will you trust in the Lord,
broth-er, will you trust in the Lord, broth-er, will you trust in the Lord,
preach-er, will you trust in the Lord, preach-er, will you trust in the Lord,

I will trust in the Lord, till I die.
sis-ter, will you trust in the Lord, till you die.
broth-er, will you trust in the Lord, till you die.
preach-er, will you trust in the Lord, till you die.

WORDS: African American spiritual (Ps. 37:3)
MUSIC: African American spiritual; adapt. and arr. William Farley Smith
Adapt. and arr. © 1989 The United Methodist Publishing House, admin. The Copyright Co.

I WILL TRUST
Irr.

오 놀라운 구세주

WORDS: Fanny J. Crosby (Ps. 95:1); Korean trans. The United Methodist Korean Hymnal Committee
MUSIC: William J. Kirkpatrick
Korean trans. © 2001 The United Methodist Publishing House, admin. The Copyright Co.

HE HIDETH MY SOUL
11.8.11.8.11.8.11.8.8.

293 A Wonderful Savior Is Jesus My Lord

1. A won-der-ful Sav-ior is Je-sus my Lord,
2. A won-der-ful Sav-ior is Je-sus my Lord,
3. With num-ber-less bless-ings each mo-ment he crowns,
4. When clothed in his bright-ness, trans-port-ed I rise

a won-der-ful Sav-ior to me;
he tak-eth my bur-den a-way;
and filled with his full-ness di-vine,
to meet him in clouds of the sky,

he hid-eth my soul in the cleft of the rock,
he hold-eth me up, and I shall not be moved,
I sing in my rap-ture, oh, glo-ry to God
his per-fect sal-va-tion, his won-der-ful love,

where riv-ers of plea-sure I see.
he giv-eth me strength as my day.
for such a Re-deem-er as mine!
I'll shout with the mil-lions on high.

Ps. 95:1

HE HIDETH MY SOUL
11.8.11.8.11.8.11.8.8.

Refrain

He hid - eth my soul in the cleft of the rock

that shad - ows a dry, thirst - y land;

he hid - eth my life in the depths of his love,

and co - vers me there with his hand,

and co - vers me there with his hand.

294

주 안에 있는 나에게

1. 주 안 에 있 는 나 에 게 딴 근 심 있 으 랴 -
2. 그 두 려 움 이 변 하 여 내 기 도 되 었 고 며 -
3. 주 하 나 님 의 사 랑 이 늘 지 켜 주 시 며 -
4. 주 보 좌 앞 에 나 가 면 큰 위 로 주 시 고 -

십 자 가 밑 에 나 아 가 내 짐 을 풀 었 네 네
전 날 의 한 숨 이 변 하 여 내 노 래 되 었 네 네 네 리
나 필 요 하 는 모 든 것 다 내 채 워 주 시 네 리
그 강 한 팔 로 붙 드 사 내 짐 을 지 시 리 -

후렴

주 님 을 찬 송 하 면 서 할 렐 루 야 할 렐 루 야

주 의 길 걸 어 가 겠 네 주 내 짐 을 벗 기 셨 네

WORDS: Eliza E. Hewitt (Ps. 119:54); Korean trans. The United Methodist Korean Hymnal Committee
MUSIC: William J. Kirkpatrick
Korean trans. © 2001 The United Methodist Publishing House, admin. The Copyright Co.

SINGING I GO
8.6.8.8.8.8.

The Trusting Heart to Jesus Clings

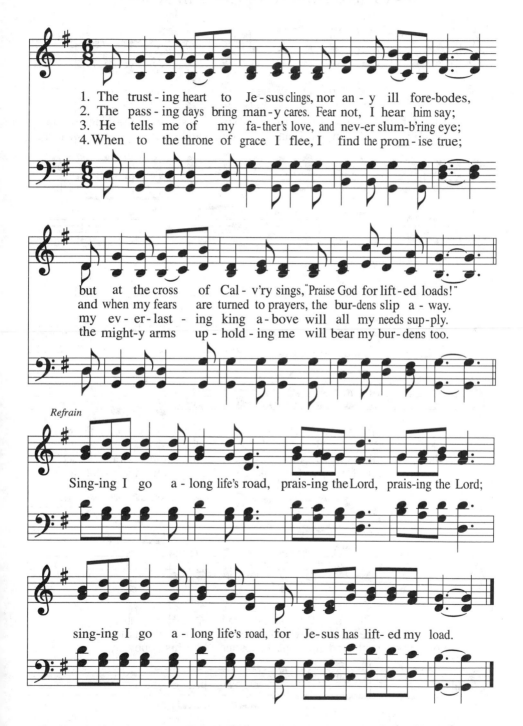

1. The trust-ing heart to Je-sus clings, nor an-y ill fore-bodes,
2. The pass-ing days bring man-y cares. Fear not, I hear him say;
3. He tells me of my fa-ther's love, and nev-er slum-b'ring eye;
4. When to the throne of grace I flee, I find the prom-ise true;

but at the cross of Cal-v'ry sings, "Praise God for lift-ed loads!"
and when my fears are turned to prayers, the bur-dens slip a-way.
my ev-er-last-ing king a-bove will all my needs sup-ply.
the might-y arms up-hold-ing me will bear my bur-dens too.

Refrain

Sing-ing I go a-long life's road, prais-ing the Lord, prais-ing the Lord;

sing-ing I go a-long life's road, for Je-sus has lift-ed my load.

WORDS: Eliza E. Hewitt (Ps. 119:54)
MUSIC: William J. Kirkpatrick

SINGING I GO
8.6.8.8.8.8.

295

내 진정 사모하는
I Have Found a Friend in Jesus

1. 내 진정 사모하는 주 예수 내 친구
2. 내 모든 쓰라림을 주 담당하시고
1. I have found a friend in Je - sus, he's ev - ery-thing to me,
2. He all my grief has ta - ken, and all my sor-rows borne;

이 땅 위에 비길 것이 없어라
시험 당할 때에 방패 되시네
he's the fair - est of ten thou-sand to my soul;
in temp - ta - tion he's my strong and might - y tower;

내 주는 저 산 밑에 한 송이 백합화
나 모든 것을 바쳐 내 주를 섬기니
the lil - y of the val - ley, in him a-lone I see
I have all for him for-sak - en, and all my i-dols torn

나를 온전하고 정케 하시네
크신 권능으로 지켜 주시네
all I need to cleanse and make me ful - ly whole.
from my heart and now he keeps me by his power.

WORDS: Charles W. Fry; Korean trans. The United Methodist Korean Hymnal Committee
MUSIC: William S. Hays; adapt. Charles W. Fry
Korean trans. © 2001 The United Methodist Publishing House, admin. The Copyright Co.

SALVATIONIST
Irr.

후렴 (Refrain)

3. 나 믿음으로 살며 주뜻을 따르면
   주는 길이 길이 함께 하시니
   이세상 어느것도 나 두렵지 않네
   나의 주린 영혼 채워 주시리
   저 생명강가에서 나 영광에 싸여
   내 주의 귀한 얼굴 뵈오리

3. He will never, never leave me, nor yet forsake me
   here, while I live by faith and do his blessed will;
   a wall of fire about me, I've nothing now to fear,
   with his manna he my hungry soul shall fill.
   Then sweeping up to glory to see his blessed face,
   where rivers of delight shall ever roll;

296

저 장미꽃 위에 이슬
In the Garden
(I Come to the Garden Alone)

1. 저 장미꽃 위에 이 슬 – 아 직 맺 혀 있 는 그
2. 그 청아한 주의 음 성 – 울 던 새 도 잠 잠 케
3. 밤 깊도록 동산 안 에 – 주 와 함 께 있 으 려

1. I come to the gar-den a - lone while the dew is still on the
2. He speaks, and the sound of his voice is so sweet the birds hush their
3. I'd stay in the gar-den with him though the night a-round me be

때 에 귀 에 은 은 히 소 리 들 리 니 주
한 다 주 님 나 에 게 주 신 그 노 래 내
하 나 괴 론 세 상 에 할 일 많 아 서 날

ros - es, and the voice I hear fall-ing on my ear, the
sing - ing, and the mel - o - dy that he gave to me with
fall - ing, but he bids me go; thru the voice of woe his

후렴 *(Refrain)*

음 성 분 명 하 – 다
맘 에 울 리 도 – 다 다   주 가 나 와 동 행 을
가 라 명 하 신 – 다 다

Son of God dis - clos - es.
in my heart is ring - ing.   And he walks with me, and he
voice to me is call - ing.

WORDS: C. Austin Miles (Jn. 20:11-18); Korean trans. The United Methodist Korean Hymnal Committee
MUSIC: C. Austin Miles; adapt. Charles H. Webb
Korean trans. © 2001 The United Methodist Publishing House, admin. The Copyright Co.

GARDEN
89.557 with Refrain

하 면 서 나 의 친 구 되 시 오 니 -
talks with me, and he tells me I am his own,

우 리 서 로 받 은 그 기 쁨 은 알
and the joy we share as we tar - ry there, none

사 람 이 없 도 - 다 -
oth - er has ev - er known.

297

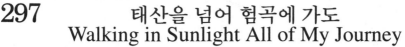

태산을 넘어 험곡에 가도
Walking in Sunlight All of My Journey

1. 태 산 을 넘 어 험 곡 에 가 도
2. 캄 캄 한 밤 에 다 닐 지 라 도
3. 광 명 한 그 빛 마 음 에 받 아

1. Walk - ing in sun - light, all of my jour - ney;
2. Shad - ows a - round me, shad - ows a - bove me,
3. In the bright sun - light, ev - er re - joic - ing,

빛 가 운 데 로 걸 어 가 면 ─
주 께 서 나 의 길 되 시 고 ─
기 쁘 게 천 국 향 해 가 며 ─

o - ver the moun - tains, through the deep vale;
nev - er con - ceal my Sav - ior and guide;
press - ing my way to man - sions a - bove;

주 께 서 항 상 지 키 시 기 로
나 에 게 밝 은 빛 이 되 시 니
할 렐 루 야 를 힘 차 게 불 러

Je - sus has said, "I'll nev - er for - sake thee,"
he is the light, in him is no dark - ness;
sing - ing his prais - es glad - ly I'm walk - ing,

WORDS: H. J. Zelley (1 Jn. 1:7); Korean trans. The Christian Literature Society of Korea
MUSIC: George Harrison Cook
Korean trans. © The Christian Literature Society of Korea

SUNLIGHT
10.9.10.9 with Refrain

주의 곁에 있을 때

WORDS: F. M. Davis (Ps. 16:9); Korean trans. The Christian Literature Society of Korea
MUSIC: F. M. Davis
Korean trans. © The Christian Literature Society of Korea

LEAD ME, SAVIOR
7.7.7.7. with Refrain

후럼

주여 주여

나 를 인 도 하 소 서

하 소 서

빠 른 세 상 살 동 안 (살 동 안) 주 여

인 도 하 소 서 (하 소 서)

298

Savior, Lead Me

1. Sav - ior, lead me, lest I stray, (lest I stray)
2. Thou the ref - uge of my soul, (of my soul)
3. Sav - ior, lead me, then at last, (then at last)

gen - tly lead me all the way; (all the way)
when life's stor - my bil - lows roll, (bil-lows roll)
when the storm of life is past, (life is past)

I am safe when by thy side, (by thy side)
I am safe when thou art high, (thou art high)
to the land of end - less day, (end-less day)

I would in thy love a - bide. (love a-bide)
all my hopes on thee re - ly. (thee re - ly)
where all tears are wiped a - way. (wiped a-way)

WORDS: F. M. Davis (Ps. 16:9)
MUSIC: F. M. Davis

LEAD ME, SAVIOR
7.7.7.7. with Refrain

299

날 대속하신 나의 구세주

TOULON
10.10.10.10

I Greet Thee, Who My Sure Redeemer Art 299

1. I greet thee, who my sure Re-deem-er art,
2. Thou art the King of mer-cy and of grace,
3. Thou art the life, by which a-lone we live,
4. Thou hast the true and per-fect gen-tle-ness,
5. Our hope is in no oth-er save in thee;

my on-ly trust and Sav-ior of my heart,
reign-ing om-nip-o-tent in ev-ery place:
and all our sub-stance and our strength re-ceive;
no harsh-ness hast thou and no bit-ter-ness:
our fa-ith is built upon thy prom-ise free;

who pain didst un-der-go for my poor sake;
so come, O King, and our whole be-ing sway;
sus-tain us by thy faith and by thy power,
O grant to us the grace we find in thee,
Lord, give us peace, and make us calm and sure,

I pray thee from our hearts all cares to take.
shine on us with the light of thy pure day.
and give us strength in ev-ery try-ing hour.
that we may dwell in per-fect u-ni-ty.
that in thy strength we ev-er-more en-dure.

WORDS: Att. John Calvin, *French Psalter*, 1545; English trans. Elizabeth Lee Smith
MUSIC: Adapt. from *Genevan Psalter*, 1551

TOULON
10.10.10.10

300 하나님의 사랑을 사모하는 자
Everyone Who Longs for
(Only Long for God)

하나 님의 사 랑을 사 모 하 는 자
님 께 찬 양과 경 배 하 는 자
Ev-'ry - one who longs for the bound-less love of God,
one who wor-ships God and sings glad songs of praise,

하 나 님 의 평 안 을 바 라 보 는 자
하 나 님 의 선 하 심 을 닮 아 가 는 자
ev -'ry - one who hopes for the com-ing of God's peace,
ev -'ry - one who fol - lows the way of God's good - ness,

너 의 모 든 것 창 조 하 신 우 리 주 님 이
the Lord God who cre-at-ed all things beau-ti-ful and good

너 를 얼 마 나 사 랑 하 시 는 지 하 나
loves you more than you can ev - er ful-ly know. Ev-'ry -

자 녀 삼 으 셨 네 하 나 님 사 랑 의 눈 으 로
now as one of God's own. God is al - ways watch-ing o -ver you,

너 를 어 느 때 나 바 라 보 시 고
God is watch-ing you with lov - ing eyes.

WORDS: Sung-ho Park; English trans. Edward Poitras
MUSIC: Sung-ho Park
© 2001 Sung-ho Park

주님의 기쁨은 나의 힘

1. 주 님 - 의 - 기 - 쁨은 나 의시
2. 상 한 - 영 - 치 - 유하 시시
3. 주 내 - 게 - 생 - 수주 시

힘 주 님 - 의 - 기 - 쁨은 나 의시
네 상 한 - 영 - 치 - 유하 시시
네 주 내 - 게 - 생 - 수주 시

힘 주 님 - 의 - 기 - 쁨은 나 의시
네 상 한 - 영 - 치 - 유하 시시
네 주 내 - 게 - 생 - 수주 시시

힘 주 님 의 기 쁨 나 - 의 - 힘 -
네 주 님의기쁨 나 - 의 - 힘 -
네 주 님의기쁨 나 - 의 - 힘

WORDS: Alliene G. Vale (Neh. 8:10); Korean trans. The United Methodist Korean Hymnal Committee
MUSIC: Alliene G. Vale
© 1971, Korean trans. © 2001 Mutisongs/His Eye Music/Joy of the Lord Publishing, admin. EMI Christian Music Group

THE JOY OF THE LORD
8.8.7.7.8.

The Joy of the Lord

1. The joy of the Lord is my
2. He heals the bro-ken-heart-ed and they cry no
3. He gives me liv-ing wa-ter and I thirst no

strength, the joy of the Lord is my
more, he heals the bro-ken-heart-ed and they cry no
more, he gives me liv-ing wa-ter and I thirst no

strength, the joy of the Lord is my
more, he heals the bro-ken-heart-ed and they cry no
more, he gives me liv-ing wa-ter and I thirst no

strength, the joy of the Lord is my strength.
more, the joy of the Lord is my strength.
more, the joy of the Lord is my strength.

WORDS: Alliene G. Vale (Neh. 8:10)
MUSIC: Alliene G. Vale

THE JOY OF THE LORD
8.8.7.7.8.

302

독수리 높은 둥지에
The Care the Eagle Gives Her Young

1. 독　수　리　높　은　둥　지　에
2. 때　되　면　새　끼　독　수　리
1. The care the ea - gle gives her young,
2. As when the time to ven - ture comes,

그　새 - 끼　지　내　키　듯　이
다　몰 - 아　내　키　듯　이
safe in her loft - y nest,
she stirs them out to flight,

그　부 - 드　러　운　사 - 랑　을
우　리 - 도　용　기　내 - 어　서
is like the ten - der love of God
so we are pressed to bold - ly try,

주　보　으 - 여　주　셨　네
날　보　으 - 라　하　시　네
for us made man - i - fest.
to strive for dar - ing height.

3. 힘 없이 버둥 대다가
　　떨어지려 할 때
　　하나님 힘찬 날개가
　　날 태워 주시네

3. And if we flutter helplessly,
　　as fledgling eagles fall,
　　beneath us lift God's mighty wings
　　to bear us, one and all.

WORDS: R. Deane Postlethwaite (Dt. 32:11); Korean trans. The United Methodist Korean Hymnal Committee
MUSIC: Jesse Seymour Irvine; harm. TCL. Pritchard
Korean trans. © 2001 The United Methodist Publishing House, admin. The Copyright Co.;
harm. by permission of Oxford University Press

CRIMOND
CM

아름답게 하셨네
Something Beautiful

아 름 답 게　　하 셨 네
Some - thing beau-ti-ful,　　some-thing good;

내 모 든 약-함　　아 시 는 주
all my con-fu-sion　　he un-der-stood;

나 의 상 한 심 령 을　　주 받 아 주 시
all I had to of-fer him　　was bro-ken-ness and

고 내 삶을 아 름　　답 게 하 셨 네 -
strife, but he made some-thing beau-ti-ful of my life.

WORDS: Gloria Gaither; Korean trans. The United Methodist Korean Hymnal Committee
MUSIC: William J. Gaither
© 1971, Korean trans. © 2001 William J. Gaither, Inc., admin. Gaither Copyright Management

SOMETHING BEAUTIFUL
Irr.

304 내 평생에 가는 길
When Peace, Like a River, Attendeth My Way

WORDS: Horatio G. Spafford (Ps. 23:6); Korean trans. The United Methodist Korean Hymnal Committee
MUSIC: Philip P. Bliss
Korean trans. © 2001 The United Methodist Publishing House, admin. The Copyright Co.

VILLE DU HAVRE
11 8.11 9 with Refrain

후렴(Refrain)

305

네 마음에 근심 있느냐
O Soul, Are You Weary?
(Turn Your Eyes Upon Jesus)

1. 네 마음에 근심 있느냐
2. 저 죽음을 이기신 예수
3. 변치않는 주님의 예약

1. O soul, are you wea-ry and trou-bled?
2. Thru death in-to life ev-er-last-ing
3. His word shall not fail you he prom-ised;

어둠 속을 헤매느냐
우리들도 따라가네
그 말씀을 의지하라

No light in the dark-ness you see?
he passed, and we fol-low him there;
be-lieve him and all will be well;

주 예수를 바라볼 때
죄악에서 세상에 우나
죽어가는 세상에 나가

There's light for a look at the Sav-ior,
o-ver us sin no more hath do-min-ion
then go to a world that is dy-ing,

참 주 빛을 찾으리하라
밝안은에 서승리하네
주원을 선포하라

and life, more a-bund-ant and free!
for more than con-qu'rors we are!
his per-fect sal-va-tion to tell!

WORDS: Helen H. Lemmel;
Korean trans. The United Methodist Korean Hymnal Committee
MUSIC: Helen H. Lemmel

LEMMEL
Irr.

후렴 (Refrain)

눈을 주님께 돌려
Turn your eyes up - on Je - sus,

그 찬란한 얼굴보라
look full in his won - der - ful face;

세상 모든 부귀와 영광은
and the things of earth will grow strange - ly dim

주님 앞 에서 빛을 잃네
in the light of his glo - ry and grace.

306

수고한 자 오라
Come All Ye That Labor

수 고 한 - 자 오 라 너
Come all ye that la - bor, and

쉬 게 하 - 리 라 짐 진
I will give you rest, come ye

자 도 오 라 너 쉬 게 하 - 리
heav - y la - den and I will give you

라 나 의 멍 - 에 메
rest. Take my yoke up - on

WORDS: Bruce Ballinger (Mt. 11:28-30); Korean trans. The United Methodist Korean Hymnal Committee
MUSIC: Bruce Ballinger
© 1989, Korean trans. © 2001 Univesal-MCA Music Publishing

잠잠하라
Be Still, My Soul

1. 잠 잠 하 라 주 네 편 되 시 니 –
2. 잠 잠 하 라 주 너 의 앞 길 을 –
3. 잠 잠 하 라 그 때 가 다 가 와 –

1. Be still, my soul: the Lord is on your side.
2. Be still, my soul: your God will un - der - take
3. Be still, my soul: the hour is has - tening on

슬 픔 고 통 잘 참 고 견 디 며
전 과 같 이 늘 인 도 하 시 리
영 원 토 록 주 함 께 살 리 라

Bear pa - tient - ly the cross of grief or pain;
to guide the fu - ture, as in a - ges past.
when we shall be for - ev - er with the Lord,

네 모 든 것 다 주 께 맡 기 어 라
소 망 과 확 신 항 상 굳 게 하 라
실 망 과 슬 픔 두 렴 사 라 지 고

leave to your God to or - der and pro - vide;
Your hope, your con - fi - dence let noth - ing shake;
when dis - ap - point - ment, grief, and fear are gone;

WORDS: Katharina von Schlegel (Ps. 46:10); English trans. Jane Borthwick;
Korean trans. The United Methodist Korean Hymnal Committee
MUSIC: Jean Sibelius; arr. from *The Hymnal, 1933*
Arr. © 1933, renewed 1961, Korean trans. © 2001 Presbyterian Board of Christian Education

FINLANDIA
11 10.11 10.11 10

영 원 토 록 　 주 신 실 하 시 리
이 모 든 신 　 비 밝 혀 지 리 라
사 랑 의 기 　 쁨 회 복 되 리 라

in ev-ery change 　 God faith-ful will re - main.
all now mys - te - rious shall be bright at last.
sor-row for - got, 　 love's pur-est joys re - stored.

잠 잠 하 라 　 네 친 구 되 신 주 님
잠 잠 하 라 　 능 력 의 구 주 예 수
잠 잠 하 라 　 이 눈 물 지 나 가 면

Be still, my soul: 　 your best, your heaven-ly friend
Be still, my soul: 　 the waves and winds still know
Be still, my soul: 　 wnen change and tears are past,

기 쁨 으 로 　 널 인 도 하 시 리
파 도 와 바 　 람 다 스 리 셨 네
평 안 과 축 　 복 함 께 누 리 리

through thorn-y ways leads to a joy - ful end.
the Christ who ruled them while he dwelt be - low.
all safe and bless - ed we shall meet at last.

308

내 주를 가까이 하려함은

WORDS: Sarah F. Adams (Gen. 28:10-22); Korean trans. The United Methodist Korean Hymnal Committee
MUSIC: Lowell Mason
Korean trans. © 2001 The United Methodist Publishing House, admin. The Copyright Co.

BETHANY
64.64.6664

Nearer, My God, to Thee

1. Near - er, my God, to thee, near - er to thee!
2. Though like the wan - der - er the sun gone down,
3. There let the way ap - pear, steps un - to heaven;
4. Then, with my wak - ing thoughts bright with thy praise,

E'en though it be a cross that rais - eth me,
dark - ness be o - ver me, my rest a stone;
all that thou send - est me in mer - cy given;
out of my ston - y griefs Beth - el I'll raise;

still all my song shall be near - er, my God, to thee;
yet in my dreams I'd be near - er, my God, to thee;
an - gels to beck - on me near - er, my God, to thee;
so by my woes to be near - er, my God, to thee;

near - er, my God, to thee, near - er to thee!

WORDS: Sarah F. Adams (Gen. 28:10-22)
MUSIC: Lowell Mason

BETHANY
64.64.6664

309

예수여 나의 손 꼭 잡고 가소서

1. 예 수 여 나 의 손 꼭 잡 고 가 소 서
2. 인 생 이 힘 들 고 고 난 이 겹 칠 때
3. 인 생 의 밝 은 날 모 두 다 지 나 고

약 하 고 피 곤 한 이 몸 을
예 수 여 날 도 와 주 소 서
어 두 운 밤 깊 어 갈 때 에

어 둔 밤 풍 랑 속 빛 으 로 이 끄 사
외 치 는 이 소 리 주 께 서 들 으 사
강 가 에 서 있 는 나 의 손 꼭 잡 고

후렴

본 향 에 날 인 도 하 소 서

WORDS: Thomas A. Dorsey; Korean trans. The United Methodist Korean Hymnal Committee
MUSIC: George N, Allen; arr. Thomas A. Dorsey
© 1938 Hill & Range Songs, Inc., renewed Unichappell Music, Inc.; Korean trans. © 2001 Hill & Range Songs, Inc.

PRECIOUS LORD
Irr.

Precious Lord, Take My Hand

1. Pre-cious Lord, take my hand, lead me on, let me stand,
2. When my way grows drear, pre-cious Lord, lin-ger near,
3. When the dark - ness ap-pears and the night draws near,

I am tired, I am weak, I am worn;
when my life is al - most gone,
and the day is past and gone,

thru the storm, thru the night, lead me on to the light:
hear my cry, hear my call, hold my hand lest I fall:
at the riv - er I stand, guide my feet, hold my hand:

Refrain

take my hand, pre - cious Lord, lead me home.

WORDS: Thomas A. Dorsey
MUSIC: George N, Allen; arr. Thomas A. Dorsey
© 1938 Hill & Range Songs, Inc., renewed Unichappell Music, Inc.

PRECIOUS LORD
Irr.

우리의 삶은 예수 안에서
When We Are Living

Unison

1. 우 리 의 삶 은 — 예수안 에 서 —
2. 우 리 의 열 매 — 주께드 리 며 —
1. When we are liv - ing, it is in Christ Je - sus,
2. Thru all our liv - ing, we our fruits must give.

우 리 죽 음 도 — 예수안 에 서 —
섬 김 의 수 고 — 주께바 치 세 —
and when we're dy - ing, it is in the Lord.
Good works of ser - vice are for of - fer - ing.

살 아 갈 때 도 — 죽 을 때 에 도
드 릴 때 에 도 — 받 을 때 에 도
Both in our liv - ing and in our dy - ing,
When we are giv - ing, or when re - ceiv - ing,

WORDS: St. 1 anon. (Rom. 14:8), English trans. Elise S. Eslinger; sts. 2, 3, 4 Roberto Escamilla,
English trans. George Lockwood; Korean trans. The United Methodist Korean Hymnal Committee
MUSIC: Trad. Spanish melody; harm. from *Celebremos*
English trans. © 1989, Korean trans. © 2001 The United Methodist Publishing House, admin. The Copyright Co.

SOMOS DEL SENOR
Irr.

후렴 (Refrain)

last time to Coda

우린주 의 것 - 우린주 의 것
we be-long to God, we be-long to God.

Coda

우 린 주 의 것 - 우린주 의 것
We be-long to God, we be-long to God.

3. 슬퍼할 때와 고통 당할 때
아름다움과 사랑 느낄 때
괴로울 때나 즐거울 때나
우린 주의 것 우린 주의 것

3. 'Mid times of sorrow and in times of pain,
when sensing beauty or in love's embrace,
whether we suffer, or sing rejoicing,
we belong to God, we belong to God.

4. 평화 모르고 울부짖는 자
이 세상 안에 항상 있으니
도와 줄 때나 먹여 줄 때나
우린 주의 것 우린 주의 것

4. Across this wide world, we shall always find
those who are crying with no peace of mind
but when we help them, or when we feed them,
we belong to God, we belong to God.

311

새로운 삶을 시작하는

* 성찬식을 위한 가사

WORDS: Brian Wren; alt. (Rev. 21:5); Korean trans. The United Methodist Korean Hymnal Committee
MUSIC: Carlton R. Young
© 1987, Korean trans. © 2001 Hope Publishing Co.

BEGINNINGS
98. 98

This Is a Day of New Beginnings

1. This is a day of new be-gin-nings,
2. For by the life and death of Je-sus,
3. Then let us, with the Spir-it's dar-ing,
4. Christ is a-live, and goes be-fore us
*5. In faith we'll gath-er round the ta-ble

time to re-mem-ber and move on,
God's might-y Spir-it, now as then,
step from the past and leave be-hind
to show and share what love can do.
to taste and share what love can do.

time to be-lieve what love is bring-ing,
can make for us a world of dif-ference,
our dis-ap-point-ment, guilt, and griev-ing,
This is a day of new be-gin-nings;
This is a day of new be-gin-nings;

[1~3]

lay-ing to rest the pain that's gone.
as faith and hope are born a-gain.
seek-ing new paths, and sure to find.

[4 or 5]

our God is mak-ing all things new.
our God is mak-ing all things new.

* *Alternate text for Holy Communion*

WORDS: Brian Wren; alt. (Rev. 21:5)
MUSIC: Carlton R. Young
© 1987 Hope Publishing Co.

BEGINNINGS
98. 98

312

나의 삶을 주 위해
Take My Life, and Let It Be

1. 나 의 삶 을 주 위 해 성 별 하 여
2. 나 의 음 성 주 님 만 찬 송 하 게
3. 나 의 뜻 이 온 전 히 주 뜻 되 게

1. Take my life, and let it be con - se - cra - ted,
2. Take my voice, and let me sing al - ways, on - ly,
3. Take my will, and make it thine; it shall be no

주 시 고 나 의 모 든 순 간 에
하 시 고 나 의 입 술 복 음 만
하 시 고 나 의 마 음 주 님 의

Lord, to thee. Take my mo - ments and my days;
for my King. Take my lips, and let them be
long - er mine. Take my heart, it is thine own;

찬 양 하 게 하 소 서 나 의 손 을
전 파 하 게 하 소 서 나 의 가 진
보 좌 되 게 하 소 서 나 의 모 든

let them flow in cease - less praise. Take my hands, and
filled with mes - sag - es from thee. Take my sil - ver
it shall be thy roy - al throne. Take my love, my

WORDS: Frances R. Havergal (Rom. 12:1); Korean trans. The United Methodist Korean Hymnal Committee
MUSIC: Louis J. F. Hérold; arr. George Kingsley
Korean trans. © 2001 The United Methodist Publishing House, admin. The Copyright Co.

MESSIAH
77.77 D

이 끄 사 주 의 사 랑 전 하 고
은 과 금 모 두 받 아 주 시 고
사 랑 을 주 발 앞 에 쏟 으 며

let them move at the im - pulse of thy love.
and my gold; not a mite would I with-hold.
Lord, I pour at thy feet its trea - sure-store.

나 의 발 을 주 위 해 민 첩 하 게 하 소 서
나 의 힘 과 지 혜 를 주 뜻 대 로 쓰 소 서
주 만 위 해 살 리 니 나 를 받 아 주 소 서

Take my feet, and let them be swift and beau-ti - ful for thee.
Take my in - tel - lect, and use ev - ery power as thou shalt choose.
Take my -self, and I will be ev - er, on - ly, all for thee.

313

내 마음 주께 바치옵니다

1. 내 마음 주께 바치옵니다
2. 내 맘에 성령 임하옵소서
3. 내 맘의 친구 주여 오소서

주께서 말씀하이 셨다
시험을 모두 이기게
시험을 모두 이기게

내게 로이 오계 라실 오성 직전 내게 삼닥 게으칠 로사 때
주 님의 순 간 내게 삼닥 게으칠 로사 때
죽 음이의 순 간 내게

그 성승 말결리 씀케를 따하주 라소 서서서
승 서서

WORDS: Soon Sae Kim
MUSIC: Soon Sae Kim
© Soon Sae Kim

313

My Heart I Give Unto You

1. My heart I give un-to you, my dear Lord,
2. My heart fill it Spir-it, my dear Lord,
3. My heart waits for you, O Lord, my dear friend,

for you have called me lov-ing-ly:
that I may o-ver-come temp-ta-tion:
that I may o-ver-come temp-ta-tion.

"Come un-to me, be-lov-ed, come to me."
This bo-dy sanc-ti-fied, your tem-ple be,
When I face death and my last mo-ment comes,

Yes, Lord, I'll fol-low you.
come, Ho-ly Spir-it, dwell.
I will be vic-to-rious.

WORDS: Soon Sae Kim English trans. Edward Poitras
MUSIC: Soon Sae Kim
© Soon Sae Kim

My heart I give un-to you, Lord
To serve you with my heart and soul
For I will rest in your bo - som

this bo - dy, liv - ing sa - cri - fice.
I pray that I may love you more.
and rest in Sab - bath e - ter - nal.

My heart I give un-to you, my dear Lord

un - to you, my dear Lord.

하늘 향해 올라가네

WORDS: African American spiritual (Gen. 28:10-17);
Korean trans. The United Methodist Korean Hymnal Committee
MUSIC: African American spiritual
Adapt. and arr. © 1989, Korean trans. © 2001 The United Methodist Publishing House, admin. The Copyright Co.

JACOB'S LADDER

Irr.

We Are Climbing Jacob's Ladder

1. We are climb-ing Ja-cob's lad-der; we are
2. Ev-ery round goes high-er, high-er; ev-ery
3. Sin-ner, do you love my Je-sus? Sin-ner,
4. If you love him, why not serve him? If you
5. We are climb-ing high-er, high-er; we are

(yes, Lord)

climb-ing Ja-cob's lad-der, we are climb-ing
round goes high-er, high-er, ev-ery round goes
do you love my Je-sus? Sin-ner, do you
love him, why not serve him? If you love him,
climb-ing high-er, high-er, we are climb-ing

(yes, Lord)

Ja-cob's lad-der; sol-diers of the cross.
high-er, high-er; sol-diers of the cross.
love my Je-sus? Sol-diers of the cross.
why not serve him? Sol-diers of the cross.
high-er, high-er; sol-diers of the cross.

WORDS: African American spiritual (Gen. 28:10-17)
MUSIC: African American spiritual
Adapt. and arr. © 1989 The United Methodist Publishing House, admin. The Copyright Co.

JACOB'S LADDER
Irr.

315

겸손히 주를 섬길 때

WORDS: Washington Gladden (Heb. 12:1); Korean trans. The United Methodist Korean Hymnal Committee
MUSIC: H. Percy Smith
Korean trans. © 2001 The United Methodist Publishing House, admin. The Copyright Co.

MARYTON
LM

O Master, Let Me Walk with Thee **315**

1. O Master, let me walk with thee
2. Help me the slow of heart to move
3. Teach me thy patience; still with thee
4. In hope that sends a shining ray

in lowly paths of service free;
by some clear, winning word of love;
in closer, dearer company,
far down the future's broad'ning way,

tell me thy secret; help me bear the
teach me the wayward feet to stay, and
in work that keeps faith sweet and strong, in
in peace that only thou canst give, with

strain of toil, the fret of care.
guide them in the homeward way.
trust that triumphs over wrong.
thee, O Master let me live.

WORDS: Washington Gladden (Heb. 12:1)
MUSIC: H. Percy Smith

MARYTON
LM

나 주의 도움 받고자

1. 나 주 의 도움 받고 자 주 예 수 님께 빕니 다
2. 큰 죄 에 빠져 죽게 된 날 위 해 피 흘렸으 니니
3. 내 힘 과 결심 약하 여늘 깨 어 지 기 쉬우 니
4. 내 구 세 주의 발앞 에 엎 드 린 나 를 보시 고

그 구 원 내 게 베 푸 사 날 받 으 옵 소 서
주 형 상 대 로 빛 으 사 날 받 으 옵 소 서
주 이 름 으 로 구 하 사 날 받 으 옵 소 서
그 크 신 역 사 이 루 어 날 받 으 옵 소 서

후렴

내 모 습 이 대 로 주 받 으 옵 소 서

날 위 해 돌 아 가 신 주 날 받 으 옵 소 서

WORDS: Eliza H. Hamilton (Lk. 5:11); Korean trans. The United Methodist Korean Hymnal Committee
MUSIC: Ira David Sankey
Korean trans. © 2001 The United Methodist Publishing House, admin. The Copyright Co.

TAKE ME AS I AM
8.8.8.6.

Jesus, My Lord, to Thee I Cry

1. Je - sus, my Lord, to thee I cry; un - less thou help me I must die,
2. Help - less I am, and full of guilt; but yet for me thy blood was spilt,
3. No prep - ar - a - tion can I make, my best re - solves I on - ly break,
4. Be - hold me, Sav - ior, at thy feet, deal with me as thou see - est meet;

Oh, bring thy free sal - va - tion nigh, and take me as I am.
and thou canst make me what thou wilt, and take me as I am.
yet save me for thine own name's sake, and take me as I am.
thy work be - gin, thy work com - plete, and take me as I am.

Refrain

And take me as I am, and take me as I am,

my on - ly plea Christ died for me! Oh, take me as I am.

WORDS: Eliza H. Hamilton (Lk. 5:11)
MUSIC: Ira David Sankey

TAKE ME AS I AM
8.8.8.6.

317

내게 있는 향유 옥합
To My Precious Lord

후렴 (Refrain)

내 게 있 는 향 유 옥 합 주 께 가 져 와
To my pre-cious Lord I bring my flask of frag-rant oil

그 발 위 에 입 맞 추 고 깨 뜨 립 니 다
kneel-ing down, I kiss his feet, a - noint them with the oil.

1. 나 를 위 해 험 한 산 길 오 르 신 예 수
2. 나 를 위 해 십 자 가 에 오 르 신 그 발
3. 주 님 다 시 이 땅 위 에 임 하 실 그 때

1. Je - sus, who for me suf-fered the road to Cal - va - ry,
2. Je - sus, who for me had his feet nailed on to the cross,
3. When in glo - ry you with clouds come back to earth a - gain,

걸 음 마 다 크 신 사 랑 새 겨 놓 았 네
흘 린 피 로 나 의 죄 를 대 속 하 셨 네
주 의 크 신 사 랑 으 로 날 받 아 주 소 서

on each step he im-print-ed his wond-rous love for me.
with his blood he washed a - way my sins and made me whole.
Je - sus, with your love, ac-cept me, hold me in your arms.

WORDS: Chung Kwan Park (Lk. 7:37-38), English trans. Edward Poitras
MUSIC: Chung Kwan Park
© Chung Kwan Park; English trans. © 2001 The United Methodist Publishing House, admin. The Copyright Co.

내 구주 예수를 더욱 사랑
More Love to Thee, O Christ

1. 내 구주 예수를 더 욱 사 랑
2. 이 전엔 세 상 낙 기 뻤 어 도
3. 이 세 상 떠 날 때 찬 양 하 고

1. More love to thee, O Christ, more love to thee!
2. Once earth-ly joy I craved, sought peace and rest;
3. Then shall my lat - est breath whis - per thy praise;

엎 드 려 비 는 말 들 으 소 서
지 금 내 기 쁨 은 오 직 예 수
숨 질 때 하 는 말 이 것 일 세

Hear thou the prayer I make on bend - ed knee.
now thee a - lone I seek, give what is best.
this be the part - ing cry my heart shall raise;

내 진 정 소 원 이 내 내 구 주 예 수 를
다 만 내 기 도 는 내 내 구 주 예 수 를
다 만 내 기 도 는 내 구 주 예 수 를

This is my ear - nest plea: more love, O Christ, to thee;
This all my prayer shall be: more love, O Christ, to thee;
this still its prayer shall be: more love, O Christ, to thee;

더 욱 사 랑 더 욱 사 랑
더 욱 사 랑 더 욱 사 랑
더 욱 사 랑 더 욱 사 랑

more love to thee, more love to thee!
more love to thee, more love to thee!
more love to thee, more love to thee!

WORDS: Elizabeth P. Prentiss (Mt. 22:37); Korean trans. The Christian Literature Society of Korea
MUSIC: William H. Doane
Korean trans. © The Christian Literature Society of Korea

MORE LOVE TO THEE
64.64.66.44

319

부름 받아 나선 이 몸
Call'd of God, We Honor the Call

1. 부 름 받 아 나 선 이 몸 어 디 든 지
2. 아 골 골 짝 빈 들 에 도 복 음 들 고
3. 존 귀 영 광 모 든 권 세 주 님 홀 로

1. Call'd of God, we hon-or the call; Lord, we'll go wher-
2. Ach-or's vale, or des-o-late waste, there we'd bear the
3. Hon-or, glo-ry, pow-er and praise, Lord, to you, you

가 오 리 다 괴 로 우 나 즐 거 우 나
가 오 리 다 소 돔 같 은 거 리 에 도
받 으 소 서 멸 시 천 대 십 자 가 는

ev-er you say. Where you lead, come pain or plea-sure,
Gos-pel you gave, car-ry love through streets like Sod-om's
on-ly are due! Shame and scorn and cross you car-ried;

주 만 따 라 가 오 리 니 어 느 누 가 막 으 리 까
사 랑 안 고 찾 아 가 서 종 의 몸 에 지 닌 것 도
제 가 지 고 가 오 리 다 이 름 없 이 빛 도 없 이

we would fol-low you ev-'ry day. Who shall turn us back from you, Lord?
an-y-where, to seek and to save! Or a-gree a slave to be, Lord,
grant us grace to car-ry them too, with-out name or fame, but, oh, Lord,

WORDS: Ho Woon Lee (1 Cor. 4:1-2); English trans. John T. Underwood
MUSIC: Yoo Sun Lee
© The Korean Hymnal Society

CALLED OF GOD
8.8.8.8.

320

예수 따라가며
When We Walk with the Lord

WORDS: John H. Sammis (1 Jn. 1:7); Korean trans. The Christian Literature Society of Korea
MUSIC: Daniel B. Towner
Korean trans. © The Christian Literature Society of Korea

TRUST AND OBEY
669 D with Refrain

후렴 (Refrain)

의 지 하 고 순 종 하 는 길 은 예 수
Trust and o - bey, for there's no oth - er way to be

안 에 즐 겁 고 복 된 길 이 로 다
hap - py in Je - sus, but to trust and o - bey.

5. 주의 발 앞에서 깊이 친교하며
   주의 곁에서 걸어가리
   주를 의지하며 항상 순종하고
   명령 따라서 살아가리

5. Then in fellowship sweet
   we will sit at his feet,
   or we'll walk by his side in the way;
   what he says we will do,
   where he sends we will go; never fear,
   only trust and obey.

내 주되신 주를 참 사랑하고

WORDS: William R. Featherstone (Jn. 21:15); Korean trans. The United Methodist Korean Hymnal Committee
MUSIC: Adoniram J. Gordon
Korean trans. © 2001 The United Methodist Publishing House, admin. The Copyright Co.

GORDON
11 11.11 11

My Jesus, I Love Thee

1. My Je - sus, I love thee, I know thou art mine;
2. I love thee be - cause thou hast first lov - ed me,
3. I'll love thee in life, I will love thee in death;
4. In man - sions of glo - ry and end - less de - light,

for thee all the fol - lies of sin I re - sign.
and pur - chased my par - don on Cal - va - ry's tree.
and praise thee as long as thou lend - est me breath;
I'll ev - er a - dore thee in heav - en so bright;

my gra - cious Re - deem - er, my Sav - ior art thou;
I love thee for wear - ing the thorns on thy brow;
and say when the death - dew lies cold on my brow;
I'll sing with the glit - ter - ing crown on my brow;

if ev - er I loved thee, my Je - sus, 'tis now.
if ev - er I loved thee, my Je - sus, 'tis now.
if ev - er I loved thee, my Je - sus, 'tis now.
if ev - er I loved thee, my Je - sus, 'tis now.

WORDS: William R. Featherstone (Jn. 21:15)
MUSIC: Adoniram J. Gordon

GORDON
11 11.11 11

주 크신 사랑 가운데

1. 주 크 신 사 랑 가 운 데 – 내 곤 한
2. 늘 함 께 하 는 주 의 빛 – 내 내 어 둔 의
3. 나 고 통 당 할 때 에 도 – 주 나 의
4. 날 위 해 지 신 십 자 가 – 나 어 찌

영 혼 쉬 리 라 – 내 삶 을 주 께 드 리 니 – 주
길 을 비 추 네 – 내 내 마 음 빛 을 찾 으 니 – 주
기 쁨 되 시 네 – 나 소 망 잃 지 않 으 니 – 주
주 를 떠 날 까 – 이 세 상 욕 심 버 리 니 – 그

사 랑 안 에 더 욱 풍 성 하 게 하 소 서
광 명 안 에 더 욱 밝 아 지 게 하 하 시 리
약 속 하 신 대 로 밝 은 아 침 주 시 리 서
영 원 하 신 생 명 주 여 내 게 주 소 서

WORDS: George Matheson; Korean trans. The United Methodist Korean Hymnal Committee
MUSIC: Albert L. Peace
Korean trans. © 2001 The United Methodist Publishing House, admin. The Copyright Co.

ST. MARGARET
88.8886

O Love That Wilt Not Let Me Go

1. O Love that wilt not let me go, I rest my
2. O Light that fol-lowest all my way, I yield my
3. O Joy that seek-est me through pain, I can - not
4. O Cross that lift - est up my head, I dare not

wea-ry soul in thee; I give thee back the life I owe, that
flick-ering torch to thee; my heart re - stores its bor-rowed ray, that
close my heart to thee; I trace the rain-bow thru the rain, and
ask to fly from thee; I lay in dust life's glo-ry dead, and

in thine o - cean depths its flow may rich-er, full - er be.
in thy sun-shine's blaze its day may bright-er fair - er be.
feel the prom-ise is not vain, that morn shall tear - less be.
from the ground there blos-soms red life that shall end - less be.

WORDS: George Matheson
MUSIC: Albert L. Peace

ST. MARGARET
88.886

323

주 사랑해
I Love the Lord, Who Heard My Cry

1. 주 사 랑 해 - 내 눈 - 물 과 -
2. 주 사 랑 해 - 내 눈 - 물 과 -
1. I love the Lord, who heard my cry
2. I love the Lord, who heard my cry

내 - 아 픔 아 신 주 나 의 -
내 - 슬 픔 씻 긴 주 기 도 -
and pit-ied ev-ery groan. Long
and chased my grief a-way. O

삶 에 며 - 시 련 올 때 -
하 며 - 사 는 동 안 -
as I live and trou-bles rise,
let my heart no more de-spair

주 께 로 향 하 으 리 -
절 망 치 않 하 으 리 -
I'll has-ten to God's throne.
while I have breath to pray.

WORDS: African American spiritual (Ps. 116:1-2); Korean trans. The United Methodist Korean Hymnal Committee
MUSIC: African American spiritual; adapt. and arr. Lonnie Goode
Adapt. and Korean trans. © 2001 The United Methodist Publishing House, admin. The Copyright Co.; arr. © 2001 Abingdon Press

고요한 안식 있는 곳
There Is a Place of Quiet Rest

1. 고 요 한 안 식 있 는 곳 하 나 님 품 일 세
2. 따 뜻 한 위 로 있 는 곳 하 나 님 품 일 세
3. 완 전 한 자 유 있 는 곳 하 나 님 품 일 세

1. There is a place of qui-et rest, near to the heart of God;
2. There is a place of come-fort sweet, near to the heart of God;
3. There is a place of full re-lease, near to the heart of God;

죄 괴 롭 힘 이 없 는 곳 하 나 님 품 일 세
내 구 주 별 수 있 는 곳 하 나 님 품 일 세
기 쁨 과 평 화 가 득 한 하 나 님 품 일 세

a place where sin can-not mo-lest, near to the heart of God.
a place where we our Sav-ior meet, near to the heart of God.
a place where all is joy and peace, near to the heart of God.

후렴 (Refrain)

오 예 수 복 된 구 주 하 나 님 선 물

O Je-sus, blest Re-deem-er, sent from the heart of God,

주 님 의 품 에 우 리 안 아 주 소 서

hold us who wait be-fore thee near to the heart of God.

WORDS: Cleland B. McAfee; Korean trans. The United Methodist Korean Hymnal Committee
MUSIC: Cleland B. McAfee
Korean trans. © 2001 The United Methodist Publishing House, admin. The Copyright Co.

McAFEE
CM with Refrain

우리의 삶을 주관하시는 주

1. 우 리 의 삶 을 주관하시 는 주 하 나 님
2. 전 에 도 항 상 동행하신 주 함 께 하 사 리
3. 우 리 의 앞 길 알지못해 도 주 따 르 리

지 나 간 세 월 지켜주신 주 의 지 하 리 서
약 속 의 땅 과 소망의 길 로 이 끄 소 서
피 난 처 되 신 우리하나 님 도 우 소 서

새 로 운 아 침 맞 을 때 마 다 니
축 복 의 아 침 식 내 려 주 시 고
일 용 할 양 식 내 려 주 시 고

주 믿 신 자 길 비 을 내 려 주 시 이 리 네
주 음 향 집 에 인 도 하 소 서

WORDS: Hugh Thomas Kerr; alt.; Korean trans. The United Methodist Korean Hymnal Committee
MUSIC: Charles Henry Purday; harm. John Weaver
Words © 1928 F. M. Braselman; renewed 1956, Korean trans. © 2001 Presbyterian Board of Christian Education;
harm. © 1990 Hope Publishing Co.

SANDON
10.4.10.4.10.10

God of Our Life

1. God of our life, thru all the cir-cling years, we trust in thee;
2. God of the past, our times are in thy hand; with us a - bide.
3. God of the com - ing years, thru paths un- known we fol - low thee;

in all the past, thru all our hopes and fears; thy hand we see.
Lead us by faith to hope's true prom-ised land; be thou our guide.
when we are strong, Lord, leave us not a - lone; our ref - uge be.

With each new day, when morn - ing lifts the veil,
With thee to bless, the dark - ness shines as light,
Be thou for us in life our dai - ly bread,

we own thy mer - cies, Lord, which nev- er fail.
and faith's fair vi - sion chan- ges in - to sight.
our heart's true home when all our years have sped.

WORDS: Hugh Thomas Kerr; alt.
MUSIC: Charles Henry Purday; harm. John Weaver
Words © 1928 F. M. Braselman; renewed 1956 Presbyterian Board of Christian Education;
harm. © 1990 Hope Publishing Co.

SANDON
10.4.10.4.10.10

326

주여 바로 접니다
It's Me, It's Me, O Lord

WORDS: African American spiritual; Korean trans. The United Methodist Korean Hymnal Committee
MUSIC: African American spiritual; arr. William Farley Smith
Arr. © 1989, Korean trans. © 2001 The United Methodist Publishing House, admin. The Copyright Co.

PENITENT
Irr.

2. 목사님도 집사님도 아닌 접니다 기도해야 할 사람
3. 아버지도 어머니도 아닌 접니다 기도해야 할 사람

2. Not the preacher, not the deacon,
3. Not my father, not my mother,

주님의 뜻을 이루소서

WORDS: Adelaide A. Pollard (Jer. 18:6); Korean trans. The Christian Literature Society of Korea
MUSIC: George C. Stebbins
Koean trans. © The Christian Literature Society of Korea

ADELAIDE
54.54. D

Have Thine Own Way, Lord!

1. Have thine own way, Lord! Have thine own way!
2. Have thine own way, Lord! Have thine own way!
3. Have thine own way, Lord! Have thine own way!
4. Have thine own way, Lord! Have thine own way!

Thou art the pot - ter; I am the clay.
Search me and try me, Sav - ior to - day!
Wound - ed and wea - ry, help me I pray!
Hold o'er my be - ing ab - so - lute sway!

Mold me and make me af - ter thy will,
Wash me just now, Lord, wash me just now,
Pow - er, all pow - er, sure - ly is thine!
Fill with thy Spir - it till all shall see

while I am wait - ing, yield - ed and still.
as in thy pres - ence hum - bly I bow.
Touch me and heal me, Sav - ior di - vine!
Christ on - ly, al - ways, liv - ing in me!

WORDS: Adelaide A. Pollard (Jer. 18:6)
MUSIC: George C. Stebbins

ADELAIDE
54.54. D

우리를 고쳐주소서

WORDS: William Cowper (Mk. 9:14-27; Mt. 9:20-22; Mk. 5:25-34; Lk.8:43-48);
Korean trans. The United Methodist Korean Hymnal Committee
MUSIC: Johann Crüger
Korean trans. © 2001 The United Methodist Publishing House, admin. The Copyright Co.

GRÄFENBERG
CM

Heal Us, Emmanuel, Hear Our Prayer 328

1. Heal us, Emmanuel, hear our prayer; we wait to feel thy touch; deep-wounded souls to thee repair, and Savior, we are such.
2. Our faith is feeble, we confess we faintly trust thy word; but wilt thou pity us the less? Be that far from thee, Lord!
3. Remember him who once applied with trembling for relief; "Lord, I believe," with tears he cried; "O help my unbelief!"
4. She, too, who touched thee in the press and healing virtue stole, was answered, "Daughter, go in peace: thy faith hath made thee whole."
5. Like her, with hopes and fears we come to touch thee if we may; O send us not despairing home; send none unhealed away.

WORDS: William Cowper (Mk. 9:14-27; Mt. 9:20-22; Mk. 5:25-34; Lk.8:43-48)
MUSIC: Johann Crüger

GRÄFENBERG
CM

나는 비록 약하나

WORDS: African American spiritual (2 Cor. 12:9-10);
Korean trans. The United Methodist Korean Hymnal Committee
MUSIC: African American spiritual
Korean trans. © 2001 The United Methodist Publishing House, admin. The Copyright Co.

CLOSER WALK
Irr.

I Am Weak But Thou Art Strong

329

(Just a Closer Walk with Thee)

1. I am weak but thou art strong;
2. Thro' this world of toil and snares,
3. When my fee - ble life is o'er,

Refrain Just a clos - er walk with thee,

Je - sus, keep me from all wrong;
if I fal - ter, Lord, who cares?
time for me will be no more;

grant it, Je - sus, is my plea,

I'll be sat - is - fied as long
Who with me my bur - den shares?
guide me gent - ly, safe - ly o'er

dai - ly, walk - ing close to thee,

D. C. for Refrain

as I walk, let me walk close to thee.
None but thee, dear Lord, none but thee.
to thy king - dom shore, to thy shore.

let it be, dear Lord, let it be.

WORDS: African American spiritual (2 Cor. 12:9-10)
MUSIC: African American spiritual

CLOSER WALK
Irr.

내 기도하는 그 시간

WORDS: William Walford; Korean trans. The United Methodist Korean Hymnal Committee
MUSIC: William B. Bradbury
Korean trans. © 2001 The United Methodist Publishing House, admin. The Copyright Co.

SWEET HOUR
LMD

330

Sweet Hour of Prayer

1. Sweet hour of prayer! Sweet hour of prayer! That
2. Sweet hour of prayer! Sweet hour of prayer! The
3. Sweet hour of prayer! Sweet hour of prayer! Thy
4. Sweet hour of prayer! Sweet hour of prayer! Our

calls me from a world of care,
joys I feel, the bliss I share
wings shall my pe - ti - tion bear
Lord him - self knew glad - ness there;

and bids me at my Fa - ther's throne make
of those whose anx - ious spir - its burn with
to him whose truth and faith - ful - ness en -
and of - ten-times, when thronged a - bout, would

all my wants and wish - es known.
strong de - sires for thy re - turn!
gage the wait - ing soul to bless.
slip a - way and seek it out,

WORDS: William Walford
MUSIC: William B. Bradbury

SWEET HOUR
LMD

331

나를 보내소서
Send Me, Lord

인도자 (*Leader*)

보 내소서
Send me, Lord.

다같이 (*All*)

1. 나를 보내 소 서 주 여, 나를
   이 끄 소 서 주 여, 나를
   채 우 소 서 주 여, 나를

1. Send me, Je-sus, send me, Je - sus, send me,
   Je-sus, lead me, Je - sus, lead me,
   Je-sus, fill me, Je - sus, fill me,

1~2　　　　3

2. 이 끄소 서
3. 채 우소 서
2. Lead me, Lord.
3. Fill me, Lord.

1~2　　　　3

보 내 주 소 서 2. 나 를
인 도 하 소 서 3. 나 를
채 워 주 소　　　　　　　서
Je-sus,　send me,　Lord.　2. Lead me,
Je-sus,　lead me,　Lord.　3. Fill me,
Je-sus,　fill me,　　　　　Lord.

WORDS: Trad. South African (Is. 6:8); Korean trans. The United Methodist Korean Hymnal Committee
MUSIC: Trad. South African
© 1984, Korean trans. © 2001 Utryck

THUMA MINA
Irr.

여기 오소서
Kum Ba Yah
(Come by Here)

1. 여 기 오 소 서 내 주 여 여 기
1. Kum ba yah, my Lord, kum ba yah. Kum ba

오 소 서 내 주 여 여 기 오 소 서
yah, my Lord, kum ba yah. Kum ba yah, my Lord,

내 주 여 오 주 여 오 소 서
kum ba yah Oh, Lord, kum ba yah!

2. 기도 드리네 주님께
3. 울며 외치네 주님께
4. 도와 주소서 내 주여
5. 노래 부르네 주님께
6. 찬양 드리세 주님께

2. Someone's praying, Lord.
3. Someone's crying, Lord.
4. Someone needs you, Lord.
5. Someone's singing, Lord.
6. Let us praise the Lord.

WORDS: African American spiritual; Korean trans. The United Methodist Korean Hymnal Committee
MUSIC: African American spiritual; harm. Carlton R. Young
© 1989, Korean trans. © 2001 The United Methodist Publishing House, admin. The Copyright Co.

DESMOND
Irr.

333

죄짐 맡은 우리 구주

1. 죄 짐맡은우리구 주 어 찌좋은친 군 지
2. 시 험걱정모든괴 롬 없 는사람누 군 가
3. 근 심걱정무거운짐 아 니진자누 군 가

걱 정근심무거운 짐 우 리주께맡 기 세
우 리낙심하지말 고 기 도드려아 뢰 세
피 난처는우리예 수 주 께기도드 리 세

아 픈상처위로하 며 평 화내려주 시 니 까
이 런진실하신친 구 어 디다시있 을 까
세 상친구멸시하 고 너 를조롱하 여 도

우 리주께기도하 여 모 든짐을맡 기 세
우 리약함아시오 니 주 께기도드 리 세
예 수품에안기어 서 참 된위로받 겠 네

WORDS: Joseph M. Scriven (Jn. 16:23); Korean trans. The United Methodist Korean Hymnal Committee
MUSIC: Charles C. Converse
Korean trans. © 2001 The United Methodist Publishing House, admin. The Copyright Co.

CONVERSE
87.87. D

What a Friend We Have in Jesus

333

1. What a friend we have in Je - sus, all our sins and griefs to bear!
2. Have we tri - als and temp - ta - tions? Is there trou - ble an - y - where?
3. Are we weak and heav - y la - den, cum - bered with a load of care?

What a priv - i - lege to car - ry ev - 'ry-thing to God in prayer!
We should nev - er be dis - cour - aged; take it to the Lord in prayer.
Pre - cious Sav - ior, still our ref - uge; take it to the Lord in prayer.

O what peace we of - ten for - feit, O what need-less pain we bear,
Can we find a friend so faith - ful who will all our sor-rows share?
Do thy friends de-spise, for-sake thee? Take it to the Lord in prayer!

all be-cause we do not car - ry ev - 'ry-thing to God in prayer.
Je - sus knows our ev - ry weak - ness; take it to the Lord in prayer.
In his arms he'll take and shield thee; thou wilt find a sol-ace there.

WORDS: Joseph M. Scriven (Jn. 16:23)
MUSIC: Charles C. Converse

CONVERSE
87.87. D

334

주 예수여 은혜를

WORDS: Anonymous
MUSIC: Anonymous

HEART LONGINGS
11.8.11.8. with Refrain

후렴

주 예 수 여 충 만 한 은 혜

내 영 혼 에 부 으 소 서 -

주 예 수 만 나 의 힘 되 고

내 만 족 함 됩 니 다 -

334   Heart Longings, Lord Jesus

1. Heart long - ings, Lord Je - sus, I lift to the throne:
2. Lord Je - sus, break from me the bonds of my sin,
3. Lord Je - sus, grant faith such as Ja - cob's that night,
4. Lord Je - sus, let love like the love in thy heart
5. Lord Je - sus, I know that thy Spir - it, who came

for grace, and for full - ness of soul;
that I may be pure, ev - 'ry part;
to wres - tle in pray'r and not cease;
be mine with-out let or al - loy
to live in my heart, there will dwell.

while, hun - gry and thirst - y, my heart asks a - lone
let earth - ly de - ceits have no lodg - ing with - in,
and though the world's bil - lows mount high in their might,
un - til I am fill'd to the ut - ter-most part,
Now grant the great gift in the strength of thy name

thy Spir - it, pour'd forth to make whole.
no crev - ice to hide in my heart.
still grant me the gift of thy peace.
to live in thy love and thy joy.
that I may but serve my Lord well.

WORDS: Anonymous; trans. John T. Underwood
MUSIC: Anonymous

HEART LONGINGS
11.8.11.8. with Refrain

Refrain

Lord Je - sus, grant grace in its full - ness

brim - full in my heart to be pour'd;

thou only my st - rength and my whole - ness,

thou, thou art my plen - ty, Lord!

335

둥지 안의 새들
Children of the Heavenly Father

1. 둥지 안의 새들 보시나니 하늘
2. 주가 친히 돌보심이나 믿음의
3. 생명이거나 죽음보심이나 주버리
4. 주시거나 취하시나 버리

1. Chil-dren of the heaven-ly Fa - ther safe-ly
2. God his own doth tend and nour-ish; in his
3. Nei-ther life nor death shall ev - er from the
4. Though he giv - eth or he tak-eth, God his

위으로 별들라보나다네 하나님에 자녀키
의로 사랑끊지않으못해네 죄악신은의서지베거
시지 않으시네 순결하 고 거룩

in his bos-om gath - er; nest-ling bird nor star in
ho - ly courts they flour - ish; from all e - vil thing she
Lord his chil-dren sev - er, un - to them his grace he
chil dren ne'er for - sak - eth; his the lov - ing pur-pose

들 을 주님품에 안으 시 네
시고며 강우지키시기아시도다
하게 키시시기 원하시네

heav - en such a ref - uge e'er was giv - en.
spares them; in his might - y arms she bears them.
show - eth, and their sor - rows all he know - eth.
sole - ly to pre - serve them pure and ho - ly.

WORDS: Caroline V. Sandell-Berg; English trans. Ernest W. Olson;
Korean trans. The United Methodist Korean Hymnal Committee
MUSIC: Swedish melody
Words © 1925, renewed 1953, Korean trans. © 2001 Board of Publication,
Lutheran Church in America, admin. Augsburg Fortress

TRYGARE KAN INGEN VARA
88.88

아이들아 주를 찬송하라
Praise Him, All Ye Little Children

1. 아 이 들 아   주 를 찬 송 하 라
1. Praise him, praise him, all ye lit-tle chil-dren,

사 랑 의   하 나 님
God is love, God is love;

아 이 들 아   주 를 찬 송 하 라
praise him, praise him, all ye lit-tle chil-dren,

사 랑 의   하 나 님
God is love, God is love.

2. 아이들아 주를 사랑하라

3. 아이들아 주께 감사하라

2. Love him, love him, all ye little children,
God is love, God is love;

3. Thank him, thank him, all ye little children,
God is love, God is love;

WORDS: Anonymous (Mt. 21:16); Korean trans. The United Methodist Korean Hymnal Committee
MUSIC: Carey Bonner
Korean trans. © 2001 The United Methodist Publishing House, admin. The Copyright Co.

BONNER
10.6.10.6.

세상 모든 어린이를
Jesus Loves the Little Children

WORDS: C. H. Woolston, alt.; Korean trans. The United Methodist Korean Hymnal Committee
MUSIC: George F. Root
Word alt. © 1991, Korean trans. © 2001 Broadman Press

CHILDREN
Irr.

이 작은 나의 빛
This Little Light of Mine

1. 이 작은 나 의 빛 - 비 추 게 하 리 라
1. This lit-tle light of mine, I'm goin'-a let it shine,

이 작은 나 의 빛 - 비 추 게 하 리 라
this lit-tle light of mine, I'm goin'-a let it shine;

이 작은 나 의 빛 - 비 추 게 하 리 라
this lit-tle light of mine, I'm goin'-a let it shine,

비 추 리 비 추 리 비 추 리 (비 추 리)
let it shine, let it shine, let it shine. (let it shine)

2. 나 어디 가든지　　　2. Everywhere I go

3. 온 밤이 새도록　　　3. All through the night

WORDS: African American spiritual (Mt. 5:14-16); Korean trans. The United Methodist Korean Hymnal Committee
MUSIC: African American spiritual; adapt. William Farley Smith
Adapt. © 1989, Korean trans. © 2001 The United Methodist Publishing House, admin. The Copyright Co.

LATTIMER
Irr.

사철에 봄바람 불어 잇고

WORDS: Young Taik Chun
MUSIC: Doo Hoe Koo
© The Korean Hymnal Society

후렴

고 마 와 라　　임 마 누 엘

예 - 수 만 섬 기 는 우 리 집

고 마 와 라　　임 마 누 엘

복 - 되 고 즐 거 운 하 루 하 - 루

339

All Year in Our Home

1. All year in our home the spring breez-es blow,
2. Our par-ents, gen-tle with strong, ten-der care!
3. Our house-hold, work-ing till all work is done,

since God our Fa-ther a-bides with us here.
Bro-ther and sis-ter, love-link'd from our youth!
mor-ning and ev'n-ing in love and good cheer;

Firm faith the bed-rock un-shak-en be-low,
Here where all griev-ing and glad-ness we share,
one ta-ble, with food and drink shar'd as one

our home's a gar-den of glad-ness all year.
one thatch-roof room, and it's heav-en in truth.
this is our Gar-den of E-den right here!

WORDS: Young Taik Chun; English trans. John T. Underwood
MUSIC: Doo Hoe Koo
© The Korean Hymnal Society

Refrain

How we thank him, Im - man - u - el!

Our home his, his, to serve Christ al - way!

How we thank him, Im - man - u - el!

Such joy and bless - ed-ness, day up - on day!

주 말씀 배우는 믿음의 가정

WORDS: Baylus Benjamin McKinney; Korean trans. The United Methodist Korean Hymnal Committee
MUSIC: Baylus Benjamin McKinney
Korean trans. © 2001 The United Methodist Publishing House, admin. The Copyright Co.

CHRISTIAN HOME
Irr.

God, Give Us Christian Homes

1. God, give us Chris - tian homes! Homes where the Bi - ble is
2. God, give us Chris - tian homes! Homes where the fa - ther is
3. God, give us Chris - tian homes! Homes where the moth-er, in
4. God, give us Chris - tian homes! Homes where the chil-dren are

loved and taught, homes where the Mas - ter's will is sought,
true and strong, homes that are free from the blight of wrong,
car - ing quest, strives to show oth - ers your way is best,
led to know Christ in his beau - ty who loves them so,

homes crowned with beau-ty your love has wrought; God, give us
homes that are joy - ous with love and song; God, give us
homes where the Lord is an hon - ored guest; God, give us
homes where the al - tar fires burn and glow; God, give us

Chris - tian homes; God, give us Chris - tian homes!
Chris - tian homes; God, give us Chris - tian homes!
Chris - tian homes; God, give us Chris - tian homes!
Chris - tian homes; God, give us Chris - tian homes!

WORDS: Baylus Benjamin McKinney
MUSIC: Baylus Benjamin McKinney

CHRISTIAN HOME
Irr.

천사처럼 말하여서

1. 천 사 처 럼 – 말 하 여 서 – 감 동 케 할 – 힘 있 어 도 – 사 랑 없 인 – 헛 되 리 라 – 소 리 나 는 – 징 과 같 네 라
2. 나 가 진 것 – 내 어 주 고 – 나 의 사 랑 – 고 백 해 도 – 사 랑 없 이 – 내 어 주 면 – 아 무 유 익 – 없 으 리 라
3. 성 령 이 여 – 우 리 영 을 – 온 전 하 게 – 주 장 하 사 – 사 랑 으 로 – 예 배 하 며 – 자 유 얻 게 – 하 옵 소 서

WORDS: Hal Hopson (1 Cor. 13:1-3); Korean trans. The United Methodist Korean Hymnal Committee
MUSIC: Trad. English melody; adapt. Hal Hopson
© 1972, Korean trans. © 2001 Hope Publishing Co.

GIFT OF LOVE
LM

Though I May Speak with Bravest Fire

341

1. Though I may speak with brav-est fire,
   and have the gift to all in - spire,
   and have not love, my words are vain,
   as sound-ing brass, and hope-less gain.

2. Though I may give all I pos - sess,
   and striv-ing so my love pro - fess,
   but not be given by love with - in,
   the prof - it soon turn strange-ly thin.

3. Come, Spir-it, come, our hearts con - trol,
   our spir - its long to be made whole.
   Let in-ward love guide ev - ery deed;
   by this we wor - ship, and are freed.

WORDS: Hal Hopson (1 Cor. 13:1-3)
MUSIC: Trad. English melody; adapt. Hal Hopson
© 1972 Hope Publishing Co.

GIFT OF LOVE
LM

예수 사랑하심은

WORDS: St. 1 Anna B. Warner; sts. 2-3 David Rutherford McGuire;
Korean trans. The United Methodist Korean Hymnal Committee
MUSIC: William B. Bradbury
Korean trans. © 2001 The United Methodist Publishing House, admin. The Copyright Co.

JESUS LOVES ME
77.77 with Refrain

Jesus Loves Me

1. Je - sus loves me! This I know, for the Bi - ble tells me so.
2. Je - sus loves me! He who died heav-en's gate to o - pen wide;
3. Je - sus loves me! Loves me still, though I'm ver - y weak and ill;
4. Je - sus loves me! He will stay close be-side me all the way;

Lit - tle ones to him be - long; they are weak but he is strong.
he will wash a - way my sin, let his lit - tle child come in.
from his shin-ing throne on high comes to watch me whence I lie.
if I love him, when I die he will take me home on high.

Refrain

Yes, Je - sus loves me! Yes, Je - sus loves me!

Yes, Je - sus loves me! The Bi - ble tells me so.

WORDS: St. 1 Anna B. Warner; sts. 2-3 David Rutherford McGuire
MUSIC: William B. Bradbury

JESUS LOVES ME
77.77 with Refrain

사랑하고 바라면서

WORDS: Brian Wren; Korean trans. The United Methodist Korean Hymnal Committee
MUSIC: Trad. English melody; adapt. Hal Hopson
Words © 1983, Korean trans. © 2001 Hope Publishing Co.; music © 1972 Hope Publishing Co.

GIFT OF LOVE
LM

When Love Is Found

1. When love is found and hope comes home,
2. When love has flowered in trust and care,
3. When love is tried as loved ones change,
4. When love is torn and trust be - trayed,
5. Praise God for love, praise God for life,

sing and be glad that two are one.
build both each day, that love may dare
hold still to hope though all seems strange,
pray strength to love till tor - ments fade,
in age or youth, in hus - band, wife.

When love ex - plodes and fills the sky,
to reach be - yond home's warmth and light,
till ease re - turns, and love grows wise
till lov - ers keep no score of wrong,
Lift up your hearts, let love be fed

praise God and share our Mak - er's joy.
to serve and strive for truth and right.
through lis - tening ears and o - pened eyes.
but hear through pain love's Eas - ter song.
through death and life in bro - ken bread.

WORDS: Brian Wren
MUSIC: Trad. English melody; adapt. Hal Hopson
Words © 1983 Hope Publishing Co.; music © 1972 Hope Publishing Co.

GIFT OF LOVE
LM

344

예수 우리 참된 기쁨
Jesus, Joy of Our Desiring

1. 예 수 우 리 참 된 기 쁨
2. 소 망 따 라 가 는 길 에

1. Je - sus, joy of our de - sir - ing,
2. Through the way where hope is guid - ing,

하 늘 지 혜 귀 한 사 랑
평 화 로 운 찬 미 소 리

ho - ly wis - dom, love most bright;
hark, what peace - ful mu - sic rings;

영 원 하 신 참 빛 으 로
주 따 르 는 양 의 무 리

drawn by thee, our souls as - pir - ing
where the flock, in thee con - fid - ing

우 리 영 혼 이 끄 시 네
생 명 샘 물 마 시 겠 네

soar to un - cre - at - ed light.
drink of joy from death - less springs.

WORDS: Martin Janus; English trans. anonymous;
Korean trans. The United Methodist Korean Hymnal Committee
MUSIC: Johann Schop; arr. J. S. Bach
Korean trans. © 2001 The United Methodist Publishing House, admin. The Copyright Co.

JESU, JOY OF MAN'S DESIRING
87.87.88.77

345

아주 먼 옛날
Very Long Ago Up in Heav'n Above

아 주 먼 옛 날 - 하 늘 에 서 - 는
하 나 님 께 - 서 - 바 라 보 시 - 고
Ve - ry long a - go up in heav'n a - bove
God looked at the world made so long a - go

당 신 을 향 - 한 - 계 획 있 었 - 죠
좋 았 더 라 - 고 - 말 씀 하 셨 - 네
came a spe - cial plan that was just for you,
and God said, "How good that I made you, too,

이 세 상
this world that

그 무 엇 - 보 - 다 - 귀 하 게 - 나 의
I have made, in my own way I

손 으 로 - 창 조 하 였 - 노 - 라 -
love and val - ue more than I can say

WORDS: Tae-hyuk Chun and Kyong Chun; English trans. Edward Poitras
MUSIC: Tae-hyuk Chun and Kyong Chun
© Tae-hyuk Chun and Kyong Chun; English trans. © 2001 The United Methodist Publishing House

VERY LONG AGO
Irr.

주 안의 깊은 평안

WORDS: Charles Wesley; Korean trans. The United Methodist Korean Hymnal Committee
MUSIC: Att. Dimitri S. Bortniansky
Korean trans. © 2001 The United Methodist Publishing House, admin. The Copyright Co.

ST. PETERSBURG
88.88.88

Thou Hidden Source of Calm Repose 346

1. Thou hid - den source of calm re - pose, thou all suf - fi - cient
2. Thy might - y name sal - va - tion is, and keeps my hap - py
3. Je - sus, my all in all thou art, my rest in toil, my
4. In want my plen - ti - ful sup - ply, in weak - ness my al -

love di - vine, my help and ref - uge from my foes, se -
soul a - bove; com - fort it brings, and power and peace, and
ease in pain, the heal - ing of my bro - ken heart, in
might - y power, in bonds my per - fect lib - er - ty, my

cure I am if thou art mine; and lo! from sin and
joy and ev - er - last - ing love; to me with thy dear
war my peace, in loss my gain, my smile be - neath the
light in Sa - tan's dark - est hour, in grief my joy un -

grief and shame I hide me, Je - sus, in thy name.
name are given par - don and ho - li - ness and heaven.
ty - rant's frown, in shame my glo - ry and my crown.
speak - a - ble, my life in death, my heaven in hell.

WORDS: Charles Wesley
MUSIC: Att. Dimitri S. Bortniansky

ST. PETERSBURG
88.88.88

347

우리 다시 만날 때까지
God Be with You till We Meet Again

우리 다시 만날 때 까지

1. 주　　님
2. 날　　개
3. 위　　태
4. 사　　랑

God be with you till we meet a-gain;

1. by his
2. neath his
3. when life's
4. keep love's

너　를 인 도 - 하 며　안 전 하 게　보 내 리 -
아　래 품 으 - 시 고　하 늘 만 나　내 내 리 -
한　일 당 할 - 때 에　주 의 팔 로　안 아 -
으　로 지 키 - 시 며　죽 음 권 세　물 리 -

coun - sels guide, up - hold you, with his sheep se - cure - ly
wings se - cure - ly hide you, dai - ly man - na still pro -
per - ils thick con - found you, put his arms us - fail - ing
ban - ner float - ing o'er you, smite death's threat-ening wave be -

하　　사
시　　며 사
주　　치
하　　고

함 께 하 시 기 를 바 라 네

fold you;
vide you;
round you;
fore you;

God be with you till we meet a - gain.

WORDS: Jeremiah E. Rankin; Korean trans. The United Methodist Korean Hymnal Committee
MUSIC: Ralph Vaughan Williams
Korean trans. © 2001 The United Methodist Publishing House, admin. The Copyright Co.;
music © Oxford University Press

RANDOLPH
98.89

주 성전 안에
The Lord Is in His Holy Temple

주 성 전 안에 계 시 도 - 다 주 성 전 안에 계 시
The Lord is in his ho-ly tem - ple, the Lord is in his ho-ly

도 - 다 온 땅은 잠 잠 하 라 온 땅은 잠 잠 하 라 주
tem - ple; let all the earth keep si-lence, let all the earth keep si-lence be-

앞 에 잠 잠 해 잠 잠 해 주 앞 - 에
fore him, keep si-lence, keep si-lence be-fore him.

WORDS: Habakkuk 2:20; Korean trans. The United Methodist Korean Hymnal Committee
MUSIC: George F. Root
Korean trans. © 2001 The United Methodist Publishing House, admin. The Copyright Co.

QUAM DILECTA
Irr.

349

자비 베푸소서
Lord, Have Mercy

자 비 베 푸 소 서   자 비 베 푸 소 서
Ky - ri - e   e - lei - son.   Ky - ri - e   e - lei - son.

주 여 자 비 베 - 푸 소 서
Ky - ri - e   e - le - - i - son.

350

주여 자비 베푸소서
Kyrie Eleison

주 여 자 비 베 푸 소 서
Ky - ri - e,   Ky - ri - e,   e - le - i - son.

창조주 하나님께
Glory to God, the Creator

창 조 주 하 나 님 께 성 자 와 성 령
Glo - ry to God, the Cre - a - tor, the Son, and the

님 - 께 - 영 광 할 렐 루 -
Ho - ly Spir - it. Hal - le - lu -

야 할 렐 루 - - 야 할 렐 루
jah, Hal - le - lu - jah, Hal - le - lu -

야 아 - - 멘
jah! A - - men.

WORDS: Carol Ann Bradley; Korean trans. The United Methodist Korean Hymnal Committee
MUSIC: Carol Ann Bradley
Korean trans. © 2001 The United Methodist Publishing House, admin. The Copyright Co.; music © Carol Ann Bradley

352

만복의 근원 하나님
Praise God, from Whom All Blessings Flow

Unison

만 복 의 근 원 하 나 님 만 물 아
Praise God, from whom all bless-ings flow; praise God, all

Harmony

찬 양 하 여 라 알 렐 루 야 알 렐 루 야
crea-tures here be - low; Al - le - lu - ia! Al - le - lu - ia!

Unison

복 주 시 는 주 하 나 님 힘 주 시
Praise God, the source of all our gifts! Praise Je - sus

Harmony

는 주 예 수 님 주 의 성 령 찬 양 하 라
Christ, whose power up - lifts! Praise the Spir - it, Ho-ly Spir - it!

WORDS: Thomas Ken; adapt. Gilbert H. Vieira;
Korean trans. The United Methodist Korean Hymnal Committee
MUSIC: *Geistliche Kirchengesänge*, 1623; harm. Ralph Vaughan Williams
Adapt. © 1989, Korean trans. © 2001 The United Methodist Publishing House, admin. The Copyright Co.;
harm. © 1906 Oxford University Press

LASST UNS ERFREUEN
88.44.88 with Refrain

알 렐 루 야 알 렐 루 야 알 렐 루 야
Al-le - lu - ia! Al-le - lu - ia! Al-le-lu - ia!

기도 · 축복송

영광 영광
Gloria, Gloria

① ②
영 - 광 영 - 광 높 이계 신 주 께
Glo - ri - a, glo - ri - a, in ex-cel - sis De - o!

③ ④
영 - 광 영 - 광 알 렐 루 야 알 렐 루 야
Glo - ri - a, glo - ri - a, Al-le -lu -ia! Al-le-lu - ia!

돌림노래 (May be sung as a canon)

WORDS: Luke 2:14; Korean trans. The United Methodist Korean Hymnal Committee
MUSIC: Jacques Berthier and the Taizé Community
© 1979, Korean trans. © 2001 Les Presses de Taizé (France), admin. GIA Publications, Inc.

GLORIA CANON
Irr.

354

할렐루야
Heleluyan
(Alleluia)

할렐 루야 할렐루야 할렐 할렐 루 - 야
He - le - lu-yan, he - le - lu-yan; he - le, he - le - lu - yan;

할렐 루야 할렐루야 할렐할렐 루 - 야
he - le - lu - yan, he - le - lu - yan; he - le, he - le - lu - yan.

WORDS: Trad. Muscogee (Creek) Indian;
Korean trans. The United Methodist Korean Hymnal Committee
MUSIC: Trad. Muscogee (Creek) Indian; trans. Charles H. Webb
Trans. © 1989, Korean trans. © 2001 The United Methodist Publishing House, admin. The Copyright Co.

HELELUYAN
Irr.

355

알렐루야
Alleluia

1. 알 렐 루 야 알렐 루 야 알렐루 야 알렐 루 야
1. Al - le - lu - ia, al - le - lu - ia, al - le - lu - ia, al - le - lu - ia,

알렐 루 야 알렐 루 야 알렐루 야 알렐 루 야
al - le - lu - ia, al - le - lu - ia, al - le - lu - ia, al - le - lu - ia,

2. 구원의 주   2. He's my Savior
3. 주를 찬양   3. I will praise him

WORDS: Jerry Sinclair; Korean trans. The United Methodist Korean Hymnal Committee
MUSIC: Jerry Sinclair
© 1972, renewed 2000, Korean trans. © 2001 Manna Music, Inc.

ALLELUIA
Irr.

우리는 주님만 바라봅니다
Our Eyes Are on the Lord Jesus
(Occuli Nostri)

우 리 는 주 님 만 바 라 봅 니 다
Our eyes are on the Lord Je-sus, our Sa-vior.

언 제 나 주 님 만 바 라 봅 니 다
Our eyes are on the Lord Je-sus, our Sa-vior.

WORDS: Occuli nostri; Korean and English trans. The United Methodist Korean Hymnal Committee
MUSIC: The Community of Taizé
Trans. © 2001 The United Methodist Publishing House, admin. The Copyright Co.;
music © Les Presses de Taizé, admin. GIA Publications, Inc.

OCCULI NOSTRI
6.5.6.5

357

주여 나를 감동하게
Move Me

주 여 나 를 감 동 하 게 하 사
Move me, move me; move me to do thy will.

주 의 뜻 을 행 하 게 하 소 서
Move me, move me; move me to do thy will.

WORDS: Richard Alan Henderson; Korean trans. The United Methodist Korean Hymnal Committee
MUSIC: Richard Alan Henderson
© 1978, Korean trans. © 2001 Richard Alan Henderson

MOVE ME
Irr.

358

들으소서 우리 기도 드릴 때
Hear Us, O Lord

들 으소서 우리 기도드릴
Hear us, O Lord, as we come now in

때 기 쁨과고 통 함께나눌 때
prayer, shar - ing our joys, our trou-bles, and our cares.

WORDS: Don Besig and Nancy Price; Korean trans. The United Methodist Korean Hymnal Committee
MUSIC: Don Besig and Nancy Price
© 1988, Korean trans. © 2001 Harold Flammer Music, Inc.

도 우 소 서 주 의 말 씀 따 라 서 믿
Help us, O Lord, to be o - pen to your Word, and

음 으 로 살 게 하 소 서 아 멘
teach us to put our trust in you. A - men.

359

아멘
Amen

아 - 멘　　아 - 멘　　아 - 멘
A - men.　　A - men.　　A - men.

WORDS: Korean trans. The United Methodist Korean Hymnal Committee
MUSIC: Marty Haugen
Music © 1984, Korean trans. © 2001 GIA Publications, Inc.

360

주 앞에 바친 예물
Bless Thou the Gifts

주 앞 에 바 친 예 - 물 과 계
Bless thou the gifts our hands have brought; bless

획 한 모 - 든 일 들 을 주 께 서 축 복
thou the work our hearts have planned. Ours is the faith, the

하 - 시 고 뜻 대 - 로 인 - 도 하 소 서
will, the thought; the rest, O God, is in thy hand.

WORDS: Samuel Longfellow; Korean trans. The United Methodist Korean Hymnal Committee
MUSIC: Grenoble Antiphoner, 1753; adapt. Ralph Vaughan Williams; harm. Basil Harwood
Korean trans. © 2001 The United Methodist Publishing House, admin. The Copyright Co.;
adapt. © Oxford University Press

DEUS TUORUM MILITUM
LM

샬롬을 비네
Shalom to You

WORDS: Elise S. Eslinger; Korean trans. The United Methodist Korean Hymnal Committee
MUSIC: Anon.; harm. Carlton R. Young
Words © 1983, Korean trans. © 2001, harm. © 1989 The United Methodist Publishing House, admin. The Copyright Co.

SOMOS DEL SENOR
Irr.

362

샬롬 카베림
Shalom

1. 샬 롬 카베림 샬 롬카베림 샬 롬 샬 롬
2. 안 녕 친구여 안 녕친구여 안 녕 안 녕
1. Sha - lom cha-ve-rim, sha - lom cha-ve-rim. Sha - lom, sha - lom.
2. Fare - well, dear friends, stay safe, dear friends, have peace, have peace.

레 힛 라 옷 레 힛 라 옷 샬 롬 샬 롬
다 시 만 나 리 다 시 만 나 리 안 녕 안 녕
Le - hit - ra - ot, le - hit - ra - ot, sha - lom, sha - lom.
We'll see you a-gain, we'll see you a-gain, have peace, have peace.

돌림노래 (May be sung as a canon)

WORDS: Trad. Hebrew blessing; English trans. Roger N. Deschner;
Korean trans. The United Methodist Korean Hymnal Committee
MUSIC: Israeli melody
English trans. © 1982, Korean trans. © 2001 The United Methodist Publishing House, admin. The Copyright Co.

SHALOM
Irr.

363

주 안에서 평안하라
Go Now in Peace

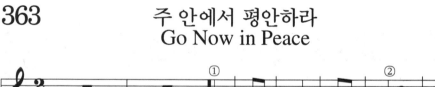

Keyboard, handbells,
and/or Orff instruments

주 안에서 평 안하라 주 의 사 랑
Go now in peace, go now in peace, may the love of

함 께 하 - 사 어 디 를 가 든 지 평 안 해
God sur-round you ev -'ry-where, ev -'ry-where you may go.

(⌢) Fine

돌림노래 (May be sung as a canon)

WORDS: Natalie Sleeth (Lk. 2:29); Korean trans. The United Methodist Korean Hymnal Committee
MUSIC: Natalie Sleeth
© 1976, Korean trans. © 2001 Hinshaw Music, Inc.

GO IN PEACE
Irr.

예수 내 주여
Jesus, Remember Me

예 수　내 주 여　　그 나 라 에 임 하 실 때
Je-sus,　re-mem-ber me　when you come in-to your king-dom.

예 수　내 주 여　　나 를 기 억 하 옵 소 서
Je-sus,　re-mem-ber me　when you come in-to your king-dom.

WORDS: Luke 23:42; Korean trans. The United Methodist Korean Hymnal Committee
MUSIC: Jacques Berthier and the Taizé Community
Music © 1981, Korean trans. © 2001 Les Presses de Taizé (France), admin. GIA Publications, Inc.

REMEMBER ME
Irr.

365

주 예수의 크신 은혜
Grace, Love, and Peace Abide

주　예 수 의　크 신　은 혜 와　사
Grace, love,　and peace　a - bide,　now, with you:　thru

랑 과　평 화 함 께 하　소　서　아　멘
Je - sus Christ, our dear Re - deem　-　er.　A - men.

WORDS: Ann Brown (Ep. 6:23-24); Korean trans. The United Methodist Korean Hymnal Committee
MUSIC: W. Hines Sims
© 1951, renewed 1979, Korean trans. © 2001 Broadman Press

MERIDIAN
Irr.

큰 축복을 받고
Sent Forth by God's Blessing

1. 큰 축 복 을 받 고 믿 음 고 백 하 며
2. 영 원 하 신 주 께 감 사 찬 송 하 며

1. Sent forth by God's bless-ing, our true faith con - fess-ing,
2. With praise and thanks - giv-ing to God ev - er liv - ing,

주 백 성 들 성 전 을 떠 나 갈 때
새 힘 얻 어 날 마 다 살 아 가 리

the peo - ple of God from this dwell-ing take leave.
the tasks of our ev - ery - day life we will face.

주 믿 는 자 마 다 그 생 활 속 에 서
이 믿 음 나 누 고 서 로 사 랑 하 며

The ser - vice is end - ed, O now be ex - tend - ed
Our faith ev - er shar-ing, in love ev - er car - ing,

이 예 배 의 열 매 를 맺 으 리 라
온 세 계 의 이 웃 을 품 어 주 리

the fruits of our wor - ship in all who be - lieve.
em - brac - ing God's chil - dren of each tribe and race.

WORDS: Omer Westendorf; Korean trans. The United Methodist Korean Hymnal Committee
MUSIC: Welsh folk tune; harm. Leland Sateren
Words © 1964, Korean trans. © 2001 World Library Publications, Inc

THE ASH GROVE
6 6 11.6 6 11 D

주께서 함께 계셔
May the Lord Go with You

Unison

주 께서 함께
May the Lord go

계 셔 나 의손 잡으사
with you. Let him take your hand.

WORDS: Don Besig and Nancy Price; Korean trans. The United Methodist Korean Hymnal Committee
MUSIC: Don Besig and Nancy Price
© 1988, Korean trans. © 2001 Harold Flammer, Inc.

주 의 사 랑 안 - 에 늘 지 켜 주 시 리
Keep his love with-in you un-til we meet a-gain.

아 - - - 멘 -
A men.

368

우리 주 예수의 크신 은혜
May the Grace of the Lord

우 리 주 예 수 의 크 신 은 혜 가 함 께 하 며
May the grace of the Lord, may the grace of the Lord Je-sus Christ,

주 하 나 님 의 – 크 신 사 랑 과 성 령 교 통
and the love of God, and the fel-low-ship of the Ho-ly

하 심 – 함 께 하 리 라 아 멘 –
Spir - it, be with you all. A - men.

WORDS: 2 Cor. 13:14; Korean trans. The United Methodist Korean Hymnal Committee
MUSIC: Ken Barker
© 1986, Korean trans. © 2001 Word Music, Inc.

PAUL
Irr.

저 아침해 뜰 때
When Morning Gilds the Skies

1. 저 아침 해 뜰 때 - 내 마음 외치네
2. 주 찬양 할 때에 - 밤 도 낮이 되리라
3. 온 세 상 만물들 - 기 쁘게 외쳐라
4. 나 사는 동안에 - 늘 부를 찬송은

1. When morn-ing gilds the skies   my heart a-wak-ing cries:
2. The night be-comes as   day   when from the heart we say:
3. Let   all   the earth a - round   ring joy-ous with the sound:
4. Be   this, while life   is   mine,   my can-ti-cle di - vine:

주 예 수 찬 양 해   나 의 삶 가 운 데
주 예 수 찬 양 해   어 두 움 의 권 세
주 예 수 찬 양 해   가 영 원 아 름 다 운
주 예 수 찬 양 해   가 영 원 무 궁 토 록

May Je - sus Christ   be praised!   A - like at work and prayer,
May Je - sus Christ   be praised!   The powers of dark-ness fear
May Je - sus Christ   be praised!   In heaven's e - ter - nal bliss
May Je - sus Christ   be praised!   Be   this th'e - ter - nal song

예 수 만 의 지 해 - 주 예 수 찬 양 해
다 물 러 가 리 라 - 주 예 수 찬 양 해
천 국 의 노 래 는 - 주 예 수 찬 양 해
불 리 워 질 노 래 - 주 예 수 찬 양 해

to   Je - sus I re - pair: May Je - sus Christ be   praised!
when this sweet chant they hear: May Je - sus Christ be   praised!
the love-li-est strain is   this: May Je - sus Christ be   praised!
through all the a - ges   long: May Je - sus Christ be   praised!

WORDS: *Katholisches Gesangbuch*; sts. 1, 2, 4 English trans. Edward Caswall; st. 3 Robert S. Bridges;
Korean trans. The United Methodist Korean Hymnal Committee
MUSIC: Joseph Barnby
Korean trans. © 2001 The United Methodist Publishing House, admin. The Copyright Co.

LAUDES DOMINI
666.666

첫 아침처럼

1. 첫 아 침 처 럼 밝 아 온 아 침
2. 맑 은 빗 방 울 반 짝 거 리 네
3. 햇 빛 과 아 침 내 게 주 셨 네

깨 어 난 새 들 노 래 하 네 -
풀 잎 에 내 린 이 슬 처 럼 -
에 덴 의 동 산 지 으 신 주 -

새 로 운 노 래 은 새 로 운 아 침 산
촉 촉 히 젖 래 찬 양 드 리 세
목 소 리 높 여 찬 양 드 리 세

배 풀 어 주 다 신 움 주 를 찬 양 세 주
그 아 름 이 날 찬 양 하 양 지 으 신 주
새 로 운 이

WORDS: Eleanor Farjeon (Lam. 3:22-23); Korean trans. The United Methodist Korean Hymnal Committee
MUSIC: Trad. Gaelic melody; harm. Carlton R. Young
Words by permission of David Higham Associates, Ltd.;
harm. © 1989 The United Methodist Publishing House, admin. The Copyright Co.

BUNESSAN
55.54 D

Morning Has Broken

1. Morn-ing has bro - ken like the first morn - ing;
2. Sweet the rain's new fall sun - lit from heav - en,
3. Mine is the sun - light! Mine is the morn - ing

black-bird has spo - ken like the first bird.
like the first dew - fall on the first grass.
born of the one light E - den saw play!

Praise for the sing - ing! Praise for the morn - ing!
Praise for the sweet - ness of the wet gar - den,
Praise with e - la - tion, praise ev-ery morn - ing,

Praise for them, spring - ing fresh from the Word!
sprung in com - plete - ness where his feet pass.
God's re - cre - a - tion of the new day!

WORDS: Eleanor Farjeon (Lam. 3:22-23)
MUSIC: Trad. Gaelic melody; harm. Carlton R. Young
Words by permission of David Higham Associates, Ltd.;
harm. © 1989 The United Methodist Publishing House, admin. The Copyright Co.

BUNESSAN
55.54 D

새벽하늘 밝히는

1.새 벽 하 늘 밝 히 는 붉 은 저 태 양 고
2.아 버 지 여 이 몸 을 지 켜 주 시 고
3.예 수 사 랑 베 푸 사 축 복 하 소 서

힘 차 구 나 그 선 모 습 아 름 다 와 라 서 네
온 유 하 고 내 마 음 자 유 하 언 었
죄 악 에 서 한 삶 살 게 소

높 이 나 는 새 들 며 향 기 로 운 꽃 쳐 니
어 른 공 경 하 시 자 녀 가 우 르
나 를 입 히 시 고 먹 여 주 시

은 혜 의 빛 입 고 서 힘 써 일 하 리
주 나 의 진 필 요 주 께 서 채 워 주 기 네
의 리 요 며 섬 시

WORDS: Chao Tzu-ch'en; Korean trans. The United Methodist Korean Hymnal Committee
MUSIC: Hu Te-ai; arr. Bliss Wiant

LE P'ING
55.55

Rise to Greet the Sun

1. Rise to greet the sun, red-dening in the sky,
2. Fa - ther, I im - plore, safe - ly keep this child;
3. May this day be blest; trust - ing Je - sus' love,

war - rior - like and strong, come - ly as a groom;
make my con-duct good, ac - tions calm and mild:
my heart's freed from ill; fair blue skies a - bove.

birds pass high in flight, fra-grant flowers now bloom;
ven - er - at - ing age, hum-bly teach-ing youth,
Glad for cot - ton coat, plain food sat - is - fies;

with the gra-cious light I my toil re - sume.
al-ways serv-ing thee, shar-ing thy rich truth.
all my count-less needs thy kind hand sup - plies.

WORDS: Chao Tzu-ch'en; English trans. Mildred A. Wiant and Bliss Wiant
MUSIC: Hu Te-ai; arr. Bliss Wiant
English trans © 1965 Bliss Wiant

LE P'ING
55.55

땅 위에도 바다에도
Now, on Land and Sea Descending

WORDS: Samuel Longfellow; Korean trans. The United Methodist Korean Hymnal Committee
MUSIC: A Selection of Popular National Airs, 1818
Korean trans. © 2001 The United Methodist Publishing House, admin. The Copyright Co.

VESPER HYMN
87.87.86.87

기 뻐 하 라 아 - 멘 우 리 들 의
기 뻐 하 라 아 - 멘 창 조 주 격 의
기 뻐 하 라 아 - 멘 근 심 격 정
기 뻐 하 라 아 - 멘 민 음 소 망
Ju - bi - la - te! A - men! Let our ves - per
Ju - bi - la - te! A - men! Tell - ing still the
Ju - bi - la - te! A - men! Cease we fear - ing
Ju - bi - la - te! A - men! Hope and faith and

저 녁 찬 송 고 요 하 게 퍼 지 네
변 함 없 는 크 하 신 사 랑 노 래 해
사 라 지 고 하 늘 안 식 깃 드 네
사 랑 의 빛 우 리 맘 에 빛 나 네
hymn be blend - ing with the ho - ly calm a - round.
an - cient sto - ry, their Cre - a - tor's change-less love.
cease we griev - ing; touched by God our bur - dens fall.
love rise glo - rious, shin - ing in the Spir - it's skies.

고요히 머리숙여
Jesus, I Think of You Now

1. 고 요 히 머 리 숙 여
2. 고 요 히 머 리 숙 여
3. 고 요 히 머 리 숙 여

1. Je - sus, I think of you now,
2. As I bow qui - et - ly now,
3. As I pray qui - et - ly now,

주 님 생 - 각 합 니 다
하 루 생 - 각 합 니 다
이 웃 생 - 각 합 니 다

Lord whom I trust and a - dore,
look - ing back on a day of life,
help me think of my friends in need,

머 리 둘 곳 도 없 이
지 은 죄 과 많 괴 사 롬 중 에
슬 픔 과 괴 롬 중 에

no place to lay your tired head,
my sins are ma - ny and grave,
be with all those who are sad,

WORDS: Chung Woon Suh; English trans. Edward Poitras
MUSIC: Sang Soo Kwak
© The Korean Hymnal Society

A BEDTIME PRAYER
7.7.

374

빛과 어둠 땅과 하늘
God, That Madest Earth and Heaven

1. 빛 과 어둠 땅 과 하늘 지 으 신 주
2. 아 침 햇살 온 누리에 밝 아 올 때

1. God, that mad-est earth and heav-en, dark - ness and light,
2. When the con-stant sun re-turn-ing un - seals our eyes,

낮 의수고 밤 의안식 주 시 었 네 주 의
새 로운삶 시 작하게 하 옵 소 서 무 슨

who the day for toil hast giv-en, for rest the night: may thine
may we, born a - new like morn-ing, to la - bor rise. Gird us

천 사 보 호 하 사 단 잠 자 게 하 옵 시 고
일 을 만 나 든 지 힘 과 지 혜 주 시 어 서

an - gel guards de - fend us, slum - ber sweet thy mer - cy send us;
for the task that calls us, let not ease and self en-thrall us,

이 밤 에 도 꿈 과 소 망 주 옵 소 서
나 의 소 명 감 당 하 게 하 옵 소 서

ho - ly dreams and hopes at-tend us, this live - long night.
strong through thee what - e'er be-fall us, O God most wise!

WORDS: St. 1, Reginald Heber (Gen. 1:1-15); st. 2, Frederick Lucian Hosmer;
Korean trans. The United Methodist Korean Hymnal Committee
MUSIC: Trad. Welsh melody; harm. Luther Orlando Emerson
Korean trans. © 2001 The United Methodist Publishing House, admin. The Copyright Co.

AR HYD Y NOS
84.84.888.4

낮이 지나가고
Now the Day Is Over

1. 낮 이 지 나 가 고   밤 이 다 가 와 -
2. 지 친 자 들 에 게   안 식 주 시 고 -
3. 고 통 받 는 자 들   위 로 하 시 고 -
4. 새 아 침 이 밝 아   일 어 날 때 에 -

1. Now the day is o - ver, night is draw-ing nigh,
2. Je-sus, give the wea - ry calm and sweet re - pose;
3. Com-fort those who suf - fer, watch-ing late in pain;
4. When the morn-ing wak - ens, then may I a - rise

저 녁 하 늘 가 득   어 둠 덮 이 네
주 의 축 복 속 에   자 게 하 소 서
죄 악 으 로 부 터   지 켜 주 소 서
주 님 보 시 기 에   정 결 하 겠 네

shad-ows of the eve - ning steal a-cross the sky.
with thy ten-derest bless - ing may mine eye-lids close.
those who plan some e - vil from their sin re-strain.
pure, and fresh, and sin - less in thy ho-ly eye.

WORDS: Sabine Baring-Gould; alt.; Korean trans. The United Methodist Korean Hymnal Committee
MUSIC: Joseph Barnby
Korean trans. © 2001 The United Methodist Publishing House, admin. The Copyright Co.

MERRIAL
6.5.6.5

주여 오늘 하루가

WORDS: George W. Doane; Korean trans. The United Methodist Korean Hymnal Committee
MUSIC: Louis M. Gottshalk; arr. Edwin P. Parker
Korean trans. © 2001 The United Methodist Publishing House, admin. The Copyright Co.

SEYMOUR
7.7.7.7

Softly Now the Light of Day

1. Soft - ly now the light of day
2. Thou, whose all per - va - ding eye
3. Soon from us the light of day

fades up - on our sight a - way;
naught es - capes, with - out, with - in,
shall for - e - ver pass a - way;

free from care, from la - bor free,
par - don each in - fir - mi - ty,
then, from sin and sor - row free,

Lord, we would com - mune with thee.
o - pen fault, and se - cret sin.
take us, Lord, to dwell with thee.

WORDS: George W. Doane
MUSIC: Louis M. Gottshalk; arr. Edwin P. Parker

SEYMOUR
7.7.7.7

377

해 지는 저편
Beyond the Sunset

1. 해 지는 저 편   새 하늘에 는   우 리 주
2. 해 지는 저 편   구 름 도 없 고   무 서 운

1. Be-yond the sun-set,   O bliss-full morn-ing,   when with our
2. Be-yond the sun-set,   no clouds will gath-er,   no storms will

예 수 계 시 는 곳   고 난 은 가 고   찬 란 한
폭 풍 없 으 리 니   즐 거 운 그 날   영 원 한

Sav-ior heav-en is be-gun; earth's toil-ing end-ed,   O glo-rious
threat-en, no fears an-noy;   O day of glad-ness,   O day un-

새 벽 영 광 의 날 이   밝 으 리 라
그 날 영 원 한 기 쁨   넘 치 리 라

dawn-ing, be-yond the sun-set, when day is done.
end-ing, be-yond the sun-set, e-ter-nal joy!

3. 해 지는 저편 그 영광 중에
먼저 간 성도 만나뵈리
영원한 본향 아름다운 곳
이별의 슬픔 없으리라

3. Beyond the sunset, O glad reunion,
with our dear loved ones who've gone before;
in that fair homeland we'll know no parting,
beyond the sunset, forevermore!

WORDS: Virgil P. Brock; Korean trans. The United Methodist Korean Hymnal Committee
MUSIC: Blanche Kerr Brock
© 1936, renewed 1965, Korean trans. © 2001 Word Music, Inc.

주께로 가려네
Steal Away to Jesus

후렴 (*Refrain*)

주 께로　가 려네　예 수께로　가 네
Steal a-way, steal a-way; steal a-way to Je-sus.

하 늘의　본향으로　나 여 기 떠 나 려 네
Steal a-way, steal a-way home. I ain't got long to stay here.

Fine

1. 천 둥 소 리 로 주 나 를 부 르 시 네 내
2. 산 천 과 초 목 죄 인 들 떨 고 있 네 내
3. 번 개 빛 으 로 주 나 를 부 르 시 네 내

1. My Lord he calls me, he calls me by the thun-der; the
2. Green trees a-bend-ing, poor sin-ners stand a-trem-bling; the
3. My Lord he calls me, he calls me by the light-ning; the

D. C.

영 혼 에 주 나 팔 울 려 나 여 기 떠 나 려 네
trum-pet sounds with-in-a my soul. I ain't got long to stay here.

WORDS: African American spiritual (1 Cor. 15:51-52);
Korean trans. The United Methodist Korean Hymnal Committee
MUSIC: African American spiritual; adapt. and arr. William Farley Smith
Adapt. and arr. © 1989, Korean trans. © 2001 The United Methodist Publishing House, admin. The Copyright Co.

STEAL AWAY
57.87 with Refrain

믿음의 선한 싸움

1. 믿음의 - 선한싸움 싸워이긴 성도들이
2. 위대하고 놀랍도다 주님께서 하시는일
3. 지극히 - 거룩한분 주님밖에 없으시며

유리같이 맑고맑은 바닷가에 둘러앉아
모든나라 왕의왕은 우리주님뿐이로다
주님의 - 의로우심 높이높이 드러났네

하 나님이 내 려주신 거 문고 둥 둥타며
하 나님을 두 려워치 않 을자 누 구이며
모 든나라 민 족들이 주 님께 경 배하며

어 린양 의 노 래를 부르고 - 있 습 니 다
주 의능 력 찬 양하지 않을사 람 그 누 구랴
구 원받은 성 도들이 감 사찬송 드 립 니 다

WORDS: Yoo Yun Kim (Rev. 15:2-3)
MUSIC: Sung Mo Moon
© The Korean Hymnal Society

All the Saints Who've Fought

1. All the saints who've fought the bat-tle and have won the vic - to-ry
2. Al-ways great   e - ver wond-rous are the works of God   our Lord,
3. There is none who shines in glo-ry as the Lamb who reigns on the throne,

gath-er round the glas-sy o -cean, clear as far as eye can see,
King of kings of all   the na-tions, God a-lone who gives   the word
prais- es rise to high-est heav-en giv-ing praise to him   a - lone,

play-ing harps that   God has giv-en, lost in joy and   har - mo-ny,
all must stand in   awe be-fore him, Lamb of God   up - on his throne,
all the na-tions join in wor-ship, lost in won-der, rapt   in praise

stand be-fore the throne of heav-en prais-ing God   in me - lo-dy.
in the light of such great glo-ry   all shall sing   with sweet-est tone.
all the saints who know sal-va-tion sing their hymns thru end-less days.

WORDS: Yoo Yun Kim (Rev. 15:2-3); English trans. Edward Poitras
MUSIC: Sung Mo Moon
© The Korean Hymnal Society

승리의 예수여

1. 승 리 의 예 수 여 주 믿 는 성 도
2. 영 원 한 하 나 님 창 조 의 주 님
3. 흙 에 서 왔 으 니 흙 으 로 가 리

저 흙 밝 으 은 로 곳 에 우 리 서 말 씀 쉽 지 하 주 으 소 셨 서 네 으 나
태 초 에 우 주 말 씀 하 으 셨 으 나

슬 픔 과 애 통 과 탄 연 - 식 다 약 가 한 의 육 고 찬 신 송
귀 무 하 덤 게 을 지 울 리 기 - 쁨 의 찬 송

영 흙 원 으 한 로 생 되 되 명 을 돌 누 아 가 리 리 네 라 야
알 렐 - 루 야 알 렐 루 야

WORDS: Carl P. Daw, Jr.; Korean trans. The United Methodist Korean Hymnal Committee
MUSIC: Alexis Lvov
Words © 1982, Korean trans. © 2001 Hope Publishing Co.

RUSSIAN HYMN
11 10.11 9

Christ the Victorious

380

1. Christ the Vic - to - ri - ous, give to your ser - vants
2. On - ly im - mor - tal One, might - y Cre - a - tor!
3. God - spo - ken proph - e - cy, word at cre - a - tion:

rest with your saints in the re - gions of light.
We are your crea - tures and chil - dren of earth.
"You came from dust and to dust shall re - turn."

Grief and pain end - ed, and sigh - ing no long - er,
From earth you formed us, both glo - rious and mor - tal,
Yet at the grave shall we raise up our glad song,

there may they find ev - er - last - ing life.
and to the earth shall we all re - turn.
"Al - le - lu - ia, al - le - lu - ia!"

WORDS: Carl P. Daw, Jr.
MUSIC: Alexis Lvov
Words © 1982 Hope Publishing Co.

RUSSIAN HYMN
11 10.11 9

새 하늘과 새 땅

381

주 예수의 크신 사랑
Sing the Wondrous Love of Jesus

1. 주 예 수 의 크 신 사 랑 그 의 자 비
2. 순 례 의 길 걸 어 갈 때 어 둔 구 름
3. 한 결 같 은 믿 음 으 로 충 성 하 며

1. Sing the won-drous love of Je - sus; sing his mer - cy
2. While we walk the pil - grim path-way, clouds will o - ver -
3. Let us then be true and faith-ful, trust - ing, serv - ing

찬 양 해 밝 고 복 된 하 늘 처 소
덮 여 도 우 리 여 정 마 칠 때 에
섬 기 세 영 광 중 에 주 를 볼 때

and his grace. In the man - sions bright and bless - ed
spread the sky; but when trav - eling days are o - ver,
ev - ery day; just one glimpse of him in glo - ry

후렴 (Refrain)

예 비 하 여 주 시 네 천 국 에 들 어
밝 은 하 늘 주 시 리
수 고 갚 아 주 시 리

he'll pre - pare for us a place.
not a shad-ow, not a sigh. When we all get to
will the toils of life re - pay.

WORDS: Eliza E. Hewitt; Korean trans. The United Methodist Korean Hymnal Committee
MUSIC: Emily D. Wilson
Korean trans. © 2001 The United Methodist Publishing House, admin. The Copyright Co.

HEAVEN
87.87 with Refrain

가 서 우 리 주 예 수 얼 굴 뵈 올 때
heav - en, what a day of re - joic - ing that will be!

모 두 기 뻐 하 며 승 리 의 노 래 부 르 리
When we all see Je - sus, we'll sing and shout the vic - to - ry!

4. 면류관을 향해 가세 주의 얼굴 뵈리니
진주 문에 들어가서 황금 길을 걸으리

4. Onward to the prize before us!
Soon his beauty we'll behold;
soon the pearly gates will open;
we shall tread the streets of gold.

영화로운 성도들과

1. 영화로운 성도들과 부활 찬송 부르세며 죽음 슬픔 어둠 권세 없던 모두 지나갔도다 검은 구름 사라지고 폭풍 우가 그치니 주의 자녀 깨어나서 하늘 평화 누리리

2. 우리 눈이 볼 수 없던 하늘 영광 누리세며 우리 맘이 알 수 없던 하늘 기쁨 맛보리 언약하사 예비하신 하늘 처소 있으니 부활하신 예수께서 우리 맞아 주시리

3. 영생하신 구주 예수 온 하늘이 기뻐해 주의 자녀 성도들과 기쁨으로 찬양해
   하나님을 경외하던 우리 믿음 조상들 열망하던 주의 영광 모두 함께 누리리

4. 주의 성도 심판 날에 보좌 앞에 설 때에 놀라우신 영생축복 하늘 기쁨 맛보리
   영광의 문 들어가서 빛난 하늘 볼 때에 영원하신 구주 예수 밝히 알게 되리라

WORDS: William J. Irons (1 Cor. 15:20); Korean trans. The United Methodist Korean Hymnal Committee
MUSIC: Ludwig van Beethoven; arr. Edward Hodges
Korean trans. © 2001 The United Methodist Publishing House, admin. The Copyright Co.

HYMN TO JOY
87.87 D

Sing with All the Saints in Glory

1. Sing with all the saints in glory, sing the res-ur-rec - tion song! Death and sor - row, earth's dark sto - ry, to the for - mer days be-long. All a - round the clouds are break-ing, soon the storms of time shall cease; in God's like-ness we, a-wak-ing, know the ev - er - last-ing peace.

2. O what glo - ry, far ex - ceed - ing all that eye has yet per-ceived! Ho - liest hearts, for a - ges plead-ing, nev - er that full joy con-ceived. God has prom-ised, Christ pre - pares it, there on high our wel - come waits. Ev - ery hum-ble spir -it shares it; Christ has passed th'e - ter - nal gates.

3. Life eternal! Heaven rejoices: Jesus lives, who once was dead. Join we now the deathless voices: child of God, lift up your head! Patriarchs from the distant ages, saints all longing for their heaven, prophets, psalmists, seers, and sages, all await the glory given.

4. Life eternal! O what wonders crowd on faith; what joy unknown, when, amidst earth's closing thunders, saints shall stand before the throne! O to enter that bright portal, see that glowing firmament; know, with thee, O God Immortal, "Jesus Christ whom thou has sent!

WORDS: William J. Irons (1 Cor. 15:20)
MUSIC: Ludwig van Beethoven; arr. Edward Hodges

HYMN TO JOY
87.87 D

383

꿈을 꾸세 평화의 자녀
Dream on, Dream on

1. 꿈 을 꾸 세 평 화 의 자 녀
2. 소 망 하 세 부 활 의 자 녀

1. Dream on, dream on, chil-dren of peace;
2. Hope on, hope on, Eas - ter peo - ple,

주 의 나 라 이 르 도 록
어 둠 후 에 아 침 오 리

till on earth God's king - dom come.
b'yond the cross, a dawn, sun - rise.

양 과 늑 대 함 - 께 놀 고
평 화 주 신 구 - 주 예 수

Th'wolf and lamb will feed to - geth - er,
Christ our peace, broke down all bar - riers,

사 자 들 도 풀 - 을 뜯 으 며
우 리 장 벽 모 - 두 허 무 사

li - ons like ox will eat straw.
na - tions, cul - tures, and of race.

WORDS: Hae-Jong Kim
MUSIC: Sunkyung Lee
© 2001 The United Methodist Publishing House, admin. The Copyright Co.

DREAM ON
Irr.

독 사 들 도 흙 을 먹 고　상 처 주 지 않　는 곳
하 나 님 과 화 목 하 며　하 나 되 게 하 셨 네
Dust shall be the ser-pent's food, they shall not hurt or des-troy.
Rec-on-cil-ing us to God, Christ made us one hu-man race.

8va⌐ *(Descant)*

서　로　다　른　모　–　든　백　성
정　의　평　화　자　–　유　주　신
Chil-dren of earth in all col-ors,
Jus-tice peace, and li-be-ra-tion,

평　화　롭　게　살　리　라
참　된　소　망　주　예　수
live in peace and har-mo-ny.
Christ, the hope for hu-man-kind.

3. 올라가세 독수리 같이
구름 너머 하늘높이
슬픔 근심 사라지고
눈물 고통 모두 이기리
피곤하여 넘어져도
주가 새 힘 주시리
걸어가세 달려가세
쓰러지지 않으리

3. Mount on, mount on, like an eagle,
to the heights, beyond the clouds.
Strife and sorrows, shall not stop you,
pains and tears shall weary you not.
Youth grow tired, young may stumble,
wait on th'Lord, strength to renew.
Thou shall soar on wings of eagles,
run on, walk on, shall not faint.

384 오라 하늘의 수레

오 라 하 늘 의수레 본향에날데려가 오

오 라 하 늘 의 수레 본향에날 데 려가 오

1. 저 내 요 단 서 건 너 난 내 보 았 네 여 때 날
2. 내 앞 기 때 나 내 친 구 슬 프 던
3. 나 뻘 생 가 장 또 기 뺐 던
4. 내 일

본 향 에날데려가 오

날 곧 늘 주
맞 나 천 예
이 도 국 수
하 따 바 내
는 라 라 죄

천 사 들 라
가 리 다 네
셋 은 날

본 향 에날데려가 오

WORDS: African American spiritual (2 Kg. 2:11);
Korean trans. The United Methodist Korean Hymnal Committee
MUSIC: African American spiritual; arr. Sunkyung Lee
Arr., Korean trans. © 2001 The United Methodist Publishing House, admin. The Copyright Co.

SWING LOW
10 8.10 8 with Refrain

Swing Low, Sweet Chariot

Refrain

Swing low, sweet char-i-ot, com-ing for to car-ry me home;

swing low, sweet char-i-ot, com-ing for to car-ry me home.

Fine

1. I looked o-ver Jor-dan, and what did I see,
2. If you get there be-fore I do,
3. I'm some-times up, I'm some-times down,
4. The bright-est day that I can say,

com-ing for to car-ry me home?   A band of an-gels
com-ing for to car-ry me home;   tell all my friends I'm
com-ing for to car-ry me home;   but still my soul feels
com-ing for to car-ry me home;   when Je-sus washed my

D. C.

com-ing af-ter me,   com-ing for to car-ry me home.
com-ing too,   com-ing for to car-ry me home.
heav-en-ly bound,   com-ing for to car-ry me home.
sins a-way,   com-ing for to car-ry me home.

WORDS: African American spiritual (2 Kg. 2:11)
MUSIC: African American spiritual; arr. Sunkyung Lee
Arr. © 2001 The United Methodist Publishing House, admin. The Copyright Co.

SWING LOW
10 8.10 8 with Refrain

385

머지 않아서
Soon and Very Soon

2. 죽음 없는 곳 우리 왕을 보겠네　　　2. No more dying there,
3. 눈물 없는 곳 우리 왕을 보겠네　　　3. No more crying there,

WORDS: Andraé Crouch (Rev. 21:3-4); Korean trans. The United Methodist Hymnal Committee
MUSIC: Andraé Crouch; adapt. William Farley Smith
© 1976, Korean trans. © 2001 Bud John Song, Inc./Crouch Music Corp.

VERY SOON
Irr.

주여 좋은 아침
My Lord, What a Morning

후렴 (Refrain)

주 여 좋 은 아 침   주 여 좋 은 아 침
My Lord, what a morn-ing; my Lord, what a morn-ing;

오   주 여 좋 은 아 침 별 들 사 라 질 때 에
Oh, my Lord, what a morn-ing, when the stars be-gin to fall.

Fine

1. 저 나 팔 소 리 - 에 -
2. 저 죄 인 신 음 - 에 - 온 천 지 깨 어 나 리 라
3. 저 성 도 외 침 - 에 -

1. You'll hear the trum-pet sound,
2. You'll hear the sin-ner moan, to wake the na-tions un-der-ground,
3. You'll hear the Chris-tian shout,

주 의 오 른 손 보 리   별 들 사 라 질 때 에
look-ing to my God's right hand, when the stars be-gin to fall.

D. C.

WORDS: African American spiritual (1 Cor. 15:51-52; Rev. 6:12-17);
Korean trans. The United Methodist Korean Hymnal Committee
MUSIC: African American spiritual; adapt. and arr. William Farley Smith
Adapt. and arr. © 1989, Korean trans. © 2001 The United Methodist Publishing House, admin. The Copyright Co.

BURLEIGH
Irr.

저 하늘 성도들과
Come, Let Us Join Our Friends

1. 저 하늘 성 도 들 과 우 리 하 나
2. 하 나 님 안 에 거 하 는 우 리 는
3. 수 많 은 사 람 지 금 도 본 향 을

1. Come, let us join our friends a - bove who have ob -
2. One fam - i - ly we dwell in him, one church a -
3. Ten thou-sand to their end - less home this sol - emn

되 어 서 저 하 늘 높 이 올 라 가 큰
한 가 족 하 늘 과 땅 나 뉘 어 도 우
향 하 네 우 리 도 하 늘 본 향 에 곧

tained the prize, and on the ea - gle wings of love to
bove, be - neath, though now di - vid - ed by the stream, the
mo - ment fly, and we are to the mar - gin come, and

기 쁨 나 누 세 회 하 늘 과 땅 의
리 는 한 교 회 라 주 님 의 명 의
들 어 가 리 라 지 금 도 민 음

joys ce - les - tial rise. Let saints on earth u -
nar - row stream of death; one ar - my of the
we ex - pect to die. E'en now by faith we

WORDS: Charles Wesley; Korean trans. The United Methodist Korean Hymnal Committee
MUSIC: Trad. English melody; arr. Ralph Vaughan Williams
Korean trans. © 2001 The United Methodist Publishing House, admin. The Copyright Co.;
arr. © Oxford University Press

FOREST GREEN
CMD

성 도 들 함 께 찬 양 하 라 주 섬 기
따 르 는 주 님 의 한 군 대 먼 저 간
안 에 서 그 들 과 손 잡 고 영 원 한

nite to sing with those to glo - ry gone, for all the
liv - ing God, to his com-mand we bow; part of his
join our hands with those that went be - fore, and greet the

는 자 누 구 나 다 하 나 됨 이 라
주 의 성 도 들 곧 만 나 뵈 리 라
생 명 강 가 에 서 맞 이 하 리 라

ser - vants of our King in earth and heaven are one.
host have crossed the flood, and part are cross - ing now.
blood be sprin - kled bands on the e - ter - nal shore.

4. 그들과 같이 우리 영혼 면류관 쓰고
   주 하나님의 나팔소리 듣게 되리라
   오 주여 여기 오셔서 그 말씀 주시고
   저 천국으로 우리 모두 인도 하소서

4. Our spirits too shall quickly join,
   like theirs with glory crowned,
   and shout to see our Captain's sign,
   to hear his trumpet sound.
   O that we now might grasp our
   Guide! O that the word were given!
   Come, Lord of Hosts, the waves divide,
   and land us all in heaven.

새 하늘과 새 땅

388

안식하는 하늘의 성도들

WORDS: William W. How (Heb. 12:1); Korean trans. The United Methodist Korean Hymnal Committee
MUSIC: Ralph Vaughan Williams
Korean trans. © 2001 The United Methodist Publishing House, admin. The Copyright Co.;
music © Oxford University Press

SINE NOMINE
10 10 10 with Alleluias

*무반주 4절

후렴

알 - 렐 루 야 알 - 렐 루 야

Harmony

*4. 약 한 우 리 빛 나 는 성 도 와

거 룩 한 교 제 함 께 나 눌 때

주 안 에 모 두 하 나 되 었 네

알 - 렐 루 야 알 - 렐 루 야

388

For All the Saints

Unison

1. For all the saints, who from their la-bors rest, who
2. Thou wast their rock, their for-tress, and their might; thou,
3. O may thy sol - diers, faith-ful, true, and bold,
*4. O blest com - mu - nion, fel-low-ship di - vine!
5. And when the strife is fierce, the war-fare long,
6. From earth's wide bounds, from o-cean's far-thest coast, through

thee by faith be - fore the world con - fessed, thy
Lord, their cap - tain in the well-fought fight;
fight as the saints who no - bly fought of old, and
we fee-bly strug - gle, they in glo-ry shine; yet
steals on the ear the dis - tant tri-umph song, and
gates of pearl streams in the count-less host,

name, O Je - sus, be for - ev - er blest.
thou, in the dark - ness drear, their one true light.
win with them the vic - tor's crown of gold.
all are one in thee, for all are thine.
hearts are brave a - gain, and arms are strong.
sing - ing to Fa - ther, Son, and Ho - ly Ghost:

WORDS: William W. How (Heb. 12:1)
MUSIC: Ralph Vaughan Williams

SINE NOMINE
10 10 10 with Alleluias

Refrain

Al – le-lu – ia, Al – le-lu – ia!

Harmony

*4. O blest com – mu – nion, fel-low-ship di – vine!

We fee-bly strug – gle, they in glo-ry shine;

yet all are one in thee, for all are thine.

Al – le-lu – ia, Al – le-lu – ia!

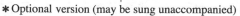
* Optional version (may be sung unaccompanied)

강가에서 만나보자

WORDS: Robert Lowry (Rev. 22:1-5); Korean trans. The United Methodist Korean Hymnal Committee
MUSIC: Robert Lowry
Korean trans. © 2001 The United Methodist Publishing House, admin. The Copyright Co.

HANSON PLACE
87.87 with Refrain

Shall We Gather at the River

1. Shall we gath-er at the riv - er, where bright an-gel feet have
2. On the mar-gin of the riv - er, wash-ing up its sil-ver
3. Ere we reach the shin-ing riv - er, lay we ev-ery bur-den
4. Soon we'll reach the shin-ing riv - er, soon our pil-grim-age will

trod, with its crys-tal tide for- ev - er flow-ing
spray, we will walk and wor-ship ev - er, all the
down; grace our spir- its will de - liv - er, and pro-
cease; soon our hap - py hearts will quiv - er with the

Refrain

by the throne of God? Yes, we'll gath-er at the riv - er,
hap - py gold - en day.
vide a robe and crown.
mel - o - dy of peace.

the beau - ti-ful, the beau - ti-ful riv - er; gath-er with the

saints at the riv - er that flows by the throne of God.

WORDS: Robert Lowry, 1864 (Rev. 22:1-5)
MUSIC: Robert Lowry, 1864

HANSON PLACE
87.87 with Refrain

어린양 다스리시는

1. 어린양 다스리시는 그 거룩한 성에 그 곳엔 어둠 없으며 고통 이려 없도다네
2. 죄악과 불의가 가득한 이 세상 보아라 그 이웃에게 모질게 큰 상처 주도다
3. 저 거리마다 욕심에 다 눈이 어두워 그 저여인들과 아이 속의 그 저 그 절망

주치외 시솟침 니는을 더그왜 슬픔든 식지못 겠소하 네리나

4. 다 사랑하고 섬기는 그 거룩한 성을 곧 이룩할 수 있도록 큰 능력 주소서
   그 곳에 주의 은혜가 늘 밝게 빛나리

5. 주 예비하신 그 성은 참 아름다우니 담대한 영혼들에게 큰 도전 되도다
   그 거룩한 성 영광을 세우라 하시네

WORDS: Walter Russell Bowie (Rev. 21:1-22:5)
MUSIC: Wyeth's *Repository of Sacred Music, Part Second*, 1813; harm. Charles H. Webb
Harm. © 1989, Korean trans. © 2001 The United Methodist Publishing House, admin. The Copyright Co.

MORNING SONG
86.86.86

O Holy City, Seen of John

1. O ho-ly cit-y, seen of John, where Christ, the
2. Hark, how from men whose lives are held more cheap than
3. O shame to us who rest con-tent while lust and

Lamb, doth reign, with-in whose four-square walls shall come no
mer-chan-dise, from wom-en strug-gling sore for bread, from
greed for gain in street and shop and ten-e-ment wring

night, nor need, nor pain, and where the tears are
lit-tle chil-dren's cries, there swells the sob-bing
gold from hu-man pain, and bit-ter lips in

wiped from eyes that shall not weep a-gain.
hu-man plaint that bids thy walls a-rise.
blind de-spair cry, "Christ hath died in vain!"

4. Give us, O God, the strength to build the city that hath stood too long a
   dream, whose laws are love, whose crown is servanthood, and where the
   sun that shineth is God's grace for human good.

5. Already in the mind of God that city riseth fair: lo, how its splendor
   challenges the souls that greatly dare; yea, bids us seize the whole of
   life and build its glory there.

WORDS: Walter Russell Bowie (Rev. 21:1-22:5)
MUSIC: Wyeth's *Repository of Sacred Music, Part Second*, 1813; harm. Charles H. Webb

MORNING SONG
86.86.86

새 하늘과 새 땅

391

저 높은 곳을 향하여

WORDS: Johnson Oatman, Jr. (Col. 3:2); Korean trans. The United Methodist Korean Hymnal Committee
MUSIC: Charles H. Gabriel
Korean trans. © 2001 The United Methodist Publishing House, admin. The Copyright Co.

HIGHER GROUND
8.8.8.8 with Refrain

후렴

내 주 여 내 발 붙 드 사

그 곳 에 서 게 하 소 서

그 곳 은 빛 과 사 랑 이

언 제 나 넘 치 옵 니 다

391   I'm Pressing on the Upward

1. I'm press-ing on the up-ward way,
2. My heart has no de-sire to stay
3. I want to live a-bove the world,
4. I want to scale the ut-most height
5. My Lord I'll fol-low, till I stand

new heights I'm gain - ing ev - 'ry day;
wh're doubts a - rise and fears dis - may;
tho' Sa - tan's darts at me are hurled;
and catch a gleam of glo - ry bright;
e - rect up - on that loft - y land;

still pray - ing as I'm on - ward bound,
tho' some may dwell where these a - bound,
for faith has caught the joy - ful sound,
but still I'll pray till heav'n I've found,
and, blest for - ev - er, sing his grace,

"Lord, plant my feet on high - er ground."
my prayer, my aim, is high - er ground.
the song of saints on high - er ground.
"Lord, lead me on to high - er ground."
who led and set me in this place.

WORDS: Johnson Oatman, Jr. (Col. 3:2)
MUSIC: Charles H. Gabriel

HIGHER GROUND
8.8.8.8 with Refrain

봉오리에 꽃 한송이

1. 봉 오 리 에 꽃 한 송 이 씨 앗 속 사 과 나 무
2. 침 묵 속 에 노 래 있 어 찬 양 울 려 나 오 리
3. 우 리 삶 이 끝 이 날 때 영 생 시 작 되 리 라

누 에 속 에 숨 은 약 속 나 비 되 어 날 으 리 네
모 든 어 둠 속 에 새 벽 우 리 회 망 주 시 네
의 심 속 에 서 도 믿 음 우 리 삶 속 의 영 원

추 운 겨 울 눈 속 에 도 봄 이 기 다 리 듯 이
미 래 속 에 담 겨 있 는 하 나 님 의 신 비 함
죽 음 속 에 서 도 부 활 최 후 승 리 하 리 니

때 가 차 면 이 뤄 지 리 하 나 님 만 아 시 네

WORDS: Natalie Sleeth; Korean trans. The United Methodist Korean Hymnal Committee
MUSIC: Natalie Sleeth
© 1986, Korean trans. © 2001 Hope Publishing Co.

PROMISE
87.87.D

In the Bulb There Is a Flower
(Hymn of Promise)

392

Unison

1. In the bulb there is a flow-er; in the seed, an ap-ple tree;
2. There's a song in ev-ery si-lence, seek-ing word and mel-o-dy;
3. In our end is our be-gin-ning; in our time, in-fin-i-ty;

in co-coons, a hid-den prom-ise; but-ter-flies will soon be free!
there's a dawn in ev-ery dark-ness, bring-ing hope to you and me.
in our doubt there is be-liev-ing; in our life, e-ter-ni-ty.

In the cold and snow of win-ter there's a spring that waits to be,
From the past will come the fu-ture; what it holds, a mys-ter-y,
In our death, a res-ur-rec-tion; at the last, a vic-to-ry,

un-re-vealed un-til its sea-son, some-thing God a-lone can see.

WORDS: Natalie Sleeth
MUSIC: Natalie Sleeth
© 1986 Hope Publishing Co.

PROMISE
87.87.D

시편 1

1 복 있는 사람은
　　악인들의 꾀를 따르지 아니하며
죄인들의 길에 서지 아니하며
　　오만한 자들의 자리에 앉지 아니하고
2 오직 여호와의 율법을 즐거워하여
그의 율법을 주야로 묵상하는도다
3 그는 시냇가에 심은 나무가
　　철을 따라 열매 맺으며
　　그 잎사귀가 마르지 아니함 같으니
그가 하는 모든 일이 다 형통하리로다
4 악인들은 그렇지 아니함이여
　　오직 바람에 나는 겨와 같도다
5 **그러므로 악인들은 심판을 견디지 못하며**
　　죄인들이 의인들의 모임에 들지 못하리로다
6 무릇 의인들의 길은 여호와께서 인정하시나
악인들의 길은 망하리로다

Psalm 1

1 Happy are those
　　who do not follow the advice of the wicked,
or take the path that sinners tread,
　　or sit in the seat of scoffers;
2 but their delight is in the law of the Lord,
and on his law they meditate day and night.
3 They are like trees planted by streams of water,
　　which yield their fruit in its season,
　　and their leaves do not wither.
In all that they do, they prosper.
4 The wicked are not so,
　　but are like chaff that the wind drives away.
5 **Therefore the wicked will not stand in the judgment,**
　　nor sinners in the congregation of the righteous;
6 for the Lord watches over the way of the righteous,
but the way of the wicked will perish.

시편 3

1 여호와여 나의 대적이 어찌 그리 많은지요
　　일어나 나를 치는 자가 많으니이다
2 **많은 사람이 나를 대적하여 말하기를**
　　그는 하나님께 구원을 받지 못한다 하나이다
3 여호와여 주는 나의 방패시요 나의 영광이시요
　　나의 머리를 드시는 자이시니이다
4 **내가 나의 목소리로 여호와께 부르짖으니**
　　그의 성산에서 응답하시는도다
5 내가 누워 자고 깨었으니 여호와께서 나를 붙드심이로다
6 **천만인이 나를 에워싸 진 친다하여도**
　　나는 두려워하지 아니하리이다
7 여호와여 일어나소서 나의 하나님이여 나를 구원하소서
　　주께서 나의 모든 원수의 뺨을 치시며
　　　악인의 이를 꺾으셨나이다
8 구원은 여호와께 있사오니
　　주의 복을 주의 백성에게 내리소서

Psalm 3

1 O Lord, how many are my foes!
　　Many are rising against me;
2 **many are saying to me,**
　　"There is no help for you in God."
3 But you, O Lord, are a shield around me,
　　my glory, and the one who lifts up my head.
4 **I cry aloud to the Lord,**
　　and he answers me from his holy hill.
5 I lie down and sleep;
　　I wake again, for the Lord sustains me.
6 **I am not afraid of ten thousands of people**
　　who have set themselves against me all around.
7 Rise up, O Lord! Deliver me, O my God!
　　For you strike all my enemies on the cheek;
　　you break the teeth of the wicked.
8 Deliverance belongs to the Lord;
　　may your blessing be on your people!

시편 4

1 내 의의 하나님이여 내가 부를 때에 응답하소서
곤란 중에 나를 너그럽게 하셨사오니
  내게 은혜를 베푸사 나의 기도를 들으소서
2 인생들아 어느 때까지 나의 영광을 바꾸어 욕되게 하며
헛된 일을 좋아하고 거짓을 구하려는가
3 여호와께서 자기를 위하여
    경건한 자를 택하신 줄 너희가 알지어다
내가 그를 부를 때에 여호와께서 들으시리로다
4 너희는 떨며 범죄하지 말지어다
자리에 누워 심중에 말하고 잠잠할지어다
5 의의 제사를 드리고 여호와를 의지할지어다
6 **여러 사람의 말이 우리에게 선을 보일 자 누구뇨 하오니**
    여호와여 주의 얼굴을 들어 우리에게 비추소서
8 내가 평안히 눕고 자기도 하리니
나를 안전히 살게 하시는 이는 오직 여호와이시니이다

Psalm 4

1 Answer me when I call, O God of my right!
    You gave me room when I was in distress.
  Be gracious to me, and hear my prayer.
2 How long, you people, shall my honor suffer shame?
  How long will you love vain words,
      and seek after lies?
3 But know that the Lord has set apart
      the faithful for himself;
  the Lord hears when I call to him.
4 When you are disturbed, do not sin;
  ponder it on your beds, and be silent.
5 Offer right sacrifices, and put your trust in the Lord.
6 **There are many who say,**
      "O that we might see some good!
      Let the light of your face shine on us, O Lord!"
8 I will both lie down and sleep in peace;
  for you alone, O Lord,
      make me lie down in safety.

시편 8

1 여호와 우리 주여
　　주의 이름이 온 땅에서 어찌 그리 아름다운지요
주의 영광이 하늘을 덮었나이다

3 주의 손가락으로 만드신 주의 하늘과
　　주께서 베풀어 두신 달과 별들을 내가 보오니

4 **사람이 무엇이기에 주께서 그를 생각하시며**
　　인자가 무엇이기에 주께서 그를 돌보시나이까

5 그를 하나님보다 조금 못하게 하시고
영화와 존귀로 관을 씌우셨나이다

6 주의 손으로 만드신 것을 다스리게 하시고
　　만물을 그의 발 아래에 두셨으니

8 **공중의 새와 바다의 물고기와 바닷길에 다니는 것이니이다**

9 여호와 우리 주여
주의 이름이 온 땅에 어찌 그리 아름다운지요

Psalm 8

1 O Lord, our Sovereign,
　　how majestic is your name in all the earth!
You have set your glory above the heavens.

3 When I look at your heavens, the work of your fingers,
　　the moon and the stars that you have established;

4 **what are human beings that you are mindful of them,**
　　mortals that you care for them?

5 You have made them a little lower than God,
and crowned them with glory and honor.

6 You have given them dominion
　　over the works of your hands;
　　you have put all things under their feet.

8 **the birds of the air, and the fish of the sea,**
　　whatever passes along the paths of the seas.

9 O Lord, our Sovereign,
how majestic is your name in all the earth!

시편 9

11 너희는 시온에 계신 여호와를 찬송하며
그의 행사를 백성 중에 선포할지어다
12 피 흘림을 심문하시는 이가 그들을 기억하심이여
가난한 자의 부르짖음을 잊지 아니하시도다
13 여호와여 내게 은혜를 베푸소서
나를 사망의 문에서 일으키시는 주여
　　　나를 미워하는 자에게서 받는
　　　나의 고통을 보소서
14 그리하시면 내가 주의 찬송을 다 전할 것이요
딸 시온의 문에서 주의 구원을 기뻐하리이다
16 여호와께서 자기를 알게 하사 심판을 행하셨음이여
악인은 자기가 손으로 행한 일에 스스로 얽혔도다
17 악인들이 스올로 돌아감이여
하나님을 잊어버린 모든 이방 나라들이 그리하리로다

Psalm 9

11 Sing praises to the Lord, who dwells in Zion.
Declare his deeds among the peoples.
12 For he who avenges blood is mindful of them;
he does not forget the cry of the afflicted.
13 Be gracious to me, O Lord.
See what I suffer from those who hate me;
　　　you are the one who lifts me up
　　　from the gates of death,
14 so that I may recount all your praises,
and, in the gates of daughter Zion,
　　　rejoice in your deliverance.
16 The Lord has made himself known,
　　　he has executed judgment;
the wicked are snared in the work
　　　of their own hands.
17 The wicked shall depart to Sheol,
all the nations that forget God.

시편 10

12 여호와여 일어나옵소서
   하나님이여 손을 드옵소서
   가난한 자들을 잊지 마옵소서
13 **어찌하여 악인이 하나님을 멸시하여**
   그의 마음에 이르기를
   주는 감찰하지 아니하리라 하나이까
14 주께서는 보셨나이다 주는 재앙과 원한을 감찰하시고
   주의 손으로 갚으려 하시오니
   외로운 자가 주를 의지하나이다
   주는 벌써부터 고아를 도우시는 이시니이다
16 여호와께서는 영원무궁하도록 왕이시니
   이방 나라들이 주의 땅에서 멸망하였나이다
17 여호와여 주는 겸손한 자의 소원을 들으셨사오니
   그들의 마음을 준비하시며 귀를 기울여 들으시고
18 고아와 압제 당하는 자를 위하여 심판하사
   세상에 속한 자가 다시는 위협하지 못하게 하시리이다

Psalm 10

12 Rise up, O Lord; O God, lift up your hand;
   do not forget the oppressed.
13 **Why do the wicked renounce God, and say in their hearts,**
   "You will not call us to account"?
14 But you do see!
   Indeed you note trouble and grief,
   that you may take it into your hands;
   the helpless commit themselves to you;
   you have been the helper of the orphan.
16 The Lord is king forever and ever;
   the nations shall perish from his land.
17 O Lord, you will hear the desire of the meek;
   you will strengthen their heart,
   you will incline your ear
18 to do justice for the orphan and the oppressed,
   so that those from earth
   may strike terror no more.

시편 13

1 여호와여
　　어느 때까지니이까 나를 영원히 잊으시나이까
주의 얼굴을 나에게서 어느 때까지 숨기시겠나이까
2 나의 영혼이 번민하고
　　종일토록 마음에 근심하기를 어느 때까지 하오며
내 원수가 나를 치며 자랑하기를
　어느 때까지 하리이까
3 여호와 내 하나님이여 나를 생각하사 응답하시고
나의 눈을 밝히소서
　두렵건대 내가 사망의 잠을 잘까 하오며
4 두렵건대 나의 원수가 이르기를
　　내가 그를 이겼다 할까 하오며
내가 흔들릴 때에
　나의 대적들이 기뻐할까 하나이다
5 나는 오직 주의 사랑을 의지하였사오니
나의 마음은 주의 구원을 기뻐하리이다
6 내가 여호와를 찬송하리니
이는 주께서 내게 은덕을 베푸심이로다

Psalm 13

1 How long, O Lord?
　　Will you forget me forever?
How long will you hide your face from me?
2 How long must I bear pain in my soul,
　　and have sorrow in my heart all day long?
How long shall my enemy be exalted over me?
3 Consider and answer me, O Lord my God!
Give light to my eyes,
　or I will sleep the sleep of death,
4 and my enemy will say, "I have prevailed";
my foes will rejoice because I am shaken.
5 But I trusted in your steadfast love;
my heart shall rejoice in your salvation.
6 I will sing to the Lord,
because he has dealt bountifully with me.

시편 14

1 어리석은 자는 그의 마음에 이르기를
       하나님이 없다 하는도다
  그들은 부패하고 그 행실이 가증하니
       선을 행하는 자가 없도다
2 여호와께서 하늘에서 인생을 굽어살피사
       지각이 있어 하나님을 찾는 자가 있는가 보려 하신즉
3 **다 치우쳐 함께 더러운 자가 되고**
       선을 행하는 자가 없으니 하나도 없도다
4 죄악을 행하는 자는 다 무지하냐
       그들이 떡 먹듯이 내 백성을 먹으면서
       여호와를 부르지 아니하는도다
5 **그러나 거기서 그들은 두려워하고 두려워하였으니**
       하나님이 의인의 세대에 계심이로다
6 너희가 가난한 자의 계획을 부끄럽게 하나
       오직 여호와는 그의 피난처가 되시도다
7 **이스라엘의 구원이 시온에서 나오기를 원하도다**

Psalm 14

1 Fools say in their hearts, "There is no God."
  They are corrupt, they do abominable deeds;
       there is no one who does good.
2 The Lord looks down from heaven on humankind
       to see if there are any who are wise,
       who seek after God.
3 **They have all gone astray,**
       they are all alike perverse;
       there is no one who does good, no, not one.
4 Have they no knowledge,
       all the evildoers who eat up my people as they eat bread,
       and do not call upon the Lord?
5 **There they shall be in great terror,**
       for God is with the company of the righteous.
6 You would confound the plans of the poor,
       but the Lord is their refuge.
7 **O that deliverance for Israel would come from Zion!**

시편 15

1 여호와여 주의 장막에 머무를 자 누구오며
  주의 성산에 사는 자 누구오니이까
2 정직하게 행하며 공의를 실천하며
  그의 마음에 진실을 말하며
3 **그의 혀로 남을 허물하지 아니하고**
  그의 이웃에게 악을 행하지 아니하며
  그의 이웃을 비방하지 아니하며
4 그의 눈은 망령된 자를 멸시하며
  여호와를 두려워하는 자들을 존대하며
  그의 마음에 서원한 것은
  해로울지라도 변하지 아니하며
5 이자를 받으려고 돈을 꾸어 주지 아니하며
  뇌물을 받고 무죄한 자를 해하지 아니하는 자이니
  이런 일을 행하는 자는
  영원히 흔들리지 아니하리이다

Psalm 15

1 O Lord, who may abide in your tent?
  Who may dwell on your holy hill?
2 Those who walk blamelessly,
  and do what is right,
  and speak the truth from their heart;
3 **who do not slander with their tongue,**
  and do no evil to their friends,
  nor take up a reproach against their neighbors;
4 in whose eyes the wicked are despised,
  but who honor those who fear the Lord;
  who stand by their oath even to their hurt;
5 who do not lend money at interest,
  and do not take a bribe against the innocent.
  Those who do these things shall never be moved.

시편 16

5 여호와는 나의 산업과 나의 잔의 소득이시니
   나의 분깃을 지키시나이다
6 내게 줄로 재어 준 구역은
     아름다운 곳에 있음이여
   나의 기업이 실로 아름답도다
7 나를 훈계하신 여호와를 송축할지라
     밤마다 내 양심이 나를 교훈하도다
8 **내가 여호와를 항상 내 앞에 모심이여**
     그가 나의 오른쪽에 계시므로
     내가 흔들리지 아니하리로다
9 이러므로 나의 마음이 기쁘고 나의 영도 즐거워하며
   내 육체도 안전히 살리니
10 이는 주께서 내 영혼을 스올에 버리지 아니하시며
   주의 성도를 멸망시키지 않으실 것임이니이다
11 주께서 생명의 길을 내게 보이시리니
   주의 앞에는 충만한 기쁨이 있고
     주의 오른쪽에는 영원한 즐거움이 있나이다

Psalm 16

5 The Lord is my chosen portion and my cup;
   you hold my lot.
6 The boundary lines have fallen for me in pleasant places;
   I have a goodly heritage.
7 I bless the Lord who gives me counsel;
     in the night also my heart instructs me.
8 **I keep the Lord always before me;**
     because he is at my right hand, I shall not be moved.
9 Therefore my heart is glad,
     and my soul rejoices;
   my body also rests secure.
10 For you do not give me up to Sheol,
   or let your faithful one see the Pit.
11 You show me the path of life.
   In your presence there is fullness of joy;
     in your right hand are pleasures forevermore.

시편 17

1 여호와여 의의 호소를 들으소서
    나의 울부짖음에 주의하소서
  거짓 되지 아니한 입술에서 나오는
    나의 기도에 귀를 기울이소서
2 주께서 나를 판단하시며
  주의 눈으로 공평함을 살피소서
3 주께서 내 마음을 시험하시고 밤에 내게 오시어서
    나를 감찰하셨으나 흠을 찾지 못하셨사오니
    내가 결심하고 입으로 범죄하지 아니하리이다
5 **나의 걸음이 주의 길을 굳게 지키고**
    실족하지 아니하였나이다
6 하나님이여 내게 응답하시겠으므로 내가 불렀사오니
  내게 귀를 기울여 내 말을 들으소서
7 주께 피하는 자들을 그 일어나 치는 자들에게서
    오른손으로 구원하시는 주여 주의 기이한 사랑을 나타내소서
15 **나는 의로운 중에 주의 얼굴을 뵈오리니**
    깰 때에 주의 형상으로 만족하리이다

Psalm 17

1 Hear a just cause, O Lord; attend to my cry;
  give ear to my prayer from lips free of deceit.
2 From you let my vindication come;
  let your eyes see the right.
3 If you try my heart, if you visit me by night,
    if you test me, you will find no wickedness in me;
    my mouth does not transgress.
5 **My steps have held fast to your paths;**
    my feet have not slipped.
6 I call upon you, for you will answer me, O God;
  Incline your ear to me, hear my words.
7 Wondrously show your steadfast love,
    O savior of those who seek refuge
    from their adversaries at your right hand.
15 **As for me, I shall behold your face in righteousness;**
    when I awake I shall be satisfied, beholding your likeness.

시편 19

1 하늘이 하나님의 영광을 선포하고
궁창이 그의 손으로 하신 일을 나타내는도다
7 여호와의 율법은 완전하여 영혼을 소성시키며
여호와의 증거는 확실하여 우둔한 자를 지혜롭게 하며
8 여호와의 교훈은 정직하여 마음을 기쁘게 하고
여호와의 계명은 순결하여 눈을 밝게 하시도다
9 여호와를 경외하는 도는 정결하여 영원까지 이르고
여호와의 법도 진실하여 다 의로우니
10 금 곧 많은 순금보다 더 사모할 것이며
꿀과 송이꿀보다 더 달도다
11 **또 주의 종이 이것으로 경고를 받고**
이것을 지킴으로 상이 크니이다
14 내 입의 말과 마음의 묵상이
주님 앞에 열납되기를 원하나이다
나의 반석이시요 나의 구속자이신 여호와여

Psalm 19

1 The heavens are telling the glory of God;
and the firmament proclaims his handiwork.
7 The law of the Lord is perfect, reviving the soul;
the decrees of the Lord are sure,
making wise the simple;
8 the precepts of the Lord are right, rejoicing the heart;
the commandment of the Lord is clear, enlightening the eyes;
9 the fear of the Lord is pure, enduring forever;
the ordinances of the Lord
are true and righteous altogether.
10 More to be desired are they than gold, even much fine gold;
sweeter also than honey,
and drippings of the honeycomb.
11 **Moreover by them is your servant warned;**
in keeping them there is great reward.
14 Let the words of my mouth
and the meditation of my heart be acceptable to you,
O Lord, my rock and my redeemer.

시편 23

1 여호와는 나의 목자시니
　　내게 부족함이 없으리로다
2 **그가 나를 푸른 풀밭에 누이시며**
　　쉴 만한 물 가로 인도하시는도다
3 내 영혼을 소생시키시고
　　자기 이름을 위하여 의의 길로 인도하시는도다
4 내가 사망의 음침한 골짜기로 다닐지라도
　　해를 두려워하지 않을 것은
　　주께서 나와 함께 하심이라
　　주의 지팡이와 막대기가 나를 안위하시나이다
5 주께서 내 원수의 목전에서 내게 상을 차려 주시고
　　기름을 내 머리에 부으셨으니
　　내 잔이 넘치나이다
6 내 평생에 선하심과 인자하심이
　　반드시 나를 따르리니
　　내가 여호와의 집에 영원히 살리로다

Psalm 23

1 The Lord is my shepherd, I shall not want.
2 **He makes me lie down in green pastures;**
　　he leads me beside still waters;
3 he restores my soul.
　　He leads me in right paths for his name's sake.
4 Even though I walk through the darkest valley,
　　I fear no evil;
　　for you are with me;
　　your rod and your staff—they comfort me.
5 You prepare a table before me
　　in the presence of my enemies;
　　you anoint my head with oil; my cup overflows.
6 Surely goodness and mercy shall follow me
　　all the days of my life,
　　and I shall dwell in the house of the Lord
　　my whole life long.

시편 27

1 여호와는 나의 빛이요 나의 구원이시니
    내가 누구를 두려워하리요
여호와는 내 생명의 능력이시니 내가 누구를 무서워하리요

4 내가 여호와께 바라는 한 가지 일 그것을 구하리니
    곧 내가 내 평생에 여호와의 집에 살면서
        여호와의 아름다움을 바라보며
        그의 성전에서 사모하는 그것이라

5 여호와께서 환난 날에 나를 그의 초막 속에 비밀히 지키시고
    그의 장막 은밀한 곳에 나를 숨기시며
        높은 바위 위에 두시리로다

7 여호와여 내가 소리 내어 부르짖을 때에 들으시고
    또한 나를 긍휼히 여기사 응답하소서

9 주의 얼굴을 내게서 숨기지 마시고
        주의 종을 노하여 버리지 마소서
        주는 나의 도움이 되셨나이다
나의 구원의 하나님이시여 나를 버리지 마시고 떠나지 마소서

Psalm 27

1 The Lord is my light and my salvation; whom shall I fear?
The Lord is the stronghold of my life;
    of whom shall I be afraid?

4 One thing I asked of the Lord, that will I seek after;
    to live in the house of the Lord all the days of my life,
        to behold the beauty of the Lord,
        and to inquire in his temple.

5 For he will hide me in his shelter in the day of trouble;
    he will conceal me under the cover of his tent;
        he will set me high on a rock.

7 Hear, O Lord, when I cry aloud,
    be gracious to me and answer me!

9 Do not hide your face from me.
        Do not turn your servant away in anger,
        you who have been my help.
Do not cast me off, do not forsake me,
    O God of my salvation!

시편 28

1 여호와여 내가 주께 부르짖으오니
　　나의 반석이여 내게 귀를 막지 마소서
주께서 내게 잠잠하시면
　　내가 무덤에 내려가는 자와 같을까 하나이다
2 내가 주의 지성소를 향하여 나의 손을 들고 주께 부르짖을 때에
나의 간구하는 소리를 들으소서
3 악인과 악을 행하는 자들과 함께 나를 끌어내지 마옵소서
그들은 그 이웃에게 화평을 말하나 그들의 마음에는 악독이 있나이다
5 그들은 여호와께서 행하신 일과
　　손으로 지으신 것을 생각하지 아니하므로
여호와께서 그들을 파괴하고 건설하지 아니하시리로다
6 여호와를 찬송함이여 내 간구하는 소리를 들으심이로다
7 **여호와는 나의 힘과 나의 방패이시니 내 마음이 그를 의지하여**
　　도움을 얻었도다 그러므로 내 마음이 크게 기뻐하며
　　내 노래로 그를 찬송하리로다

Psalm 28

1 To you, O Lord, I call; my rock, do not refuse to hear me,
for if you are silent to me,
　　I shall be like those who go down to the Pit.
2 As I cry to you for help,
　　as I lift up my hands toward your most holy sanctuary,
hear the voice of my supplication.
3 Do not drag me away with the wicked,
　　with those who are workers of evil,
who speak peace with their neighbors,
　　while mischief is in their hearts.
5 Because they do not regard the works of the Lord,
　　or the work of his hands,
he will break them down and build them up no more.
6 Blessed be the Lord,
　　for he has heard the sound of my pleadings.
7 **The Lord is my strength and my shield; in him my heart trusts;**
　　so I am helped, and my heart exults,
　　and with my song I give thanks to him.

시편 29

1 너희 권능 있는 자들아
    영광과 능력을 여호와께 돌리고 돌릴지어다
2 **여호와께 그의 이름에 합당한 영광을 돌리며**
    거룩한 옷을 입고 여호와께 예배할지어다
3 여호와의 소리가 물 위에 있도다
    영광의 하나님이 우렛소리를 내시니
    여호와는 많은 물 위에 계시도다
4 **여호와의 소리가 힘 있음이여**
    여호와의 소리가 위엄차도다
7 여호와의 소리가 화염을 가르시도다
8 **여호와의 소리가 광야를 진동하심이여**
    여호와께서 가데스 광야를 진동시키시도다
10 여호와께서 홍수 때에 좌정하셨음이여
    여호와께서 영원하도록 왕으로 좌정하시도다
11 여호와께서 자기 백성에게 힘을 주심이여
    여호와께서 자기 백성에게 평강의 복을 주시리로다

Psalm 29

1 Ascribe to the Lord, O heavenly beings,
    ascribe to the Lord glory and strength.
2 **Ascribe to the Lord the glory of his name;**
    worship the Lord in holy splendor.
3 The voice of the Lord is over the waters;
    the God of glory thunders,
    the Lord, over mighty waters.
4 **The voice of the Lord is powerful;**
    the voice of the Lord is full of majesty.
7 The voice of the Lord flashes forth flames of fire.
8 **The voice of the Lord shakes the wilderness;**
    the Lord shakes the wilderness of Kadesh.
10 The Lord sits enthroned over the flood;
    the Lord sits enthroned as king forever.
11 May the Lord give strength to his people!
    May the Lord bless his people with peace!

시편 30

4 주의 성도들아 여호와를 찬송하며
그의 거룩함을 기억하며 감사하라
5 그의 노염은 잠깐이요 그의 은총은 평생이로다
저녁에는 울음이 깃들일지라도
아침에는 기쁨이 오리로다
6 내가 형통할 때에 말하기를
영원히 흔들리지 아니하리라 하였도다
7 여호와여 주의 은혜로 나를 산 같이 굳게 세우셨더니
주의 얼굴을 가리시매 내가 근심하였나이다
8 여호와여 내가 주께 부르짖고 여호와께 간구하기를
10 여호와여 들으시고 내게 은혜를 베푸소서
여호와여 나를 돕는 자가 되소서
11 주께서 나의 슬픔이 변하여 내게 춤이 되게 하시며
나의 베옷을 벗기고 기쁨으로 띠 띠우셨나이다

Psalm 30

4 Sing praises to the Lord,
    O you his faithful ones,
    and give thanks to his holy name.
5 For his anger is but for a moment;
    his favor is for a lifetime.
    Weeping may linger for the night,
    but joy comes with the morning.
6 As for me, I said in my prosperity,
    "I shall never be moved."
7 By your favor, O Lord,
    you had established me as a strong mountain;
    you hid your face; I was dismayed.
8 To you, O Lord, I cried,
    and to the Lord I made supplication:
10 hear, O Lord, and be gracious to me!
    O Lord, be my helper!
11 You have turned my mourning into dancing;
    you have taken off my sackcloth
        and clothed me with joy.

시편 31

1 여호와여 내가 주께 피하오니
   나를 영원히 부끄럽게 하지 마시고
   주의 공의로 나를 건지소서
2 내게 귀를 기울여 속히 건지시고
   내게 견고한 바위와 구원하는 산성이 되소서
3 **주는 나의 반석과 산성이시니**
   그러므로 주의 이름을 생각하셔서
   나를 인도하시고 지도하소서
7 내가 주의 인자하심을 기뻐하며 즐거워할 것은
   주께서 나의 고난을 보시고
   환난 중에 있는 내 영혼을 아셨으며
8 나를 원수의 수중에 가두지 아니하셨고
   내 발을 넓은 곳에 세우셨음이니이다
15 나의 앞날이 주의 손에 있사오니
   내 원수들과 나를 핍박하는 자들의 손에서 나를 건져 주소서
16 주의 얼굴을 주의 종에게 비추시고
   주의 사랑하심으로 나를 구원하소서

Psalm 31

1 In you, O Lord, I seek refuge;
   do not let me ever be put to shame;
   in your righteousness deliver me.
2 Incline your ear to me; rescue me speedily.
   Be a rock of refuge for me, a strong fortress to save me.
3 **You are indeed my rock and my fortress;**
   for your name's sake lead me and guide me,
7 I will exult and rejoice in your steadfast love,
   because you have seen my affliction;
   you have taken heed of my adversities,
8 and have not delivered me into the hand of the enemy;
   you have set my feet in a broad place.
15 My times are in your hand;
   deliver me from the hand of my enemies and persecutors.
16 Let your face shine upon your servant;
   save me in your steadfast love.

시편 33

1 너희 의인들아 여호와를 즐거워하라
찬송은 정직한 자들이 마땅히 할 바로다

3 새 노래로 그를 노래하며
즐거운 소리로 아름답게 연주할지어다

4 **여호와의 말씀은 정직하며**
그가 행하시는 일은 다 진실하시도다

5 그는 공의와 정의를 사랑하심이여
세상에는 여호와의 인자하심이 충만하도다

6 여호와의 말씀으로 하늘이 지음이 되었으며
그 만상을 그의 입 기운으로 이루었도다

8 **온 땅은 여호와를 두려워하며**
세상의 모든 거민들은 그를 경외할지어다

20 우리 영혼이 여호와를 바람이여
그는 우리의 도움과 방패시로다

22 **여호와여 우리가 주께 바라는 대로**
주의 인자하심을 우리에게 베푸소서

Psalm 33

1 Rejoice in the Lord, O you righteous.
Praise befits the upright.

3 Sing to him a new song;
play skillfully on the strings, with loud shouts.

4 **For the word of the Lord is upright,**
and all his work is done in faithfulness.

5 He loves righteousness and justice;
the earth is full of the steadfast love of the Lord.

6 By the word of the Lord
the heavens were made,
and all their host by the breath of his mouth.

8 **Let all the earth fear the Lord; let all the**
inhabitants of the world stand in awe of him.

20 Our soul waits for the Lord;
he is our help and shield.

22 **Let your steadfast love, O Lord,**
be upon us, even as we hope in you.

시편 36

5 여호와여 주의 인자하심이 하늘에 있고
  주의 진실하심이 공중에 사무쳤으며
6 주의 공의는 하나님의 산들과 같고
  주의 심판은 큰 바다와 같으니이다
  여호와여 주는 사람과 짐승을 구하여 주시나이다
7 하나님이여 주의 인자하심이
  어찌 그리 보배로우신지요
  사람들이 주의 날개 그늘 아래에 피하나이다
8 그들이 주의 집에 있는 살진 것으로 풍족할 것이라
  주께서 주의 복락의 강물을 마시게 하시리이다
9 진실로 생명의 원천이 주께 있사오니
  주의 빛 안에서 우리가 빛을 보리이다
10 주를 아는 자들에게
   주의 인자하심을 계속 베푸시며
   마음이 정직한 자에게 주의 공의를 베푸소서
11 교만한 자의 발이 내게 이르지 못하게 하시며
   악인들의 손이 나를 쫓아내지 못하게 하소서

Psalm 36

5 Your steadfast love, O Lord, extends to the heavens,
  your faithfulness to the clouds.
6 Your righteousness is like the mighty mountains,
    your judgments are like the great deep;
  you save humans and animals alike, O Lord.
7 How precious is your steadfast love, O God!
  All people may take refuge in the shadow of your wings.
8 They feast on the abundance of your house,
  and you give them drink
    from the river of your delights.
9 For with you is the fountain of life;
  in your light we see light.
10 O continue your steadfast love to those who know you,
   and your salvation to the upright of heart!
11 Do not let the foot of the arrogant tread on me,
   or the hand of the wicked drive me away.

시편 37

1 악을 행하는 자들 때문에 불평하지 말며
불의를 행하는 자들을 시기하지 말지어다
2 그들은 풀과 같이 속히 베임을 당할 것이며
푸른 채소 같이 쇠잔할 것임이로다
3 **여호와를 의뢰하고 선을 행하라**
땅에 머무는 동안 그의 성실을 먹을 거리로 삼을지어다
4 또 여호와를 기뻐하라
그가 네 마음의 소원을 네게 이루어 주시리로다
5 **네 길을 여호와께 맡기라 그를 의지하면 그가 이루시고**
6 네 의를 빛 같이 나타내시며
네 공의를 정오의 빛 같이 하시리로다
7 여호와 앞에 잠잠하고 참고 기다리라
자기 길이 형통하며
악한 꾀를 이루는 자 때문에 불평하지 말지어다
18 여호와께서 온전한 자의 날을 아시나니
그들의 기업은 영원하리로다

Psalm 37

1 Do not fret because of the wicked;
do not be envious of wrongdoers,
2 for they will soon fade like the grass,
and wither like the green herb.
3 **Trust in the Lord, and do good;**
so you will live in the land, and enjoy security.
4 Take delight in the Lord,
and he will give you the desires of your heart.
5 **Commit your way to the Lord;**
trust in him, and he will act.
6 He will make your vindication shine like the light,
and the justice of your cause like the noonday.
7 Be still before the Lord, and wait patiently for him;
do not fret over those who prosper in their way,
over those who carry out evil devices.
18 The Lord knows the days of the blameless,
and their heritage will abide forever.

시편 46

1 하나님은 우리의 피난처이시요 힘이시니
　　환난 중에 만날 큰 도움이시라
4 **한 시내가 있어 나뉘어 흘러**
　　하나님의 성 곧 지존하신 이의 성소를 기쁘게 하도다
5 하나님이 그 성 중에 계시매
　　성이 흔들리지 아니할 것이라
　　새벽에 하나님이 도우시리로다
7 만군의 여호와께서 우리와 함께 하시니
　　야곱의 하나님은 우리의 피난처시로다
8 와서 여호와의 행적을 볼지어다
　　그가 땅을 황무지로 만드셨도다
9 **그가 땅 끝까지 전쟁을 쉬게 하심이여**
　　활을 꺾고 창을 끊으며 수레를 불사르시는도다
10 너희는 가만히 있어 내가 하나님 됨을 알지어다.
　　내가 뭇 나라 중에서 높임을 받으리라
　　내가 세계 중에서 높임을 받으리라 하시도다.

Psalm 46

1 God is our refuge and strength,
　　a very present help in trouble.
4 **There is a river whose streams**
　　make glad the city of God,
　　the holy habitation of the Most High.
5 God is in the midst of the city; it shall not be moved;
　　God will help it when the morning dawns.
7 The Lord of hosts is with us;
　　the God of Jacob is our refuge.
8 Come, behold the works of the Lord;
　　see what desolations he has brought on the earth.
9 **He makes wars cease to the end of the earth;**
　　he breaks the bow, and shatters the spear;
　　he burns the shields with fire.
10 "Be still, and know that I am God!
　　I am exalted among the nations,
　　I am exalted in the earth."

시편 62

5 나의 영혼아 잠잠히 하나님만 바라라
    무릇 나의 소망이 그로부터 나오는도다
6 **오직 그만이 나의 반석이시요 나의 구원이시요**
    나의 요새이시니 내가 흔들리지 아니하리로다
7 나의 구원과 영광이 하나님께 있음이여
    내 힘의 반석과 피난처도 하나님께 있도다
8 백성들아 시시로 그를 의지하고
    그의 앞에 마음을 토하라
        하나님은 우리의 피난처시로다
9 아, 슬프도다 사람은 입김이며 인생도 속임수이니
    저울에 달면 그들은 입김보다 가벼우리로다
11 하나님이 한두 번 하신 말씀을 내가 들었나니
    권능은 하나님께 속하였다 하셨도다
12 **주여 인자함은 주께 속하오니**
    주께서 각 사람이 행한 대로 갚으심이니이다

Psalm 62

5 For God alone my soul waits in silence,
    for my hope is from him.
6 **He alone is my rock and my salvation, my fortress;**
    I shall not be shaken.
7 On God rests my deliverance and my honor;
    my mighty rock, my refuge is in God.
8 Trust in him at all times, O people;
    pour out your heart before him;
        God is a refuge for us.
9 Those of low estate are but a breath,
    those of high estate are a delusion;
    in the balances they go up;
        they are together lighter than a breath.
11 Once God has spoken;
    twice have I heard this:
    that power belongs to God,
12 **and steadfast love belongs to you, O Lord.**
    For you repay to all according to their work.

시편 63

1 하나님이여 주는 나의 하나님이시라
   내가 간절히 주를 찾되
   물이 없어 마르고 황폐한 땅에서
   내 영혼이 주를 갈망하며
   내 육체가 주를 앙모하나이다
2 내가 주의 권능과 영광을 보기 위하여
   이와 같이 성소에서 주를 바라보았나이다
3 **주의 인자하심이 생명보다 나으므로**
   내 입술이 주를 찬양할 것이라
4 이러므로 나의 평생에 주를 송축하며
   주의 이름으로 말미암아 나의 손을 들리이다
5 골수와 기름진 것을 먹음과 같이 나의 영혼이 만족할 것이라
   나의 입이 기쁜 입술로 주를 찬송하되
6 내가 나의 침상에서 주를 기억하며
   새벽에 주의 말씀을 작은 소리로 읊조릴 때에 하오리니
7 **주는 나의 도움이 되셨음이라**
   내가 주의 날개 그늘에서 즐겁게 부르리이다

Psalm 63

1 O God, you are my God,
   I seek you, my soul thirsts for you;
   my flesh faints for you, as in a dry and weary land
   where there is no water.
2 So I have looked upon you in the sanctuary,
   beholding your power and glory.
3 **Because your steadfast love is better than life,**
   my lips will praise you.
4 So I will bless you as long as I live;
   I will lift up my hands and call on your name.
5 My soul is satisfied as with a rich feast,
   and my mouth praises you with joyful lips
6 when I think of you on my bed,
   and meditate on you in the watches of the night;
7 **for you have been my help,**
   and in the shadow of your wings I sing for joy.

시편 67

1 하나님은 우리에게 은혜를 베푸사 복을 주시고
    그의 얼굴 빛을 우리에게 비추사

2 **주의 도를 땅 위에,**
    주의 구원을 모든 나라에게 알리소서

3 하나님이여 민족들이 주를 찬송하게 하시며
    모든 민족들이 주를 찬송하게 하소서

4 온 백성은 기쁘고 즐겁게 노래할지니
    주는 민족들을 공평히 심판하시며
      땅 위의 나라들을 다스리실 것임이니이다

5 하나님이여 민족들이 주를 찬송하게 하시며
    모든 민족으로 주를 찬송하게 하소서

6 땅이 그의 소산을 내어 주었으니
    하나님 곧 우리 하나님이
      우리에게 복을 주시리로다

7 하나님이 우리에게 복을 주시리니
    땅의 모든 끝이 하나님을 경외하리로다

Psalm 67

1 May God be gracious to us and bless us
    and make his face to shine upon us,

2 **that your way may be known upon earth,**
    your saving power among all nations.

3 Let the peoples praise you, O God;
    let all the peoples praise you.

4 Let the nations be glad and sing for joy,
    for you judge the peoples with equity
      and guide the nations upon earth.

5 Let the peoples praise you, O God;
    let all the peoples praise you.

6 The earth has yielded its increase;
    God, our God, has blessed us.

7 May God continue to bless us;
    let all the ends of the earth revere him.

시편 70

1 하나님이여 나를 건지소서
여호와여 속히 나를 도우소서

2 나의 영혼을 찾는 자들이
수치와 무안을 당하게 하시며
나의 상함을 기뻐하는 자들이
뒤로 물러가 수모를 당하게 하소서

3 아하, 아하 하는 자들이 자기 수치로 말미암아
뒤로 물러가게 하소서

4 **주를 찾는 모든 자들이**
주로 말미암아 기뻐하고 즐거워하게 하시며
주의 구원을 사랑하는 자들이 항상 말하기를
하나님은 위대하시다 하게 하소서

5 나는 가난하고 궁핍하오니
하나님이여 속히 내게 임하소서
주는 나의 도움이시오 나를 건지시는 이시오니
여호와여 지체하지 마소서

Psalm 70

1 Be pleased, O God, to deliver me.
O Lord, make haste to help me!

2 Let those be put to shame and confusion
who seek my life.
Let those be turned back
and brought to dishonor who desire to hurt me.

3 Let those who say, "Aha, Aha!"
turn back because of their shame.

4 **Let all who seek you**
rejoice and be glad in you.
Let those who love your salvation
say evermore, "God is great!"

5 But I am poor and needy;
hasten to me, O God!
You are my help and my deliverer;
O Lord, do not delay!

시편 71

1 여호와여 내가 주께 피하오니
 내가 영원히 수치를 당하게 하지 마소서

2 주의 공의로 나를 건지시며 나를 풀어 주시며
 주의 귀를 내게 기울이사 나를 구원하소서

3 주는 내가 항상 피하여 숨을 바위가 되소서
 주께서 나를 구원하라 명령하셨으니
 　　이는 주께서 나의 반석이시요 나의 요새이심이니이다

4 나의 하나님이여 나를 악인의 손
 　　곧 불의한 자와 흉악한 자의 장중에서 피하게 하소서

5 **주 여호와여 주는 나의 소망이시요 내가 어릴 때부터 신뢰한 이시라**

6 내가 모태에서부터 주를 의지하였으며
 　　나의 어머니의 배에서부터 주께서 나를 택하셨사오니
 나는 항상 주를 찬송하리이다

7 나는 무리에게 이상한 징조 같이 되었사오나
 　　주는 나의 견고한 피난처시오니

8 **주를 찬송함과 주께 영광 돌림이 종일토록 내 입에 가득하리이다**

Psalm 71

1 In you, O Lord, I take refuge;
 let me never be put to shame.

2 In your righteousness deliver me and rescue me;
 incline your ear to me and save me.

3 Be to me a rock of refuge, a strong fortress,
 to save me, for you are my rock and fortress.

4 Rescue me, O my God, from the hand of the wicked,
 　　from the grasp of the unjust and cruel.

5 **For you, O Lord, are my hope, my trust,**
 　　O Lord, from my youth.

6 Upon you I have leaned from my birth;
 　　it was you who took me from my mother's womb.
 My praise is continually of you.

7 I have been like a portent to many,
 　　but you are my strong refuge.

8 **My mouth is filled with your praise,**
 　　and with your glory all day long.

시편 72

1 하나님이여 주의 판단력을 왕에게 주시고
주의 공의를 왕의 아들에게 주소서
2 그가 주의 백성을 공의로 재판하며
주의 가난한 자를 정의로 재판하리니
3 공의로 말미암아 산들이 백성에게 평강을 주며
작은 산들도 그리하리로다
4 **그가 가난한 백성의 억울함을 풀어 주며**
궁핍한 자의 자손을 구원하며 압박하는 자를 꺾으리로다
11 모든 왕이 그의 앞에 부복하며
모든 민족이 다 그를 섬기리로다
17 그의 이름이 영구함이여 그의 이름이 해와 같이 장구하리로다
사람들이 그로 말미암아 복을 받으리니
모든 민족이 다 그를 복되다 하리로다
19 그 영화로운 이름을 영원히 찬송할지라
온 땅에 그의 영광이 충만할지어다
아멘 아멘

Psalm 72

1 Give the king your justice, O God,
and your righteousness to a king's son.
2 May he judge your people with righteousness,
and your poor with justice.
3 May the mountains yield prosperity for the people,
and the hills, in righteousness.
4 **May he defend the cause of the poor of the people,**
give deliverance to the needy, and crush the oppressor.
11 May all kings fall down before him,
all nations give him service.
17 May his name endure forever,
his fame continue as long as the sun.
May all nations be blessed in him;
may they pronounce him happy.
19 Blessed be his glorious name forever;
may his glory fill the whole earth.
Amen and Amen.

시편 80

1 요셉을 양 떼 같이 인도하시는 이스라엘의 목자여
귀를 기울이소서
그룹 사이에 좌정하신 이여 빛을 비추소서
2 에브라임과 베냐민과 므낫세 앞에서
주의 능력을 나타내사 우리를 구원하러 오소서
3 하나님이여 우리를 돌이키시고
주의 얼굴빛을 비추사
우리가 구원을 얻게 하소서
4 만군의 하나님 여호와여
주의 백성의 기도에 대하여
어느 때까지 노하시리이까
5 **주께서 그들에게 눈물의 양식을 먹이시며**
많은 눈물을 마시게 하셨나이다
6 우리를 우리 이웃에게 다툼 거리가 되게 하시니
우리 원수들이 서로 비웃나이다
7 **만군의 하나님이여 우리를 회복하여 주시고**
주의 얼굴의 광채를 비추사
우리가 구원을 얻게 하소서

Psalm 80

1 Give ear, O Shepherd of Israel,
    you who lead Joseph like a flock!
You who are enthroned upon the cherubim, shine forth
2 before Ephraim and Benjamin and Manasseh.
Stir up your might, and come to save us!
3 Restore us, O God;
let your face shine, that we may be saved.
4 O Lord God of hosts,
    how long will you be angry with your people's prayers?
5 **You have fed them with the bread of tears,**
    and given them tears to drink in full measure.
6 You make us the scorn of our neighbors;
    our enemies laugh among themselves.
7 **Restore us, O God of hosts;**
    let your face shine, that we may be saved.

시편 81

8 내 백성이여 들으라 내가 네게 증언하리라
    이스라엘이여 내게 듣기를 원하노라

9 **너희 중에 다른 신을 두지 말며**
    이방 신에게 절하지 말지어다

10 나는 너를 애굽 땅에서 인도하여 낸
    여호와 네 하나님이니
    네 입을 크게 열라 내가 채우리라 하였으나

11 내 백성이 내 소리를 듣지 아니하며
    이스라엘이 나를 원하지 아니하였도다.

12 그러므로 내가 그의 마음을
    완악한 대로 버려 두어
    그의 임의대로 행하게 하였도다

13 **내 백성아 내 말을 들으라**
    이스라엘아 내 도를 따르라

14 그리하면 내가 속히 그들의 원수를 누르고
    내 손을 돌려 그들의 대적들을 치리라

Psalm 81

8 Hear, O my people, while I admonish you;
    O Israel, if you would but listen to me!

9 **There shall be no strange god among you;**
    you shall not bow down to a foreign god.

10 I am the Lord your God,
    who brought you up out of the land of Egypt.
    Open your mouth wide and I will fill it.

11 But my people did not listen to my voice;
    Israel would not submit to me.

12 So I gave them over to their stubborn hearts,
    to follow their own counsels.

13 **O that my people would listen to me,**
    that Israel would walk in my ways!

14 Then I would quickly subdue their enemies,
    and turn my hand against their foes.

시편 82

1 하나님은 신들의 모임 가운데에 서시며
   하나님은 그들 가운데에서 재판하시느니라
2 **너희가 불공평한 판단을 하며**
   악인의 낯 보기를 언제까지 하려느냐
3 가난한 자와 고아를 위하여 판단하며
   곤란한 자와 빈궁한 자에게 공의를 베풀지며
4 **가난한 자와 궁핍한 자를 구원하여**
   악인들의 손에서 건질지니라 하시는도다
5 그들은 알지도 못하고 깨닫지도 못하여
   흑암 중에 왕래하니 땅의 모든 터가 흔들리도다
6 **내가 말하기를 너희는 신들이며**
   다 지존자의 아들들이라 하였으나
7 그러나 너희는 사람처럼 죽으며
   고관의 하나 같이 넘어지리로다
8 **하나님이여 일어나사 세상을 심판하소서**
   모든 나라가 주의 소유이기 때문이니이다

Psalm 82

1 God has taken his place in the divine council;
   in the midst of the gods he holds judgment:
2 **"How long will you judge unjustly**
   and show partiality to the wicked?
3 Give justice to the weak and the orphan;
   maintain the right of the lowly and the destitute.
4 **Rescue the weak and the needy;**
   deliver them from the hand of the wicked."
5 They have neither knowledge nor understanding,
   they walk around in darkness;
   all the foundations of the earth are shaken.
6 **I say, "You are gods,**
   children of the Most High, all of you;
7 nevertheless, you shall die like mortals
   and fall like any prince."
8 **Rise up, O God, judge the earth;**
   for all the nations belong to you!

시편 85

1 여호와여 주께서 주의 땅에 은혜를 베푸사
    야곱의 포로 된 자들이 돌아오게 하셨으며
2 **주의 백성의 죄악을 사하시고**
    그들의 모든 죄를 덮으셨나이다
3 주의 모든 분노를 거두시며
    주의 진노를 돌이키셨나이다
4 **우리 구원의 하나님이여 우리를 돌이키시고**
    우리에게 향하신 주의 분노를 거두소서
5 주께서 우리에게 영원히 노하시며 대대에 진노하시겠나이까
6 **주께서 우리를 다시 살리사 주의 백성이**
    주를 기뻐하도록 하지 아니하시겠나이까
7 여호와여 주의 인자하심을 우리에게 보이시며
    주의 구원을 우리에게 주소서
10 **인애와 진리가 같이 만나고 의와 화평이 서로 입맞추었으며**
11 **진리는 땅에서 솟아나고 의는 하늘에서 굽어보도다**

Psalm 85

1 Lord, you were favorable to your land;
    you restored the fortunes of Jacob.
2 **You forgave the iniquity of your people;**
    you pardoned all their sin.
3 You withdrew all your wrath;
    you turned from your hot anger.
4 **Restore us again, O God of our salvation,**
    and put away your indignation toward us.
5 Will you be angry with us forever?
    Will you prolong your anger to all generations?
6 **Will you not revive us again,**
    so that your people may rejoice in you?
7 Show us your steadfast love, O Lord,
    and grant us your salvation.
10 Steadfast love and faithfulness will meet;
    righteousness and peace will kiss each other.
11 **Faithfulness will spring up from the ground,**
    and righteousness will look down from the sky.

시편 91

1 지존자의 은밀한 곳에 거주하며
전능자의 그늘 아래에 사는 자여,
2 나는 여호와를 향하여 말하기를
그는 나의 피난처요 나의 요새요
내가 의뢰하는 하나님이라 하리니
3 **이는 그가 너를 새 사냥꾼의 올무에서와**
심한 전염병에서 건지실 것임이로다
4 그가 너를 그의 깃으로 덮으시리니
네가 그의 날개 아래에 피하리로다
그의 진실함은 방패와 손방패가 되시나니
9 네가 말하기를 여호와는 나의 피난처시라 하고
지존자를 너의 거처로 삼았으므로
10 화가 네게 미치지 못하며
재앙이 네 장막에 가까이 오지 못하리니
16 내가 그를 장수하게 함으로 그를 만족하게 하며
나의 구원을 그에게 보이리라 하시도다

Psalm 91

1 You who live in the shelter of the Most High,
who abide in the shadow of the Almighty,
2 will say to the Lord,
"My refuge and my fortress;
my God, in whom I trust."
3 **For he will deliver you**
from the snare of the fowler
and from the deadly pestilence;
4 he will cover you with his pinions,
and under his wings you will find refuge;
his faithfulness is a shield and buckler.
9 Because you have made the Lord your refuge,
the Most High your dwelling place,
10 no evil shall befall you,
no scourge come near your tent.
16 With long life I will satisfy them,
and show them my salvation.

시편 92

1 가장 높으신 하나님께 감사를 드리며
　　　주의 이름을 찬양하고
2 **아침마다 주의 인자하심을 알리며**
　　　밤마다 주의 성실하심을 베풂이 좋으니이다
3 십현금과 비파와 수금으로 찬양함이 좋으니이다
4 **여호와여 주께서 행하신 일로 나를 기쁘게 하셨으니**
　　　주의 손이 행하신 일로 말미암아
　　　내가 높이 외치리이다
5 여호와여
　　　주께서 행하신 일이 어찌 그리 크신지요
　　　주의 생각이 매우 깊으시니이다
6 **어리석은 자도 알지 못하며**
　　　무지한 자도 이를 깨닫지 못하나이다
7 악인들은 풀 같이 자라고
　　　악을 행하는 자들은 다 흥왕할지라도
　　　영원히 멸망하리이다
8 **여호와여 주는 영원토록 지존하시니이다**

Psalm 92

1 It is good to give thanks to the Lord,
　　　to sing praises to your name, O Most High;
2 **to declare your steadfast love in the morning,**
　　　and your faithfulness by night,
3 to the music of the lute and the harp,
　　　to the melody of the lyre.
4 **For you, O Lord, have made me glad by your work;**
　　　at the works of your hands I sing for joy.
5 How great are your works, O Lord!
　　　Your thoughts are very deep!
6 **The dullard cannot know,**
　　　the stupid cannot understand this:
7 though the wicked sprout like grass
　　　and all evildoers flourish,
　　　they are doomed to destruction forever,
8 **but you, O Lord, are on high forever.**

시편 95

1 오라 우리가 여호와께 노래하며
　우리의 구원의 반석을 향하여 즐거이 외치자
2 우리가 감사함으로 그 앞에 나아가며
　　시를 지어 즐거이 그를 노래하자
3 **여호와는 크신 하나님이시요**
　　모든 신들보다 크신 왕이시기 때문이로다
4 땅의 깊은 곳이 그의 손 안에 있으며
　　산들의 높은 곳도 그의 것이로다
5 **바다도 그의 것이라 그가 만드셨고**
　　육지도 그의 손이 지으셨도다
6 오라 우리가 굽혀 경배하며
　　우리를 지으신 여호와 앞에 무릎을 꿇자
7 **그는 우리의 하나님이시요**
　　우리는 그가 기르시는 백성이며
　　그의 손이 돌보시는 양이기 때문이라

Psalm 95

1 O come, let us sing to the Lord;
　let us make a joyful noise
　　to the rock of our salvation!
2 Let us come into his presence with thanksgiving;
　let us make a joyful noise to him
　　with songs of praise!
3 For the Lord is a great God,
　and a great King above all gods.
4 In his hand are the depths of the earth;
　　the heights of the mountains are his also.
5 **The sea is his, for he made it,**
　　and the dry land,
　　which his hands have formed.
6 O come, let us worship and bow down,
　　let us kneel before the Lord, our Maker!
7 **For he is our God,**
　　and we are the people of his pasture,
　　and the sheep of his hand.

시편 99

1 여호와께서 다스리시니 만민이 떨 것이요
  여호와께서 그룹 사이에 좌정하시니
      땅이 흔들릴 것이로다
2 시온에 계시는 여호와는 위대하시고
      모든 민족보다 높으시도다
3 **주의 크고 두려운 이름을 찬송할지니**
      그는 거룩하심이로다
4 능력 있는 왕은 정의를 사랑하느니라
  주께서 공의를 견고하게 세우시고
      주께서 야곱에게 정의와 공의를 행하시나이다
5 너희는 여호와 우리 하나님을 높여
  그의 발등상 앞에서 경배할지어다
      그는 거룩하시도다
9 너희는 여호와 우리 하나님을 높이고
      그 성산에서 예배할지어다
  여호와 우리 하나님은 거룩하심이로다

Psalm 99

1 The Lord is king; let the peoples tremble!
  He sits enthroned upon the cherubim;
      let the earth quake!
2 The Lord is great in Zion;
      he is exalted over all the peoples.
3 **Let them praise your great**
      and awesome name. Holy is he!
4 Mighty King, lover of justice,
      you have established equity;
  you have executed justice
      and righteousness in Jacob.
5 Extol the Lord our God;
  worship at his footstool. Holy is he!
9 Extol the Lord our God,
      and worship at his holy mountain;
  for the Lord our God is holy.

시편 100
(일반주일 혹은 감사절)

1 온 땅이여
    여호와께 즐거운 찬송을 부를지어다
2 **기쁨으로 여호와를 섬기며**
    노래하면서 그의 앞에 나아갈지어다
3 여호와가 우리 하나님이신 줄 너희는 알지어다
  그는 우리를 지으신 이요
    우리는 그의 것이니 그의 백성이요
    그의 기르시는 양이로다
4 감사함으로 그의 문에 들어가며
    찬송함으로 그의 궁정에 들어가서
  그에게 감사하며
    그의 이름을 송축할지어다
5 여호와는 선하시니
    그의 인자하심이 영원하고
  그의 성실하심이 대대에 이르리로다

Psalm 100
(Regular Sundays or Thanksgiving)

1 Make a joyful noise to the Lord, all the earth.
2 **Worship the Lord with gladness;**
    come into his presence with singing.
3 Know that the Lord is God.
  It is he that made us, and we are his;
    we are his people,
    and the sheep of his pasture.
4 Enter his gates with thanksgiving,
    and his courts with praise.
  Give thanks to him, bless his name.
5 For the Lord is good;
    his steadfast love endures forever,
  and his faithfulness to all generations.

시편 102

1 여호와여 내 기도를 들으시고
나의 부르짖음을 주께 상달하게 하소서
12 여호와여 주는 영원히 계시고
주에 대한 기억은 대대에 이르리이다
13 주께서 일어나사 시온을 긍휼히 여기시리니
지금은 그에게 은혜를 베푸실 때라
정한 기한이 다가옴이니이다
25 주께서 옛적에 땅의 기초를 놓으셨사오며
하늘도 주의 손으로 지으신 바니이다
26 천지는 없어지려니와 주는 영존하시겠고
그것들은 다 옷 같이 낡으리니
의복 같이 바꾸시면 바뀌려니와
27 주는 한결같으시고 주의 연대는 무궁하리이다
28 주의 종들의 자손은 항상 안전히 거주하고
그의 후손은 주 앞에 굳게 서리이다 하였도다

Psalm 102

1 Hear my prayer, O Lord;
let my cry come to you.
12 But you, O Lord, are enthroned forever;
your name endures to all generations.
13 You will rise up and have compassion on Zion,
for it is time to favor it;
the appointed time has come.
25 Long ago you laid the foundation of the earth,
and the heavens are the work of your hands.
26 They will perish, but you endure;
they will all wear out like a garment.
You change them like clothing,
and they pass away;
27 but you are the same,
and your years have no end.
28 The children of your servants shall live secure;
their offspring shall be established
in your presence.

시편 105

1 여호와께 감사하고 그의 이름을 불러 아뢰며
　　그가 하는 일을 만민 중에 알게 할지어다

2 **그에게 노래하며 그를 찬양하며**
　　그의 모든 기이한 일들을 말할지어다

3 그의 거룩한 이름을 자랑하라
　　여호와를 구하는 자들은 마음이 즐거울지로다

4 **여호와와 그의 능력을 구할지어다**
　　그의 얼굴을 항상 구할지어다

5 그의 종 아브라함의 후손 곧 택하신 야곱의 자손

6 **너희는 그가 행하신 기적과 그의 이적과**
　　그의 입의 판단을 기억할지어다

7 그는 여호와 우리 하나님이시라
　　그의 판단이 온 땅에 있도다

8 **그는 그의 언약**
　　곧 천 대에 걸쳐 명령하신 말씀을
　　영원히 기억하셨도다

Psalm 105

1 O give thanks to the Lord, call on his name,
　　make known his deeds among the peoples.

2 **Sing to him, sing praises to him;**
　　tell of all his wonderful works.

3 Glory in his holy name,
　　let the hearts of those who seek the Lord rejoice.

4 **Seek the Lord and his strength;**
　　seek his presence continually.

5 Remember the wonderful works he has done,
　　his miracles, and the judgments he uttered,

6 **O offspring of his servant Abraham,**
　　children of Jacob, his chosen ones.

7 He is the Lord our God;
　　his judgments are in all the earth.

8 **He is mindful of his covenant forever,**
　　of the word that he commanded,
　　for a thousand generations.

시편 112

1 할렐루야,

여호와를 경외하며

    그의 계명을 크게 즐거워하는 자는 복이 있도다

2 그의 후손이 땅에서 강성함이여

    정직한 자들의 후손에게 복이 있으리로다

3 **부와 재물이 그의 집에 있음이여**

    그의 공의가 영구히 서 있으리로다

4 정직한 자들에게는 흑암 중에 빛이 일어나나니

    그는 자비롭고 긍휼이 많으며 의로운 이시로다

5 은혜를 베풀며 꾸어 주는 자는 잘 되나니

    그 일을 정의로 행하리로다

6 **그는 영원히 흔들리지 아니함이여 의인은 영원히 기억되리로다**

7 그는 흉한 소문을 두려워하지 아니함이여

    여호와를 의뢰하고 그의 마음을 굳게 정하였도다

8 그의 마음이 견고하여 두려워하지 아니할 것이라

    그의 대적들이 받는 보응을 마침내 보리로다

Psalm 112

1 Praise the Lord!

Happy are those who fear the Lord,

    who greatly delight in his commandments.

2 Their descendants will be mighty in the land;

    the generation of the upright will be blessed.

3 **Wealth and riches are in their houses,**

    and their righteousness endures forever.

4 They rise in the darkness as a light for the upright;

    they are gracious, merciful, and righteous.

5 It is well with those who deal generously and lend,

    who conduct their affairs with justice.

6 For the righteous will never be moved;

    they will be remembered forever.

7 They are not afraid of evil tidings;

    their hearts are firm, secure in the Lord.

8 Their hearts are steady, they will not be afraid;

    in the end they will look in triumph on their foes.

시편 113

1 할렐루야,
  여호와의 종들아 찬양하라
      여호와의 이름을 찬양하라
2 이제부터 영원까지
      여호와의 이름을 찬송할지로다
3 **해 돋는 데에서부터 해 지는 데에까지**
      여호와의 이름이 찬양을 받으시리로다
4 여호와는 모든 나라보다 높으시며
  그의 영광은 하늘보다 높으시도다
5 여호와 우리 하나님과 같은 이가 누구리요
      높은 곳에 앉으셨으나
6 **스스로 낮추사 천지를 살피시고**
7 가난한 자를 먼지 더미에서 일으키시며
      궁핍한 자를 거름 더미에서 들어 세워
8 **지도자들 곧 그의 백성의 지도자들과**
      함께 세우시는도다

Psalm 113

1 Praise the Lord!
  Praise, O servants of the Lord;
      praise the name of the Lord.
2 Blessed be the name of the Lord
      from this time on and forevermore.
3 **From the rising of the sun to its setting**
      the name of the Lord is to be praised.
4 The Lord is high above all nations,
  and his glory above the heavens.
5 Who is like the Lord our God,
      who is seated on high,
6 **who looks far down on the heavens**
      and the earth?
7 He raises the poor from the dust,
      and lifts the needy from the ash heap,
8 **to make them sit with princes,**
      with the princes of his people.

시편 115

1 여호와여 영광을 우리에게 돌리지 마옵소서
　　우리에게 돌리지 마옵소서
오직 주는 인자하시고 진실하시므로
　　주의 이름에만 영광을 돌리소서
2 어찌하여 뭇 나라가
　　그들의 하나님이 이제 어디 있느냐 말하게 하리이까
3 **오직 우리 하나님은 하늘에 계셔서**
　　원하시는 모든 것을 행하셨나이다
4 그들의 우상들은 은과 금이요 사람이 손으로 만든 것이라
5 **입이 있어도 말하지 못하며 눈이 있어도 보지 못하며**
6 귀가 있어도 듣지 못하며 코가 있어도 냄새 맡지 못하며
7 **손이 있어도 만지지 못하며 발이 있어도 걷지 못하며**
　　목구멍이 있어도 작은 소리조차 내지 못하느니라
8 우상들을 만드는 자들과 그것을 의지하는 자들이
　　다 그와 같으리로다
9 **이스라엘아 여호와를 의지하라**
　　그는 너희의 도움이시요 너희의 방패시로다

Psalm 115

1 Not to us, O Lord, not to us, but to your name give glory,
for the sake of your steadfast love and your faithfulness.
2 Why should the nations say, "Where is their God?"
3 **Our God is in the heavens;**
　　he does whatever he pleases.
4 Their idols are silver and gold, the work of human hands.
5 **They have mouths, but do not speak;**
　　eyes, but do not see.
6 They have ears, but do not hear; noses, but do not smell.
7 **They have hands, but do not feel;**
　　feet, but do not walk;
　　they make no sound in their throats.
8 Those who make them are like them;
　　so are all who trust in them.
9 **O Israel, trust in the Lord!**
　　He is their help and their shield.

시편 116

5 여호와는 은혜로우시며 의로우시며
우리 하나님은 긍휼이 많으시도다

6 여호와께서는 순진한 자를 지키시나니
내가 어려울 때에 나를 구원하셨도다

8 주께서 내 영혼을 사망에서, 내 눈을 눈물에서,
내 발을 넘어짐에서 건지셨나이다

9 **내가 생명이 있는 땅에서**
여호와 앞에 행하리로다

10 내가 크게 고통을 당하였다고 말할 때에도
나는 믿었도다

12 **내게 주신 모든 은혜를**
내가 여호와께 무엇으로 보답할까

13 내가 구원의 잔을 들고
여호와의 이름을 부르며

14 **여호와의 모든 백성 앞에서**
나는 나의 서원을 여호와께 갚으리로다

Psalm 116

5 Gracious is the Lord, and righteous;
our God is merciful.

6 The Lord protects the simple;
when I was brought low, he saved me.

8 For you have delivered my soul from death,
my eyes from tears,
my feet from stumbling.

9 **I walk before the Lord**
in the land of the living.

10 I kept my faith, even when I said,
"I am greatly afflicted."

12 **What shall I return to the Lord**
for all his bounty to me?

13 I will lift up the cup of salvation
and call on the name of the Lord,

14 **I will pay my vows to the Lord**
in the presence of all his people.

시편 118

1 여호와께 감사하라 그는 선하시며
그의 인자하심이 영원함이로다

14 여호와는 나의 능력과 찬송이시요
또 나의 구원이 되셨도다

20 이는 여호와의 문이라 의인들이 그리로 들어가리로다

21 **주께서 내게 응답하시고 나의 구원이 되셨으니**
내가 주께 감사하리이다

22 건축자가 버린 돌이 집 모퉁이의 머릿돌이 되었나니

23 **이는 여호와께서 행하신 것이요**
우리 눈에 기이한 바로다

24 이 날은 여호와께서 정하신 것이라
이 날에 우리가 즐거워하고 기뻐하리로다

25 **여호와여 구하옵나니 이제 구원하소서**
여호와여 우리가 구하옵나니 이제 형통하게 하소서

28 주는 나의 하나님이시라 내가 주께 감사하리이다
주는 나의 하나님이시라 내가 주를 높이리이다

Psalm 118

1 O give thanks to the Lord, for he is good;
his steadfast love endures forever!

14 The Lord is my strength and my might;
he has become my salvation.

20 This is the gate of the Lord;
the righteous shall enter through it.

21 **I thank you that you have answered me**
and have become my salvation.

22 The stone that the builders rejected
has become the chief cornerstone.

23 **This is the Lord's doing; it is marvelous in our eyes.**

24 This is the day that the Lord has made;
let us rejoice and be glad in it.

25 **Save us, we beseech you, O Lord!**
O Lord, we beseech you, give us success!

28 You are my God, and I will give thanks to you;
you are my God, I will extol you.

시편 121

1 내가 산을 향하여 눈을 들리라
　　　나의 도움이 어디서 올까
2 **나의 도움은 천지를 지으신 여호와에게서로다**
3 여호와께서
　　　너를 실족하지 아니하게 하시며
　　　너를 지키시는 이가 졸지 아니하시리로다
4 **이스라엘을 지키시는 이는 졸지도 아니하시고**
　　　주무시지도 아니하시리로다
5 여호와는 너를 지키시는 이시라
　　　여호와께서 네 오른쪽에서 네 그늘이 되시나니
6 **낮의 해가 너를 상하게 하지 아니하며**
　　　밤의 달도 너를 해치지 아니하리로다
7 여호와께서 너를 지켜
　　　모든 환난을 면하게 하시며
　　　또 네 영혼을 지키시리로다
8 **여호와께서 너의 출입을**
　　　지금부터 영원까지 지키시리로다

Psalm 121

1 I lift up my eyes to the hills—
　　　from where will my help come?
2 **My help comes from the Lord,**
　　　who made heaven and earth.
3 He will not let your foot be moved;
　　　he who keeps you will not slumber.
4 **He who keeps Israel will neither slumber nor sleep.**
5 The Lord is your keeper;
　　　the Lord is your shade at your right hand.
6 **The sun shall not strike you by day,**
　　　nor the moon by night.
7 The Lord will keep you from all evil;
　　　he will keep your life.
8 **The Lord will keep your going out**
　　　and your coming in
　　　from this time on and forevermore.

시편 138

1 내가 전심으로 주께 감사하며
신들 앞에서 주께 찬송하리이다
2 내가 주의 성전을 향하여 예배하며 주의 인자하심과
성실하심으로 말미암아 주의 이름에 감사하오리니
이는 주께서 주의 말씀을
주의 모든 이름보다 높게 하셨음이라
3 내가 간구하는 날에 주께서 응답하시고
내 영혼에 힘을 주어 나를 강하게 하셨나이다
6 **여호와께서는 높이 계셔도 낮은 자를 굽어살피시며**
멀리서도 교만한 자를 아심이니이다
7 내가 환난 중에 다닐지라도 주께서 나를 살아나게 하시고
주의 손을 펴사 내 원수들의 분노를 막으시며
주의 오른손이 나를 구원하시리이다
8 여호와께서 나를 위하여 보상해 주시리이다
여호와여 주의 인자하심이 영원하오니
주의 손으로 지으신 것을 버리지 마옵소서

Psalm 138

1 I give you thanks, O Lord, with my whole heart;
before the gods I sing your praise;
2 I bow down toward your holy temple
and give thanks to your name
for your steadfast love and your faithfulness;
for you have exalted your name
and your word above everything.
3 On the day I called, you answered me,
you increased my strength of soul.
6 **For though the Lord is high, he regards the lowly;**
but the haughty he perceives from far away.
7 Though I walk in the midst of trouble,
you preserve me against the wrath of my enemies;
you stretch out your hand, and your right hand delivers me.
8 The Lord will fulfill his purpose for me;
your steadfast love, O Lord endures forever.
Do not forsake the work of your hands.

시편 139

1 여호와여 주께서 나를 살펴 보셨으므로 나를 아시나이다
2 **주께서 내가 앉고 일어섬을 아시고**
멀리서도 나의 생각을 밝히 아시오며
3 나의 모든 길과 내가 눕는 것을 살펴 보셨으므로
나의 모든 행위를 익히 아시오니
4 **여호와여 내 혀의 말을 알지 못하시는 것이**
하나도 없으시니이다
7 내가 주의 영을 떠나 어디로 가며
주의 앞에서 어디로 피하리이까
8 **내가 하늘에 올라갈지라도 거기 계시며**
스올에 내 자리를 펼지라도 거기 계시니이다
9 내가 새벽 날개를 치며 바다 끝에 가서 거주할지라도
10 **거기에서도 주의 손이 나를 인도하시며**
주의 오른손이 나를 붙드시리이다
23 하나님이여 나를 살피사 내 마음을 아시며
나를 시험하사 내 뜻을 아옵소서

Psalm 139

1 O Lord, you have searched me and known me.
2 **You know when I sit down and when I rise up;**
you discern my thoughts from far away.
3 You search out my path and my lying down,
and are acquainted with all my ways.
4 **Even before a word is on my tongue,**
O Lord, you know it completely.
7 Where can I go from your spirit?
Or where can I flee from your presence?
8 **If I ascend to heaven, you are there;**
if I make my bed in Sheol, you are there.
9 If I take the wings of the morning
and settle at the farthest limits of the sea,
10 **even there your hand shall lead me,**
and your right hand shall hold me fast.
23 Search me, O God, and know my heart;
test me and know my thoughts.

시편 141

1 여호와여 내가 주를 불렀사오니
　　속히 내게 오시옵소서
내가 주께 부르짖을 때에
　　내 음성에 귀를 기울이소서
2 나의 기도가 주의 앞에 분향함과 같이 되며
나의 손 드는 것이
　　저녁 제사 같이 되게 하소서
3 여호와여 내 입에 파수꾼을 세우시고
　　내 입술의 문을 지키소서
4 내 마음이 악한 일에 기울어
　　죄악을 행하는 자들과 함께
　　악을 행하지 말게 하시며
　　그들의 진수성찬을 먹지 말게 하소서
5 의인이 나를 칠지라도 은혜로 여기며
　　책망할지라도 머리의 기름 같이 여겨서
내 머리가 이를 거절하지 아니할지라
　　그들의 재난 중에도 내가 항상 기도하리로다

Psalm 141

1 I call upon you, O Lord;
　　come quickly to me;
give ear to my voice when I call to you.
2 Let my prayer be counted as incense before you,
and the lifting up of my hands
　　as an evening sacrifice.
3 Set a guard over my mouth, O Lord;
　　keep watch over the door of my lips.
4 **Do not turn my heart to any evil,**
　　to busy myself with wicked deeds
　　in company with those who work iniquity;
　　do not let me eat of their delicacies.
5 Let the righteous strike me;
　　let the faithful correct me.
Never let the oil of the wicked anoint my head,
　　for my prayer is continually
　　against their wicked deeds.

시편 145

3 여호와는 위대하시니 크게 찬양할 것이라
그의 위대하심을 측량하지 못하리로다

8 여호와는 은혜로우시며 긍휼이 많으시며
노하시기를 더디 하시며 인자하심이 크시도다

9 **여호와께서는 모든 것을 선대하시며**
그 지으신 모든 것에 긍휼을 베푸시는도다

10 여호와여 주께서 지으신 모든 것들이 주께 감사하며
주의 성도들이 주를 송축하리이다

15 모든 사람의 눈이 주를 앙망하오니
주는 때를 따라 그들에게 먹을 것을 주시며

16 손을 펴사 모든 생물의 소원을 만족하게 하시나이다

17 **여호와께서는 그 모든 행위에 의로우시며**
그 모든 일에 은혜로우시도다

18 여호와께서는 자기에게 간구하는 모든 자
곧 진실하게 간구하는 모든 자에게 가까이 하시는도다

19 그는 자기를 경외하는 자들의 소원을 이루시며
또 그들의 부르짖음을 들으사 구원하시리로다

Psalm 145

3 Great is the Lord, and greatly to be praised;
his greatness is unsearchable.

8 The Lord is gracious and merciful, slow to anger
and abounding in steadfast love.

9 **The Lord is good to all,**
and his compassion is over all that he has made.

10 All your works shall give thanks to you, O Lord,
and all your faithful shall bless you.

15 The eyes of all look to you,
and you give them their food in due season.

16 You open your hand, satisfying the desire of every living thing.

17 **The Lord is just in all his ways, and kind in all his doings.**

18 The Lord is near to all who call on him,
to all who call on him in truth.

19 He fulfills the desire of all who fear him;
he also hears their cry, and saves them.

시편 146

1 할렐루야 내 영혼아 여호와를 찬양하라
2 **나의 생전에 여호와를 찬양하며**
   나의 평생에 내 하나님을 찬송하리로다
3 귀인들을 의지하지 말며
   도울 힘이 없는 인생도 의지하지 말지니
4 **그의 호흡이 끊어지면 흙으로 돌아가서**
   그 날에 그의 생각이 소멸하리로다
5 야곱의 하나님을 자기의 도움으로 삼으며
   여호와 자기 하나님에게
   자기의 소망을 두는 자는 복이 있도다
6 여호와는 천지와 바다와 그 중의 만물을 지으시며
   영원히 진실함을 지키시며
7 **억눌린 사람들을 위해 정의로 심판하시며**
   주린 자들에게 먹을 것을 주시는 이시로다
   여호와께서는 갇힌 자들에게 자유를 주시는도다
9 여호와께서 나그네들을 보호하시며
   고아와 과부를 붙드시고 악인들의 길을 굽게 하시는도다

Psalm 146

1 Praise the Lord! Praise the Lord, O my soul!
2 **I will praise the Lord as long as I live;**
   I will sing praises to my God all my life long.
3 Do not put your trust in princes,
   in mortals, in whom there is no help.
4 **When their breath departs, they return to the earth;**
   on that very day their plans perish.
5 Happy are those whose help is the God of Jacob,
   whose hope is in the Lord their God,
6 who made heaven and earth, the sea,
   and all that is in them; who keeps faith forever;
7 **who executes justice for the oppressed; who gives food**
   to the hungry. The Lord sets the prisoners free.
9 The Lord watches over the strangers;
   he upholds the orphan and the widow,
   but the way of the wicked he brings to ruin.

시편 147

1 할렐루야
  우리 하나님을 찬양하는 일이 선함이여
  　　찬송하는 일이 아름답고 마땅하도다
2 여호와께서 예루살렘을 세우시며
  　　이스라엘의 흩어진 자들을 모으시며
3 **상심한 자들을 고치시며 그들의 상처를 싸매시는도다**
4 그가 별들의 수효를 세시고
  　　그것들을 다 이름대로 부르시는도다
5 **우리 주는 위대하시며 능력이 많으시며**
  　　그의 지혜가 무궁하시도다
6 여호와께서 겸손한 자들은 붙드시고
  악인들은 땅에 엎드러뜨리시는도다
7 감사함으로 여호와께 노래하며
  　　수금으로 하나님께 찬양할지어다
11 **여호와는 자기를 경외하는 자들과**
  　　그의 인자하심을 바라는 자들을 기뻐하시는도다

Psalm 147

1 Praise the Lord!
  　　How good it is to sing praises to our God;
  for he is gracious, and a song of praise is fitting.
2 The Lord builds up Jerusalem;
  　　he gathers the outcasts of Israel.
3 **He heals the brokenhearted,**
  　　and binds up their wounds.
4 He determines the number of the stars;
  　　he gives to all of them their names.
5 **Great is our Lord, and abundant in power;**
  　　his understanding is beyond measure.
6 The Lord lifts up the downtrodden;
  he casts the wicked to the ground.
7 Sing to the Lord with thanksgiving;
  　　make melody to our God on the lyre.
11 **The Lord takes pleasure in those who fear him,**
  　　in those who hope in his steadfast love.

시편 148

1 할렐루야
  하늘에서 여호와를 찬양하며
  높은 데서 그를 찬양할지어다
2 그의 모든 천사여 찬양하며
  모든 군대여 그를 찬양할지어다
3 **해와 달아 그를 찬양하며 밝은 별들아 다 그를 찬양할지어다**
5 그것들이 여호와의 이름을 찬양함은
  그가 명령하시므로 지음을 받았음이로다
6 **그가 또 그것들을 영원히 세우시고**
  폐하지 못할 명령을 정하셨도다
10 짐승과 모든 가축과 기는 것과 나는 새며
11 **세상의 왕들과 모든 백성들과 고관들과**
  땅의 모든 재판관들이며
12 총각과 처녀와 노인과 아이들아
13 **여호와의 이름을 찬양할지어다 그의 이름이 홀로 높으시며**
  그의 영광이 땅과 하늘 위에 뛰어나심이로다

Psalm 148

1 Praise the Lord!
  Praise the Lord from the heavens;
  praise him in the heights!
2 Praise him, all his angels; praise him, all his host!
3 **Praise him, sun and moon;**
  praise him, all you shining stars!
5 Let them praise the name of the Lord,
  for he commanded and they were created.
6 **He established them forever and ever;**
  he fixed their bounds, which cannot be passed.
10 Wild animals and all cattle, creeping things and flying birds!
11 **Kings of the earth and all peoples,**
  princes and all rulers of the earth!
12 Young men and women alike, old and young together!
13 **Let them praise the name of the Lord,**
  for his name alone is exalted;
  his glory is above earth and heaven.

시편 150

1 할렐루야
  그의 성소에서 하나님을 찬양하며
    그의 권능의 궁창에서 그를 찬양할지어다
2 그의 능하신 행동을 찬양하며
  그의 지극히 위대하심을 따라 찬양할지어다
3 나팔 소리로 찬양하며
    비파와 수금으로 찬양할지어다
4 소고 치며 춤 추어 찬양하며
  현악과 퉁소로 찬양할지어다
5 큰 소리 나는 제금으로 찬양하며
  높은 소리 나는 제금으로 찬양할지어다
6 호흡이 있는 자마다 여호와를 찬양할지어다
  할렐루야

Psalm 150

1 Praise the Lord!
  Praise God in his sanctuary;
    praise him in his mighty firmament!
2 Praise him for his mighty deeds;
  praise him according to his surpassing greatness!
3 Praise him with trumpet sound;
    praise him with lute and harp!
4 Praise him with tambourine and dance;
    praise him with strings and pipe!
5 Praise him with clanging cymbals;
  praise him with loud clashing cymbals!
6 Let everything that breathes praise the Lord!
  Praise the Lord!

시편 25
(일반주일 혹은 강림절)

1 여호와여 나의 영혼이 주를 우러러보나이다
4 **여호와여 주의 도를 내게 보이시고 주의 길을 내게 가르치소서**
5 주의 진리로 나를 지도하시고 교훈하소서
   주는 내 구원의 하나님이시니 내가 종일 주를 기다리나이다
6 여호와여 주의 긍휼하심과 인자하심이 영원부터 있었사오니
      주여 이것들을 기억하옵소서
7 **여호와여 내 젊은 시절의 죄와 허물을 기억하지 마시고**
      주의 인자하심을 따라 주께서 나를 기억하시되
      주의 선하심으로 하옵소서
8 여호와는 선하시고 정직하시니
      그러므로 그의 도로 죄인들을 교훈하시리로다
9 **온유한 자를 정의로 지도하심이여**
      온유한 자에게 그의 도를 가르치시리로다
21 내가 주를 바라오니
   성실과 정직으로 나를 보호하소서

Psalm 25
(Regular Sundays or Advent)

1 To you, O Lord, I lift up my soul.
4 **Make me to know your ways, O Lord; teach me your paths.**
5 Lead me in your truth, and teach me,
   for you are the God of my salvation; for you I wait all day long.
6 Be mindful of your mercy, O Lord, and of your steadfast love,
      for they have been from of old.
7 **Do not remember the sins of my youth or my transgressions;**
      according to your steadfast love remember me,
      for your goodness' sake, O Lord!
8 Good and upright is the Lord;
      therefore he instructs sinners in the way.
9 **He leads the humble in what is right,**
      and teaches the humble his way.
21 May integrity and uprightness preserve me,
   for I wait for you.

시편 89 (일반주일 혹은 강림절)

1 내가 여호와의 인자하심을 영원히 노래하며
    주의 성실하심을 내 입으로 대대에 알게 하리이다
2 내가 말하기를 인자하심을 영원히 세우시며
    주의 성실하심을 내 입으로 대대에 알게 하리이다
5 여호와여 주의 기이한 일을 하늘이 찬양할 것이요
    주의 성실도 거룩한 자들의 모임 가운데서 찬양하리이다
13 주의 팔에 능력이 있사오니 주의 손은 강하고
        주의 오른손은 높이 들리우셨나이다.
14 **공의와 정의가 주의 보좌의 기초라**
        인자함과 진실함이 주 앞에 있나이다
15 즐겁게 소리칠 줄 아는 백성은 복이 있나니
        여호와여 그들이 주의 얼굴 빛 안에서 다니리로다
16 **그들은 종일 주의 이름 때문에 기뻐하며**
    주의 공의로 말미암아 높아지리이다
52 여호와를 영원히 찬송할지어다
    아멘 아멘

Psalm 89
(Regular Sundays or Advent)

1 I will sing of your steadfast love, O Lord, forever;
    with my mouth I will proclaim your faithfulness to all generations.
2 I declare that your steadfast love is established forever;
    your faithfulness is as firm as the heavens.
5 Let the heavens praise your wonders, O Lord,
    your faithfulness in the assembly of the holy ones.
13 You have a mighty arm;
        strong is your hand, high your right hand.
14 **Righteousness and justice are the foundation of your throne;**
        steadfast love and faithfulness go before you.
15 Happy are the people who know the festal shout,
        who walk, O Lord, in the light of your countenance;
16 **they exult in your name all day long,**
    and extol your righteousness.
52 Blessed be the Lord forever.
    Amen and Amen.

이사야 11장 (강림절)

1 이새의 줄기에서 한 싹이 나며
　　그 뿌리에서 한 가지가 나서 결실할 것이요
2 **그의 위에 여호와의 영 곧 지혜와 총명의 영이요 모략과 재능의 영이요**
　　지식과 여호와를 경외하는 영이 강림하시리니
6 그 때에 이리가 어린 양과 함께 살며
　　표범이 어린 염소와 함께 누우며
　　송아지와 어린 사자와 살진 짐승이 함께 있어 어린 아이에게 끌리며
8 **젖 먹는 아이가 독사의 구멍에서 장난하며**
　　젖 뗀 어린 아이가 독사의 굴에 손을 넣을 것이라
9 내 거룩한 산 모든 곳에서 해 됨도 없고 상함도 없을 것이니
　　이는 물이 바다를 덮음 같이
　　여호와를 아는 지식이 세상에 충만할 것임이니라
10 그 날에 이새의 뿌리에서 한 싹이 나서 만민의 기치로 설 것이요
　　열방 그에게로 돌아오리니 그가 거한 곳이 영화로우리라

Isaiah 11 (Advent)

1 A shoot shall come out from the stump of Jesse,
　　and a branch shall grow out of his roots.
2 **The spirit of the Lord shall rest on him, the spirit of wisdom**
　　and understanding, the spirit of counsel and might,
　　the spirit of knowledge and the fear of the Lord.
6 The wolf shall live with the lamb,
　　the leopard shall lie down with the kid,
　　the calf and the lion and the fatling together,
　　and a little child shall lead them.
8 **The nursing child shall play over the hole of the asp,**
　　and the weaned child shall put its hand on the adder's den.
9 They will not hurt or destroy on all my holy mountain;
　　for the earth will be full of the knowledge of the Lord
　　as the waters cover the sea.
10 On that day the root of Jesse shall stand
　　as a signal to the peoples;
　　the nations shall inquire of him,
　　and his dwelling shall be glorious.

이사야 61장
(일반주일 혹은 강림절)

1   주 여호와의 영이 내게 내리셨으니
      이는 여호와께서 내게 기름을 부으사
  가난한 자에게 아름다운 소식을 전하게 하려 하심이라
    나를 보내사 마음이 상한 자를 고치며
    포로된 자에게 자유를, 갇힌 자에게 놓임을 선포하며

2   여호와의 은혜의 해와 우리 하나님의 보복의 날을 선포하여
  모든 슬픈 자를 위로하되

10 내가 여호와로 말미암아 크게 기뻐하며
    내 영혼이 나의 하나님으로 말미암아 즐거워하리니
    이는 그가 구원의 옷을 내게 입히시며
  공의의 겉옷을 내게 더하심이 신랑이 사모를 쓰며
  신부가 자기 보석으로 단장함 같게 하셨음이라

11 땅이 싹을 내며 동산이 거기 뿌린 것을 움돋게 함 같이
  주 여호와께서 공의와 찬송을 모든 나라 앞에 솟아나게 하시리라

Isaiah 61
(Regular Sundays or Advent)

1   The spirit of the Lord God is upon me,
      because the Lord has anointed me;
  he has sent me to bring good news to the oppressed,
    to bind up the brokenhearted, to proclaim
    liberty to the captives, and release to the prisoners;

2   to proclaim the year of the Lord's favor,
      and the day of vengeance of our God;
  to comfort all who mourn.

10 For he [God] has clothed me with the garments of salvation,
      he has covered me with the robe of righteousness,
  I will greatly rejoice in the Lord,
    my whole being shall exult in my God.

11 For as the earth brings forth its shoots,
      and as a garden causes what is sown in it to spring up,
  so the Lord God will cause righteousness
    and praise to spring up before all the nations.

요한복음 1장 (강림절)

1　태초에 말씀이 계시니라
　　이 말씀이 하나님과 함께 계셨으니 이 말씀은 곧 하나님이시니라
2　그가 태초에 하나님과 함께 계셨고
3　**만물이 그로 말미암아 지은 바 되었으니**
　　　　지은 것이 하나도 그가 없이는 된 것이 없느니라
4　그 안에 생명이 있었으니 이 생명은 사람들의 빛이라
9　**참 빛 곧 세상에 와서 각 사람에게 비추는 빛이 있었나니**
10　그가 세상에 계셨으며 세상은 그로 말미암아 지은 바 되었으되
　　　세상이 그를 알지 못하였고
11　자기 땅에 오매 자기 백성이 영접하지 아니하였으나
12　**영접하는 자 곧 그 이름을 믿는 자들에게는**
　　　　하나님의 자녀가 되는 권세를 주셨으니
18　본래 하나님을 본 사람이 없으되
　　아버지 품 속에 있는 독생하신 하나님이 나타내셨느니라

John 1 (Advent)

1　In the beginning was the Word,
　　and the Word was with God, and the Word was God.
2　He was in the beginning with God.
3　**All things came into being through him,**
　　　　and without him not one thing came into being.
　　　　What has come into being in him was life,
　　　　and the life was the light of all people.
4　in him was life, and the life was the light of all people.
9　**The true light, which enlightens everyone,**
　　　was coming into the world.
10　He was in the world, and the world came into being through him;
　　　yet the world did not know him.
11　He came to what was his own,
　　　　and his own people did not accept him.
12　**But to all who received him, who believed in his name,**
　　　he gave power to become children of God,
18　No one has ever seen God.
　　It is God the only Son, who is close to the Father's heart,
　　　who has made him known.

시편 96
(일반주일 혹은 성탄절)

1 새 노래로 여호와께 노래하라 온 땅이여 여호와께 노래할지어다
2 **여호와께 노래하여 그의 이름을 송축하며**
　　그의 구원을 날마다 전파할지어다
3 그의 영광을 백성들 가운데에,
　　그의 기이한 행적을 만민 가운데에 선포할지어다
4 **여호와는 위대하시니 지극히 찬양할 것이요**
　　모든 신들보다 경외할 것임이여
5 만국의 모든 신들은 우상들이지만
　　여호와께서는 하늘을 지으셨음이로다
6 **존귀와 위엄이 그의 앞에 있으며**
　　능력과 아름다움이 그의 성소에 있도다
7 만국의 족속들아 영광과 권능을 여호와께 돌릴지어다
　　여호와께 돌릴지어다
13 **그가 의로 세계를 심판하시며**
　　그의 진실하심으로 백성을 심판하시리로다

Psalm 96
(Regular Sundays or Christmas)

1 O sing to the Lord a new song; sing to the Lord, all the earth.
2 **Sing to the Lord, bless his name;**
　　tell of his salvation from day to day.
3 Declare his glory among the nations,
　　his marvelous works among all the peoples.
4 **For great is the Lord, and greatly to be praised;**
　　he is to be revered above all gods.
5 For all the gods of the peoples are idols,
　　but the Lord made the heavens.
6 **Honor and majesty are before him;**
　　strength and beauty are in his sanctuary.
7 Ascribe to the Lord, O families of the peoples,
　　ascribe to the Lord glory and strength.
13 **He will judge the world with righteousness,**
　　and the peoples with his truth.

누가복음 2장
(성탄절)

8 그 지역에 목자들이 밤에 밖에서 자기 양 떼를 지키더니

9 **주의 사자가 곁에 서고**
    주의 영광이 그들을 두루 비추매 크게 무서워하는지라

10 천사가 이르되 무서워하지 말라
    보라 내가 온 백성에게 미칠 큰 기쁨의 좋은 소식을 너희에게 전하노라

11 오늘 다윗의 동네에 너희를 위하여 구주가 나셨으니
    곧 그리스도 주시니라

12 너희가 가서 강보에 싸여 구유에 뉘어 있는 아기를 보리니
    이것이 너희에게 표적이니라 하더니

13 홀연히 수많은 천군이
    그 천사들과 함께 하나님을 찬송하여 이르되

14 **지극히 높은 곳에서는 하나님께 영광이요**
    땅에서는 하나님이 기뻐하신 사람들 중에 평화로다 하니라

Luke 2
(Christmas)

8 In that region there were shepherds living in the fields,
    keeping watch over their flock by night.

9 **Then an angel of the Lord stood before them,**
    and the glory of the Lord shone around them,
    and they were terrified.

10 But the angel said to them, "Do not be afraid;
    for see—I am bringing you good news
    of great joy for all the people:

11 to you is born this day in the city of David a Savior,
    who is the Messiah, the Lord.

12 You will find a child wrapped in bands of cloth
    and lying in a manger.
    This will be a sign for you."

13 And suddenly there was with the angel
    a multitude of the heavenly host, praising God and saying,

14 **"Glory to God in the highest heaven,**
    and on earth peace among those whom he favors!"

요한복음 3장
(성탄절)

16 하나님이 세상을 이처럼 사랑하사 독생자를 주셨으니
이는 그를 믿는 자마다 멸망하지 않고 영생을 얻게 하려 하심이라
17 하나님이 그 아들을 세상에 보내신 것은
세상을 심판하려 하심이 아니요
그로 말미암아 세상이 구원을 받게 하려 하심이라
18 그를 믿는 자는 심판을 받지 아니하는 것이요
믿지 아니하는 자는 하나님의 독생자의 이름을 믿지 아니하므로
벌써 심판을 받은 것이니라
19 그 정죄는 이것이니 곧 빛이 세상에 왔으되
사람들이 자기 행위가 악하므로 빛보다 어둠을 더 사랑한 것이니라
21 진리를 따르는 자는 빛으로 오나니
이는 그 행위가 하나님 안에서 행한 것임을 나타내려 함이라 하시니라

John 3
(Christmas)

16 For God so loved the world that he gave his only Son,
so that everyone who believes in him may not perish
but may have eternal life.
17 Indeed, God did not send the Son
into the world to condemn the world,
but in order that the world might be saved through him.
18 Those who believe in him are not condemned;
but those who do not believe
are condemned already,
because they have not believed
in the name of the only Son of God.
19 And this is the judgment,
that the light has come into the world,
and people loved darkness rather than light
because their deeds were evil.
21 But those who do what is true come to the light,
so that it may be clearly seen
that their deeds have been done in God.

시편 98
(일반주일 혹은 주현절)

1 새 노래로 여호와께 찬송하라 그는 기이한 일을 행하사
그의 오른손과 거룩한 팔로 자기를 위하여 구원을 베푸셨음이라
2 여호와께서 그의 구원을 알게 하시며
그의 공의를 뭇 나라의 목전에서 명백히 나타내셨도다
3 그가 이스라엘의 집에 베푸신 인자와 성실을 기억하셨으므로
땅 끝까지 이르는 모든 것이 우리 하나님의 구원을 보았도다
4 온 땅이여 여호와께 즐거이 소리칠지어다
소리 내어 즐겁게 노래하며 찬송할지어다
5 수금으로 여호와를 노래하라 수금과 음성으로 노래할지어다
6 **나팔과 호각 소리로 왕이신 여호와 앞에 즐겁게 소리칠지어다**
7 바다와 거기 충만한 것과
세계와 그 중에 거주하는 자는 다 외칠지어다

Psalm 98
(Regular Sundays or Epiphany)

1 O sing to the Lord a new song,
    for he has done marvelous things.
His right hand and his holy arm
    have gotten him victory.
2 The Lord has made known his victory;
he has revealed his vindication in the sight of the nations.
3 He has remembered his steadfast love
    and faithfulness to the house of Israel.
All the ends of the earth have seen
    the victory of our God.
4 Make a joyful noise to the Lord, all the earth;
break forth into joyous song and sing praises.
5 Sing praises to the Lord with the lyre,
    with the lyre and the sound of melody.
6 **With trumpets and the sound of the horn**
    make a joyful noise before the King, the Lord.
7 Let the sea roar, and all that fills it;
the world and those who live in it.

시편 111
(일반주일 혹은 주현절)

2 여호와께서 행하시는 일들이 크시오니
이를 즐거워하는 자들이 다 기리는도다

3 그의 행하시는 일이 존귀하고 엄위하며
그의 공의가 영원히 서 있도다

4 **그의 기적을 사람이 기억하게 하셨으니**
여호와는 은혜로우시고 자비로우시도다

7 그의 손이 하는 일은 진실과 정의이며 그의 법도는 다 확실하니

8 **영원무궁토록 정하신 바요 진실과 정의로 행하신 바로다**

9 여호와께서 그의 백성을 속량하시며 그의 언약을 영원히 세우셨으니
그의 이름이 거룩하고 지존하시도다

10 여호와를 경외함이 지혜의 근본이라
그의 계명을 지키는 자는 다 훌륭한 지각을 가진 자이니
여호와를 찬양함이 영원히 계속되리로다

Psalm 111
(Regular Sundays or Epiphany)

2 Great are the works of the Lord,
studied by all who delight in them.

3 Full of honor and majesty is his work,
and his righteousness endures forever.

4 **He has gained renown by his wonderful deeds;**
the Lord is gracious and merciful.

7 The works of his hands are faithful and just;
all his precepts are trustworthy.

8 **They are established forever and ever,**
to be performed with faithfulness
and uprightness.

9 He sent redemption to his people;
he has commanded his covenant forever.
Holy and awesome is his name.

10 The fear of the Lord is the beginning of wisdom;
all those who practice it have a good understanding.
His praise endures forever.

시편 51
(일반주일 혹은 재의 수요일)

1 하나님이여 주의 인자를 따라 내게 은혜를 베푸시며
   주의 많은 긍휼을 따라 내 죄악을 지워 주소서
2 나의 죄악을 말갛게 씻으시며 나의 죄를 깨끗이 제하소서
3 **무릇 나는 내 죄과를 아오니 내 죄가 항상 내 앞에 있나이다**
6 보소서 주께서는 중심이 진실함을 원하시오니
   내게 지혜를 은밀히 가르치시리이다
7 우슬초로 나를 정결케 하소서 내가 정하리이다
   나의 죄를 씻어 주소서 내가 눈보다 희리이다
8 내게 즐겁고 기쁜 소리를 들려 주시사
   주께서 꺾으신 뼈들도 즐거워하게 하소서
10 하나님이여 내 속에 정한 마음을 창조하시고
   내 안에 정직한 영을 새롭게 하소서

Psalm 51
(Regular Sundays or Ash Wednesday)

1 Have mercy on me, O God,
     according to your steadfast love;
   **according to your abundant mercy
       blot out my transgressions.**
2 Wash me thoroughly from my iniquity,
     and cleanse me from my sin.
3 **For I know my transgressions,
     and my sin is ever before me.**
6 You desire truth in the inward being;
   **therefore teach me wisdom
       in my secret heart.**
7 Purge me with hyssop, and I shall be clean;
   wash me, and I shall be whiter than snow.
8 Let me hear joy and gladness;
   let the bones that you have crushed rejoice.
10 Create in me a clean heart, O God,
   **and put a new
       and right spirit within me.**

시편 22
(일반주일 혹은 사순절)

1 내 하나님이여 내 하나님이여 어찌 나를 버리셨나이까
어찌 나를 멀리 하여 돕지 아니하시오며
   내 신음 소리를 듣지 아니하시나이까

2 내 하나님이여 내가 낮에도 부르짖고
   밤에도 잠잠하지 아니하오나 응답하지 아니하시나이다

4 **우리 조상들이 주께 의뢰하고 의뢰하였으므로 그들을 건지셨나이다**

5 그들이 주께 부르짖어 구원을 얻고
주께 의뢰하여 수치를 당하지 아니하였나이다

6 나는 벌레요 사람이 아니라
사람의 비방 거리요 백성의 조롱 거리니이다

9 오직 주께서 나를 모태에서 나오게 하시고
내 어머니의 젖을 먹을 때에 의지하게 하셨나이다

24 그는 곤고한 자의 곤고를 멸시하거나 싫어하지 아니하시며
그의 얼굴을 그에게서 숨기지 아니하시고
   그가 울부짖을 때에 들으셨도다

Psalm 22
(Regular Sundays or Lent)

1 My God, my God, why have you forsaken me?
Why are you so far from helping me,
   from the words of my groaning?

2 O my God, I cry by day, but you do not answer,
   and by night, but find no rest.

4 **In you our ancestors trusted; they trusted, and you delivered them.**

5 To you they cried, and were saved;
in you they trusted, and were not put to shame.

6 But I am a worm, and not human;
scorned by others, and despised by the people.

9 Yet it was you who took me from the womb;
you kept me safe on my mother's breast.

24 For he did not despise
   or abhor the affliction of the afflicted;
he did not hide his face from me, but heard when I cried to him.

시편 42
(일반주일 혹은 사순절)

1 하나님이여 사슴이 시냇물을 찾기에 갈급함 같이
   내 영혼이 주를 찾기에 갈급하니이다
2 내 영혼이 하나님 곧 살아 계시는 하나님을 갈망하나니
   내가 어느 때에 나아가서 하나님의 얼굴을 뵈올까
3 사람들이 종일 내게 하는 말이
   네 하나님이 어디 있느뇨 하오니
   내 눈물이 주야로 내 음식이 되었도다
4 내가 전에 성일을 지키는 무리와 동행하여
   기쁨과 감사의 소리를 내며
   그들을 하나님의 집으로 인도하였더니
   이제 이 일을 기억하고 내 마음이 상하는도다
11 내 영혼아 네가 어찌하여 낙심하며
   어찌하여 내 속에서 불안해하는가
   너는 하나님께 소망을 두라
   나는 그가 나타나 도우심으로 말미암아
   내 하나님을 여전히 찬송하리로다

Psalm 42
(Regular Sundays or Lent)

1 As a deer longs for flowing streams,
   so my soul longs for you, O God.
2 My soul thirsts for God, for the living God.
   When shall I come and behold the face of God?
3 While people say to me continually, "Where is your God?"
   my tears have been my food day and night.
4 These things I remember, as I pour out my soul:
   how I went with the throng, and led them in procession
   to the house of God, with glad shouts and songs
   of thanksgiving, a multitude keeping festival.
11 Why are you cast down,
   O my soul, and why are you disquieted within me?
   Hope in God; for I shall again praise him,
   my help and my God.

시편 103
(일반주일 혹은 사순절)

1　내 영혼아 여호와를 송축하라 내 속에 있는 것들아
　　　다 그의 거룩한 이름을 송축하라
2　**내 영혼아 여호와를 송축하며 그의 모든 은택을 잊지 말지어다**
3　그가 네 모든 죄악을 사하시며 네 모든 병을 고치시며
4　**네 생명을 파멸에서 속량하시고 인자와 긍휼로 관을 씌우시며**
5　좋은 것으로 네 소원을 만족하게 하사
　　　네 청춘을 독수리 같이 새롭게 하시는도다
6　**여호와께서 공의로운 일을 행하시며**
　　　억압 당하는 모든 자를 위하여 심판하시는도다
8　여호와는 긍휼이 많으시고 은혜로우시며
　　　노하기를 더디 하시고 인자하심이 풍부하시도다
17　여호와의 인자하심은 자기를 경외하는 자에게
　　　영원부터 영원까지 이르며
　　　그의 공의는 자손의 자손에게 이르리라

Psalm 103
(Regular Sundays or Lent)

1　Bless the Lord, O my soul,
　　　and all that is within me, bless his holy name.
2　**Bless the Lord, O my soul,**
　　　and do not forget all his benefits—
3　who forgives all your iniquity, who heals all your diseases,
4　**who redeems your life from the Pit,**
　　　who crowns you with steadfast love and mercy,
5　who satisfies you with good as long as you live
　　　so that your youth is renewed like the eagle's.
6　**The Lord works vindication**
　　　and justice for all who are oppressed.
8　The Lord is merciful and gracious,
　　　slow to anger and abounding in steadfast love.
17　But the steadfast love of the Lord is from everlasting
　　　to everlasting on those who fear him,
　　　and his righteousness to children's children.

시편 130
(일반주일 혹은 사순절)

1 여호와여 내가 깊은 곳에서 주께 부르짖었나이다
2 **주여 내 소리를 들으시며**
   나의 부르짖는 소리에 귀를 기울이소서
3 여호와여 주께서 죄악을 지켜보실진대 주여 누가 서리이까
4 **그러나 사유하심이 주께 있음은 주를 경외하게 하심이니이다**
5 나 곧 내 영혼은 여호와를 기다리며
   나는 주의 말씀을 바라는도다
6 **파수꾼이 아침을 기다림보다 내 영혼이 주를 더 기다리나니**
   참으로 파수꾼이 아침을 기다림보다 더하도다
7 이스라엘아 여호와를 바랄지어다
   여호와께서는 인자하심과 풍성한 속량이 있음이라
8 **그가 이스라엘을 그의 모든 죄악에서 속량하시리로다**

Psalm 130
(Regular Sundays or Lent)

1 Out of the depths I cry to you, O Lord.
2 **Lord, hear my voice!**
   Let your ears be attentive
   to the voice of my supplications!
3 If you, O Lord, should mark iniquities,
   Lord, who could stand?
4 **But there is forgiveness with you,**
   so that you may be revered.
5 I wait for the Lord, my soul waits,
   and in his word I hope;
6 **my soul waits for the Lord**
   more than those who watch for the morning,
   more than those who watch for the morning.
7 O Israel, hope in the Lord!
   For with the Lord there is steadfast love,
   and with him is great power to redeem.
8 **It is he who will redeem Israel**
   from all its iniquities.

이사야 53장 (성금요일)

4 그는 실로 우리의 질고를 지고 우리의 슬픔을 당하였거늘
　　우리는 생각하기를 그는 징벌을 받아
　　　　하나님께 맞으며 고난을 당한다 하였노라
5 그가 찔림은 우리의 허물 때문이요
　　　　그가 상함은 우리의 죄악 때문이라
　　그가 징계를 받으므로 우리는 평화를 누리고
　　그가 채찍에 맞으므로 우리는 나음을 받았도다
6 우리는 다 양 같아서 그릇 행하여 각기 제 길로 갔거늘
　　여호와께서는 우리 모두의 죄악을 그에게 담당시키셨도다
7 그가 곤욕을 당하여 괴로울 때에도 그의 입을 열지 아니하였음이여
　　마치 도수장으로 끌려 가는 어린 양과 털 깎는 자 앞에서
　　　　잠잠한 양 같이 그의 입을 열지 아니하였도다
8 그는 곤욕과 심문을 당하고 끌려갔으나
　　　　그 세대 중에 누가 생각하기를
　　　　그가 살아 있는 자들의 땅에서 끊어짐은
　　마땅히 형벌 받을 내 백성의 허물 때문이라 하였으리요

Isaiah 53 (Good Friday)

4 Surely he has borne our infirmities and carried our diseases;
　　yet we accounted him stricken, struck down by God, and afflicted.
5 But he was wounded for our transgressions,
　　　　crushed for our iniquities;
　　upon him was the punishment that made us whole,
　　　　and by his bruises we are healed.
6 All we like sheep have gone astray;
　　　　we have all turned to our own way,
　　and the Lord has laid on him the iniquity of us all.
7 He was oppressed, and he was afflicted,
　　　　yet he did not open his mouth;
　　like a lamb that is led to the slaughter, and like a sheep
　　　　that before its shearers is silent, so he did not open his mouth.
8 By a perversion of justice he was taken away.
　　　　Who could have imagined his future?
　　For he was cut off from the land of the living,
　　　　stricken for the transgression of my people.

스가랴 9장
(종려주일)

9 시온의 딸아 크게 기뻐할지어다
  예루살렘의 딸아 즐거이 부를지어다
  보라 네 왕이 네게 임하시나니
  그는 공의로우시며 구원을 베푸시며
  겸손하여서 나귀를 타시나니
  나귀의 작은 것 곧 나귀 새끼니라
10 내가 에브라임의 병거와 예루살렘의 말을 끊겠고
  전쟁하는 활도 끊으리니
  그가 이방 사람에게 화평을 전할 것이요
  그의 통치는 바다에서 바다까지 이르고
  유브라데 강에서 땅 끝까지 이르리라
16 이 날에 그들의 하나님 여호와께서
  그들을 자기 백성의 양 떼 같이 구원하시리니
  그들이 왕관의 보석 같이 여호와의 땅에 빛나리로다

Zechariah 9
(Palm Sunday)

9 Rejoice greatly, O daughter Zion!
   Shout aloud, O daughter Jerusalem!
   Lo, your king comes to you;
   triumphant and victorious is he,
   humble and riding on a donkey, on a colt,
   the foal of a donkey.
10 He will cut off the chariot from Ephraim
   and the war horse from Jerusalem;
   and the battle bow shall be cut off,
   and he shall command peace to the nations;
   his dominion shall be from sea to sea,
   and from the River to the ends of the earth.
16 On that day the Lord their God will save them
   for they are the flock of his people;
   for like the jewels of a crown
   they shall shine on his land.

빌립보서 2장
(고난주간)

5 너희 안에 이 마음을 품으라 곧 그리스도 예수의 마음이니
6 그는 근본 하나님의 본체시나
   하나님과 동등됨을 취할 것으로 여기지 아니하시고
7 오히려 자기를 비워 종의 형체를 가지사 사람들과 같이 되셨고
8 사람의 모양으로 나타나사 자기를 낮추시고
   죽기까지 복종하셨으니 곧 십자가에 죽으심이라
9 이러므로 하나님이 그를 지극히 높여
   모든 이름 위에 뛰어난 이름을 주사
10 하늘에 있는 자들과 땅에 있는 자들과 땅 아래에 있는 자들로
   모든 무릎을 예수의 이름에 꿇게 하시고
11 모든 입으로 예수 그리스도를 주라 시인하여
   하나님 아버지께 영광을 돌리게 하셨느니라

Philippians 2
(Holy Week)

5 Let the same mind be in you
   that was in Christ Jesus,
6 **who, though he was in the form of God,**
   did not regard equality with God
   as something to be exploited,
7 but emptied himself, taking the form of a slave,
   being born in human likeness.
8 **And being found in human form,**
   he humbled himself
   and became obedient to the point of death—
   even death on a cross.
9 Therefore God also highly exalted him
   and gave him the name that is above every name,
10 so that at the name of Jesus every knee should bend,
   in heaven and on earth and under the earth,
11 **and every tongue should confess**
   that Jesus Christ is Lord,
   to the glory of God the Father.

로마서 8
(부활)

31 그런즉
이 일에 대하여 우리가 무슨 말 하리요
만일 하나님이 우리를 위하시면
누가 우리를 대적하리요

32 **자기 아들을 아끼지 아니하시고**
우리 모든 사람을 위하여 내주신 이가
어찌 그 아들과 함께 모든 것을
우리에게 주시지 아니하겠느냐

33 누가 능히 하나님께서 택하신 자들을 고발하리요
의롭다 하신 이는 하나님이시니

34 **누가 정죄하리요**
죽으실 뿐 아니라 다시 살아나신 이는 그리스도 예수시니
그는 하나님 우편에 계신 자요
우리를 위하여 간구하시는 자시니라

35 누가 우리를 그리스도의 사랑에서 끊으리요
환난이나 곤고나 박해나 기근이나
적신이나 위험이나 칼이랴

36 기록된 바
우리가 종일 주를 위하여 죽임을 당하게 되며
도살 당할 양 같이 여김을 받았나이다 함과 같으니라

37 **그러나 이 모든 일에**
우리를 사랑하시는 이로 말미암아
우리가 넉넉히 이기느니라

38 내가 확신하노니
사망이나 생명이나 천사들이나 권세자들이나
현재 일이나 장래 일이나 능력이나

39 **높음이나 깊음이나 다른 어떤 피조물이라도**
우리를 우리 주 그리스도 예수 안에 있는
하나님의 사랑에서 끊을 수 없으리라

Romans 8
(Resurrection)

31 What then are we to say about these things?
    If God is for us, who is against us?

32 **He who did not withhold his own Son,**
    but gave him up for all of us,
    will he not with him also give us everything else?

33 Who will bring any charge against God's elect?
    It is God who justifies.

34 **Who is to condemn?**
    It is Christ Jesus, who died,
    yes, who was raised,
    who is at the right hand of God,
    who indeed intercedes for us.

35 Who will separate us from the love of Christ?
Will hardship, or distress, or persecution,
    or famine, or nakedness, or peril, or sword?

36 As it is written,
    "For your sake we are being killed all day long;
    we are accounted as sheep to be slaughtered."

37 **No, in all these things**
    we are more than conquerors
    through him who lovd us.

38 For I am convinced that neither death,
    nor life, nor angels, nor ruler, nor things present,
    nor thing to come, nor powers,

39 **nor height, nor depth,**
    nor anything else in all creation,
    will be able to separate us
    from the love of God in Christ Jesus our Lord.

고린도전서 15장
(부활)

17 그리스도께서 다시 살아나신 일이 없으면
　너희의 믿음도 헛되고
　　　너희가 여전히 죄 가운데 있을 것이요
18 또한 그리스도 안에서 잠자는 자도 망하였으리니
19 만일 그리스도 안에서 우리가 바라는 것이
　　　이 세상의 삶뿐이면
　모든 사람 가운데 우리가 더욱 불쌍한 자이리라
20 그러나 이제 그리스도께서 죽은 자 가운데서 다시 살아나사
　　　잠자는 자들의 첫 열매가 되셨도다
21 사망이 한 사람으로 말미암았으니
　　죽은 자의 부활도 한 사람으로 말미암는도다
22 아담 안에서 모든 사람이 죽은 것 같이
　　　그리스도 안에서 모든 사람이 삶을 얻으리라
42 죽은 자의 부활도 그와 같으니 썩을 것으로 심고
　썩지 아니할 것으로 다시 살아나며
43 욕된 것으로 심고 영광스러운 것으로 다시 살아나며
　약한 것으로 심고 강한 것으로 다시 살아나며
44 육의 몸으로 심고 신령한 몸으로 다시 살아나나니
　육의 몸이 있은즉 또 영의 몸도 있느니라
49 우리가 흙에 속한 자의 형상을 입은 것 같이
　또한 하늘에 속한 이의 형상을 입으리라
50 형제들아 내가 이것을 말하노니
　　　혈과 육은 하나님 나라를 이어 받을 수 없고
　또한 썩는 것은 썩지 아니하는 것을
　　유업으로 받지 못하느니라
54 이 썩을 것이 썩지 아니함을 입고
　　　이 죽을 것이 죽지 아니함을 입을 때에는
　사망을 삼키고 이기리라고 기록된 말씀이 이루어지리라
55 사망아 너의 승리가 어디 있느냐
　　　사망아 네가 쏘는 것이 어디 있느냐
56 사망이 쏘는 것은 죄요 죄의 권능은 율법이라
57 우리 주 예수 그리스도로 말미암아
　우리에게 승리를 주시는 하나님께 감사하노라

1 Corinthians 15
(Resurrection)

17 If Christ has not been raised,
> your faith is futile and you are still in your sins.

18 **Then those also who have died in Christ have perished.**

19 If for this life only we have hoped in Christ,
> **we are of all people most to be pitied.**

20 But in fact Christ has been raised from the dead,
> he first fruits of those who have died.

21 **For since death came through a human being,**
> **the resurrection of the dead**
> **has also come through a human being;**

22 For as all die in Adam, so all will be made alive in Christ.

42 **So it is with the resurrection of the dead.**
> **What is sown is perishable,**
> **what is raised is imperishable.**

43 It is sown in dishonor, it is raised in glory.
> **It is sown in weakness, it is raised in power.**

44 It is sown a physical body, it is raised a spiritual body.
> **If there is a physical body, there is also a spiritual body.**

49 Just as we have borne the image of the man of dust,
> **we will also bear the image of the man of heaven.**

50 Flesh and blood cannot inherit the kingdom of God,
> **nor does the perishable inherit the imperishable.**

54 When this perishable body puts on imperishability,
> and this mortal body puts on immortality,
> then the saying that is written will be fulfilled:
"Death has been swallowed up in victory."

55 "Where, O death, is your victory?
> Where, O death, is your sting?"

56 **The sting of death is sin,**
> **and the power of sin is the law.**

57 But thanks be to God,
who gives us the victory
> **through our Lord Jesus Christ.**

시편 47
(일반주일 혹은 승천일)

1 너희 만물들아 손바닥을 치고
 즐거운 소리로 하나님께 외칠지어다
5 하나님께서 즐거운 함성 중에 올라가심이여
 여호와께서 나팔 소리 중에 올라가시도다
6 찬송하라 하나님을 찬송하라
 찬송하라 우리 왕을 찬송하라
7 하나님은 온 땅의 왕이심이라
 지혜의 시로 찬송할지어다
8 하나님이 뭇 백성을 다스리시며
 하나님이 그의 거룩한 보좌에 앉으셨도다
9 뭇 나라의 고관들이 모임이여
 아브라함의 하나님의 백성이 되도다
 세상의 모든 방패는 하나님의 것임이여
 그는 높임을 받으시리로다

Psalm 47
(Regular Sundays or Ascension)

1 Clap your hands, all you peoples;
 shout to God with loud songs of joy.
5 God has gone up with a shout,
 the Lord with the sound of a trumpet.
6 Sing praises to God, sing praises;
 sing praises to our King, sing praises.
7 For God is the king of all the earth;
 sing praises with a psalm.
8 God is king over the nations;
 God sits on his holy throne.
9 The princes of the peoples gather
 as the people of the God of Abraham.
 For the shields of the earth
 belong to God;
 he is highly exalted.

시편 104
(일반주일 혹은 성령강림주일)

1 내 영혼아 여호와를 송축하라
  여호와 나의 하나님이여 주는 심히 위대하시며
    존귀와 권위로 옷 입으셨나이다
2 주께서 옷을 입음 같이 빛을 입으시며 하늘을 휘장 같이 치시며
3 **물에 자기 누각의 들보를 얹으시며**
    구름으로 자기 수레를 삼으시고 바람 날개로 다니시며
4 바람을 자기 자신으로 삼으시고
    불꽃으로 자기 사역자를 삼으시며
5 **땅에 기초를 넣으사 영원히 흔들리지 아니하게 하셨나이다**
24 여호와여 주께서 하신 일이 어찌 그리 많은지요
  주께서 지혜로 그들을 다 지으셨으니
    주께서 지으신 것들이 땅에 가득하나이다
30 주의 영을 보내어 그들을 창조하사 지면을 새롭게 하시나이다
31 **여호와의 영광이 영원히 계속하리로다**

Psalm 104
(Regular Sundays or Pentecost)

1 Blessed the Lord, O my soul.
  O Lord my God, you are very great.
    You are clothed with honor and majesty,
2 wrapped in light as with a garment.
    You stretch out the heavens like a tent,
3 **you set the beams of your chambers on the waters,**
    you make the clouds your chariot,
    you ride on the wings of the wind,
4 you make the winds your messengers, fire and flame your ministers.
5 **You set the earth on its foundations, so that it shall never be shaken.**
24 O Lord, how manifold are your works!
  In wisdom you have made them all;
    the earth is full of your creatures.
30 When you send forth your spirit they are created;
    and you renew the face of the ground.
31 **May the glory of the Lord endure forever.**

시편 24
(일반주일 혹은 종교개혁주일)

1 땅과 거기에 충만한 것과 세계와 그 가운데에 사는 자들은
   다 여호와의 것이로다
3 **여호와의 산에 오를 자가 누구며**
   그의 거룩한 곳에 설 자가 누구인가
4 곧 손이 깨끗하며 마음이 청결하며
   뜻을 허탄한 데에 두지 아니하며
   거짓 맹세하지 아니하는 자로다
5 그는 여호와께 복을 받고
   구원의 하나님께 공의를 얻으리니
6 이는 여호와를 찾는 족속이요
   야곱의 하나님의 얼굴을 구하는 자로다
7 문들아 너희 머리를 들지어다 영원한 문들아 들릴지어다
   영광의 왕이 들어가시리로다
8 **영광의 왕이 누구시냐 강하고 능한 여호와시요**
   전쟁에 능한 여호와시로다

Psalm 24
(Regular Sundays or Reformation Sunday)

1 The earth is the Lord's and all that is in it,
   the world, and those who live in it.
3 **Who shall ascend the hill of the Lord?**
   And who shall stand in his holy place?
4 Those who have clean hands and pure hearts,
   who do not lift up their souls to what is false,
   and do not swear deceitfully.
5 They will receive blessing from the Lord,
   and vindication from the God of their salvation.
6 Such is the company of those who seek him,
   who seek the face of the God of Jacob.
7 Lift up your heads, O gates! and be lifted up,
   O ancient doors! that the King of glory may come in.
8 **Who is the King of glory?**
   The Lord, strong and mighty, the Lord, mighty in battle.

시편 34
(일반주일 혹은 성도추모일)

1 내가 여호와를 항상 송축함이여
　　내 입술로 항상 주를 찬양하리이다
2 **내 영혼이 여호와를 자랑하리니**
　　곤고한 자들이 이를 듣고 기뻐하리로다
3 나와 함께 여호와를 광대하시다 하며 함께 그의 이름을 높이세
4 **내가 여호와께 간구하매 내게 응답하시고**
　　내 모든 두려움에서 나를 건지셨도다
5 그들이 주를 앙망하고 광채를 내었으니
　　그들의 얼굴은 부끄럽지 아니하리로다
6 **이 곤고한 자가 부르짖으매 여호와께서 들으시고**
　　그의 모든 환난에서 구원하셨도다
7 여호와의 천사가 주를 경외하는 자를 둘러 진 치고
　　그들을 건지시는도다
8 **너희는 여호와의 선하심을 맛보아 알지어다**
　　그에게 피하는 자는 복이 있도다

Psalm 34
(Regular Sundays or All Saints Day)

1 I will bless the Lord at all times;
　　his praise shall continually be in my mouth.
2 **My soul makes its boast in the Lord;**
　　let the humble hear and be glad.
3 O magnify the Lord with me, and let us exalt his name together.
4 **I sought the Lord, and he answered me,**
　　and delivered me from all my fears.
5 Look to him, and be radiant;
　　so your faces shall never be ashamed.
6 **This poor soul cried, and was heard by the Lord,**
　　and was saved from every trouble.
7 The angel of the Lord encamps around
　　those who fear him, and delivers them.
8 **O taste and see that the Lord is good;**
　　happy are those who take refuge in him.

시편 65
(일반주일 혹은 감사절)

4 주께서 택하시고 가까이 오게 하사
　　주의 뜰에 살게 하신 사람은 복이 있나이다
우리가 주의 집 곧 주의 성전의 아름다움으로 만족하리이다
9 땅을 돌보사 물을 대어 심히 윤택하게 하시며
하나님의 강에 물이 가득하게 하시고
　　이같이 땅을 예비하신 후에 그들에게 곡식을 주시나이다
10 주께서 밭고랑에 물을 넉넉히 대사 그 이랑을 평평하게 하시며
또 단비로 부드럽게 하시고 그 싹에 복을 주시나이다
11 주의 은택으로 한 해를 관 씌우시니
주의 길에는 기름 방울이 떨어지며
12 들의 초장에도 떨어지니
작은 산들이 기쁨으로 띠를 띠었나이다
13 초장은 양 떼로 옷 입었고 골짜기는 곡식으로 덮였으매
그들이 다 즐거이 외치고 또 노래하나이다

Psalm 65
(Regular Sunday or Thanksgiving)

4 Happy are those whom you choose
　　and bring near to live in your courts.
We shall be satisfied with the goodness of your house, your holy temple.
9 You visit the earth and water it, you greatly enrich it;
the river of God is full of water;
　　you provide the people with grain,
　　for so you have prepared it.
10 You water its furrows abundantly, settling its ridges,
softening it with showers, and blessing its growth.
11 You crown the year with your bounty;
your wagon tracks overflow with richness.
12 The pastures of the wilderness overflow,
the hills gird themselves with joy,
13 the meadows clothe themselves with flocks,
the valleys deck themselves with grain,
　　they shout and sing together for joy.

시편 136
(일반주일 혹은 감사절)

1 여호와께 감사하라
  그는 선하시며 그 인자하심이 영원함이로다

2 신들 중에 뛰어난 주께 감사하라
  그 인자하심이 영원함이로다

3 주들 중에 뛰어난 주께 감사하라
  그 인자하심이 영원함이로다

23 우리를 비천한 가운데에서도
  기억해 주신 이에게 감사하라
  그 인자하심이 영원함이로다

24 우리를 우리의 대적에게서 건지신 이에게 감사하라
  그 인자하심이 영원함이로다

25 모든 육체에게 먹을 것을 주신 이에게 감사하라
  그 인자하심이 영원함이로다

26 하늘의 하나님께 감사하라
  그 인자하심이 영원함이로다

Psalm 136
(Regular Sundays or Thanksgiving)

1 Give thanks to the Lord,
  for he is good, for his steadfast love endures forever.

2 O give thanks to the God of gods,
  for his steadfast love endures forever.

3 O give thanks to the Lord of lords,
  for his steadfast love endures forever.

23 It is he who remembered us in our low estate,
  for his steadfast love endures forever;

24 and rescued us from our foes,
  for his steadfast love endures forever;

25 who gives food to all flesh,
  for his steadfast love endures forever.

26 O give thanks to the God of heaven,
  for his steadfast love endures forever.

요한계시록 21장
(일반주일 혹은 송구영신 · 신년)

1 또 내가 새 하늘과 새 땅을 보니
　　처음 하늘과 처음 땅이 없어졌고
　　바다도 다시 있지 않더라
2 **또 내가 보매 거룩한 성 새 예루살렘이**
　　하나님께로부터 하늘에서 내려오니
　　그 준비한 것이 신부가 남편을 위하여
　　단장한 것 같더라
3 내가 들으니 보좌에서 큰 음성이 나서 이르되
　보라 하나님의 장막이 사람들과 함께 있으매
　　하나님이 그들과 함께 계시리니
　　그들은 하나님의 백성이 되고
　　하나님은 친히 그들과 함께 계셔서
4 모든 눈물을 그 눈에서 닦아 주시니
　　다시는 사망이 없고
　　애통하는 것이나 곡하는 것이나 아픈 것이
　　다시 있지 아니하리니
　처음 것들이 다 지나갔음이러라
5 보좌에 앉으신 이가 이르시되
　　　보라 내가 만물을 새롭게 하노라 하시고
　　　또 이르시되
　이 말은 신실하고 참되니 기록하라 하시고
6 또 내게 말씀하시되 이루었도다
　　　나는 알파와 오메가요 처음과 마지막이라
　내가 생명수 샘물을
　　목마른 자에게 값없이 주리니
7 이기는 자는 이것들을 상속으로 받으리라
　나는 그의 하나님이 되고
　　그는 내 아들이 되리라

Revelation 21
(Regular Sundays or Watch Night · New Year)

1 Then I saw a new heaven and a new earth;
    for the first heaven and the first earth had passed away,
    and the sea was no more.
2 **And I saw the holy city, the new Jerusalem,**
    coming down out of heaven from God,
    prepared as a bride adored for her husband.
3 And I heard a loud voice from the throne saying,
"See, the home of God is among mortals.
    He will dwell with them;
    they will be his peoples,
    and God himself will be with them;
4 he will wipe every tear from their eyes.
    Death will be no more;
    mourning and crying and pain will be no more,
for the first things have passed away."
5 And the one who was seated on the throne said,
    "See, I am making all things new."
    Also he said,
"Write this. for these words are trustworthy and true."
6 Then he said to me,
    "It is done! I am the Alpha and the Omega,
    the beginning and the end.
To the thirsty I will give water as a gift
    from the spring of the water of life.
7 Those who conquer will inherit these things,
and I will be their God
    and they will be my children.

시편 90
(일반주일 혹은 신년)

1 주여 주는 대대에 우리의 거처가 되셨나이다

2 산이 생기기 전, 땅과 세계도 주께서 조성하시기 전
곧 영원부터 영원까지 주는 하나님이시니이다

3 주께서 사람을 티끌로 돌아가게 하시고
말씀하시기를
너희 인생들은 돌아가라 하셨사오니

4 주의 목전에는 천 년이 지나간 어제 같으며
밤의 한 순간 같을 뿐임이니이다

5 주께서 그들을 홍수처럼 쓸어가시나이다
그들은 잠깐 자는 것 같으며
아침에 돋는 풀 같으니이다

6 풀은 아침에 꽃이 피어 자라다가
저녁에는 시들어 마르나이다

7 우리는 주의 노에 소멸되며
주의 분내심에 놀라나이다

8 주께서 우리의 죄악을 주 앞에 놓으시며
우리의 은밀한 죄를
주의 얼굴 빛 가운데 두셨나이다

9 우리의 모든 날이 주의 분노 중에 지나가며
우리의 평생이 순식간에 다하였나이다

10 우리의 연수가 칠십이요 강건하면 팔십이라도,
그 연수의 자랑은 수고와 슬픔뿐이요,
신속히 가니 우리가 날아가나이다

11 누가 주의 노여움의 능력을 알며
누가 주의 진노의 두려움을 알리이까

12 우리에게 우리 날 계수함을 가르치사
지혜로운 마음을 얻게 하소서

13 여호와여 돌아오소서 언제까지니이까
주의 종들을 불쌍이 여기소서

14 아침에 주의 인자하심이
우리를 만족하게 하사
우리를 일생 동안 즐겁고 기쁘게 하소서

Psalm 90
(Regular Sundays or New Year)

1 Lord,
  you have been our dwelling place in all generations.

2 **Before the mountains were brought forth,**
  or ever you had formed the earth and the world,
  from everlasting to everlasting you are God.

3 You turn us back to dust, and say,
  "turn back, you mortals."

4 **For a thousand years in your sight are like yesterday**
  when it is past, or like a watch in the night.

5 You sweep them away; they are like a dream,
  like grass that is renewed in the morning;

6 **in the morning it flourished and is renewed;**
  in the evening it fades and withers.

7 For we are consumed by your anger;
  by your wrath we are overwhelmed.

8 **You have set our iniquities before you,**
  our secret sins in the light of your countenance.

9 For all our days pass away under your wrath;
  our years come to an end like a sigh.

10 **The days of our life are seventy years,**
   or perhaps eighty, if we are strong;
   even then their span is only toil and trouble;
   they are soon gone, and we fly away.

11 Who considers the power of your anger?
   Your wrath is as great as the fear that is due you.

12 **So teach us to count our days**
   that we may gain a wise heart.

13 Turn, O Lord! How long?
   Have compassion on your servants!

14 Satisfy us in the morning with your steadfast love,
   so that we may rejoice and be glad all our days.

신명기 6장
(기독교교육)

1 이는 곧 너희의 하나님 여호와께서 너희에게 가르치라고
　　명하신 명령과 규례와 법도라
　　너희가 건너가서 차지할 땅에서 행할 것이니
2 곧 너와 네 아들과 네 손자들이 평생에 네 하나님 여호와를 경외하며
　　내가 너희에게 명한 그 모든 규례와 명령을 지키게
　　하기 위한 것이며 또 네 날을 장구하게 하기 위한 것이라
3 이스라엘아 듣고 삼가 그것을 행하라
　　그리하면 네가 복을 받고 네 조상들의 하나님 여호와께서 네게
　　허락하심같이 젖과 꿀이 흐르는 땅에서 네가 크게 번성하리라
4 이스라엘아 들으라
　　우리 하나님 여호와는 오직 유일한 여호와이시니
5 너는 마음을 다하고 뜻을 다하고 힘을 다하여
　　네 하나님 여호와를 사랑하라

Deuteronomy 6
(Christian Education)

1 Now this is the commandment—the statutes and the ordinances—
　　that the Lord your God charged me
　　to teach you to observe in the land
　　that you are about to cross into and occupy,
2 so that you and your children and your children's children,
　　may fear the Lord your God all the days of your life,
　　and keep all his decrees and his commandments
　　that I am commanding you, so that your days may be long.
3 Hear therefore, O Israel, and observe them diligently,
　　so that it may go well with you,
　　and so that you may multiply greatly in a
　　land flowing with milk and honey, as the Lord,
　　the God of your ancestors, has promised you.
4 Hear, O Israel:
　　The Lord is our God, the Lord alone.
5 You shall love the Lord your God with all your heart,
　　and with all your soul, and with all your might.

에베소서 4장
(기독교교육)

11 그가 어떤 사람은 사도로, 어떤 사람은 선지자로,
어떤 사람은 복음 전하는 자로,
    어떤 사람은 목사와 교사로 삼으셨으니

12 이는 성도를 온전하게 하며 봉사의 일을 하게 하며
    그리스도의 몸을 세우려 하심이라

13 **우리가 다 하나님의 아들을 믿는 것과**
    아는 일에 하나가 되어 온전한 사람을 이루어
    그리스도의 장성한 분량이 충만한 데까지 이르리니

14 이는 우리가 이제부터 어린 아이가 되지 아니하여
    사람의 속임수와 간사한 유혹에 빠져
    온갖 교훈의 풍조에 밀려 요동하지 않게 하려 함이라

15 **오직 사랑 안에서 참된 것을 하여**
    범사에 그에게까지 자랄지라
    그는 머리니 곧 그리스도라

Ephesians 4
(Christian Education)

11 The gifts he gave were that some would be apostles,
some prophets, some evangelists,
    some pastors and teachers,

12 to equip the saints for the work of ministry,
    for building up the body of Christ,

13 **until all of us come to the unity of the faith**
    and of the knowledge of the Son of God,
    to maturity, to the measures of
    the full stature of Christ.

14 We must no longer be children, tossed to and fro
    and blown about by every wind of doctrine,
    by people's trickery, by their craftiness
    in deceitful scheming.

15 **But speaking the truth in love,**
    we must grow up in every way
    into him who is the head, into Christ.

시편 119
(일반주일 혹은 교사임명식)

97 내가 주의 법을 어찌 그리 사랑하는지요
    내가 그것을 종일 작은 소리로 읊조리나이다
98 주의 계명들이 항상 나와 함께 하므로
    그것들이 나를 원수보다 지혜롭게 하나이다.
101 내가 주의 말씀을 지키려고 발을 금하여
    모든 악한 길로 가지 아니하였사오며
102 주께서 나를 가르치셨으므로
    내가 주의 규례들에서 떠나지 아니하였나이다
103 주의 말씀의 맛이 내게 어찌 그리 단지요
    내 입에 꿀보다 더 다나이다
104 주의 법도로 말미암아 내가 명철하게 되었으므로
    모든 거짓 행위를 미워하나이다
105 주의 말씀은 내 발에 등이요
    내 길에 빛이니이다

Psalm 119
(Regular Sundays or Installation of Teachers)

97 Oh, how I love your law!
    It is my meditation all day long.
98 Your commandment makes me wiser than my enemies,
    for it is always with me.
101 I hold back my feet from every evil way,
    in order to keep your word.
102 I do not turn away from your ordinances,
    for you have taught me.
103 How sweet are your words to my taste,
    sweeter than honey to my mouth!
104 Through your precepts I get understanding;
    therefore I hate every false way.
105 Your word is a lamp to my feet
    and a light to my path.

로마서 12장
(일반주일 혹은 임직)

1 그러므로 형제들아
　　내가 하나님의 모든 자비하심으로 너희를 권하노니
　　　너희 몸을 하나님이 기뻐하시는 거룩한 산 제물로 드리라
　이는 너희가 드릴 영적 예배니라
2 너희는 이 세대를 본받지 말고
　　오직 마음을 새롭게 함으로 변화를 받아
　하나님의 선하시고 기뻐하시고 온전하신 뜻이
　　무엇인지 분별하도록 하라
3 내게 주신 은혜로 말미암아 너희 각 사람에게 말하노니
　　마땅히 생각할 그 이상의 생각을 품지 말고
　오직 하나님께서 각 사람에게 나누어 주신
　　믿음의 분량대로 지혜롭게 생각하라
4 우리가 한 몸에 많은 지체를 가졌으나
　　모든 지체가 같은 기능을 가진 것이 아니니
5 **이와 같이 우리 많은 사람이 그리스도 안에서**
　　한 몸이 되어 서로 지체가 되었느니라
6 우리에게 주신 은혜대로 받은 은사가 각각 다르니
　　혹 예언이면 믿음의 분수대로
7 혹 섬기는 일이면 섬기는 일로,
　　혹 가르치는 자면 가르치는 일로,
8 **혹 위로하는 자면 위로하는 일로,**
　　구제하는 자는 성실함으로,
　　다스리는 자는 부지런함으로,
　　긍휼을 베푸는 자는 즐거움으로 할 것이니라
9 사랑에는 거짓이 없나니 악을 미워하고 선에 속하라
10 **형제를 사랑하여 서로 우애하고**
　　존경하기를 서로 먼저 하며
11 부지런하여 게으르지 말고
　열심을 품고 주를 섬기라
12 소망 중에 즐거워하며
　　환난 중에 참으며 기도에 항상 힘쓰며
13 **성도들의 쓸 것을 공급하며 손 대접하기를 힘쓰라**

Romans 12
(Regular Sundays or Installation of Officers)

1 I appeal to you therefore, brothers and sisters,
   by the mercies of God,
   to present your bodies as a living sacrifice,
   holy and acceptable to God,
which is your spiritual worship.

2 Do not be conformed to this world,
   but be transformed by the renewing of your minds,
**so that you may discern what is the will of God—
   what is good and acceptable and perfect.**

3 For by the grace given to me I say to everyone among you
   not to think of yourself more highly
   than you ought to think,
**but to think with sober judgment,
   each according to the measure of faith that God has assigned.**

4 For as in one body we have many members,
   and not all the members have the same function,

5 **so we, who are many, are one body in Christ,
   and individually we are members one of another.**

6 We have gifts that differ according to the grace given to us:
   prophecy, in proportion to faith;

7 ministry, in ministering; the teacher, in teaching;

8 **the exhorter, in exhortation; the giver, in generosity;
   the leader, in diligence;
   the compassionate, in cheerfulness.**

9 Let love be genuine; hate what is evil,
   hold fast to what is good;

10 **Love one another with mutual affection;
   outdo one another in showing honor.**

11 Do not lag in zeal,
be ardent in spirit, serve the Lord.

12 Rejoice in hope, be patient in suffering, persevere in prayer.

13 **Contribute to the needs of the saints; extend hospitality.**

골로새서 1
(임직)

25 내가 교회의 일꾼 된 것은 하나님이 너희를 위하여
　　내게 주신 직분을 따라 하나님의 말씀을 이루려 함이니라
26 **이 비밀은 만세와 만대로부터 감추어졌던 것인데**
　　이제는 그의 성도들에게 나타났고
27 하나님이 그들로 하여금 이 비밀의 영광이
　　이방인 가운데 얼마나 풍성하지를 알게 하려 하심이라
이 비밀은 너희 안에 계신 그리스도시니
곧 영광의 소망이니라
28 우리가 그를 전파하여 각 사람을 권하고
　　모든 지혜로 각 사람을 가르침은
　　각 사람을 그리스도 안에서 완전한 자로 세우려 함이니
29 **이를 위하여 나도 내 속에서 능력으로 역사하시는 이의**
　　역사를 따라 힘을 다하여 수고하노라

Colossians 1
(Installation of Officers)

25 I became its servant according to God's commission
　　that was given to me for you,
　　to make the word of God fully known,
26 **the mystery that has been hidden**
　　throughout the ages and generations
　　but has now been revealed to his saints.
27 to them God chose to make known
　　how great among the Gentiles
　　are the riches of glory of this mystery,
which is Christ in you, the hope of glory.
28 It is he whom we proclaim,
　　warning everyone and teaching everyone in all wisdom,
　　so that we may present every mature in Christ.
29 **For this I toil and struggle with all the energy**
　　that he powerfully inspires within me.

시편 126
(일반주일 혹은 국가기념일)

1 여호와께서 시온의 포로를 돌려 보내실 때에
　　우리는 꿈꾸는 것 같았도다
2 **그 때에 우리 입에는 웃음이 가득하고**
　　우리 혀에는 찬양이 찼었도다
　　그 때에 뭇 나라 가운데서 말하기를
　　여호와께서 그들을 위하여
　　큰 일을 행하셨도다 하였도다
3 여호와께서 우리를 위하여
　　큰 일을 행하셨으니 우리는 기쁘도다
4 **여호와여**
　　우리의 포로를 남방 시내들 같이 돌려 보내소서
5 눈물을 흘리며 씨를 뿌리는 자는 기쁨으로 거두리로다
6 **울며 씨를 뿌리러 나가는 자는**
　　반드시 기쁨으로 그 곡식 단을 가지고 돌아오리라

Psalm 126
(Regular Sundays or National Holidays)

1 When the Lord restored the fortunes of Zion,
　　we were like those who dream.
2 **Then our mouth was filled with laughter,**
　　and our tongue with shouts of joy;
　　then it was said among the nations,
　　"The Lord has done great things for them."
3 The Lord has done great things for us,
　　and we rejoiced.
4 **Restore our fortunes, O Lord,**
　　like the watercourses in the Negeb.
5 May those who sow in tears
　　reap with shouts of joy.
6 **Those who go out weeping,**
　　bearing the seed for sowing,
　　shall come home with shouts of joy,
　　carrying their sheaves.

시편 137
(일반주일 혹은 국가기념일)

1 우리가 바벨론의 여러 강변 거기에 앉아서
    시온을 기억하며 울었도다
2 **그 중의 버드나무에 우리가 우리의 수금을 걸었나니**
3 이는 우리를 사로잡은 자가 거기서 우리에게 노래를 청하며
    우리를 황폐하게 한 자가 기쁨을 청하고
    자기들을 위하여 시온의 노래 중 하나를 노래하라 함이로다
4 **우리가 이방 땅에서 어찌 여호와의 노래를 부를까**
5 예루살렘아 내가 너를 잊을진대
    내 오른손이 그의 재주를 잊을지로다
6 **내가 예루살렘을 기억하지 아니하거나**
    내가 가장 즐거워하는 것보다 더 즐거워하지 아니할진대
    내 혀가 내 입천장에 붙을지로다
7 여호와여 예루살렘이 멸망하던 날을 기억하시고 에돔 자손을 치소서
    그들의 말이 헐어 버리라 헐어 버리라
    그 기초까지 헐어 버리라 하였나이다

Psalm 137
(Regular Sundays or National Holidays)

1 By the rivers of Babylon—there we sat down
    and there we wept when we remembered Zion.
2 **On the willows there we hung up our harps.**
3 For there our captors asked us for songs,
    and our tormentors asked for mirth,
    saying, "Sing us one of the songs of Zion!"
4 **How could we sing the Lord's song in a foreign land?**
5 If I forget you, O Jerusalem, let my right hand wither!
6 **If I do not remember you,**
    if I do not set Jerusalem above my highest joy,
    let my tongue cling to the roof of my mouth.
7 Remember, O Lord,
    against the Edomites the day of Jerusalem's fall,
    how they said, "Tear it down!
    Tear it down! Down to its foundations!"

시편 127
(일반주일 혹은 가정)

1 여호와께서 집을 세우지 아니하시면
　　세우는 자의 수고가 헛되며
　여호와께서 성을 지키지 아니하시면
　　파수꾼의 깨어 있음이 헛되도다
2 너희가 일찍이 일어나고 늦게 누우며
　　수고의 떡을 먹음이 헛되도다
　그러므로 여호와께서 그의 사랑하시는 자에게는
　　잠을 주시는도다
3 보라 자식들은 여호와의 기업이요
　　태의 열매는 그의 상급이로다
4 **젊은 자의 자식은 장사의 수중의 화살 같으니**
5 이것이 그의 화살통에 가득한 자는 복되도다
　그들이 성문에서 그들의 원수와 담판할 때에
　　수치를 당하지 아니하리로다

Psalm 127
(Regular Sundays or Home)

1 Unless the Lord builds the house,
　　those who build it labor in vain.
　Unless the Lord guards the city,
　　the guard keeps watch in vain.
2 It is in vain that you rise up early
　　and go late to rest,
　　eating the bread of anxious toil;
　for he gives sleep to his beloved.
3 Sons are indeed a heritage from the Lord,
　　the fruit of the womb a reward.
4 **Like arrows in the hand of a warrior**
　　are the sons of one's youth.
5 Happy is the man
　　who has his quiver full of them.
　He shall not be put to shame
　　when he speaks with his enemies in the gate.

시편 128
(일반주일 혹은 가정)

1 여호와를 경외하며
     그의 길을 걷는 자마다 복이 있도다
2 **네가 네 손이 수고한 대로 먹을 것이라**
     네가 복되고 형통하리로다
3 네 집 안방에 있는 네 아내는
     결실한 포도나무 같으며
     네 식탁에 둘러 앉은 자식들은
     어린 감람나무 같으리로다
4 **여호와를 경외하는 자는**
     이같이 복을 얻으리로다
5 여호와께서 시온에서 네게 복을 주실지어다
     너는 평생에 예루살렘의 번영을 보며
6 **네 자식의 자식을 볼지어다**
     이스라엘에게 평강이 있을지로다

Psalm 128
(Regular Sundays or Home)

1 Happy is everyone who fears the Lord,
     who walks in his ways.
2 **You shall eat the fruit of the labor of your hands;**
     you shall be happy,
     and it shall go well with you.
3 Your wife will be like a fruitful vine
     within your house;
     your children will be like olive shoots
     around your table.
4 **Thus shall the man be blessed who fears the Lord.**
5 The Lord bless you from Zion.
     May you see the prosperity of Jerusalem
     all the days of your life.
6 **May you see your children's children.**
     Peace be upon Israel!

고린도전서 13 (사랑)

1 내가 사람의 말과 방언과 천사의 말을 할지라도
사랑이 없으면 소리 나는 구리와 울리는 꿱과리가 되고

2 내가 예언하는 능력이 있어
　　모든 비밀과 모든 지식을 알고
　　또 산을 옮길 만한 모든 믿음이 있을지라도
사랑이 없으면 내가 아무것도 아니요

3 내가 내게 있는 모든 것으로 구제하고
　　또 내 몸을 불사르게 내어 줄지라도
사랑이 없으면 내게 아무 유익이 없느니라

4 사랑은 오래 참고 사랑은 온유하며 시기하지 아니하며
사랑은 자랑하지 아니하며 교만하지 아니하며

5 무례히 행하지 아니하며 자기의 유익을 구하지 아니하며
　　성내지 아니하며 악한 것을 생각하지 아니하며

6 **불의를 기뻐하지 아니하며 진리와 함께 기뻐하고**

7 모든 것을 참으며 모든 것을 믿으며
　　모든 것을 바라며 모든 것을 견디느니라

8 **사랑은 언제까지나 떨어지지 아니하되**
　　예언도 폐하고 방언도 그치고 지식도 폐하리라

9 우리는 부분적으로 알고 부분적으로 예언하니

10 **온전한 것이 올 때에는 부분적으로 하던 것이 폐하리라**

11 내가 어렸을 때에는 말하는 것이 어린 아이와 같고
　　깨닫는 것이 어린 아이와 같고
　　생각하는 것이 어린 아이와 같다가
장성한 사람이 되어서는 어린 아이의 일을 버렸노라

12 우리가 지금은 거울로 보는 것 같이 희미하나
　　그 때에는 얼굴과 얼굴을 대하여 볼 것이요
지금은 내가 부분적으로 아나
　　그 때에는 주께서 나를 아신 것 같이
　　내가 온전히 알리라

13 그런즉 믿음 소망 사랑
　　이 세 가지는 항상 있을 것인데
그 중의 제일은 사랑이이라

1 Corinthians 13 (Love)

1 If I speak in the tongues of mortals and of angels,
but do not have love, I am a noisy gong or a clanging cymbal.
2 And if I have prophetic powers,
  and understand all mysteries and all knowledge,
  and If I have all faith, so as to remove mountains,
but do not have love, I am nothing.
3 If I give away all my possessions,
  and if I hand over my body so that I may boast,
but do not have love, I gain nothing.
4 Love is patient; love is king;
love is not envious or boastful or arrogant or rude.
5 It does not insist on its own way;
  it is not irritable or resentful;
6 **it does not rejoice in wrongdoing,**
  but rejoices in the truth.
7 It bears all things, believes all things,
  hopes all things, endures all things.
8 **Love never ends. But as for prophecies, they will cease;**
  as for knowledge, it will come to an end.
9 For we know only in part, and we prophesy only in part;
10 **but when the complete comes,**
  the partial will come to an end.
11 When I was a child, I spoke like a child,
  I thought like a child, I reasoned like a child;
when I became an adult,
  I put an end to childish ways
12 For now we see in a mirror;
  dimly, but then we will see face to face.
Now I know only in part; then I will know fully,
  even as I have been fully known.
13 And now faith, hope, and love abide, these three;
and the greatest of these is love.

요한1서 4장
(일반주일 혹은 사랑)

7 사랑하는 자들아 우리가 서로 사랑하자
    사랑은 하나님께 속한 것이니
사랑하는 자마다 하나님으로부터 나서 하나님을 알고

8 사랑하지 아니하는 자는 하나님을 알지 못하나니
이는 하나님은 사랑이심이라

9 하나님의 사랑이 우리에게 이렇게 나타난 바 되었으니
    하나님이 자기의 독생자를 세상에 보내심은
그로 말미암아 우리를 살리려 하심이라

10 사랑은 여기에 있으니
    우리가 하나님을 사랑한 것이 아니요
    하나님이 우리를 사랑하사
    우리 죄를 속하기 위하여 화목 제물로
    그 아들을 보내셨음이라

11 **사랑하는 자들아**
    하나님이 이같이 우리를 사랑하셨은즉
    우리도 서로 사랑하는 것이 마땅하도다

1 John 4
(Regular Sundays or Love)

7 Beloved, let us love one another,
    because love is from God;
everyone who loves is born of God
    and knows God.

8 Whoever does not love does not know God,
for God is love.

9 God's love was revealed among us in this way:
    God sent his only Son into the world
so that we might live through him.

10 In this is love, not that we loved God
    but that he loved us and sent his Son
    to be the atoning sacrifice for our sins.

11 **Beloved, since God loved us so much,**
    we also ought to love one another.

시편 84
(일반주일 혹은 입당·헌당예배)

1 만군의 여호와여 주의 장막이 어찌 그리 사랑스러운지요
2 **내 영혼이 여호와의 궁정을 사모하여 쇠약함이여**
   내 마음과 육체가 살아 계시는 하나님께 부르짖나이다
3 나의 왕, 나의 하나님, 만군의 여호와여
   주의 제단에서 참새도 제 집을 얻고
   제비도 새끼 둘 보금자리를 얻었나이다
4 **주의 집에 사는 자들은 복이 있나니**
   그들이 항상 주를 찬송하리이다
5 주께 힘을 얻고
   그 마음에 시온의 대로가 있는 자는 복이 있나이다
6 **그들이 눈물 골짜기로 지나갈 때에**
   그 곳에 많은 샘이 있을 것이며
   이른 비가 복을 채워 주나이다
7 그들은 힘을 얻고 더 얻어 나아가
   시온에서 하나님 앞에 각기 나타나리이다
8 **만군의 하나님 여호와여 내 기도를 들으소서**
   야곱의 하나님이여 귀를 기울이소서
9 우리 방패이신 하나님이여
   주께서 기름 부으신 자의 얼굴을 살펴 보옵소서
10 주의 궁정에서의 한 날이
   다른 곳에서의 천 날보다 나은즉
   악인의 장막에 사는 것보다
   내 하나님의 성전 문지기로 있는 것이 좋사오니
11 여호와 하나님은 방패이시라
   여호와께서 은혜와 영화를 주시며
   정직하게 행하는 자에게 좋은 것을
   아끼지 아니하실 것임이니이다
12 **만군의 여호와여 주께 의지하는 자는 복이 있나이다**

Psalm 84
(Regular Sundays or Dedication of a Building)

1 How lovely is your dwelling place, O Lord of hosts!

2 **My soul longs,**
>   **indeed it faints for the courts of the Lord;**
>   **my heart and my flesh**
>   **sing for joy to the living God.**

3 Even the sparrow finds a home,
>   and the swallow a nest for herself,
>   where she may lay her young, at your altars,
>   O Lord of hosts, my King and my God.

4 **Happy are those who live in your house,**
>   **ever singing your praise.**

5 Happy are those whose strength is in you,
>   in whose heart are the highways to Zion.

6 **As they go through the valley of Baca**
>   **they make it a place of springs;**
>   **the early rain also covers it with pools.**

7 They go from strength to strength;
>   the God of gods will be seen in Zion.

8 **O Lord God of hosts, hear my prayer;**
>   **give year, O God of Jacob!**

9 Behold our shield, O God;
>   **look on the face of your anointed.**

10 For a day in your courts is better
>   than a thousand elsewhere.
>   **I would rather be a doorkeeper in the house of my God**
>   **than live in the tents of wickedness.**

11 For the Lord God is a sun and shield;
>   he bestows favor and honor.
>   No good thing does the Lord withhold
>   from those who walk uprightly.

12 **O Lord of hosts,**
>   **happy is everyone who trusts in you.**

마태복음 28장
(전도 · 선교)

18 예수께서 나아와 말씀하여 이르시되
  하늘과 땅의 모든 권세를 내게 주셨으니
19 그러므로 너희는 가서
     모든 민족을 제자로 삼아
     아버지와 아들과 성령의 이름으로 세례를 베풀고
20 **내가 너희에게 분부한 모든 것을 가르쳐 지키게 하라**
     볼지어다 내가 세상 끝까지
     너희와 항상 함께 있으리라 하시니라

Matthew 28
(Evangelism · Mission)

18 And Jesus came and said to them,
  "All authority in heaven and on earth
     has been given to me.
19 Go therefore and make disciples of all nations,
     baptizing them
     in the name of the Father
     and of the Son
     and of the Holy Spirit,
20 **and teaching them to obey everything**
     that I have commanded you.
     And remember,
     I am with you always,
     to the end of the age."

결혼 예문

부름

사람들이 입장하는 동안 악기를 연주하거나 찬송이나 노래를 부른다.

주례목사의 선언

이제부터 신랑 000 군과 신부 000 양의 혼인예식을 거행하겠습니다.

신랑 신부 입장

신랑이 먼저 주례목사 앞에 나아와 목례하고 주례자의 왼쪽에 서서 회중을 향하여 선다.
신부가 주악에 맞추어 부모나 혹은 친지와 함께 들어오면 신랑이 그를 맞이하여 주례목사를 향하여 선다.

예식사

사랑하는 여러분,
오늘 우리는 하나님과 여러 증인들 앞에서
000 군과 000 양을 위한 혼인예식을
　기독교 전통에 따라 거행하고자 합니다.
혼인은 하나님께서 한 남자와 한 여자를 지으시고, 축복하사,
　서로 사랑하고, 보살피며 살 수 있도록
　언약으로 제정하여 주신 것입니다.
예수께서는 갈릴리 가나 혼인잔치에 참예하사,
　물을 포도주로 만드는 이적을 행하여 주심으로
　결혼의 귀중함을 보여 주셨습니다.
그리고 예수께서는 자신을 희생하시기까지
　사람들을 사랑하심으로써 남편과 아내가 실천해야 할
　희생적인 사랑의 본을 보여 주셨습니다.
000 군과 000 양이 이 거룩한 혼인예식을 통하여
　서로가 일생을 나누기로 서약하고자 하오니
　여러분은 이 두 사람의 혼인예식을
　마음껏 축복해 주시기 바랍니다.

[찬송]

[기도}

[성경 봉독 (마태복음 19:4-6)]

[ ] 부분은 경우에 따라 생략이 가능함

혼인 의사 선포

주례목사가 신랑 신부에게 다음과 같이 말한다:

예수 그리스도께서 여러분과 하나가 되기 위하여 세례를 통하여
부르신 은혜를 힘입어 두 분은 서로 하나가 되고자 하는 의사를
하나님과 이 증인들 앞에서 선포하시기 바랍니다.

주례목사가 신부에게 다음과 같이 묻는다:

000 양,
당신이 000 군을 남편으로 맞으니
하나님의 명령을 따라 아내된 책임을 다하여
그를 사랑하고 도와주며 귀중히 여기고 보호하며
병들거나 건강하거나 오직 이 신랑으로만 남편을 삼아
평생토록 이 혼인의 언약을 지키며 살겠습니까?
신부: **예, 그렇게 살겠습니다.**

주례목사가 신랑에게 묻는다:

000 군,
당신이 000 양을 아내로 맞으니
하나님의 명령을 따라 남편된 책임을 다하여
그를 사랑하고 도와주며 귀중히 여기고 보호하며
병들거나 건강하거나 오직 이 신부로만 아내를 삼아
평생토록 이 혼인의 언약을 지키며 살겠습니까?
신랑: **예, 그렇게 살겠습니다.**

가족과 회중의 응답

주례목사가 가족과 회중에게 말한다:

000 군과 000 양의 혼인은 그들의 가족을 연합하여 주며
또 하나의 새로운 가족을 이루어 줍니다.
여러분은 이 두 사람의 혼인예식을 축복해 주시기를 바랍니다.

부모와 친척이 일어나서 말한다.

우리는 이 두 사람이 하나됨을 진심으로 기뻐하며
하나님께서 이 두 사람을 크게 축복해 주시기를 기도합니다.

주례목사가 회중에게 묻는다:

여러분은 하나님의 은혜에 힘입어 최선을 다하여
이 두 사람을 붙들어 주고 보살펴 주시겠습니까?
회중: **예, 우리가 그렇게 하겠습니다.**

기도

기도합시다.

만물을 창조하신 거룩하신 하나님,
주님은 모든 사람에게 빛을 골고루 비추어 주는 참 빛이시며,
주님은 우리들에게 길과 진리와 생명이 되십니다.
주님은 우리가 그릇된 길을 갈지라도
우리를 끊임없이 사랑하여 주시고
우리의 삶 속에 오셔서 성령으로 지켜 주시며
살아 역사하여 주시니 감사합니다.
특별히 이 혼인서약을 통하여
우리와 함께 하시는 주님께 찬양을 드립니다.
우리 주 예수 그리스도의 이름으로 기도합니다.
아멘.

성경 봉독

적절한 성경구절을 봉독한다.
성경을 봉독하기 전후로 특별찬양을 해도 좋다.

설교

중보기도

주례자가 다음과 같은 기도를 하거나 혹은 상황에 맞추어 준비한 기도를 한다.

기도합시다.

우리의 생명을 창조하고 섭리하시며,
우리를 은혜로 구원하여 주시는 영원하신 하나님,
오늘 결혼하는 000 군과 000 양에게
성령으로 축복하여 주시고, 성별하여 주소서.
주님의 풍성한 사랑 안에서 저들이 맺은 서약을
서로 지킬 수 있도록 도와주소서.
저들로 하여금 삶이 다하는 날까지
주님의 사랑과 평화 안에서
성장할 수 있도록 도와주시고,
저들이 이웃에게 관심을 가지며
그들을 섬길 수 있도록 도와주소서.
예수 그리스도의 이름으로 기도합니다.
아멘.

혼인 서약

신랑과 신부가 서로 손을 마주 잡는다. 신랑이 주례목사를 따라 다음과 같이 서약한다.

나 000는 그대 000를
내 아내로 맞아 이제부터 평생토록
즐거우나 괴로우나 가난할 때나 부할 때나
병들거나 건강하거나
어떤 환경에서라도 당신을 귀중히 여기고 사랑하며
죽음이 우리를 나눌 때까지 오늘의 이 서약을 지키기로
하나님과 여러 증인들 앞에서 굳게 다짐합니다.

신부가 주례목사를 따라 다음과 같이 서약한다.

나 000는 그대 000를
내 남편으로 맞아 이제부터 평생토록
즐거우나 괴로우나 가난할 때나 부할 때나
병들거나 건강하거나
어떤 환경에서라도 당신을 귀중히 여기고 사랑하며
죽음이 우리를 나눌 때까지 오늘의 이 서약을 지키기로
하나님과 여러 증인들 앞에서 굳게 다짐합니다.

반지 교환

주례목사가 다음과 같이 말한다.

이 반지는 예수 그리스도와 그의 몸된 교회가 하나되는
내적인 신비를 상징하는 외적인 표시입니다.

주례목사가 반지를 들고 축복기도를 한다.

오 주님,
저들이 이 반지를 주고받은 후, 반지를 낄 때에
주님의 평화 안에서 살면서 평생토록
주님의 사랑 안에 거하도록 축복하여 주소서.
우리 주 예수 그리스도의 이름으로 기도합니다.
아멘.

주례목사가 준비된 반지를 신랑에게 줄 때 신랑으로 하여금 신부의 왼손 무명지에 반지를 끼우면서 다음과 같이 따라 말하게 한다.

000,
내가 성부와 성자와 성령의 이름을 받들어
이 반지를 나의 사랑의 표로 삼아 당신에게 드리고
나의 모든 것을 다하여 사랑하겠습니다.

신부가 신랑의 왼손 무명지에 반지를 끼우면서 다음과 같이 따라 말하게 한다.

000,
내가 성부와 성자와 성령의 이름을 받들어
이 반지를 나의 사랑의 표로 삼아 당신에게 드리고
나의 모든 것을 다하여 사랑하겠습니다.

혼인 선포

주례목사는 신랑 신부가 서로 손을 잡게 한 후,
신랑 신부의 손 위에 오른손을 얹고 다음과 같이 선언한다.

이 두 사람은 하나님과 여러 증인들 앞에서
서로 엄숙하게 혼인서약을 하였습니다.
하나님께서 이 혼인을 확증하여 주시고
은혜를 베풀어주시기 바랍니다.

주례목사가 회중에게 말한다.

000 군과 000 양이 서로 손을 잡고 서로 엄숙하게 서약하며
   거룩한 혼인예식을 거행하였으니
내가 성부와 성자와 성령의 이름으로
이 두 사람이 부부가 되었음을 선포합니다.
무릇 하나님이 짝지어 주신 것을 사람이 나누지 못할 것입니다.
아멘.

[하나뵘의 촛불을 이 시간에 점화할 수 있다.]

혼인 축복기도

주례자가 축복기도를 하는 동안 신랑과 신부는 무릎을 꿇는다.

오 하나님,
주님께서는 그리스도와 그의 몸된 교회 사이에 맺은
언약을 통하여 혼인을 거룩하게 하셨습니다.
그러므로 000 군과 000 양이 서로 맺은 서약을
지킬 수 있도록 축복하여 주소서.
사랑 안에서 저들이 성숙할 수 있게 도와주시고
서로 협력하여 평화로운 가정을 이루게 하소서.
우리 주 예수 그리스도의 이름으로 기도합니다.
아멘.

[성만찬을 거행할 경우에는 이 시간에 한다.]

보냄

[축가]

인사

신랑 신부가 회중을 향하여 인사한다.

[광고]

축도

주례목사가 신랑과 신부에게:

영원하신 하나님께서
사랑으로 두 분을 평생 지켜 주시고,
예수 그리스도의 은혜와 평화가
새 가정에 함께 하시기를 축원합니다.

주례자가 회중에게:

주 안에서 하나가 된 성도 여러분,
사랑 받기를 원하는 사람들이
여러분으로부터 관대한 사랑을 체험할 수 있도록
세상 속에서 하나님의 사랑을 증거하시기 바랍니다.
주 예수 그리스도의 은혜와 하나님의 사랑과
성령의 교통하심이 여러분과 함께 하시기를 축원합니다.
아멘.

신랑 신부 퇴장

후주

신랑 신부와 사람들이 퇴장하는 동안 찬송과 노래를 부르거나
혹은 악기를 연주한다.

A SERVICE OF CHRISTIAN MARRIAGE

ENTRANCE

GATHERING

While the people gather, instrumental or vocal music may be offered.
During the entrance of the wedding party, separately or together, there may be instrumental music, or a hymn, or an anthem.

GREETING

Pastor to people:

Friends, we are gathered together in the sight of God
    to witness and bless the joining together of *Name* and *Name*
    in Christian marriage.
The covenant of marriage was established by God,
    who created us male and female for each other.
With his presence and power
    Jesus graced a wedding at Cana of Galilee,
    and in his sacrificial love gave us the example
    for the love of husband and wife. *Name* and *Name*
    come to give themselves to one another in this holy covenant.

[HYMN]

[PRAYER]

[SCRIPTURE LESSON   Matthew 19:4-6]

DECLARATION OF INTENTION

DECLARATION BY THE MAN AND THE WOMAN

Pastor to the persons who are to marry:

I ask you now, in the presence of God and these people,
to declare your intention to enter into union with one another
through the grace of Jesus Christ, who calls you
into union with himself as acknowledged in your baptism.

[ ] means optional

Pastor to the woman:

Name, will you have *Name* to be your husband,
    to live together in holy marriage?
Will you love him, comfort him, honor and keep him,
    in sickness and in health,
and forsaking all others,
    be faithful to him as long as you both shall live?
Woman: **I will.**

Pastor to the man:

Name, will you have *Name* to be your wife,
    to live together in holy marriage?
Will you love her, comfort her, honor and keep her,
    in sickness and in health,
and forsaking all others,
    be faithful to her as long as you both shall live?
Man: **I will.**

RESPONSE OF THE FAMILIES AND PEOPLE

Pastor to people:

The marriage of *Name* and *Name* unites their families
    and creates a new one. They ask for your blessing.

Parents or other representatives of the families may respond:

We rejoice in your union, and pray God's blessing upon you.

Pastor to people:

Will all of you, by God's grace, do everything in your power
    to uphold and care for these two persons in their marriage?
People: **We will.**

PRAYER

Let us pray.

God of all peoples,
you are the true light illumining everyone.
You show us the way, the truth, and the life.
You love us even when we are disobedient.
You sustain us with your Holy Spirit.

We rejoice in your life in the midst of our lives.
We praise you for your presence with us,
and especially in this act of solemn covenant;
through Jesus Christ our Lord.
Amen.

SCRIPTURE LESSON(S)

Read an appropriate scripture. A hymn or other music may be offered before or after the readings.

SERMON

INTERCESSORY PRAYER

An extemporaneous prayer may be offered, or the following may be prayed by the pastor:

Let us pray.

Eternal God, creator and preserver of all life,
　　author of salvation, giver of all grace:
Bless and sanctify with your Holy Spirit
Name and *Name*, who come now to join in marriage.
Grant that they may give their vows to each other
　　in the strength of your steadfast love.
Enable them to grow in love and peace
　　with you and with one another all their days,
　　that they may reach out in concern and service to the world;
through Jesus Christ our Lord. **Amen.**

THE MARRIAGE

EXCHANGE OF VOWS

The woman and man face each other, joining hands.

Man to woman:

In the name of God,
I, *Name*, take you, *Name*, to be my wife,
　　to have and to hold from this day forward,
　　for better, for worse, for richer, for poorer,
　　in sickness and in health, to love and to cherish,
　　until we are parted by death.
This is my solemn vow.

Woman to man:

In the name of God,
I, *Name*, take you, *Name*, to be my husband,
  to have and to hold from this day forward,
  for better, for worse, for richer, for poorer,
  in sickness and in health, to love and to cherish,
  until we are parted by death.
This is my solemn vow.

BLESSING AND EXCHANGE OF RINGS

The pastor may say:

These rings (symbols) are the outward
  and visible sign of an inward and spiritual grace,
signifying to us the union between Jesus Christ and his church.

The pastor may bless the giving of rings or other symbols of the marriage:

Bless, O Lord,
the giving of these rings (symbols),
that they who wear them may live in your peace
  and continue in your favor all the days of their life;
through Jesus Christ our Lord.
Amen.

Man to Woman:

Name, I give you this ring as a sign of my vow,
and with all that I am, and all that I have,
I honor you; in the name of the Father,
  and of the Son, and of the Holy Spirit.

Woman to Man:

Name, I give you this ring
  as a sign of my vow,
and with all that I am, and all that I have,
I honor you; in the name of the Father,
  and of the Son, and of the Holy Spirit.

DECLARATION OF MARRIAGE

The wife and husband join hands. The pastor may place a hand on their joined hands.

The pastor to husband and wife:

You have declared your consent and vows before God
  and this congregation.
May God confirm your covenant
  and fill you both with grace.

Pastor to people:

Now that *Name* and *Name*
  have given themselves to each other
  by solemn vows, with the joining of hands,
  [and the giving and receiving of rings,]

I announce to you that they are husband and wife:
in the name of the Father,
and of the Son,
and of the Holy Spirit.
Those whom God has joined together,
let no one put asunder.
Amen.

A doxology or other hymn may be sung. Intercessions may be offered for the church and for the world.

[The husband and wife may have the unity candlelight service.]

BLESSING OF THE MARRIAGE

The husband and wife may kneel, as the pastor prays:

O God, you have so consecrated
  the covenant of Christian marriage
  that in it is represented the covenant
  between Christ and his church.
Send therefore your blessing upon *Name* and *Name*,
  that they may surely keep their marriage covenant,
and so grow in love and godliness together
  that their home may be a haven of blessing and peace:
through Jesus Christ our Lord.
Amen.

[If the Holy Communion is to be celebrated, the service continues with a Service of Word and Table II.]

In either event, the service concludes with the sending forth.

SENDING FORTH

Here may be sung a hymn or psalm.

DISMISSAL WITH BLESSING

Pastor to wife and husband:

God the Eternal keep you in love with each other,
  so that the peace of Christ may abide in your home.
Go to serve God and your neighbor in all that you do.

Pastor to people:

Bear witness to the love of God in this world,
  so that those to whom love is a stranger
  will find in you generous friends.
The grace of the Lord Jesus Christ,
  and the love of God,
  and the communion of the Holy Spirit
  be with you all.
Amen.

THE PEACE

The peace of the Lord be with you always.
And also with you.

The couple and pastor(s) may greet each other, after which greetings may be exchanged
through the congregation.

GOING FORTH

A hymn may be sung or instrumental music played as the couple,
the wedding party, and the people leave.

죽음과 부활 예문
(장례 예문)

사람들이 예배실이나 혹은 장례식장에 들어오는 동안 조용하게 악기를 연주하거나 찬송을 부른다.
관이나 유골단지가 미리 예배실이나 장례식장에 놓여있지 않았으면 이 시간에 목사가 앞에 서서 인도한다.

목사가 다음과 같이 말한다:

예수 그리스도는 죽음을 직접 체험하시면서
    우리의 죽음을 멸하셨고,
예수 그리스도는 죽은 자 가운데서 직접 살아나시면서
    우리의 생명을 부활시키셨으며,
예수 그리스도는 영광 중에 다시 오실 것입니다.
000는 세례 받았을 때에 그리스도의 옷을 입은 것처럼,
000가 그리스도 안에서
    영광의 옷을 입게 될 것입니다.
지금 이 자리에 앉아 있는 우리 모두는
    하나님의 자녀들입니다.
우리가 장래에 어떻게 될지
    아직 나타나지 아니하였으나,
그리스도가 나타나시면
    우리는 그의 참 모습을 보게 될 것이며.
    우리는 그대로 그의 참 모습을 닮게 될 것입니다.
이러한 믿음과 소망을 가진 사람들에게는
    그리스도가 정결하신 것처럼
    우리들도 정결하게 될 것입니다.

은혜의 말씀

예수께서 이르시되 나는 부활이요 생명이니
나를 믿는 자는 죽어도 살겠고
무릇 살아서 나를 믿는 자는 영원히 죽지 아니하리라.

나는 알파와 오메가라
이제도 있고 전에도 있었고 장차 올 자요 전능한 자라.

내가 전에 죽었었노라
볼지어다 이제 세세토록 살아 있어
사망과 음부의 열쇠를 가졌노라.

이는 내가 살아 있고 너희도 살아 있겠음이라.

예식사

사랑하는 성도 여러분,
우리는 000의 일생을 돌보아 주신
　　하나님께 감사하고,
　　우리의 믿음을 증거하며,
　　하나님께 찬양 드리기 위하여 이 자리에 모였습니다.
우리는 000가 우리 곁을 떠나서 슬퍼합니다.
하나님께서 우리의 아픈 마음을 위로하여 주시고,
　　슬픈 마음에 소망을 주시고,
　　죽음에서 부활을 체험할 수 있도록
　　역사하여 주시기를 기원합니다.

찬송

목사: 주님께서 함께 하시기를 바랍니다.
회중: **주님께서 우리와 함께 하심을 믿습니다.**

다음의 기도문들 중에서 하나나 둘을 선택하여 다같이 기도한다.

(기도문 1)

다같이 기도합시다.

우리에게 생명을 허락하여 주신 하나님,
주님께서는 우리가 기도하기 전에
　　우리의 기도를 들어줄 준비가 되어 계시고,
우리가 구하기 전에 무엇을 원하는지
　　아는 분이시기에 기도합니다.
우리가 죽음의 신비 앞에서 움츠리고 있을 때에,
　　영생을 체험할 수 있도록
　　우리에게 은혜를 베풀어 주소서.
이 시간 주님의 뜻하신 삶과 죽음의 엄숙한 의미를
우리에게 다시 한번 말씀하여 주소서.
죽음의 두려움에 사로잡히지 않고 살 수 있도록 도와주소서.
우리의 생명이 다하는 날,
　　주님의 품 안에 안기기 위하여
　　앞서간 사람들의 믿음을 본받을 수 있도록 도와주소서.
우리가 살든지 죽든지
　　우리 주 예수 그리스도 안에 있는 하나님의 사랑에서
　　끊어지지 않게 하여 주소서.
아멘.

(기도문 2)

영원하신 하나님,
우리는 믿음의 길을 다 가고,
　할 일을 다 마친 후,
　편히 쉬고 있는 큰 무리를 인하여
　주님께 감사드립니다.
우리가 마음 속으로 이름을 부르며 아뢰는
　사랑하는 이들을 위하여 주님께 감사드립니다.
특별히 자비스러운 마음으로
　주님이 계신 곳으로 받아 주신
　000를 인하여 감사드립니다.
여기에 모여 있는 우리 모두에게
　주님의 평화를 내려 주소서.
슬픔과 절망에 싸여 있는 자들에게
　영원한 소망의 빛을 비추어 주셔서
　우리가 아직 가보지 못한 곳을
　믿을 수 있게 도와주소서.
주님께서 우리와 함께 하시면서
　우리의 날들을 인도하여 주시고,
　마지막 날에 주님께서 손수 지으신
　영원한 하늘나라에 있는 즐거운 집에 거하는
　사람들과 함께 거할 수 있도록 이끌어 주소서.
우리 주 예수 그리스도의 이름으로 기도합니다.
아멘.

누가 정죄하리요
죽으실 뿐 아니라 다시 살아나신 이는
그리스도 예수시니
그는 하나님의 우편에 계신 자요
우리를 위하여 간구하시는 자시니라.
우리 주 예수 그리스도로 말미암아
　우리에게 승리를 주시는 하나님께 감사하노라.

시편 130

여호와여
내가 깊은 곳에서 주께 부르짖었나이다
주여 내 소리를 들으시며
　나의 부르짖는 소리에 귀를 기울이소서

여호와여 주께서 죄악을 지켜 보실진대
　주여 누가 서리이까
그러나 사유하심이 주께 있음은
　주를 경외하게 하심이니이다
나 곧 내 영혼은 여호와를 기다리며
　나는 주의 말씀을 바라는도다
파수꾼이 아침을 기다림보다
　내 영혼이 주를 더 기다리나니
　참으로 파수꾼이 아침을 기다림보다 더하도다
이스라엘아 여호와를 바랄지어다
　여호와께서는 인자하심과
　풍성한 속량이 있음이라
그가 이스라엘을
　그의 모든 죄악에서 속량하시리로다.

선포와 응답

구약성경

시편 23

여호와는 나의 목자시니
　내게 부족함이 없으리로다
그가 나를 푸른 풀밭에 누이시며
　쉴 만한 물 가로 인도하시는도다
내 영혼을 소생시키시고
　자기 이름을 위하여 의의 길로 인도하시는도다
내가 사망의 음침한 골짜기로 다닐지라도
　해를 두려워하지 않을 것은
　주께서 나와 함께 하심이라
주의 지팡이와 막대기가 나를 안위하시나이다
주께서 내 원수의 목전에서
　내게 상을 차려 주시고
　기름을 내 머리에 부으셨으니
　내 잔이 넘치나이다
내 평생에 선하심과 인자하심이
　반드시 나를 따르리니
　내가 여호와의 집에 영원히 살리로다.

신약성경

설교

약력

별세한 이의 약력을 나눈다.

추도사

별세한 이에 대하여 생각나는 것들을 서로 나눈다.

찬송

사도신경

영혼 위탁

기도

기도하시겠습니다.

우리를 사랑하여 주시는 하나님, 우리 모두가
　　다 주님을 버려도 주님은 끝까지 우리를 사랑하십니다.
여기에 사랑하는 이를 잃고 슬퍼하는 사람들과 원근 각처에서
　　우리들과 함께 슬퍼하는 이들을 위하여 기도합니다.
의심하는 자에게 지혜의 빛을 비추어 주시고
　　약한 자에게 강건함을 주소서.
죄 지은 자에게 긍휼을 베푸시고,
　　슬퍼하는 자에게 주님의 위로와 평화를 주소서.
사랑만이 우리의 삶을 풍성하게 한다는 것을
　　변함없는 사실로 간직하게 하시고,
우리가 사는 날까지 주님을 의지하게 하여 주소서.
이 땅의 교회와 하늘나라의 성도들이
　　당신께 존귀와 영광을 영원히 돌리나이다.
아멘.

목사가 관이나 유골단지에 손을 얹고 다음의 기도문들 중에서 하나를 선택한다.

(기도문 1)

000를 주님의 자비로우신 팔에 안아 주시고

OOO를 주님의 백성과 함께 부활시켜 주소서.
우리도 받아 주시고, 새 생명 가운데 살게 하여 주소서.
우리로 하여금 다가오는 하늘나라의 기쁨에 참여할 수 있도록
주님과 이웃을 사랑하고 섬길 수 있게 도와주소서. **아멘.**

(기도문 2)

오 자비로우신 구세주시여,
　주님의 종 OOO를 주님의 손에 맡기나이다.
우리가 간절히 간구하옵기는
　주님의 우리 안에 있는 한 양으로 받아 주시고,
　양떼 중의 한 어린 양으로 받아 속량하신 죄인으로 받아 주소서.
OOO를 주님의 자비로우신 품에 안기게 하여 주시고,
영원한 평화 가운데 쉬게 하시며 하늘나라 성도들의 영광스러운 무리에
　함께 할 수 있도록 영접하여 주소서. **아멘.**

[성만찬을 거행할 경우, 24-25쪽에 있는 성만찬 예문 II를 이 시간에 사용하면 된다.]

감사의 기도

사랑의 하나님,
오늘 이 시간까지 저희들을 축복하여 주시니 감사합니다.
우리들이 건강하고 힘이 있을 때에,
　기쁨을 선물로 허락하여 주시니 감사합니다.
우리들이 고통과 슬픔 가운데 있을 때에도,
　우리와 함께 하여 주시고, 항상 함께 하심을 약속하여 주시니 감사합니다.
우리의 가정과 친구를 인하여 감사합니다.
우리에게 세례를 베풀어 주셔서 이제까지 신실하게 신앙생활을 하다가 죽은
　모든 사람들과 함께 할 수 있는 자리를 교회 안에 주심을 감사합니다.
무엇보다도 우리의 슬픔을 아셨고, 우리들을 위하여 죽으셨고,
　다시 사셨고, 지금도 살아 계시면서 우리를 위하여 기도하시는
　예수님을 인하여 감사드립니다.

다같이 주님께서 가르쳐 주신 기도를 드리겠습니다.

주기도문

찬송

축도

하관 예배가 장지에서 이어진다.

하관식 예문

하관식(예배)을 위한 예문이지만, 화장 혹은 수장이나 시신을 병원에 기증할 때에 드리는 예배에도
이 예문을 수정하여 사용할 수 있다.

그리스도 예수를 죽은 자 가운데서 살리신 이가
너희 안에 거하시는 그의 영으로 말미암아
　너희 죽을 몸도 살리시리라.
　　　　　(로마서 8:11)

보라 내가 너희에게 비밀을 말하노니
우리가 다 잠 잘 것이 아니요
　마지막 나팔에 순식간에 홀연히 다 변화되리니
이 썩을 것이 반드시 썩지 아니 할 것을 입겠고
이 죽을 것이 죽지 아니함을 입으리로다
이 썩을 것이 썩지 아니함을 입고
이 죽을 것이 죽지 아니함을 입을 때에는
　사망을 삼키고 이기리라고 기록된 말씀이 이루어지리라
사망아 너의 승리가 어디 있느냐
사망아 네가 쏘는 것이 어디 있느냐
우리 주 예수 그리스도로 말미암아
　우리에게 승리를 주시는 하나님께 감사하노라
　　(고린도전서 15:51, 53, 54 하반절-55, 57).

기도하시겠습니다.

오 하나님,
주님께서는 우주의 질서를 창조하여 주시고,
　하늘과 땅에 있는 모든 것들을 알고 계십니다.
밤이나 낮이나, 언제 어디서나,
현재의 삶과 장차 다가올 삶 속에서
우리 자신과 우리가 사랑하는 사람들을
하나님과 끊을 수 없는 사랑에 주저함 없이
맡길 수 있는 믿음을 허락해 주소서.
아멘.

다음의 성경구절들 중에서 하나를 선택하든가 아니면 성경에서 다른 구절을 읽는다.

우리 주 예수 그리스도의 아버지 하나님을 찬송하리로다
그의 많으신 긍휼대로

예수 그리스도를 죽은 자 가운데서
부활하게 하심으로 말미암아 우리를 거듭나게 하사
산 소망이 있게 하시며 썩지 않고 더럽지 않고
쇠하지 아니하는 유업을 잇게 하시나니
곧 너희를 위하여 하늘에 간직하신 것이라
너희는 말세에 나타내기로 예비하신
　구원을 얻기 위하여 믿음으로 말미암아
　하나님의 능력으로 보호하심을 받았느니라
그러므로 너희가 이제 여러 가지 시험으로 말미암아
　잠깐 근심하게 되지 않을 수 없으나
　오히려 크게 기뻐하는도다
너희 믿음의 확실함은 불로 연단하여도
　없어질 금보다 더 귀하여
　예수 그리스도께서 나타나실 때에
　칭찬과 영광과 존귀를 얻게 할 것이니라
예수를 너희가 보지 못하였으나 사랑하는도다
　이제도 보지 못하나 믿고 말할 수 없는
　영광스러운 즐거움으로 기뻐하니
　믿음의 결국 곧 영혼의 구원을 받음이라
　　　　　　　　（베드로전서 1:3-9）.

관의 머리 방향에 서서 관을 보면서 목사가 기도한다.
(또는 이 때에 관을 내리는 동안 다음의 기도를 할 수 있다.)

전능하신 하나님,
부활의 확실한 소망 안에서
우리 주 예수 그리스도로 말미암은 영생을 누릴 수 있도록
주님의 자녀 000를
하나님의 자비하신 팔에 위탁합니다.
아멘.

우리가 이 시신을 땅에 장사하매
　흙은 흙으로, 재는 재로, 티끌은 티끌로
　돌아가도록 맡기나이다.

지금 이후로 주 안에서 죽는 자들은 복이 있도다 하시매
　성령이 이르시되 그러하다
　그들이 수고를 그치고 쉬리니 이는 그들의 행한 일이 따름이라
　　　　　　　　（요한계시록 14:13）.

다음의 기도 중에서 한두 가지 선택한다.

(기도문 1)

은혜로우신 하나님,
우리가 사랑하나 더 이상 볼 수 없게 된 이들의 삶을 감사드립니다.
주님의 품 안으로 000를 받아 주소서.
주님의 팔 안으로 받아 주소서.
하늘나라 사역에 쓰임 받도록 주님을 아는 지혜와 사랑을 더하여 주소서.
우리 주 예수 그리스도의 이름으로 기도합니다. **아멘.**

(기도문 2)

영원하신 하나님,
주님께서는 우리들과 함께 살아온 000의 삶을 주관하셨습니다.
오늘의 우리가 될 수 있도록 우리와 함께 살아 온 000와
우리의 삶 속에서 지금도 살아서 영향을 주고 있는 것들과
주님의 사랑 안에서 영원히 사라지지 않을 000의 삶을
  기억하며 감사드립니다.
지금 000이 주님의 팔에 안길 때에, 우리들의 외로움을 달래주시고,
  우리들의 약함을 강건하게 하여 주시며,
  두려움 없이 미래를 맞이할 수 있도록 용기를 주소서.
이 땅에 머물러 있는 우리들이
  좀더 서로 가깝게 살 수 있도록 모아 주시고,
  서로가 서로를 섬기며 살 수 있게 하사
  영생의 기쁨과 평안을 맛볼 수 있게 하여 주소서.
우리 주 예수 그리스도의 이름으로 기도합니다. **아멘.**

주기도문

찬송

축도

여러분을 보호하사 거침이 없게 하시고
여러분을 그 영광 앞에 흠이 없이 기쁨으로 서게 하실 이
곧 우리 구주 홀로 하나이신 하나님께
우리 주 예수 그리스도로 말미암아 영광과 위엄과 권력과 권세가
영원 전부터 이제와 영원토록 있을지어다.
아멘.   (유다서 24-25 참조)

A SERVICE OF DEATH AND RESURRECTION

GATHERING

The pastor may greet the family.
Music for worship may be offered while the people gather.
Hymns and songs of faith may be sung during the gathering.
The pall may be placed on the coffin or urn with these words:

Dying, Christ destroyed our death.

Rising, Christ restored our life.

Christ will come again in glory.

As in baptism *Name* put on Christ,
　so in Christ may *Name* be clothed with glory.

Here and now, dear friends,
　we are God's children.

What we shall be has not yet been revealed;
but we know that when he appears,
　we shall be like him,
　for we shall see him as he is.

Those who have this hope purify themselves
　as Christ is pure.

The coffin or urn may be carried into the place of worship in procession,
　the pastor going before it and saying the word of grace, the congregation standing.
Or, if the coffin or urn is already in place, the pastor says the following from
　in front of the congregation.

THE WORD OF GRACE

Jesus said, I am the resurrection and I am the life.
Those who believe in me,
　even though they die, yet shall they live,
　and whoever lives and believes in me shall never die.

I am Alpha and Omega, the beginning and the end,
　the first and the last.

I died, and behold I am alive for evermore,
　and I hold the keys of hell and death.

Because I live, you shall live also.

GREETING

Friends, we have gathered here to praise God
　　and to witness to our faith as we celebrate the life of *Name*.
We come together in grief,
　　acknowledging our human loss.
May God grant us grace,
　　that in pain we may find comfort,
　　in sorrow hope, in death resurrection.

HYMN OR SONG

PRAYER

The following or other prayers may be offered, in unison if desired.
Petition for God's help, thanksgiving for the communion of saints,
confession of sin, and assurance of pardon are appropriate here.

The Lord be with you.
And also with you.

Let us pray together.

O God, who gave us birth,
you are ever more ready to hear
　　than we are to pray.
You know our needs before we ask,
　　and our ignorance in asking.
Give to us now your grace,
　　that as we shrink before the mystery of death,
　　we may see the light of eternity.
Speak to us once more
　　your solemn message of life and of death.
Help us to live
　　as those who are prepared to die.
And when our days here are accomplished,
　　enable us to die as those who go forth to live,
　　so that living or dying, our life may be in you,
　　and that nothing in life or in death
　　will be able to separate us from your great love
　　in Christ Jesus our Lord.
Amen.

and/or

Eternal God,
we praise you for the great company of all those
  who have finished their course in faith
  and now rest from their labor.
We praise you for those dear to us
  whom we name in our hearts before you.
Especially we praise you for *Name*,
  whom you have graciously received into your presence.
To all of these, grant your peace.
Let perpetual light shine upon them;
and help us so to believe where we have not seen,
  that your presence may lead us through our years,
  and bring us at last with them into the joy of your home
    not made with hands but eternal in the heavens;
through Jesus Christ our Lord.   Amen.

Who is in a position to condemn?
  Only Christ, Christ who died for us, who rose for us,
    who reigns at God's right hand and prays for us.
  Thanks be to God who gives us the victory
    through our Lord Jesus Christ.

PSALM 130

Out of depths I cry unto thee, O Lord!
  Lord, hear my cry.
Let thine ears be attentive
  to the voice of my supplication.
If thou, Lord, should mark iniquities, Lord, who could stand?
But there is forgiveness with thee, that thou may be feared.
I wait for the Lord,
  my soul waits, and in his word do I hope.
My soul waits for the Lord
  more than those who watch for the morning.
O Israel, hope in the Lord!
  For with the Lord is great mercy.
With him is plenteous redemption,
  and he will redeem Israel from all their sins.

PROCLAMATION AND RESPONSE

OLD TESTAMENT LESSON

PSALM 23

The Lord is my shepherd; I shall not want.
He maketh me to lie down in green pastures:
  he leadeth me beside the still waters.
He restoreth my soul:
  he leadeth me in the paths of righteousness for his name's sake.
Yea, though I walk through the valley of the shadow of death,
  I will fear no evil: for thou art with me;
  thy rod and thy staff they comfort me.
Thou preparest a table before me in the presence of mine enemies;
thou anointest my head with oil; my cup runneth over.
Surely goodness and mercy shall follow me all the days of my life:
  and I will dwell in the house of the Lord for ever.

NEW TESTAMENT LESSON

PSALM OR HYMN

GOSPEL LESSON

SERMON

A sermon may be preached, proclaiming the gospel in the face of death.
It may lead into, or include, the following acts of naming and witness.

NAMING

The life and death of the deceased may be gathered up by the reading of a memorial or appropriate statement,
  or in other ways, by the pastor or others.

WITNESS

Family, friends, and members of the congregation may briefly voice their thankfulness to God
  for the grace they have received in the life of the deceased and their Christian faith and joy.
Signs of faith, hope, and love may be exchanged.

HYMN OR SONG

CREED OR AFFIRMATION OF FAITH

If the creed has not been preceded by, it may be followed by, a hymn or musical response.

COMMENDATION

PRAYERS

One or more of the following prayers may be offered, or other prayers may be used.

God of us all, your love never ends.
When all else fails, you still are God.
We pray to you for one another in our need,
　and for all, anywhere, who mourn with us this day.
To those who doubt, give light:
　to those who are weak, strength:
　to all who have sinned, mercy:
　to all who sorrow, your peace.
Keep true in us the love with which we hold one another.
In all our ways we trust you.
And to you,
　with your church on earth and in heaven,
　we offer honor and glory, now and for ever.
Amen.

O God, all that you have given us is yours.
As first you gave *Name* to us,
　so now we give *Name* back to you.

Here the pastor, with others, standing near the coffin or urn,
may lay hands on it, continuing:

Receive *Name* into the arms of your mercy.
Raise *Name* up with all your people.
Receive us also, and raise us into a new life.
Help us so to love and serve you in this world
　that we may enter into your joy in the world to come.
Amen.

Into your hands, O merciful Savior,
　we commend your servant *Name.*
Acknowledge, we humbly beseech you,
　a sheep of your own fold,
　a lamb of your own flock,
　a sinner of your own redeeming.

Receive *Name* into the arms of your mercy,
   into the blessed rest of everlasting peace,
   and into the glorious company of the saints of light.
Amen.

The pastor may administer Holy Communion to all present who wish to share at the Lord's
table, using Service of Word and Table II on page 26–27. Otherwise, the service continues as follows:

PRAYER OF THANKSGIVING

God of love, we thank you for all with which
   you have blessed us even to this day:
for the gift of joy in days of health and strength,
   and for the gifts of your abiding presence
   and promise in days of pain and grief.
We praise you for home and friends,
   and for our baptism and place in your church
   with all who have faithfully lived and died.
Above all else we thank you for Jesus,
   who knew our griefs,
   who died our death and rose for our sake,
   and who lives and prays for us.

And as he taught us, so now we pray.

THE LORD'S PRAYER

HYMN

DISMISSAL WITH BLESSING

A service of committal follows at the final resting place.

A SERVICE OF COMMITTAL

This order is intended primarily for burial in the ground.
However, it can be adapted for cremation or the interment of ashes, for burial above ground
　or at sea, or for donation of the body for medical purposes.

God who raised Christ from the dead
　will give life to your mortal bodies also
　through the Spirit that dwells in you
　　　　　　　　　　　(Romans 8:11).

Listen, I will tell you a mystery!
We will not all die, but we will all be changed.
For this perishable body must put on imperishability,
　and this mortal body must put on immortality.
Then the saying that is written will be fulfilled:
　"Death has been swallowed up in victory."
　"Where, O death, is your victory?
　Where, O death, is your sting?"
But thanks be to God, who gives us the victory
　　　through our Lord Jesus Christ (1 Corinthians 15:51, 53, 54b-55, 57).

The following prayer is offered:

Let us pray.

O God, you have ordered this wonderful world
　and know all things in earth and in heaven.
Give us such faith that by day and by night,
　at all times and in all places,
　we may without fear commit ourselves
　and those dear to us to your never-failing love,
　in this life and in the life to come. **Amen.**

One of the following or other scriptures may be read:

Blessed be the God and Father of our Lord Jesus Christ!
By his great mercy we have been born anew
　to a living hope through the resurrection of Jesus Christ
　from the dead, and to an inheritance
　which is imperishable, undefiled and unfading,
　kept in heaven for you.

In this you rejoice,
   though now for a little while you suffer trials
   so that the genuineness of your faith
   may prove itself worthy
     at the revelation of Jesus Christ.
Without having seen him, yet you love him;
though you do not now see him, you believe in him
   and rejoice with unutterable and exalted joy.
As the harvest of your faith you reap
   the salvation of your souls
(1 Peter 1:3-9).

Standing at the head of the coffin and facing it (preferably casting earth upon it as it is lowered into the grave) the pastor says:

Almighty God,
   into your hands we commend
   your *son/daughter Name*,
   in sure and certain hope of resurrection to eternal life
   through Jesus Christ our Lord.
Amen.

This body we commit to the ground
   earth to earth, ashes to ashes, dust to dust.

"Blessed are the dead who die in the Lord.
Yes, says the Spirit, they will rest from their labors
   for their deeds follow them"
(Revelation 14:13).

One or more of the following or other prayers is offered:

Gracious God,
   we thank you for those we love but see no more.
Receive into your arms your servant *Name*,
   and grant that increasing
   in knowledge and love of you,
   he/she may go from strength to strength
     in service to your heavenly kingdom;
through Jesus Christ our Lord.
Amen.

For all that *Name* has given us
  to make us what we are,
  for that of *him/her*
  which lives and grows in each of us,
  and for *his/her* life
  that in your love will never end,
  we give you thanks.
As now we offer *Name* back into your arms,
  comfort us in our loneliness,
  strengthen us in our weakness,
  and give us courage to face the future unafraid.
Draw those of us who remain in this life
  closer to one another,
  make us faithful to serve one another,
  and give us to know
    that peace and joy which is eternal life;
through Jesus Christ our Lord.
Amen.

The Lord's Prayer may follow.

A hymn or song may be sung.

The pastor dismisses the people with the following or another blessing:

Now to the One who is able to keep you from falling,
  and to make you stand without blemish
    in the presence of God's glory with rejoicing,
to the only God our Savior,
  through Jesus Christ our Lord,
  be glory, majesty, power, and authority,
    before all time and now and forever.
Amen.

(Jude 24-25)

아침 찬양과 기도

이 예문은 아침 기도회를 위한 것이다.

찬양에로의 부름

인도자: 주님, 저희들의 입을 열어 주소서.
회　중: **우리가 주님께 찬양하리이다.**

찬송

아침에 적절한 찬송을 부른다.

감사기도

다음의 기도를 하든가 아니면 다른 적절한 기도를 한다.

빛을 창조하신 하나님,
주님은 사랑으로 날마다 새로운 아침을 창조하십니다.
주님께서는 온종일 세상에서 선을 이루십니다.
주님을 섬기고 이웃과 평화롭게 살며
하루하루 주님의 아들 우리 주 예수 그리스도께
헌신하는 삶을 살도록 우리의 마음을 움직여 주소서.
예수 그리스도의 이름으로 기도합니다.　아멘.

성경 봉독

시편 51, 63, 95; 신명기 6:4-9; 이사야 55:1-3; 요한복음 1:1-5, 9-14;
로마서 12:1-2; 혹은 아침, 계절, 교회력, 특별한 날과 특별한 경우와 관련된 성경구절을 읽는다.

묵상

봉독한 성경구절에 대하여 명상한다. 그리고 짤막하게 기도한다.

찬양

시편이나 적절한 찬송을 선택하여 부른다.

회중의 기도

인도자가 기도제목을 제안함에 따라 회중 가운데 한 사람씩 짧은 중보의 기도나
청원의 기도를 소리내어 하든가, 각자가 묵상으로 기도하면
인도자가 "주여, 긍휼히 여겨주소서" 라고 매 기도의 끝을 맺고,
회중들은 "우리의 기도를 들어주소서" 라고 기도한다.

다음과 같은 기도제목으로 함께 기도한다.

우리 교회의 교인들을 위하여 . . .

고난으로 인하여 어려움 중에 있는 사람들을 위하여 . . .

우리가 살고 있는 지역사회를 위하여 . . .

세계에 흩어져 사는 한국 사람들을 위하여 . . .

세상, 세상 사람들, 세상의 지도자들을 위하여 . . .

세계에 있는 모든 그리스도 교회, 지도자들,
   교인들, 선교를 위하여 . . .

성도들의 교제를 위하여 . . .

기도가 끝난 후 찬송가에서 적절한 찬송을 선택하여 부른다.

주기도문

폐회기도

지도자: 오늘 예수 그리스도의 은총과 평강이
       여러분을 인도해 주시기 바랍니다.
회 중: **하나님께 감사드립니다.**

평화의 인사

성도들은 화해와 사랑의 표시로 주위 사람들과 인사를 나눈다.

AN ORDER FOR
MORNING PRAISE AND PRAYER

This service is for groups as they begin their day in prayer.

CALL TO PRAISE AND PRAYER

O Lord, open our lips.
And we shall declare your praise.

HYMN

A hymn appropriate to the morning may be sung.

PRAYER OF THANKSGIVING

The following or other prayer of thanksgiving may be said:

New every morning is your love, great God of light,
   and all day long you are working for good in the world.
Stir up in us desire to serve you,
   to live peacefully with our neighbors,
   and to devote each day to your Son,
   our Savior, Jesus Christ the Lord.
Amen.

SCRIPTURE

Psalm 51, 63, or 95; Deuteronomy 6:4-9; Isaiah 55:1-3; John 1:1-5, 9-14;
Romans 12:1-2; or other readings appropriate to the morning, or to the day
or season of the Christian year, or to the nature of the occasion, may be used.

SILENCE

Silent meditation on the Scripture that has been read.
This may be concluded with a short prayer.

SONG OF PRAISE

Appropriate hymn may be sung.

PRAYERS OF THE PEOPLE

The following or other litany of intercession may be prayed, during which any

person may offer a brief prayer of intercession or petition.
After each prayer, the leader may conclude: Lord, in your mercy,
and all may respond: Hear our prayer.

Together, let us pray for

the people of this congregation . . .

those who suffer and those in trouble . . .

the concerns of this local community . . .

the Koreans who live throughout the world . . .

the world, its people, and its leaders . . .

the church universal—
its leaders, its members, and its mission . . .

the communion of saints . . .

Following these prayers, all may sing appropriate morning hymn(s).

THE LORD'S PRAYER

BLESSING

May the grace of Jesus Christ guide you today.
Go in peace.
People: **Thanks be to God.**

THE PEACE

Signs of peace may be exchanged.

저녁 찬양과 기도

이 예문은 하루의 일과를 마치고 저녁 기도회를 위한 것이다.

빛의 선포

촛불이 준비되어 있으면 킨다.

인도자: 예수 그리스도 안에 나타난 빛과 평화에 대하여
회　중: **하나님께 감사합시다.**

찬송

저녁에 적절한 찬송을 부른다.

감사기도

다음에 적혀 있는 기도를 하든가 아니면 다른 적절한 기도를 한다.

오 하나님,
시작과 끝이 없는 무한하신 주님께 찬양과 감사를 드립니다.
그리스도를 통하여 하나님께서는 모든 것을 창조하셨고,
**　또한 지금도 모든 것을 섭리하고 계십니다.**
빛이 일할 수 있도록 낮을 창조하셨고,
몸과 마음이 쉴 수 있도록 밤을 창조하셨습니다.
예수 그리스도 안에서 저희를 지켜 주시고,
**　죄에 물들지 않는 평온한 밤을 저희들에게 주소서.**
저희들로 하여금 하늘나라에 이르도록 인도하여 주소서.
그리스도를 통하여 그리고 성령 안에서
**　영광과 존귀와 찬양을 당신께 영원히 드리나이다.**
예수 그리스도의 이름으로 기도합니다.　아멘.

성경 봉독

시편 23, 90, 121, 141; 창세기 1:1-5, 14-19; 출애굽기 13:21-22; 마태복음 25:1-13;
로마서 5:6-11; 데살로니가전서 5:2-10; 요한계시록 22:1-5;
혹은 저녁, 계절, 교회력, 특별한 날과 특별한 경우와 관련된 성경구절을 읽는다.

묵상

봉독한 성경구절에 대하여 명상한다. 그리고 짤막하게 기도한다.

찬양

시편이나 적절한 찬송을 선택하여 부른다.

회중의 기도

인도자가 기도제목을 제안함에 따라 회중 가운데 한 사람씩 짧은 중보의 기도나
청원의 기도를 소리내어 하든가, 각자가 묵상으로 기도하면
인도자가 "주여, 긍휼히 여겨주소서" 라고 매 기도의 끝을 맺고,
회중들은 "우리의 기도를 들어주소서" 라고 기도한다.

다음과 같은 기도제목으로 함께 기도한다.

우리 교회의 교인들을 위하여 . . .

고난으로 인하여 어려움 중에 있는 사람들을 위하여 . . .

우리가 살고 있는 지역사회를 위하여 . . .

세계에 흩어져 사는 한국 사람들을 위하여 . . .

세상, 세상 사람들, 세상의 지도자들을 위하여 . . .

세계에 있는 모든 그리스도 교회, 지도자들,
    교인들, 선교를 위하여 . . .

성도들의 교제를 위하여 . . .

기도가 다 끝난 후 적절한 찬송을 선택하여 부른다.

주기도문

폐회기도

지도자: 오늘밤 예수 그리스도의 은총과 평강이
        여러분을 보호해 주시기 바랍니다.
회 중: **하나님께 감사드립니다.**

평화의 인사

성도들은 화해와 사랑의 표시로 주위 사람들과 인사를 나눈다.

AN ORDER FOR
EVENING PRAISE AND PRAYER

This service is for groups as they end their day in prayer.

PROCLAMATION OF THE LIGHT

A candle may be lit and lifted in the midst of the community.
The following may be sung or spoken:

Light and peace in Jesus Christ.
Thanks be to God.

HYMN

A hymn appropriate to the evening may be sung.

PRAYER OF THANKSGIVING

The following or other prayer of thanksgiving may be said:

We praise and thank you, O God,
  for you are without beginning and without end.
Through Christ,
  you created the whole world;
through Christ, you preserve it.
You made the day for the works of light
  and the night for the refreshment of our minds and our bodies.
Keep us now in Christ; grant us a peaceful evening,
  a night free from sin;
  and bring us at last to eternal life.
Through Christ and in the Holy Spirit,
  we offer you all glory, honor, and worship,
  now and for ever.
Amen.

SCRIPTURE

Psalm 23, 90, 121, 141; Genesis 1:1-5, 14-19; Exodus 13:21-22;
Matthew 25:1-13; Romans 5:6-11; 1 Thessalonians 5:2-10; Revelation 22:1-5;
or other readings appropriate to the evening, or to the day or season of the
Christian year, or to the nature of the occasion, may be used.

SILENCE

Silent meditation on the Scripture that has been read.
This may be concluded with a short prayer.

SONG OF PRAISE

Appropriate hymn may be sung.

PRAYERS OF THE PEOPLE

The following or other litany of intercession may be prayed,
during which any person may offer a brief prayer of intercession or petition.
After each prayer, the leader may conclude: "Lord, in your mercy,"
and all may respond: "Hear, our prayer."

Together, let us pray for

the people of this congregation . . .

those who suffer and those in trouble . . .

the concerns of this local community . . .

the Koreans who live throughout the world . . .

the world, its people, and its leaders . . .

the church universal—
its leaders, its members, and its mission . . .

the communion of saints . . .

Or, prayers of confession and words of pardon may be offered.
Following these prayers, all may sing appropriate evening hymn(s).

THE LORD'S PRAYER

BLESSING

The grace of Jesus Christ enfold you this night.
Go in peace.
Thanks be to God.

THE PEACE

Signs of peace may be exchanged, or all may depart in silence.

니케야 신조

한 분이신 하나님을 저희는 믿나이다.
전능하신 아버지, 하늘과 땅과 유형 무형한 만물의 창조주를 믿나이다.
또한 한 분이신 주 예수 그리스도, 하나님의 외아들
영원으로부터 성부에게서 나신 분을 믿나이다.
하나님에게서 나신 하나님, 빛에서 나신 빛,
참 하나님에게서 나신 참 하나님으로서, 창조되지 않고 나시어
성부와 한 본체로서 만물을 창조하셨음을 믿나이다.

성자께서는 저희 인간을 위하여, 저희 구원을 위하여
하늘에서 내려 오셨음을 믿나이다.
또한 성령으로 인하여 동정 마리아에게서
육신을 취하시어 사람이 되셨음을 믿나이다.

본디오 빌라도 통치 아래서 저희를 위하여
십자가에 못박혀 고난 받고 묻히셨으며
성경 말씀대로 삼일만에 부활하시어
하늘에 올라 성부 오른편에 앉아 계심을 믿나이다.
그분께서는 산 자와 죽은 자를 심판하러
영광 속에 다시 오시리니
그분의 나라는 끝이 없으리이다.

또한 주님이시며 생명을 주시는 성령을 믿나이다.
성령께서는 성부와 성자에게서 발하시고
성부와 성자와 더불어 영광과 예배를 받으시며
예언자들을 통하여 말씀하셨나이다.
하나이고 거룩하고 보편되며
사도로서 이어오는 교회를 믿나이다.
죄를 씻는 유일한 세례를 믿으며,
죽은 자들의 부활과 내세의 삶을 기다리나이다.
아멘.

THE NICENE CREED

We believe in one God,
  the Father, the Almighty,
  maker of heaven and earth,
  of all that is, seen and unseen.
We believe in one Lord, Jesus Christ,
  the only Son of God,
  eternally begotten of the Father,
  God from God, Light from Light,
  true God from true God,
  begotten, not made, of one Being with the Father;
  through him all things were made.
For us and for our salvation
  he came down from heaven,
  was incarnate of the Holy Spirit and the Virgin Mary
  and became truly human.
  For our sake he was crucified under Pontius Pilate;
  he suffered death and was buried.
  On the third day he rose again
  in accordance with the Scriptures;
  he ascended into heaven
  and is seated at the right hand of the Father.
  He will come again in glory
  to judge the living and the dead,
  and his kingdom will have no end.
We believe in the Holy Spirit, the Lord, the giver of life,
  who proceeds from the Father and the Son,
  who with the Father and the Son
    is worshiped and glorified,
  who has spoken through the prophets.
  We believe in the one holy catholic and apostolic church.
  We acknowledge one baptism for the forgiveness of sins.
  We look for the resurrection of the dead,
    and the life of the world to come.
Amen.

사도신경

전능하사 천지를 만드신 하나님 아버지를 내가 믿사오며,
그 외아들 우리 주 예수 그리스도를 믿사오니,
　이는 성령으로 잉태하사 동정녀 마리아에게 나시고,
　본디오 빌라도에게 고난을 받으사
　십자가에 못박혀 죽으시고,*
　장사한지 사흘만에 죽은 자 가운데서 다시 살아나시며,
　하늘에 오르사, 전능하신 하나님 우편에 앉아 계시다가,
　저리로서 산 자와 죽은 자를 심판하러 오시리라.
성령을 믿사오며,
　거룩한 공회와, 성도가 서로 교통하는 것과,
　죄를 사하여 주시는 것과, 몸이 다시 사는 것과,
　영원히 사는 것을 믿사옵나이다.　**아멘.**

(이 번역은 초대교회 때부터 사용되어진 사도신경을 참작하여 수정된 것임.)

THE APOSTLES' CREED

I believe in God the Father Almighty,
　maker of heaven and earth.
And in Jesus Christ his only Son our Lord:
　who was conceived by the Holy Spirit,
　　born of the Virgin Mary,
　　suffered under Pontius Pilate,
　　was crucified, dead, and buried;
　　he descended to the dead.
　the third day he rose from the dead;
　he ascended into heaven,
　　and sitteth at the right hand of God the Father Almighty;
　from thence he shall come to judge the quick and the dead.
I believe in the Holy Spirit,
　the holy catholic church,
　the communion of saints,
　the forgiveness of sins,
　the resurrection of the body,
　and the life everlasting.
Amen.

기독교대한감리회 신앙고백

우리는 만물의 창조자시요 섭리자시며
　온 인류의 아버지시요
　모든 선과 미와 애와 진의 근원이 되시는
　오직 하나이신 하나님을 믿으며,

우리는 하나님이 육신으로 나타나사
　우리의 스승이 되시고 모범이 되시며
　대속자가 되시고 구세주가 되시는
　예수 그리스도를 믿으며,

우리는 하나님이 우리와 같이 계시사
　우리의 지도와 위안과 힘이 되시는
　성령을 믿으며,

우리는 사랑과 기도의 생활을 믿으며
　죄를 용서하심과 모든 요구에 넉넉하신
　은혜를 믿으며,

우리는 구약과 신약에 있는 하나님의 말씀이
　신앙과 실행의 충분한 표준이 됨을 믿으며,

우리는 살아계신 주 안에서
　하나이 된 모든 사람들이
　예배와 봉사를 목적하여 단결된
　교회를 믿으며,

우리는 하나님의 뜻이 실현된
　인류사회가 천국임을 믿으며
　하나님 아버지 앞에
　모든 사람이 형제됨을 믿으며,

우리는 의의 최후 승리와 영생을 믿노라.
아멘.

A STATEMENT OF FAITH OF THE KOREAN METHODIST CHURCH

We believe in the one God,
   creator and sustainer of all things,
   Father of all nations,
   the source of all goodness and beauty,
   all truth and love,

We believe in Jesus Christ,
   God manifest in the flesh,
   our teacher, example, and Redeemer,
   the Savior of the world.

We believe in the Holy Spirit,
   God present with us for guidance, for comfort,
   and for strength.

We believe in the forgiveness of sins,
   in the life of love and prayer,
   and in grace equal to every need.

We believe in the Word of God
   contained in the Old and New Testaments
   as the sufficient rule both of faith and of practice.

We believe in the church,
   those who are united in the living Lord
   for the purpose of worship and service.

We believe in the reign of God
   as the divine will realized in human society,
   and in the family of God,
   where we are all brothers and sisters,

We believe in the final triumph of righteousness
   and in the life everlasting.
Amen.

주기도문

하늘에 계신 우리 아버지여,
　이름이 거룩히 여김을 받으시오며,
　나라이 임하옵시며,
　뜻이 하늘에서 이룬 것 같이 땅에서도 이루어지이다.
오늘날 우리에게 일용할 양식을 주옵시고,
우리가 우리에게 죄 지은 자를 사하여 준 것 같이
　우리 죄를 사하여 주옵시고,
우리를 시험에 들게 하지 마옵시고,
　다만 악에서 구하옵소서.
대개 나라와 권세와 영광이 아버지께
　영원히 있사옵나이다.
아멘.

THE LORD'S PRAYER

Our Father, who art in heaven,
　hallowed be thy name.
　Thy kingdom come,
　thy will be done on earth as it is in heaven.
Give us this day our daily bread.
And forgive us our trespasses,
　as we forgive those who trespass against us.
And lead us not into temptation,
　but deliver us from evil.
For thine is the kingdom, and power, and the glory,
　forever.
Amen.

색인
INDEXES

ACKNOWLEDGMENTS

Use of copyrighted material is gratefully acknowledged by the publisher. Every effort has been made to locate the administrator of each copyright. The publisher would be pleased to have any errors or omissions brought to the attention. All copyright notices include the following declarations: All rights reserved. International copyright secured. Used with permission.

United Methodist and Presbyterian Church (U.S.A.) congregations may reproduce for worship and educational purposes any single item from *Come, Let Us Worship* for one-time use, as in a bulletin, special program, or lesson resource, provided the item bears a United Methodist Publishing House or Abingdon Press or Geneva Press copyright notice; that the copyright notice as shown on the page is included in the reproduction; and that *Come, Let Us Worship* is acknowledged as the source. Permission requests for use of more than one *Come, Let Us Worship* item should be addressed to Permission Offices of the respective owners. Music, respective publisher who owns the copyrighted music; *The Korean-English United Methodist Book of Worship*, The United Methodist Publishing House; 201 8th Avenue South, Nashville, TN 37202; *The Korean-English Presbyterian Hymnal and Service Book*; Geneva Press, .100 Witherspoon Street, Louisville, Kentucky 40202.

Scripture, unless otherwise indicated, is adapted from *THE HOLY BIBLE, Old and New Testaments, New Korean Revised Version*, © 1998 Korean Bible Society and *The New Revised Standard Version*, © 1989 Division of Christian Education of the National Council of the Churches of Christ in the United States of America and is used by permission.

The Korean-English United Methodist Hymnal and Book of United Methodist Worship
Pages 1-58, 393-531, containing the General Services of The United Methodist Church are copyrighted as follows:
1-8 *The Basic Pattern of Worship*, © 1976 Abingdon Press; © 1980, 1984, 1989 The United Methodist Publishing House.
9-23 *A Service of Word and Table I*, © 1972, 1980, 1985, 1989 The United Methodist Publishing House.
24-27 *A Service of Word and Table II*, © 1980, 1985, 1989 The United Methodist Publishing House.
28-58 *Baptismal Covenants I, II*, © 1976, 1980, 1985, 1989 The United Methodist Publishing House.
393-531 The Liturgical Psalter, based on *The Holy Bible, New Korean Revised Version*, © 1998 and *The New Revised Standard Version*.
494-505 *A Service of Christian Marriage*, © Abingdon Press; 1980, 1985, 1989 The United Methodist Publishing House; 506-523 *A Service of Death and Resurrection*, © Abingdon Press; © 1980, 1985, 1989 The United Methodist Publishing House; 524-531 *Orders of Daily Praise and prayer*, © 1989 The United Methodist Publishing House.

Permission for use of items controlled by other copyright owners must be obtained from the respective owners listed below.
English Language Liturgical Consultation;
1522 "K" St., NW, #1000; Washington, D.C. 20005-1202, revision of ICET translations:
The Lord's Prayer 22; The Apostles' Creed pp. 18, 41-42, 46, 55, 534; The Nicene Creed 533; Sursam Corda, pp 17, 20, 26; The Nicene Creed in Korean, 532; Catholic Bishop's Conference of Korea 82-2-460-7500; Fax 82-2-460-7505

International Commission on English in the Liturgy; 1522 K St. NW, #1202; Washington, D.C. 20005-1202: Memorial Acclamation, pp 22, 27 from the Roam Missal © 1973 ICEL International Commission on English in the Liturgy; 1275 K St. NW, #1202; Washington, D.C. 20005-1202, translations 1975: The Lord's Prayer, Ecumenical Text, pp. 22 Sanctus and Benedictus, pp 21, 26

The Book of Common Prayer, 1979:
Opening prayer, p. 17, Declaration of Intention 500-1, Marriage Vow, Exchange of Rings, 502-3, Blessing 504

The Upper Room Worshipbook, © 1985 The Upper Room; P. O. Box 189; Nashville, TN 37203.
Prayer of Thanksgiving, p. 530

The Korean-English Presbyterian Hymnal And Service Book.
Sundays and Festivals is taken from *The Revised Common Lectionary.* © 1992 by the Consultation on Common Texts (CCT), P.O. Box 34003, Room 381, Nashville, TN 37203-0003. Used with Permission.

Permission for use of items controlled by other copyright owners must be obtained from the respective owners listed below.
English Language Liturgical Consultation;
1522 "K" St., NW, #1000; Washington, D.C. 20005-1202, revision of ICET translations: The Lord's Prayer 24; The Apostles' Creed 16; The Nicene Creed 14 Sanctus and Benedictus 20 22

The metric Psalm texts in Korean were written by Keun Won Park. The English response texts were written by Paul Junggap Huh. The response settings were written by Seung Nam Kim, Hyun Chul Lee, and Paul Junggap Huh.

Psalm 33, 113: United Methodist Liturgical Psalter ©. 1989, by Beck, Holbert, Kingbrough and Luff. The United Methodist Publishing House. Adapted and used by permission.

22 Grail Psalms: © 1991 by Ladies of the Grail (England). Used by permission of G.I.A. Publications, Inc., exclusive agent. (PC U.S.A.)

Text adaptations of Psalm 63m 104, and 138 used by permission of Arlo D. Duba. (PC U.S.A.)

59 Words: © 1983 Concordia Publishing; 3558
S. Jefferson Ave; St. Louis, MO 63118-3968;
Fax 314-268-1329; music ©1983 G.I.A. Publications
Inc., 7404 S. Mason Ave., Chicago, IL 60638;
800-GIA-1358; Fax 708-496-3828

60 Korean trans. © 2001 The United Methodist
Publishing House, admin. The Copyright Co.;
40 Music Square E., Nashville, TN 37203
615-244-5588; Fax 615-244-5591

61 © 1953 S. K. Hine, renewed 1981 Manna
Music, Inc.; Korean Trans. .© 2001 Manna
Music, Inc.; 25510 Ave., Stanford, Suite
101-102, Valencia, CA 91355

62 Korean trans. © The Christian Literature
Society of Korea, 169-1 Sam Sung Dong,
Kang Nam Ku, Seoul, Korea; Fax 82-2-3453-1639

63 Korean trans. © The United Methodist
Publishing House, admin. The Copyright Co. (see 60)

64 Words © 1967, .Hope Publishing. Korean
trans. © 2001 Hope Publishing Company;
380 S Main Pl; Carol Stream, IL 60188;
800-323-1049; Fax 630-665-2552

65 Korean trans. © The United Methodist
Publishing House (see 60); arr. © Oxford
University Press; Great Clarendon St.; Oxford OX2
6DP, UK; Fax 441-865-267749

66 Arr. © 1943 Church Pension Fund; Korean trans. .
© 2001 The United Methodist Publishing House (60)

67 Music © 1976 Resource Publications, Inc.;
160 E. Virginia St., #290; San Jose, CA 95112
Arr. © 1983 The United Methodist Publishing House;
English trans. © 1989 Korean trans. © 2001
The United Methodist Publishing House (see 60)

68 Korean trans. © The Christian Literature Society
of Korea (see 62)

69 Words and music © 2001 The United Methodist
Publishing House, admin. The Copyright Co. (see 60)

70 Korean trans. © 2001 The United Methodist
Publishing House (see 60)

71 Harm © 1986 G.I.A. Publications, Inc.(see 59); Korean
trans. © 2001 The United Methodist Publishing House,
admin. The Copyright Company (see 60)

72 Arr. © renewed 1963 Abingdon Press (see 60)

73 Words © 1980 Korean trans. 2001 William Boyd Grove;
900 Washington St., E; Charleston, WV 25301

74-75 Korean trans. © 2001 The United Methodist
Publishing House, admin. The Copyright Co. (see 60)

76 Words and Music © Sung Mo Moon; 26-6 Jang Choong
Dong 1 Ga, Joong Ku, Seoul, Korea; 02-2274-0161

77 © 1981, LITA Music; Attn; Justin Peters; 3609 Donna
Kay Dr.; Nashville, TN 37211. Korean trans. © 2001,
Mole End Music. admin. by Word Music; Acuff-Rose
Music Publishing, Inc.; 65 Music Square, West;
Nashville, TN 37203; Fax 615-327-0560

78 Korean trans. © The United Methodist
Publishing House (see 60)

79 Korean trans. © The Christian Literature
Society of Korea (see 62)

80 Korean trans. © 2001 The United Methodist
Publishing House (see 60)

81 © 1923, renewed 1951, Korean trans. © 2001
Hope Publishing Company (see 64)

82 Arr. © 1991 McKinney, Inc.; Korean trans.
© 2001 The United Methodist Publishing House,
admin. The Copyright Company (see 60)

83 © 1979, 1989, Korean trans. © 2001 North
American Liturgy Resources; 10802 N. 23rd
Ave.; Phoenix, AZ 85029; 602-864-1980

84 Words and music © The Korean Hymnal Society

85 © 1984 Scripture in Song (a div. of Integrity
Music, Inc.; Korean trans. © 2001 Scripture in Song;
1000 Cody Road.; Mobile, AL 36695; Fax 334-633-9998

86 Korean trans. © The United Methodist
Publishing House (60)

87 © 1989, Korean trans. © 2001 All Nations
Music, admin. CopyCare Korea

88 Korean trans. © 2001 The United Methodist
Publishing House (see 60)

89 Words © The Korean Hymnal Society; Music ©
Chai Hoon Park; Chai Hoon Park, 610-1360 Rathburn
Road East, Mississauga, ON14WH4, Canada

90 © 1979, Korean trans. © 2001 Ediciones Paulina;
English trans. © 1989 The United Methodist
Publishing House (see 60); harm. © 1987 Skinner
Chavez-Melo; 200 W. 79th, #12-F; NY, NY 10024

91 © 1979, Korean trans. © 2001 Mercy/Vineyard
Publishing; c/o Music Services; 209 Chapelwood Dr.;
Franklin, TN 37069; 615-794-9015; Fax 615-794-0793

92 © 1939 Eugene M. Bartlett, renewed 1967 Mrs. Eugene
M Bartlett, assigned to Albert E. Brumley & Sons,
Inc., admin. ICG; Korean trnas. © 2001 Albert E.
Brumley, Inc.; Down in Memory Valley; Powell, MO 65730

93 Korean trans. © 2001 The United Methodist
Publishing House, admin. The Copyright Co. (see 60)

94 Korean trans. © The Christian Literature
Society of Korea (see 62)

95-96 Korean trans. © 2001 The United Methodist
Publishing House (see 60)

97 Words © 1976, Korean trans. © 2001, Music
© 1960, renewed 1988 Hope Publishing Co. (see 64)

98 Adapt and arr. © 1989 Korean trans. © 2001
The United Methodist Publishing House (see 60)

99 © 1924, renewed 1952, Korean trans. © 2001
Hope Publishing Company (see 64)

100-1 © 1983, Korean trans. © 2001 The United
Methodist Publishing House (see 60)

102 © 1970, 1975, Korean trans © 2001 Celebration,
admin. Maranath! Music (see 60)

103 Korean trans. © The Christian Literature
Society of Korea (see 62)

104 Adapt © 1989, Korean trans. © 2001 The
United Methodist Publishing House (see 60)

105 English trans. and arr. by permission of Christian
Conference of Asia; Tainan Theological College and
Seminary, Tung-men road, Section 1, Tainan, Taiwan

106 Music © Woon Yong Na

107 Korean trans. © 2001 The United Methodist
Publishing House (see 60); Arr. © 1991 McKinney
Music, Inc, admin. Genevox Music Group

108 Korean trans. © 2001 The United Methodist
Publishing House (60)

109 © 1984 Meadowgreen Music Co./Word Music, Inc.
54 Music Square E., Suite 305, Nashville; Brentwood,
TN 37203

110 Korean trans.© Christian Literature Society of Korea (see 62)

111 Korean trans. © 2001 The United Methodist Publishing House (see 60)

112 Words © The Korean Hymnal Society; music © Soon Sae Kim; English trans. © The Korean Hymnal Society

113 © 1967, The Hymnal Committee of The United Church of Japan; 2-3-18 Nishiwaseda; Shinjuku, Tokyo, Japan; English trans. © 1983, Korean trans. © 2001 The United Methodist Publishing House (see 60)

114 Korean trans. © Christian Literature Society of Korea (see 62)

115 Korean trans. © 2001 The United Methodist Publishing House (see 60); harm. © Oxford University Press (see 65)

116 © 1984, Korean trans. 2001 Maranatha! Praise, Inc., administered The Copyright Co. (see 60)

117 Korean trans. © Christian Literature Society of Korea (see 62)

118 Korean trans. © 2001 The United Methodist Publishing House, admin. The Copyright Co. (see 60)

119 © 1990 Sound The Bamboo; Christian Conference of Asia, Tainan Theological College and Seminary, Tung-men road, Section 1, Tainan, Taiwan

120-1 © 1984, Korean trans. © 2001 Les Presses de Taize (France), admin. G.I.A. Publications, Inc. (see 59)

122 Korean trans. © The Christian Literature Society of Korea (see 62)

123 Harm.© 1964 The United Methodist Publishing House (see 60)

124 Korean trans. © 2001 The United Methodist Publishing House (see 60)

125 © Geonyong Lee; c/o St. Paul Church; 2-20-1 Megura, Gohonggi; Tokyo, Japan 153-0053; Fax 82-2-520-8109

126-128 Korean trans. © 2001 The United Methodist Publishing House (see 60)

129 Words © 1972 Hope Publishing Co. (see 64)

130 Korean trans. © 2001 The United Methodist Publishing House (see 60)

131 Korean trans. © The United Methodist Publishing House; arr. © 2001 Abingdon Press (see 60)

132 © 1985, Korean trans. © 2001 Mercy/Vineyard Publishing (see 91)

133 © Young Jo Lee

134 © Kyung Dong Presbyterian Church (see 76)

135 Korean trans. © 2001 The United Methodist Publishing House (see 60)

136 © 1972 Maranatha Music (see 60)

137 © 1955, assigned to Jan-Lee Music; renewed 1983; Korean trans. © 2001 Jan-Lee Music

138 © 1971, Korean trans. © 2001 J. A. Oliver, Miguel Manzano and San Pablo International-SSP; English trans. © 1980 The United Methodist Publishing House (see 60)

139 Korean trans. © 2001 The United Methodist Publishing House (see 60)

140 Adapt. © 1989, Korean trans. © 2001 The United Methodist Publishing House (see 60)

141 © 1984, Korean trans. © 2001 Les Presses de Taize, admin. by G.I.A. Publications, Inc. (see 59)

142 Korean trans. © 2001 The United Methodist Publishing House (see 60)

143 Korean trans. © The Christian Literature Society of Korea (see 62)

144 Words © Jane Parker Huber; Korean trans. © 2001 Jane Parker Huber

145 Korean trans. © 2001 The United Methodist Publishing House (see 60)

146 Words and music © Hyung Sun Ryu; Fax 82-41-634-8700

147 © 1986, Korean trans. © 2001 Word Music (see 77)

148 © 1988, Korean trans. © 2001 Geonyong Lee (125)

149-50 © The Korean Hymnal Society; English trans. © 2001 The United Methodist Publishing House (see 60)

151 © 1984, Korean trnas. © 2001 Hope Pub. (see 64)

152 Korean trans. © 2001 The United Methodist Publishing House (see 60)

153 © 1963, 1980, Korean trans. © 2001 Walter Ehret and George K. Evans, Viking Penguin (a div. of Penguin Book USA, Inc.)

154 Korean trans. © 2001 The United Methodist Publishing House, admin. The Copyright Co. (see 60)

155-7 Korean trans. © 2001; harm. © 1989 The United Methodist Publishing House (see 60)

158 Words © 1956, 1958, Korean trans. © 2001 Gordon V. Thompson, Ltd., Toronto, Canada; Used by permission of Carl Fisher, Inc., New York, agents on behalf of Alta Lind Cook and Gordon V. Thompson,

159 Korean trans. © 2001 The United Methodist Publishing House (see 60)

160 Korean trans. © The Christian Literature Society of Korea (see 62)

161-162 Korean trans. © 2001 The United Methodist Publishing House (see 60)

163 Korean trans. © 2001 The United Methodist Publishing House (see 60); Harm. © 1941 Ronald Stafford, executor of the estate of Leo Sowerby

164-165 © The Korean Hymnal Society

166 Korean trans. © 2001 The United Methodist Publishing House (see 60); harm by permission of Oxford University Press (see 65)

167-9 Korean trans. © 2001 The United Methodist Publishing House (see 60)

170-1 Words and adpt © 1963, Korean trans. © 2001 Stainer & Bell, Ltd., admin. Hope Publishing Co. (see 64)

172-3 Korean trans. © 2001 The United Methodist Publishing House (see 60)

174 Words and music © 1974, Korean trans. © 2001 Hope Publishing Company (see 64)

175 © Chai Hoon Park, 610-1360 Rathburn Road East, Mississauga, ON14WH4, Canada

176 Words © 1979, Korean trans. © 2001 Stainer & Bell, Ltd., admin. by Hope Publishing Company (see 64); harm. © 1989 The United Methodist Publishing House (see 60)

177 Korean trans. © 2001 The United Methodist Publishing House (see 60)

178 © 1972, 1979, 1989, Korean trans. © 2001 The United Methodist Publishing House (see 60)

179 © 1969, 1989, Korean trans. © 2001 Hope Publishing Company (see 64)

180-3 Korean trans. © 2001; harm. © 1989 The United Methodist Publishing House (see 60)

184 Words © 1973, Korean trans. © 2001 Hope Publishing Co. (see 64); arr. Oxford University Press (see 65)

185-9 Korean trans. © 2001 The United Methodist Publishing House, admin. The Copyright Co. (see 60).

190 Words © 1975, rev. 1995, Korean trans. ©2001 Hope Publishing Company (see 64)

191 © 1984 Jubilate Hymns Ltd., Korean trans. © 2001 admin. Hope Publishing Company (see 64)

192-194 Korean trans. © The Christian Literature Society of Korea (see 62)

195 Wores © The Korean Hymnal Society; music © Woon Young Na

196 Korean trans. © 2001 The United Methodist Publishing House (see 60); music used by permission of Oxford University Press from The English Hymnal, 1906 (see 65).

197 Words, arr. © 1986, Korean trans. © 2001 Word Music (see 77)

198-9 Korean trans. © 2001 The United Methodist Publishing House, admin. The Copyright Co. (see 60)

200 Words and music © 1984, Korean trnas. © 2001 Kingsway's Thank You Music; admin. EMI Christian Music Group; P. O. Box 5085; 101 Winners Circle; Brentwood, TN 37024-5085; 615-371-4300

201 © 1973, Korean trans. © 2001 The Word of God Music, admin. The Copyright Co. (see 60)

202 © 1976, Korean trans. © 2001 Universal-MCA Music 15800 Northwest 48th Ave.; Miami, FL 33014

203 © 1959, renewed 1987, Korean trans. © 2001 Manna Music, Inc.; 22510 Ave., Stanford, Suite 101-102, Valencia, CA 91355

204 © 1981, Korean trans. © 2001 Rocksmith Music; c/o Trust Music Management, Inc. (see 202)

205 Words © 1922, renewed 1950, Korean trans © 2001; Music © 1939, renew. 1968 Word Music (see 77)

206 © 1973, Korean trans. © 2001 William J. Gaither, admin. Gaither Copyright Management; P.O. Box 737; Alexandria, IN 46001; Fax 765-724-8290

207 © 1988, Korean trans. © 2001 Thank You Music, admin. EMI Christian Music Group (see 200)

208 © 1985, Korean trans. © 2001 Mercy/Vineyard (see 91)

209 © 1922 Universal (see 202)

210 © 1984, 1987, Korean trans. © 2001 Acts Music, admin. EMI Christian Music Group (see 200)

211 © 1976, Korean trans. © 2001 C. A. Music, admin. Music Services, Inc. (div of C. A. Records, Inc.) (see 91)

212 © 1974, Korean trans. © 2001 Al Carmines; 400 W 43rd St., #24 N. New York, NY 10036

213 Adapt. and arr. © 1989, Korean trans. © 2001 The United Methodist Publishing House (see 60)

214 © 1935, renewed 1963, Korean trans. © 2001 Birdwing Music; see EMI Christian Music Group (see 200)

215 © 1977, Korean trans. © 2001 Lanny Wolfe Music, admin. Gaither Copyright Management (see 206)

216 Words © 1989 The United Methodist Publishing House, admin. by The Copyright Co. (see 60)

217 Words © 1971, Korean trans. © 2001 Faber Music Ltd.; music © 1960 renewed 1988 Hope Publishing Company (see 64)

218-9 Korean trans. © 2001 The United Methodist Publishing House, admin. The Copyright Co. (see 60)

220 © 1962, renewed 1990, Korean trans. © 2001 Manna Music, Inc. (see 203)

221 © 1978, Korean trans. © 2001 James K. Manley; 690 Persian Dr., #67; Sunnyvale, CA 94089; 408-747-0667

222 Words © 1971, Korean trans. © 2001 Hope Publishing Company (see 64)

223 Korean trans. © 2001, adapt. © 1989 The United Methodist Publishing House (see 60)

224 Korean trans. © 2001 The United Methodist Publishing House (see 60); music © 1937, renewed 1965 Broadman Press; Fax 615-251-2869.

225 © 1972, Korean trans. © 2001 Maranatha! Music, admin. by The Copyright Co. (see 60)

226 Korean trans. © 2001 The United Methodist Publishing House, admin. The Copyright Co. (see 60)

227 English trans. by permission of Christian Conference of Asia; Korean trans. © 2001 The United Methodist Publishing House, (see 60)

228 © 1976, 1981, Korean trans. © 2001 Maranatha! Music, admin. The Copyright Co. (see 60)

229 © 1972, Korean trans. © 2001 Bud John Songs, Inc., admin. EMI Christian Music Group (see 200)

230 Words © 1982, Korean trans. © 2001 H. Francis Yardley; harm. by permission of Oxford University Press (see 65)

231 Words © 1981, Korean trans. © 2001 John Brownlow Geyer; 5 Wealey Hill; Birmingham, England B29 4AA

232 Words © 1981, Korean trans. © 2001 Ronald S. Cole-Turner; Memphis Theological Seminary, 168 Parkway Sl, Memphis, TN 38104

233 Adapt. © 1985, GIA Publication (see 59); Korean trans. © 2001 The United Methodist Publishing House, admin. The Copyright Co. (see 60)

234 Korean trans. © 2001 The United Methodist Publishing House; harm. © 1981 Abingdon Press (see 60)

235 Korean trans. © 2001 The United Methodist Publishing House (see 60); music © 1960, renewed 1988 Hope Publishing Company (see 64)

236 Korean trans. © 2001, adapt. and arr. © 1989 The United Methodist Publishing House (see 60)

237 © 1978, 1989, Korean trans. © 2001 John B. Foley, SJ and New Dawn Music

238 © 1966, Korean trans. © 2001 Joe Wise, admin. by G.I.A. Publications, Inc. (see 59)

239 © 1975, Korean trans. © 2001 Hope Pub. (see 64)

240-1 Korean trans. © 2001 The United Methodist Publishing House (see 60)

242 Words © 2001 The United Methodist Publishing House (see 60); music © Kyung Dong Presbyterian Church (see 76)

243 Words © The Korean Hymnal Society; music © Chai Hoon Park (see 175)

244 © The Christian Literature Society of Kore (see 62)

245 Words © The Korean Hymnal Society; music © Woon Young Na

246 Korean trans. © 2001 The United Methodist Publishing House (see 60)

247 © 1978, Korean trans. © 2001 Integrity's
    Hosanna! Music; c/o Integrity Music; 1000
    Cody Rd; Mobile, AL 36695-3425; Fax 334-633-9998
248 Korean trans. © 2001 The United Methodist
    Publishing House, admin. The Copyright Co.;
    harm. © 1964 Abingdon Press (see 60)
249 Words © 1954, renewed 1982, Korean trans.
    © 2001 The Hymn Society of America,
    admin. by Hope Publishing Company (see 64)
250-1 Korean trans. © 2001 The United Methodist
    Publishing House, admin. The Copyright Co. (see 60)
252 © 1972, Korean trans. © 2001 Hope Pub. (see 64)
253 Words © 1975, Korean trans. © 2001, music
    © 1977 Hope Publishing Company (see 64)
254 Korean trans. © 2001 The United Methodist
    Publishing House, admin. .The Copyright Co. (see 60)
255 Korean trans. © The Christian Literature
    Society of Korea (see 62).
256 Korean trans. © 2001 The United Methodist
    Publishing House, admin. The Copyright Co. (see 60)
257 © 1966 F.E.L Publications, assigned 1991 to
    the Lorenz Corp; Korean trans. © 2001 The
    Lorenz Corp; 501 E. Third St.; Dayton, OH
    45402-2118; 937-228-6118; Fax 937-223-2042
258 © 1972, Korean trans. © 2001 Bud John Songs, Inc.
    admin. EMI Christian Music Group (see 200)
259 Words and music © Seog Kyun Kim;
    Fax 82-2-6265-3950
260 Korean trans. © 2001 The United Methodist
    Publishing House, admin. The Copyright Co. (see 60)
261 Words © 1964 Abingdon Press; Korean trans. © 2001
    The United Methodist Publishing House (see 60)
262 © 1969, Korean trans. © 2001 EMI Christian Music
    Group (see 200)
263 © 1981, 1983, 1989, Korean trans. © Daniel
    L. Schutte and New Dawn Music
264 © 1987, Korean trans. © 2001 Make Way
    Music Ltd., admin. by Music Services (see 91)
265 © 1977 Words, Music, Inc. (see 77)
266 Korean trans. © The Christian Literature
    Society of Korea (see 62)
267 Korean trans. © 2001 The United Methodist
    Publishing House, admin. The Copyright Co. (see 60)
268 © Jang Hee Lee, icmkey@hotmail.com; English trans.
    © The United United Methodist Publishing House
    (see 60)
269 Korean trans. © 2001 The United Methodist
    Publishing House, admin. The Copyright Co. (see 60)
270 © Jang Hee Lee (see 268)
271 Korean trans. © 2001 The United Methodist
    Publishing House, admin. The Copyright Co. (see 60)
272 © 1989, 2001 The United Methodist Publishing
    House, admin. The Copyright Co. (see 60)
273 Korean trans. © 2001 The United Methodist
    Publishing House, admin. The Copyright Co. (see 60)
274 Korean trans. © 2001 The United Methodist
    Publishing House (see 60); arr. © 1986 Word Music,
    Inc. (see 77)
275-7 Korean trans. © The Christian Literature Society
    of Korea (see 62)
278 © 1982, Korean trans. © 2001 Mercy/Vineyard
    Publishing (see 91).

279 © 1971, renewed 1999, Korean trans. © 2001
    Manna Music, Inc. (see 203)
280-2 Korean trans. © 2001 The United Methodist
    Publishing House (see 60)
283 © 1972, Korean trans. © 2001 Word Music; arr.
    Word Music, Inc. (see 77).
284 Korean trans. © 2001 The United Methodist
    Publishing House (see 60)
285-6 © 1971, Korean trans. © 2001 William J. Gaither,
    Inc. (see 215)
287-93 Korean trans. © 2001 The United Methodist
    Publishing House (see 60)
297-8 Korean trans. © The Christian Literature Society
    of Korea (see 62)
299 Korean trans. © 2001 The United Methodist
    Publishing House (see 60)
300 Words, Music; © English trans. © 2001 Sung-ho Park
301 © 1971, Korean trans. © 2001 Multisongs/His Eye
    Music/Joy of the Lord Publishing., admin. EMI
    Christian Music Group (see 200)
302 Korean trans. © 2001 The United Methodist
    Publishing House (see 60); harm. Oxford University
    Press (see 65)
303 © 1971, Korean trans. © 2001 William J. Gaither, Inc.,
    admin. Gaither Copyright Management (see 215)
304-5 Korean trans. © 2001 The United Methodist
    Publishing House (see 60)
306 © 1989, Korean trans. © 2001 Universal-MCA Music
    Publishing (see 202)
307 Korean trans. © 2001, arr. © 1933, renewed
    1961 Presbyterian Board of Christian
    Education; c/o Westminster John Knox
    Press; 100 Whitherspoon St.; Louisville, KY
    40202; 502-569-5342; Fax 502-569-5113
308 Korean trans. © 2001 The United Methodist
    Publishing House (see 60)
309 © 1938 Hill & Range Songs, Inc., renewed
    Unichappell Music, Inc.; Korean trans. © 2001 Hill &
    Range Songs, Inc.; c/o Hal Leonard Corp.777 W.
    Bluemound Rd.; Milwaukee, WI 53213
310 English trans. © 1989, Korean trans. © 2001
    The United Methodist Publishing House (see 60)
311 Words © 1987, Korean trans. © 2001 Hope Pub. (see 64)
312 Korean trans. © 2001 The United Methodist
    Publishing House (see 60)
313 © Soon Sae Kim; Valley Korean UMC, 10408
    Balboa Blvd., Granada Hills, CA 91344
314 Adapt and arr. © 1989 The United Methodist
    Publishing House (see 60)
315-6 Korean trans. © 2001 The United Methodist
    Publishing House (see 60)
317 © Chung Kwan Park; English trans. © 2001 The
    United Methodist Publishing House (see 60)
318 Korean trans. © The Christian Literature Society of
    Korea (see 62)
319 Words and Music © The Korean Hymnal Society
320-2 Korean trans. © 2001 The United Methodist
    Publishing House (see 60)
323-4 Adapt and Korean trans. © 2001 The United
    Methodist Publishing House; arr. © 2001 Abingdon
    Press, admin. The Copyright Co. (see 60)
325 Words © 1928 F. L. Braselman, renewed 1956,

Korean trans. © 2001 Presbyterian Board of Christian Education (see 307); harm. © 1990 Hope Publishing Company (see 64)

326 Korean trans. © 2001, arr. © 1989 The United Methodist Publishing House (see 60)

327 Korean trans. © The Christian Literature Society of Korea (see 62)

328–30 Korean trans. © 2001 The United Methodist Publishing House (see 60)

331 © 1984, Korean trans. © 2001 Utryck; c/o Walton Music corp.; P.O. Box 167; Bynum, NC 27228; 919-542-5548; Fax 919-542-5527

332–333 Korean trans. © 2001 The United Methodist Publishing House (see 60)

334 Korean trans. © The Christian Literature Society of Korea (see 62)

335 Words © 1925, renewed 1953, Korean trans. © 2001 Board of Lutheran Church in America, admin. Augsburg/Fortress; P.O. Box 1209; Minneapolis, MN 55440-1209; 612-330-3300

336 Korean trans. © 2001 The United Methodist Publishing House (see 60)

337 Alt. © 1991, Korean trans. © Boardman Press, admin. Van Ness Press, Inc., Fax 615-251-2869

338 Korean trans. © 2001; adapt. © 1989 The United Methodist Publishing House (see 60)

339 Words and Music © The Korean Hymnal Society

340 Korean trans. © 2001 The United Methodist Publishing House (see 60)

341 © 1972, Korean trans. © 2001 Hope Publishing Co. (see 64)

342 Korean trans. © 2001 The United Methodist Publishing House (see 60)

343 Words © 1983, Korean trans. © 2001, music © Hope Publishing Company (see 64)

344 Korean trans. © 2001 The United Methodist Publishing House (see 60)

345 Words and music © Tae-hyuck Chun & Kyong Jin; English trans. © 2001 The United Methodist Publishing House (see 60)

346 Korean trans. © 2001 The United Methodist Publishing House (see 60)

347 Korean trans. © 2001 The United Methodist Publishing House (see 60); music © Oxford University Press (65)

348-9 Korean trans. © 2001 The United Methodist Publishing House (see 60)

350 Korean trans. © 2001 The United Methodist Publishing House (see 60); music © 1970 Les Presses de Taize (France), admin. by G.I.A. Publications (see 59).

351 Korean trans. © 2001 The United Methodist Publishing House, admin. The Copyright Co. (see 60)

352 Adapt. © 1989, Korean trans. © The United Methodist Publishing House (see 60); harm. © 1906 Oxford University Press (see 65)

353 © 1979, Korean trans. © 2001 Les Presses de Taize (France), admin. by G.I.A. Publications, Inc. (see 59)

354 Transcription © 1989, Korean trans. © 2001 The United Methodist Publishing House (see 60)

355 © 1972, renewed 2000, Korean trans. © 2001 Manna Music, Inc. (see 203)

356 Music © Les Presses de Taize de Taize (France), admin. by G.I.A. Publications, Inc.; Korean trans. © 2001 The United Methodist Publishing House (see 60)

357 © 1978, Korean trans. © 2001 Richard Alan Henderson; P.O. Box 45; Anderson, IN 46015

358 © 1988, Korean trans. © 2001 Harold Flammer, Inc.; 49 Waring Dr.; Delaware Water Gap, PA 18327-0690; Fax 717-476-5247

359 © Music © 1984, Korean trans. © 2001 G.I.A. Publications, Inc. (see 59)

360 Korean trans. © 2001 The United Methodist Publishing House, admin. The Copyright Co. (see 60)

361 Words © 1983, Korean trans. © 2001, harm, © 1989 The United Methodist Publishing House admin. by The Copyright Co. (see 60)

362 English trans. © 1982, Korean trans. © 2001 The United Methodist Publishing House (see 60)

363 1976, Korean trans. © 2001 Hinshaw Music, Inc.; P.O. Box 470; Chapel Hill, NC 27514

364 © 1981, Korean trans. © 2001 Les Presses de Taize (France), admin. by G.I.A. Publications, Inc. (see 59)

365 © 1951, renewed 1979, Korean trans. © 2001 Broadman Press;c/o Van Ness Press, Inc.; Fax 615-251-2869

366 Words © 1964, Korean trans. © 2001 World Library Publications, Inc.; 3815 N. Willow Rd.; Schiller Park, IL 60176

367 © 1988, Korean trans. © 2001 Harold Flammer, Inc. (see 358).

368 © 1986, Korean trans. © 2001 Word Music (see 77)

369-70 Korean trans. © 2001 The United Methodist Publishing House (see 60)

371 English trans. © 1965 Bliss Wiant; Executor; 325 Gudrun Rd; Columbus, Oh 43202

372 Korean trans. © 2001 The United Methodist Publishing House (see 60)

373 © The Korean Hymnal Society

374-6 Korean trans. © 2001 The United Methodist Publishing House (see 60)

377 © 1936, renewed 1964, Korean trans. © 2001 Word Music (see 205)

378 Adapt. and arr. © 1989, Korean trans. © 2001 The United Methodist Publishing House, admin. The Copyright Co. (see 60)

379 © The Korean Hymnal Society

380 Words © 1982, Korean trans. © 2001 Hope Publishing Company (see 64)

381–3 Korean trans. © 2001 The United Methodist Publishing House (see 60)

384 Adapt. and arr. © 1989, Korean trans. © 2001 The United Methodist Publishing House (see 60)

385 © 1978, Korean trans. © 2001 Bud John Song, Inc., (see 200)

386 Adapt. and arr. © 1989, Korean trans. © 2001 The United Methodist Publishing House,(see 60)

387–88 Korean trans. © 2001 The United Methodist Publishing House (see 60); arr. © Oxford University Press (see 65)

389-91 Korean trans. © 2001 The United Methodist Publishing House (see 60)

392 © 1986 Hope Publishing Co. (see 64).

AUTHORS, COMPOSERS, ARRANGERS, AND TRANSLATORS

Abbey, Alonzo J. (1858) 111
Adams, Sarah F. (1841) 308
Adkins, Donna (1940) 228
Adkins, Leon M. (1955) 261
Ahle, Johann R. (1664) 108
Akers, Doris (1962), 220
Alexander, Cecil F. (1848) 63 96 159
Alford, Henry (1844) 241
Allen, David 283
Allen, George N. (1844) 309
Allen, H. B. (1938) 267
Amerson,Stephen 209
Asuncion, Francisca (1983) 100
Avery, Richard K. (1972) 252
Avila, Ruben Ruiz (1972) 178
Babcock, M. D. (1901) 62
Bach, J. S. (1723) 344
Ballinger, Bruce (1945) 202 306
Baring-Gould, Sabine (1865) 375
Barker, Ken 368
Barnby, Joseph (1868) 222 369 375
Bartlett, Eugene M. (1939) 92
Baughen, Michael (1980) 191
Beck, John Ness (1977) 253
Beethoven, Ludwig van, (1824) 75 382
Bennett, William (1864) 68
Bell, Maurice F. (1906) 60
Benson, Louis F. (1924) 235
Berthier, Jacques (1979) 121 141 349
                         353 364
Besig, Don 358 367
Blackith, H. H. (1893) 110
Bliss, Philip P. (1876) 304
Bonner, Carey (1859-1938) 336
Borthwick, Jane (1855) 307
Bortniansky Dimitri S. (1825) 122 346
Bourgeois, Louis (1551) 118
Bowie, Walter Russell (1909) 390
Bradbury, William B. (1858) 117 182
                         328 342
Bradley, Carol Ann 351
Brahms, Johannes (1833-1897)
Breviary, Sarum (1495) 169
Bridges, Robert (1899) 186 369
Bridgers, Luther B. (1910) 289 369
Brock, Blanche Kerr 377
Brook, Virgil P. 377
Brown, Ann (1908-1988) 365
Brown, Phoebe H. (1818) 111
Buchanan, Anabel Morris (1938) 181
Budry, Edmond (1904) 194
Burton, John (1773-1822) 110
Calvin, John 299
Cameron, Catherine (1967) 64
Campbell, Thomas (1835) 280
Cantinoes, Pae (1582) 158

Card, Michael (1981) 75
Carmines, Al (1973) 212
Carter, Sydney (1963) 170
Cason, Don 147
Cassel, E. T. (1902) 95
Caswall, Edward (1854) 369
Challinor, Frederick A. (1903) 177
Chao, Tzu-chen (1931) 371
Chavez-Melo, Skinner (1987) 88
Chisholm, Thomas O. (1923) 81
Cho, Ki Tak (1995) 149
Chorale Book England, (1864)
Chun, Tae-hyuck 345
Chun, Young Taik (1894-1968) 272 339
Chung, Se Yeon 147
Clarke, H. D. (1888-1957) 99
Clausnitzer, Tobias (1663) 108
Cleveland, J. Jefferson (1981) 234
Cloninger, Claire 147
Coelho, Terrye (1952) 225
Cole-Turner, Ronald S. (1981) 232
Colvin, Tom (1969) 179
Converse, Charles C. (1868) 333
Cook, George H. (1899) 297
Cook, Joseph S. (1919) 158
Copes, V. Earle (1960) 97 123 217 235
Cowper, William, (1779) 328
Cox, Frances E. (1864) 60
Cropper, Margaret (1975) 176
Crosby, Fanny J. (1875) 78 101 183
                         271 287 293
Crotch, William (1836) 128 288
Crouch, Andrae (1971) 278 385
Crueger Johann (1647) 186, 326
Davidica, Lyra (1708) 193
Davis, F. M. (1882) 298
Daw, Carl P. Jr. (1982) 380
Dix, William C. (1865) 154 196
Doane, George W. (1799-1859) 380
Doane, William (1875) 78 183 271 318
Doran, Carol (1984) 172
Dorsey, Thomas A. (1932) 309
Douglas, C. Winfred (1940) 66 163
Douglas, Robert 274
Dyke, H. Van (1907) 75
Dykes, John B. (1861) 79
Edwards, Rusty (1983) 151
Ehret, Walter (1918) 153
Elliott, Emily E. S. (1864) 172
Elvery, George (1858) 241
Emerson, Luther Orlando (1906)
Escamilla, Roberto (1983) 67, 310
Eslinger, Elise S. (1983) 67, 310, 361
Espinosa, Eddie 278
Evans, David (1927) 230
Evans, George K. (1917) 153

Everest, Charles W. (1833) 145
Farjeon, Elanor (1931) 370
Featherstone, William R. (1864) 321
Fellingham, Daved 207
Fetke, Tom 264
Fishel, Donald (1973) 201
Fitts, Bob 85
Foley, Brian 217
Foley, John B. (1978) 237
Franz, Ignaz (18th century) 80
Frazier, Phillip (1929) 71
Frostenson, Anders (1960) 97
Fry, Charles W. (1881) 295
Gabarain, Cesareo 90
Gabriel, Charles H. (1905) 93, 391
Gaither, Gloria (1971) 206 303
Gaither, William J. (1971) 206 286
Gardiners William (1815) 145
Gauntlett, Henry J. (1849) 159 232
Gerhardt, Paul (1653) 282
Geyer, John Bornwlow (1969) 231
Giardini, Felice de (1769) 260
Gibbons, Orlando (1623) 250 273
Gladden, W. (1879) 315
Glaeser, Carl G. (1780) 226
Gordon, Anthony J. (1876) 321
Goss, John (1869) 73
Gottshalk, Louis M. (1829-1869) 376
Grant, Amy (1984) 109
Gray, Marie 107
Green, Fred Pratt (1971) 129 184 222
Greiter, Matthaus (1525) 123
Grenoable Antiphoner (1753)
Grindal, Gracia (1983) 151
Grove, William Boyd (1980) 73
Grueber, Franz (1818) 160
Grueger, Johann (1647) 169
Guierrez-Achon, Raquel (1987) 90
Hagen, F. F. (1818-1907) 166
Hah, Stephen 87
Hahn, Jung Hee (1993) 164
Hamilton E. H. (19th Cent) 316
Hanaoka, Nobuaki (1983) 113
Handel, G. F. (1747) 161 194
Harkness, Robert 180
Harvey, Bennet, Jr. (1885) 166
Harwood, Basil (1908) 360
Hastings, T (1830) 143
Hatch, Edwin 224
Hatton, John (1793) 126
Haugen, Marty (1984) 364
Haultman, J. A. (1861-1942) 246
Havergal, William H. (1847) 254 281
Haydn, Franz Joseph (1780) 72, 256
Hayford Jack (1981) 204
Hays, William S. (1907) 295
Heber, Reginald (1826) 79, 240, 374
Henderson, Gerald S 197
Henderson, Richard Allen (1978) 357
Hernaman, Claudia F. (1873) 181

Herold, Louis J.F. (1839) 312
Herrmann, J. (1630) 186
Hewitt, Eliza E. (1898) 294 381
Hierro, Jude Del 208
Hine, Stuart K. (1899) 61
Hodges, Edward (1796-1867) 75, 382
Hodges, John S. (1868) 240
Hofkappelle, H. (1784) 249
Hoffman, Elisha A. (1839-1929) 277 291
Holmes, John Haynes (1913) 139
Hopkinson, A. S. (1989)
Hopson, Hal (1972) 341 343
Hosmer, Frederick L. (1912) 378
How, William W. (1864) 388
Hu, Te-ai 371
Huber, Jane Parker (1976) 144
Im, Jong Rack (1993) 244
Im, Song Suk 119
Imakoma, Yasushige (1965) 113
Irons, William, J. (1873) 382
Irvine, Jesse Seymour (1872) 115 302
Iverson, Daniel (1926) 214
Jackson, Jill 137
Janus, Martin (1661) 344
Johnson, Nelsie, T. (1988) 173
Joncas, Michael (1979) 83
Jones, J. E. 266
Jude, William H. (1874) 96
Kaan, Fred (1972) 97, 239, 253
Kaiser, Kurt (1969) 262
Kang, Eun Soo (1995) 134
Kang, Mahn-Hee 62 223
Kang, Won Young (1995) 134
Kempen, Andre 135
Ken Thomas (1674) 352
Kendrick, Graham 264
Kerr, Hugh Thomson (1916) 325
Kethe, William (1561) 118
Kim, Do Wan (1978) 165
Kim, Hae-Jong (1989) 69 383
Kim, Hee Bo (1957) 112
Kim, Jung Joon (1967) 84
Kim, Soon Sae (1982) 112 313
Kim, Seog Kyun 259
Kim, Sung Ho (1990) 195
Kim, Yoo Yun (1951) 379
Kingsley, George (1839) 312
Kirkpatrick, William (1885) 157 293 294
Kitchin, George William (1916) 174
Knapp, Phoebe P. (1873) 287
Knapp, William (1738) 169
Koizumi, Isao (1958) 252
Koo, Doo Hoe (1967) 339
Koyama, Shozo (1965) 113
Kwak, Sang Soo (1967) 84 373
Lafferty, Karen (1972) 136
Larcom, Lucy (1893) 103
Lee, Chul Joo 133
Lee, Geonyong 125 148
Lee, Ho Woon (1951) 319

Lee, Jang Hee 268 270
Lee, Kae Joon (1978) 165
Lee, Moon Seung (1995) 149
Lee, Song-Ch'on 119
Lee, Sum Sook (1993) 244
Lee, Sun Kyung (2001) 69 383
Lee, Yoo Sun (1967) 319
Leech, Bryan Jeffery (1931)
Lehman, F. M. 86
Lewis, J. E. 266
Lim, Ok In (1967) 243
Lincoln, C. Eric (1987) 216
Lloyd, William (1840) 139
Lockwood, George (1987) 90 138 310
Longfellow, Samuel (1859-1914) 360 372
Lowry, R. (1826-1899) 101 192 275 389
Lvov, Alexis (1833) 380
MacMillan, Ernest C. (1930) 158
Maker, Henry Williams (1859) 68
Manley, James K. (1975) 221
Manzano, Miguel 138
Maquiso, Elena G. (1961) 227
Marsh, Donald S. (1972 252
Martinez, Raquel Mora 69
Mason, Lowell (1792-1872) 143 144 161
　　　　219 226 254
Matheson, George (1882) 322
Matthews, Timothy (1876) 173
Matthews, Timothy R. (1826-1910)
McAfee, Cleland B. (1903) 324
McGee, Bob (1976) 211
McGranahan, J. (1883) 290
McKinney, B. (1886-1952) 224 267 340
Medema, Ken 283
Messiter, Arthur H. (1889) 130
Mieir, Audrey (1959) 203
Miles, C. Austin (1913) 296
Miller, F. S. (1905) 242
Miller, R. F. (1922) 205
Miller, Sy 137
Minchin, James 119
Mohr, Joseph (1818) 160
Monsell, John S. P. (1811-1875)
Montgomery, James (1820) 128 187
Moon, Sung Mo (1989) 76 379
Moore, William (1825) 64
Morgan, Patricia 200
Morley, Frederick B. (1953) 249
Moultrie, Gerard 150
Na, Wong Yong (1979) 245
Na, Woon Young (1967) 106 131 195 245
Na, Young Soo (1971) 242 356
Neale, John M. (1854) 66 155 169 188
Neander, Joachim (1650-1680) 68
Neidlinger, William H. (1863-1924) 162
Newbolt, Michael Robert (1916) 174
Newton, Bill 82
Newton, John (1779) 94, 256
Nicholson, Sydney Hugo (1916) 174
Niles, D. T. (1963) 105 227

Nystrom, Martin 116
Oakeley, Frederick (1841) 162
Oatman, Johnson. Jr. (1898) 391
Olivar, J. A. 138
Olson, Ernst W. (1925)
Orr, J. Edwin 274
Ovin (1946) 106
Owens, Carol (1972) 258
Owens, Jimmy (1972) 229
Page, Kate Stearns (1932) 72
Park, Sung-Ho 300
Park, Chung Kwan 317
Park, Chai-Hoon (1967) 89 175 243 272
Park, J. Edgar (1913) 168
Park, Sung Won (1989) 76
Parker, Edwin (1836-1925) 376
Parker, William H. (1885) 177
Peace, Alvert L. (1884) 322
Phillips, Keith 109
Pieters, A. A, (1898) 114
Plumptre, Edward H. (1865) 130
Pollard, Adelaide A. (1902) 327
Pope, Marion 148
Postlethwaite, R. Deane 302
Potter, Doreen (1975) 241
Prentiss Elizabeth P. (1869) 318
Prichard, Rowland H. (1830) 196
Pritchard, TCL (1929) 112
Proulx, Richard (1986) 71, 233
Prudentius, Aurelisu C. (348-413) 66
Psalmodia Evangelica (1789)
Pucket, Martha (1927-1994) 158
Purday, Charles Henry (1860) 325
Purifoy, John (1952) 265
Rankin, Jeremiah E. (1880) 347
Rasanayagam, Shantil (1962) 103
Reed, Edith M.G. (1926) 152
Renville, Joseph R. (1846) 71
Roberts, John (1839) 74
Robinson, Robert (1758) 127
Root, George F. (1820-1895) 337 348
Rosas, Carlos (1983) 67
Runyan, William M. (1923) 81
Ryu, Hyung Seaon 146
Sammis, John H. (1887) 320
Sandell-Berg, Caroline V. (1855) 335
Sankey, I. D. (1840-1908) 316
Sasao, T. 89
Sateren, Leland (1972) 366
Schalk, Carl F. (1983) 59
Scheffler, Johann (1624-1677) 167
Schlegel, Katharina von (1752) 307
Scholtes, Peter 257
Schop, Johann 344
Schubert, Franz 233
Schuetz, Johann (1675) 60
Schutmaat, Alvin 138 178
Schutte, Daniel L. (1981) 263
Scriven, J. (1855) 333
Shaw, Martin (1928) 166

Shea, George B. (1909-) 205
Sheppard, F. L. (1915) 62
Showalter, Anthony. J. (1887) 291
Sibelius, Jean (1899) 307
Sims, W. Hines (1907-1997) 365
Sinclair, Jerry (1972) 355
Sleeper, William T. (1887) 276
Sleeth, Natalie (1976) 363 392
Smallwood, Richard (1975) 323
Smart, Henry T. (1835) 188 261
Smith, Alfred Morton (1941) 216
Smith, Elizabeth Lee (1868) 399
Smith, Gary Alan (1988) 155 237
Smith, Henry Percy. (1874) 247 315
Smith, Michael W. (1984) 109
Smith, Peter D. (1979) 171
Smith, Walter Chalmers (1867) 74
Smith, William Farley (1986) 98 104
　　　　　140 189 213 223 236, 292
　　　　　314 324 338 384 386
Spafford, Horation G. (1828-1888) 304
Stanford, Charles Villiers (1904)
　　　　　129 231
Staford, Ronald (1941) 163
Starr, Richard 70
Stebbins, George C. (1907) 276 327
Stockton, John H. (1813-77) 277
Stone, Samuel J. (1868) 255
Storm, August L. (1862) 246
St. James (4th Cent) 149
Suh, Byung Joo (1991) 164
Suh, Chung Woon (1966) 373
Suk, Jin Young 175
Sullivan, Arthur S. (11842-900) 103
Suppe, Gertrude C. (1987) 90, 178
Tannous, Arthur 210
Tzize 120 121 141 349 353 364
Thomas, Edith Lowell (1935) 72
Thomas, Eugene (1981) 204
Thomerson, Kathleen (1966) 102
Thompson, John (1981) 77
Thompson, Michael (1981) 77
Thompson, Will L. (1880) 284
Tinio, Rolando 115
Towner, Daniel (1887) 320
Troeger, Thomas (1984) 172
Tucker, F. Bland (1982) 77
Turner, Herbert B. (1907) 168
Tuttle, Carl 132
Uckeet, Paul (1923) 158
Underwood, John T. (1988) 334 339
Vajda, Jaroslav J. (1983) 59
Vale, Alliene G. 301
Vieira, Gilbert H. (1978) 352
Wade, John (1743) 162
Walford, William W. (1842) 330
Walter, William H. (1894) 282
Walworth, Clarence (1853) 80
Warner, Anna B. (1859) 342
Watts, Issac (1719) 65 123 126 161 323

Weaver, John (1986) 325
Webb, Charles. H. (1988) 137 179 181
　　　　　227 296 354
Werners J. G. (1815) 281
Wesley, Charles (1743) 88 124 182
　　　　　185 187 193 199 218 226
　　　　　248 250 254 269 273 280
　　　　　281 288 346 387
Wesley, John (1737) 121, 270, 282
Wesley, Samuel S. (1872) 255 269
Westendorf, Omer (1964) 366
Whitfield, Fredrick (1855) 198
Whittle, Daniel W. (1883) 290
Wiant, Mildred A. & Bliss (1946) 371
Willcox, J. H. (1849) 114
Williams, Ralph. Vaughan (1906) 65, 184
　　　　　196 347 388
Williams, Thomas (1789) 144
Wilson, Emily D. (1898) 381
Wimber, John (1979) 91
Winkworth, Catherine (1863) 68 108
Wise, Joe (1966) 238
Witt, C. F. (1715) 232
Wolcott, Samuel (1869) 260
Wolfe, Lanny (1977) 215
Woodbury, Isaac B. (1850) 185, 187
Woolston, C. H. (1856-1927) 337
Wordsworth, C (1862) 111
World Library Publications (1964)
Wren, Brian (1968) 190 311 343
Yamaguchi, Tokuo (1958) 251
Yardley, H. Francis (1982) 230
Young, Carlton (1988) 83 156 176 248,
　　　　　311 330 362 370
Zelley, H. J. (1899) 297

TRANSLATORS

Cho, Sang Yean
Chun, Sang Eui
Chun, Young Ho
Ham, Jong Taik
Han Se Hee
Hong, Hyesung
Hong, Yeon Pyo
Huh, Paul Junggap
Hwang, In Sook
Hwang Mee Kyung
Juhn, Youngstone
Jung, Hee Soo
Kang, Keumhee
Kang, Mahn Hee
Kim, Eun Sook
Kim, Hae Jong
Kim, Hea Sun
Kim, Jin Ho
Kim, Seung Nam
Kim, Sun Bae
Kim, Woong Min
Kim, Young Joo

Kwon, Kyoung Ho
Lee, Hoo Sug
Lee, Hyeran
Lee, Jai Sook
Lee, Joung Suk
Lee, Keyong Hee
Lee, San Young
Lee, Seung Woo
Lee, Sun Kyung
Lee, Won Wha
Lim, Hakchoon
Paik, Miyoung
Paik, Seung Bae
Park, Hankyu
Poitras, Edward
Shin, Young Cheol
Shin, Young Kak
Won, Dal Joon
Yoon, Dae Sob
Yu, Bohyun
Yun, Sam
Yun, Won Kyung

성경 인용

창세기
1:1-15 374
1:1-5, 14-19 528
1:31 63
28:10-17 314
28:10-22 308

출애굽기
13:21-22 528
13:22 256
19:4 83

레위기
6:13 269

신명기
6:1-5 478
6:4-9 524
32:2 112
32:3 60
31:11 302
33:27 291

사무엘상
7:12 127

열왕기상
18:44-45 248

열왕기하
2:11 384

느헤미야
8:10 301
9:5 128

시편
1:1-6 393
3:1-8 394
4:1-8 395
8:1, 3-9 396
9:11-17 397
10:12-14, 16-18 398
13:1-6 399
14:1-7 400
15:1-5 401
16:5-11 402
16:9 298
17:1-7, 15 403
19 67

19:1, 7-11, 14 404
20:1 114
20:4 130
22:1, 2, 4, 5, 6, 9, 24
         457
23 115
23:6 107 304
23:1-6 405 509 528
24:1-8 470
25:1-9, 21 446
27:1, 4, 5, 7, 9 406
28:1-7 407
29:1-4, 7-8, 10-11
         408
30:4-8, 10-11 409
31:1-3, 7-8, 15-16
         410
33:1, 3-6, 8, 20, 22
         411
34:1-8 471
36:5-11 412
37:1-7, 18 413
37:3 292
37:5 282
42:1 116
42:1-4, 11 458
46:1, 4-5, 7-10 414
46:10 307
47:1 121
47:1-9 468
51 524
51:1-3, 6-8, 10 456
61 105
62:5-9, 11-12 415
63 524
63:1-7 416
65:4, 9-13 472
67:1 117
67:1-7 417
70:1-5 418
71:1-8 419
72:1-4, 11, 17, 19 420
80:1-7 421
81:8-14 422
82:1-8 423
84:1-12 491
85:1-7, 10-11 424
87:3 256
89:1-2, 5, 13-16 52
         447
90:1-14 476 528
91:1-4, 9-10, 16 425

92:1-8 426
95:1-2 131
95:1-7 427 524
96:1-7, 13 451
98:1-7 454
98:4-9 161
99:1-5, 9 428
100 118
100:1-5 429
100:2-3 121
101:1-9 68
102:1, 12-13, 25-28
         430
103 120
103:1-6 68
103:1-8 17 459
104:1-5, 24, 30-31
         469
104:24-30 71
105:1-8 431
111:2-4, 7-10 455
112:1-8 432
113:1-8 433
115:1-9 434
116:1-2 323
116:5-6, 8-10, 12-14
         435
117 121 126
118:1, 14, 20-25, 28
         436
119:11 110
119:54 294
119:97-98, 101-105
         480
119:105 109
121 119
121:1-8 437 528
122:1 202
126:1-6 484
127:1-5 486
128:1-6 487
130:1 122
130:1-8 460 508
136:1-3, 23-26 473
137:1-7 485
138:1-3, 6-8 438
139:1-10, 23 439
141:1-5 440 528
145:3, 8-10, 15-19
         441
146:1-9 442
147:1-7, 11 443

148:1-3, 5-6, 10-13
         444
150:1-6 445

이사야
1:18 283
6:8 139 263 265 329
11:1-2, 6, 8-10 448
33:20-21 256
40:3 141
52:10 141
53:4-8, 12 461
55:1-3 524
60:1 143
61:1, 2, 10-11 449

예레미야
8:22 98
10:12-13 71
18:6 327
23:5 162

예레미야애가
3:22-23 81 370

하박국
2:20 348

스가랴
9:9-10, 16 462

마태복음
1:23 210
2:1-12 154 166
4:1-11 181
4:18-22 90 96
5:14-16 337
6:24 205
6:26 242
6:33 136
7:7 136
8:3 286
9:20-22 328
10:8 258
11:28-30 306
13:36-43 241
15:16-20 184
16:24-25 145
17:1-8 169
18:10 50
19:4-6 494

19:13-15　177
19:14　337
21:8-9　178
21:16　335
22:37　318
25:1-13　528
25:31-46　138
26:26-29　13　235
27:27-31　184
28:1-10　192
28:6-7　197
28:7　193
28:18-20　258　491
28:19-20　95　261

마가복음
1:12-13　181
1:16-20　90
1:21　171
1:41　286
4:26-29　241
5:25-34　328
8:34-35　145
9:2-8　169
9:14-27　328
10:13-16　177
10:14　50
11:8-10　178
14:22-25　235
14:26　129
15:16-20　184

누가복음
1:26-38　151
2:6-20　152　154
2:7　159
2:8-14　452
2:8-20　166
2:12　160
2:14　353
2:29　363
3:21-22　230
4:1-13　181
4:31-37　171
5:1-11　90
5:11　316
5:13　286
7:37-38　317
8:43-48　328
9:23-24　145
9:28-36　169
12:49　248
14:16-24　88
15:15-20　275
15:18-24　272

17:5　103
19:36-38　178
22:15-20　235
22:41-44　93
23:42　234　364

요한복음
1:1-4, 9-12, 18　450
1:1-5, 9-14　524
1:9　264
1:11　172
2:12-13　178
3:16　86
3:16-21　368　453
4:23-24　84
6:35-58　150　240
6:51　24
8:12　106
12:13　177
13:1-17　179
13:35　257
14:27　272
15:8　244
15:9　343
15:12　253
19:1-5　184
19:30　182
20:11-18　296
20:22　224
21:15　205

사도행전
1:8　266
1:14　328
2:5-11　249
2:42　236
6:4　260
11:15　214
14:17　243
16:26　280

로마서
4:25　194
5:6-11　528
6:3-11　231
6:9　195
8:11　512
8:15-17　213
8:28　89
8:31-39　464
8:34　508
12:1　312
12:1-2　524
12:1-13　481
14:8　310

고린도전서
2:2　254
3:11　255
4:1-2　319
10:16-17　24　237
11:23-26　21　235
12　237
12:1　312
12:4-31　250
13:1-3　341
13:1-13　488
15:17-22,　42-44,　49-50,
　　　　　　54-57　467
15:20　382
15:51-52　386
15:51, 53, 54, 55, 57　512

고린도후서
4:6　297
12:9-10　329
13:13　23　368

갈라디아서
2:20　287
3:27-28　250
3:28　237

에베소서
2:5　94
2:16　183
3:17-19　99
3:19　225
4:11-15　479
5:19　226
6:4　50
6:23-24　356

빌립보서
1:11　111
2:5-11　463
2:9-11　199
3:8　205
4:4　130
4:13　327

골로새서
1:20　277
1:25-29　483
3:2　391

데살로니가전서
5:2-10　528

디모데전서
1:17　74

디모데후서
1:12　290
4:7　101

히브리서
11　97
12:1　315　388
13:8　105

베드로전서
1:3-9　513
2:20-24　752
5:10　34

요한1서
1:7　320
4:7-9　24
4:7-11　490

유다서
24-25　514

요한계시록
3:20　24
4　82　150
4:8-11　79
6:12-17　386
14:13　513
19:6-7　196
21:1-5　392
21:1-7　474
21:1—22:5　390
21:3-4　385
21:5　311
22:1-5　389　528
22:12　147

(주: 392쪽 이후는
연합감리교회만 적용됨.)

INDEX OF SCRIPTURE

Genesis
1:1-15 374
1:1-5, 14-19 530
1:31 63
28:10-17 314
28:10-22 308

Exodus
13:21-22 530
13:22 256
19:4 83

Leviticus
6:13 269

Deuteronomy
6:1-5 478
6:4-9 526
32:2 112
32:3 60
31:11 302
33:27 291

1 Samuel
7:12 127

1 Kings
18:44-45 248

2 Kings
2:11 384

Nehemiah
8:10 301
9:5 128

Psalms
1:1-6 393
3:1-8 394
4:1-8 395
8:1, 3-9 396
9:11-17 397
10:12-14, 16-18 398
13:1-6 399
14:1-7 400
15:1-5 401
16:5-11 402
16:9 298
17:1-7, 15 403

19 67
19:1, 7-11, 14 404
20:1 114
20:4 130
22:1, 2, 4, 5, 6, 9, 24 457
23 115
23:6 107 304
23:1-6 405 518 530
24:1-8 470
25:1-9, 21 446
27:1, 4, 5, 7, 9 406
28:1-7 407
29:1-4, 7-8, 10-11 408
30:4-8, 10-11 409
31:1-3, 7-8, 15-16 410
33:1, 3-6, 8, 20, 22 411
34:1-8 471
36:5-11 412
37:1-7, 18 413
42:1 116
42:1-4, 11 458
46:1, 4, 5, 7-10 414
46:10 307
47:1 121
47:1-9 468
51 526
51:1-3, 6-8, 10 456
61 105
62:5-9, 11-12 415
63 526
63:1-7 416
65:4, 9-13 472
67:1 117
67:1-7 417
70:1-5 418
71:1-8 419
72:1-4, 11, 17, 19 420
80:1-7 421
81:8-14 422
82:1-8 423
84:1-12 492
85:1-7, 10-11 424
87:3 256
89:1-2, 5, 13-16, 52 447
90:1-14 477 530

91:1-4, 9-10, 16 425
92:1-8 426
95 526
95:1-2 131
95:1-7 427
96:1-7, 13 451
98:1-7 454
98:4-9 161
99:1-5, 9 428
100 118
100:1-5 429
100:2-3 121
101:1-9 68
102:1, 12-13, 25-28 430
103 120
103:1-6 68
103:1-8, 17 459
104:1-5, 24, 30-31 469
104:24-30 71
105:1-8 431
111:2-4, 7-10 455
112:1-8 432
113:1-8 433
115:1-9 434
116:1-2 323
116:5-6, 8-10, 12-14 435
117 121 126
118:1, 14, 20-25, 28 436
119:11 110
119:54 294
119:97-98, 101-105 480
121:1-8 437 530
122 119
126:1-6 484
127:1-5 486
128:1-6 487
130:1 122
130:1-8 460 517
136:1 245
136:1-3, 23-26 473
137:1-7 485
138:1-3, 6-8 438
138:2 228
139:1-10, 23 439
139:23 274
141:1-10 440 530

145:3, 8-10, 15-19 444
146 123
146:1-7, 9 442
147:1 130
147:1-7, 11 443
148:1-3, 5-6, 10-13 444
150 68 124 125
150:1-6 445

Isaiah
1:18 283
6:8 139 263 265 329
11:1-2, 6, 8-10 448
33:20-21 256
40:3 141
52:10 141
53:4-8, 12 461
55:1-3 526
60:1 143
61:1, 2, 10-11 449

Jeremiah
8:22 98
10:12-13 71
18:6 327
23:5 162

Lamentations
3:22-23 81 370

Habakkuk
2:20 348

Zechariah
9:9-10, 16 462

Matthew
1:23 210
2:1-12 154 166
4:1-11 181
4:18-22 90 96
5:14-16 337
6:24 205
6:26 242
6:33 136
7:7 136
8:3 286
9:20-22 328

10:8 258
11:28-30 306
13:36-43 241
15:16-20 184
16:24-25 145
17:1-8 169
19:4-6 500
19:13-15 177
19:14 337
21:8-9 178
21:16 335
22:37 318
25:1-13 530
25:31-46 138
26:26-29 21 235
27:27-31 184
28:1-10 192
28:6-7 197
28:7 193
28:18-20 258 493
28:19-20 95 261

Mark
1:12-13 181
1:16-20 90
1:21 171
1:41 286
4:26-29 241
5:25-34 328
8:34-35 145
9:2-8 169
9:14-27 328
9:28-36 169
10:13-16 177
11:8-10 178
14:22-25 235
14:26 129
15:16-20 184

Luke
1:26-38 151
2:6-20 152 154
2:7 159
2:8-14 452
2:6-20 152 154
2:7 159
2:8-20 166
2:12 160
2:14 353
2:29 363
3:21-22 230
4:1-13 181
4:31-37 171
5:1-11 90

5:11 316
5:13 286
7:37-38 317
8:43-48 328
9:23-24 145
9:28-36 169
12:49 248
14:16-24 88
15:15-20 275
15:18-24 272
17:5 103
19:36-38 178
22:15-20 235
22:41-44 93
23:42 234 364

John
1:1-4, 9-12 450
1:1-18 526
1:9 264
1:11 172
2:12-13 178
3:16 86
3:16-21 453
4:23-24 84
6:35-58 150 240
6:51 26
8:12 106
12:13 177
13:1-17 179
13:35 257
14:27 271
15:8 244
15:9 342
15:12 253
19:1-5 184
19:30 182
20:11-18 296
20:22 224
21:15 205

Acts
1:8 266
1:14 328
2:5-11 249
2:42 236
6:4 260
11:15 214
14:17 243
16:26 280

Romans
4:25 194
5:6-11 530

6:3-11 231
6:9 195
8:11 757
8:15-17 213
8:28 89
8:31-39 465
8:34 517
12:1 312
12:1-2 526
12:1-13 482
14:8 310

1 Corinthians
2:2 254
3:11 255
4:1-2 319
10:16-17 26 237
11:23-26 13 237
12 237
12:1 312
12:4-31 250
13:1-3 341
13:1-13 489
15:17-22, 42-44, 49-50,
         54-57 467
15:20 382
15:51-52 386
15:51, 53-55, 57 521

2 Corinthians
4:6 297
12:9-10 329
13:3 23 368

Galatians
2:20 287
3:27-28 250
3:28 237

Ephesians
2:5 94
2:16 183
3:17-19 99
3:19 225
4:11-15 479
5:19 226
6:23-24 356

Philippians
1:11 111
2:5-11 463
2:9-11 199
3:8 205
4:4 130

4:13 327

Colossians
1:20 277
1:25-29 483
3:2 391

1 Thessalonians
5:2-10 530

1 Timothy
1:17 74

2 Timothy
1:12 290
4:7 101

Hebrews
11 97
12:1 315 388
13:8 105

1 Peter
1:3-9 522
2:20-24 752
5:10 44

1 John
1:7 320
4:7-9 26
4:7-11 490

Jude
24-25 523

Revelation
3:20 26
4 82 150
4:8-11 79
14:13 522
19:6-7 196
21:1-5 289
21:1-7 475
21:1—22:5 390
21:3-4, 385
22:1-5 389 530
22:12 147

(Note: After number 392,
all numbers are only
applicable to the United
Methodist Hymnal.)

제목 분류

가르침 말씀과 가르침 참조

가정
335 둥지 안의 새들보다
343 사랑하고 바라면서
339 사철에 봄바람 불어 잇고
311 새로운 삶을 시작하는
337 세상 모든 어린이를
336 아이들아 주를 찬송하라
338 이 작은 나의 빛
340 주 말씀 배우는 믿음의 가정
253 주 우릴 받아주심 본받게
232 축복하신 주의 자녀

간구와 응답
132 눈을 들어
224 성령이여 오셔서 정결케 하소서
281 온 하늘에 가득히 주의 영광
322 주 크신 사랑 가운데
97 꽃이 필 때 믿음으로

감사(절)
241 감사하는 성도여
247 거룩하신 하나님 주께 감사
114 내가 환난 당할 때에
246 대속하신 주께 감사
352 만복의 근원 하나님
244 봄이 오면 밭고랑에
243 산마다 불이 탄다 고운 단풍에
371 새벽 하늘 밝히는
201 알렐루야 알렐루야
360 주 앞에 바친 예물
67 주 찬양 드리세
245 주의 형상 따라서
366 큰 축복을 받고
242 하늘 나는 새를 보라
71 하늘과 땅을 지으신 주
59 하늘의 새와 물고기

강림 교회력: 강림절 참조

개회 찬송
80 거룩하신 하나님 이름 높여
75 기뻐하며 경배하세
60 높이 계신 주 찬양
174 높이 들라 사랑의 십자가
68 다 찬양하여라
283 다 함께 오라
123 숨 쉬는 동안 주 찬양
74 신비롭고 영원한 지혜의 주
212 영광스런 주님 전능하신 주

126 온 천하 거하는 만물아
118 온 땅의 모든 사람들
190 주 사셨다
348 주 성전 안에
72 주의 백성 찬양
370 첫 아침처럼
178 흥분한 군중들이

결혼
75 기뻐하며 경배하세
73 사랑으로 다스리는
343 사랑하고 바라면서
345 아주 먼 옛날
342 예수 사랑하심은
344 예수 우리의 참된 기쁨
341 천사처럼 말하여서

경건
234 기억하소서
358 들으소서 우리 기도 드릴 때
352 만복의 근원 하나님
319 부름 받아 나선 이 몸
362 샬롬 카베림
361 샬롬을 비네
359 아멘
355 알렐루야
353 영광 영광
364 예수 내 주여
281 온 땅에 가득히 주의 영광
368 우리 주 예수의 크신 은혜가
349 자비 베푸소서
348 주 성전 안에
363 주 안에서 평안하라
365 주 예수의 크신 은혜
350 주여 자비 베푸소서
367 주께서 함께 게서
357 주여 나를 감동하게
351 창조주 하나님께
366 큰 축복을 받고
76 하나님을 찬양하세
354 할렐루야

경배와 찬양
79 거룩 거룩 거룩
82 거룩 거룩 거룩하신 주
80 거룩하신 하나님 이름 높여
75 기뻐하며 경배하세
207 기뻐하며 왕께 노래 부르리
129 노래로 주께 영광 돌리며
124 높은 곳에 계신 주님
60 높이 계신 주 찬양해

132　눈을 들어
131　다 와서 노래하자
200　다 와서 찬양해
68　다 찬양하여라
135　두 손 들고 찬양합니다
226　만 입이 내게 있으면
352　만복의 근원 하나님
116　목마른 사슴
127　복의 근원 강림하사
73　사랑으로 다스리는
134　사랑으로 천지 만물
85　사랑하는 나의 아버지
123　숨 쉬는 동안 주 찬양
74　신비롭고 영원한 지혜의 주
336　아이들아 주를 찬송하라
355　알렐루야
77　엘샤다이
353　영광 영광
169　오 놀랍고 아름다운
81　오 신실하신 주
87　왕이신 나의 하나님
126　온 천하 거하는 만물아
118　온 땅의 모든 사람들
133　좋은 날 기쁜 날
83　주 너를 독수리 날개 위에
188　주 부활하신 이 날
67　주 찬양 드리세
121　주 찬양하여라
61　주 하나님 지으신 세계
65　주 하나님의 능력
115　주는 나의 목자 되시니
128　주님의 사람들
91　주님의 사랑과 그 영이
210　주를 찬양하리라
100　주여 나를 이끄사
72　주의 백성 찬양
64　찬란하고 빛난 하늘
62　참 아름다와라
230　창조주 하나님 감사 찬송
370　첫 아침처럼
228　하나님 사랑과 경배 드립니다
76　하나님을 찬양하세
78　하나님께 영광을
71　하늘과 땅을 지으신 주
84　하늘에 가득찬 영광의 하나님
59　하늘의 새와 물고기
227　하늘의 주님 내려주소서
354　할렐루야
202　함께 주의 이름으로

종려주일 · 고난주일
　　교회력: 종려주일 · 고난주일　참조

고난주간
185　거룩한 사랑의 주님
186　거룩한 예수 무슨 죄가 있어
187　겟세마네 동산의 구세주
182　다 이루었다
183　예수 나를 위하여
179　예수 예수
184　주 가시관을 쓰시고
178　흥분한 군중들이
　　성만찬 참조

고백　죄와 고백 참조

교독 기도　기도 · 축복송 · 기타 참조

교회
255　교회의 참된 터는
268　나 비록 연약하지만
252　나는 교회 너도 교회
266　빛의 사자들이여
257　성령 안에서 우리 하나
256　시온성과 같은 교회
143　시온의 영광이 빛나는 아침
254　오 우릴 연합하시는
249　오 하나님의 교회
267　온 세상 위하여
250　완전하게 하시는 복의 근원 예수여
248　은혜 작은 불꽃이
222　주 믿는 성도들 날마다 기도해
360　주 앞에 바친 예물
253　주 우릴 받아주심 본받게
251　주의 종들 여기에 모여

교회력
강림절
152　거룩하신 아기 예수
147　구주여 오소서
154　마리아 무릎 위에
162　베들레헴 작은 그 마을
165　사랑의 주님 예수
167　새벽 별 오 기쁜 빛
148　오소서
150　인생들아 잠잠하라
211　임마누엘 임마누엘
151　저 동정녀 마리아
141　주의 길 예비하라
113　주의 말씀 내리소서
102　주의 빛 따르기 원합니다
149　평화의 나라 임하시니

성탄(절)
152　거룩하신 아기 예수
160　고요한 밤 거룩한 밤
153　고요히 그 아기 잠자네
158　구유 안에 누이신 마리아의 아기

157   그 어린 주 예수
161   기쁘다 구주 오셨네
154   마리아 무릎 위에
162   베들레헴 작은 그 마을
165   사랑의 주님 예수
155   성도여 기뻐 찬양해
166   성탄 노래하세
156   아기 예수 나셨네
159   어느 옛날 다윗 성에
172   주님 보좌와 영광
164   하나님의 아들이 사람 몸을 입으사
163   흰눈이 쌓이고 별 빛날 때

주현절

152   거룩하신 아기 예수
162   베들레헴 작은 그 마을
167   새벽 별 오 기쁜 빛
155   성도여 기뻐 찬양해
166   성탄 노래하세
156   아기 예수 나셨네
159   어느 옛날 다윗 성에
281   온 땅에 가득히 주의 영광

주 변모일

169   오 놀랍고 아름다운
281   온 땅에 가득히 주의 영광

재의 수요일

180   골짜기 외로운 길
181   사십일 동안 주님께서

사순절

185   거룩한 사랑의 주님
186   거룩한 예수 무슨 죄가 있어
187   겟세마네 동산의 구세주
180   골짜기 외로운 길
277   구주의 십자가 보혈로
174   높이 들라 사랑의 십자가
182   다 이루었다
181   사십일 동안 주님께서
183   예수 나를 위하여
184   주 가시관을 쓰시고
178   흥분한 군중들이

종려·고난주일 (주간)

185   거룩한 사랑의 주님
186   거룩한 예수 무슨 죄가 있어
187   겟세마네 동산의 구세주
277   구주의 십자가 보혈로
182   다 이루었다
183   예수 나를 위하여
179   예수 예수
177   예수님 이야기 내게 들려주오
184   주 가시관을 쓰시고
178   흥분한 군중들이

부활절

192   무덤에 머물러
195   사랑하는 우리 예수
355   알렐루야
197   알렐루야 예수 다시 사셨네
201   알렐루야 알렐루야
196   알렐루야 찬양하라
382   영화로운 성도들과
193   예수 부활했으니
281   온 땅에 가득히 주의 영광
296   저 장미꽃 위에 이슬
188   주 부활하신 이 날
190   주 사셨다
189   주 예수 십자가에
285   주 하나님 독생자 예수
191   주님은 죽음 이기시고
194   주님께 영광

승천

196   알렐루야 찬양하라
188   주 부활하신 이 날
190   주 사셨다
189   주 예수 십자가에

성령강림절

225   나의 하나님 나의 삶을 다해
216   내 안에 계신 온유하신 주
219   믿음의 영이여
214   살아계신 주 성령
221   성령
223   성령을 따라서 찬양하리
224   성령이여 오셔서 정결케 하소서
217   성령이여 진리 안에
220   여기 성령 함께 계시니
212   영광스런 주님 전능하신 주
218   오 성령이여 오소서
248   은혜 작은 불꽃이
222   주 믿는 성도들 날마다 기도해
191   주님은 죽음 이기시고
 91   주님의 사랑과 그 영이
215   주님의 영이 여기 함께 계시니
213   주의 성령 느낄 때
228   하나님 사랑과 경배 드립니다
227   하늘의 주님 내려주소서
     성령 참조

삼위일체 (주일)

229   거룩 거룩
 80   거룩하신 하나님 이름 높여
225   나의 하나님 나의 삶을 다해 사랑해요
226   만 입이 내게 있으면
230   창조주 하나님 감사 찬송
228   하나님 사랑과 경배 드립니다
227   하늘의 주님 내려주소서

성도추모일 (만성절)

389 강가에서 만나보자
255 교회의 참된 터는
380 승리의 예수여
388 안식하는 하늘의 성도들
387 저 하늘 성도들과
235 주님 떼어주신 떡
　새 하늘과 새 땅 참조

그리스도 왕 주일

204 경배해 위대한 주님께
207 기뻐하며 왕께 노래 부르리
203 놀라운 그 이름
201 알렐루야 알렐루야
148 오소서

교회연합운동

212 영광스런 주님 전능하신 주
387 저 하늘 성도들과
237 한 떡을 떼며

구세주 구원 참조

구원

277 구주의 십자가 보혈로
94 나 같은 죄인 살리신
104 나와 함께 걸으소서
101 나의 갈길 다 가도록
92 난 들었네 주 예수
299 날 대속하신 나의 구세주
289 내 맘속의 음악 소리는
198 내 사랑하는 그 이름
114 내가 환난 당할 때에
88 다 오라 복음 잔치에
246 대속하신 주께 감사
231 사망의 모든 권세 이기고
155 성도여 기뻐 찬양해
290 아 하나님의 은혜로
288 어찌 알 수 있나
275 여러 해 동안 주 떠나
183 예수 나를 위하여
70 온 세상 우리 주님 손 안에
107 온종일 예수와 함께
105 예수 내 주께 (싸라남 싸라남)
287 예수를 내가 주로 믿어
95 우리가 지금은 길가는 나그네
103 이 마음 주께로
93 저 나사렛 예수 앞에
99 주 예수님 내 맘에 오사
90 주 호숫가에 오셔서
91 주님의 사랑과 그 영이
327 주님의 뜻을 이루소서
100 주여 나를 이끄사
102 주의 빛 따르기 원합니다
291 주의 친절한 팔에 안기세

89 지금까지 지내온 것
96 풍랑 이는 바다 위로
278 항상 진실케
98 향유가 있는 길르앗
97 꽃이 필 때 믿음으로

그리스도 예수 그리스도 참조

그리스도 왕 (주일) 교회력: 그리스도 왕 (주일) 참조

그리스도의 공동체

252 나는 교회 너도 교회
212 영광스런 주님 전능하신 주
249 오 하나님의 교회
107 온종일 예수와 함께
250 완전하게 하시는 복의 근원 예수여
253 주 우릴 받아주심 본받게
237 한 떡을 떼며

그리스도인의 삶

175 갈릴리 맑은 바다
315 겸손히 주를 섬길 때
316 나 주의 도움 받고자
312 나의 삶을 주 위해
318 내 구주 예수를 더욱 사랑
313 내 마음 주께 바치옵니다
321 내 주 되신 주를 참 사랑하고
308 내 주를 가까이 하려 함은
88 다 오라 복음 잔치에
135 두 손 들고 찬양합니다
319 부름 받아 나선 이 몸
257 성령 안에서 우리 하나
306 수고한 자 오라
145 십자가 지라
275 여러 해 동안 주 떠나
320 예수 따라가며
284 예수가 우리를 부르는 소리
272 어서 돌아오오
103 이 마음 주께로
296 저 장미꽃 위에 이슬
146 정의가 강물처럼
333 죄짐 맡은 우리 구주
294 주 안에 있는 나에게
90 주 호숫가에 오셔서
301 주님의 기쁨은 나의 힘
91 주님의 사랑과 그 영이
291 주의 친절한 팔에 안기세
89 지금까지 지내온 것
144 큰 소망 중에 살리라
297 태산을 넘어 험곡에 가도
149 평화의 나라 임하시니
96 풍랑 이는 바다 위로
314 하늘에 올라가네
97 꽃이 필 때 믿음으로
　헌신 참조

기도

324 고요한 안식 있는 곳
147 구주여 오소서
234 기억하소서
329 나는 비록 약하나
292 나는 주를 의지하리
329 나를 보내소서
279 나의 삶 속에서
318 내 구주 예수를 더욱 사랑
332 내 기도하는 그 시간
332 여기 오소서
364 예수 내 주여
309 예수여 나의 손 꼭 잡고 가소서
107 온종일 예수와 함께
325 우리의 삶을 주관하시는 주
328 우리를 고쳐주소서
349 자비 베푸소서
333 죄짐 맡은 우리 구주
222 주 믿는 성도들 날마다 기도해
323 주 사랑해
334 주 예수여 은혜를
322 주 크신 사랑 가운데
327 주님의 뜻을 이루소서
357 주여 나를 감동하게
326 주여 바로 접니다
350 주여 자비 베푸소서
227 하늘의 주님 내려주소서

기도·축복송·기타

358 들으소서 우리 기도 드릴 때
352 만복의 근원 하나님
362 샬롬 카베림
361 샬롬을 비네
359 아멘
173 아멘 아멘
355 알렐루야
368 우리 주 예수의 크신 은혜
356 우리는 주만 바라봅니다
353 영광 영광
364 예수 내 주여
349 자비 베푸소서
348 주 성전 안에
363 주 안에서 평안하라
360 주 앞에 바친 예물
365 주 예수의 크신 은혜
367 주님께서 함께 계셔
357 주여 나를 감동하게
350 주여 자비 베푸소서
367 주께서 함께 계셔
351 창조주 하나님께
366 큰 축복을 받고
354 할렐루야

교독 기도

104 나와 함께 걸으소서
214 살아계신 주 성령
108 예수 말씀 듣고자

기도송

355 알렐루야
77 엘 샤다이
91 주님의 사랑과 그 영이
357 주여 나를 감동하게
142 주의 평화 내리소서

기도·축복송·기타 참조

기도로의 부름

324 고요한 안식 있는 곳
234 기억하소서
308 내 주를 가까이 하려 함은
214 살아계신 주 성령
330 여기 오소서
238 우리의 삶을 받아주소서
333 죄짐 맡은 우리 구주
378 주께로 가려네

말씀의 깨달음을 위한 기도

219 믿음의 영이여
214 살아계신 주 성령
108 예수 말씀 듣고자
218 오 성령이여 오소서
109 주 말씀은 나의 발에 등

평화의 인사

362 샬롬 카베림
361 샬롬을 비네
237 한 떡을 떼며

기쁨

75 기뻐하며 경배하세
114 내가 환난 당할 때에
130 맘 정결한 자들
155 성도여 기뻐 찬양해
260 세상의 구주께
382 영화로운 성도들과
344 예수 우리의 참된 기쁨
126 온 천하 거하는 만물아
118 온 땅의 모든 사람들
286 죄와 수치 무거운 짐
190 주 사셨다
189 주 예수 십자가에
334 주 예수여 은혜를
381 주 예수의 크신 사랑
301 주님의 기쁨은 나의 힘
91 주님의 사랑과 그 영이
62 참 아름다와라

돌림 노래

348 영광 영광
363 주 안에서 평안하라
141 주의 길 예비하라
142 주의 평화 내리소서

말씀과 가르침

110 거룩하다 성경은
108 예수 말씀 듣고자
112 이슬을 내리시듯 말씀을 내리소서
109 주 말씀은 나의 발에 등
111 주 하나님의 말씀이
113 주의 말씀 내리소서

말씀의 깨달음을 위한 기도
기도 · 축복송 · 기타 참조

믿음

315 겸손히 주를 섬길 때
279 나의 삶 속에서
282 두려움을 떨치고 소망을
335 둥지 안의 새들보다
219 믿음의 영이여
392 봉오리에 꽃 한 송이
73 사랑으로 다스리시는
307 잠잠하라
83 주 너를 독수리 날개 위에
301 주님의 기쁨은 나의 힘
78 하나님께 영광을
97 꽃이 필 때 믿음으로
그리스도인의 삶 참조

보혈 예수 그리스도: 예수의 보혈 참조

보호 인도 참조

봉사 제자의 도리와 봉사 참조

부활(절) 교회력 참조

빛

74 신비롭고 영원한 지혜의 주
281 온 땅에 가득히 주의 영광
338 이 작은 나의 빛
113 주의 말씀 내리소서
102 주의 빛 따르기 원합니다

사랑

175 갈릴리 맑은 바다
185 거룩한 사랑의 주님
86 그 크신 하나님의 사랑
68 다 찬양하여라
302 독수리 높은 둥지에
343 사랑하고 바라면서
290 아 하나님의 은혜로

345 아주 먼 옛날
220 여기 성령 함께 계시니
342 예수 사랑하심은
344 예수 우리의 참된 기쁨
273 주의 깊은 그 자비
341 천사처럼 말하여서

사순절 교회력 참조

사회 참여 정의 참조

삼위일체 (주일) 교회력 참조

새 하늘과 새 땅

389 강가에서 만나보자
324 고요한 안식 있는 곳
385 머지 않아서
379 믿음의 선한 싸움
392 봉오리에 꽃 한 송이
380 승리의 예수여
388 안식하는 하늘의 성도들
390 어린양 다스리시는
382 영화로운 성도들과
384 오라 하늘의 수레
391 저 높은 곳을 향하여
387 저 하늘 성도들과
381 주 예수의 크신 사랑
386 주여 좋은 아침
378 주께로 가려네
377 해 지는 저편
383 꿈을 꾸세 평화의 자녀

새로운 피조물

75 기뻐하며 경배하세
231 사망의 모든 권세 이기고
217 성령이여 진리 안에
287 예수를 내가 주로 믿어
286 죄와 수치 무거운 짐
체험 참조

새해

309 예수여 나의 손 꼭 잡고 가소서
325 우리의 삶을 주관하시는 주

선교와 봉사

138 가난해도 이웃에게
269 거룩한 불꽃 주시려
268 나 비록 연약하지만
261 너 가서 모든 자로
259 많은 사람들 참된 진리를
263 바다와 하늘의 주
266 빛의 사자들이여
260 세상의 구주께
270 예수 그리스도 모든 문제의 해결자
258 예수 이름으로

249 오 하나님의 교회
267 온 세상 위하여
 95 우리가 지금은 나그네 되어도
338 이 작은 나의 빛
262 작은 불꽃 하나가
360 주 앞에 바친 예물
265 주여 내가 여기 있나이다
264 주여 사랑의 빛을
　　전도 참조

선포 증거 참조

섬김 제자의 도리와 봉사; 증거 참조

섭리
101 나의 갈길 다 가도록
330 내 기도하는 그 시간
 60 높이 계신 주 찬양해
302 독수리 높은 둥지에
282 두려움을 떨치고 소망을
335 둥지 안의 새들보다
374 빛과 어둠 땅과 하늘
123 숨 쉬는 동안 주 찬양
325 우리 삶을 주관하시는
 83 주 너를 독수리 날개 위에
115 주는 나의 목자 되시니
291 주의 친절한 팔에 안기세
 62 참 아름다와라

성경
110 거룩하다 성경은
108 예수 말씀 듣고자
218 오 성령이여 오소서
112 이슬을 내리시듯 말씀을 내리소서
109 주 말씀은 나의 발에 등
111 주 하나님의 말씀이

성경 이야기
308 내 주를 가까이 하려 함은
181 사십일 동안 주님께서
342 예수 사랑하심은
179 예수 예수
177 예수님 이야기 내게 들려주오
169 오 놀랍고 아름다운
248 은혜 작은 불꽃이
151 저 동정녀 마리아
340 주의 말씀 배우는 믿음의 가정
314 하늘 향해 올라가네

성도의 사역 제자의 도리와 봉사 참조

성도추모일 (만성절) 교회력: 성도추모일 (만성절)

성령
225 나의 하나님 나의 삶을 다해

216 내 안에 계신 온유하신 주
219 믿음의 영이여
214 살아계신 주 성령
221 성령
223 성령을 따라서 찬양하리
224 성령이여 오셔서 정결케 하소서
217 성령이여 진리 안에
220 여기 성령 함께 계시니
212 영광스런 주님 전능하신 주
218 오 성령이여 오소서
222 주 믿는 성도들 날마다 기도해
 91 주님의 사랑과 그 영이
215 주님의 영이 여기 함께 계시니
213 주의 성령 느낄 때
　　교회력: 성령강림절; 삼위일체 (주일) 참조

성령강림(절) 교회력 참조

성만찬
 79 거룩 거룩 거룩
233 거룩 거룩 거룩 전능하신 주
234 기억하소서
239 모든 은사와 언어로
214 살아계신 주 성령
173 아멘 아멘
238 우리 삶을 받아주소서
150 인생들아 잠잠하라
240 자비로 그 몸 찢기시고
253 주 우릴 받아주심 본받게
360 주님 앞에 바친 예물
235 주님 떼어 주신 떡
191 주님은 죽음 이기시고
366 큰 축복을 받고
237 한 떡을 떼며
236 함께 주님의 떡을 나누세
9-27 **연합감리교회 한영찬송가**
5-28 **장로교 한영찬송가**

성육신
152 거룩하신 아기 예수
219 믿음의 영이여
162 베들레헴 작은 그 마을
165 사랑의 주님 예수
156 아기 예수 나셨네
201 알렐루야 알렐루야
211 임마누엘 임마누엘
164 하나님의 아들이 사람 몸을 입으사

성장 그리스도인의 삶 참조

성탄 교회력: 성탄 참조

세례
231 사망의 모든 권세 이기고
230 창조주 하나님 감사 찬송하세
232 축복하신 주의 자녀

28-58 연합감리교회 한영찬송가
29-40 장로교 한영찬송가

속죄
80   거룩하신 하나님 이름 높여
88   다 오라 복음 잔치에
182   다 이루었다
183   예수 나를 위하여
384   오라 하늘의 수레
93   저 나사렛 예수 앞에
78   하나님께 영광을
     구원 참조

송영   기도·축복송·기타 참조

순종
175   갈릴리 맑은 바다
223   성령을 따라서 순종하리
145   십자가 지라
320   예수 따라가며
287   예수를 내가 주로 믿어
96   풍랑 이는 바다 위로

슬픔
308   내 주를 가까이 하려 함은
60   높이 계신 주 찬양
380   승리의 예수여
105   예수 내 주께 (싸라남 싸라남)
309   예수여 나의 손 꼭 잡고 가소서
346   주 안의 깊은 평안

승리
389   강가에서 만나보자
75   기뻐하며 경배하세
174   높이 들라 사랑의 십자가
380   승리의 예수여
140   승리하리라
388   안식하는 하늘의 성도들
390   어린양 다스리시는
386   주여 좋은 아침
297   태산을 넘어 험곡에 가도

승천(일)   교회력: 승천 참조

시련과 극복
234   기억하소서
104   나와 함께 걸으소서
289   내 맘속의 음악 소리는
308   내 주를 가까이 하려 함은
304   내 평생에 가는 길
114   내가 환난 당할 때에
305   네 마음에 근심 있느냐
302   독수리 높은 둥지에
306   수고한 자 오라
140   승리하리라

303   아름답게 하셨네
105   예수 내 주께 (싸라남 싸라남)
342   예수 사랑하심은
309   예수여 나의 손 꼭 잡고 가소서
284   예수가 우리를 부르는 소리
307   잠잠하라
333   죄짐 맡은 우리 구주
301   주님의 기쁨은 나의 힘
98   향유가 있는 길르앗

시편
292   나는 주를 의지하리
295   내 진정 사모하는
304   내 평생에 가는 길
122   내가 깊은 곳에서
119   내가 산을 향하여
114   내가 환난 당할 때에
124   높은 곳에 계신 주님
130   맘 정결한 자들
116   목마른 사슴
123   숨 쉬는 동안 주 찬양
125   어하라디야 상사디야
293   오 놀라운 구세주
148   오소서
126   온 천하 거하는 만물아
118   온 땅의 모든 사람들
271   인애하신 구세주여
307   잠잠하라
323   주 사랑해
294   주 안에 있는 나에게
67   주 찬양 드리세
121   주 찬양하여라
115   주는 나의 목자 되시니
128   주님의 사람들
117   주여 우리 무리를
120   찬양하여라

신뢰와 확신
324   고요한 안식 있는 곳
280   구주 예수 피 흘리심
147   구주여 오소서
234   기억하소서
94   나 같은 죄인 살리신
329   나를 보내소서
279   나의 삶 속에서
318   내 구주 예수를 더욱 사랑
330   내 기도하는 그 시간
289   내 맘속의 음악 소리는
304   내 평생에 가는 길
299   날 대속하신 나의 구세주
283   다 함께 오라
302   독수리 높은 둥지에
282   두려움을 떨치고 소망을
335   둥지 안의 새들보다
385   머지 않아서

116   목마른 사슴
392   봉오리에 꽃 한 송이
319   부름받아 나선 이 몸
140   승리하리라
290   아 하나님의 은혜로
302   아름답게 하셨네
288   어찌 알 수 있나
332   여기 오소서
364   예수 내 주여
105   예수 내 주께 (싸라남 싸라남)
344   예수 우리의 참된 기쁨
320   예수 따라가며
284   예수가 우리를 부르는 소리
287   예수를 내가 주로 믿어
309   예수여 나의 손 꼭 잡고 가소서
293   오 놀라운 구세주
81   오 신실하신 주
281   온 하늘에 가득히 주의 영광
107   온종일 예수와 함께
271   인애하신 구세주여
349   자비 베푸소서
307   잠잠하라
394   저 높은 곳을 향하여
296   저 장미꽃 위에 이슬
286   죄와 수치 무거운 짐
83   주 너를 독수리 날개 위에
294   주 안에 있는 나에게
322   주 크신 사랑 가운데
285   주 하나님 독생자 예수
301   주님의 기쁨은 나의 힘
350   주여 자비 베푸소서
357   주여 나를 감동하게
298   주의 곁에 있을 때
291   주의 친절한 팔에 안기세
333   죄짐 맡은 우리 구주
297   태산을 넘어 험곡에 가도
300   하나님의 사랑을 사모하는 자
227   하늘의 주님 내려주소서
97   꽃이 필 때 믿음으로
    확신; 믿음 참조

신앙고백 (연합감리교회 한영찬송가)
532   니케야 신조
534   사도신경
535   기독교대한감리회 신앙고백
537   주기도문

신앙고백 (장로교 한영찬송가)
14   니케야 신조
15   사도신조
23   주님의 기도

심판
80   거룩하신 하나님 이름 높여

386   주여 좋은 아침
378   주께로 가려네

십자가
185   거룩한 사랑의 주님
186   거룩한 예수 무슨 죄가 있어
187   겟세마네 동산의 구세주
180   골짜기 외로운 길
277   구주의 십자가 보혈로
174   높이 들라 사랑의 십자가
182   다 이루었다
181   사십일 동안 주님께서
196   알렐루야 찬양하라
183   예수 나를 위하여
184   주 가시관을 쓰시고
59   하늘의 새와 물고기
178   흥분한 군중들이
    교회력: 사순절 참조

아침
80   거룩하신 하나님 이름 높여
299   날 대속하신 나의 구세주
371   새벽 하늘 밝히는
118   온 땅의 모든 사람들
369   저 아침해 뜰 때
370   첫 아침처럼

안수
261   너 가서 모든 자로
263   바다와 하늘의 주
319   부름 받아 나선 이 몸
380   승리의 예수여
254   오 우릴 연합하시는
265   주여 내가 여기 있나이다

어린이
337   세상 모든 어린이를
336   아이들아 주를 찬양하라
177   예수님 이야기 내게 들려주오

어린이 합창곡
153   고요히 그 아기 잠자네
158   구유 안에 누이신 마리아의 아기
229   거룩 거룩
157   그 어린 주 예수
252   나는 교회 너도 교회
198   내 사랑하는 그 이름
335   둥지 안의 새들보다
362   샬롬 카베림
361   샬롬을 비네
223   성령을 따라서 찬양하리
156   아기 예수 나셨네
173   아멘 아멘
159   어느 옛날 다윗 성에
332   여기 오소서

353 영광 영광
342 예수 사랑하심은
177 예수님 이야기 내게 들려주오
137 이 땅에 주의 평화
109 주 말씀은 나의 발에 등
65 주님의 능력
100 주여 나를 이끄사
213 주의 성령 느낄 때
62 참 아름다와라
370 첫 아침처럼
178 흥분한 군중들이
314 하늘 향해 올라가네
59 하늘의 새와 물고기
354 할렐루야
163 흰눈이 쌓이고 별 빛날 때

영생

130 맘 정결한 자들
385 머지 않아서
392 봉오리에 꽃 한 송이
123 숨 쉬는 동안 주 찬양
380 승리의 예수여
388 안식하는 하늘의 성도들
382 영화로운 성도들과
309 예수여 나의 손 꼭 잡고 가소서
384 오라 하늘의 수레
310 우리의 삶 예수 안에서
307 잠잠하라
188 주 부활하신 이 날
189 주 예수 십자가에
381 주 예수의 크신 사랑
285 주 하나님 독생자 예수
115 주 나의 목자 되시니
378 주께로 가려네

예배 시작

80 거룩하신 하나님 이름 높여
75 기뻐하며 경배하세
299 날 대속하신 나의 구세주
60 높이 계신 주 찬양해
174 높이 들라 사랑의 십자가
68 다 찬양하여라
283 다 함께 오라
123 숨 쉬는 동안 주 찬양
74 신비롭고 영원한 지혜 주
212 영광스런 주님 전능하신 주
126 온 천하 거하는 만물아
118 온 땅의 모든 사람들
190 주 사셨다
348 주 성전 안에
72 주의 백성 찬양
370 첫 아침처럼
178 흥분한 군중들이

예배로의 부름

80 거룩하신 하나님 이름 높여
204 경배해 위대한 주님께
207 기뻐하며 왕께 노래부르리
299 날 대속하신 나의 구세주
220 여기 성령 함께 계시니
126 온 천하 거하는 만물아
348 주 성전 안에
128 주님의 사람들
215 주님의 영이 여기 함께 계시니
141 주의 길 예비하라
370 첫 아침처럼

예수 그리스도

175 갈릴리 맑은 바다
204 경배해 위대한 주님께
101 나의 갈 길 다 가도록
206 내 모든 장래 지난 날
198 내 사랑하는 그 이름
295 내 진정 사모하는
305 네 마음에 근심 있느냐
317 내게 있는 향유 옥합
203 놀라운 그 이름
174 높이 들라 사랑의 십자가
200 다 와서 찬양해
130 맘 정결한 자들
173 아멘 아멘
369 아침해 솟을 때
355 알렐루야
201 알렐루야 알렐루야
196 알렐루야 찬양하라
270 예수 그리스도 모든 문제의 해결자
179 예수 예수
342 예수 사랑하심은
284 예수가 우리를 부르는 소리
199 예수는 가장 높으신
176 예수님 두 손 친절하신 손
177 예수님 이야기 내게 들려주오
168 예수를 보리
169 오 놀랍고 아름다운
281 온 땅에 가득히 주의 영광
328 우리를 고쳐주소서
170 이 세상이 시작되던
211 임마누엘 임마누엘
209 주 안에 평안 있고
346 주 안의 깊은 평안
205 주 예수보다 더 귀한 것은 없네
171 주 예수님 갈릴리 지나실 때
172 주님 보좌와 영광
210 주를 찬양하리라
113 주의 말씀 내리소서
341 천사처럼 말하여서

202 함께 주의 이름으로
178 흥분한 군중들이
      교회력: 강림절; 성탄절; 주현절 참조

예수 사랑
186 거룩한 예수 무슨 죄가 있어
187 겟세마네 동산의 구세주
280 구주 예수 피 흘리심
198 내 사랑하는 그 이름
355 알렐루야
342 예수 사랑하심은
272 어서 돌아오오
248 은혜 작은 불꽃이
346 주 안의 깊은 평안
381 주 예수의 크신 사랑
285 주 하나님 독생자 예수
333 죄짐 맡은 우리 구주

예수의 보혈
280 구주 예수 피 흘리심
 92 난 들었네 주 예수
219 믿음의 영이여
196 알렐루야 찬양하라
288 어찌 알 수 있나
183 예수 나를 위하여
287 예수를 내가 주로 믿어
 93 저 나사렛 예수 앞에
 78 하나님께 영광을

예수의 생애와 사역
175 갈릴리 맑은 바다
174 높이 들라 사랑의 십자가
173 아멘 아멘
196 알렐루야 찬양하라
179 예수 예수
199 예수는 가장 높으신
176 예수님 두 손 친절하신 손
177 예수님 이야기 내게 들려주오
168 예수를 보리
169 오 놀랍고 아름다운
170 이 세상이 시작되던
171 주 예수님 갈릴리 지나실 때
172 주님 보좌와 영광
178 흥분한 군중들이
      예수의 십자가 참조

예수의 이름
204 경배해 위대한 주님께
198 내 사랑하는 그 이름
203 놀라운 그 이름
 60 높이 계신 주 찬양해
174 높이 들라 사랑의 십자가
226 만 입이 내게 있으면
258 예수 이름으로
199 예수는 가장 높으신

296 저 장미꽃 위에 이슬
346 주 안의 깊은 평안
 91 주님의 사랑과 그 영이
 72 주의 백성 찬양

예수의 주권
152 거룩하신 아기 예수
 60 높이 계신 주 찬양해
219 믿음의 영이여
156 아기 예수 나셨다
201 알렐루야 알렐루야

예수 찬양
204 경배해 위대한 주님께
207 기뻐하며 왕께 노래부르리
206 내 모든 장래 지난 날
198 내 사랑하는 그 이름
203 놀라운 그 이름
200 다 와서 찬양해
355 알렐루야
201 알렐루야 알렐루야
208 예수 사랑해요
199 예수는 가장 높으신
211 임마누엘 임마누엘
209 주 안에 평안 있고
205 주 예수보다 더 귀한 것은 없네
210 주를 찬양하리라
202 함께 주의 이름으로

용기
104 나와 함께 걸으소서
216 내 안에 계신 온유하신 주
302 독수리 높은 둥지에
282 두려움을 떨치고 소망을
140 승리하리라
105 예수 내 주께 (싸라남 싸라남)
307 잠잠하라

용서
373 고요히 머리 숙여
276 고통의 멍에 벗으려고
280 구주 예수 피 흘리심
274 살피소서 내 맘을
311 새로운 삶을 시작하는
303 아름답게 하셨네
271 인애하신 구세주여
273 주의 깊은 그 자비
288 어찌 알 수 있나
275 여러 해 동안 주 떠나
258 예수 이름으로
 81 오 신실하신 주
310 우리의 삶은 예수 안에서
286 죄와 수치 무거운 짐
253 주 우릴 받아주심 본받게
285 주 하나님 독생자 예수

327 주님의 뜻을 이루소서
265 주여 내가 여기 있나이다
326 주여 바로 접니다
376 주여 햇빛 저무니
78 하나님께 영광을
278 항상 진실케
377 해 지는 저편
　회개 참조

은혜와 평안

94 나 같은 죄인 살리신
304 내 평생에 가는 길
127 복의 근원 강림하사
290 아 하나님의 은혜로
342 예수 사랑하심은
284 예수가 우리를 부르는 소리
287 예수를 내가 주로 믿어
293 오 놀라운 구세주
347 우리 다시 만날 때까지
310 우리의 삶 예수 안에서
333 죄짐 맡은 우리 구주
346 주 안의 깊은 평안
90 주 호숫가에 오셔서
91 주님의 사랑과 그 영이
326 주여 바로 접니다
273 주의 깊은 그 자비
144 큰 소망 중에 살리라
59 하늘의 새와 물고기

인도

315 겸손히 주를 섬길 때
104 나와 함께 걸으소서
101 나의 갈 길 다 가도록
105 예수 내 주께 (싸라남 싸라남)
344 예수 우리의 참된 기쁨
81 오 신실하신 주
107 온종일 예수와 함께
334 우리 다시 만날 때까지
103 이 마음 주께로
115 주 나의 목자 되시니
100 주여 나를 이끄사
102 주의 빛 따르기 원합니다
64 찬란하고 빛난 하늘
106 캄캄한 밤중에 빈들에서
　평안 참조

일치단결

252 나는 교회 너도 교회
254 오 우릴 연합하시는
249 오 하나님의 교회
250 완전하게 하시는 복의 근원 예수여
253 주 우릴 받아주심 본받게
251 주의 종들 여기 모여

임명식·임직

263 바다와 하늘의 주
319 부름 받아 나선 이 몸
266 빛의 사자들이여
267 온 세상 위하여
360 주 앞에 바친 예물
265 주여 내가 여기 있나이다

임재　예수 그리스도; 성령 참조

입당·헌당

252 나는 교회 너도 교회
256 시온성과 같은 교회
360 주 앞에 바친 예물

자비

70 온 세상 우리 주님 손 안에
118 온 땅의 모든 사람들
273 주의 깊은 그 자비
　사랑 참조

자연

118 온 땅의 모든 사람들
346 주 안의 깊은 평안
67 주 찬양 드리세
65 주 하나님의 능력
64 찬란하고 빛난 하늘
370 첫 아침처럼
71 하늘과 땅을 지으신 주
59 하늘의 새와 물고기

자유

280 구주 예수 피 흘리심
182 다 이루었다
140 승리하리라

장례와 추도식

389 강가에서 만나보자
255 교회의 참된 터는
86 그 크신 하나님의 사랑
385 머지 않아서
392 봉오리에 꽃 한 송이
123 숨 쉬는 동안 주 찬양
380 승리의 예수여
388 안식하는 하늘의 성도들
390 어린양 다스리시는
382 영화로운 성도들과
309 예수여 나의 손 꼭 잡고 가소서
384 오라 하늘의 수레
307 잠잠하라
381 주 예수의 크신 사랑
115 주 나의 목자 되시니
391 저 높은 곳을 향하여
387 저 하늘 성도들과
386 주여 좋은 아침

378 주께로 가려네
297 태산을 넘어 험곡에 가도
377 해 지는 저편
영생; 새 하늘과 새 땅 참조

재의 수요일 교회력: 재의 수요일 참조

저녁
373 고요히 머리숙여
375 낮이 지나가고
374 빛과 어둠 땅과 하늘
362 샬롬 카베림
361 샬롬을 비네
363 주 안에서 평안하라
376 주여 오늘 하루가
142 주의 평화 내리소서
366 큰 축복을 받고
377 해 지는 저편
372 땅 위에도 바다에도

전도와 선교
269 거룩한 불꽃 주시려
268 나 비록 연약하지만
265 내가 여기 있나이다
261 너 가서 모든 자로
259 많은 사람들 참된 진리를
263 바다와 하늘의 주
266 빛의 사자들이여
260 세상의 구주께
270 예수 그리스도 모든 문제의 해결자
258 예수 이름으로
267 온 세상 위하여
 95 우리가 지금은 나그네 되어도
262 작은 불꽃 하나가
265 주여 내가 여기 있나이다
264 주여 사랑의 빛을

정의
138 가난해도 이웃에게
261 너 가서 모든 자로
136 너희는 먼저 주의 나라와
260 세상의 구주께
140 승리하리라
143 시온의 영광이 빛나는 아침
145 십자가 지라
148 오소서
137 이 땅에 주의 평화
146 정의가 강물처럼
139 주 하나님의 음성이 우리를 부르네
141 주의 길 예비하라
142 주의 평화 내리소서
144 큰 소망 중에 살리라
149 평화의 나라 임하시니

제자의 도리와 봉사
315 겸손히 주를 섬길 때
277 구주의 십자가 보혈로
268 나 비록 연약하지만
316 나 주의 도움 받고자
312 나의 삶을 주 위해
318 내 구주 예수를 더욱 사랑
313 내 마음 주께 바치옵니다
321 내 주 되신 주를 참 사랑하고
308 내 주를 가까이 하려 함은
214 살아계신 주 성령
257 성령 안에서 우리 하나
260 세상의 구주께
306 수고한 자 오라
145 십자가 지라
320 예수 따라가며
284 예수가 우리를 부르는 소리
168 예수를 보리
107 온종일 예수와 함께
347 우리 다시 만날 때까지
310 우리의 삶은 예수 안에서
103 이 마음 주께로
391 저 높은 곳을 향하여
333 죄짐 맡은 우리 구주
294 주 안에 있는 나에게
 90 주 호숫가에 오셔서
301 주님의 기쁨은 나의 힘
291 주의 친절한 팔에 안기세
 89 지금까지 지내온 것
 64 찬란하고 빛난 하늘
144 큰 소망 중에 살리라
149 평화의 나라 임하시니
 96 풍랑 이는 바다 위로
314 하늘 향해 올라가네
 97 꽃이 필 때 믿음으로
헌신; 그리스도인의 삶 참조

죄와 고백
276 고통의 멍에 벗으려고
277 구주의 십자가 보혈로
274 살피소서 내 맘을
272 어서 돌아오오
275 여러 해 동안 주 떠나
271 인애하신 구세주여
273 주의 깊은 그 자비
276 항상 진실케

죄와 참회 죄와 고백 참조

종려 · 고난주일 (주간)
교회력: 종려 · 고난주일 (주간) 참조

주님의 만찬
성만찬 참조

주 변모일

교회력: 주 변모일 참조

주현절

교회력: 주현절 참조

죽음　장례와 추도식 참조

중생　회개 참조

증거

315　겸손히 주를 섬길 때
255　교회의 참된 터는
292　나는 주를 의지하리
312　나의 삶을 주 위해
198　내 사랑하는 그 이름
216　내 안에 계신 온유하신 주
261　너 가서 모든 자로
174　높이 들라 사랑의 십자가
226　만 입이 내게 있으면
260　세상의 구주께
201　알렐루야 알렐루야
258　예수 이름으로
199　예수는 가장 높으신
338　이 작은 나의 빛
262　작은 불꽃 하나가
205　주 예수보다 더 귀한 것은 없네
61　주 하나님 지으신 세계
301　주님의 기쁨은 나의 힘
128　주님의 사람들
72　주의 백성 찬양
366　큰 축복을 받고
98　향유가 있는 길르앗

찬미

80　거룩하신 하나님 이름 높여
75　기뻐하며 경배하세
207　기뻐하며 왕께 노래 부르리
225　나의 하나님 나의 삶을 다해
317　내게 있는 향유 옥합
129　노래로 주께 영광 돌리며
132　눈을 들어
131　다 나와서 노래하자
200　다 와서 찬양해
135　두 손 들고 찬양합니다
259　많은 사람들 참된 진리를
130　맘 정결한 자들
127　복의 근원 강림하사
134　사랑으로 천지 만물
345　아주 먼 옛날
87　왕이신 나의 하나님
133　좋은 날 기쁜 날
128　주님의 사람들
210　주를 찬양하리라

참회의 기도

280　구주 예수 피 흘리심
364　예수 내 주여
310　우리의 삶은 예수 안에서
286　죄와 수치 무거운 짐
285　주 하나님 독생자 예수
326　주여 바로 접니다
273　주의 깊은 그 자비

　　회개 참조

창조

80　거룩하신 하나님 이름 높여
75　기뻐하며 경배하세
225　나의 하나님 나의 삶을 다해
124　높은 곳에 계신 주님
60　높이 계신 주 찬양해
68　다 찬양하여라
302　독수리 높은 둥지에
335　둥지 안의 새들보다
352　만복의 근원 하나님
69　빛 있으라
73　사랑으로 다스리시는
123　숨 쉬는 동안 주 찬양
74　신비롭고 영원한 지혜의 주
63　아름다운 모든 것
66　아버지의 사랑으로
77　엘샤다이
212　영광스런 주님 전능하신 주
70　온 세상 우리 주님 손 안에
126　온 천하 거하는 만물아
118　온 땅의 모든 사람들
325　우리의 삶을 주관하시는
83　주 너를 독수리 날개 위에
67　주 찬양 드리세
61　주 하나님 지으신 세계
65　주 하나님의 능력
64　찬란하고 빛난 하늘
62　참 아름다와라
78　하나님께 영광을
71　하늘과 땅을 지으신 주
59　하늘의 새와 물고기
227　하늘의 주님 내려오소서

　　하나님 참조

창조주 하나님　창조; 하나님 참조

천국

389　강가에서 만나보자
385　머지 않아서
390　어린양 다스리시는
384　오라 하늘의 수레
387　저 하늘 성도들과
381　주 예수의 크신 사랑
378　주께로 가려네

213 주의 성령 느낄 때
377 해 지는 저편
　　영원; 하나님 나라; 새 하늘과 새 땅 참조

청지기
360 주 앞에 바친 예물
97 꽃이 필 때 믿음으로

체험
280 구주 예수 피 흘리심
88 다 오라 복음 잔치에
219 믿음의 영이여
214 살아계신 주 성령
303 아름답게 하셨네
258 예수 이름으로
262 작은 불꽃 하나가

초청　그리스도인의 삶 참조

추수　감사(절) 참조

출애굽　구원; 인도 참조

충성　헌신; 제자의 도리와 봉사 참조

치유
176 예수님 두 손 친절하신 손
168 예수를 보리
328 우리를 고쳐주소서
171 주 예수님 갈릴리 지나실 때
98 향유가 있는 길르앗

친교
255 교회의 참된 터는
252 나는 교회 너도 교회
257 성령 안에서 우리 하나
212 영광스런 주님 전능하신 주
249 오 하나님의 교회
107 온종일 예수와 함께
250 완전하게 하시는 복의 근원 예수여
253 주 우릴 받아주심 본받게

친구
295 내 진정 사모하는
296 저 장미꽃 위에 이슬
333 죄짐 맡은 우리 구주

평안
324 고요한 안식 있는 곳
214 살아계신 주 성령
362 샬롬 카베림
361 샬롬을 비네
347 우리 다시 만날 때까지
220 여기 성령 함께 계시니
307 잠잠하라

346 주 안의 깊은 평안
113 주의 말씀 내리소서
142 주의 평화 내리소서
373 땅 위에도 바다에도

평안과 위로
324 고요한 안식 있는 곳
292 나는 주를 의지하리
304 내 평생에 가는 길
305 네 마음에 근심 있느냐
302 독수리 높은 둥지에
335 둥지 안의 새들보다
392 봉오리에 꽃 한 송이
214 살아계신 주 성령
362 샬롬 카베림
361 샬롬을 비네
306 수고한 자 오라
123 숨 쉬는 동안 주 찬양
220 여기 성령 함께 계시니
105 예수 내 주께 (싸라남 싸라남)
309 예수여 나의 손 꼭 잡고 가소서
347 우리 다시 만날 때까지
307 잠잠하라
83 주 너를 독수리 날개 위에
346 주 안의 깊은 평안
115 주 나의 목자 되시니
301 주님의 기쁨은 나의 힘
113 주의 말씀 내리소서
142 주의 평화 내리소서
377 해 지는 저편
372 땅 위에도 바다에도

평화
138 가난해도 이웃에게
347 고요한 안식 있는 곳
174 높이 들라 사랑의 십자가
214 살아계신 주 성령
362 샬롬 카베림
361 샬롬을 비네
220 여기 성령 함께 계시니
148 오소서
334 우리 다시 만날 때까지
137 이 땅에 주의 평화
307 잠잠하라
346 주 안의 깊은 평안
113 주의 말씀 내리소서
142 주의 평화 내리소서
144 큰 소망 중에 살리라
372 땅 위에도 바다에도
　　평안과 위로 참조

평화의 인사　기도·축복송·기타 참조

하나님
229 거룩 거룩

79   거룩 거룩 거룩
233   거룩 거룩 거룩 전능하신 주
82   거룩 거룩 거룩하신 주
80   거룩하신 하나님 이름 높여
86   그 크신 하나님의 사랑
75   기뻐하며 경배하세
225   나의 하나님 나의 삶을 다해
124   높은 곳에 계시 주님
60   높이 계신 주 찬양해
68   다 찬양하여라
302   독수리 높은 둥지에
352   만복의 근원 하나님
73   사랑으로 다스리시는
85   사랑하는 나의 아버지
123   숨 쉬는 동안 주 찬양
74   신비롭고 영원한 지혜의 주
63   아름다운 모든 것
66   아버지의 사랑으로
77   엘샤다이
353   영광 영광
212   영광스런 주님 전능하신 주
81   오 신실하신 주
70   온 세상 우리 주님 손 안에
118   온 땅의 모든 사람들
87   왕이신 나의 하나님
325   우리의 삶을 주관하시는
83   주 너를 독수리 날개 위에
67   주 찬양 드리세
61   주 하나님 지으신 세계
65   주 하나님의 능력
72   주의 백성 찬양
64   찬란하고 빛난 하늘
62   참 아름다와라
228   하나님 사랑과 경배 드립니다
76   하나님을 찬양하세
78   하나님께 영광을
71   하늘과 땅을 지으신 주
84   하늘에 가득찬 영광의 하나님
59   하늘의 새와 물고기
227   하늘의 주님 내려주소서
354   할렐루야

하나님 나라

138   가난해도 이웃에게
80   거룩하신 하나님 이름 높여
255   교회의 참된 터는
136   너희는 먼저 주의 나라와
256   시온성과 같은 교회
143   시온의 영광이 빛나는 아침
145   십자가 지라
390   어린양 다스리시는
137   이 땅에 주의 평화
139   주 하나님의 음성이 우리를 부르네
100   주여 나를 이끄사

62   참 아름다와라
    새 하늘과 새 땅 참조

하나됨

252   나는 교회 너도 교회
254   오 우릴 연합하시는
249   오 하나님의 교회
250   완전하게 하시는 복의 근원 예수여
253   주 우릴 받아주심 본받게
251   주의 종들 여기에 모여

합창과 후렴

204   경배해 위대한 주님께
234   기억하소서
279   나의 삶 속에서
136   너희는 먼저 주의 나라와
203   놀라운 그 이름
283   다 함께 오라
214   살아계신 주 성령
303   아름답게 하셨네
355   알렐루야
220   여기 성령 함께 계시니
211   임마누엘 임마누엘
83   주 너를 독수리 날개 위에
91   주님의 사랑과 그 영이
357   주여 나를 감동하게
228   하나님 사랑과 경배 드립니다
237   한 떡을 떼며
354   할렐루야
    돌림 노래 참조

해방   자유 참조

헌신

315   겸손히 주를 섬길 때
316   나 주의 도움 받고자
331   나를 보내소서
312   나의 삶을 주 위해
299   날 대속하신 나의 구세주
318   내 구주 예수를 더욱 사랑
313   내 마음 주께 바치옵니다
321   내 주 되신 주를 참 사랑하고
317   내게 있는 향유 옥합
319   부름 받아 나선 이 몸
311   새로운 삶을 시작하는
145   십자가 지라
320   예수 따라가며
254   오 우릴 연합하시는
310   우리의 삶은 예수 안에서
238   우리의 삶을 받아주소서
338   이 작은 나의 빛
137   이 땅에 주의 평화
391   저 높은 곳을 향하여
322   주 크신 사랑 가운데
357   주여 나를 감동하게

265　주여 내가 여기 있나이다
102　주의 빛 따르기 원합니다
96　풍랑 이는 바다 위로
300　하나님의 사랑을 사모하는 자
314　하늘 향해 올라가네
　　신뢰 참조

화해

343　사랑하고 바라면서
311　새로운 삶을 시작하는
362　샬롬 카베링
361　샬롬을 비네
253　주 우릴 받아주심 본받게

확신

279　나의 삶 속에서
289　내 맘속의 음악 소리는
136　너희는 먼저 주의 나라와
335　둥지 안의 새들보다
288　어찌 알 수 있나
342　예수 사랑하심은
199　예수는 가장 높으신
293　오 놀라운 구세주
70　온 세상 우리 주님 손 안에
93　저 나사렛 예수 앞에
322　주 크신 사랑 가운데
65　주 하나님의 능력
115　주 나의 목자 되시니
142　주의 평화 내리소서
62　참 아름다와라
144　큰 소망 중에 살리라
98　향유가 있는 길르앗

환난 시련 참조

회개

276　고통의 멍에 벗으려고
280　구주 예수 피 흘리심
274　살피소서 내 맘을
311　새로운 삶을 시작하는
303　아름답게 하셨네
258　예수 이름으로
288　어찌 알 수 있나
275　여러 해 동안 주 떠나

81　오 신실하신 주
310　우리의 삶 예수 안에서
271　인애하신 구세주여
286　죄와 수치 무거운 짐
253　주 우릴 받아주심 본받게
285　주 하나님 독생자 예수
327　주님의 뜻을 이루소서
265　주여 내가 여기 있나이다
326　주여 바로 접니다
376　주여 햇빛 저무니
273　주의 깊은 그 자비
278　항상 진실케
　　용서 참조

희망

269　거룩한 불꽃 주시려
324　고요한 안식 있는 곳
147　구주여 오소서
234　기억하소서
94　나 같은 죄인 살리신
292　나는 주를 의지하리
279　나의 삶 속에서
318　내 구주 예수를 더욱 사랑
330　내 기도하는 그 시간
358　들으소서 우리 기도 드릴 때
385　머지 않아서
392　봉오리에 꽃 한 송이
140　승리하리라
364　예수 내 주여
344　예수 우리의 참된 기쁨
309　예수여 나의 손 꼭 잡고 가소서
81　오 신실하신 주
107　온종일 예수와 함께
222　주 믿는 성도들 날마다 기도해
322　주 크신 사랑 가운데
357　주여 나를 감동하게
326　주여 바로 접니다
350　주여 자비 베푸소서
213　주의 성령 느낄 때
97　꽃이 필 때 믿음으로

희생

그리스도인의 삶; 헌신; 제자의 도리와 봉사;
청지기; 증거 참조

TOPICS AND CATEGORIES

ADORATION AND PRAISE

118	All people that on earth do dwell
355	Alleluia
116	As the Deer
133	Blessed day, happy day
200	Come on and celebrate
131	Come one and all
127	Come, thou fount of every blessing
100	Dear Lord, lead me day by day
77	El Shaddai
225	Father, I adore you
228	Father, we love you (Glorify thy name)
85	Father in heaven how we love you
126	From all that dwell below the skies
247	Give thanks
353	Gloria, gloria
59	God of the sparrow God of the whale
134	God who created all
64	God, who stretched the spangled heavens
73	God, whose love is reigning o'er us
81	Great is thy faithfulness
354	Heleluyan (Alleluia)
80	Holy God, we praise thy name
79	Holy, holy, holy! Lord God almighty
82	Holy, holy, holy is the Lord
210	I just want to praise you
135	I lift my hands
65	I sing the almighty power of God
123	I'll praise my maker while I've breath
74	Immortal, invisible, God only wise
75	Joyful, joyful, we adore thee
67	Let's sing unto the Lord
84	Lord God, thy glory
71	Many and Great, O God
370	Morning has broken
87	My Savior, my King
226	O for a thousand tongues to sing
227	O God in Heaven
61	O Lord my God (How great thou art)
169	O wondrous sight! O vision fair
83	On Eagle's Wings
132	Open your eyes
230	Praise and thanksgiving be to God
352	Praise God, from whom all blessings
336	Praise him, all ye little children
124	Praise the Lord who reigns above
76	Praise to the Lord
68	Praise to the Lord, the almighty
207	Shout for joy and sing
60	Sing praise to God who reigns above

91	Spirit song (O let the Son of God)
121	Sing, praise and bless the Lord
128	Stand up and bless the Lord
188	The day of resurrection
115	The Lord's my shepherd, I'll not want
62	This is my Father's world
78	To God be the glory
202	We have come into his house
72	We, thy people, praise thee
291	What a fellowship, what a joy divine
129	When in our music God is glorified

ADVENT See Christian Year

AFFIRMATION OF FAITH

The Korean-English United Methodist Hymnal

533	The Nicene Creed
534	The Apostles' Creed
536	A Statement of Faith of The Korean Methodist Church
537	The Lord's Prayer

The Korean-English Presbyterian Hymnal

14	The Nicene Creed
16	The Apostles' Creed
24	The Lord's Prayer

AFFLICTION AND COMFORT

307	Be still, my soul
306	Come all ye that labor
104	I want Jesus to walk with me
342	Jesus loves me!
105	Jesus, Savior, Lord (Saranam, Saranam)
308	Nearer, my God, to thee
305	O soul, are you weary?
309	Precious Lord, take my hand
234	Remember Me
284	Softly and tenderly Jesus is calling
303	Something beautiful
302	The care the eagle gives her young
301	The joy of the Lord
114	The Lord hear thee
98	There is a balm in Gilead
289	There's within my heart a melody
140	We shall overcome
333	What a friend we have in Jesus
304	When peace, like a river, attendeth

ALL SAINTS DAY See Christian Year

ASCENSION See Christian Year

ASH WEDNESDAY See Christian Year

ASPIRATION AND RESOLVE
281 Christ, whose glory fills the skies
97 Faith, while trees are still in blossom
224 Holy Spirit, breathe on me
322 O love that wilt not let me go
132 Open your eyes

ASSURANCE
293 A wonderful Savior is Jesus my Lord
335 Children of the heavenly Father
142 Dona nobis pacem
70 He's got the whole world in his hands
288 How can we sinners know
65 I sing the almighty power of God
93 I stand amazed in the presence
342 Jesus loves me!
199 Jesus! the name high over all
144 Live into hope
322 O love that wilt not let me go
136 Seek ye first
115 The Lord's my shepherd, I'll not want
98 There is a balm in Gilead
289 There's within my heart a melody
62 This is my Father's world
279 Through it all

ATONEMENT See Jesus Christ

BAPTISM
232 Child of blessing, child of promise
230 Praise and thanksgiving be to God
231 We Know that Christ is raised
22-58 The Korean-English UM Hymnal
30-41 The Korean-English Presbyterian Hymnal

BIBLE
111 Almighty God, your word is cast
112 As dew falls gently at night
108 Blessed Jesus, at thy word
218 Come, Holy Ghost, our hearts inspire
110 Holy Bible, Book divine
109 Thy word is a lamp

BIBLICAL NARRATIVE
340 God, give us Christian homes
179 Jesu, Jesu
342 Jesus loves me!
181 Lord, who throughout these forty
308 Nearer, my God, to thee
169 O wondrous sight! O vision fair
248 See how great a flame aspires

177 Tell me the stories of Jesus
151 To a maid engaged to Joseph
314 We are climbing Jacob's ladder

BLOOD OF JESUS See Jesus Christ

CALL TO PRAYER
See Service Music: Invitation to Prayer

CALL TO CHRISTIAN LIFE See Christian Life

CALL TO WORSHIP See Service Music

CALMNESS AND SERENITY
307 Be still, my soul
142 Dona nobis pacem
347 God be with you till we meet again
372 Now, on land and sea descending
113 Send your word
362 Shalom
361 Shalom to you
214 Spirit of the living God
324 There is a place of quiet rest
(Near to the heart of God)
220 There is a sweet, sweet Spirit
346 Thou hidden source of calm repose

CHILDREN
337 Jesus loves the little children
336 Praise him, all ye little children
177 Tell me the stories of Jesus

CHILDREN'S CHOIR SELECTION
173 Amen, Amen
157 Away in a manger
335 Children of the heavenly Father
100 Dear Lord, lead me day by day
213 Every time I feel the Spirit
178 Filled with excitement
158 Gentle Mary laid her child
353 Gloria, gloria
59 God of the sparrow God of the whale
156 He is born
354 Heleluyan (Alleluia)
229 Holy, holy
252 I am the church! You are the church
65 I sing the almighty power of God
223 I'm goin'a sing when the spirit says
342 Jesus loves me!
332 Kum ba yah (Come by here)
137 Let there be peace on earth
370 Morning has broken
159 Once in royal David's city
362 Shalom
361 Shalom to you

153 Still, still, still
177 Tell me the stories of Jesus
163 The snow lay on the ground
198 There is a name I love
62 This is my Father's world
109 Thy word is a lamp
314 We are climbing Jacob's ladder

CHORUSES AND REFRAINS
355 Alleluia
283 Come, let us reason
211 Emmanuel, Emmanuel
228 Father, we love you (Glorify thy name)
354 Heleluyan (Alleluia)
203 His name is wonderful
204 Majesty, worship his majesty
357 Move me
83 On eagle's wings
237 One bread, one body
234 Remember me
136 Seek ye first
303 Something beautiful
214 Spirit of the living God
91 Spirit song (O let the Son of God)
220 There's a sweet, sweet Spirit
279 Through it all
    See also Rounds

CHRIST   See Jesus Christ

CHRISTIAN EXPERIENCE
280 And can it be that I should gain
88 Come, sinners, to the gospel feast
258 God forgave my sin (Freely, freely)
262 It only takes a spark (Pass it on)
303 Something beautiful
219 Spirit of faith, come down
214 Spirit of the living God

CHRISTIAN LIFE
319 Called of God, we honor the call
306 Come all ye that labor
272 Come back quickly to the Lord
88 Come, sinners, to the gospel feast
103 Draw thou my soul, O Christ
97 Faith, while trees are still in blossom
275 Far from the Lord I wandered
149 God brings the kingdom
334 Heart longings, Lord Jesus
135 I lift my hands
296 In the garden (I come to the garden)
96 Jesus calls us
316 Jesus, my Lord, to thee I cry
146 Justice comes as river water flow
144 Live into hope

90 Lord, you have come to the lakeshore
318 More love to thee
313 My heart I give unto you
175 My heart is little Galilee
321 My Jesus, I love thee
308 Nearer, my God, to thee
315 O master, let me walk with thee
89 O, the help that God has given
284 Softly and tenderly Jesus is calling
91 Spirit song (O let the Son of God enfold)
312 Take my life, and let it be
145 Take up thy cross
301 The joy of the Lord
294 The trusting heart to Jesus clings
297 Walking in sunlight all of my journey
314 We are climbing Jacob's ladder
257 We are one in the Spirit
291 What a fellowship, what a joy divine
333 What a friend we have in Jesus
320 When we walk with the Lord
    See also Commitment

CHRISTIAN YEAR
Advent
148 Come, now, O Price of peace
211 Emmanuel, Emmanuel
149 God brings the kingdom
102 I want to walk as a child of the light
152 Infant holy, infant lowly
150 Let all mortal flesh keep silence
165 Loving Lord Jesus
167 Morning Star, O Cheering Sight
141 Prepare the way of the Lord
113 Send your word
151 To a maid engaged to Joseph
162 In the little village of Bethlehem
154 What child is this
147 While we are waiting, come

Christmas
157 Away in a manger
158 Gentle Mary laid her child
164 God who came in human form
    (God almighty, ruling the world)
155 Good Christian friends, rejoice
156 He is born
162 In the little village of Bethlehem
152 Infant holy, infant lowly
161 Joy to the world
165 Loving Lord Jesus
159 Once in royal David's city
160 Silent night! Holy night!
166 Sing we now of Christmas
153 Still, still, still
163 The snow lay on the ground

172   Thou didst leave thy throne
154   What child is this

Epiphany

281   Christ, whose glory fills the skies
155   Good Christian friends, rejoice
156   He is born
162   In the little village of Bethlehm
152   Infant holy, infant lowly
159   Once in royal David's city
166   Sing we now of Christmas

Transfiguration

281   Christ, whose glory fills the skies
169   O wondrous sight! o vision fair

Ash Wednesday

180   Jesus walked this lonesome valley
181   Lord, who throughout these forty days

Lent

186   Ah, holy Jesus
277   Down at the cross
178   Filled with excitement
187   Go to dark Gethsemane
183   Jesus shed his blood for me
180   Jesus walked this lonesome valley
174   Lift high the cross
181   Lord, who throughout these forty days
185   O love divine, what has thou done
182   'Tis finished! the Messiah dies
184   To mock your reign, O dearest Lord
    See also Cross

Passion · Palm Sunday

186   Ah, holy Jesus
277   Down at the cross
178   Filled with excitement
187   Go to dark Gethsemane
183   Jesus shed his blood for me
185   O love divine, what has thou done
177   Tell me the stories of Jesus
182   'Tis finished! the Messiah dies
184   To mock your reign, O dearest Lord

Holy Week

186   Ah, holy Jesus
178   Filled with excitement
187   Go to dark Gethsemane
179   Jesu, Jesu
183   Jesus shed his blood for me
185   O love divine, what hast thou done
182   'Tis finished! the messiah dies
184   To mock your reign, o dearest
    See also Holy Communion

Easter

355   Alleluia
201   Alleluia, Alleluia
197   Alleluia! Christ is risen
         (Resurrection canon)
196   Alleluia! Sing to Jesus
191   Because he died and is risen
190   Christ is alive!
193   Christ the Lord is risen today
281   Christ, whose glory fills the skies
285   God sent his Son (Because he lives)
296   In the garden (I come to the garden)
195   Jesus, beloved Lord
192   Low in the grave he lay
382   Sing with all the saints in glory
188   The day of resurrection
189   They crucified my Savior (He rose)
194   Thine be the glory

Ascension

196   Alleluia! Sing to Jesus
190   Christ is alive!
188   The day of resurrection
189   They crucified my Savior (He rose)

Pentecost

191   Because he died and is risen
218   Come, Holy Ghost, our hearts inspire
213   Every time I feel the Spirit
225   Father, I adore you
228   Father, we love you
224   Holy Spirit, breathe on me
217   Holy Spirit, come, confirm us
216   How like gentle Spirit
223   I'm goin' a sing when the Spirit says
222   Let every Christian pray
212   Many gifts, one Spirit
227   O God in heaven
248   See how great a flame aspires
221   Spirit
219   Spirit of faith, come down
214   Spirit of the living God
 91   Spirit song
         (O let the Son of God)
215   Surely the presence of the Lord
220   There's a sweet, sweet Spirit
    See also Holy Spirit

Trinity (Sunday)

225   Father, I adore you
228   Father, we love you
 80   Holy God, we praise thy name
229   Holy, holy
226   O for a thousand tongues to sing

227   O God in heaven
230   Praise and thanksgiving be to God

All Saints Day
380   Christ the Victorious
387   Come, let us join our friends
388   For all the saints
235   For the bread which you have broken
389   Shall we gather at the river
255   The church's one foundation
      See New Heaven and New Earth

Christ the King
201   Alleluia, Alleluia
148   Come now, O Prince of peace
203   His name is wonderful
204   Majesty, worship his majesty
207   Shout for joy and sing

CHRISTMAS See Christian Year

CHURCH
360   Bless thou the gifts
254   Blest be the dear uniting love
267   Christ for the whole wide world
250   Christ, from whom all blessings flow
268   Even though I'm forever weak
256   Glorious things of thee are spoken
143   Hail to the brightness
253   Help us accept each other
266   Heralds of light, speed away
251   Here, O Lord, your servants gather
252   I am the church! You are the church
222   Let every Christian pray
249   O church of God, united
248   See how great a flame aspires
255   The church's one foundation
257   We are one in the Spirit

Community in Christ
107   All day long
250   Christ, from whom all blessings flow
253   Help us accept each other
252   I am the church! You are the church
212   Many gifts, one Spirit
249   O Church of God, united
237   One bread, one body

Dedication of a Building
360   Bless thou the gifts
256   Glorious things of thee are spoken
252   I am the church! you are the church

Ecumenism
387   Come, let us join our friends

212   Many gifts, one Spirit
237   One bread, one body

COMFORT AND ENCOURAGEMENT
307   Be still, my soul
377   Beyond the sunset
335   Children of the heavenly Father
306   Come all ye that labor
142   Dona nobis pacem
347   God be with you till we meet again
292   I will trust in the Lord
392   In the bulb there is a flower
123   I'll praise my maker while I've breath
105   Jesus, Savior, Lord (Saranam, Saranam)
372   Now, on land and sea descending
305   O soul, are you weary?
 83   On eagle's wings
309   Precious Lord, take my hand
113   Send your word
362   Shalom
361   Shalom to you
113   Spirit of the living God
302   The care the eagle gives her young
301   The joy of the Lord
115   The Lord's my shepherd, I'll not want
324   There is a place of quiet rest
      (Near to the heart of God)
220   There is a sweet, sweet Spirit
346   Thou hidden source of calm repose
304   When peace, like a river, attendeth
      See also Affliction and Comfort

COMMITMENT
254   Blest be the dear uniting love
319   Call'ed of God, we honor the call
300   Everyone who longs for
265   Here am I, send me
299   I greet thee, who my sure redeemer art
102   I want to walk as a child of the light
391   I'm pressing on the upward way
 96   Jesus calls us
316   Jesus, my Lord, to thee I cry
137   Let there be peace on earth
318   More love to thee, O Christ
357   Move me
313   My heart I give unto you
321   My Jesus, I love thee
322   O love that wilt not let me go
315   O master, let me walk with thee
331   Send me, Lord
312   Take my life, and let it be
238   Take our bread
145   Take up thy cross
311   This is a day of new beginning
338   This little light of mine

317　To my precious Lord
314　We are climbing Jacob's ladder
310　When we are living
320　When we walk with the Lord
　　See also Trust

COMMUNION　See Holy Communion

COMMUNION OF THE SAINTS
　See New Heaven and New Earth

COMMUNITY IN CHRIST　See Church

CONFESSION　See also Sins

COURAGE
307　Be still, my soul
282　Give to the winds thy fears
216　How like a gentle Spirit
104　I want Jesus to walk with me
105　Jesus, Savior, Lord (Saranam, Saranam)
302　The care the eagle gives
91　Spirit song (O let the Son of God)
140　We shall overcome

CREATION
118　All people that on earth do dwell
63　All things bright and beautiful
335　Children of the heavenly Father
77　El Shadai
225　Father, I adore you
126　From all that dwell below the skies
325　God of our life
59　God of the sparrow God of the whale
64　God, who stretched the spangled heavens
73　God, whose love is reigning o'er us
70　He's got the whole world in his hands
80　Holy God, we praise thy name
65　I sing the almighty power of God
123　I'll praise my maker
74　Immortal, invisible, God only wise
75　Joyful, joyful, we adore thee
69　Let there be light
67　Let's sing unto the Lord
71　Many and great, O God
212　Many gifts, one spirit
227　O God in heaven
61　O Lord my God (How great thou art)
66　Of the Father's love begotten
83　On eagle's wings
352　Praise God, from whom all blessings
124　Praise the Lord who reigns above
68　Praise to the Lord, the almighty
60　Sing praise to God who reigns above
302　The care he eagle gives her young

62　This is my Father's world
78　To God be the glory
　　See also God

CROSS OF JESUS　See Jesus Christ

DEATH
　See also Funeral and Memorial Service

DEDICATION OF A BUILDING
　See Church: Dedication of a Building

DEVOTION
355　Alleluia
359　Amen
319　Call'd of God, we honor the call
281　Christ, whose glory fills the skies
351　Glory to God, the Creator
353　Gloria, gloria
363　Go now in peace
365　Grace, love, and peace abide
354　Heleluyan (Alleluia)
358　Hear us, O Lord (Before prayer)
364　Jesus, remember me
350　Kyrie Eleison
349　Lord, have mercy
368　May the grace of the Lord
367　May the Lord go with you
357　Move me
352　Praise God, from whom all blessings
76　Praise to the Lord and glory to God
234　Remember me
366　Sent forth by God's blessing
362　Shalom
361　Shalom to you
348　The Lord is in his temple

DISCIPLESHIP AND SERVICE
107　All day long
260　Christ for the world we sing
306　Come all ye that labor
277　Down at the cross
103　Draw thou my soul, O Christ
268　Even though I'm forever weak
97　Faith, while trees are still in blossom
347　God be with you till we meet again
149　God brings the kingdom
64　God, who stretched the spangled heavens
391　I'm pressing on the upward way
96　Jesus calls us
316　Jesus, my Lord, to thee I cry
144　Live into hope
90　Lord, you have come to the lakeshore
318　More love to thee, O Christ
313　My heart I give unto you

321 My Jesus, I love thee
308 Nearer, my God, to thee
315 O master, let me walk with thee
89 O, the help that God has given
284 Softly and tenderly Jesus is calling
214 Spirit of living God (O let the Son of God)
312 Take my life, and let it be
145 Take up thy cross
301 The joy of the Lord
294 The trusting heart to Jesus clings
314 We are climbing Jacob's ladder
257 We are one in the Spirit
168 We would see Jesus
291 What a fellowship, what a joy divine
333 What a friend we have in Jesus
310 When we are living
320 When we walk with the Lord
　　See also Commitment; Christian Life

DOXOLOGY　See Service Music

EASTER　See Christian Year

ECUMENISM　See Church

EDUCATION　See Church

EPIPHANY　See Christian Year

ETERNAL LIFE
307 Be still, my soul
380 Christ the Victorious
388 For all the saints
285 God sent his Son (Because he lives)
123 I'll praise my maker while I've breath
392 In the bulb there is a flower
309 Precious Lord, take my hand
130 Rejoice, ye pure in heart
381 Sing the wondrous love of Jesus
382 Sing with all the saints
385 Soon and very soon
378 Steal away to Jesus
384 Swing low, sweet chariot
188 The day of resurrection
115 The Lord's my shepherd, I'll not want
189 They crucified my Savior (He rose)
310 When we are living

EVANGELISM AND MISSION
267 Christ for the whole wide world
260 Christ for the world we sing
268 Even though I'm forever weak
261 Go, make of all disciples
258 God forgave my sin (Freely, freely)

266 Heralds of light, speed away
265 Here am I, send me
95 I am a stranger here
263 I, the Lord of sea and sky (Here I am), 262
　　It only takes a spark (Pass it on)
270 Jesus, he is the Christ
264 Lord, the light of your love (Shine, Jesus)
269 O thou who camest from above
259 Though so many have gone astray
　　See also Mission and Outreach

EVENING
377 Beyond the sunset
142 Dona nobis pacem
363 Go now in peace
373 Jesus, I think of you now
375 Now the day is over
372 Now, on land and sea descending
366 Sent forth by God's blessing
362 Shalom
361 Shalom to you
376 Softly now the light of day

EXODUS　See Salvation

EXPERIENCE　See Christian Experience

FAITH
307 Be still, my soul
335 Children of the heavenly Father
97 Faith, while trees are still in blossom
282 Give to the winds thy fears
73 God, whose love is reigning o'er us
392 In the bulb there is a flower
315 O master, let me walk with thee
83 On eagle's wings
219 Spirit of faith, come down
301 The joy of the Lord
279 Through it all
78 To God be the glory
　　See also Christian Life

FAMILY　See Home

FELLOWSHIP
107 All day long
250 Christ, from whom all blessings flow
253 Help us accept each other
252 I am the church! You are the church
212 Many gifts, one Spirit
249 O Church of God, united
237 One bread, one body
255 The church's one foundation
257 We are one in the Spirit

FORGIVENESS

280	And can it be that I should gain
377	Beyond the sunset
278	Change my heart, Oh God
273	Depth of mercy
275	Far from the Lord I wandered
258	God forgave my sin
	(Freely, freely)
285	God sent his Son
81	Great is thy faithfulness
327	Have thine own way, Lord
253	Help us accept each other
265	Here am I, send me
288	How can we sinners know
326	It's me, it's me, O Lord
373	Jesus, I think of you now
276	Out of my bondage
271	Pass me not, O gentle Savior
274	Search me, O God
	(Cleanse me)
286	Shackled by a heavy burden
303	Something beautiful
311	This is a day of new beginnings
78	To God be the glory
310	When we are living

See also Repentance

FREEDOM

280	And can it be that I should gain
182	'Tis finished! the Messiah dies
140	We shall overcome

FUNERAL AND MEMORIAL SERVICE

307	Be still, my soul
377	Beyond the sunset
380	Christ the Victorious
387	Come, let us join our friends above
388	For all the saints
123	I'll praise my maker while I've breath
391	I'm pressing on the upward way
392	In the bulb there is a flower
386	My Lord, what a morning
390	O holy city, seen of John
309	Precious Lord, take my hand
389	Shall we gather at the river
381	Sing the wondrous love of Jesus
	(When we all get to heaven)
382	Sing with all the saints in glory
385	Soon and very soon
378	Steal away to Jesus
384	Swing low, sweet chariot
255	The church's one foundation
115	The Lord's my shepherd, I'll not want
86	The love of God

324	There is a place of quiet rest
297	Walking in sunlight all of my journey

See also Eternal Life; New Heaven and New Earth

GOD

118	All people that on earth do dwell
63	All things bright and beautiful
77	El Shaddai
85	Father in heaven how we love you
225	Father, I adore you
228	Father, we love you (Glorify thy name)
353	Gloria, gloria
325	God of our life
59	God of the sparrow God of the whale
73	God, whose love is reigning o'er us
81	Great is thy faithfulness
70	He's got the whole world in his hands
354	Heleluyan (Alleluia)
80	Holy God, we praise thy name
229	Holy, holy
233	Holy, holy, holy Lord
79	Holy, holy, holy! Lord God almighty
82	Holy, holy, holy is the Lord
65	I sing the almighty power of God
123	I'll praise my maker while I've breath
74	Immortal, invisible, God only wise
75	Joyful, joyful, we adore thee
67	Let's sing unto the Lord
84	Lord God, thy glory
71	Many and great, O God
212	Many gifts, one Spirit
87	My Savior, my King
227	O God in heaven
61	O Lord my God (How great thou art)
66	Of the Father's love begotten
83	On eagle's wings
352	Praise God, from whom all blessings
124	Praise the Lord who reigns above
76	Praise to the Lord
68	Praise to the Lord, the almighty
60	Sing praise to God who reigns above
302	The care the eagle give her young
86	The love of God
62	This is my Father's world
78	To God be the glory
72	We, thy people, praise thee
129	When in our music god is glorified

GOD THE CREATOR See Creation; God

GRACE AND CALMNESS

293	A wonderful Savior is Jesus my Lord
93	Amazing grace, how sweet the sound
287	Blessed assurance, Jesus is mine
127	Come, though found of every blessing

273　Depth of mercy
347　God be with you till we meet again
59　God of the sparrow God of the whale
334　Heart longings, Lord Jesus
290　I know not why God's wondrous grace
326　It's me, it's me, O Lord
342　Jesus loves me!
144　Live into hope
90　Lord, you have come to the lakeshore
284　Softly and tenderly Jesus is calling
91　Spirit song (O let the Son of God)
346　Thou hidden source of calm repose
333　What a friend we have in Jesus
304　When peace, like a river, attendeth
310　When we are living

GRATITUDE
201　Alleluia, Alleluia
360　Bless thou the gifts
243　Every hill seems to be aflame
247　Give thanks
59　God of the sparrow God of the whale
67　Let's sing unto the Lord
71　Many and great, O God
352　Praise God, from whom all blessings
371　Rise to greet the sun
242　See the birds as they fly
366　Sent forth by God's blessing
244　Soft rains of spring flow
246　Thanks to God for my redeemer
114　The Lord hear thee
245　We who bear the image of God
　　See Christian Year: Thanksgiving Day

GRIEF
380　Christ the Victorious
308　Nearer, my God, to thee
309　Precious Lord, take my hand
105　Jesus, Savior, Lord (Sarnam, Saranam)
60　Sing praise to God who reigns above
346　Thou hidden source of calm repose

GROWTH　See Christian Life

GUIDANCE
107　All day long
101　All the way my Savior leads me
100　Dear Lord, lead me day by day
103　Draw thou my soul, O Christ
347　God be with you till we meet again
64　God, who stretched the spangled heavens
81　Great is thy faithfulness
104　I want Jesus to walk with me
102　I want to walk as a child of the light
106　In deepest darkness I wandered alone

344　Jesus, joy of our desiring
105　Jesus, Savior, Lord (Saranam, Saranam)
315　O master, let me walk with thee
115　The Lord is my shepherd, I'll not want

HEALING
328　Heal us, Emmanuel, hear our prayer
176　Jesus' hands were kind hands
98　There is a balm in Gilead
168　We would see Jesus
171　When Jesus the healer passed

HEAVEN
377　Beyond the sunset
387　Come, let us join our friends
213　Every time I feel the Spirit
390　O holy city, seen of John
389　Shall we gather at the river
381　Sing the wondrous love of Jesus
385　Soon and very soon
378　Steal away to Jesus
384　Swing low, sweet chariot
324　There is a place of quiet rest
　　See also Eternal Life; Kingdom of God; New Heaven
　　and New Earth

HOLY COMMUNION
173　Amen, Amen
191　Because he died and is risen
360　Bless thou the gifts
240　Bread of the world
235　For the bread which you have broken
253　Help us accept each other
79　Holy, holy, holy! Lord God almighty
233　Holy, holy, holy Lord
150　Let all mortal flesh keep silence
236　Let us break bread together
239　Let us talents and tongues employ
237　One bread, one body
234　Remember me
366　Sent forth by God's blessing
214　Spirit of the living God
238　Take our bread
9-58　The Korean-English U. Methodist Hymnal
6-59　The Korean-English Presbyterian Hymnal

HOLY SPIRIT
218　Come, Holy Ghost, our hearts inspire
213　Every time I feel the Spirit
225　Father, I adore you
228　Father, we love you
224　Holy Spirit, breathe on me
217　Holy Spirit, come, confirm us
216　How like a gentle Spirit
223　I'm goin'a sing when the Spirit says

222   Let every Christian pray
212   Many gifts, one Spirit
221   Spirit
219   Spirit of faith, come down
214   Spirit of the living God
91   Spirit song (O let the Son of God)
215   Surely the presence of the Lord
220   There's a sweet, sweet Spirit
     See also Christian Year; Pentecost; Trinity

HOLY WEEK   See Christian Year: Holy Week

HOME AND FAMILY
232   Child of blessing, child of promise
335   Children of the heavenly Father
340   God, give us Christian homes
253   Help us accept each other
337   Jesus loves the little children
336   Praise him, all ye little children
339   Spring breezes blow gently
311   This is a day of new beginnings
338   This little light of mine
343   When love is found

HOPE
107   All day long
94   Amazing grace, how sweet the sound
213   Every time I feel the Spirit
97   Faith, while trees are still in blossom
81   Great is thy faithfulness
358   Hear us, O Lord
292   I will trust in the Lord
392   In the bulb there is a flower
326   It's me, it's me, O Lord
344   Jesus, joy of our desiring
364   Jesus, remember me
332   Kum ba yah (Come by here)
350   Kyrie Eleison
222   Let every Christian pray
318   More love to thee, O Christ
357   Move me
322   O love that wilt not let me go
269   O thou who camest from above
309   Precious Lord, take my hand
234   Remember me
385   Soon and very soon
330   Sweet hour of prayer
324   There is a place of quiet rest
     (Near to the heart of God)
279   Through it all
140   We shall overcome
147   While we are waiting, come

INCARNATION
     See Jesus Christ: Incarnation

INSTALLATION SERVICES
360   Bless thou the gifts
319   Call'd of God, we honor the call
267   Christ for the whole wide world
266   Heralds of light, speed away
265   Here am I, send me
263   I, the Lord of sea and sky

INVITATION   See Call to Christian Life

JESUS CHRIST
206   All my tomorrows, all my past
101   All the way my Savior leads me
355   Alleluia
201   Alleluia, Alleluia
196   Alleluia! Sing to Jesus
173   Amen, Amen
281   Christ, whose glory fills the skies
200   Come on and celebrate
211   Emmanuel, Emmanuel
178   Filled with excitement
328   Heal us, Emmanuel, hear our prayer
203   His name is wonderful
170   I danced in the Lord
     (Lord of the dance)
295   I have found a friend in Jesus
210   I just want to praise you
205   I'd rather have Jesus
209   In his name
179   Jesu, Jesu
176   Jesus' hands were kind hands
342   Jesus loves me!
199   Jesus! the name high over all
270   Jesus, he is the Christ
174   Lift high the cross
204   Majesty, worship his majesty
175   My heart is little Galilee
305   O soul, are you weary?
169   O wondrous sight! O vision fair
130   Rejoice, ye pure in heart
113   Send your word
207   Shout for joy and sing
284   Softly and tenderly Jesus is calling
91   Spirit song
     (O let the Son of God enfold you)
177   Tell me the stories of Jesus
198   There is a name I love
172   Thou didst leave thy throne
346   Thou hidden source of calm repose
341   Though I may speak
259   Though so many have gone astray far
317   To my precious Lord
202   We have come into his house
168   We would see Jesus

171   When Jesus the healer passed
369   When morning gilds the skies
      See also Christian Year: Advent; Christmas; Epiphany

Atonement
88   Come, sinners, to the gospel feast
80   Holy God, we praise thy name
93   I stand amazed in the presence
183   Jesus shed his blood for me
384   Swing low, sweet chariot
182   'Tis finished! the Messiah dies
78   To God be the glory
      See also Salvation

Blood
196   Alleluia! Sing to Jesus
280   And can it be that I should gain
287   Blessed assurance, Jesus is mine
288   How can we sinners know
92   I heard an old, old story
      (Victory in Jesus)
93   I stand amazed in the presence
183   Jesus shed his blood for me
219   Spirit of faith, come down
198   There is a name I love
78   To God be the glory

Cross
186   Ah, holy Jesus
196   Alleluia! Sing to Jesus
277   Down at the cross
178   Filled with excitement
187   Go to dark Gethsemane
59   God of the sparrow god of the whale
183   Jesus shed his blood for me
180   Jesus walked this lonesome valley
174   Lift high the cross
181   Lord, who throughout these forty days
185   O love divine, what hast thou done
182   'Tis finished! The Messiah dies
184   To mock your reign, O dearest Lord
      See also Christian Year: Lent

Friend
295   I have found a friend in Jesus
296   In the garden
      (I come to the garden alone)
333   What a friend we have in Jesus

Incarnation
201   Alleluia, Alleluia
211   Emmanuel, Emmanuel
164   God who came in human form
      (God almighty, ruling the world)
156   He is born

162   In the little village of Bethlehem
152   Infant holy, infant lowly
165   Loving Lord Jesus
219   Spirit of faith, come down

Life and Ministry
196   Alleluia! Sing to Jesus
173   Amen, Amen
178   Filled with excitement
170   I dance in the morning
      (Lord of the dance)
179   Jesu, Jesu
199   Jesus! The name high over all
176   Jesus' hands were kind hands
174   Lift high the cross
175   My heart is little Galilee
169   O wondrous sight! O vision fair
177   Tell me the stories of Jesus
172   Thou didst leave thy throne
168   We would see Jesus
171   When Jesus the healer passed

Lordship
201   Alleluia, Alleluia
156   He is born
152   Infant holy, infant lowly
60   Sing praise to God who reigns above
219   Spirit of faith, come down

Love for
186   Ah, holy Jesus
355   Alleluia
280   And can it be that I should gain
272   Come back quickly to the Lord
275   Far from the Lord I wandered
187   Go to dark Gethsemane
285   God sent his Son (Because he lives)
342   Jesus loves me!
248   See how great a flame aspires
381   Sing the wondrous love of Jesus
198   There is a name I love
      (O how I love Jesus)
346   Thou hidden source of calm repose
333   What a friend we have in Jesus

Name of
258   God forgave my sin (Freely, freely)
203   His name is wonderful
296   In the garden (I come to the garden)
199   Jesus! The name high over all
174   Lift high the cross
204   Majesty, worship his majesty
226   O for a thousand tongue to sing
198   O how I love Jesus
60   Sing praise to God who reigns above

91   Spirit song (O let the Son of God)
198   There is a name I love (O how I love) 346
      Thou hidden source of calm repose
72   We, thy people, praise thee
      Resurrection See Christian Year: Easter

Savior See Salvation

JOY
118   All people that on earth do dwell
260   Christ for the world we sing
190   Christ is alive!
126   From all that dwell below the skies
155   Good Christian friends rejoice
334   Heart longings, Lord Jesus
344   Jesus, joy of our desiring
75   Joyful, joyful, we adore thee
130   Rejoice, ye pure in heart
286   Shackled by a heavy burden
      (He touched)
381   Sing the wondrous love of Jesus
382   Sing with all the saints in glory
91   Spirit song
      (O let the Son of God)
301   The joy of the Lord
114   The Lord hear thee
189   They crucified my Savior (He rose)
62   This is my Father's world

JUDGMENT
80   Holy God, we praise thy name
386   My Lord, what a morning
378   Steal away to Jesus

JUSTICE
260   Christ for the world we sing
148   Come now, O Prince of peace
142   Dona nobis pacem
261   Go, make of all disciples
149   God brings the kingdom
143   Hail to the brightness
179   Jesu, Jesu
146   Justice comes as river water flow
137   Let there be peace on earth
144   Live into hope
141   Prepare the way of the Lord
136   Seek ye first
145   Take up thy cross
139   The voice of God is calling
140   We shall overcome
138   When the poor ones
      See also Social Concerns

KINGDOM OF GOD
100   Dear Lord, lead me day by day
256   Glorious things of thee are spoken
143   Hail to the brightness
80   Holy God, we praise thy name
137   Let there be peace on earth
390   O holy city, seen of John
136   Seek ye first
145   Take up thy cross
255   The church's one foundation
139   The voice of God is calling
62   This is my Father's world
138   When the poor ones
      See also Heaven; New Heaven and New Earth

LENT See Christian Year: Lent

LIBERATION   See Freedom

LIGHT
281   Christ, whose glory fills the skies
102   I want to walk as a child of the light
74   Immortal, invisible, God only wise
113   Send your word
338   This little light of mine

LORD'S SUPPER
9-27 The Korean-English United Methodist
6-29 The Korean-English Presbyterian

LOVE
273   Depth of mercy
290   I know not why God's wondrous grace
344   Jesus, joy of our desiring
342   Jesus loves me!
175   My heart is little Galilee
185   O love divine, what has thou done
68   Praise to the Lord, the almighty
302   The care the eagle gives her young
86   The love of God
220   There's a sweet, sweet Spirit
341   Though I may speak
345   Very long ago up in heav'n above
343   When love is found

LOYALTY
      See Commitment; Discipleship and Service

MARRIAGE
73   God, whose love is reigning o'er us
344   Jesus, joy of our desiring
342   Jesus loves me!
75   Joyful, joyful, we adore thee
341   Though I may speak
345   Very long ago up in heav'n above
343   When love is found

MERCY

118 All people that on earth do dwell
273 Depth of mercy
70 He's got the whole world in his hands

MINISTRY OF ALL　See Discipleship and Service

MISSION AND OUTREACH

360 Bless thou the gifts
267 Christ for the whole wide world
260 Christ for the world we sing
268 Even though I'm forever weak
261 Go, make of all disciples
258 God forgave my sin (Freely, freely)
266 Heralds of light, speed away
265 Here am I, send me
95 I am a stranger here
263 I, the Lord of sea and sky (Here am I), 262
　　It only takes a spark (Pass it on)
270 Jesus, he is the Christ
264 Lord, the light of your love (Shine, Jesus)
249 O church of God, united
269 O thou who camest from above
338 This little light of mine
259 Though so many have gone astray
138 When the poor ones
　　See also Evangelism

MORNING

118 All people that on earth do dwell
80 Holy God, we praise thy name
299 I greet thee, who my sure redeemer art
370 Morning has broken
371 Rise to greet the sun
369 When morning gilds the skies

NAME OF JESUS　See Jesus Christ: Name of

NATURE

118 All people that on earth do dwell
59 God of the sparrow God of the whale
64 God, who stretched the spangled
65 I sing the almighty power of God
67 Let's sing unto the Lord
71 Many and great, O God
370 Morning has broken
346 Thou hidden source of calm repose

NEW CREATION

287 Blessed assurance, Jesus is mine
217 Holy Spirit, come, confirm us
75 Joyful, joyful, we adore thee
286 Shackled by a heavy burden (He touched)
231 We know that Christ is raised
　　See also Christian Experience

NEW HEAVEN AND NEW EARTH

379 All the saints who've fought
377 Beyond the sunset
380 Christ the Victorious
387 Come, let us join our friends
383 Dream on, dream on
388 For all the saints
391 I'm pressing on the upward way
392 In the bulb there is a flower
386 My Lord, what a morning
390 O holy city, seen of John
389 Shall we gather at the river
381 Sing the wondrous love of Jesus
382 Sing with all the saints in glory
385 Soon and very soon
378 Steal away to Jesus
384 Swing low, sweet chariot
324 There is a place of quiet rest

NEW YEAR

325 God of our life
309 Precious Lord, take my hand

OBEDIENCE

287 Blessed assurance, Jesus is mine
223 I'm goin'a sing when the Spirit says
96 Jesus calls us
175 My heart is little Galilee
145 Take up thy cross
320 When we walk with the Lord

OFFERING　See Service Music

OPENING HYMNS

118 All people that on earth do dwell
190 Christ is alive!
283 Come, let us reason
178 Filled with excitement
126 From all that dwell below the skies
80 Holy God, we praise thy name
123 I'll praise my maker while I've breath
74 Immortal, invisible, God only wise
75 Joyful, joyful, we adore thee
174 Lift high the cross
212 Many gifts, one Spirit
370 Morning has broken
68 Praise to the Lord, the almighty
60 Sing praise to God who reigns above
348 The Lord is in his holy temple
72 We, thy people, praise thee

ORDINATION

254 Blest be the dear uniting love
319 Call'd of God, we honor the call
380 Christ the Victorious

261   Go, make of all disciples
265   Here am I, send me
263   I, the Lord of sea and sky (Here I am),
     See also Installation

PARDON

280   And can it be that I should gain
377   Beyond the sunset
278   Change my heart, Oh God
273   Depth of mercy
275   Far from the Lord I wandered
258   God forgave my sin (Freely, freely)
285   God sent his Son (Because he lives)
 81   Great is thy faithfulness
327   Have thine own way, Lord
253   Help us accept each other
265   Here am I, send me
288   How can we sinners know
326   It's me, it's me, O Lord
373   Jesus, I think of you now
276   Out of my bondage, sorrow, and night
274   Search me, O God (Cleanse me)
271   Pass me not, O gentle Savior
286   Shackled by a heavy burden
     (He touched)
376   Softly now the light of day
303   Something beautiful
311   This is a day of new beginnings
 78   To God be the glory
310   When we are living
     See also Forgiveness

PASSION/PALM SUNDAY

     See Christian Year: Passion/Palm Sunday

PEACE

307   Be still, my soul
148   Come now, O prince of peace
142   Dona nobis pacem
347   God be with you till we meet again
334   Heart longings, Lord Jesus
137   Let there be peace on earth
174   Lift high the cross
144   Live into hope
372   Now, on land and sea descending
113   Send your word
362   Shalom
361   Shalom to you
214   Spirit of the living God
324   There is a place of quiet rest
220   There's a sweet, sweet spirit
346   Thou hidden source of calm repose
138   When the poor ones
     See also Calmness; Comfort and Encouragement

PENITENCE   See Sins

PENTECOST   See Christian Year: Pentecost

PRAISE

133   Blessed day, happy day
127   Come, thou fount of every blessing
200   Come on and celebrate
131   Come one and all, come join in sing
225   Father, I adore you
134   God who created all
125   Hallelujah, in God's Temple
 80   Holy God, we praise thy name
210   I just want to praise you
135   I lift my hands
 75   Joyful, joyful, we adore thee
 87   My Savior, my King
132   Open your eyes
130   Rejoice. ye pure in heart
207   Shout for joy and sing
128   Stand up and bless the Lord
259   Though so many have gone astray
317   To my precious Lord
345   Very long ago up in heav'n above
129   When in our music God is glorified

PRAISE JESUS CHRIST

206   All my tomorrows, all my past
355   Alleluia
201   Alleluia, Alleluia
200   Come on and celebrate
211   Emmanuel, Emmanuel
203   His name is wonderful
210   I just want to praise you
205   I'd rather have Jesus
209   In his name
208   Jesus, I love you
204   Majesty, worship his majesty
207   Shout for joy and sing
 91   Spirit song
     (O let the Son of God)
198   There is a name I love
     (O how I love Jesus)
202   We have come into his house

PRAYER

107   All day long
325   God of our life
327   Have thine own way, Lord
328   Heal us, Emmanuel, hear our prayer
334   Heart longings, Lord Jesus
329   I am weak but thou art strong
323   I love the Lord, who heard my cry
292   I will trust in the Lord
326   It's me, it's me, O Lord

332	Kum ba yah (Come by here)
364	Jesus, remember me
332	Kum ba yah (Come by here)
350	Kyrie Eleison
349	Lord, have mercy
222	Let every Christian pray
318	More love to thee, O Christ
357	Move me
227	O God in heaven
322	O love that wilt not let me go
309	Precious Lord, take my hand
234	Remember me
329	Send me, Lord
330	Sweet hour of prayer
324	There is a place of quiet rest
279	Through it all
333	What a friend we have in Jesus
147	While we are waiting, come

PRAYER RESPONSE See Service Music

PRESENCE See Jesus Christ and Holy Spirit

PROCLAMATION See Testimony and Witness

PROTECTION See Guidance

PROVIDENCE

101	All the way my Savior leads me
335	Children of the heavenly Father
282	Give to the winds thy fears
325	God of our life
374	God, that madest earth and heaven
123	I'll praise my maker while I've
83	On eagle's wings
60	Sing praise to God who reigns above
330	Sweet hour of prayer
302	The care the eagle gives her young
115	The Lord's my shepherd i'll not want
62	This is my Father's world
291	What a fellowship, what a joy divine

PSALMS

293	A wonderful Savior is Jesus my Lord
118	All people that on earth do dwell
116	As the deer
307	Be still, my soul
120	Bless the Lord
148	Come now, O Prince of peace
126	From all that dwell below the skies
122	From the depths, O Lord, I cry
117	God, be merciful to us
295	I have found a friend in Jesus
323	I love the Lord, who heard my cry
292	I will trust in the Lord

123	I'll praise my maker while I've
67	Let's sing unto the Lord
125	Hallelujah, in God's temple
271	Pass me not, O gentle Savior
124	Praise the Lord who reigns above
130	Rejoice, ye pure in heart
121	Sing, praise bless the Lord
128	Stand up and bless the Lord
114	The Lord hear thee
115	The Lord's my shepherd, I'll not want
294	The trusting heart to Jesus clings
119	To the high and kindly hills
304	When peace, like a river, attendeth

REBIRTH See Forgiveness

RECONCILIATION

253	Help us accept each other
362	Shalom
361	Shalom to you
311	This is a day of new beginnings
343	When love is found

REDEMPTION See Salvation

REPENTANCE

280	And can it be that I should gain
278	Change my heart, Oh God
273	Depth of mercy
275	Far from the Lord I wandered
258	God forgave my sin (Freely, freely)
285	God sent his Son (Because he lives)
81	Great is thy faithfulness
327	Have thine own way, Lord
253	Help us accept each other
265	Here am I, send me
288	How can we sinners know
326	It's me, it's me, O Lord
276	Out of my bondage, sorrow, and night
271	Pass me not, O gentle Savior
274	Search me, O God
286	Shackled by a heavy burden (He touched)
376	Softly now the light of day
303	Something beautiful
311	This is a day of new beginnings
310	When we are living
	See Forgiveness

RESURRECTION See Jesus Christ: Easter

ROUNDS

142	Dona nobis pacem
353	Gloria, gloria
363	Go now in peace
141	Prepare the way of the Lord

SACRIFICE

See Christian Life; Commitment; Discipleship; Service;
Stewardship; Testimony

SALVATION

107　All day long
101　All the way my Savior leads me
94　Amazing grace, how sweet the sound
287　Blessed assurance, Jesus is mine
278　Change my heart, Oh God
99　Come into my heart, blessed Jesus
88　Come, sinners, to the gospel feast
100　Dear Lord, lead me day by day
277　Down at the cross
103　Draw thou my soul, O Christ
97　Faith, while trees are still blossom
275　Far from the Lord I wandered
155　Good Christian friends, rejoice
327　Have thine own way, Lord
70　He's got the whole world in his hands
288　How can we sinners know
95　I am a stranger here
299　I greet thee, who my sure redeemer art
92　I heard an old, old story (Victory in Jesus)
290　I know not why God's wondrous grace
93　I stand amazed in the presence
104　I want Jesus to walk with me
102　I want to walk as a child of the light
96　Jesus calls us
183　Jesus shed his blood for me
105　Jesus, Savior, Lord (Saranam, Saranam)
90　Lord, you have come to the lakeshore
89　O, the help that God has given
91　Spirit song (O let the Son of God)
246　Thanks to God for my redeemer
114　The Lord hear thee
98　There is a balm in Gilead
198　There is a name I love (O how I love) 289
　　　There's within my heart a melody
231　We know that Christ is raised
291　What a fellowship, what a joy divine

SCRIPTURE　See also Bible

SENDING FORTH

See Service Music

SERENITY

See Calmness and Serenity

SERVANTHOOD

See also Commitment; Discipleship and Service;
Ministry; Stewardship; Testimony

SERVICE MUSIC

355　Alleluia
359　Amen
173　Amen, Amen
360　Bless thou the gifts
353　Gloria, gloria
351　Glory to God, the Creator
363　Go now in peace
365　Grace, love, and peace abide
358　Hear us, O Lord
354　Heleluyan (Alleluia)
358　Hear us, O Lord
364　Jesus, remember me
350　Kyrie Eleison
349　Lord, have mercy
368　May the grace of the Lord
367　May the Lord go with you
357　Move me
356　Our eyes are on the Lord Jesus
352　Praise God, from whom all blessings flow
366　Sent forth by God's blessing
362　Shalom
361　Shalom to you
348　The Lord is in his holy temple

Greeting · Call to Worship · Opening Hymns

126　From all that dwell below the skies
80　Holy God, we praise thy name
299　I greet thee, who my sure redeemer
204　Majesty, worship his majesty
370　Morning has broken
141　Prepare the way of the Lord
207　Shout for joy and sing
128　Stand up and bless the Lord
215　Surely the presence of the Lord
220　There's a sweet, sweet Spirit
348　The Lord is in his holy temple

Prayer for Illumination

108　Blessed Jesus, at thy word
218　Come, Holy Ghost, our hearts inspire
219　Spirit of faith, come down
214　Spirit of the living God
109　Thy word is a lamp

Invitation to Prayer

332　Kum ba yah (Come by here)
308　Nearer, my God, to thee
234　Remember me
214　Spirit of the living God
378　Steal away to Jesus
324　There is a place of quiet rest
　　　(Near to the heart of God)
238　Take our bread
333　What a friend we have in Jesus

Litany Prayer
108 Blessed Jesus, at thy word
104 I want Jesus to walk with me
214 Spirit of the living God

Confession and Pardon Prayer
280 And can it be that I should gain
273 Depth of Mercy
285 God sent his Son (Becasue he lives)
326 It's me, it's me, O Lord
364 Jesus, remember me
286 Shackled by a heavy burden
   (He touched me)
310 When we are living
 See also Confession

Prayer Responses
355 Alleluia
142 Dona nobis pacem
77 El Shaddai
357 Move me
91 Spirit song
   (O let the Son of God)

Peace, Passing of
237 One bread, one body
362 Shalom
361 Shalom to you

SERVICE TO OTHERS
 See Discipleship and Service

SINS AND CONFESSION
278 Change my heart, O God
272 Come back quickly to the Lord
273 Depth of mercy
277 Down at the cross
275 Far from the Lord I wandered
334 Heart longings, Lord Jesus
183 Jesus shed his blood for me
276 Out of my bondage
271 Pass me not, O gentle Savior
274 Search me, O God (Cleanse me)
 See also Penitence

SOCIAL CONCERNS
 See Justice

SPIRIT See Holy Spirit

SPIRITUAL HERITAGE
280 And can it be that I should gain
250 Christ, from whom all blessings flow
218 Come, Holy Ghost, our hearts inspire
 See also Christian Experience

STEWARDSHIP
360 Bless thou the gifts
97 Faith, while trees are still in blossom

SUFFERING
 See Affliction and Tribulation

STRENGTH
 See Courage

TEACHING
 See Word and Teaching

TESTIMONY AND WITNESS
201 Alleluia, Alleluia
260 Christ for the world we sing
261 Go, make of all disciples
258 God forgave my sin (Freely, freely)
216 How like a gentle Spirit
292 I will trust in the Lord
205 I'd rather have Jesus
262 It only takes a spark (Pass it on)
199 Jesus! The name high over all
174 Lift high the cross
249 O church of God, united
226 O for a thousand tongues to sing
61 O Lord my God (How great thou art)
315 O master, let me walk with thee
366 Sent forth by God's blessing
128 Stand up and bless the Lord
312 Take my life, and let it be
255 The church's one foundation
301 The joy of the Lord
98 There is a balm in Gilead
198 There is a name I love
338 This little light of mine
72 We, thy people, praise thee

THANKSGIVING (DAY)
360 Bless thou the gifts
243 Every hill seems to be aflame
247 Give thanks
242 See the birds as they fly
244 Soft rains of spring flow
246 Thanks to God for my redeemer
245 We who bear the image of God
 See also Gratitude

TRANSFIGURATION
 See Christian Year: Transfiguration

TRIBULATION
 See Affliction and Tribulation; Suffering

TRINITY (SUNDAY)
See Christian Year: Trinity

TRIUMPH
380	Christ the Victorious
388	For all saints
75	Joyful, joyful, we adore thee
174	Lift high the cross
386	My Lord, what a morning
390	O holy city, seen of John
389	Shall we gather at the river
297	Walking in sunlight all of my journey
140	We shall overcome

TRUST AND ASSURANCE
293	A wonderful Savior is Jesus my Lord
107	All day long
94	Amazing grace, how sweet the sound
280	And can it be that I should gain
116	As the deer
307	Be still, my soul
287	Blessed assurance, Jesus is mine
319	Call'd of God, we honor the call
335	Children of the heavenly Father
281	Christ, whose glory fills the skies
283	Come, let us reason
300	Everyone who longs for
97	Faith, while tree are still in blossom
282	Give to the winds thy fears
285	God sent his Son (Because he lives)
81	Great is thy faithfulness
288	How can we sinners know
299	I greet thee, who my sure Redeemer
295	I have found a friend in Jesus
290	I know not why God's wondrous grace
292	I will trust in the Lord
392	In the bulb there is a flower
296	In the garden (I come to the garden)
326	It's me, it's me, O Lord
391	I'm pressing on the upward way
344	Jesus, joy of our desiring
364	Jesus, remember me
105	Jesus, Savior, Lord (Saranam, Saranam)
332	Kum ba yah (Come by here)
350	Kyrie Eleison
349	Lord, have mercy

318	More love to thee, O Christ
357	Move me
227	O God in heaven
322	O love that wilt not let me go
83	On eagle's wings (And God will raise you up)
271	Pass me not, O gentle Savior
309	Precious Lord, take my hand
234	Remember me
298	Savior, lead me
331	Send me, Lord
286	Shackled by a heavy burden (He touched me)
284	Softly and tenderly Jesus is calling
302	Something beautiful
385	Soon and very soon
330	Sweet hour of prayer
302	The care the eagle gives her young
301	The joy of the Lord
294	The trusting heart to Jesus clings
289	There's within my heart a melody
279	Through it all
297	Walking in sunlight all of my journey
140	We shall overcome
291	What a fellowship, what a joy divine
333	What a friend we have in Jesus
304	When peace, like a river, attendeth
320	When we walk with the Lord
147	While we are waiting, come

See also Assurance; Faith

UNITED
254	Blest be the dear uniting love
250	Christ, from whom all blessings flow
253	Help us accept each other
251	Here, O Lord, your servants gather
252	I am the church! You are the church!
249	O church of God, united

WORD AND TEACHING
111	Almighty God, your word is cast
112	As dew falls gently at night
108	Blessed Jesus, at thy word
110	Holy Bible, Book divine
113	Send your word
109	Thy word is a lamp

가사 첫 줄 차례

138	가난해도 이웃에게
175	갈릴리 맑은 바다
	(내 마음 작은 갈릴리)
241	감사하는 성도여
389	강가에서 만나보자
229	거룩 거룩
79	거룩 거룩 거룩
233	거룩 거룩 거룩 전능하신 주
82	거룩 거룩 거룩하신 주
110	거룩하다 성경은
152	거룩하신 아기 예수
80	거룩하신 하나님 이름 높여
247	거룩하신 하나님 주께 감사
269	거룩한 불꽃 주시려
185	거룩한 사랑의 주님
186	거룩한 예수 무슨 죄가 있어
187	겟세마네 동산의 구세주
315	겸손히 주를 섬길 때
204	경배해 위대한 주님께
160	고요한 밤 거룩한 밤
324	고요한 안식 있는 곳
153	고요히 그 아기 잠자네
373	고요히 머리 숙여 (잠들기 전에)
276	고통의 멍에 벗으려고
180	골짜기 외로운 길
255	교회의 참된 터는
158	구유 안에 누이신 마리아의 아기
280	구주 예수 피 흘리심
147	구주여 오소서
277	구주의 십자가 보혈로
157	그 어린 주 예수
86	그 크신 하나님의 사랑
75	기뻐하며 경배하세
207	기뻐하며 왕께 노래 부르리
161	기쁘다 구주 오셨네
234	기억하소서
94	나 같은 죄인 살리신
329	나는 비록 약하나
268	나 비록 연약하지만
	(우리는 언약의 백성)
316	나 주의 도움 받고자
252	나는 교회 너도 교회
292	나는 주를 의지하리
331	나를 보내소서
104	나와 함께 걸으소서
101	나의 갈 길 다 가도록
279	나의 삶 속에서
312	나의 삶을 주 위해
225	나의 하나님 나의 삶을 다해 사랑해요
92	난 들었네 주 예수
299	날 대속하신 나의 구세주
375	낮이 지나가고
318	내 구주 예수를 더욱 사랑
330	내 기도하는 그 시간
313	내 마음 주께 바치옵니다
289	내 맘속의 음악 소리는
206	내 모든 장래 지난 날
198	내 사랑하는 그 이름
216	내 안에 계신 온유하신 주
321	내 주되신 주를 참 사랑하고
308	내 주를 가까이 하려 함은
295	내 진정 사모하는
304	내 평생에 가는 길
122	내가 깊은 곳에서
119	내가 산을 향하여
114	내가 환난 당할 때에
317	내게 있는 향유 옥합
261	너 가서 모든 자로
136	너희는 먼저 주의 나라와
305	네 마음에 근심 있느냐
129	노래로 주께 영광 돌리며
203	놀라운 그 이름
124	높은 곳에 계신 주님
60	높이 계신 주 찬양해
174	높이 들라 사랑의 십자가
132	눈을 들어
131	다 나와서 노래하자
88	다 오라 복음 잔치에
200	다 와서 찬양해
182	다 이루었다
68	다 찬양하여라
283	다 함께 오라
246	대속하신 주께 감사
302	독수리 높은 둥지에
135	두 손 들고 찬양합니다
282	두려움 떨치고 소망을 가지세
335	둥지 안의 새들
358	들으소서 우리 기도 드릴 때
154	마리아 무릎 위에
226	만 입이 내게 있으면

352 만복의 근원 하나님
259 많은 사람들 참된 진리를
(예수가 좋다오)
130 맘 정결한 자들
385 머지 않아서
239 모든 은사와 언어로
116 목마른 사슴
192 무덤에 머물러
379 믿음의 선한 싸움
219 믿음의 영이여
263 바다와 하늘의 주
(내가 여기 있나이다)
162 베들레헴 작은 그 마을
127 복의 근원 강림하사
244 봄이 오면 밭고랑에 (하나님의 선물)
392 봉오리에 꽃 한 송이 (약속의 찬미)
319 부름 받아 나선 이 몸
69 빛 있으라
374 빛과 어둠 땅과 하늘
266 빛의 사자들이여
73 사랑으로 다스리는
134 사랑으로 천지만물
165 사랑의 주님 예수
343 사랑하고 바라면서
85 사랑하는 나의 아버지
195 사랑하는 우리 예수
231 사망의 모든 권세 이기고
181 사십일 동안
339 사철에 봄바람 불어 잇고
243 산마다 불이 탄다 고운 단풍에
214 살아계신 주 성령
274 살피소서 내 맘을
311 새로운 삶을 시작하는
371 새벽하늘 밝히는
167 새벽 별 오 기쁜 빛
362 샬롬 카베림
361 샬롬을 비네
155 성도여 기뻐 찬양해
221 성령
257 성령 안에서 우리 하나
223 성령을 따라서 찬양하리
224 성령이여 오셔서 정결케 하소서
217 성령이여 진리 안에
166 성탄 노래하세
337 세상 모든 어린이를
260 세상의 구주께
306 수고한 자 오라
123 숨 쉬는 동안 주 찬양

380 승리의 예수여
140 승리하리라
256 시온성과 같은 교회
143 시온의 영광이 빛나는 아침
74 신비롭고 영원한 지혜의 주
145 십자가 지라
290 아 하나님의 은혜로
156 아기 예수 나셨네
63 아름다운 모든 것
303 아름답게 하셨네
359 아멘
173 아멘 아멘
66 아버지의 사랑으로
336 아이들아 주를 찬송하라
345 아주 먼 옛날
369 아침 해 솟을 때
388 안식하는 하늘의 성도들
355 알렐루야
201 알렐루야 알렐루야
197 알렐루야 예수 다시 사셨네
196 알렐루야 찬양하라
159 어느 옛날 다윗 성에
390 어린양 다스리시는
272 어서 돌아오오
288 어찌 알 수 있나
125 어하라디야 상사디야
77 엘샤다이
220 여기 성령 함께 계시니
332 여기 오소서
275 여러 해 동안 주 떠나
353 영광 영광
212 영광스런 주님 전능하신 주
382 영화로운 성도들과
270 예수 그리스도 모든 문제의 해결자
(예수 전하세)
183 예수 나를 위하여
105 예수 내 주께 (싸라남, 싸라남)
364 예수 내 주여
108 예수 말씀 듣고자
193 예수 부활했으니
342 예수 사랑하심은
208 예수 사랑해요
179 예수 예수
344 예수 우리 참된 기쁨
258 예수 이름으로
320 예수 따라가며
284 예수가 우리를 부르는 소리
199 예수는 가장 높으신

177	예수님 이야기 내게 들려주오	387	저 하늘 성도들과
176	예수님의 두 손 친절하신 손	146	정의가 강물처럼
287	예수를 내가 주로 믿어	133	좋은 날 기쁜 날
168	예수를 보리	286	죄와 수치 무거운 짐
309	예수여 나의 손 꼭 잡고 가소서	333	죄짐 맡은 우리 구주
335	오 나의 자비로운 주	184	주 가시관을 쓰시고
293	오 놀라운 구세주	115	주 나의 목자 되시니
169	오 놀랍고 아름다운	83	주 너를 독수리 날개 위에
218	오 성령이여 오소서	340	주 말씀 배우는 믿음의 가정
81	오 신실하신 주	109	주 말씀은 나의 발에 등
254	오 우릴 연합하시는	222	주 믿는 성도들 날마다 기도해
249	오 하나님의 교회	188	주 부활하신 이 날
384	오라 하늘의 수레	323	주 사랑해
148	오소서	190	주 사셨다
70	온 세상 우리 주님 손 안에	348	주 성전 안에
267	온 세상 위하여	294	주 안에 있는 나에게
126	온 천하 거하는 만물아	209	주 안에 평안 있고
281	온 하늘에 가득히 주의 영광	363	주 안에서 평안하라
118	온 땅의 모든 사람들	346	주 안의 깊은 평안
107	온종일 예수와 함께	360	주 앞에 바친 예물
250	완전하게 하시는 복의 근원 예수여	189	주 예수 십자가에
87	왕이신 나의 하나님	171	주 예수님 갈릴리 지나실 때
347	우리 다시 만날 때까지	99	주 예수님 내 맘에 오사
238	우리 삶을 받아주소서	205	주 예수보다 더 귀한 것은 없네
368	우리 주 예수의 크신 은혜	334	주 예수여 은혜를
95	우리가 지금은 나그네 되어도	381	주 예수의 크신 사랑
356	우리는 주만 바라봅니다	365	주 예수의 크신 은혜
328	우리를 고쳐주소서	253	주 우릴 받아주심 본받게
310	우리의 삶은 예수 안에서	67	주 찬양 드리세
325	우리의 삶을 주관하시는 주	121	주 찬양하여라
248	은혜 작은 불꽃이	322	주 크신 사랑 가운데
103	이 마음 주께로	285	주 하나님 독생자 예수
170	이 세상이 시작되던	61	주 하나님 지으신 모든 세계
338	이 작은 나의 빛	65	주 하나님의 능력
137	이 땅에 주의 평화	111	주 하나님의 말씀이
112	이슬을 내리시듯 말씀을 내리소서	139	주 하나님의 음성 우리를 부르네
150	인생들아 잠잠하라	90	주 호숫가에 오셔서
271	인애하신 구세주	172	주님 보좌와 영광
211	임마누엘 임마누엘	235	주님 떼어주신 떡
349	자비 베푸소서	191	주님은 죽음 이기고
240	자비로 그 몸 찢기시고	301	주님의 기쁨은 나의 힘
262	작은 불꽃 하나가	128	주님의 사람들
307	잠잠하라	91	주님의 사랑과 그 영이
93	저 나사렛 예수 앞에	215	주님의 영이 여기 함께 하시니
391	저 높은 곳을 향하여	327	주님의 뜻을 이루소서
151	저 동정녀 마리아	194	주님께 영광
369	저 아침해 뜰 때	210	주를 찬양하리라
296	저 장미꽃 위에 이슬	357	주여 나를 감동하게

100	주여 나를 이끄사
265	주여 내가 여기 있나이다
326	주여 바로 접니다
264	주여 사랑의 빛을 (비추소서)
376	주여 오늘 하루가
117	주여 우리 무리를
350	주여 자비 베푸소서
386	주여 좋은 아침
298	주의 곁에 있을 때
141	주의 길 예비하라
273	주의 깊은 그 자비
113	주의 말씀 내리소서
72	주의 백성 찬양
102	주의 빛 따르기 원합니다
213	주의 성령 느낄 때
251	주의 종들 여기에 모여
291	주의 친절한 팔에 안기세
142	주의 평화 내리소서
245	주의 형상 따라서
378	주께로 가려네
367	주께서 함께 계셔 (축복송)
89	지금까지 지내 온 것
64	찬란하고 빛난 하늘
120	찬양하여라
62	참 아름다와라
351	창조주 하나님께
230	창조주 하나님 감사 찬송하세
341	천사처럼 말하여서
370	첫 아침처럼
232	축복하신 주의 자녀

106	캄캄한 밤중에 빈들에서
144	큰 소망 중에 살리라
366	큰 축복을 받고
297	태산을 넘어 험곡에 가도
149	평화의 나라 임하시니
96	풍랑 이는 바다 위로
228	하나님 사랑과 경배 드립니다
76	하나님을 찬양하세
300	하나님의 사랑을 사모하는 자 (주만 바라볼찌라)
164	하나님의 아들이 사람 몸을 입으사
78	하나님께 영광을
242	하늘 나는 새를 보라
314	하늘 향해 올라가네
71	하늘과 땅을 지으신 주
84	하늘에 가득찬 영광의 하나님
59	하늘의 새와 물고기
227	하늘의 주님 내려주소서
237	한 떡을 떼며
354	할렐루야
236	함께 주님의 떡을 나누세
202	함께 주의 이름으로
278	항상 진실케
377	해 지는 저편
98	향유가 있는 길르앗
178	흥분한 군중들이
163	흰눈이 쌓이고 별 빛날 때
97	꽃이 필 때 믿음으로
383	꿈을 꾸세 평화의 자녀
372	땅 위에도 바다에도

INDEX OF FIRST LINES AND COMMON TITLES

293	A wonderful Savior is Jesus my Lord
186	Ah, holy Jesus
107	All day long
206	All my tomorrows, all my past
118	All people that on earth do dwell
379	All the saints who've fought
101	All the way my Savior leads me
63	All things bright and beautiful
355	Alleluia
201	Alleluia, Alleluia
197	Alleluia! Christ is risen (Resurrection canon)
196	Alleluia! Sing to Jesus
111	Almighty God, your word is cast
94	Amazing grace! How sweet the sound
359	Amen
173	Amen, Amen
280	And can it be that I should gain
112	As dew falls gently at night
116	As the deer
157	Away in a manger
307	Be still, my soul
191	Because he died and is risen
377	Beyond the sunset
120	Bless the Lord
360	Bless thou the gifts
287	Blessed assurance, Jesus is mine
133	Blessed day, happy day
108	Blessed Jesus, at thy word
254	Blest be the dear uniting love
240	Bread of the world
319	Call'd of God, we honor the call
278	Change my heart, Oh God
232	Child of blessing, child of promise
335	Children of the heavenly Father
267	Christ for the whole wide world
260	Christ for the world we sing
190	Christ is alive!
193	Christ the Lord is risen today
380	Christ the Victorious
250	Christ, from whom all blessings flow
281	Christ, whose glory fills the skies
306	Come all ye that labor
272	Come back quickly to the Lord
99	Come into my heart, blessed Jesus
148	Come now, O Prince of peace
200	Come on and celebrate
131	Come one and all, come join in song
218	Come, Holy Ghost, our hearts inspire
387	Come, let us join our friends
283	Come, let us reason
88	Come, sinners, to the gospel feast
127	Come, thou fount of every blessing
241	Come, ye thankful people, come
273	Depth of mercy
100	Dear Lord, lead me day by day
142	Dona nobis pacem
277	Down at the cross
103	Draw thou my soul, O Christ
383	Dream on, dream on
77	El Shaddai
211	Emmanuel, Emmanuel
268	Even though I'm forever weak
243	Every hill seems to be aflame
213	Every time I feel the Spirit
300	Everyone who longs for
97	Faith, while trees are still in blossom
275	Far from the Lord I wandered
85	Father in heaven how we love you
225	Father, I adore you
228	Father, we love you
178	Filled with excitement (Mantos y palmas esparciendo)
388	For all the saints
235	For the bread which you have broken
126	From all that dwell below the skies
122	From the depths, O Lord, I cry
158	Gentle Mary laid her child
247	Give thanks
282	Give to the winds thy fears
353	Gloria, gloria
256	Glorious things of thee are spoken
351	Glory to God, the Creator
363	Go now in peace
187	Go to dark Gethsemane
261	Go, make of all disciples
347	God be with you till we meet again
149	God brings the kingdom
258	God forgave my sin (Freely, Freely)
325	God of our life

59	God of the sparrow God of the whale
285	God sent his Son (Because he lives)
164	God who came in human form (God almighty, ruling the world)
134	God who created all
117	God, be merciful to us
340	God, give us Christian homes
374	God, that madest earth and heaven
64	God, who stretched the spangled
73	God, whose love is reigning o'er us
155	Good Christian friends, rejoice
365	Grace, love, and peace abide
81	Great is thy faithfulness
143	Hail to the brightness
125	Hallelujah, in God's temple,
327	Have thine own way, Lord
156	He is born
328	Heal us, Emmanuel, hear our prayer
358	Hear us, O Lord
334	Heart longings, Lord Jesus
70	He's got the whole world in his hands
354	Heleluyan (Alleluia)
253	Help us accept each other
266	Heralds of light, speed away
265	Here am I, send me
251	Here, O Lord, your servants gather
203	His name is wonderful
110	Holy Bible, Book divine
80	Holy God, we praise thy name
229	Holy, holy
233	Holy, holy, holy Lord
79	Holy, holy, holy! Lord God almighty
82	Holy, holy, holy is the Lord
224	Holy Spirit, breathe on me
217	Holy Spirit, come, confirm us
288	How can we sinners know
216	How like a gentle Spirit
95	I am a stranger here
252	I am the church! You are the church!
329	I am weak but thou art strong
170	I danced in the morning (Lord of the dance)
299	I greet thee, who my sure redeemer art
295	I have found a friend in Jesus (The lily of the valley)
92	I heard an old, old story (Victory in Jesus)
210	I just want to praise you
290	I know not why God's wondrous grace
135	I lift my hands
323	I love the Lord, who heard my cry
65	I sing the almighty power of God
93	I stand amazed in the presence
104	I want Jesus to walk with me
102	I want to walk as a child of the light
292	I will trust in the Lord
263	I, the Lord of sea and sky (Here I Am, Lord)
205	I'd rather have Jesus
123	I'll praise my maker while I've breath
223	I'm goin'a sing when the Spirit says
391	I'm pressing on the upward way
74	Immortal, invisible, God only wise
106	In deepest darkness I wandered alone
209	In his name
392	In the bulb there is a flower (Hymn of promise)
296	In the garden (I come to the garden alone)
162	In the little village of Bethlehem
152	Infant holy, infant lowly
262	It only takes a spark (Pass it on)
326	It's me, it's me, O Lord
179	Jesu, Jesu
96	Jesus calls us
176	Jesus' hands were kind hands
342	Jesus loves me!
337	Jesus loves the little children
183	Jesus shed his blood for me
199	Jesus! The name high over all
180	Jesus walked this lonesome valley
195	Jesus, beloved Lord
270	Jesus, he is the Christ
208	Jesus, I love you (Alleluia)
373	Jesus, I think of you now
344	Jesus, joy of our desiring
316	Jesus, my Lord, to thee I cry
364	Jesus, remember me
105	Jesus, Savior, Lord (Saranam, Saranam)
161	Joy to the world
75	Joyful, joyful, we adore thee
146	Justice comes as river water flow
332	Kum Ba Yah (Come by here)
350	Kyrie Eleison

150	Let all mortal flesh keep silence	89	O, the help that God has given
222	Let every Christian pray	66	Of the Father's love begotten
69	Let there be light	83	On Eagle's Wings
137	Let there be peace on earth		(And God will raise you up)
236	Let us break bread together	159	Once in royal David's city
239	Let us talents and tongues employ	237	One bread, one body
67	Let's sing unto the Lord	132	Open your eyes
174	Lift high the cross	356	Our eyes are on the Lord
144	Live into hope	276	Out of my bondage
84	Lord God, thy glory	271	Pass me not, O gentle Savior
115	Lord, as the earth welcomes shower	230	Praise and thanksgiving be to God
349	Lord, have mercy	352	Praise God, from whom all blessings
264	Lord, the light of your love	336	Praise him, all ye little children
	(Shine, Jesus, shine)	124	Praise the Lord who reigns above
181	Lord, who throughout these forty days	76	Praise to the Lord
90	Lord, you have come to the	68	Praise to the Lord, the almighty
	lakeshore (Tu Has Venito a la)	309	Precious Lord, take my hand
165	Loving Lord Jesus	141	Prepare the way of the Lord
192	Low in the grave he lay	130	Rejoice, ye pure in heart
204	Majesty, worship his majesty	234	Remember me
71	Many and great, O God	371	Rise to greet the sun
212	Many gifts, one Spirit	298	Savior, lead me
368	May the grace of the Lord	274	Search me, O God
367	May the Lord go with you		(Cleanse me)
318	More love to thee, O Christ	248	See how great a flame aspires
370	Morning has broken	242	See the birds as they fly
167	Morning Star, O Cheering Sight	136	Seek ye first
357	Move me	331	Send me, Lord
313	My heart I give unto you	113	Send your word
175	My heart is little Galilee	366	Sent forth by God's blessing
321	My Jesus, I love thee	286	Shackled by a heavy burden
386	My Lord, what a morning		(He touched me)
87	My Savior, my King	389	Shall we gather at the river
308	Nearer, my God, to thee	362	Shalom
375	Now the day is over	361	Shalom to you
372	Now, on land and sea descending	207	Shout for joy and sing
249	O church of God, united	160	Silent night! Holy night!
226	O for a thousand tongues to sing	60	Sing praise to God who reigns above
227	O God in heaven	381	Sing the wondrous love of Jesus
390	O holy city, seen of John		(When we all get to heaven)
61	O Lord My God!	166	Sing we now of Christmas
	(How Great Thou Art)	382	Sing with all the saints in glory
185	O love divine, what has thou done	121	Sing, praise and bless the Lord
322	O love that wilt not let me go	244	Soft rains of spring flow
315	O master, let me walk with thee	376	Softly now the light of day
305	O soul, are you weary?	284	Softly and tenderly Jesus is calling
269	O thou who camest from above	303	Something beautiful
169	O wondrous sight! O vision fair	385	Soon and very soon

221	Spirit	311	This is a day of new beginnings
219	Spirit of faith, come down	62	This is my Father's world
214	Spirit of the living God	338	This little light of mine
91	Spirit Song	172	Thou didst leave thy throne
	(O let the Son of God enfold you)	346	Thou hidden source of calm repose
339	Spring breezes blow gently	341	Though I may speak
	(Our home)	259	Though so many have gone astray
128	Stand up and bless the Lord	279	Through it all
378	Steal away to Jesus	109	Thy word is a lamp
153	Still, still, still	182	'Tis finished! the Messiah dies
215	Surely the presence of the Lord	151	To a maid engaged to Joseph
330	Sweet hour of prayer	78	To God be the glory
384	Swing low, sweet chariot	184	To mock your reign, O dearest Lord
312	Take my life, and let it be	317	To my precious Lord
238	Take our bread	119	To the high and kindly hills
145	Take up thy cross	345	Very long ago up in heaven's above
177	Tell me the stories of Jesus	297	Walking in sunlight all of my journey
246	Thanks to God for my redeemer	314	We are climbing Jacob's ladder
302	The care the eagle gives her young	257	We are one in the Spirit
255	The church's one foundation	202	We have come into his house
188	The day of resurrection	231	We know that Christ is raised
301	The joy of the Lord	140	We shall overcome
114	The Lord hear thee	245	We who bear the image of God
348	The Lord is in his holy temple	168	We would see Jesus
115	The Lord's my shepherd, I'll not want	72	We, thy people, praise thee
86	The love of God	291	What a fellowship, what a joy divine
163	The snow lay on the ground	333	What a friend we have in Jesus
294	The trusting heart to Jesus clings	154	What child is this
139	The voice of God is calling	129	When in our music God is glorified
98	There is a balm in Gilead	171	When Jesus the healer passed
198	There is a name I love	343	When love is found
	(O how I love Jesus)	369	When morning gilds the skies
324	There is a place of quiet rest	304	When peace, like a river, attendeth
	(Near to the heart of God)	138	When the poor ones
220	There's a sweet, sweet Spirit		(Cuando el pobre)
289	There's within my heart a melody	310	When we are living
189	They crucified my Savior		(Pues si vivimos)
	(He rose)	320	When we walk with the Lord
194	Thine be the glory	147	While we are waiting, come